Computational Psycholinguistics

Computational Psycholinguistics

AI and Connectionist Models of Human Language Processing

Edited by
Ton Dijkstra
University of Nijmegen, The Netherlands
and
Koenraad de Smedt
University of Bergen, Norway

Taylor & Francis
Publishers since 1798

| UK | Taylor & Francis Ltd, 1 Gunpowder Square, London EC4A 3DE |
| USA | Taylor & Francis Inc., 1900 Frost Road, Suite 101, Bristol, PA 19007 |

First published 1996

A catalogue record for this book is available from the British Library

ISBN 0–7484–0465–1 (hbk)
ISBN 0–7484–0466–X (pbk)

Library of Congress Cataloging-in-Publication Data are available on request

Cover design by Barking Dog Art

Typeset by RGM, The Mews, Birkdale Village, Southport

Printed in Great Britain by SRP Ltd, Exeter

10072728401 A

Contents

Foreword

Psycholinguistics is the study of how we produce and understand language and how we acquire these skills. Among the skills that are universal to our species, these linguistic capacities are doubtless the most complex ones. When we speak, listen to spoken language or read, we are constantly accessing a huge mental lexicon, which is a repository of tens of thousands of words. We generate and parse these words at speeds that easily exceed four syllables, 10 phonemes or 20 letters per second. We are also constantly processing the syntactic relations among the words that we access. As a speaker we produce utterances that are surprisingly well-formed syntactically. In fact, this *on-line* computation of syntax is a crucial step in the generation of natural, fluent prosody. And as a listener or a reader, we simply cannot inhibit the automatic syntactic parsing that is always at work when we attend to linguistic input. This parsing steadily interacts with the construction of meaning. After all, the ultimate step in language understanding is to interpret what we hear or read, to derive the intention of the speaker or the author. And meaning is at the core of all language use. As speakers/listeners, but also as readers/writers, we are always in the process of negotiating meaning. We are using a rich arsenal of rhetorical devices in order to generate effective utterances or texts and to be co-operative listeners or readers. In short, processing language is a multi-levelled cognitive skill of bewildering complexity.

Computational modelling, one would suppose, is an obvious tool for coping with this complexity. Even if component systems, such as lexical selection, are theoretically well understood, their interaction in the fluent generation and perception of language will be unpredictable from these partial theories. Many sciences, such as economics or meteorology, share this problem and they have naturally moved to computational modelling as soon as hard- and soft-ware of sufficient power became available. Surprisingly, no comparable development has taken place in psycholinguistics. If one skims through the *Handbook of Psycholinguistics* (Gernsbacher, 1994), it is immediately apparent that computational modelling is *not* a major tool in psycholinguistics. On a highly generous interpretation of *computational*, no more than 5 per cent of this almost 1200-page handbook is concerned with computational modelling. It is, moreover, largely restricted to just two domains of theorizing, lexical access and mental discourse models.

Clearly, there is something to be developed here. To the best of my knowledge, the present book is the first of its kind in psycholinguistics. It presents a representative range of computational models in psycholinguistics, both symbolic and subsymbolic.

The editors have managed to keep a balance between models of perception and models of production, one that is typically absent from psycholinguistic texts or handbooks, where language production tends to be a marginal subject. There are good computational reasons for spreading attention evenly here. There is a tacit belief among many of my colleagues that language production is roughly language comprehension in reverse. In comprehension you go from an input utterance to some derived meaning, with the mental grammar and lexicon somehow mediating. In production you go from some initial notion to an output utterance, with the same grammar and lexicon somehow mediating. This picture is, however, far too simple. The computational requirements are deeply different for production and comprehension. An ideal delivery in production requires completeness and well-formedness at all linguistic levels involved. The pragmatics should be precisely tuned to the discourse situation. The words, phrases, sentences should be accurate and complete renditions of the information to be expressed. Syntax and morphology have to be complete and well-formed and the same holds for the segmental and suprasegmental phonology of an utterance. Finally, the phonetic realization has to conform to the standards of intelligibility, rate, formality of the speech environment. The ideal speaker is kind of a decathlete, a master of myriad linguistic crafts. The ideal writer must add well-formedness at the graphemic level. It is a special computational challenge to generate these well-defined linguistic structures completely and on the fly, 'from left to right' as language producers do.

The computational problem is a rather different one for the listener. Whereas a produced utterance has to be linguistically complete at all levels, that requirement does not hold in parsing. Almost every utterance that we encounter is multiply ambiguous, phonetically (*I scream*), lexically (*the organ was removed*), syntactically (*I enjoy visiting colleagues*), semantically (*there are two tables with four chairs here*) or otherwise. As listeners we hardly notice this. We typically do not compute all possible well-formed parses of an utterance, even though ambiguities can produce momentary ripples in comprehension. Parsing is hardly ever complete. Rather, we go straight to the one most likely interpretation, given the discourse situation. This is due to powerful context effects and a major computational problem is precisely to model these *top-down* effects in language understanding. So, where linguistic completeness is a main requirement for production modelling, contextual robustness is a major challenge for comprehension modelling. As language users we are experts on both, and so should be the ultimate computational models in psycholinguistics.

I have no doubt that this timely book will find its way into the psycholinguistic classroom and laboratory. Its chapters can also enrich courses in computational linguistics by adding a processing (or *performance*) dimension to the more traditional structural (or *competence*) approach. And more generally, it will be a rich fund of ideas, methods and references for any student or professional in cognitive science who has a core interest in language.

Willem J. M. Levelt
Nijmegen, 1995

Reference

GERNSBACHER, M. A. (Ed.) (1994) *Handbook of Psycholinguistics*, San Diego, CA: Academic Press.

Preface

This book grew out of a need we felt year after year during the preparation of our one-semester course on computational psycholinguistics. Finding relevant research articles in the literature was not a problem. However, having our students read a multitude of articles with different degrees of detail and originating in different research traditions often resulted in misunderstandings on the side of the students and in extra efforts on our side. Therefore, time and again, we conducted an exhaustive and exhausting search for a suitable advanced textbook, but did not come across any that provided a broad overview of psycholinguistics at a more advanced level while at the same time paying special attention to the wide range of computer models in the field. Given this situation, we were delighted when we were asked to edit an advanced textbook. Our need was apparently shared by many other university lecturers in different countries — an impression which was confirmed several times during this project in the form of positive feedback.

From the foregoing it is clear that this book is intended for a specific audience. The book is written for graduate and advanced undergraduate students of psychology, linguistics, and cognitive science. It aims to provide a solid overview of computational psycholinguistics, presented in a scientifically as well as educationally motivated way. The book can serve as a main text in courses on computational psycholinguistics. Alternatively, it can be a recommended or complementary text on computational models in advanced level courses in general psycholinguistics. The modular organization of the book allows a selection of chapters dependent on course load or thematic restrictions. Finally, the book is also aimed at researchers in the different subfields of psycholinguistics who want to broaden their horizons by looking at developments in computer modelling.

The reader should also be aware what the book is *not* intended to be. It is not intended as a primer, but has a level of exposition that presumes some background in psycholinguistics. Nevertheless, we have tried to keep the book readable by defining many specialized terms where they occur in the text and including an extensive subject index at the end. Neither is the book intended as a comprehensive handbook or an encyclopaedia. It focuses on a broad but nevertheless limited range of computational models that are illustrative and representative for particular subdomains. The models have proven their heuristic value for theory development and their relationship to empirical data. Finally, and regrettably, the present book is not a 'how to' book. Although we would very much have liked to include practical exercises and even computer programs, the lack of time and resources in relation to the multitude of models in each subdomain forced us to confine ourselves to a more expository style.

With respect to its coverage, the book deals with language comprehension and production in normal adult humans, covering a large group of subfields in which we point out interrelations and contrasts. At the same time, we consciously leave out several specialized topics in psycholinguistics, notably language acquisition and language disorders. Despite these limitations, we hope to capture three important current trends in psycholinguistics. First, the book underscores the relevance of computer models for psycholinguistic theories. Second, the book takes a multidisciplinary approach, highlighting some of the recent contributions to psycholinguistics by researchers in different fields, in particular psychology, linguistics, cognitive science, and computer science. Third, the book pays attention to the competition between different modelling approaches, in particular the traditional symbol manipulation models, inspired by Artificial Intelligence (AI), and the newer connectionist approach, inspired by the neurophysiology of the human brain.

We have attempted to realize these objectives by editing a volume in three parts. The first part provides some background knowledge on modelling in general and on techniques from AI and connectionism in particular. The second and third parts of the book contain chapters on selected topics in language comprehension and language production, respectively. Each of these chapters focuses on the use of computer simulation models in a particular subdomain of psycholinguistics. The book as a whole thus presents and compares a substantial range of computer models. To ensure that the book is globally coherent, the structure of each individual chapter is more or less similar, consisting of an introduction and a review of empirical evidence, followed by a description, comparison and evaluation of at least two different computer models that cover the subdomain in question.

Many people have given us their support in this project and we feel very grateful to them all. First of all, we thank the authors not only for their willingness to write, and many times rewrite, their chapters to fit our conception of the book, but also for their willingness to review previous versions of other chapters and to comment on the book as a whole. We would also like to express our gratitude — also on behalf of the authors — to the following external reviewers for their precious comments on previous versions of chapters: Ab de Haan, Alain Content, Alice Dijkstra, Alistair Knott, Anne Cutler, Antje Meyer, Arnold Thomassen, Berndt Abb, Carel van Wijk, Carol Fowler, Christina Burani, Colin Brown, Dennis Norris, Don Mitchell, Eduard Hovy, Elisabeth Maier, Frank van der Velde, Gerald Gazdar, Gezinus Wolters, Hans-Leo Teulings, Henk Haarmann, Henk van Jaarsveld, Herbert Schriefers, James McQueen, Jan-Peter de Ruiter, Kai Lebeth, Kathryn Bock, Len Katz, Louis Pols, Matt Crocker, Merrill Garrett, Michael Cohen, Michael Gasser, Nigel Ward, Norbert Reithinger, Pascal van Lieshout,

Patrick Hudson, Peter Hagoort, Peter Wittenburg, Piero Morasso, Richard Sproat, Robert Dale, Robert Hartsuiker, Robert Shillcock, Ruud van der Plaats, Sally Andrews, Theo Vosse, Wido La Hey, Wilbert Spooren, Wim Simons, and Wolfgang Finkler. Last but not least, we thank Carla Huls (University of Nijmegen) for her tremendous help in scrutinizing the prefinal manuscript.

We hope that this intense co-operation has resulted in a book which is informative for students and leads to a better mutual understanding between the researchers who are together paving new ways in the study of human language processing.

Koenraad de Smedt
Ton Dijkstra
Leiden/Nijmegen, 1995

Acknowledgements

The writing and editing of this book as a whole has been financially and administratively supported by the Nijmegen Institute for Cognition and Information (NICI) of the University of Nijmegen and by the Unit of Experimental and Theoretical Psychology of Leiden University.

The research reported in Chapter 4 and the writing of this chapter were supported, in part, by grants from the Public Health Service (PHS R01 NS 20314), the National Science Foundation (BNS 8812728), and the graduate division of the University of California at Santa Cruz.

Part of the work of Chapter 5 was carried out while the author was at the Max-Planck Institute for Psycholinguistics in Nijmegen.

The writing of Chapter 6 was supported by a grant from the NFS-fund for Dutch-French collaboration (Netherlands Organization for Scientific Research NWO, The Netherlands) to the Nijmegen Institute for Cognition and Information (NICI).

The author of Chapter 8 is indebted to Theo Vosse (Leiden University) for numerous helpful discussions and for generating the SLR(1) control table underlying Tables 8.2 and 8.3.

Preparation of Chapter 12 was supported by a grant to the author from the Netherlands Organization for Scientific Research (NWO). It was largely written while the author was a post-doctoral fellow at the Department of Brain and Cognitive Sciences of MIT, Cambridge, USA.

Preparation of Chapter 13 was supported by NIH grant DC–00191. The authors thank Linda May for help with the manuscript. Figures 13.1 and 13.4 are reprinted with permission from Ablex Publishing Corporation. Figures 13.2 and 13.3 are copyright 1986 by the American Psychological Association (APA).

Preparation of Chapter 15 was supported by ESPRIT Project P5204.

Part I
Computer Modelling

Chapter 1

Computer Models in Psycholinguistics: An Introduction

Ton Dijkstra and Koenraad de Smedt

Introduction

In a scientific tradition that is over a century old, psycholinguists have studied human language processing in all its forms, from reading and listening to speaking and writing. Innumerable studies have collected evidence about language perception and production by means of well-established research methods of observation and experimentation. Overviews of this large body of empirical work form the bulk of the material in numerous textbooks and handbooks (Garman, 1990; Taylor and Taylor, 1990; Miller, 1991; Carroll, 1994; Gernsbacher, 1994).

Over the years, many models have been developed to describe language processing in particular subdomains, giving rise to a rough conception of the architecture of the human language processing system and its components. In the last decades, our understanding of the time course of language processing has grown considerably because of the development of more precise on-line measurement techniques which allow the collection of more exact data. However, verbal models, which are only informally specified, have not been able to take full advantage of the technological innovations. For example, verbal models can not easily make quantitative predictions, and they allow only marginal checks with respect to their completeness and consistency, which hampers their comparison to empirical data and their theoretical sophistication, respectively.

It is therefore fortunate that the same technological advances that have resulted in better measurement techniques have also stimulated theoretical developments in the form of computer modelling and simulation. Indeed, recently, the number of psycholinguistic articles that present computer models in combination with empirical and theoretical work has steadily grown. Due to the increasing complexity of linguistic and psycholinguistic theory and thanks to advances in computer science and technology, we have now reached a point where computer models can no longer be ignored as scientific instruments in the study of human language processing. In this chapter, we highlight the general role of computer models in present-day psycholinguistics and give an overview of the models in the remainder of this book.

Computer Models

Cognitive science considers human language processing as a form of information processing. Language perception and production are analyzed conceptually into a number of processing steps which recode representations of the incoming information from one form into another, in order to transform the speech signal into an idea or vice versa (cf. Hillgard and Bower, 1975, p. 431). In the context of a psycholinguistic theory, a *model* can be seen as a precise and operationalized rendering of this type of process for a restricted domain of human language processing.

Even though a model may be described *verbally* in ordinary terms, a precise description often requires a *formal* notation borrowed from mathematics or computer science. Insofar as formal models specify a series of computations (algorithm) in the terminology of information processing, they are called *computational*. Well-specified computational models can be implemented as computer programs, written in a particular programming language, that embody the model's algorithm(s) and can be executed on a computer (see also Pylyshyn, 1986, pp. 88–89). We will call such programs *computer models*. In practice, this proposed distinction between computational models (algorithms) and computer models (implemented programs) is not always made, and the two terms are often used interchangeably.

Models are necessary and useful *simplifications* of the real world, which enhance our understanding of the world by revealing the abstract (and perhaps simple) principles underlying its bewildering complexity. In making the world's opaque nature transparent, modelling provides a kind of X-ray vision. Ideally, models abstract away from those aspects of reality that are circumstantial and irrelevant, while highlighting other aspects that are fundamental in explaining what is under investigation. The simplifying assumptions and abstractions can be taken at various levels. It must be decided which aspects of reality should be represented in terms of the model's architecture, which as representational units or their connections, which as steps in the computational process, which as variables or parameters, and which should simply be left out.

Given adequate input and suitable parameter settings, computer models perform computations, the outcomes of which correspond to predictions in accordance with the underlying theory. For example, presenting a language comprehension model with a word or sentence may result in the identification of that word or the interpretation of that sentence. Furthermore, models can also predict error rates and response latencies in specific experimental paradigms.

The model thus *simulates* part of the real world, i.e., the model's behaviour is intended to be similar to that observed in real-life and experimental conditions. A comparison of simulation results and experimental data can be expected to lead to a revision or further refinement of theoretical insights. This, in turn, leads to further adaptations in the model and perhaps to more experiments, etc. As a result of the introduction of models, the classical empirical cycle is extended to the form as shown in Figure 1.1.

Figure 1.1: The empirical cycle including computer modelling

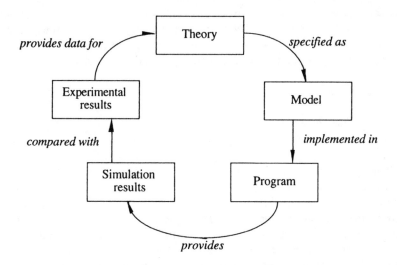

Both computer models and humans can be considered as (more or less complex) information processing systems. Marr (1982) distinguished three levels at which an information processing device can be understood: the level of computational theory, that of representation and algorithm, and that of the hardware implementation. The most general level is a *computational theory* in Marr's sense, specifying what is the goal of the computation, why it is appropriate, and what is the general strategy. With respect to natural language processing, Marr assigns theories of linguistic competence at this level, for example Chomsky's (1980) transformational grammar, because transformations in this theory define abstract mappings between linguistic descriptions, not operations of cognitive processes. Such operations are specified as *algorithms* at the second level. Distinctions such as the relative speed of various algorithms, their sensitivity to inaccuracies in the data, or whether they run in parallel or serially play a role here. We use the term *computational* to refer to the operations at this algorithmic level (as witnessed by the title of this book), rather than to refer to Marr's first level. The third level specifies the *physical realization* of the machine executing the algorithm. The wiring and other physical properties of this machine may put severe restrictions on, for instance, speed and parallelism of realizable algorithms, as well as on memory capacity.

The computational models in this book are mainly described at the theoretical level of representation and algorithm. To be interesting for psycholinguistics, such models may abstract away from the human hardware (or rather, wetware) implementation, but they must still be correct and specific about the algorithm underlying a particular cognitive process and the representations involved in it. Such computational models must also give accounts of cognitive errors and response latencies. In this respect, psycholinguistic models are different from models that are product-oriented and based on technological solutions. Such models (perhaps 'programs' is a better term) do not care about the particular algorithm underlying a linguistic process, as long as input and output representations are optimal. For instance, in reading aloud the newspaper to a blind person, a machine does not need to use the same series of algorithms as a human reader, it just has to perform the task optimally and efficiently.

Simulation

Implementing a model on a computer has practical advantages over only formally specifying a computational model. The automaticity, speed, and precision of computers make it possible to run fast and accurate simulations with the implemented model. In the most general sense, a psycholinguistic computer model is designed to reach an outcome similar to that of human language processing. A sentence parser is meant to process those types of sentence that a human can process under various conditions. For example, whether a sentence can be parsed or not may depend on the number of embedded clauses (see Chapter 8). Going further, the model could be made to predict not only qualitative aspects of parsing behaviour, but also quantitative aspects, for example, that one parsing is preferred over another (ordinal scale) and how strong this preference is (interval scale). Other quantitative simulations concern the success rate of parsing for different sentences and the time needed to parse these (interval scale).

Due to the increasing complexity of scientific theories, simulation is not only practical, but even indispensable in many fields, including psycholinguistics. We list some important uses of computer simulation and their advantages.

First, without computer simulation it is practically impossible to check whether the model is complete and the different parts of the model are internally consistent (in the sense that they do not produce contradictions). It is often impossible to test a verbal model by manually computing its results when it is applied to sample situations, let alone by performing exhaustive tests on a comprehensive set of data. This is even so for formally specified or mathematical (*closed-form*) models, for example when these predict probabilistic behaviour or yield complex response distributions.

Second, simulation may sometimes be essential in the interpretation of empirical results. Simulations can reveal that data which *prima facie* seem to contradict verbal theory may in fact be consistent with it. This case was illustrated in language production by Levelt *et al.* (1991a, b), whose computer implementation of the so-called *standard theory* (assuming two autonomous serial processing stages in production) could be reconciled with what appeared to be conflicting empirical data (see Chapter 13 for a discussion of this issue from a different viewpoint).

Moreover, predictions made on the basis of a verbal theory for different experimental conditions may be fine-tuned by the computer model to the actually used stimulus material. As has been observed already by Cutler (1981), it is becoming more and more difficult for experimenters to run experiments using stimuli that have been controlled for the increasing number of characteristics that are considered relevant. For example, in the domain of word recognition, relevant factors include word frequency, bigram frequency, number of neighbours, frequency of the neighbours, familiarity, concreteness, etc. (see Chapters 5 and 6). If one of these factors is the topic of investigation, the experimenter wants to match the stimulus material with respect to the other factors. However, given the large number of relevant factors, the experimenter must often use less stringent criteria on stimulus matching than she would have liked to, simply because the optimal word material does not exist in the language. This results in stimulus material that may to some extent be suboptimal or noisy, and in experimental data that will deviate to an unknown extent from what would have occurred under ideal circumstances.

In this case, computer simulation can be applied as a tool to evaluate the effects of variability in the material that is uncontrolled for or unavoidable. Suppose the experimenter adheres to the assumptions on the architecture and process of visual word recognition that are incorporated in the Interactive Activation (IA) model (discussed in Chapter 6), and that the model is run with the stimuli selected for the test conditions. If the assumptions underlying the model are correct, then different stimulus conditions should result in the differential behaviour that was expected on the basis of the verbal theory, since the model is assumed to be a specification of this theory. For example, in a very precise way the model takes into account how bigram frequency, target frequency, and frequency and number of neighbours interact. The actual pattern of simulation results can therefore be considered to reflect more precise predictions *tuned to this particular stimulus material* than those made on the basis of the verbal theory (cf., Van Heuven, Dijkstra, and Grainger, in prep.). If only a verbal model were available, it would have been impossible to obtain predictions that are corrected for the inherent biases in the stimulus material.

Even if the model's predictions indicate that the stimulus material deviates in some respects from the theoretically motivated criteria, later collected empirical data can still be compared to the model's performance. Though the material does not reflect the theoretically distinct dimensions completely, the results of the simulation may still be considered to be predictions based on the cognitive architecture and processes assumed by the theory and implemented in the model.

Third, modelling not only results in predictions of linguistic behaviour under empirically known conditions, taking into account many different aspects of the stimulus material simultaneously, but even under previously unknown conditions. This may lead to ideas for new experiments which can then check the predictions made by the simulations. As an example, consider a semantic priming situation in which a target word (e.g., *nurse*) is presented at different temporal intervals (Stimulus Onset Asynchronies or SOAs) after a prime stimulus (e.g., *doctor*). When fit to empirical data for a particular range of SOAs, a computer model can predict target latencies for an as yet untested SOA between prime and target. The heuristic value of computer models is further enhanced by the use of computer models as practical tools that support research by visualizing processes and representations (cf., Lakoff and Johnson, 1980; Gentner and Stevens, 1983; Chandrasekaran, Hari Narayanan and Iwasaki, 1993). In the earlier example, a suitable new SOA might be suggested by examining a visual display of the simulation results for already tested or simulated SOAs.

Fourth, even manipulations which cannot be performed in a direct way on human subjects are amenable to simulation. For example, one may simulate successive degrees of lesions to a computer model to invoke effects of aphasia (e.g., Patterson, Seidenberg and McClelland, 1989; Haarmann and Kolk, 1991). Although obvious ethical considerations make the replication of such manipulations in an experimental way impossible, simulation results can nevertheless be compared to observable facts ('nature's own experiments') in the real world. A similar role for simulation is common in other scientific fields, for instance in astronomy, where it is impossible to experiment by manipulating real galaxies, but where computer simulations of galaxy formation are compared to observed galaxies in different stages.

These advantages of computer modelling are widely discussed and are obviously shared by the authors and editors of this book. We hope that, by studying the various computer models described in this book, the reader will be infected by our enthusiasm and become convinced of the exciting possibilities offered by simulation studies. However, to warn for potential pitfalls in modelling, we now address the difficult issue of *how to specify* a computational model.

Model Specification

Even though computational models are becoming increasingly complex, with many different parameters and constructs at different hierarchical levels, they still simplify human behaviour to a tremendous degree, not in the least because simulation tests of the model are subject to practical and theoretical limitations. These simplifications become apparent if we compare the architecture and behaviour of a particular model to what is known about the cognitive subsystems serving a similar purpose in humans. The organization of the model reflects the choices and restrictions made by the modeller with respect to the representation of reality in terms of (at least) structure, process, task, and resources and strategies (cf., McCloskey, 1991).

Structural choices in computer models are made with respect to input and output *representations* of messages, as well as to internal representations within the processing system. Some of the choices are willingly made simplifications that help to avoid irrelevant complexity ('nuisance factors') in the model. It may not be very useful, for example, to incorporate letter features within a model that focuses on general aspects of text representation, despite the observation that changing a single letter feature could make a difference to the meaning of the word, sentence, and even the text it belongs to.

Sometimes structural simplifications are forced because not enough is known about human cognitive architecture to provide the model with empirically motivated and thus 'realistic' representations. Some representational choices cannot be avoided because either the output or the input of the model cannot be directly observed. For example, we cannot directly observe the semantic representations that are the product of language comprehension or that lie at the origin of language production, so that models at these levels must use abstract, 'invented' (even if plausible) semantic representations.

More generally, in order to be able to operate at all, computer models require *ad hoc* solutions to deal with the underspecification of less central parts of the model. Such underspecifications may become painfully apparent especially during the model's implementation phase, and remedies to this problem may to some extent depend on the characteristics of the chosen computer environment. One must beware of theoretically unmotivated 'patchwork' since the implemented solutions may affect the model's performance.

To summarize this point, most current computational models can be criticized in that they incorporate only a crude and possibly disfigured replica of some central part of human cognitive architecture, while they disregard less salient aspects.

In this respect, *process* simplifications are even more apparent. Most available computer models are static in the sense that they tend to focus on the end-products of processing (Parisi and Burani, 1988). Even when models have an explicit architecture, many are still like black boxes in the sense that they do not allow the *on-line* examination of the developing linguistic process they are meant to mimic. Moreover, since we often cannot precisely know the input or output of human processing, we do not even know where certain processes start and end.

This indicates how difficult — if not impossible — it is to distinguish cognitively motivated from technologically motivated (e.g., pure AI) or behaviourist accounts of input–output relationships (cf., Pylyshyn, 1989; Anderson, 1983, 1991). However, the currently available experimental and clinical evidence from different disciplines concerning human information processing constrains the number of possible human mental architectures in many more ways than product-oriented approaches take into account. Also, the cognitive relationship between input and output representations is so complex that modelling is indispensable as a powerful heuristic means to chart potential intermediate mental processes, representations, and knowledge sources.

Furthermore, the time-course of the mental process and the informational pathways taken depend on the representational units in the model and the way they are linked up. Consider a network model in which two parameters regulate the amount of the forward and backward spreading activation between representations of a letter and the word in which it occurs (cf., Chapter 6). When a model includes these or other parameters with a variable strength, a particular implemented version of a verbally or formally specified model is in fact but one possible realization of a general class of models. It is possible that some parameter settings may result in model behaviour that is not only quantitatively but also qualitatively different from that emerging with other settings. For several models found in the literature, this has led to the wise decision to restrict empirical investigations to one particular model with a fixed set of parameters and parameter settings, or alternatively to experimentally vary these parameter settings (cf., Jacobs and Grainger, 1992).

Task specifications are unfortunately often lacking in computer models. The input-output associations established by computer models are seldom explicitly linked to particular tasks. Little is known about which task simplifications can be allowed in a computer model without seriously deforming the similarity between model and human processing. Whereas the human mind is characterized by flexibility and seems to have at its disposal complex task-dependent identification and decision processes, most models at best embody a simple decision process that operates in the same rigid manner in different tasks on a common task-independent identification process (cf., Jacobs and Grainger, 1994). Admittedly, the task dependence of human language processing is still an open issue. The question is whether, for instance, human syntactic parsing operates differently depending on the task, which may vary from 'deep' understanding to skimming, correcting and reading aloud. It would be useful if modellers would give standard specifications for which particular tasks their models are appropriate and to which extent they believe the models are generalizable to other task situations.

Human flexibility is also prominent in issues relating to *mental resources* and *strategic decisions*. Very few of the current models account for attentional constraints on information processing, e.g., limitations in working memory capacity in relation to mental processing load. In addition, a subject's resort to particular *strategies* in a particular task may sometimes be related to such resource limitations as well, or may in other cases be related to attempts to obtain an over-all benefit in task performance (Stone and Van Orden, 1993). However, such extraordinary flexibility of subjects is unaccounted for by practically all models. Recent approaches to language processing have just started to pay attention to these issues, sometimes in relation to interindividual differences in task performance (e.g., King and Just, 1991; Just and Carpenter, 1992). One interesting idea that has been brought forward is to implement strategic control as a form of control over parameter settings. Even though paying attention to strategic factors may currently seem to require a considerable investment of modelling efforts, 'rigorous treatments of strategy may, in the long run, simplify rather than complicate the big picture' (Stone and Van Orden, 1993, p. 771).

In the foregoing, we have elaborated on the choices the modelling researcher must make during implementation for several reasons. Each choice with respect to structure, process, and other characteristics of the model not only constrains and co-determines the actual behaviour of a complete and operative model, but also necessarily implies a simplification of the real world. Furthermore, as we shall see in more detail below, each choice can be used in the process of evaluating the model. If the model's behaviour is not sufficiently similar to the empirical data, this could be due to incorrect assumptions with respect to fundamental model characteristics such as the model's architecture (e.g., interactivity, or lack of it) and the representations it uses (cf., Lachter and Bever's, 1988, and Besner *et al.*'s, 1990, criticisms concerning the use of Wickeltriples in models of language acquisition and word recognition). Trying to improve the fit between the model's behaviour and empirical data by fiddling with parameter settings may not be as illuminative or useful as examining the simplifying choices that are made with respect to different model components.

Furthermore, the modeller will ideally not build the model just to account for one data set, but will have an open eye for the research context and potential future developments. Keeping this broader perspective in mind, a modeller should, from the very beginning, take into account those aspects that will allow generalization to different materials, tasks, and subjects in future research. A model with many simplifications may be very useful on a small-scale, but in order to generalize it while keeping the same underlying explanatory constructs it may be necessary to improve the description of structural, process, task, resource, or strategic aspects.

In our opinion the advantages of computer models far outweigh the model design problems we have just signalled. Computer models are tools, and tools can be useful even if they are not perfect, as long as we remain aware of their limitations. The remainder of this book therefore pays attention not only to the achievements, but also the shortcomings of computational psycholinguistic models.

Model Evaluation

There are several criteria by which to judge the adequacy of a model. One obviously essential step of model evaluation lies in the comparison of the model's results with appropriate *empirical data*. But as already hinted at above, such a comparison can only be considered as a rather weak test of the model if the empirical results were previously known and the model was constructed to account for those data in the first place. In particular, models that try to fit their results with the help of many parameters may amount to rather trivial views of mental processing. Researchers in the field of simulation are familiar with the saying that 'a good scientist can draw an elephant with three parameters, and with four he can tie a knot in its tail' (Miller, Galanter and Pribram, 1960, p. 182). A stronger test consists in having an already existing model produce predictions for untested conditions. Subsequent empirical tests can then falsify or verify these predictions. Though pure model predictions for new stimulus material are seldom made (see Chapter 12 for a notable exception in the domain of lemma retrieval), researchers do often check if their models generalize to data sets which were not taken into account during model construction.

We would like to point out that in an optimal situation, the stimulus material tested in the experiments would be nominally identical to that used in the computer simulations. In this case, the results of the experiments can be related to the model behaviour without making the implicit assumption that differences in simulation and experiment are not due to unknown stimulus differences. So, in practice, models and experiments impose restrictions on each other. We recommend building new models in combination with planning experiments, while making sure the models can handle the stimulus material to be used in experiments. This approach seems to ensure an optimal coordination between, on the one hand, the top-down, hypothetico–deductive theory development which is typically enforced by the modelling effort and, on the other hand, the bottom-up development of theory on the basis of experimental data.

Clearly, a model may try to account for *multiple* aspects of human language behaviour at once, and may thus be evaluated on several dimensions. For instance, learning connectionist models typically include a training phase before testing the output. If the language learning process is assumed to be similar to that in human subjects, this provides an extra criterion to evaluate the model, in addition to the evaluation of the learned behaviour. Therefore, when models become more complex, there may on the one hand be more ways to 'solve' deviations with respect to the data, but on the other hand the more complex models may offer more dimensions to be tested and evaluated upon. When the model's performance range is enlarged, the chance that there is real convergence between the computational model and human processing may also be enlarged.

In scientific practice, models are often evaluated also in a *model to model comparison*. But the comparison of several models for the same domain should be done carefully, taking into account the specific simplifications and assumptions in each of the models. In addition, models often cut the cognitive pie in very different pieces, even when they relate to the same subdomain, so that even input and output are often hardly comparable.

A general set of evaluation criteria is discussed by Jacobs and Grainger (1994) under the headings of *descriptive and explanatory adequacy*, *simplicity*, *generality*, and *falsifiability*. These criteria, originally conceived for evaluating models of visual word recognition, can be usefully applied to computer models of psycholinguistic processes at large. In addition to these criteria which relate models to the empirical data they wish to simulate, Jacobs and Grainger also mention other criteria such as *modifiability*, *equivalence class*, *completeness*, and *research generativity* of models. The main motivation behind this last set of criteria is that models that can more easily be tested or changed, or that are based on more abstract principles, should be preferable to others. We refer the reader to this article for detailed discussion and confine ourselves to a few remarks, starting with descriptive adequacy.

We consider a model to be *descriptively adequate* in a qualitative way, if the model, despite several simplifications and abstractions, nevertheless retains essential properties of the human cognitive processing system and the representations it uses. This suggests a model evaluation in terms of the implementation choices previously described. However, this reveals an implicit conflict: on the one hand, a simple model is preferable to a complex one in order to be more easily controllable and to avoid Bonini's paradox ('the simulation turns out to be no easier to understand than the real-world processes it is supposed to illuminate'). On the other hand, a good model must retain enough of the essential complexity of human behaviour. We would consider a model's input representation to be sufficient and acceptable if it incorporates just the right amount and kind of simplification compared to the signals a human uses as input, while the model still results in the same behaviour as that of the humans. However, in the current state of psycholinguistics, it is very hard to define 'the right amount and kind of simplification' or even 'the same behaviour'. As a rough guideline, models that are based upon widely accepted empirical assumptions are preferable to models that make *ad hoc* assumptions.

However, Jacobs and Grainger (1994) use the term *descriptive adequacy* of a model in a more quantitative way, referring to the degree of accuracy with which a model can predict a data set. This, by the way, is unfortunately often the main or only criterion used in practice. Jacobs and Grainger point out that while verbal models should be formulated to allow predictions at the level of an ordinal scale, algorithmic models should enable us to compute goodness-of-fit indices at an interval scale. These predictions of course depend on how well units on a model scale correspond to those in reality. For instance, activation values (see Chapter 3) in the model may be transformed into response probabilities, or time measurements in terms of the model's processing cycles may be transformed into reaction times.

While descriptive adequacy amounts to an 'in depth' criterion, models can also be judged with respect to their 'breadth' in terms of *generalizability* to other stimulus sets, tasks, and response measures. Sure enough, models that are more generally applicable are often more useful than models operating in a restricted domain, but benefits in generality often bring about costs in terms of depth of analysis or in terms of model complexity. A tough problem in model comparison here is that, even though we sometimes count the number of free parameters in determining a model's goodness-of-fit, we do not yet have a good means to evaluate the implicit 'theoretical degrees of freedom' which a model consumes in terms of aspects of its architecture (cf., Newell *et al.*, 1989, p. 126; Massaro and

Cohen, 1991). Some first suggestions on how to obtain a 'simplicity rating' for computer models are given by Jacobs and Grainger (1994).

Approaching model evaluation from a practical perspective, we suggested to the authors of Parts II and III to keep in mind a number of aspects of the computer models in their discussion. First, relating to the section on model specification are the following aspects: the quality of the model input compared to that of human language; the psychological validity of the processing assumptions; the types of internal representation used during processing; the quality of the model output compared to that of humans; the assumed types of decision process. Second, relating to the current section on model evaluation are the following: the coverage of the available experimental data, e.g., the range of data sets accounted for (generalizability); and the goodness-of-fit (descriptive adequacy). Third, models should also be evaluated in terms of the types of problem that remain as yet unsolved, which may lead to suggestions for improvements in future research.

Organization of the Book

This book is organized in three parts. Part I is about computational modelling as a new approach to psycholinguistics in general. Part II discusses models in the various subdomains of language comprehension, and Part III does the same for language production.

Overview of Part I: Modelling Paradigms

Part I consists of three chapters of which the current introductory chapter is the first. The two remaining chapters each deal with a broad group of paradigms for cognitive modelling.

In Chapter 2, Daelemans and De Smedt introduce the paradigms of mainstream Artificial Intelligence (AI), based on symbolic representations of mental states and concepts. Computation in an AI model is driven by an algorithm that manipulates symbols and is itself also symbolically specified. The chapter describes a number of formalisms for the representation of knowledge, including semantic or associative networks, frames, inheritance mechanisms, marker passing, conceptual dependency structures and conceptual graphs, production systems and logic, as well as various types of grammar.

Chapter 3 by Murre and Goebel introduces the connectionist approach, which is inspired by ideas of how the human brain works, even though the majority of the resulting neural network models in psycholinguistics do not make neurophysiological claims. The chapter distinguishes between *localist* and *distributed* neural networks. In the former, also referred to as Interactive Activation (IA) networks, concepts to be modelled (including linguistic notions) are represented by single network nodes, as in associative networks, and the weights on connections are usually preprogrammed. Distributed models, also called Parallel Distributed Processing (PDP) models, are based on networks in which concepts are associated with activation patterns over several nodes simultaneously and the system itself can often learn to categorize and generalize. Connectionist models in general are characterized by the fact that regular behaviour arises not from hard rules, but from the interaction of many small influences. Among other things, Chapter 3 describes various network architectures and system dynamics, and a number of widely-used learning rules, such as the Hebb-rule, the delta rule, and backpropagation.

The Language User Framework

Parts II and III discuss prominent computer models, organized by the subdomains in psycholinguistics to which they belong. Given the limited scope of this book, no attempt at completeness has been made, neither with respect to the subdomains nor with respect to modelling techniques. In particular, accounts of language learning and language disorders are limited in this book. Nevertheless, we hope to present a sufficiently wide range of representative computational models to give an indication of their importance for psycholinguistics. Furthermore, each chapter in these parts has roughly the same structure, proceeding from an overview of basic concepts and phenomena to empirical and theoretical work and then to a number of computer models, which are explained in some detail and evaluated.

As an overall framework to subdivide psycholinguistics in convenient sections, we use the language user framework proposed by Dijkstra and Kempen (1994, 1983; see also Levelt, 1989) and depicted in Figure 1.2. Like the human body which comprises a number of organs that each have a different function, the language user system can be conceived as consisting of functionally different mechanisms (cf., Chomsky, 1980, pp. 38-9). Thus, to understand human language processing, we distinguish a number of subsystems or (in loose terminology) *modules*, each of which deals with a specific subtask (see also Stone and Van Orden, 1993). For example, the task of the Word Recognition subsystem is to identify morphemes or words that can be used by the Parser to construct a syntactic representation of a sentence. The Word Recognition system and the Parser make use of specialized linguistic knowledge stored in a specific part of the language user system (e.g., the Mental Lexicon and the Grammar). Figure 1.2 shows the various components or mechanisms of the language user framework grouped around the knowledge sources containing representations of linguistic units and rules.

Figure 1.2: The language user framework which serves to organize the book

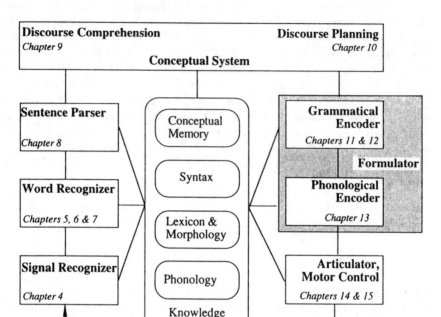

The language user framework can be subdivided in several ways. First, a distinction can be made between the linguistic knowledge that is stored in long-term memory (middle of the model), and the mechanisms (situated at the edges) that use that knowledge to transform the incoming or outgoing representations into new formats. To some extent, this distinction corresponds to the traditional subdivision of linguistics and psycholinguistics.

Second, the model contains modules for both language perception (left) and language production (right), and makes the simplifying assumption that these employ representations from a common database, even though the processes underlying production and perception may necessarily be very different (see Zwitserlood, 1994, for a recent analysis of the viability of this position with respect to phonological representations of lexical form; also see Foreword).

Third, the framework contains (horizontal) layers that roughly correspond to linguistic units of different sizes: letter–phoneme, morpheme–word, sentence, and discourse. To these units correspond different linguistic subdisciplines: phonetics and phonology, morphology and lexicology, syntax, and semantics and pragmatics.

The framework purposely leaves open the complicated issue of whether information between modules flows unidirectionally or bidirectionally between modules, e.g., only from speech signal to concept in language comprehension or with feedback. In fact, some researchers may stress the interactions between different components to such an extent that they subdivide the language user system in a different way. Some may even find the whole enterprise of specifying modules within the linguistic system futile. However, the language user framework offers a convenient classification to structure Parts II and III of this book. For this reason, Figure 1.2 indicates the mapping between modules and chapters.

The models discussed in Parts II and III are for the most part psychologically inspired models that are not only well-known in their domain but describe a special, restricted set of phenomena that have attracted attention from many researchers. For example, the IA-model for visual word recognition (Chapter 6) is discussed not only because it is a 'classic' model in its subdomain, but also because it makes psychologically interesting predictions with respect to the influence of competing word candidates on target recognition. Other thematic choices include the discussion of syntactic preferences in sentence understanding (Chapter 8), incremental processing in sentence production (Chapter 11), and speech errors in phonological encoding (Chapter 13). In other cases, the authors chose particular models in a domain because they were the only models available, even though these models currently have little psychological motivation. This was the case, for instance, in the area of text planning (Chapter 10), where most available models are mainly product-oriented. In still other cases, the authors chose the only implemented models that are currently available for a specific task, and which often happened to be their own models. A case in point is the modelling of handwriting (Chapter 15).

Overview of Part II: Language Comprehension

In Chapter 4, Massaro presents two well-known computer models in the area of speech perception and evaluates these with respect to a number of prominent factors that affect processing. These models are his own Fuzzy Logic Model of Perception (FLMP) and the IA-model TRACE. The models are discussed in the light of the question of which perceptual units should be considered most important in speech perception. Massaro argues that the syllable is a likely candidate representation.

While the TRACE model is considered at the sublexical level in Chapter 4, it is reconsidered by Frauenfelder in Chapter 5 from the perspective of word recognition. Frauenfelder systematically compares the architecture and (simulation) behaviour of TRACE with that of two influential verbal models of auditory word recognition, COHORT I and COHORT II, and with SHORTLIST, a hybrid connectionist model. Empirical evidence and theoretical considerations are presented to evaluate the different ways the models handle the positive and negative effects of competing lexical candidates in the time-course of auditory word recognition and the way they select the final candidate.

Many of the same issues with respect to representational units, interactivity, and competitor effects return in Chapter 6 on visual word recognition. Grainger and Dijkstra give an overview of the empirical literature in search for relevant constraints on computer models. Two implemented computer models are described next, the IA-model of McClelland and Rumelhart and Seidenberg and McClelland's more recent PDP-model. Even though both are connectionist models, comparing them is not easy, since they differ on several dimensions, particularly with respect to the experimental tasks to which they have been applied.

While the models described by Grainger and Dijkstra can handle only the recognition of morphologically monomorphemic words, Baayen and Schreuder in Chapter 7 consider models that deal with morphologically complex words. The chapter gives a brief but useful overview of morphology, and proceeds to the discussion of linguistically oriented models, taking into account linguistic considerations, as well as psycholinguistic models that take empirical evidence into account. Apart from a discussion of verbal psycholinguistic models (such as the AAM and MRM), the chapter pays attention to the recently implemented connectionist PDP-model of Gasser.

In Chapter 8, the book's attention moves up to the sentence level. Considering parsing from a more general psychological point of view than is usually done, Kempen discusses the need for parallel, incremental, and interactive sentence processing. Several linguistic and psycholinguistic parsers that have been proposed in the last decades are described and compared, among which Augmented Transition Networks (ATNs), shift-reduce parsers, Marcus's PARSIFAL, race-based parsers and, finally, Kempen and Vosses's Unification Space model. Kempen concludes his chapter by stating that he expects a future perspective for dynamically oriented parsers, perhaps in the guise of connectionist models.

Competition between AI-based linguistic models and connectionist based psycholinguistics models can also be observed in Chapter 9, in which Garnham contrasts Kintsch's construction-integration model of discourse comprehension with the connectionist model of text comprehension by Sharkey. The models are discussed after a review of theoretical constraints and empirical findings about the interrelationship of sentences with respect to inference processes, anaphorical expressions, and nonliteral meaning. Both implemented models are discussed in the light of the mental models theory of discourse.

Overview of Part III: Language Production

Both Chapter 9 on discourse understanding and Chapter 10 on discourse planning are oriented more towards the visual modality (written text) than towards the spoken modality (conversation). However, in the area of discourse planning, the existing computer models are to a much larger extent application-oriented, as witnessed, for instance, by a system that answers questions about ships in a naval data base. In Chapter 10, Andriessen, De Smedt, and Zock review a number of psycholinguistic constraints on models of discourse planning, and then discuss three models that are application-oriented but show an increasingly psycholinguistic orientation: the TEXT schema-based model of McKeown, Hovy's RST-based text structurer, and a recent model of Moore and Paris on planning text for advisory dialogues.

In Chapter 11, De Smedt discusses how speakers compose their sentences in language production, a process technically called 'grammatical encoding', paying special attention to the incremental (piecemeal) syntactic construction of sentences. Interesting theoretical relationships can be found between this chapter and those on parsing and discourse planning. De Smedt first considers conceptual, lexical, and syntactic factors that affect the construction of sentence frames, and then discusses a number of computational models for incremental sentence generation: the AI-based models IPG, IPF, and POPEL, and a connectionist model called FIG.

The construction of sentence frames that De Smedt describes goes hand in hand with the selection of word material at an abstract level called the *lemma*. In Chapter 12, Roelofs gives an account on lemma retrieval in which he discusses a number of different views on how particular lexical items can be found for the conceptual content that needs to be uttered. He describes his own implemented computer model, a hybrid model which incorporates symbolic notions (such as flagging of current nodes), together with mathematical notions (application of a hazard rate) and connectionist notions (spreading activation). Support for the model is provided by reviewing empirical data.

In Chapter 13, Dell and Juliano describe two computational approaches that account for the process of phonological encoding, which is the attribution of a speech form to retrieved lemmas. Giving the verbal symbolic standard theory as background, Dell's well-known spreading activation model is presented and compared with a recent learning distributed connectionist model. In this chapter, the authors focus on speech error evidence as a major empirical data source for modelling phonological encoding.

In Chapter 14, Boves and Cranen consider the last stage in language production, that of articulation. After explaining the basic concepts of speech articulation and speech acoustics, they describe how the actual execution of articulation commands by the speech apparatus can be captured by Articulatory Synthesis (as implemented by the *task-dynamics* model) and Terminal Analog Synthesis. The chapter makes clear we still have only rather limited knowledge about the intricacies of the speech production system. Furthermore, this chapter is to some extent complementary to that on Speech Perception by Massaro. For example, the authors also discuss the issue of what are the basic unit(s) in speech, but approach it from a more phonetically oriented angle. While Massaro argues for an important role of the syllable in speech perception, Boves and Cranen pay much attention to phonemic and subphonemic types of representation in speech production.

In Chapter 15, the last chapter of the book, Schomaker and Van Galen also consider the last stage of language production, but in the written mode, dealing with the hand movements in the process of connected, cursive handwriting. The major empirical issues in this domain, often neglected in textbooks on psycholinguistics, are first discussed within a general framework that is remarkably compatible with the language user framework presented earlier in the current chapter. In the light of this framework, the chapter explains an implemented symbolic model (named the Cursive Connections Grammar) that simulates the process of concatenating cursive characters. Next comes a discussion of two variants of a connectionist model that focuses on the actual trajectory formation (articulation) of individual letters. Though these models differ to some extent in focus and in content from the other psycholinguistic models presented in earlier chapters, similar issues arise with respect to the modelling of discrete or continuous time and value dimensions.

To conclude, the models in this book are samples stemming from different traditions. Traditional AI-models have stimulated computational modelling from the 1960s onwards. Linguistic information processing is specified in AI in terms of symbol manipulation (Chapter 2). From the 1980s onward, the AI-models have been getting tough competition from connectionist models, which consider information processing in terms of a brain-based metaphor (Chapter 3). The clash between these two types of model is evident in sometimes fierce discussions (cf., Rumelhart and McClelland, 1986, MacWhinney and Leinbach, 1991, Plunkett and Marchman, 1991, vs. Lachter and Bever, 1988, Pinker and Mehler, 1989, Pinker and Prince, 1988; Fodor and Pylyshyn, 1988, Fodor and McLaughlin, 1990, vs. McClelland, 1993, Rumelhart, 1989, Seidenberg, 1994, Smolensky, 1988; Seidenberg and McClelland, 1989, 1990, vs. Besner *et al.*, 1990, and Coltheart *et al.*, 1993; Levelt *et al.*, 1991a, 1991b, vs. Dell and O'Seaghda, 1991; and, to some extent, Massaro, 1988, 1989, Massaro and Cohen, 1991, vs. McClelland, 1991, McClelland and Elman, 1986). In this book we do not take sides, but merely report on the achievements of individual models in particular subdomains.

As a consequence of the confrontation of radically different paradigms for human cognitive processing, the field has become sensitized to new creative modelling approaches that go beyond the established ones. Hybrid models are starting to appear that combine advantages and characteristics of two or more approaches (Lehnert, 1991; Gutknecht, 1992; Stone, in press). In this book, the number of such models is still rather limited. For example, the non-decompositional spreading activation model in Chapter 12 combines features from the classical symbolic, mathematical, and connectionist paradigms. Another example is the Unification Space model in Chapter 8, which incorporates a symbolic grammar, but also makes use of a new connectionist optimization method (simulated annealing) within the framework of an unexpected metaphor (that of chemistry and physics). In the literature at large, more and more models start to appear that deviate from the mainstream, describing cognitive and psycholinguistic models from as yet less familiar viewpoints such as adaptive dynamic systems theory (see, e.g., Grossberg, 1980, on resonance; Smolensky, 1986, on harmony theory; and Van Orden and Goldinger, in press, on covariant learning) and genetic algorithms (Holland, 1975).

Almost a century ago, brave pioneers contrived all sorts of amazing contraptions in an attempt to fulfill man's desire to fly. Perhaps, in our age, at the brink of the twenty-first century, computer models are the devices that stimulate man's imagination. As before, of all the amazing models that are devised, only time can tell which will fall and which will fly.

References

ANDERSON, J. R. (1983) *The Architecture of Cognition*, Cambridge, MA: Harvard University Press.

ANDERSON, J. R. (1991) *The Adaptive Character of Thought*, Hillsdale, NJ: Lawrence Erlbaum.

BESNER, D., TWILLEY, L., McCANN, R. S. and SEERGOBIN, K. (1990) 'On the association between connectionism and data: Are a few words necessary?', *Psychological Review*, 97, pp. 432–46.

CARROLL, D. W. (1994) *Psychology of Language*, Belmont, CA: Brooks/Cole.

CHANDRASEKARAN, B., HARI NARAYANAN, N. and IWASAKI, Y. (1993) 'Reasoning with diagrammatic representations', *AI Magazine*, 14, 2, pp. 49–56.

CHOMSKY, N. (1980) *Rules and Representations*, Oxford: Blackwell.

COLTHEART, M., CURTIS, B., ATKINS, P. and HALLER, M. (1993) 'Models of reading aloud: Dual-route and parallel-distributed-processing approaches', *Psychological Review*, 100, pp. 589–608.

CUTLER, A. (1981) 'Making up materials is a confounded nuisance, or: Will we be able to run any psycholinguistic experiments at all in 1990?', *Cognition*, 10, pp. 65–70.

DELL, G. S. and O'SEAGHDA, P. G. (1991) 'Mediated and convergent lexical priming in language production: A comment on Levelt *et al.* (1991)', *Psychological Review*, 98, pp. 604–14.

DIJKSTRA, A. and KEMPEN, G. (1984) *Taal in Uitvoering*, Groningen, The Netherlands: Wolters-Noordhoff.

DIJKSTRA, A. and KEMPEN, G. (1993) *Taalpsychologie*, Groningen, The Netherlands: Wolters-Noordhoff.

FODOR, J. A. and McLAUGHLIN, B. (1990) 'Connectionism and the problem of systematicity: why Smolensky's solution doesn't work', *Cognition*, 35, pp. 183–204.

FODOR, J. A. and PYLYSHYN, Z. (1988) 'Connectionism and cognitive architecture: A critical analysis', *Cognition*, 28, pp. 3–71.

GARMAN, M. (1990) *Psycholinguistics*, Cambridge: Cambridge University Press.

GENTNER, D. and STEVENS, A. L. (Eds.), (1983) *Mental Models*, Hillsdale, NJ: Lawrence Erlbaum.

GERNSBACHER, M. A. (Ed.) (1994) *Handbook of Psycholinguistics*, San Diego, CA: Academic Press.

GROSSBERG, S. (1980) 'How does the brain build a cognitive code?', *Psychological Review*, 87, pp. 1–51.

GUTKNECHT, M. (1992) 'The "Postmodern Mind": Hybrid models of cognition', *Connection Science*, 4, pp. 339–64.

HAARMANN, H. J. and KOLK, H. H. J. (1991) 'A computer model of the temporal course of agrammatic sentence understanding: The effects of variation in severity and sentence complexity', *Cognitive Science*, 15, pp. 49–87.

HILLGARD, E. R. and BOWER, G. H. (1975) *Theories of Learning*, Englewood Cliffs, NJ: Prentice Hall.

HOLLAND, J. H. (1975) *Adaptation in Natural and Artificial Systems*, Ann Arbor, MI: University of Michigan Press.

JACOBS, A. M. and GRAINGER, J. (1992) 'Testing a semi-stochastic variant of the interactive activation model in different word recognition experiments', *Journal of Experimental Psychology: Human Perception and Performance*, 18, pp. 1174–88.

JACOBS, A. M. and GRAINGER, J. (1994) 'Models of visual word recognition: Sampling the state of the art', *Journal of Experimental Psychology: Human Perception and Performance*, 20, pp. 1311–34.

JUST, M. A. and CARPENTER, P. A. (1992) 'A capacity theory of comprehension: Individual differences in working memory', *Psychological Review*, 99, pp. 122–49.

KING, J. and JUST, M. A. (1991) 'Individual differences in syntactic processing: The role of working memory', *Journal of Memory and Language*, 30, pp. 580–602.

LACHTER, J. and BEVER, T. (1988) 'The relation between linguistic structure and associative theories of language learning: A constructive critique of some connectionist learning models', *Cognition*, 28, pp. 195–247.

LAKOFF, G. and JOHNSON, M. (1980) *Metaphors We Live By*, Chicago: University of Chicago Press.

LEHNERT, W. (1991) 'Symbolic/subsymbolic sentence analysis — Exploiting the best of two worlds', in BARNDEN, J. A. and POLLACK, J. B. (Eds) *High-Level Connectionist Models*, Norwood, NJ: Ablex.

LEVELT, W. J. M. (1989) *Speaking: From Intention to Articulation*, Cambridge, MA: MIT Press.

LEVELT, W. J. M., SCHRIEFERS, H., VORBERG, D., MEYER, A. S., PECHMANN, Th. and HAVINGA, J. (1991a) 'The time course of lexical access in speech production: A study of picture naming', *Psychological Review*, 98, pp. 122–42.

LEVELT, W. J. M., SCHRIEFERS, H., VORBERG, D., MEYER, A. S., PECHMANN, Th. and HAVINGA, J. (1991b) 'Normal and deviant lexical processing: Reply to Dell and O'Seaghda (1991)', *Psychological Review*, 98, pp. 122–42.

MACWHINNEY, B. and LEINBACH, J. (1991) 'Implementations are not conceptualizations: Revising the verb learning model', *Cognition*, 40, pp. 121–57.

MARR, D. (1982) *Vision: A Computational Investigation into the Human Representation and Processing of Visual Information*, New York: Freeman.

MASSARO, D. W. (1988) 'Some criticisms of connectionist models of human performance', *Journal of Memory and Language*, 27, pp. 213–34.

MASSARO, D. W. (1989) 'Testing between the TRACE model and the Fuzzy Logical Model of Perception', *Cognitive Psychology*, 21, pp. 398–421.

MASSARO, D. W. and COHEN, M. M. (1991) 'Integration versus interactive activation: The joint influence of stimulus and context in perception', *Cognitive Psychology*, 23, pp. 558–614.

MCCLELLAND, J. L. (1991) 'Stochastic interactive processes and the effect of context on perception', *Cognitive Psychology*, 23, pp. 1–44.

MCCLELLAND, J. L. (1993) 'Toward a theory of information processing in graded, random, and interactive networks', in MEYER, D. E. and KORNBLUM, (Eds), *Attention and Performance XIV: Synergies in Experimental Psychology, Artificial Intelligence, and Cognitive Neuroscience*, Cambridge, MA: MIT Press, pp. 655–88.

MCCLELLAND, J. L. and ELMAN, J. L. (1986) 'The TRACE model of speech perception', *Cognitive Psychology*, 18, pp. 1–86.

MCCLOSKEY, M. (1991) 'Networks and theories: The place of connectionism in cognitive science', *Psychological Science*, 2, pp. 387–95.

MILLER, G. (1991) *The Science of Words*, New York: Freeman & Company.

MILLER, G. A., GALANTER, E. and PRIBRAM, K. H. (1960) *Plans and the Structure of Behavior*, London: Holt, Rinehart, & Winston.

NEWELL, A., ROSENBLOOM, P. S. and LARD, J. E. (1989) 'Symbolic architectures for cognition', in POSNER, M.I. (Ed), *Foundations of Cognitive Science*, Cambridge, MA: MIT Press, pp. 93–131.

PARISI, D. and BURANI, C. (1988) 'Observations on theoretical models in neuropsychology of language', in DENES, G., SEMENZA, C. and BISACCHI, P. (Eds), *Perspectives on Cognitive Neuropsychology*, London: Lawrence Erlbaum.

PATTERSON, K.E., SEIDENBERG, M.S. and McCLELLAND, J.L. (1989) 'Connections and disconnections: Acquired dyslexia in a computational model of reading processes', in MORRIS, R.G.M., (Ed), *Parallel Distributed Processing: Implications for Psychology and Neurobiology*, Oxford: Clarendon, pp. 131–81.

PINKER, S. and MEHLER, J. (1989) *Connections and Symbols*. Cambridge, MA: MIT Press.

PINKER, S. and PRINCE, A. (1988) 'On language and connectionism: Analysis of a Parallel Distributed Processing model of language acquisition', *Cognition*, 28, pp. 73–193.

PLUNKETT, K. and MARCHMAN, V. (1991) 'U-shaped learning and frequency effects in a multilayered perceptron: Implications for child language acquisition', *Cognition*, 38, pp. 43–102.

POSNER, M.I. (Ed). (1989) *Foundations of Cognitive Science*, Cambridge MA: MIT Press.

PYLYSHYN, Z.W. (1986) *Computation and Cognition: Toward a Foundation of Cognitive Science*, Cambridge, MA: Bradford Books.

PYLYSHYN, Z.W. (1989) 'Computing in cognitive science', in POSNER, M.I. (Ed), *Foundations of Cognitive Science*, Cambridge, MA: MIT Press, pp. 49–91.

RUMELHART, D.E. (1989) 'The architecture of mind: A connectionist approach', in POSNER, M.I. (Ed), *Foundations of Cognitive Science*, Cambridge, MA: MIT Press, pp. 133–59).

RUMELHART, D.E. and McCLELLAND, J.L. (1986) 'On learning the past tenses of English verbs', in McCLELLAND, J.L., RUMELHART, D.E. and the PDP RESEARCH GROUP, *Parallel Distributed Processing: Explorations in the Microstructure of Cognition: Vol. 2. Psychological and Biological Models*, Cambridge, MA: MIT Press, pp. 216–71.

SEIDENBERG, M.S. (1994) 'Language and connectionism: The developing interface', *Cognition*, 50, pp. 385–441.

SEIDENBERG, M.S. and McCLELLAND, J.L. (1989) 'A distributed, developmental model of word recognition and naming', *Psychological Review*, 96, pp. 523–68.

SEIDENBERG, M.S. and McCLELLAND, J.L. (1990) 'More words but still no lexicon. Reply to Besner *et al.* (1990)', *Psychological Review*, 97, pp. 447–52.

SMOLENSKY, P. (1986) 'Information processing in dynamical systems: Foundations of harmony theory', in RUMELHART, D.E. and McCLELLAND, J.L. (Eds), *Parallel Distributed Processing: Vol. 1*, Cambridge, MA: MIT Press, pp. 194–281).

SMOLENSKY, P. (1988) 'On the proper treatment of connectionism', *Behavioral and Brain Sciences*, 11, pp. 1–23.

STONE, G.O. (in press) 'Combining connectionist and symbolic properties in a single process', in CORREGAN, R., IVERSON, G. and LIMA, S. (Eds), *The Reality of Linguistic Rules*.

STONE, G.O. and VAN ORDEN, G.C. (1993) 'Strategic control of processing in word recognition', *Journal of Experimental Psychology: Human Perception and Performance*, 19, pp. 744–74.

TAYLOR, I. and TAYLOR, M.M. (1990) *Psycholinguistics: Learning and Using Language*, Englewood Cliffs, NJ: Prentice-Hall.

VAN HEUVEN, W., DIJKSTRA, A. and GRAINGER, J. (in preparation) 'Neighborhood effects in bilingual word recognition: The BIA-model and experiments'.

VAN ORDEN, G.C. and GOLDINGER, S.D. (1994) 'The interdependence of form and function in cognitive systems explains perception of printed words', *Journal of Experimental Psychology: Human Perception and Performance*, 20(6), pp. 1269–91.

ZWITSERLOOD, P. (1994) 'Access to phonological-form representations in language comprehension and production', in CLIFTON, C., FRAZIER, L. and RAYNER, K. (Eds), *Perspectives on Sentence Processing*, Hillsdale, NJ: Lawrence Erlbaum, pp. 83–106.

Chapter 2

Computational Modelling in Artificial Intelligence

Walter Daelemans and Koenraad de Smedt

Introduction

Artificial Intelligence (AI) is a branch of computer science in which methods and techniques are developed that permit intelligent computer systems to be built. These systems allow the simulation of different aspects of human and animal cognition, including perception, action, communication, problem solving, and learning. Whether these systems are really intelligent is a controversial issue which will not concern us here (see, for example, Copeland, 1993, for an overview). What is more important is that AI stimulated researchers in cognitive psychology to be more explicit in their theories about mental processes. By the very fact that AI enabled machines to somehow carry out linguistic and other cognitive tasks, researchers could no longer ignore the possibilities of computer models as a precise reflection of ideas about how humans carry out such tasks. Put briefly, AI instigated the use of a computational vocabulary and provided programming methods and tools for building working models of language processing and other aspects of cognition.

AI approaches to natural language are often referred to as *computational linguistics* (CL) or *natural language processing* (NLP), although not all computational linguists see their work as belonging to AI. For some computational linguists, the linguistic aspect is the most important: the goal of the implementation of a natural language processing program is not so much a simulation of human language processing, but rather a test of linguistic theory with respect to its principles, consistency, correctness, and linguistic coverage. For other computational linguists, the computer science aspect is more important: natural language processing presents complex information processing problems and therefore the challenge is to arrive at efficient solutions to these problems by means of powerful mathematical and computer processing techniques.

From our point of view, the problem with some AI-models of language processing is therefore that they do not seek to account for the characteristics of psycholinguistic processes in humans, but rather are meant to be in line with linguistic theory and with the state of the art in computer science. Moreover, AI researchers often pursue the construction of working systems that can be applied to solving practical problems, for example spelling and grammar checking, machine translation, human-computer communication, etc. These systems, the products of *language technology* or *linguistic engineering*, are designed only for special practical purposes. They are based on designs that disguise fundamental problems in modelling aspects of language processing, and are therefore of no real psychological interest (Garnham, 1994).

But even if many AI-models of language processing are not particularly suited or intended as psycholinguistic models, the large body of AI research is not to be dismissed as irrelevant to computational psycholinguistics for two reasons. First, even if AI researchers have somewhat different goals from psycholinguists, they also have to face the same fundamental problems, so there is no reason why AI solutions should always be wrong or irrelevant from a psycholinguistic point of view. On the contrary, to a certain extent there has been some cross-fertilization between AI and psychology. Second, the rich repertoire of modelling techniques provided by AI has proven practical and useful in building computational models of language processing that are of psychological interest, as witnessed in several chapters in Parts II and III of this volume. The aim of the current chapter is to support the readers' understanding of the models presented in those chapters by introducing the essentials of the AI methods that underlie those models.

While AI has assimilated many different computational methods including the connectionist approaches discussed in Chapter 3, the current chapter will be restricted to traditional or mainstream AI, which is based on symbol manipulation. The next section will explain this basis and will be followed by an introduction to some of the architectures, modelling principles, and formalisms offered by AI. It concludes with a discussion of the shortcomings of AI and a brief guide to the literature.

Symbol Manipulation

AI considers linguistic and other intelligent tasks as problems requiring the acquisition, representation and use of knowledge. Consequently, the use of knowledge representation and manipulation is central to AI. Much of the research in AI has led to theories of problem solving and knowledge representation in general, while language processing tasks such as the production and interpretation of utterances are often seen as particular instances of more general problem classes. The main research questions include the following: Which knowledge sources are necessary?; which strategies should be used in processing?; and how can all of this be represented and stored so as to be executed by a computer? The answers of traditional AI are based on symbolic representations of knowledge, and on processing as symbol manipulation.

The fact that computers can be seen as general symbol manipulators and not just number crunchers is due to Allen Newell, for which he received the 1975 Turing Award. With Herbert Simon, he formulated the *Physical Symbol System Hypothesis* (PSSH), a central hypothesis in both AI and cognitive science (Newell, 1980). According to the PSSH, mental processes are no more than the operations of a physical system that is capable of manipulating symbols. Not only human brains, but also computers have these capacities. The PSSH projects the mental onto the physical as follows. Mental concepts (including linguistic concepts, such as phonemes and words) are represented by physical symbols. The term *physical* means that the symbols should be implemented in some sense in physical reality, for example as electric states in a computer memory. Relations between concepts are represented by structures (groupings) of physical symbols. Mental functions are represented by physical processes notated as programs that manipulate physical symbol structures.

Programs are themselves represented as symbol structures, so that they can be manipulated by other programs or even by themselves. Because of this recursion, learning can be explained within this framework: the mind can change itself in useful ways by manipulating its own mental structures and programs through learning. According to the PSSH, the manipulation of symbol structures is both necessary and sufficient for cognition. A consequence of the PSSH is that cognition is independent of its physical realization. In other words, the hypothesis holds regardless of whether physical symbols are located in the human brain as networks of neurons, or implemented in a computer as pointers to memory locations on a silicon chip. More detailed, layered views on computation and cognition based on symbol manipulation have been put forward in the literature (Marr, 1982; Newell, 1982; Pylyshyn, 1989; Steels, 1990).

Architectures

AI approaches complex tasks by decomposing them into subtasks so as to make the modelling of the task more manageable. Figure 1.1 in Chapter 1 provides an overview of comprehension and production of natural language and their possible decomposition into modules representing subtasks. How far these modules are autonomous, and how far they interact with one another, are topics of much debate. This debate goes on not only in AI, but also in connectionism, where there has recently been a move towards more modular architectures, e.g., CALM (see Chapter 3). One extreme is a strictly *sequential* architecture, where the different modules are accessed in sequence: output of one component is input to the next component. The other extreme is to have no modules at all, but to have an *integrated* system where knowledge at all levels acts together.

Clearly, other kinds of architecture exhibiting some limited form of *interaction* between the different modules have been proposed to address certain processing issues. In the area of sentence comprehension (see Chapter 8), for instance, a strictly sequential architecture is problematic. Possible syntactic structures can run into the hundreds or thousands for normal sentences, due to the combinatory explosion of several individual lexical and structural ambiguities. However, these can often be resolved as a natural side-effect of solving semantic ambiguities. Therefore, a sequential 'syntax first' strategy, in which all possible syntactic parses are computed first and are then input to the semantic component, is impractical. Instead, a tighter interaction has been pursued by CL researchers as well as psycholinguists.

One possible interaction consists of a form of turn taking between modules in an *interleaving* architecture. This is realized, for example, in the interplay between syntax and semantics in the UNIFICATION SPACE (see Chapter 8). Another architecture consists of a direct *feedback* from a module to the previous one. This is, for example, the case in the sentence generator POPEL, where a module responsible for conceptualizing interacts with one for formulating (see Chapter 11). In *blackboard* architectures, modules do not communicate directly, but via a common channel called the blackboard. In *object-oriented* designs, objects representing parts of modules communicate with other objects via *message passing*. Parallelism can be exploited by letting a module start processing before the output of the previous one is complete. A *parallel* architecture has been proposed for some models of incremental sentence production discussed in Chapter 11.

Entirely different kinds of interactions are present in *connectionist* architectures. *Localist* connectionist systems enable direct interaction between symbols through weighted links, within and across modules. *Distributed* connectionist systems allow many symbols to be represented by different patterns of activity in a group of cells, thus making even the representation of symbols a matter of interaction. Chapter 3 provides a more in depth discussion of connectionism.

Knowledge Representation Formalisms

Within each module, the AI approach aims to put together the necessary knowledge and methods needed for that module to accomplish its task. This information needs to be captured in a formalism for the representation and manipulation of knowledge. At this point, it is useful to reflect on the role of formalisms in AI in general and in linguistic models in particular. A *formalism* is a description language with a syntax and (ideally) unambiguous semantics that provides a bridge between the computer program and the theory.

A formalism consists of two parts. A *data organization* part consists of a language for describing domain entities, properties and relations involved. In a natural language processing model, this could contain knowledge about words and grammar rules, among other things. A second part, the *inference* part, determines methods for how the data can be used to carry out a task. Specific methods include *logical resolution, if-then rule application, inheritance*, etc., which are discussed below.

In a trivial sense, most implemented representation formalisms are equivalent, because they can express any computation. In general, it will therefore always be possible to translate the knowledge represented in one formalism into another formalism. However, representation formalisms differ in the kinds of abstraction they promote, and thus differ in the ease of use for particular problems. AI has therefore been oriented toward the development of formalisms that are expressive and offer powerful abstraction mechanisms, for example, to classify information in a minimally redundant way. In addition, practical considerations of economy, readability, uniformity, and ease of maintenance (see, for example, Daelemans, De Smedt and Gazdar, 1992) may be criteria for choosing one formalism over another. However, the preference for certain representations over others should be theoretically motivated. Conflicts may occur. For example, a model of the lexicon that is linguistically felicitous removes as much redundancy as possible, but this economy is not necessarily psychologically felicitous (Stemberger and MacWhinney, 1986). The criteria of psychological realism on the one hand and linguistic abstraction on the other can thus be in conflict because they are relevant to different enterprises.

Some Modelling Principles

Having considered knowledge representation and some criteria for knowledge representation formalisms, we now briefly discuss some principles and distinctions that are common in symbolic representations of knowledge.

Procedural/Declarative Representations

Let us consider the way in which the data organization and the inference methods are represented and operationalized. Many AI models use a *declarative* architecture, where the data organization part contains factual knowledge descriptions represented, for example, as lists of words and grammar rules. Problem solving methods are then implemented separately as operations performing inferences on this knowledge. For example, a model for syntactic sentence parsing may consist of a general parsing method and a separately specified set of grammar rules for a specific language (see Chapter 8).

In a *procedural* architecture, the data organization and a specific problem solving method are integrated in the form of procedures to carry out a specific task (see Figure 2.1). Consequently, reflection on data organizations and inference methods is hardly possible. This is no problem for models of cognitive tasks that are considered automatic and unconscious activities. In Chapter 11, the IPG model is given as an example of a procedural architecture for natural language production. In this model, syntactic constituents and grammatical functions are viewed as active procedures, and the syntactic tree structure is not a data structure but a hierarchy of procedures calling other procedures.

Figure 2.1: Declarative and procedural architectures

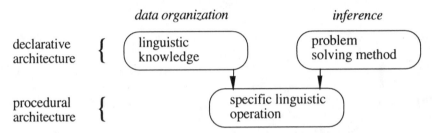

However, a procedural architecture is not always an advantage. When linguistic knowledge and problem solving methods are tied together, they are harder to manipulate, so that the learning and development of procedures present serious problems. In particular, extensions to a procedural language processing system may lead to discrepancies between existing procedures and new situations, which would require additional procedures to solve the conflict, and so on. Most AI systems for natural language processing use a declarative architecture.

Type/Token

In their data organizations, symbolic models usually distinguish between types and tokens. *Tokens* represent objects which can be identified in the real world and are unique, such as the first word you have spoken today. If this word happens to be *socks* then that occurrence of the word is unique and different from any other occurrence of the word *socks*. All occurrences are linguistic tokens of the same *type*, which is the word *socks* as it exists in the English vocabulary. The difference may be important for representational reasons. For example, in one sentence, *socks* may be the subject, whereas in another it may be the direct object. In one context, it may refer to clothing, whereas in another it may be the name of a cat. Should we want to represent both sentences at once in memory, then we can avoid conflicts by representing both tokens as separate units. Object-oriented models explicitly represent tokens as separate *instances* of types. Nevertheless, some models need to link repetitions of the same items more strongly and therefore use and reuse linguistic types rather than tokens. For example, the spreading activation model for phonological encoding by Dell (1986) discussed in Chapter 13 uses units for each type of phoneme in each positional slot in the syllable. Repeated occurrences of these units are modelled by repeated activation of the same unit through time. The TRACE model discussed in Chapter 5 uses type units to handle the occurrences of a phoneme within a certain time window.

Search

Problem solving in AI is generally based on the representation of possible situations in the search for solutions. These situations are called *states* and the set of all states, together with operators to change from one state to another, is called the *state space*. Some of the states are begin states and some are goal states. Search methods are algorithms allowing a state space to be searched for a path leading from a begin state to a goal state. When the state space involves choices between possible paths leading from one state to the next, the state space takes the shape of a tree. Chapter 7 discusses the use of a tree shaped state space for segmenting complex words. This *L-tree* or *trie* is a lexicon structure where each node is labelled with a particular grapheme or phoneme. Words are looked up by matching each successive character in an input string with a node in the L-tree.

Methods for searching a tree can be *blind*, which means that possible states are tried in a systematic but uninformed way. One kind of systematic search is *depth first*, where at each choice point between several possible next states, only the first alternative is considered, following this path as long as possible, and backtracking to the next possibility when necessary. Chapter 8 discusses a model for sentence comprehension based on ATNs with backtracking. Another kind or search is *breadth first*, where all alternatives may be considered in parallel. Examples from Chapter 8 are the Sausage Machine and race-based parsing, two models of sentence comprehension with limited forms of parallel search. These two search methods are illustrated in Figure 2.2.

Instead of being blind, search methods can make use of *heuristics*, i.e., knowledge about the domain to traverse the state space in a more efficient way (Pearl, 1984). An example of such a heuristic in sentence comprehension is *right association*: the preference to attach a new constituent to the rightmost node of a syntactic tree (see Chapter 8). One problem with heuristics is that their use can lead to a *local minimum*, which means that they may lead to a path that seems the most promising in a local context but turns out to be bad in a global context (as illustrated by *garden path* sentences). More recent and sophisticated forms of search include probabilistic methods that help to escape from local minima. In the

Figure 2.2: Depth-first search (left) and breadth-first search (right)

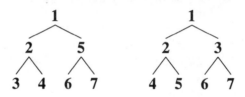

UNIFICATION SPACE, discussed in Chapter 8, the state space is searched with a probabilistic optimization technique.

Planning

Searching for a solution to a problem is often viewed as *planning* in AI work, and planning techniques from everyday life are applied in the process. These techniques include, for instance, the division of plans into separate smaller steps, each achieving a particular subgoal (*hierarchical* planning), the analysis of appropriate means to achieve certain ends (*means-ends* analysis), and on the fly modification of plans to achieve secondary goals when appropriate (*opportunistic* planning). Chapter 10 takes a strong plan-oriented approach to discourse production. The TEXT model discussed in that chapter makes use of *schemata*, which are prepackaged plans for the generation of structured discourse. In order to generate discourse defining an object, for example, TEXT chooses from several schemata, including a schema which describes parts of the object and one which lists defining characteristics.

Whereas schemata are hierarchically structured plans, more recent text planners take a more flexible approach, e.g., by assembling plans *incrementally*, in the order in which the plan elements appear in the final text, and by choosing plan elements depending on the current context (see Chapter 10). Also, the modelling of spontaneous speech, for example, requires incremental planning. This is necessary to account for the fact that people sometimes start speaking before they have delineated the complete content of their utterance. Models of incremental planning in grammatical encoding are discussed in Chapter 11.

AI Paradigms and Formalisms for Knowledge Representation

There are two opposing trends in the development of formalisms for linguistic knowledge representation. Some of the research is aimed at using and refining existing general purpose AI paradigms for the representation of all knowledge, including linguistic knowledge. A full inventory is beyond the scope of the current chapter (see our short bibliographic guide below). In the following sections we group general purpose formalisms into three main paradigms: frame-based formalisms, rule-based formalisms, and logic. Other research is aimed at the development of special purpose formalisms for language. Among these, only a limited number of grammar formalisms are discussed. The choice of formalisms and examples is mostly determined by the models discussed in later chapters of this book, while some formalisms not discussed are added because they are important.

Structured Knowledge Representation

Semantic or Associative Networks

Semantic (or *associative*) *networks* were introduced in the 1960s as models for human semantic memory (Quillian, 1968; Collins and Quillian, 1970; Collins and Loftus, 1975; Brachman, 1979). The data organization of a semantic network consists of labelled *nodes* representing concepts and labelled *links* representing relations between concepts. Nodes can be used to represent both types and tokens. The *is-a* link hierarchically relates types to types or types to tokens, *part-of* links relate concepts and their parts, and in general any relation can be the label of a link. Figure 2.3 shows the common graphical notation of an example network representing some of the knowledge underlying the utterance *Lucy weeded the vegetable garden*. Note that *Lucy* is a named individual, and *vg012* is a token whereas *garden*, for instance, is a type.

Figure 2.3: Part of a semantic network

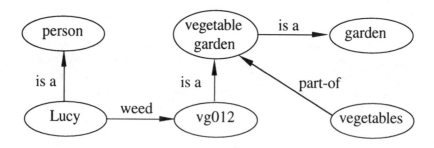

In a semantic network, each link between two nodes represents a separate proposition, e.g., the fact that Lucy is a person is a proposition separate from the fact that Lucy weeds the garden and the fact that the garden contains vegetables. But suppose we want to represent relations between more than two nodes. A solution is to allow nodes to represent situations or actions. Each such node has

Figure 2.4: A semantic network representing an action with roles

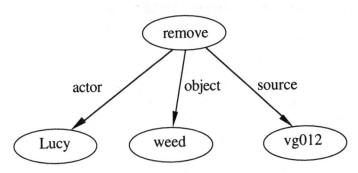

outgoing links representing *thematic roles* (or *cases*) for participants in the situation or action. An example is depicted in Figure 2.4. Semantic networks and variants thereof have been used in several psycholinguistic models. Chapter 9 discusses how networks can be used to represent the meaning of a text, e.g., in Kintsch's construction-integration model. Chapter 12 discusses Roelofs' model for non-decompositional lexical semantics, based on a network with *is-a* and other links.

Frames

In order to incorporate more structure into semantic networks, *frames* were introduced by Minsky (1975) as a representation formalism. A frame is basically a encapsulated fragment of a semantic network with conceptually related nodes and links that can be addressed as a unity. For example, one can define a frame for the *remove* action and the associated roles *actor, object* and *source*.

The term *frame* is not only used for structures representing domain knowledge, but also for structures representing linguistic knowledge. In Dell's (1986) model for phonological encoding, discussed in Chapter 13, for example, a *syllable* frame may consist of an *onset*, a *nucleus*, and a *coda*. In the syllable *best*, these roles are filled by *b*, *e*, and *st*, respectively. Several modifications have been proposed to make frames so powerful that they can be used as high-level programming languages: (1) *constraints* on the items allowed to fill each slot in the list; (2) *recursive* frames, the slots of which may contain items that are themselves frames; (3) *procedural attachment*, in which procedures are attached to roles of the frame to compute the fillers of these roles; and (4) *inheritance*, which makes inferences along *is-a* links: this is dealt with in more detail in the next section.

Inheritance

Given the enormous number of linguistic facts that are brought to bear in language processing, it is clearly important to represent this knowledge in an efficient and general way. *Inheritance* is a powerful technique to represent generalizations over descriptions in a way similar to *is-a* relations in semantic networks, and to use these generalizations to make inferences. Daelemans *et al.* (1992) motivate the use of inheritance for linguistic knowledge as follows. Imagine that we are setting out on the job of building a lexicon for English. We begin by encoding everything we know about the verb *love*, including its syntactic category and how it is conjugated. Next, we turn our attention to the verb *hate*. Although these words are antonyms, they nevertheless have a lot in common: for example, they are both transitive verbs and have past participle ending *-ed*. To save time and space, both can be categorized as transitive verbs and the common information about these kinds of word can be encoded in just one place called, say, *transitive verb*. The verb *love* then inherits information from *transitive verb*. Similarly, when we hit upon intransitive verbs, we collect all information about this kind of verb in a place *intransitive verbs*. The next step is to extract from both classes of verb the common information which is then stored in an even more abstract category *verb*. This is shown in Figure 2.5.

Figure 2.5: Inheritance hierarchy of some English verbs

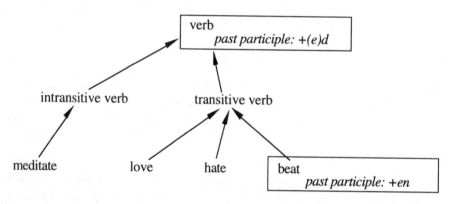

Suppose we discover the verb *beat*, which is transitive but not regular: it has a past participle ending *-en*. If we let *beat* inherit from *transitive verb*, we still need to specify the exceptional information, but then we get an inconsistency with the inherited information. The obvious solution is to let the exceptional information override inherited information. This mechanism is called *default* (or *non-monotonic*) inheritance. Default inheritance is incorporated into semantic networks and frame-based representation languages used in AI. The sentence production model IPF, discussed in Chapter 11, is implemented in a frame-based language using default inheritance. Default inheritance is also used in specific linguistic formalisms, for example DATR (Evans and Gazdar, 1989), a formalism for lexical representation.

Marker Passing and Spreading Activation

One of the inference mechanisms available in semantic networks is *marker passing*, a process with which *intersection search* can be implemented. This type of search starts from two nodes which pass a marker to those nodes which are linked to them, a process which is repeated for each of those nodes. Whenever a marker originating from one of the original nodes encounters a marker originating from the other node, a path is found representing an association between the two concepts represented by the nodes. This way, semantic associations can be modelled, but marker passing can also be used in networks representing other types of linguistic knowledge. A similar inference mechanism in networks is *spreading activation* (explained in Chapter 3), where, instead of discrete symbolic markers, a continuous (numerical) activation level is propagated along the links of a network. Chapter 12 discusses a model of lexical retrieval where a semantic network with labelled links is combined with spreading activation.

Conceptual Dependency Structures and Conceptual Graphs
Many of the early symbolic AI research on natural language understanding used semantic network or frame-based formalisms to represent its theoretical insights. Schank and his students developed *conceptual dependency theory* for the description of the meaning of sentences and texts (Schank, 1975; 1980). This theory was based on semantic networks, but defined only a limited number of node types and link types (conceptual primitives) that were deemed necessary and sufficient as a language of thought to represent meaning unambiguously. Any implicit information in the text (information that can be inferred by the reader) was to be made explicit in the conceptual dependency representation.

This goal gave rise to the development of a large number of data structures and inference mechanisms (often without well-defined semantics). Data structures included *causal chains* (a chain of states enabling or motivating actions which in turn result in, or initiate, other states), *scripts* and *scenarios* (prepackaged sequences of causal chains), and MOPs (Memory Organization Packages) (Schank and Abelson, 1977; Schank, 1982). These data structures enabled directed and efficient inference mechanisms, based on following up causal connections and associations between representations at the same and at different levels of abstraction. Work by Sowa (e.g., Sowa, 1984; 1991) on *conceptual graphs* also follows this approach. Chapter 9 discusses some models using *scripts*, *scenarios* and MOPs as data structures for discourse comprehension. One problem is that these models tend to focus on the data structure, and are vague on the inference part.

The work by Schank and his students also made clear that two sources of knowledge are indispensable for developing useful symbolic natural language understanding systems: (1) knowledge about the intentions, plans and goals of different *agents* in narratives or dialogue, and (2) knowledge about preceding discourse (*discourse representation*). In work by Allen and Perrault (1980) and others, AI planning formalisms are combined with speech act theory to model the recognition of intention, an approach which gave rise to research on speech act planning, topic structure modelling, and user modelling. This AI work has influenced psycholinguistic models of discourse comprehension (see Chapter 9) and discourse productiion (see Chapter 10).

Production Systems

Production systems are rule-based systems developed during the 1970s as models for human problem solving (Newell and Simon, 1972). They are common in models for many areas of knowledge. In this kind of formalism, knowledge is expressed as rules taking the form of condition-action pairs: *if X then do Y*. For example, in a model for language production, one of the rules for producing questions might be the following:

if the intention is to query the truth of P,
then produce a sentence about P where the finite verb of the main clause is moved up front.

Rules of this type, often called *production* rules, can only produce actual behaviour with the help of an *interpreter*, a mechanism which applies the rules to reach a given goal. In addition to the rule-base (which acts as a kind of long-term memory), a production rule system also has a short-term memory (working memory) which registers the current state of the computation, as well as current input and output states. The control structure of a production system interpreter consists of a cyclical process, where each cycle consists of three phases:

1 *Identification*. This phase determines for which rules the condition sides are currently satisfied in working memory.
2 *Selection*. It will often happen that more than one rule's condition side will be satisfied. Since in general it is not desirable for all applicable rules to fire, one or more rules are selected on the basis of a particular conflict resolution strategy.
3 *Execution*. The action part of the chosen rule is executed. Although actions can take many forms, the most typical ones involve the addition to or removal from working memory of certain facts.

This interpreter's mode of operation is called *forward chaining* or data-driven: rules are identified when states in working memory match their conditions; the execution of the rules may in their turn activate other rules, until a goal is achieved. But it is also possible to run an interpreter in a *backward chaining* or goal-driven mode: in that case, rules are identified when their actions match the current goals; their execution may add elements of their conditions as new goals when they are not present in working memory, and so on, until rules are found whose conditions match the current states in working memory. It is evident that both modes represent different kinds of search.

Rule-based architectures have been further developed toward more sophisticated cognitive architectures, for example, ACT* (Anderson, 1983) and SOAR (Laird, Newell and Rosenbloom, 1987; Rosenbloom, Laird and Newell,

1993). The ACT* system has a semantic network (see above) as part of its long-term memory.

Production systems have been used in a few psycholinguistic models, but no models based on them are discussed in this book. Anderson, Kline and Lewis (1977) describe a production system model of language processing. In PROZIN (Kolk, 1987), agrammatism effects are simulated by manipulating the processing speed of the production system interpreter and the decay rate of facts in working memory. Lewis (1993) describes a computer model of human sentence comprehension implemented in SOAR.

Logic

Logic has often been used as a formal foundation for knowledge representation in AI. For this reason it is mentioned here, even if no psycholinguistic models discussed in this book are directly based on logic. The formal properties of logic formalisms are relatively well understood and make them ideally suited as a language into which other formalisms can be translated in order to evaluate and compare them.

Data organization in predicate logic consists of a set of unambiguous constants (representing entities in the domain), a set of unambiguous predicates (representing relations between entities in the domain), a set of functions (mapping between sets), variables, quantifiers, and logical connectives. Inference in predicate logic is achieved by applying deductive inference rules, e.g., by means of *resolution*. For an introduction to the logical approach to knowledge representation, see, e.g., Ramsay (1988).

A practical computer language based on a limited version of predicate logic is PROLOG (Clocksin and Mellish, 1984). Below is a small program that expresses the fact that Socrates and Plato are human, and the rule that if x is human, then x is mortal:

```
human(socrates).
human(plato).
mortal(X) :- human(X).
```

The *interpreter* of PROLOG uses these facts and rules to derive other facts. For example, the following dialogue is possible, where we ask whether Socrates and Descartes are mortal, and who are all the mortal beings the system knows. The system infers, for instance, that Socrates and Plato are mortal. Notice that PROLOG gives a negative answer for everything that does not occur in the knowledge base.

```
|?-mortal(socrates).
yes
```

```
|?-mortal(descartes).
no
|?-mortal(X).
X = socrates;
X = plato;
no
```

Predicate logic has some severe limitations as a tool for representing linguistic knowledge which is incomplete, inconsistent, dynamically changing, or relating to time, action and beliefs. For all these problems, special purpose logics are being designed. An example is default logic, which handles exceptional information without having to modify existing general knowledge (see the section on *inheritance* above).

Grammar Formalisms

Grammar formalisms constitute a special type of formalism for natural language processing, even though they are not unrelated to the knowledge representation paradigms and formalisms discussed earlier. They often use a different terminology, due to the different background of the developers, which is linguistics, logic, and theoretical computer science rather than AI, and use special notations for linguistic strings and structures. Most grammar formalisms were developed as part of the efforts to build systems for natural language understanding, which up to now received more attention in AI than natural language generation.

Phrase Structure Grammars and Automata

The representation of grammatical knowledge as *phrase structure rules* is common for syntactic parsing in sentence comprehension (see Chapter 8), and to some extent, the recognition of complex words (see Chapter 7). The use of these rules is somewhat similar to production rules, but they operate on strings of linguistic items. Phrase structure rules basically specify how an initial symbol can be recursively expanded into a sequence of other symbols.

For example, the first rule in the rule set below specifies that a sentence (S) can be expanded into a noun phrase (NP) followed by a verb phrase (VP), or, inversely, that a noun phrase and a verb phrase can be reduced to a sentence. The selection mechanism chooses among various applicable rules. Often, a symbol can be expanded into different ways, for example in the following rule set describing how an NP can be rewritten as either an article followed by a noun, or an article followed by an adjective, followed by a noun.

$$
\begin{aligned}
S &\rightarrow \text{NP VP} \\
\text{NP} &\rightarrow \text{PRONOUN} \\
\text{NP} &\rightarrow \text{ART N} \\
\text{NP} &\rightarrow \text{ART ADJ N} \\
\text{VP} &\rightarrow \text{COPULA NP} \\
\text{PRONOUN} &\rightarrow \text{she} \\
\text{COPULA} &\rightarrow \text{is} \\
\text{ART} &\rightarrow \text{the} \\
\text{ART} &\rightarrow \text{a} \\
\text{ADJ} &\rightarrow \text{nice} \\
\text{ADJ} &\rightarrow \text{smart} \\
\text{N} &\rightarrow \text{doctor}
\end{aligned}
$$

A *deterministic* system will choose only one rule, whereas a *non-deterministic* system may search through a space of possibilities, using, for example, a parallel or backtracking search (see section on Search). Chapter 8 argues for determinism, as embodied, for example, in PARSIFAL. When a rule is chosen, the left hand side of the rule is replaced with the right hand side. Successive expansions develop the structure until a solution is reached in the form of a sequence of words. The expansion history of a particular case can be represented as a syntactic tree structure, for example, the one in Figure 2.6. Clearly, different grammars give rise to different tree structures.

Figure 2.6: A syntactic structure for She is a nice doctor

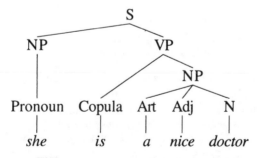

Phrase structure rules may operate in both directions, top-down, where the left hand sides of rules are rewritten as their right hand sides, or bottom-up, where the right hand sides are rewritten as the left hand sides. Depending on the form the left-hand side and the right-hand side of the phrase structure rules can take, different types of grammar can be formally defined: regular, context-free, context-sensitive, or unrestricted (see, e.g., Wall, 1972; Hopcroft and Ullman, 1979). Much research in CL is based on context-free grammars.

Languages can be described by grammars, but they can also be characterized by abstract computing devices called *automata* or *transition networks*. An automaton is an idealized machine which receives an input *tape* on which it performs operations according to given instructions. Automata have internal *states* and during computation they can make transitions from one state to another. If the automaton reaches a state designated as a final state, this may signify that the input has either been accepted or rejected. Thus, an automaton is effectively a recognizer of sentences (or other linguistic units) corresponding to a given grammar. There are four main classes of automaton, corresponding to the different grammar types (see, e.g., Wall, 1972; Hopcroft and Ullman, 1979).

One class of automata are *finite state automata*. Figure 2.7 shows a simple automaton that recognizes several kinds of sequence including those consisting of *art adj adj n*, e.g., *a nice smart doctor*. The process starts in an initial state NP1 and accepts words, which allow it to perform transitions to other states. If after the last word, a state NP3 is reached, which is designated as a final state, the process of recognition is successful. Automata can also be used to generate sentences.

Figure 2.7: A transition network for simple NPs

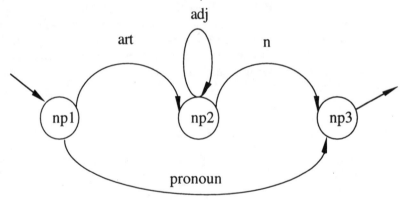

Some variants of automata have been defined and applied to parsing. In *recursive transition networks* (RTNs), not only a word can be accepted on a transition, but also a network can be called recursively in order to recognize a string of words. Chapter 8 discusses *augmented transition networks* (ATNs), which are not only recursive, but in which transitions can be coupled to tests and to operations on memory registers. This memory can be used to store information, for example, to build syntactic structures. Another variant of automata are *transducers*, which operate on several input and output tapes at the same time. Chapter 7 discusses models based on *two-tape finite state transducers* for morphological analysis.

Clearly, parsing with a transition network can be seen as a kind of search. One way in which a search can often be made more effective is by storing the results of partial computations, so that when the search fails, one does not need to

Figure 2.8: A chart containing a record of constituents found

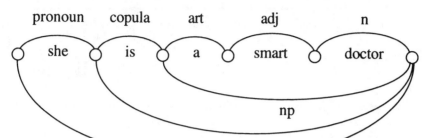

start from scratch. A *chart* parser is a device where the results of partial parses are stored in a working structure called a *chart* (e.g., Winograd, 1983). Figure 2.8 gives an example of a chart made with the grammar given above. Chapter 7 discusses a model of morphological analysis based on charts. In that model, the items between nodes are morphemes rather than words.

More Expressive Formalisms

During the last decade, many grammar formalisms have been devised that have in some way or other departed from simple phrase structure rules (see, e.g., Sells, 1985; Shieber, 1986). They have been applied primarily to syntax, although they are also used for modelling other levels of processing. For example, categories can be made more abstract by the use of wild cards, for example, XP may stand for NP as well as for PP. Another way to increase abstractness is separating information about left to right order from information about hierarchical relations (in terms of immediate dominance). In the following set of rules, for example, the first two rules representing immediate dominance are supplemented by a third rule which is an abstract ordering rule:

$$VP \rightarrow V, NP$$
$$VP \rightarrow V, NP, PP$$
$$V < XP.$$

Another way in which the rules are made more expressive is by adding tags to categories in order to represent syntactic features, for example, for number and person. In this way, information about agreement, for example, between the subject and the finite verb, is factored out. In many formalisms, feature structures (or feature graphs, or feature matrices) are the common way to represent linguistic information. A feature structure is a recursively defined structure consisting of a

Figure 2.9: Three feature structures

$$(a) \begin{bmatrix} \text{cat} = \text{NP} \\ \text{number} = \text{singular} \end{bmatrix} \quad (b) \begin{bmatrix} \text{cat} = \text{NP} \\ \text{person} = 3 \\ \text{head} = \begin{bmatrix} \text{cat} = \text{N} \\ \text{lex} = \text{girl} \end{bmatrix} \end{bmatrix} \quad (c) \begin{bmatrix} \text{cat} = \text{NP} \\ \text{person} = 3 \\ \text{number} = \text{singular} \\ \text{head} = \begin{bmatrix} \text{cat} = \text{N} \\ \text{lex} = \text{girl} \end{bmatrix} \end{bmatrix}$$

set of features and their values. A frequently used notation writes feature-value pairs as *feature = value*, and puts square brackets around the whole feature structure. Figure 2.9 gives three examples of feature structures in this notation: (a) describes singular NPs, (b) describes third person NPs with as their heads the noun *girl*, and (c) describes third person singular NPs with as their heads the noun *girl*.

Most of the new grammar formalisms based on feature structures are unification-based. Unification is prescribed as the sole information-combining operation. It can intuitively be described as a combination of two feature structures into a new one (see Shieber, 1986, for a more formal description). For example, feature structure (c) is the unification of (a) and (b). Besides the unification operation, a unification-based grammar consists of only declarative knowledge expressed in feature structures.

Kay (1979; 1984) proposed a formalism called FUNCTIONAL GRAMMAR, later called FUNCTIONAL UNIFICATION GRAMMAR (FUG), which works along the lines outlined above. A unification grammar can be described as a disjunction of feature graphs describing all possible sentence forms in a language. The processing of a sentence with such a grammar is a search for the unification of an initial description of the sentence with one of the alternatives in the grammar.

Several influential theories of language use linguistic descriptions which are feature structures, including LEXICAL FUNCTIONAL GRAMMAR (LFG: Kaplan and Bresnan, 1982), GENERALIZED PHRASE STRUCTURE GRAMMAR (GPSG; Gazdar *et al.*, 1985), and HEAD-DRIVEN PHRASE STRUCTURE GRAMMAR (HPSG; Pollard and Sag, 1987). We briefly mention some other grammar formalisms, which have been created as extensions of older formalisms by the unification operation: UNIFICATION CATEGORIAL GRAMMAR (UCG; Calder, Klein and Zeevat, 1988), and FEATURE STRUCTURES BASED TREE ADJOINING GRAMMAR (FTAG; Vijay-Shanker and Joshi, 1988).

Logic grammars view language processing as resolution in the logic sense. Because resolution can be seen as unification, there is a strong link between logic grammars and other unification based formalisms. In DEFINITE CLAUSE GRAMMAR (DCG; Pereira and Warren, 1980), for example, grammar rules are expressed in a way quite similar to phrase structure rules, but are translated into PROLOG clauses. The PROLOG resolution mechanism then executes the program. The rules of DCG have the general form of phrase structure rules (rewrite rules). Below is a small grammar for sentences of a simple form.

$$s \rightarrow np, vp.$$
$$np \rightarrow pronoun.$$

> np → determiner, noun.
> vp → copula, np.
> pronoun → [she].
> copula → [is].
> determiner → [a].
> determiner → [the].
> noun → [doctor].

The program can be used to recognize or generate sentences that conform to the grammar. Below is an example of two queries to recognize sentences.

```
|?-s([she,is,a,doctor],[])
yes
|?-s([is,she,a,doctor],[])
no
```

SEGMENT GRAMMAR (SG: Kempen, 1987; De Smedt and Kempen, 1991) is a unification-based formalism especially proposed for incremental syntactic processing. This formalism views a grammar as a collection of syntactic segments. Each segment represents a single hierarchical (immediate dominance) relation between two categories. The relation between a sentence and a noun phrase that is its subject, for example, is represented as the segment S-subject-NP (see Chapters 8 and 11 for details and examples). The essence of sentence processing in SEGMENT GRAMMAR consists of using such segments as building blocks in the construction of a syntactic structure for a sentence, joining them by unification. For example, a path S-subject-NP-head-N can be formed by unifying the NP node in an S-subject-NP and that in an NP-head-N segment. Chapter 11 discusses the IPF model for grammatical encoding, which is based on the construction of syntactic structures out of segments. Chapter 8 explains a variant of SEGMENT GRAMMAR where unification is turned into a probabilistic operation dependent not only on the feature composition of the nodes to be unified, but also on the activation levels of these nodes (see Chapter 3 for activation based paradigms).

Advantages and Disadvantages of Symbolic Systems

Symbolic approaches that are based on logic, frame-based systems, production systems, grammar formalisms, or on a combination of these representation techniques, are able to successfully perform complex natural language processing tasks. Thanks to the definition of formal operations — procedures that operate on the form of structures, irrespective of their content — symbolic systems achieve a high level of abstraction. New symbols and structures can be created dynamically during execution of a program. Moreover, symbolic structures can easily be defined recursively and can thus represent a potentially infinite number of actual structures.

However, symbolic systems have some drawbacks. First, when symbols are represented as single pointers to memory locations, a symbolic system is vulnerable when the properties of even a single symbol change. Second, symbolic systems are rigid and complex. Each exception requires additional rules and more processing. This is particularly problematic as the system is scaled up, even though the problem of scaling up can be somewhat alleviated by the use of powerful mechanisms such as default inheritance. It is this sheer complexity that makes the system vulnerable in the case of ill-formed or incomplete input and in the case of unforeseen interactions between rules. When a symbolic system goes wrong, it usually does not degrade gracefully, but breaks down completely. Third, the data and methods must generally be hand-coded by the system designer, because their complexity makes it hard to acquire them automatically. Machine learning of natural language from data like corpora or machine-readable dictionaries is therefore becoming an increasingly important topic, as it may alleviate these knowledge acquisition and robustness problems.

The PSSH goes a long way toward providing a framework for the study of *knowledge-based intelligence*, that is, intelligence based on the construction and manipulation of models. However, this is less so for *behaviour-based intelligence*, that is, intelligent behaviour based on direct associations between sensory input and motor output without intermediate models. It is an open research question whether language processing is an instance of behaviour-based or knowledge-based intelligence, or both. It also remains to be seen whether language is indeed a task much like other cognitive tasks, for example, playing chess, solving algebra problems, or recognizing visual objects, or whether it requires a mode of processing that is unique.

In this chapter we have touched upon a few topics in traditional AI, but it must be stressed that AI is continually incorporating new ideas from computer science and other disciplines such as neurology and biology. Recently, AI has seen the influence of radically new computing paradigms, including genetic algorithms, complex dynamic systems, and several kinds of brain style computing which are usually grouped under the term *connectionism*. The adoption of the new computing paradigms into mainstream AI has recently been stimulated by the availability of massively parallel hardware. Chapter 3 of this volume introduces connectionism and shows how connectionist approaches are designed to overcome the robustness and acquisition problems of traditional AI systems.

Epilogue: Finding Your Way in AI and CL

A thorough introduction to even a small subset of the formalisms, techniques and theories developed in symbolic AI and CL would require several times the size of this chapter. However, there are several good textbooks and reference works that can be used to acquire a deeper knowledge about the concepts introduced in this chapter. Two recent textbooks on AI are Winston (1992) and Luger and Stubblefield (1993), an older one is Charniak and McDermott (1985). They include chapters on CL formalisms. *The Encyclopaedia of AI* (Shapiro, 1992) and the *Handbook of AI* (Barr, Feigenbaum and Cohen, 1986–1989) provide introductions to all subfields and most concepts in AI and CL, and contain numerous references to the AI literature. There are anthologies of articles on AI (Webber and Nilsson, 1981), knowledge representation (Brachman and Levesque, 1985), and natural language processing (Grosz, Sparck Jones and Webber, 1986). The textbook by Winograd (1983) is a classic introduction to syntactic processing.

Programming is an essential skill for anyone who wants to develop AI models. Languages like LISP and PROLOG are especially suited to implementing the formalisms discussed in this chapter. Winston and Horn (1988) and Norvig (1992) are excellent textbooks for learning how to program AI formalisms in LISP. Bratko (1986) and Flach (1994) do the same for PROLOG. Excellent textbooks especially devoted to CL are Gazdar and Mellish (1989a; 1989b), which introduce the most important CL formalisms with their implementation in LISP or PROLOG, and Allen (1994). Pereira and Shieber (1987) is a classic introduction to implementation of CL formalisms in PROLOG.

References

ALLEN, J. (1994) *Natural Language Understanding*, 2nd edn., Reading, MA: Addison-Wesley.

ALLEN, J. F. and PERRAULT, C. R. (1980) 'Analyzing intention in utterances', *Artificial Intelligence*, 15, pp. 143–78.

ANDERSON, J. R. (1983) *The Architecture of Cognition*, Cambridge, MA: Harvard University Press.

ANDERSON, J. R., KLINE, P. and LEWIS, C. (1977) 'A production system model of language processing', in JUST, M. A. and CARPENTER, P. A. (Eds), *Cognitive Processes in Comprehension*, Hillsdale, NJ: Lawrence Erlbaum, pp. 271–311.

BARR, A., FEIGENBAUM, E. A. and COHEN, P. R. (1986–1989) *The Handbook of Artificial Intelligence* (Vols. 1–2: ed. by BARR, A. and FEIGENBAUM, E. A.; Vol. 3: ed. by COHEN, P. R. and FEIGENBAUM, E. A.: Vol. 4: ed. by BARR, A., COHEN, P. R. and FEIGENBAUM, E. A.), Reading, MA: Addison-Wesley.

BRACHMAN, R. J. (1979) 'On the epistemological status of semantic networks', in FINDLER, N. V. (Ed), *Associative Networks: Representation and Use of Knowledge by Computers*, New York: Academic Press, pp. 3–50.

BRACHMAN, R. J. and LEVESQUE, H. J. (Eds), (1985) *Readings in Knowledge Representation*, Los Altos, CA: Morgan Kaufmann.

BRATKO, I. (1986) *PROLOG Programming for Artificial Intelligence*, Reading, MA: Addison-Wesley.

CALDER, J., KLEIN, E. and ZEEVAT, H. (1988) 'Unification categorial grammar', in *Proceedings of the 12th International Conference on Computational Linguistics, Budapest*, Morristown, NJ: Association for Computational Linguistics, pp. 83–6.

CHARNIAK, E. and MCDERMOTT, D. (1985) *Introduction to Artificial Intelligence*, Reading, MA: Addison-Wesley.

CLOCKSIN, W. F. and MELLISH, C. S. (1984) *Programming in PROLOG, 2nd edn.*, Berlin: Springer.

COLLINS, A. M. and LOFTUS, E. F. (1975) 'A spreading-activation theory of semantic processing', *Psychological Review*, 16, pp. 399–412.

COLLINS, A. M. and QUILLIAN, M. R. (1970) 'Facilitating retrieval from semantic memory', *Acta Psychologica*, 33, pp. 304–14.

COPELAND, J. (1993) *Artificial Intelligence: A Philosophical Introduction*, Oxford: Blackwell.

DAELEMANS, W., DE SMEDT, K. and GAZDAR, G. (1992) 'Inheritance in natural language processing', *Computational Linguistics*, 18, pp. 205–18.

DELL, G. (1986) 'A spreading activation theory of retrieval in sentence production', *Psychological Review*, 93, pp. 283–321.

DE SMEDT, K. and KEMPEN, G. (1991) 'Segment grammar: A formalism for incremental sentence generation', in PARIS, C. L. and SWARTOUT, W. R. and MANN, W. C. (Eds), *Natural Language Generation in Artificial Intelligence and Computational Linguistics*, Dordrecht: Nijhoff (Kluwer), pp. 329–49.

EVANS, R. and GAZDAR, G. (1989) 'Inference in DATR', in *Proceedings of the 4th Conference of the European Chapter of the ACL, Manchester*, Morristown, NJ: Association for Computational Linguistics, pp. 66–71.

FLACH, P. A. (1994) *Simply Logical: Intelligent Reasoning by Example*, New York: Wiley.

GARNHAM, A. (1994) 'Future directions', in GERNSBACHER, M. A. (Ed), *Handbook of Psycholinguistics*, San Diego, CA: Academic Press, pp. 1123–44.

GAZDAR, G., KLEIN, E., PULLUM, G. and SAG, I. (1985) *Generalized Phrase Structure Grammar*, Oxford: Basil Blackwell.

GAZDAR, G. and MELLISH, C. (1989a) *Natural Language Processing in LISP: An Introduction to Computational Linguistics*, Reading, MA: Addison-Wesley.

GAZDAR, G. and MELLISH, C. (1989b) *Natural Language Processing in PROLOG: An Introduction to Computational Linguistics*, Reading, MA: Addison-Wesley.

GROSZ, B. J., SPARCK JONES, K. and WEBBER, B. L. (Eds), (1986) *Readings in Natural Language Processing*, Los Altos, CA: Morgan Kaufmann.

HOPCROFT, J. E. and ULLMAN, J. D. (1979) *Introduction to Automata Theory, Languages, and Computation*, Reading, MA: Addison-Wesley.

KAPLAN, R. and BRESNAN, J. (1982) 'Lexical-functional grammar: A formal system for grammatical representation', in BRESNAN, J. (Ed), *The Mental Representation of Grammatical Relations*, Cambridge, MA: MIT Press, pp. 173–381).

KAY, M. (1979) 'Functional grammar', in *Proceeding of the 5th Annual Meeting of the Berkeley Linguistic Society*, pp. 142–58).

KAY, M. (1984) 'Functional unification grammar: A formalism for machine translation', in *Proceedings of COLING84, Stanford*, Morristown, NJ: Association for Computational Linguistics, pp. 75–8.

KEMPEN, G. (1987) 'A framework for incremental syntactic tree formation', in *Proceedings of the 10th International Joint Conference on Artificial Intelligence, Milan*, Los Altos, CA: Morgan Kaufmann, pp. 655–60.

KOLK, H. (1987) 'A theory of grammatical impairment in aphasia', in KEMPEN, G. (Ed), *Natural Language Generation: New Results in Artificial Intelligence, Psychology and Linguistics*, Dordrecht: Nijhoff (Kluwer Academic Publishers), pp. 377–91.

LAIRD, J. E., NEWELL, A. and ROSENBLOOM, P. S. (1987) 'SOAR: An architecture for general intelligence', *Artificial Intelligence*, 33, pp. 1–64.

LEWIS, R. L. (1993) 'An architecturally-based theory of sentence comprehension', in *Proceedings of the 15th Annual Conference of the Cognitive Science Society*, pp. 108–13.

LUGER, G. F. and STUBBLEFIELD, W. A. (1993) *Artificial Intelligence: Structures and Strategies for Complex Problem Solving*, 2nd edn., Redwood City, CA: Benjamin Cummings.

MARR, D. (1982) *Vision*, New York: Freeman.

MINSKY, M. (1975) 'A framework for representing knowledge', in WINSTON, P. (Ed) *The Psychology of Computer Vision*, New York: McGraw-Hill, pp. 211–77.

NEWELL, A. (1980) 'Physical symbol systems', *Cognitive Science*, 4, pp. 135–83.

NEWELL, A. (1982) 'The knowledge level', *Artificial Intelligence*, 18, pp. 87–127.

NEWELL, A. and SIMON, H. A. (1972) *Human Problem Solving*, Englewood Cliffs, NJ: Prentice Hall.

NORVIG, P. (1992) *Paradigms of Artificial Intelligence Programming: Case Studies in COMMON LISP*, San-Mateo, CA: Morgan Kaufmann.

PEARL, J. (1984) *Heuristics: Intelligent Strategies for Computer Problem Solving*, Reading. MA: Addison-Wesley.

PEREIRA, F. and SHIEBER, S. (1987) *PROLOG and Natural-Language Analysis* (CSLI Lecture Notes 10), Stanford, CA: Center for the Study of Language and Information.

PEREIRA, F. and WARREN, D. (1980) 'Definite clause grammars for language analysis', *Artificial Intelligence*, 13, pp. 231–78.

POLLARD, C. and SAG, I. (1987) *Information-Based Syntax and Semantics* (CSLI Lecture Notes 13), Stanford, CA: Center for the Study of Language and Information.

PYLYSHYN, Z. (1989) 'Computing in cognitive science', in POSNER, M. I. (Ed), *Foundations of Cognitive Science*, Cambridge, MA: MIT Press, pp. 49–92.

QUILLIAN, M. R. (1968) 'Semantic memory', in MINSKY, M. (Ed), *Semantic Information Processing*, Cambridge, MA: MIT Press, pp. 227–70.

RAMSAY, A. (1988) *Formal Methods in Artificial Intelligence*, Cambridge: Cambridge University Press.

ROSENBLOOM, P. S., LAIRD, J. E. and NEWELL, A. (1993) *The SOAR Papers: Research on Integrated Intelligence*, Cambridge, MA: MIT Press.

SCHANK, R. (1975) *Conceptual Information Processing*, Amsterdam: North-Holland.

SCHANK, R. (1980) 'Language and memory', *Cognitive Science*, 4, pp. 243–84.

SCHANK, R. (1982) *Dynamic Memory: A Theory of Reminding and Learning in Computers and People*, Cambridge: Cambridge University Press.

SCHANK, R. and ABELSON, R. (1977) *Scripts, Plans, Goals and Understanding: An Inquiry into Human Knowledge Structures*, Hillsdale, NJ: Lawrence Erlbaum.

SELLS, P. (1985) *Lectures on Contemporary Syntactic Theories* (CSLI Lecture Notes 3), Stanford, CA: Center for the Study of Language and Information.

SHAPIRO, S. (1992) *Encyclopedia of Artificial Intelligence*, 2nd edn., New York: Wiley.

SHIEBER, S. M. (1986) *An Introduction to Unification-Based Approaches to Grammar* (CSLI Lecture Notes 4), Stanford, CA: Center for the Study of Language and Information.

SOWA, J. F. (1984) *Conceptual Structures: Information Processing in Mind and Machine*, Reading, MA: Addison-Wesley.

SOWA, J. F. (1991) 'Toward the expressive power of natural language', in SOWA, J. F. (Ed), *Principles of Semantic Networks*, Los Altos, CA: Morgan Kaufmann, pp. 157–90.

STEELS, L. (1990) 'Components of expertise', *AI Magazine*, 11, 2, pp. 29–49.

STEMBERGER, J. and MACWHINNEY, B. (1986) 'Frequency and the lexical storage of regularly inflected words', *Memory and Cognition*, 14, pp. 17–26.

VIJAY-SHANKER, K. and JOSHI, A. K. (1988) 'Feature structures based Tree Adjoining Grammars', in *Proceedings of the 12th International Conference on Computational Linguistics, Budapest*, Morristown, NJ: Association for Computational Linguistics, pp. 83–6.

WALL, R. (1972) *Introduction to Mathematical Linguistics*, Englewood Cliffs, NJ: Prentice Hall.

WEBBER, B. L. and NILSSON, N. J. (Eds) (1981) *Readings in Artificial Intelligence*, Los Altos, CA: Morgan Kaufmann.

WINOGRAD, T. (1983) *Language as a Cognitive Process*, Reading, MA: Addison-Wesley.

WINSTON, P. H. (1992) *Artificial Intelligence*, 3rd edn., Reading, MA: Addison-Wesley.

WINSTON, P. H. and HORN, B. K. (1988) *LISP*, 3rd edn., Reading, MA: Addison-Wesley.

Chapter 3

Connectionist Modelling

Jacob M. J. Murre and Rainer Goebel

The Brain Metaphor

Many scientists working in cognitive science realized that although symbolic models rooted in traditional AI (see Chapter 2) solved many problems, they performed poorly and slowly on some computations that the brain does rapidly and well, such as the almost immediate recognition of faces or the comprehension of speech. As a result, many researchers of cognition have turned to massively parallel and interactive systems, in particular those called *connectionist networks* or *neural networks*. Connectionist networks use interconnected computational elements (nodes) that, like neural circuits in the brain, process information in parallel. The preliminary insights that have emerged from connectionist models show that the collective workings of many simple elements may perform complex computations. The distinctiveness of the wiring of the connections between nodes, and the ability to modify this wiring through learning, allow many cognitive functions to be simulated in connectionist networks.

The biological brain possesses a great number of interacting elements: nerve cells or neurons. Neurons themselves have only limited computational powers. These systems are usually highly noise-resistant, including a high resistance to damage causing loss of elements. They are not programmed to carry out a specific task. Rather they are exposed to the environment in which they must function, and through their self-organizing capacities they are often able to acquire the necessary functional properties spontaneously. Similarly, connectionist systems have shown excellent self-organizing behaviour through learning.

The characteristics of these brain-based systems contrast sharply with the traditional approach to computing based on the Turing machine, which has a single processor and a set of explicitly programmed transition rules. These computing systems are extremely sensitive to noise and do not show self-organizing behaviour or learning.

In some connectionist networks a *symbol* is represented as an activated atomic element or node (a local representation of the symbol), in others as an activity pattern over a large number of nodes (a distributed representation of the symbol). In either case the activation patterns are not interpreted by a central processor (as in AI) but they directly evoke other activity patterns through connection weights. Each weight contributes a small influence (a *weak constraint*, a *soft rule* or a *microinference*) to the transformation from one activity pattern to the next.

Though it is only since the early 1980s that the field has enjoyed such great popularity, some of the oldest roots of connectionism can be traced back to William James (1890, see also the Introduction to Chapter 1 in Anderson and Rosenfeld, 1988) and Donald Hebb (1949). Both researchers attempted to integrate the existing knowledge of the brain into a coherent theory that could explain elementary and complex aspects of behaviour. That knowledge has vastly expanded since then. The recent upsurge in brain research has been one of the major incentives for connectionist modelling. Another has been the exponential increase in affordable computing power over the last two decades, because connectionist models are typically tested in extensive simulations that make high demands on the available computer power.

The increasing prominence of the brain metaphor of cognition is not an isolated development restricted to the field of psycholinguistics and cognitive psychology. Nature-based metaphors are becoming an increasingly important source of novel approaches to formal modelling in widely differing areas of science. Physical and biological systems such as interacting magnetic spins, annealing alloys, growing tissue, evolving species, and networks of neurons have provided modellers with an entire new domain of metaphors. Examples are connectionism or neurocomputing (Anderson and Rosenfeld, 1988), molecular computing (Conrad, 1985), simulated annealing (Kirkpatrick, Gelatt and Vecchi, 1983), and genetic algorithms (Holland, 1975).

In this chapter, we give an overview of some of the major properties of neural networks. First, we take a brief look at the main point of departure for connectionist models: the neural networks in the brain. Next, we investigate the relationship between structure and function in neural networks. We start this investigation with an example from an important class of neural networks called *Interactive Activation (IA) networks*. Additional functional principles of networks are introduced using two other examples of networks, the Hopfield network and the Boltzmann machine. The ability to learn and to adapt the network structure by presenting it with training patterns is one of the main assets of network modelling. We refer to learning connectionist networks with distributed representations as *Parallel Distributed Processing (PDP) networks*. A number of learning principles are discussed in the next two sections, where we first deal with approaches to learning inspired by the work of Hebb (1949) and then with those approaches that operate through correction of errors. We discuss the perceptron learning rule, the delta rule and backpropagation. Although learning is a powerful mechanism in adapting the structure and in achieving the desired functionality in a model, the outcome highly depends upon the initial structure of the network. In the section on neural network architectures we discuss ways in which networks can be pre-structured and advantages that may be gained by choosing particular network architectures. In the final section, we briefly discuss the modularity of subsystems and the manipulation of symbols in connectionist networks.

Connectionism and the Brain

The brain contains a very large number of *neurons*. These simple processing elements collect electrochemical pulses on their input side. If the summed total of the incoming signals is strong enough, a neuron will generate an action potential. This is a pulse that travels along a long thin fibre at its output side, the *axon*, and its branches. Many quantitative facts about the human brain still need to be verified thoroughly. For humans, a recent estimate based on quantitative analyses by Murre and Sturdy (1995) of the total number of neurons in the human brain is 40×10^9, of which about one-fifth (8.3 billion neurons) is located in the neocortex (i.e., the part of the brain thought to underlie many human cognitive activities, including aspects of language processing). The cortical neurons have an average of 4000 connections to other neurons. This gives us 3.3×10^{13} connections in the neocortex alone. Roughly 2.8×10^{13} of these are modifiable (also see Braitenberg and Schüz, 1991). These are important figures to keep in mind when considering neural network models discussed in this book. Not only are these artificial networks many orders of magnitude smaller than the brain, they are also gross — but necessary — abstractions of the complexities of brain tissue.

The similarity of a specific connectionist network model to neurobiological networks can be judged at different levels, for example, at the unit level or at the level of organization into layers and connection patterns. At node level, a single processor of a connectionist network is a simplified description of some essential functional properties of a neuron or a group of neurons (for a comparison between nodes and neurons see Crick and Asanuma, 1986). The gradual activation value of a unit is often compared with the frequency of emitted action potentials by a neuron. At the organizational level the comparison between real and connectionist networks is not taken seriously because in most cases connectionist network models address high-level cognition for which detailed neurobiological knowledge is still lacking. In some areas such as vision, this is changing, since our neurobiological knowledge is at present sufficiently developed to constrain the design of a specific model (e.g., Goebel, 1993).

The following aspects of the structure of the brain are usually taken to be most relevant for modelling:

1   A connectionist model consists of many simple processing elements, capable of transferring a unidimensional type of information, called *activation*. We call such an element a *node* to stress its highly abstracted character.

2   Each of these nodes is connected to many other nodes. The structure of the connecting network and the efficiency of the individual connections, called *weights*, determine the function of a network. The connections are the most important aspect of a model.

3   Whereas the structure of the network is mostly fixed, the efficiency of the connections can often be modified by a *learning rule*. This enables networks to learn new tasks. In this chapter we concentrate on this aspect of connectionism.

These points are of course abstractions from the 'wetware' of the brain. One can distinguish between roughly three different model types at an increasing abstraction level:

1   Neurobiological models. These aim to capture as much biological detail as possible in a given area (e.g., a model of the hippocampus).

2   Functional models. These abstract strongly from biology but typically derive much of their structure from psychology (e.g., Interactive Activation models).

3   Application-oriented models. These are highly abstracted from the biology and usually derive most of their structure from formal considerations concerning efficiency in solving a practical problem. These formal considerations can, for example, be of statistical nature (e.g., Bayesian statistics) or they can be problem specific (e.g., combinatorial optimization strategies, such as for the Travelling Salesman Problem, see below).

Almost all connectionist models discussed in the remainder of this book are of the functional type. To show the link between these types of model with application-oriented models, we give one example of the latter type below. Neurobiological models are not discussed.

In the rest of the chapter, we distinguish two types of functional connectionist models, the Interactive Activation (IA) models and the Parallel Distributed Processing (PDP) models. The IA-models make use of networks with local symbol representations and their elements (nodes) can usually be identified with linguistic units that are discerned by the modeller in the input to be processed (e.g., words, phonemes, letters, etc.). Input to these models causes a flow of *interacting activations* through the network, that usually stabilizes after a short period. The stable end configuration of activations is the basis for a solution, recognition, or response. If, for example, a single word nodes remains activated, then this node represents the word that has been recognized. IA-models do not include learning algorithms, though such algorithms may have been used to arrive at a certain network structure. The interactive activation process is only studied after learning has been completed.

The PDP-models focus on the learning process itself, and several *learning algorithms* have been developed that have important applications for practical and theoretical problems. Given the interrelation between IA- and PDP-models it seems natural to examine first the system dynamics of connectionist models in general and then discuss the algorithms that help PDP-models learn.

System Dynamics

The operation of a single node can be characterized by three basic functions (also see Figure 3.1): the propagation function, the activation function, and the output function. The propagation function computes the net input net_i of unit i based on the output values of other nodes connected to unit i. The activation function transforms the net input into the current activation value a_i which is finally transformed into the current output value o_i of the node.

Figure 3.1: Example of a node, showing input and output connections and the three internal processes

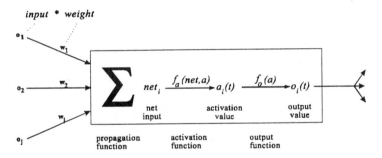

Propagation Function

The basic or net input to a particular node i is simply the sum of the influences of all the other nodes in the network connected to node i:

$$(1) \quad net_i(t) = \sum_{j=1}^{n} w_{ij} o_j(t-1)$$

Any particular node j projecting to node i contributes as its influence the value $w_{ij} o_j$ which is the product of that node's output value, o_j at time $t-1$, times the weight (strength) w_{ij} of the connection from node j to node i (see Figure 3.1). The net input of node i, then, is just the sum of all these products. Almost all connectionist network models use this propagation function for determining the net input.

Activation Function

A number of different activation functions f_a are used to transform the net input to the current activation value $a_i(t) = f_a(net_i(t))$. Three frequently used activation functions are depicted in Figure 3.2.

Figure 3.2: Graphs of three activation functions: (a) linear, (b) S-shaped (sigmoid), (c) threshold

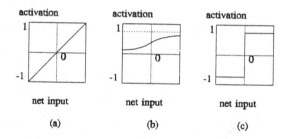

In the case of simple *linear* nodes the activation value is computed as

(2) $a_i(t) = net_i(t)$

Most activation functions, however, transform the unbounded net value into a bounded activation value. An activation function that is often used in the context of backpropagation networks (see later section on backpropagation) is the *logistic function* which produces an S-shaped (sigmoid) activation curve:

(3) $a_i(t) = s(net_i(t)) = \dfrac{1}{1 + e^{-net_i(t)}}$

Most localist connectionist networks have *recurrent connections*, leading to interactive stimulation: a node A activates a node B, which in turn activates node A. In order to get gradual changes in activation (avoiding oscillatory states), the activation function within these networks often includes the current activation value of a node as well. An example of such a function is:

(4) $a_i(t) = (1 - \Delta)a_i(t-1) + \Delta f(net_i(t))$

where Δ represents a *decay* parameter with a value between 0 and 1.

Output Function

The output function transforms the computed activation value into an output value, which is sent to other nodes: $o_i(t) = f_o(a_i(t))$. The output function often restricts the activation values to positive output values. In many cases, a simple linear output function is used:

(5) $\quad o_i(t) = a_i(t)$

Because all activation and learning rules in the remainder of this chapter use a linear output function, the output function and activation function are identical. To simplify the notation we simply write $a_i(t)$ and ignore $o_i(t)$.

Activation Schedules

In a neural network, activations can be updated according to three main activation schedules:

1 *Asynchronous random*. At each iteration, a single node is selected randomly and only its activation is updated.
2 *Synchronously*. The activations of all nodes are updated simultaneously.
3 *Sequentially*. This update mechanism is for example used with feedforward networks. The term *feedforward* means that all nodes within a given layer are updated synchronously, but that the layers themselves are updated in a strict order from input layer to output layer (see Figure 3.7). Feedforward networks cannot have recurrent connections.

In addition there are update schedules that do not fit the above classification, such as 'hard' winner-take-all, where the node that receives the highest net input is set to one, the others to zero. Only the weights to the winner are changed. We shall return to these schedules below, when discussing different approaches to learning. Before we discuss learning, however, we first consider the relationship between structure and function of nonlearning neural networks. This is important because structure determines function to a large degree in connectionist models.

Attractors and Constraints

Connectivity and Function: An Example

As an illustration of the above principles and rules, the functioning of a small neural network (see Figure 3.3) is discussed. The example is derived from the classic interactive-activation model for context-effects in letter recognition by McClelland and Rumelhart (1981; also see Chapter 6). We use it to describe the characteristics of many connectionist models: competition, distributed versus local representations, graceful degradation, parallel processing, pattern completion, and content-addressable memory.

The model contains eight nodes, divided over four *pools* or *modules*. The nodes in the upper module represent three words that can be formed from these letters. The nodes in the lower three modules represent letters-at-a-position: Z-- and C-- are at the first position, the -A- is at the second position, and --P and --R are at the third position. Within a module nodes inhibit each other, between layers of modules there is mutual excitation. The bidirectional positive (*excitatory*) connections between layers are denoted by arrow heads. Only nodes that are mutually compatible have been connected. Thus, the Z-at-the-first-position is connected to the word ZAP, but not to CAP or CAR. The negative, within-module connections, denoted with closed circles, implement the fact that at one position, only a single letter or word can be present. We assume strong inhibition that is equal between all nodes in a module. This implies that only a single node in each module can remain activated. As soon as two or more are activated, they will start to inhibit each other; they will *compete* until one of them has won. This is often called a process of *winner-take-all-competition* (Feldman and Ballard, 1982).

The words ZAP, CAP, and CAR are represented in the network by the nodes in the top module. As each node represents a single concept, we may call this type of representation *symbolic* and *local* with respect to nodes or modules. If the node for CAR were deleted, the whole concept would disappear. However, since the word nodes collect activation from the lower modules through their connections, it could be argued that they are represented in a distributed way with respect to the connections from the lower modules to the top module. The representations are distributed over the connections in the sense that the top nodes' functioning is completely dependent on the activation arriving through their incoming connections.

However, in the literature, a more frequent use of the term *distributed* rather than local for representations is when a concept consists of an activation pattern over many nodes, rather than a single node (Rumelhart *et al.*, 1986). Indeed, networks exist in which it is difficult to assign a clear function to any given node in a particular subset (e.g., in the so-called hidden layers of a backpropagation model). In that case, representations are distributed over both the nodes and the

Figure 3.3: Example network, consisting of four modules with lateral inhibition. The shading of a node is an indication for its level of activation. The arrow heads indicate excitatory connections, the black filled circles indicate inhibitory connections. Three phases of the spreading activation process are shown: (a) *Input letters C, A, and P have been presented to the network;* (b) *The word nodes are in competition;* (c) *The word node CAP has won the competition*

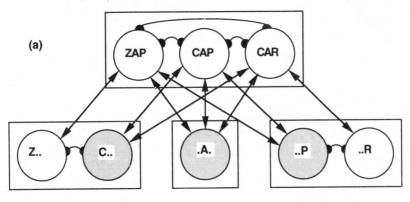

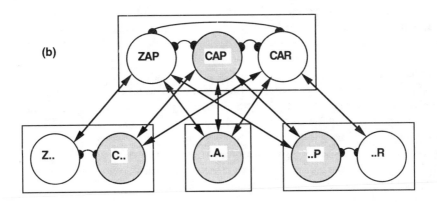

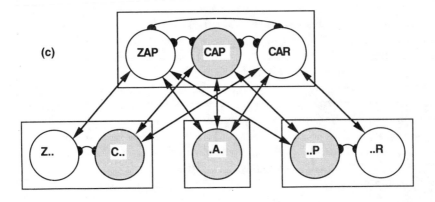

connections. Distributed representations imply that the network will not be very prone to perturbations or deletions of some of the connections. This effect, where disturbance of the connections leads to a gradual, rather than an abrupt, deterioration in performance, is often called *graceful degradation*. These characteristics of connectionist models (distributed representations and graceful degradation) can well account for the classic experiments of Karl Lashley (1950), who found that after lesioning the rat cortex, the extent of impairments of previously learned behaviour was directly related to the size of removed cortex and not to its location. The information necessary to display learning could not be stored at any single cortical location, but must be distributed throughout the cortex.

In Figure 3.3(a), the letters C, A, and P have been presented to the network by activating (*clamping*) these nodes in the lower modules. We could imagine that this activation process is carried out by another network, designed to recognize handwritten or printed letters. In Figure 3.3(b), the three word-nodes have been activated by the letter-nodes and are in competition with each other. The network would function with a wide variety of sigmoid activation rules, provided they allow only positive activation values. With negative activation values, the within-module inhibition would turn into strong excitation, and as can be seen in Figure 3.2, the activations within a module would soon become maximal and all reach a value of 1.0. Activations are exchanged in parallel and processed synchronously in this network, as would be the case with biological neurons. With the present input pattern, the CAP-node receives more input and, therefore, the network settles in a stable configuration where nodes C, A, P, and CAP are activated, as illustrated in Figure 3.3(c). Even if we would, at this point, *unclamp* nodes C, A, and P, the downward excitation from the CAP-node would be able to sustain the activation in C, A, and P. The importance of such stable states (also called *attractor* states) for connectionist modelling can hardly be exaggerated. They are the key to under-standing important characteristics of neural networks, such as pattern completion or content-addressable memory. As we see in the next section, the concept of attractor also presents an ·important theoretical perspective on activation processing in neural networks as a form of optimization.

During testing, a network gets some external stimulation via the input units. Processing proceeds until the network reaches a stable state corresponding to the system's response to that particular input. It is possible to stop the system at any time and to interpret the state of the network over some specified subset of units as an intermediate representation. The final response of an interactive network is retrieved when units no longer change their activation values by more than a certain small value from one time step to the next. In this case the network has reached a *fix-point attractor*. If one is interested in empirical phenomena, a *model reaction time* for computing the response to a specific input pattern can be based upon the number of processing cycles required to reach a fix-point attractor.

How might pattern completion operate with this example? Suppose the letter nodes were not clamped very strongly, and that we presented the network with Z, A, and an ambiguous letter R/P. The latter could be achieved, for example, by slightly activating both R and P. In a competition process similar to that of Figure 3.3, the ZAP-node would win, because it receives more excitation than the other two nodes. Through the downward connection the ZAP-node would reinforce the activation of P only. Because P and R are themselves also competing through inhibitory connections, R's activation would soon be reduced to zero. This situation is an example of *pattern completion*: an incomplete or ambiguous pattern is completed to the most similar pattern stored in the network. Another way of viewing this process of completion is by saying that such neural networks have *content-addressable memory*: part of a pattern is used to address the remainder of the pattern. This form can be contrasted with addressing through a pointer to a specific location in memory, as is the case in modern-day computers.

The ZAP example that we have just described concerns a type of localist connectionist network in which the connection strength between units is 'hard-wired' by the researcher. The properties of this type of network have been extensively explored during the last decade in various domains of psycho-linguistics. Many examples of models of this type can be found in other chapters of this book. In the perceptual domain, for example, in the areas of visual and auditory word recognition (well-known models are the Interactive Activation model in Chapter 6 and the TRACE model in Chapters 4 and 5), and in the area of discourse understanding (Sharkey's discourse model in Chapter 9). In language production, such models are discussed in the areas of grammatical encoding (FIG, Chapter 11), lemma retrieval (featural spreading activation in Chapter 12), and phonological encoding (Dell's Interactive Activation model in Chapter 13). We note that several of these models combine connectionist and symbolic features (e.g., Sharkey's model in Chapter 9), and may to some extent be considered as *hybrid* models.

Hopfield Networks

The example of recognizing an incomplete or ambiguous input (pattern completion) in the previous section demonstrates how connectivity determines function. Another important characteristic of a network is its global organization through local processing. The network relaxes into a global configuration of activity on the basis of locally defined constraints coded in the weights of the connections. In most interactive-activation networks, these constraints are coded in terms of inhibitory connections within modules and excitatory connections between modules, as in the network of Figure 3.3. Stationary configurations of activations in the network determined by such constraints are often called *attractors*, a concept derived fom physics where it refers to a state of minimal energy. In psychology, a somewhat similar concept exists in the form of a *cell assembly* (Hebb, 1949). The idea of an attractor is associated with the *energy*, E, of a network, which Hopfield and Tank (1986) define as

$$(6) \quad E = - \sum_{i>j} w_{ij} a_i a_j$$

This formula applies to networks with symmetrical connections, $w_{ij} = w_{ji}$, and with nodes that can only take values -1 and 1. The minus sign is a remnant of its physics history. The energy formula expresses formally the intuitive idea that two activated nodes connected by a positive weight are more stable (have less energy) than if they are connected by a negative weight. The connections constrain the possible stable configurations into which the network can settle.

Hopfield (1982, 1984) proved that the application of certain activation rules always guarantees a constant reduction of energy in the network. This process operates in a way comparable to the process of political decision making. For some time, people may be persuaded to change sides, until gradually two camps are formed. Encounters with friends may enforce votes, while encounters with adversaries may push votes in the opposite direction. A stable state is achieved as soon as nobody is willing to change his vote. Similarly, the energy of a Hopfield network declines as long as some neurons are still changing their activation value. The network slides progressively closer to an energy minimum, like a skier slides down a hill. Such an energy minimum is just another word for *attractor*. The precise form of the energy landscape is determined by the way in which the problem constraints are encoded in the network. Such encoding takes place by assigning values to the weights. In the network of the example, the nodes all had positive activations. If two nodes i and j were joined by a connection with a negative weight w_{ij}, their co-activation would result in an increase of the total energy, as can easily be checked. If they are joined by a positive weight, however, it would result in a reduction of the energy. Energy reduction always corresponds to satisfying the network's constraints. The search for an energy minimum can, therefore, be viewed as a form of constraint satisfaction.

Neural networks are eminently suited for finding solutions to problems with a large number of irregular and possibly conflicting constraints, and Hopfield (1982) has been eminent in drawing attention to this. As an example of a practical application, Hopfield and Tank (1986) show how a neural network can be used to solve the Traveling Salesman Problem, where a salesman must find the shortest route to visit n cities. At each stop (position) in the journey, only one city can be visited (constraint 1), and any city may be visited only once during the entire tour (constraint 2). Calculating the optimal solution to this problem takes inordinate amounts of time for large problem sizes and can therefore, in practice, only be solved optimally for a small number of cities. Neural network models can be used to reach good suboptimal solutions in a short time.

In Figure 3.4, it is shown how Hopfield and Tank (1986) propose to encode the constraints of the Traveling Salesman Problem. The network is coded such that an active node represents a visit to a city at a certain position in the tour. If a certain node is activated, for example A3, this may mean a visit to Amsterdam (A) as the third city in the tour. There would be different nodes for Amsterdam as the first, second, etc., city in the tour. The reader may note the similarity to the

Figure 3.4: Solving the Traveling Salesman Problem: (a) Eight cities A to H, to be visited one by one through the shortest possible route; (b) The neural network solution by Hopfield and Tank (1986). Each node represents a city-at-a-position-in-the-tour. Nodes in a column inhibit each other (shown with black circles), and so do nodes in a row. Nodes in neighboring columns have excitatory connections inversely proportional to their distance (connections without black circles are excitatory; the connections of only a single node are shown)

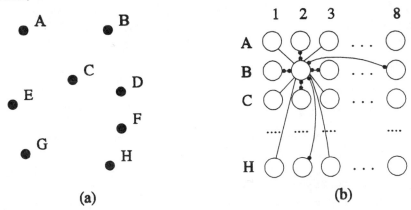

(a)   **(b)**

coding of constraints in Figure 3.3, where we have, for example, the constraint of only a single *letter* per position. Since in a column or row only one node can remain activated (due to the inhibitory connections), any fully resolved final configuration will be a solution that satisfies the two major problem constraints. To make the network find good suboptimal solutions, a third constraint has been added: After visiting city *i* it is a good strategy to visit a nearby city *j* rather than a more distant city. This heuristic constraint (i.e., one that often happens to work well) has been encoded by connecting nodes in neighbouring columns with positive connections: a node in, say, column 2 will have strong positive connections to nodes in columns 1 and 3, if these represent nearby cities. Simulations show that adding this constraint gives satisfactory results in practice. If the network is initialized by randomly activating a number of nodes, it relaxes into good suboptimal solutions most of the time.

The neural networks defined by Hopfield (1982) are strongly simplified models, well-suited for mathematical analysis. They have bidirectional, symmetrical connections: the activations take only the values −1 and 1. They function according to a simple threshold activation rule:

$$(7) \quad a_i = \begin{cases} 1 \text{ if } \sum_{j \neq i} w_{ij}\, a_j > \vartheta_i \\[2mm] -1 \text{ if } \sum_{j \neq i} w_{ij}\, a_j < \vartheta_i \\[2mm] \textit{unchanged elsewhere} \end{cases}$$

where ϑ_i is the threshold of node i [cf., Figure 3.2(c)]. This binary activation rule was first formulated by McCulloch and Pitts in an influential article in 1943. Nodes in *Hopfield networks* are updated asynchronously: one node at a time is sampled randomly and updated. This process continues until no further changes occur. Physicists have a particular interest in these models because they describe a whole range of physical processes, for example, the settling of magnetic spins. Hopfield (1984) has also shown that nodes with graded activations have similar computational properties as the binary Hopfield nodes (e.g., minimize the network's energy). These networks resemble that of Figure 3.3.

The Boltzmann Machine

Neither variety of Hopfield network guarantees an optimal problem solution. A skier may get stuck in a small and shallow valley, so that he would have to climb over a ridge to be able to continue his journey downwards. Similarly, a Hopfield network may get trapped in a *local minimum*. To deal with this problem, Ackley, Hinton and Sejnowski (1985) define a stochastic variant of the Hopfield activation rule. The resulting model is called the *Boltzmann machine*. With this stochastic activation function, the activation a_i of a node i is set to 1, regardless of the node's previous state, with probability

$$(8) \quad p_i = \frac{1}{1 + e^{\frac{-(net\ input)}{T}}} = \frac{1}{1 + e^{\frac{-\Sigma w_{ij} a_j}{T}}}$$

where T is a *temperature* parameter. If T is very high, the system functions nearly randomly and the net input to a node must take on extreme values to drive the probability of choosing one activation state over to another from chance level (i.e., $p_i \approx 0.5$). If T comes close to zero, however, rule (8) will approach (7) with $\vartheta = 0$, as the reader might care to verify. Like Hopfield networks, Boltzmann networks also try to minimize the energy in the network, but they do not follow a straight path into the nearest minimum. Instead, the stochastic component in the activation of nodes causes them to 'bounce around' in a largely random manner and this results in a greater chance of avoiding local minima. An algorithm similar to the Boltzmann machine was introduced by Metropolis *et al.* (1953) and applied to constraint satisfaction problems by Kirkpatrick *et al.* (1983). The latter showed that if the system is first run on a high temperature, which is then gradually reduced, it finds good sub-optimal solutions for many NP-complete problems. The functioning of such a 'cooling schedule' corresponds to annealing of a physical system (such as the formation of a crystal or the hardening of iron). This general approach is, therefore, often called *simulated annealing* (Kirkpatrick *et al.*, 1983). An interesting example of its application can be found the UNIFICATION

SPACE model (discussed in Chapter 8), which makes use of it in the parsing of sentences.

Hebbian Learning

The Hebb Rule

The ability of neural networks to *learn* tasks may be one of the main reasons why they form a focal point of research in psychology. From the very beginning, connectionism has been associated with learning. Hebb's influential book *The Organization of Behavior* (1949) introduces both the term *connectionism* and the famous Hebb learning rule:

> When an axon of cell A is near enough to excite a cell B and repeatedly or persistently takes place in firing it, some growth process or metabolic change takes place in one or both cells such that A's efficiency, as one of the cells firing B, is increased. (p. 62)

The origins of this important learning rule can be traced at least as far back as to William James (1890). Hebb uses it to explain the formation of *cell assemblies*, attractor-like configurations of densely connected nodes. The theory of cell assemblies was extended by Milner in 1957. Even before that publication, the ideas by Hebb and Milner were tested in what is probably the very first connectionist computer simulation in 1956 by Rochester *et al*. Connectionism has, after some ups and downs, now reached an explosive growth. The theory of cell assemblies itself, however, is still not formulated and tested in satisfactory detail. The Hebb rule has been implemented and investigated in a great variety of ways. Hebbian learning rules are all of the general form

(9) $\Delta w_{ij} = \mu f(a_i) g(a_j)$

where Δw_{ij} is the change in the weight and f and g are functions of a_i and a_j, respectively. The parameter of proportionality, μ, determines how much the weight will change at a single iteration of the network. Often, f and g are also functions of w_{ij} and of other relevant activations (e.g., Grossberg, 1976; Murre, Phaf and Wolters, 1992).

Hebbian Competitive Learning

The Hebb rule is especially well-suited for application in modular neural networks

Figure 3.5: Schematic overview of three phases in competitive learning: (a) Letters I and N have been presented; (b) Representation nodes 1 and 2 are competing; (c) Node 2 has won the competition; the connections from letter nodes I and N to node 2 are being strengthened (Hebbian learning), while the connection from 0 to 2 is being weakened (anti-Hebbian learning)

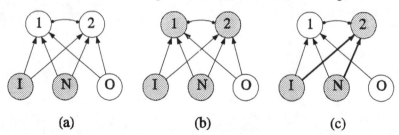

(a)   **(b)**   **(c)**

such as illustrated in Figure 3.3. To illustrate this, we have drawn a small network in Figure 3.5. This network has only two representation nodes, 1 and 2. As in Figure 3.3, these nodes strongly inhibit each other. The imput nodes are labeled I, N, and O. In this simplified network, they are not in competition and they receive no downward connections. The network is able to learn two 'words', for example, IN and NO (strictly speaking, position information is not encoded). Learning of the word NO could proceed as follows. In Figure 3.5(a), it is shown how initially all connections have equal, positive weights. The nodes I and N are activated and remain so (through clamping). In Figure 3.5(b), it can be seen how nodes 1 and 2 are in competition. Since neither of them can achieve supremacy over the other, we must assume some small random activation source that tilts the balance to, say, node 2. In Figure 3.5(c), node 2 has won the competition. Also, in this figure it is shown how Hebbian learning has strengthened the connections from I and N to node 2, whereas the connection from O to 2 has been weakened. The pattern IN has been *categorized* on node 2, and the network will retain this categorization over time. If all activations were reset to zero (but not the weights), reactivation of I and N would immediately give rise to a great competition advantage of node 2. It is necessary to also decrease the weight from O to 1, because otherwise the pattern NO would also be categorized on node 2. This approach to learning in networks with competing nodes has been formalized as *competitive learning* by Rumelhart and Zipser (1985).

The above example makes it clear that for certain applications a useful Hebb rule must also be able to *decrease* a weight, in particular, when the post-synaptic node is active while the pre-synaptic node is not active. The simplest version of the Hebb rule lacks this ability, at least when it is applied to networks with only positive activation values. When negative activations are allowed, it can also decrease the weights:

(10) $\Delta w_{ij} = \mu a_i a_j$

Already with this straightforward version of the Hebb rule, interesting results can be obtained. In a fully-connected Hopfield network with bipolar nodes (i.e., taking values −1 and 1) and with symmetrical connections, we can store a number of patterns such as digitized photographs by simply applying rule (10). If the number of patterns is not too large relative to the size of the network, the system will show recognition by pattern completion or content-addressable memory, and graceful degradation. These types of learning network have been studied intensively, in particular by the physics community, and their learning characteristics are well-established by now. An interesting learning method similar to Hopfield networks with Hebbian learning called *Bidirectional Associative Memory* (*BAM*) was defined by Kosko (1987, 1988). This type of network differs from a Hopfield network in that in BAM the activations of nodes in an entire layer can be updated in parallel, whereas in the Hopfield network updating is done one node at a time (asynchronously).

Error-Correcting Learning

Hebbian learning aims to increase association strength between correlated input patterns, and decrease this strength if the patterns are uncorrelated. The Hebbian learning paradigm illustrated in Figure 3.5 is a good example of a system that builds useful internal representations without the need for external instructions. In that model input patterns are associated with spontaneously emerging output patterns. Such learning paradigms are often called *unsupervised learning*.

In contrast, error-correcting learning tries to shape output patterns by adjusting network weights into a desired direction. For instance, when it is useful to force a particular output pattern to become correlated with an input pattern, a teaching pattern or target pattern (i.e., desired output pattern) is provided and weights are adapted to reproduce this pattern. In this way, networks can learn arbitrary correlations, for example, between a pronunciation (a phoneme string) and a written text (a grapheme string) (see Chapter 6). Because the provision of a teaching pattern can be seen as a form of supervision, telling the system what to do with the input, this approach is called *supervised learning*. All error-correction learning schemes (see below) are forms of supervised learning, because they require a teaching pattern. If in a certain application, the input vector is always equal to the output vector, we speak of *auto-associative learning*, a technique often used with Hopfield networks.

An interesting learning method is *reinforcement learning*, during which some supervisory feedback is given but 'very little'. This method was introduced by Barto, Sutton and Anderson (1983) who studied *pole balancing*. A pole is pivoting on a little cart that can move left or right to counteract the movement of the pole so that it remains upright. The task is similar to balancing a broom on one hand, but with the difference that the 'broom' is restricted to move only in the plane. Anyone who has tried this knows that it is not a trivial control task. The system receives as input only information about the angle and angle velocity of the pole, and about the position and velocity of the cart. As soon as the pole falls down or the cart falls off the rails, the system receives a failure signal. This tells the system that 'something went wrong'. The difficulty of this learning task is that the failure signal is not very informative. The system must figure out a way to find the weights responsible for the last crash, so that they can be updated. This can be viewed as reinforcement learning, because the system is reinforced positively for any action that keeps the pole in the air. As soon as the pole falls, the system is 'punished' with a negative signal. Barto, Sutton and Anderson (1983) were the first to demonstrate that a neural network can indeed learn this control on the basis of a limited reinforcement signal.

Another learning method, based on a form of error-correcting learning, is *imitation learning*. A system is simply placed in the environment in which it must learn to function. It must be able to perceive the effects of its actions and to explore its task environment. In many cases this process suffices to build a valid internal representation of the task space. The exploratory phase often proceeds through initially random actions. A walking robot could be trained, for example, by first moving its artificial limbs randomly, while perceiving the effects of its own actions. Some limb movements lead to movements to the right, others to the left, and some will not lead to any movement at all. For physical systems this is often called *motor babbling*.

A good example of motor babbling is presented by Kuperstein (1988), who describes a robot arm that learns how to grasp objects. The system receives visual information about the end position of the arm through two cameras. During the exploratory phase, the arm makes random movements (motor babbling) which are registered by the cameras and fed back to the system. This enables the neural networks, linking input to output, to acquire a sense of what type of visual input corresponds to what movements and positions. After prolonged training, presentation of a visual stimulus somewhere within its grasp will induce the arm to move towards that position. The method of motor babbling is so powerful that it even enables the system to learn stereo vision. There is, however, a problem with this general approach. If the arm can reach a certain position in two different ways (e.g., with the elbow to the right or with the elbow to the left), a single visual pattern will be associated with two arm configurations. As Jordan (in press) points out, this results in a non-zero residual error: the system will not learn to function perfectly. Extra constraints must be added to overcome this problem (e.g., 'change angle of elbow as little as possible'). A similar process might be important in human motor learning. A fascinating research question, for example, concerns the role of infant babbling in the acquisition of early speech. This issue has not yet been fully addressed in the literature (Jordan, 1990, presents a good first approach).

The Perceptron Learning Rule

Among the supervised learning schemes, the error-correction learning rules are most popular. They were pioneered by the psychologist Rosenblatt in the late 1950s. He called his model *perceptron*, a two-layer network with binary nodes of which the output node obeys the threshold activation rule (7) (Rosenblatt, 1958, 1962). The weights have random initial values and are updated according to the perceptron learning rule

(11) $\Delta w_{ij} = \mu(t_i - a_i)a_j$

where t_i is a binary *target* or *teaching signal*. The purpose of the rule is to change the weights such that an input pattern causes the network to produce an output pattern that approaches or matches a desired target pattern. Training proceeds by repeatedly presenting the network with a set of examples, each consisting of an input pattern paired with a target pattern. The learning rule can be stated verbally as follows.

> If the input a_j is 0 or if the output a_i is already equal to the target t_i, the weight is left unchanged.

> > Else, if the target activation is higher than the spontaneous output, the weights to the output node are increased by an amount μ, and if the target is lower, the weights are decreased by an amount μ.

Intuitively this makes sense. The weights are increased if the spontaneous output activation is too low. Consequently, at the next or a later presentation of the output vector, the net input to the output node may exceed its threshold, resulting in a match of the spontaneous output with the target output.

Rosenblatt proved that a perceptron will always find a set of weights that causes the network to produce the desired target for every input, *but only if such a set of weights exists*. This theorem is known as the *perceptron convergence theorem*. The *only-if*-part of this theorem is important, because a few years later, in the early 1960s, Minsky and Papert showed that in many cases such a set of weights does not in fact exist for the two-layer networks studied by Rosenblatt (1958), or for any two-layer network for that matter. A well-known case is the logical *XOR* function which is 1 (i.e., *TRUE*) if either of the two inputs but not both are 1: $XOR(0,1) = XOR(1,0) = 1$ and $XOR(0,0) = XOR(1,1) = 0$. Minsky and Papert (1969) showed that this problem, as well as a large class of similar problems known as *nonlinearly separable*, cannot be solved by a two-layer network. Because the perceptron rule applies only to two-layer networks, it seemed too limited to serve as a general learning mechanism. This finding more or less crushed the first wave of interest in connectionism generated by the exciting possibilities of powerful learning systems.

The Delta Rule or Widrow-Hoff Rule

Another limitation of the perceptron rule, is that it only uses three error signals

(-1, 0, 1). For many purposes, however, a continuous error value is required. This constraint was remedied by a learning rule by Widrow and Hoff (1960):

$$(12) \quad \Delta w_{ij} = \frac{\mu}{N} \left(t_i - \sum_{k=1}^{N} w_{ik} a_k \right) a_j$$

where N is the number of inputs to node i (i.e., irrespective of their values). In this rule, the weight is adjusted on the basis of the discrepancy between the continuous target signal and the *continuous* net input to the output node (i.e., *before* the threshold rule is applied). The nodes and targets have binary activations, but the learning process is subtler because of the continuous error values. This rule is also known as the *delta rule*. Though the biological plausibility of error-correcting rules is generally disputed (but see Hancock, Smith and Phillips, 1991), it appears to give a good description of Pavlovian conditioning (see Rescorla and Wagner, 1972, who discovered this rule independently of Widrow and Hoff).

Backpropagation

The fact that many important learning paradigms have been discovered independently by researchers in different fields illustrates that, indeed, it makes sense to establish an interdiscipline such as connectionism. The delta rule was rediscovered at least once, and linear associative memories (not discussed in this chapter) were discovered independently three times. The well-known *error backpropagation* learning rule was discovered at least *four* times: by Werbos (1974), by Parker (1982) by LeCun (1986), and also by Rumelhart, Hinton and Williams (1986). Backpropagation presents a great advance over both the perceptron rule and the Widrow-Hoff rule in that it can be used with multi-layer networks (i.e., with more than two layers) as well as with continuous activations. Most versions of backpropagation use nodes with the popular sigmoid activation rule (3; Figure 3.2), which we repeat here for convenience.

$$(13) \quad a_i = f(net_i) = \frac{1}{1 + e^{-net_i}} \text{ with } net_i = \sum_j w_{ij} a_j$$

where net_i is the net input to node a_i. A more complete specification would include a threshold ϑ_i for each node, but this can easily be circumvented by having one special node in the network with constant activation 1. The weight w_{ij} from that node can then be used as a threshold: $w_{ij}1 = \vartheta_i$. The backpropagation algorithm is formally derived from a global error function over all nodes and all examples. This derivation uses the derivative of the activation rule. For rule (13) the derivative is:

Figure 3.6: Example of a backpropagation network with one hidden layer

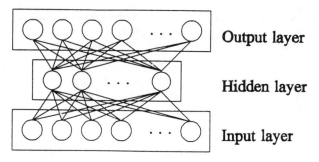

Output layer

Hidden layer

Input layer

$$(14) \quad f'(net_i) = a_i(1 - a_i)$$

A backpropagation network consists of an input layer, an output layer, and zero or more *hidden layers* where each layer is fully connected to the next (see Figure 3.6). The algorithm operates by repeatedly presenting all input-output patterns (examples) to the network and adjusting the weights. This is repeated until the spontaneous outputs approach the target outputs sufficiently closely. Each input-output pair is run through the network in two sweeps. A sweep is a 'wave' of propagating values in one direction, either forward (activations) or backward (error values). A forward sweep starts at the input nodes. A hidden node can only start calculating its activation values when it has received all its input activations. In practice this means that different layers have to be calculated successively until finally the output-layer activations can be calculated. The forward sweep produces a spontaneous output vector by a process of forward propagation of the activations from the input layer to the output layer. For the calculation of error values at the output and hidden layers this process is repeated in the opposite direction. During the backward sweep, first, the error values at the output layer are calculated. Then, these error values are used to calculate error values at the hidden layers by propagating them *backwards* through the connections. As described here, the algorithm applies only to feedforward networks (i.e., networks in which recurrent connections are not allowed, see for example Rumelhart, Hinton and Williams (1986) or Werbos (1988) for a more general description that also allows for such connections; see below for another possibility to have recurrent connections in networks).

The error values at the output layer can be calculated as the difference between the target and the spontaneous output:

$$(15) \quad \delta_i = (t_i - a_i)f'(net_i)$$

where t_i is again the external target signal provided a supervisor. The derivative of the activation is necessary for mathematical reasons. It is the result of the algorithm's formal derivation. Substitution of the expression for the derivative (14) results in

(16) $\delta_i = (t_i - a_i)a_i(1 - a_i)$

This gives us an error value for each output node. Except for the derivative of the activation rule, the algorithm is so far very similar to the perceptron rule. The difficulty comes when we consider the hidden-layer nodes. Where do we find good error values for these intermediate nodes? Backpropagation derives its name from the answer to this question: For the hidden layers, the deltas are propagated *backwards* through the connections. This can be expressed as

(17) $\delta_j = a_i(1 - a_i)\sum_{k} \delta_k w_{\overline{ki}}$

where a bar has been drawn over w_{ki} to indicate the fact that the connections *from* node i now serve as connections *to* node i.

If all error values have been calculated with rules (16) and (17), the weights can be updated. The most common method is to update the weights after each presentation of a pattern (this is called *stimulus learning*), although the original formulation of the algorithm (e.g., Rumelhart, Hinton and Williams, 1986) calls for a weight update only after accumulation of a summed error term per weight for the entire batch (set) of patterns (*batch learning*). The system must always start with random initial weights, or else it will not converge. The learning rule used with stimulus learning is:

(18) $\Delta w_{ij}(n+1) = \mu \delta_i a_j + \beta \Delta w_{ij}(n)$

where $\beta \Delta w_{ij}(n)$ is the so-called *momentum term*. A fraction of the weight change of the previous update n is added to the change calculated for the current update $n+1$. In practice, adding momentum in this way speeds up the learning process. Useful values for the parameters are $\mu = 0.4$ and $\beta = 0.9$ although the optimal values will depend on the nature of the learning task.

Backpropagation is probably the most widely applied learning algorithm for neural networks, even though it has a number of disadvantages (also see Murre, in press). For many researchers these are outweighed by its generic quality: It will usually give at least a good initial training result. This situation is similar to the application of Hopfield networks to difficult problems in combinatorial optimization such as the Traveling Salesman Problem. A Hopfield network is able to give a reasonable solution, but it can be shown that more specialized algorithms for this task are more effective. One of the early successes of backpropagation was a network called NETTALK by Sejnowski and Rosenberg (1987). This system was trained to convert English written text into strings of phonemes that can be fed into a speech synthesizer. After prolonged training, the system reached good reproduction performance, thus showing that it had extracted a significant subset of rule-like regularities from the speech corpus. It also generalized well to novel words not included in the original training corpus. Wolpert (1990), however, shows that more specialized, nonconnectionist generalizers may reach a higher generalization performance. Connectionist systems seem to offer good *general-*

Figure 3.7: A simple network as introduced by Elman (1989)

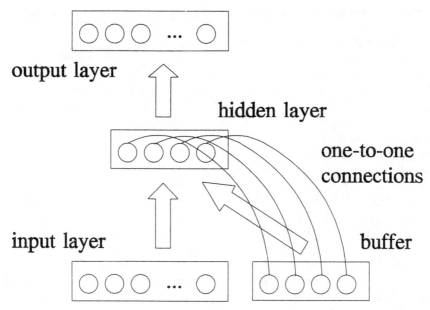

purpose solutions for a wide range of problems in optimization and learning, each of which may be optimized by *special-purpose* algorithmic systems or by neural networks tailored better to the specific task.

The above learning algorithm does not allow any recurrent connections in the network (e.g., if a node *A* is connected to a node *B*, there can not also be a connection from *B* to *A*). Several of the original articles (e.g., Rumelhart, Hinton and Williams, 1986) include a more general description of the algorithm that also works with topologies with recursive connections. Because the general variant of backpropagation is more complicated to implement, some simpler methods have been proposed that still allow for some recursive connections. Jordan (1986) proposes an architectural variant of the standard feedforward backpropagation net where values on nodes of the output layer are copied to nodes of the input layer and thus affect the hidden layer at the next time step. The recurrent links are used as a contextual memory of a particular sequence of inputs over time. Elman (1989) uses a similar architecture, but connects the *hidden* units to the input layer via recurrent links. An example of Elman's *simple recurrent networks* is given in Figure 3.7. Except for the additional copying operation, the backpropagation algorithm can be run as normal for these architectures. As can be seen, in this variant topology, the hidden-layer activations are copied to a special input buffer at each iteration (pattern presentation for activation weight update). Buffer size must equal hidden-layer size and copying is one-to-one. The one-to-one connections from the hidden layer to the buffer are fixed, but learning inter-connections exist from each node in the buffer to each node in the hidden layer. In this way, the network can keep a record of its activation history, so that serial patterns can also be encoded. This is especially relevant for language, which largely deals with serial structures. Applications of this approach include the discovery of lexical class from word order (Elman, 1989) and the learning of finite-state grammars (Cleeremans, Servan-Schreiber and McClelland, 1989).

One of the major disadvantages of almost all backpropagation networks is their slow convergence speed. It may take many thousands of iterations before a system reaches a satisfactory performance level. Another drawback is back-propagation's biological implausibility. Nowhere in the brain has it been observed that error-type signals (or any signals for that matter) are being transported *backwards* through synapses and axons. From a psychological point of view, back-propagation is most certainly not a good model for human learning and memory. These networks fail, for example, to attend selectively to the relevant dimensions of concepts (Kruschke, in press). A more serious psychological implausibility, which also limits the backpropagation's practical use, is the extent to which a newly learned batch of patterns *B* may interfere with performance of an already learned batch of patterns *A*. Learning the new patterns, without simultaneously rehearsing the old ones, will in most cases cause the latter to be overwritten completely. This problem is also known as *catastrophic interference* (McCloskey and Cohen, 1989; Ratcliff, 1990). The reason for this problem is that the representations that emerge in the hidden layers are almost completely random *between* two batches learned in succession. The resulting overlap of the hidden-layer representations induces most of the interference (French, 1991; Murre, 1992a, 1992b). Systems that are able to keep their hidden-layer representations as non-overlapping (i.e., orthogonal) as possible suffer much less from catastrophic interference. Two-layer backpropagation networks (i.e., without hidden layers), however, do show plausible degrees and types of interference, corresponding to those found in human subjects (Murre, in press).

Many distributed network models in psycholinguistics learn by the back-propagation learning rule. An example of a network trained with backpropagation is the visual word recognition and naming model by Seidenberg and McClelland (1989, discussed in Chapter 6). Examples of recurrent networks with architectures inspired by Jordan (1986) and Elman (1989) and discussed in later chapters are the morphological parser by Gasser (Chapter 7), the phonological encoding model by Dell, Juliano and Govindjee (Chapter 13), and one model for allograph patterning in handwriting by Schomaker and Van Galen (Chapter 15).

Neural Network Architectures

Learning in Modular Networks: CALM and ART

Modularity as a design principle is gaining popularity at the moment. We discuss two approaches to modular neural networks: CALM and ART. Our own approach is based on the general principles discussed above and on neuroanatomical findings. We have developed a basic building block for neural network architect-ures: a module that is able to categorize incoming patterns and to retain acquired categories over time. The building block is called *CALM*, from *Categorizing And Learning Module* (Murre, 1992a; Murre, Phaf and Wolters, 1992; Phaf, 1994). The general structure of CALM modules is not unlike that of the modules of Figure 3.3. The idea of short-range inhibition and long-range excitation can be implemented in a very natural way using a modular design. Within modules there is competition through lateral inhibition between the nodes. Between modules are learning connections that encode the structural information fed into the system. In CALM, inhibition is carried by a group of special nodes in the module. These are called *veto-nodes* because they can veto the activation of neighbouring nodes. The reason for this is that in the brain inhibition is nearly always carried out by a separate class of inhibitory neurons called *basket cells*. Rarely can a neuron be found that inhibits some neurons and excites others. CALM modules also have an arousal mechanism which enables them to adjust their local learning rate to the relative novelty of the incoming pattern. Repeated exposition of a module to the same pattern results in a habituation of the learning response: after prolonged exposure the module learns very little.

Several aspects of CALM are inspired by the work of Grossberg (1976, 1982, 1987). Since the early 1970s he and his co-workers have developed an impressive body of theories and models, addressing many important questions in cognition. Among their most well-known achievements is the Adaptive Resonance Theory (ART; see Carpenter and Grossberg (1988) for a good introduction into ART). One of the aims of ART is to remedy the stability-plasticity dilemma: How can a learning system be designed to remain plastic, or adaptive, in response to significant events and yet remain stable in response to irrelevant events? (e.g., Carpenter and Grossberg, 1988, p. 77). Plasticity is necessary for the incorporation of new representations in a network. Stability, here, means keeping old represen-tations intact, preventing for example catastrophic interference. An ART module consists of two layers called F1 and F2. The F2 layer holds top-down expectations of new patterns, which are presented at the F1 layer. A mismatch between an input pattern and the currently expected pattern causes the latter to be replaced by another candidate. This process continues until the input pattern is either categorized satisfactorily, a new category is formed, or the input pattern is rejected by the ART module. Though Adaptive Resonance Theory can be viewed as a modular approach to neural networks stressing the importance of neural network architectures, Grossberg himself has not put much emphasis on modularity.

Self-Organizing Maps

Another important approach to learning neural networks deserves mentioning here: the *self-organizing maps* by Kohonen (1989, 1990). They present an approach similar to modularity in translating delimiting constraints into neural network architectures. Similar to the modules discussed above, maps are based on local inhibition, but in addition they have a topological organization of the inhibitory connections. In many parts of the brain, neural representations show some type of topological organization. In the primary visual areas, for example, neurons representing parts of the retina are arranged so that they form an 'image' of the perceived visual scene. Their spatial arrangement corresponds to that of the cells on the retina. When Kohonen's self-organizing maps (also called *Kohonen maps*) are trained with stimuli that have spatial relations, these tend to be reproduced by the maps. Suppose, for example, that two-dimensional stimuli (x_i, y_i) are drawn from a square, say, bounded by $(0,0)$ and by $(1,1)$ and presented to a two-dimensional Kohonen map of, say, 10×10 nodes. After prolonged training with these stimuli, the nodes in the left-lower corner may become sensitive to stimuli around $(0.05, 0.05)$, whereas nodes in the right-upper corner may become sensitive to stimuli around $(0.95, 0.95)$. The stimulus space is mapped onto the nodes in a manner that preserves the original topology. Kohonen maps have been applied to many problems.

Speech recognition is a good example of domains where these maps can be applied. Vectorized speech sounds were presented to a (hexagonal) Kohonen map. This high-dimensional input (15 elements) results in a *phonotopic map*, where similar speech sounds are grouped together. A spoken word, presented to such a map, leads to a trajectory over the map, activating those nodes that represent the constituent phones (i.e., inferred 'phonemes') of the word (Kohonen, 1988). In a similar vein, Morasso *et al.*, (1990) have developed Kohonen maps showing self-organization of an allograph lexicon, a *graphotopic map* where each node represents a stroke in the sequence of movements in the production of cursive script. Ritter and Kohonen (1990) describe a method whereby words, presented to a Kohonen map as part of simple three-word sentences, self-organize on the basis of meaning. They call these *semantotopic maps*. Meaning relations are mimicked in the spatial relations in these maps. Related words can usually be found grouped together. These groupings emerge through similarities in the contexts in which the words appear. Verbs like *speaks*, *eats*, *likes*, *buys*, *hates*, etc., are grouped together on the map, because the system has encountered these words in similar contexts, such as in *Jim speaks well*, *Jim eats often*, *Jim eats bread*, or *Mary hates meat*, *Bob buys meat*. In this way, verbs will be clustered together, because they occur in the same context.

Whereas there is very strong evidence for topographical organization in the brain, no physiological evidence has been uncovered yet for semantotopic maps. Some studies suggest that higher processing stages in brain are organized on the basis of logical properties of their input items (e.g., Ojemann, 1983), but until more evidence has been accumulated we must view the simulations on semantotopic maps by Ritter and Kohonen (1990) as a challenging hypothesis, that may direct further investigations into the structure of the brain. This is one example where connectionist modelling suggests novel neurophysiological experiments. The opposite is also possible, in that facts about the brain may be used to constrain psychological and psycholinguistic models. If it is known, for example, how many neurons and interconnections are present in Broca's area and in other areas involved in speech production, these data may be used to place bounds on the size, complexity, and general form of models of speech production. There are two areas of neurobiological investigation that may provide leads for psychological models: brain connectivity and central mechanisms that modulate learning in the brain. These are discussed in the next section.

Discussion

Modularity and Modulation

As pointed out above, two main principles of network design give rise to either modules or topographical maps in networks. In the brain, dense connections are nearly found at a local level. A single neuron in the cortex is connected with about 4000 others, but most of these are located in the direct neighbourhood, say, within 0.5 cm. As with telephone calls, long-range connections are expensive, taking up a lot of space and resources in the brain. Therefore it is not surprising that we find sparse connectivity at a global or long-range level (Murre and Sturdy, 1995). In order to still be able to connect far removed areas of the brain, use is made of yet another design principle: hierarchical structures. Suppose we want to associate a picture with a word. How can this be done, when there are no direct connections between the visual and language areas? The answer seems to be that these connections are first of all made via brain areas placed high in the hierarchy. Later, with time and repetition, other indirect connections can be formed between the word and the picture, maybe through a network of intermediate areas at the same level of the hierarchy. This principle of design solves the connectivity problem, which plagues all large networks. The solution can be used to realize very large networks of processors in parallel hardware (Heemskerk and Murre, 1994). The brain seems to use the same solution. Research by Felleman and Van Essen (1991), for example, shows that many systems in the brain show a clear hierarchical structure with the hippocampus at the top of most hierarchies. We have recently used the same design principles in a model of amnesia (Murre, 1994) that explains the main characteristics of the neuropsychology of memory, for example, the fact that loss of existing memories (retrograde amnesia) affects recent memories rather than old memories (the so-called Law of Ribot).

Several connectionist models have recently been developed that focus exclusively on the question of learning, for example, on language acquisition (e.g., Broeder and Murre, in prep.). The question of how we accomplish *real-time* learning, however, has received very little attention in the psychological literature, even though it is the most typical type of learning. Rarely are we accompanied by an instructor who tells us exactly what to learn and what to ignore. We typically decide for ourselves what to learn and when. In CALM networks, introduced above, the level of competition is taken as an indication for the novelty of a pattern. A new pattern causes much competition among uncommitted nodes (i.e., that do not yet have a representation). This in turn can be used to modulate the learning rate. How much learning an incoming pattern will receive depends on its similarity to all previous patterns. If it is very similar to some previous patterns, there will be little competition; it will be considered as simply another variant pattern of a certain category. If it is different from all others, several nodes will become activated and a strong competition will ensue. This will trigger the learning mechanism and enable it to rapidly encode the new pattern. It is likely that similar mechanisms operate in the brain (see Murre 1992a, for a review). Although novelty-induced learning is a powerful mechanism, we need several other global, modulatory mechanisms in our networks, that help to decide what to learn and when. Without such mechanisms we will not be able to account for the most important aspects of human learning: its real-time and self-modulated character.

Connections and Rules

A connectionist model can mimic the behaviour of a rule-based model. For example, NETTALK was trained on a set of text-to-pronunciation examples after which its generalization performance surpassed that of the DECTALK system, which was programmed manually with explicit pronunciation rules. This, of course, does not prove that rules are worse than connections. Perhaps more and better rules might have resulted in a better DECTALK system. It does show, however, that connectionist models can be indistinguisable on the outside from rule-based models. Indeed, it has been formally proven that a neural network with sigmoid nodes can approximate any well-formed function (Hornik, Stinchcombe and White, 1989). There are, thus, at least two ways in which a system can represent (approximately) the relation between, say, the radius and the surface of a circle. A rule-based system might be given a mathematical expression as a rule, $s = \pi r^2$, and a neural network might be given a lot of examples and learn the relation from these (or some other procedure might be used to arrive at the required weight setting). In both cases, the final models would be indistinguisable.

Rule-based systems are able to keep intermediate results, and in this way they can carry out recursive functions. Before calling themselves recursively, they store their current variables. By later returning to the original point of entry and retrieving the stored variables they can continue processing. The only limit imposed on this process is the storage space available for storing intermediate results. In this way, we might construct a simple recognizer (e.g., a push-down automaton) for a context-free language such as the mirror language or the language that consists of strings with an equal number of a's and b's (also see Chapter 2). The latter language can also be recognized by a connectionist model, for example, by using the activation level of a node to 'count' the number of a's and b's, which are presented sequentially (see Murre, 1992a, p. 133). Neural networks are thus certainly not simple finite-state automata.

We assume that *selective attention* and *short-term memory* are necessary conditions for *human* symbol manipulation. The short-term retention of information and the selective access of parts of that information — independent of its content — are mechanisms which are needed to successfully handle compositionality and provide a structure-sensitive processing capacity (for a detailed argumentation, see Goebel, 1990). Goebel (in press) describes a network model possessing a selective attention mechanism and a short-term memory component. Simulation studies demonstrate that the developed system is able to perform a typical symbol manipulation task: the evaluation of simple LISP expressions. The model performs this task by *shifting attention* to relevant positions of a presented LISP expression, for instance, to the first element of an argument list and storing intermediate results in the STM-component. Indefrey and Goebel (1993) show how a network model with an auditory short-term memory component is able to learn a low-frequency morphological rule (weak noun declension in German) and to apply the acquired knowledge to novel words. In adding a short-term memory component, the model was able to 'concentrate' both on structure (detecting, for example, the end of a sequentially presented word) as well as on content (exploiting the currently active cues), combining the strength of symbolic and connectionist processing.

Neural networks have, thus far, not proved to be very good at symbol manipulation. The weaknesses of connectionist models concerning symbol manipulation and rule acquisition are expressed, for example, by Norman (1986), Fodor and Pylyshyn (1988), Pinker and Prince (1988), and Pinker (1991). But then again, humans are not very good at symbol manipulation either. Anyone who has ever tried to program in machine language knows that we are not as well adapted to symbol manipulation as is often believed. Our working memory is very limited and allows for only about two seconds worth of acoustic material to be maintained, as well as some additional visuo-spatial material (Baddeley and Hitch, 1974). This imposes strong limits on the level of recursion that can be achieved in human thinking. It is at present not clear what is the cause of this limit. It is likely that the brain is not able to sustain a greater working memory due to limitations at the neurobiological level which transpire to high-level symbol manipulations, such as, for example, repeated embeddings in sentences (see Chapter 8). The important contribution of connectionism is that it provides a new paradigm for modelling human cognitive abilities at an intermediate level which integrates major characteristics from the biological and psychological level.

Epilogue: Finding Your Way in Connectionism

In the last decade, a wealth of interesting books on connectionism has appeared.

Here we refer the reader for further reading to a few very readable and popular textbooks in the field. First, we mention the 'bible' of connectionism, the two volumes edited by Rumelhart, McClelland and the PDP Research Group (1986). These classic volumes are still a good introduction to connectionism, both with respect to IA- and to PDP-models. For the reader whose hands itch, there is the accompanying Volume 3, a manual that is accompanied by a diskette allowing the user to run simulations of different types of networks. Second, Anderson and Rosenfeld (1988) present a compilation of classic articles, each preceded by a clear introduction. Recently, a second volume of this excellent book has appeared. Last but not least, a very attractive introduction for the researcher with a psychological background is Quinlan's (1991) book on connectionism and psychology.

References

ACKLEY, D.H., HINTON, G.E. and SEJNOWSKI, T.J. (1985) 'A learning algorithm for Boltzmann machines', *Cognitive Science*, 9, pp. 147–69.

ANDERSON, J.A. and ROSENFELD, E.R. (Eds) (1988) *Neurocomputing: Foundations of Research*, Cambridge, MA: MIT Press.

BADDELEY, A.D. and HITCH, G. (1974) 'Working memory', in BOWER, G.H. (Ed) *Recent Advances in the Psychology of Learning and Motivation: Vol. VIII*, New York: Academic Press, pp. 47–90.

BARTO, A.G., SUTTON, R.S. and ANDERSON, C.W. (1983) 'Neuronlike adaptive elements that can solve difficult learning control problems', *IEEE Transactions on Systems, Man, and Cybernetics*, 13, pp. 834–46.

BRAITENBERG, V. and SCHÜZ, A. (1991) *Anatomy of the Cortex: Statistics and Geometry*, Berlin: Springer.

BROEDER, P. and MURRE, J.M.J. (Eds) (in prep.) *Cognitive Models of Language Acquisition*, Cambridge, MA: MIT Press.

CARPENTER, G.A. and GROSSBERG, S. (1988) 'The ART of adaptive pattern recognition by a self-organizing neural network', *IEEE Computer*, 21, 3, pp. 77–88.

CLEEREMANS, A., SERVAN-SCREIBER, D. and MCCLELLAND, J.L. (1989) 'Finite state automata and simple recurrent networks', *Neural Computation*, 1, pp. 372–81.

CONRAD, M. (1985) 'On design principles for a molecular computer', *Communications of the ACM*, 28, pp. 464–80.

CRICK, F.H.C. and ASANUMA, C. (1986) 'Certain aspects of the anatomy and physiology of the cerebral cortex', in MCCLELLAND, J.L. and RUMELHART, D.E. *Parallel Distributed Processing: Explorations in the Microstructure of Cognition: Vol. 2. Psychological and Biological Models*, Cambridge, MA: MIT Press, pp. 333–71.

ELMAN, J.L. (1989) 'Structured representations and connectionist models', in *Proceedings of the Eleventh Annual Conference of the Cognitive Science Society*, Hillsdale, NJ: Lawrence Erlbaum, pp. 17–25.

FELDMAN, J.A. and BALLARD, D.H. (1982) 'Connectionist models and their properties', *Cognitive Science*, 6, pp. 205–54.

FELLEMAN, D.J. and VAN ESSEN, D.C. (1991) 'Distributed hierarchical processing in the primate cerebral cortex', *Cerebral Cortex*, 1, pp. 1–47.

FODOR, J. and PYLYSHYN, P. (1988) 'Connectionism and cognitive architecture: A critical analysis', *Cognition*, 28, pp. 3–71.

FRENCH, R. M. (1991) 'Using semi-distributed representations to overcome catastrophic forgetting in connectionist networks', in *Proceedings of the Thirteenth Annual Conference of the Cognitive Science Society*, Hillsdale, NJ: Lawrence Erlbaum, pp. 173–8.

GOEBEL, R. (1990) 'Binding, episodic short-term memory, and selective attention, or why are PDP models poor at symbol manipulation?', in TOURETZKY, D. S., ELMAN, J. L., SEJNOWSKI, T. J. and HINTON, G. E. (Eds) *Connectionist Models: Proceedings of the 1990 Summer School*, San Mateo, CA: Morgan Kaufmann.

GOEBEL, R. (1993) 'Perceiving complex visual scenes: An oscillator neural network model that integrates selective attention, perceptual organisation, and invariant recognition', in GILES, C. L., HANSON, S. J. and COWAN, J. D. (Eds) *Advances in Neural Information Processing Systems 5*, San Mateo, CA: Morgan Kaufmann.

GOEBEL, R. (in press) 'The role of visual perception, selective attention, and short-term memory for symbol manipulation: A neural network model that learns to evaluate simple LISP expressions', in WENDER, K. F., SCHMALHOFER, F. and BOECKER, H. D. (Eds) *Cognition and Computer Programming*, Norwood, NJ: Ablex.

GROSSBERG, S. (1976) 'Adaptive pattern classification and universal recoding II: Feedback, expectation, olfaction, and illusions', *Biological Cybernetics*, 23, pp. 187–202.

GROSSBERG, S. (1982) *Studies of Mind and Brain: Neural Principles of Learning, Perception, Development, Cognition, and Motor Control*, Boston: Reidel.

GROSSBERG, S. (1987) *The Adaptive Brain*, Amsterdam: North-Holland.

HANCOCK, P. J. B., SMITH, L. S. and PHILLIPS, W. A. (1991) A biologically supported error-correcting learning rule, *Neural Computation*, 3, pp. 201–12.

HEBB, D. O. (1949) *The Organization of Behavior*, New York: Wiley.

HEEMSKERK, J. N. H. and MURRE, J. M. J. (1994) *Brain-Size Neurocomputers: Analyses and Simulations of Fractal Architectures*, Manuscript submitted for publication.

HOLLAND, J. H. (1975) *Adaptation in Natural and Artificial Systems*, Ann Arbor, MI: University of Michigan Press.

HOPFIELD, J. J. (1982) 'Neural networks and physical systems with emergent collective computational abilities', *Proceedings of the National Academy of Sciences, USA*, 79, pp. 2554–8.

HOPFIELD, J. J. (1984) 'Neurons with graded response have collective computational properties like those of two-state neurons', *Proceedings of the National Academy of Sciences, USA*, 81, pp. 3088–92.

HOPFIELD, J. J. and TANK, D. W. (1986) 'Computing with neural circuits: A model', *Science*, 233, pp. 625–633.

HORNIK, K., STINCHCOMBE, M. and WHITE, H. (1989) 'Multilayer feedforward networks are universal approximators', *Neural Networks*, 2, pp. 359–66.

INDEFREY, P. and GOEBEL, R. (1993) 'The learning of weak noun declension in German: Children vs. artificial neural networks', in *Proceedings of the Fifteenth Annual Conference of the Cognitive Science Society*, Hillsdale, NJ: Lawrence Erlbaum, pp. 575–80.

JAMES, W. (1890) *Psychology (Briefer Course)*, New York: Holt.

JORDAN, M. I. (1986) *Serial Order: A Parallel Distributed Processing Approach* (Technical Report 8604), La Jolla, CA: Institute for Cognitive Science, University of California.

JORDAN, M. I. (1990) 'Motor learning and the degrees of freedom problem', in JEANNEROD, M. (Ed) *Attention and Performance, XIII*, Hillsdale, NJ: Lawrence Erlbaum.

JORDAN, M. I. (in press) 'Computational aspects of motor control and motor learning', in HEUER, H. and KEELE, S. (Eds) *Handbook of Motor Control*, Berlin: Springer.

KIRKPATRICK, S., GELATT, C. D., Jr. and VECCHI, M. P. (1983) 'Optimization by simulated annealing', *Science*, 220, pp. 671–80.

KOHONEN, T. (1988) 'The "neural" phonetic typewriter', *IEEE Computer*, March, pp. 11–22.

KOHONEN, T. (1989) *Self-Organization and Associative Memory*, 3rd edn., Berlin: Springer.

KOHONEN, T. (1990) 'The self-organizing map', *Proceedings of the IEEE*, 78, pp. 1464–80.

KOSKO, B. (1987) 'Adaptive bidirectional associative memories', *Applied Optics*, 26, pp. 4947–60.

KOSKO, B. (1988) 'Bidirectional associative memories', *IEEE Transactions on Systems, Man, and Cybernetics*, SMC-18, pp. 49–60.

KRUSCHKE, J.K. (1993) 'Human category learning: Implications for backpropagation models', *Connection Science*, 5(1), 3–36.

KUPERSTEIN, M. (1988) 'Neural model of adaptive hand-eye coordination for single postures', *Science*, 239, pp. 1308–11.

LASHLEY, K.S. (1950) 'In search of the engram', in *Society of Experimental Biology Symposium, No. 4: Psychological Mechanisms in Animal Behavior*, Cambridge: Cambridge University Press, pp. 454–80.

LeCUN, Y. (1986) 'Learning processes in an asymmetric threshold network', in BIENENSTOCK, E., FOGELMAN, F. and WEISBUCH, G. (Eds) *Disordered Systems and Biological Organization*, Berlin: Springer.

McCLELLAND, J.L. and RUMELHART, D.E. (1981) 'An interactive activation model of context effects in letter perception. Part I: An account of basic findings', *Psychological Review*, 5, pp. 375–407.

McCLOSKEY, M. and COHEN, N.J. (1989) 'Catastrophic interference in connectionist networks: The sequential learning problem', in BOWER, G.H. (Ed) *The Psychology of Learning and Motivation*, New York: Academic Press.

McCULLOCH, W.S. and PITTS, W. (1943) 'A logical calculus of the ideas immanent in nervous activity', *Bulletin of Mathematical Biophysics*, 9, pp. 127–47.

METROPOLIS, N., ROSENBLUTH, A., ROSENBLUTH, M., TELLER, A. and TELLER, E. (1953) 'Equation of state calculations for fast computing machines', *Journal of Chemical Physics*, 6. p. 1087.

MILNER, P.M. (1957) 'The cell assembly: Mark II', *Psychological Review*, 64, pp. 242–52.

MINSKY, M.L. and PAPERT, S.A. (1969) *Perceptrons*, Cambridge, MA: MIT Press.

MORASSO, P., KENNEDY, J., ANTONJ, E., DI MARCO, S. and DORDONI, M. (1990) 'Self-organisation of an allograph lexicon', *International Joint Conference on Neural Networks, Lisbon*, March 1990.

MURRE, J.M.J. (1992a) *Categorization and Learning in Modular Neural Networks*, Hemel Hempstead: Harvester Wheatsheaf.

MURRE, J.M.J. (1992b) 'The effects of pattern presentation on interference in backpropagation networks', in *Proceedings of the Fourteenth Annual Conference of the Cognitive Science Society*, Hillsdale, NJ: Lawrence Erlbaum, pp. 54–9.

MURRE, J.M.J. (1994) *A Model of Amnesia*, Manuscript submitted for publication.

MURRE, J.M.J. (in press) 'Transfer of learning in backpropagation and in related neural network models', in LEVY, J., BAIRAKTARIS, D., BULLINARIA, J. and CAIRNS, P. (Eds) *Connectionist Models of Memory and Language*, London: UCL Press.

MURRE, J.M.J., PHAF, R.H. and WOLTERS, G. (1992) 'CALM: Categorizing and learning module', *Neural Networks*, 5, pp. 55–82.

MURRE, J.M.J. and STURDY, D.P.F. (1995) 'The connectivity' of the brain: multi-level quantitative analysis, *Biological Cybernetics*, 73, in press.

NORMAN, D.A. (1986) 'Reflections on cognition and parallel distributed processing', in McCLELLAND, J.L. and RUMELHART, D.E. (Eds) *Parallel Distributed Processing: Explorations in the Microstructure of Cognition: Vol. 2. Psychological and Biological Models*, Cambridge, MA: MIT Press, pp. 531–46.

OJEMANN, G.A. (1983) 'Brain organization for language from the perspective of electrical stimulation mapping', *Behavioral and Brain Sciences*, 6, pp. 189–230.

PARKER, D. (1982) *Learning Logic* (Invention report S81-64, File1), Office of Technology Licensing, Stanford University.

PHAF, R. H. (1994) *Learning in Natural and Connectionist Systems: Experiments and a Model*, Dordrecht: Kluwer Academic Publishers.

PINKER, S. (1991) 'Rules of language', *Science*, 253, pp. 530–5.

PINKER, S. and PRINCE, A. (1988) 'On language and connectionism: Analysis of a parallel distributed processing model of language acquisition', *Cognition*, 28, pp. 73–193.

QUINLAN, P. (1991) *Connectionism and Psychology: A Psychological Perspective on New Connectionist Research*, Hemel Hempstead: Harvester Wheatsheaf.

RATCLIFF, R. (1990) 'Connectionist models of recognition memory: Constraints imposed by learning and forgetting functions', *Psychological Review*, 97, pp. 285–308.

RESCORLA, R. A. and WAGNER, A. R. (1972) 'A theory of Pavlovian conditioning: Variations in the effectiveness of reinforcement and non-reinforcement', in BLACK, A. H. and PROKASY, W. F. (Eds) *Classical Conditioning II: Current Research and Theory*, New York: Appleton-Century-Crofts, pp. 64–99.

RITTER, H. and KOHONEN, T. (1990) 'Learning "semantotopic maps" from context', in *Proceedings of the International Joint Conference on Neural Networks, Washington, DC*, Vol. 1, pp. 23–6.

ROCHESTER, N., HOLLAND, J. H., HAIBT, L. H. and DUDA, W. L. (1956) 'Tests on a cell assembly theory of the action of the brain, using a large digital computer', *IRE Transactions on Information Theory*, IT-2, pp. 80–93.

ROSENBLATT, F. (1958) 'The perceptron: A probabilistic model for information storage and organization in the brain', *Psychological Review*, 65, pp. 386–408.

ROSENBLATT, F. (1962) *Principles of Neurodynamics*, Washington, DC: Spartan Books.

RUMELHART, D. E., HINTON, G. E. and WILLIAMS, R. J. (1986) 'Learning internal representations by error propagation', in RUMELHART, D. E., MCCLELLAND, J. L. and the PDP Research Group, *Parallel Distributed Processing: Explorations in the Microstructure of Cognition: Vol. 1. Foundations*, Cambridge, MA: MIT Press, pp. 318–62.

RUMELHART, D. E., MCCLELLAND, J. L. and the PDP Research Group (Eds) (1986) *Parallel Distributed Processing: Explorations in the Microstructure of Cognition* (Vols. 1–2), Cambridge, MA: MIT Press.

RUMELHART, D. E. and ZIPSER, D. (1985) 'Feature discovery by competitive learning', *Cognitive Science*, 9, pp. 75–112.

SEIDENBERG, M. S. and MCCLELLAND, J. L. (1989) 'A distributed developmental model of visual word recognition and naming', *Psychological Review*, 96, pp. 523–68.

SEJNOWSKI, T. J. and ROSENBERG, C. R. (1987) 'Parallel networks that learn to pronounce English text', *Complex Systems*, 1, pp. 145–68.

WERBOS, P. J. (1974) *Beyond Regression: New Tools for Predication and Analysis in the Behavioral Sciences*, Unpublished doctoral dissertation, Cambridge, MA: Harvard University.

WERBOS, P. J. (1988) 'Generalization of backpropagation with application to a recurrent gas market model', *Neural Networks*, 1, pp. 339–56.

WIDROW, B. and HOFF, M. E. (1960) 'Adaptive switching circuits', *1960 IRE WESCON Convention Record*, Part 4, pp. 96–104.

WOLPERT, D. H. (1990) 'Constructing a generalizer superior to NETtalk via a mathematical theory of generalization', *Neural Networks*, 3, pp. 445–52.

Part II
Models of Language Comprehension

Chapter 4

Modelling Multiple Influences in Speech Perception

Dominic W. Massaro

Introduction

Speech perception is a human skill that rivals our other impressive achievements. Even after decades of intense effort, speech recognition by machine remains far inferior to human performance. It appears that our success in recognizing speech depends on our ability to use multiple sources of information, to evaluate each source in parallel with all the others, and to integrate or combine all of these sources to achieve perceptual recognition. Recognition of spoken words in a sentence is achieved via a variety of bottom-up and top-down sources of information. Top-down sources include contextual, semantic, syntactic, lexical, and sublexical constraints, of which I consider the last two in this chapter. Bottom-up sources include audible and visible features of the spoken word.

An example of the use of multiple influences in speech perception is the following well-known effect. A senior citizen watching a talk show on television is having trouble hearing the participants. He remembers he does not have his glasses, retrieves them, and puts them on. Surprisingly, seeing the show better allows him to hear the show better.

In this chapter, two well-known computational models of speech perception are discussed. To set the stage for this discussion, I first address the questions which processing units and which architecture are supported by available empirical evidence. I argue that the (demi-)syllable is a likely processing unit and that speech perception requires an architecture in which different information sources collaborate. Next I discuss the FLMP model, then the TRACE model. These two models are compared and evaluated with respect to the processing units, the architecture, and available empirical data concerning visual speech.

Theoretical Principles

Speech perception appears to be well-described by three basic principles that are compatible with perception. These principles are: (1) perception is a process of inference, (2) perceptual inference is not deductively valid, and (3) perceptual inferences are biased (e.g., Bennett, Hoffman and Prakash, 1989). The first two assumptions go back to at least Hermann von Helmholtz and require little explanation. The third simply means that a given perceptual system prefers some interpretations relative to others. In visual perception, for example, we have a bias to see two-dimensional projections as three-dimensional scenes. In speech perception, we are biased to perceive the speech input in terms of the segments of our language and to perceive the segments as comprising a meaningful communication. These three principles describe the perceiver's solution to the inverse mapping problem: the perceiver's goal is to solve the problem of what environmental situation exists given the current sensory cues.

There is also evidence that language understanding is mediated by a sequence of processing stages. It might be helpful to describe visual perception to clarify the concept of stages of information processing (see Banks and Krajicek, 1991, for a recent review). There are at least three stages of processing (DeYoe and Van Essen, 1988): visual input is transduced by the visual system (retinal transduction), a conglomeration of sensory cues (features) is made available, and attributes of the visual world are experienced by the perceiver. In visual perception, there is both a one-to-many and a many-to-one relationship between sensory cues and perceived attributes. As an example of the former, motion provides information about both the perceived shape of an object and its perceived movement. A case of the many-to-one relationship in vision is that information about the shape of an object is enriched not only by motion, but also by perspective cues, picture cues, binocular disparity, and shading.

This same framework can be applied to speech perception and spoken language understanding. Speech perception involves transduction along the basilar membrane, sensory cues, and perceived attributes. A single cue can influence several perceived attributes. For example, the duration of a vowel provides information about vowel identity, prosodic information such as stress, and the syntactic role of the word in the sentence. Another example is that the pitch of a speaker's voice is informative about both the identity of the speaker and intonation. The best known example of multiple cues to a single perceived attribute in speech is the case of the many cues for the voicing of a medial stop consonant (Lisker, 1978; Cohen, 1979). These include the duration of the preceding vowel, the onset frequency of the fundamental (F0), the voice onset time (VOT), and the silent closure interval (the silence between the preceding vowel and the stop consonant). Another example is the impressive demonstration that both the speech sound and the visible mouth movements of the speaker influence perception of speech segments (McGurk and MacDonald, 1976). Features and perceived attributes necessarily mediate segments of the speech input. Thus, it has been of primary interest to determine the units that are functional in speech perception.

Perceptual Units in Speech Perception

Students of speech science usually assume that perception of spoken words is mediated by perceptual units which have some type of representation in long-term memory and have a relatively invariant relationship to properties of the speech signal. When we recognize speech, we experience a sequence of units whereas a language foreign to us appears like a run-together babble. Postulating just a single size of unit is scientifically parsimonious, although there is no reason why perceivers might not exploit several perceptual units. We now address the issue of which candidate best qualifies for perceptual unit in speech.

Phonemes

The first candidate we consider for the perceptual unit is the phoneme, which reflects the smallest functional difference between the meaning of two speech sounds. Consider the acoustic properties of vowel phonemes. Unlike some consonant phonemes, whose acoustic properties change over time, the wave shape of the vowel is relatively steady-state. The wave shape of the vowel repeats itself anywhere from 75 to 200 times per second. In normal running speech, vowels last between 45 and 180 ms, and even longer in citation speech in which words are pronounced singly. During this time the vowels maintain a fairly regular and unique pattern (Klatt, 1976). It follows that, by our criteria, vowels could function as perceptual units in speech.

Consonant signals, on the other hand, are more complicated than vowels and some of them do not seem to qualify as perceptual units. A perceptual unit must have a relatively invariant sound pattern in different contexts but some consonant phonemes have significantly different sound patterns in different speech contexts. For example, the stop consonant phoneme /d/ has very different acoustic representations in different vowel contexts (e.g., before /ɑ/ or /u/). Since the steady-state portion corresponds to the vowel sounds, the first part, called the transition, must be responsible for the perception of the consonant /d/. Because the acoustic pattern corresponding to the /d/ differs significantly in different syllables, one set of acoustic features would not be sufficient to recognize the consonant /d/ in the different vowel contexts. In pattern recognition terms, we say that consonant phonemes do not represent a linearly separable set: two different phonemes can be represented more closely together than two occurrences of the same phoneme. Therefore, we must either modify our definition of a perceptual unit or eliminate the stop consonant phoneme as a candidate.

Open (CV, VC, and V) Syllables

There is another reason why the consonant phoneme /d/ cannot qualify as a perceptual unit. In a successive stage model perceptual units are recognized in a successive and linear fashion. Research has shown, however, that the consonant /d/ in a consonant-vowel (CV) syllable, for example /da/, cannot be recognized before the vowel is also recognized. If the consonant were recognized before the vowel, then we should be able to decrease the duration of the vowel portion of the syllable so that only the consonant would be recognized. Experimentally, the duration of the vowel in the CV syllable is gradually decreased and the subject is asked to respond when she hears the stop consonant sound alone. The CV syllable is perceived as a complete syllable until the vowel is eliminated almost entirely (Liberman *et al.*, 1967). At that point, however, instead of the perception changing to the consonant /d/, a nonspeech whistle is heard. Even so, recognition of the C and V is still above chance, meaning that the stop consonant /d/ cannot be perceived independently of perceiving or recognizing a CV syllable. Therefore, it seems unlikely that the /d/ sound would be perceived before the vowel sound; it appears, rather, that the CV syllable is perceived as an indivisible whole or Gestalt.

One might argue that there is also significant contextual variation of a given open syllable. Using our logic, this variation would disqualify open syllables as perceptual units as well according to our invariance criterion. However, the contextual variation for open syllables is considerably less than it is for phonemes (Massaro and Oden, 1980). It has been shown that isolating a CV from a VCV utterance does not disrupt recognition of the CV, for example. If open syllables were not sufficiently invariant in different contexts, then it should not have been possible to recognize the isolated CV.

These arguments lead to the idea that CV or VC syllables function as perceptual units rather than containing two perceptual units each. Liberman *et al.* (1967) found that subjects could identify shortened versions of the CV syllables when most of the vowel portion is eliminated. It is important to distinguish between the size of a perceptual unit and the time course of its recognition. It is possible that the recognition is delayed somewhat from a perceptual unit's actual occurrence. One way to test this hypothesis is to employ the CV syllables in a recognition-masking task. One can measure the time course of recognition of a syllable by varying the amount of processing time before the onset of a second syllable, which masks the first one. If the masking syllable follows the first one soon enough, it should interfere with perception of the first. Consider the three CV syllables /ba/, /da/, and /ga/ (/a/ pronounced as in *father*), which differ from each other only with respect to the consonant phoneme. Backward recognition masking, if found with these sounds, would demonstrate that the consonant sound is not recognized before the vowel occurs and also that the CV syllable requires time to be perceived.

Backward Recognition Masking
There have been several experiments on the backward recognition masking of CV syllables (Pisoni, 1972; Massaro, 1975). Newman and Spitzer (1987) employed the three CV syllables /bɑ/, /dɑ/, and /gɑ/ as test items. These items were synthetic speech stimuli that lasted 40 msec; the first 20 msec of the item consisted of the CV transition and the last 20 msec corresponded to the steady-state vowel. The masking stimulus was the steady-state vowel /ɑ/ presented for 40 msec after a variable silent interval. In one condition, the test and masking stimuli were presented to opposite ears, that is, dichotically.

Figure 4.1 shows the percentage of correct recognitions for eight observers as a

Figure 4.1: Probability of correct recognitions of the test CV syllables as a function of the duration of the silent intersyllable interval in a backward recognition-masking task (results of Newman and Spitzer, 1987)

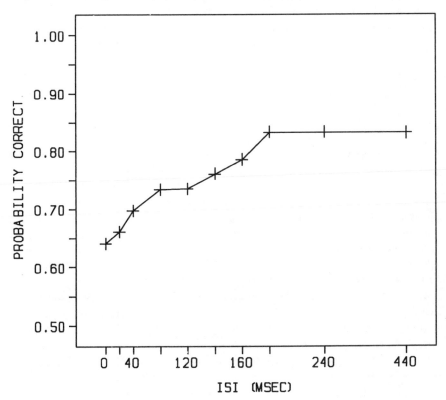

function of the silent interval between the test and masking CVs. The results show that recognition of the consonant is not complete at the end of the CV transition, nor even at the end of the short vowel presentation. Rather, correct identification of the CV syllable requires perceptual processing after the stimulus presentation. These results support the hypothesis that the CV syllable must have functioned as a perceptual unit. The features necessary for recognition must, therefore, define the complete CV unit. An analogous argument can be made for VC syllables also functioning as perceptual units.

Words and Phrases

We must also ask whether perceptual units could be larger than CV or VC syllables. Miller (1962) argued that the phrase of two or three words might function as a perceptual unit. According to our criteria for a perceptual unit, it must correspond to a prototype in long-term memory which has a list of features describing the acoustic features in the auditory storage of that perceptual unit. Accordingly, auditory storage must last for one or two seconds to hold perceptual units of the size of a phrase. But the recognition-masking studies estimate the effective duration of storage to be about 250 msec. Therefore, perceptual units must occur within this period, eliminating the phrase as the perceptual unit.

Lexical Effects

We have considered evidence for phonemes, syllables, words, and phrases as perceptual units of speech perception. There is good support for the syllable as a perceptual unit, but this does not preclude higher order sources of information from contributing to the resolution of the syllable. Lexical knowledge might facilitate syllable recognition, for example. Consistent with this expectation, detection of the first phoneme is faster in monosyllable words than in nonwords (Cutler *et al.*, 1987). This result is interpreted in terms of activation of lexical knowledge leading to the faster RT. This word advantage did not hold for bisyllabic words (Segui, Frauenfelder and Mehler, 1981). In this case, we can say that the lexical activation did not occur soon enough to facilitate processing of the first syllable. Similarly, in the same initial phoneme detection task, word frequency effects are obtained for monosyllabic but not bisyllabic words (Dupoux and Mehler, 1990). This difference is maintained even if the bisyllabic words are compressed in time. This result reveals that the first syllable is processed very quickly so that the first phoneme is detected before the recognition of the bisyllabic word.

Cross-Linguistic Differences

Cutler *et al.* (1986) have shown that segmentation appears to be language dependent. French perceivers were faster at detecting a syllable-sized segment when the segment matched exactly the first syllable of the test word. Thus, subjects were faster at detecting *pa* in *pa-lace* than in *pal-mier*. Similarly, subjects were faster at detecting *pal* in *pal-mier* than in *pa-lace*. This result does not occur in English (Cutler *et al.*, 1987). Subjects have roughly the same RT to *pa* in *pa-lace* and *pal-pitate*. Because open syllables function as perceptual units, we would also expect that the English subjects would be faster in the detection of *pa* than *pal* (which is the case, Savin and Bever, 1970). Furthermore, French subjects processed the English words in the same way they processed the French words, and similarly for the English subjects.

These results are interpreted to mean that the processing units functional in speech perception depend on the native language of the perceiver. The sources of information in language are learned in terms of the perceiver's native tongue. This result is consistent with the findings on bimodal speech perception across languages (Sekiyama and Tohkura, 1991; Massaro *et al.*, 1993).

Summary

Empirical research has appeared to solve the issue of perceptual units in speech. The recognition-masking paradigm developed to study the recognition of auditory sounds has provided a useful tool for determining the perceptual units in speech. If auditory storage is limited to 250 msec, the perceptual units must occur within this short period. This time period precludes larger units of word and phrase length, but agrees nicely with the durations of open (V, CV, and VC) syllables in normal speech. Nooteboom (1992), although having an alternative theoretical viewpoint, also concludes that the syllable is a psychologically real perceptual unit. Given some support for a functional perceptual unit in speech, we now explore the sources of information used in recognizing these units.

Multiple Sources Influence Speech Perception

Numerous studies have shown that spectral cues such as voicing during the closure of the consonant and preclosure transition are important cues, as is the duration of the preceding vowel (Lisker, 1978). These spectral and duration cues trade off with one another in an intriguing manner. For high quality stimuli, the spectral cues have the most impact on identification. If the quality of the sound is decreased, then vowel duration has a larger influence. For example, Raphael (1972) found that vowel duration has a large effect with synthetic speech, which has relatively poor spectral information. Wardrip-Fruin (1985) studied the perception of voicing in final stop consonants in natural speech and found that vowel duration was the primary influence when the test stimuli were presented against a high level of background noise. This result agrees with the trade-off idea because the noise would tend to degrade spectral cues much more than the vowel duration cue.

The study of voicing in initial stops has usually involved the variation of VOT. Several perceptual studies, on the other hand, have shown that other cues such as the F0 at the onset of voicing can influence categorization when the VOT is ambiguous (e.g., Summerfield and Haggard, 1974). Whalen *et al.* (1993) independently varied VOT and F0 in unspeeded and speeded categorization tasks. They found some evidence that the identification RTs were influenced by F0, even for VOTs that were consistently identified as one alternative or the other. This result shows that multiple information sources influence perceptual recognition, even when one of the cues is unambiguous. The influence of cues might be best understood in terms of their resolution over time, and even an asymptotic unambiguous cue necessarily begins as ambiguous and can be aided by other less influential cues.

Although perceivers find it natural to integrate the cues so that all cues contribute to the resulting percept, one might expect that the influence of a particular cue might be modified if certain constraints are placed on the perceptual process. Relevant to this issue, Gordon, Eberhardt and Rueckl (1993) showed that relative contribution of a speech cue to identification could be modulated by a secondary task. One secondary task involved the presentation of a visual display of three two-digit numbers. The subjects had to decide if the difference between first two numbers was equal to the difference between the second two. The speech stimulus was presented 150 msec after the numbers. In another secondary task, the subjects had to indicate the longer of two lines. Subjects identified speech stimuli that were independently varied along two properties. In one test, the VOT and F0 onset frequency of CV syllables were varied. The presence of a secondary task primarily reduced the influence of F0 onset frequency duration but not VOT. In another test, subjects identified vowels varying in their formant pattern and duration (for a definition of formant and other phonetic terms, see Chapter 15). The secondary task now reduced the influence of formant pattern but not vowel duration. These results reveal that cognitive processing load can lower the cue value of a source of information. This degradation might be analogous to some form of lowering the quality of the information, for instance by adding noise to the cue.

Context Effects in Speech Perception

It has been known for some time that stimulus information and context contribute to speech perception. In Bagley's (1900) seminal study, naturally spoken words were recorded and played back on Edison phonograph cylinders. These words were more easily recognized when they were placed in a sentence context. Context effects have been repeatedly rediscovered or replicated since Bagley's original demonstrations (Pollack and Pickett, 1963; Tyler and Wessels, 1983). We briefly describe just a few representative studies of context effects that will prove informative in our evaluation of contemporary models.

Figure 4.2: Average observed probability of an r response as a function of the glide F3 onset level and context (after Massaro and Cohen, Experiment 2, 1983)

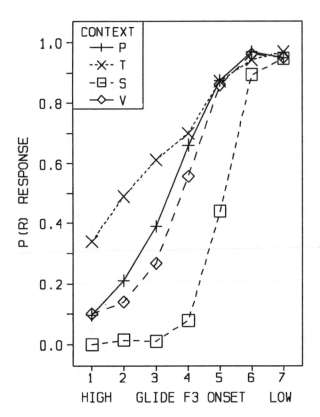

Phonological Context

Massaro and Cohen (1983) varied a top-down and a bottom-up source of information in a speech identification task. Subjects were presented with CCV syllables of which the first consonant was /p/, /t/, /s/, or /v/ the second consonant one of seven glides equally spaced on a continuum between /l/ and /r/, and the vowel /i/. The glide was changed in small steps from /l/ to /r/ by changing its initial F3 frequency from high to low. The results of this experiment are shown in Figure 4.2. Both the bottom-up glide information and the top-down phonological context influenced performance. In addition, the contribution of one source was larger when the other source was more ambiguous.

Phonemic Restoration

In the original type of phonemic-restoration study (Warren, 1970), a phoneme in a word is removed and replaced with some other stimulus, such as a tone or white noise. Subjects perceive the word as relatively intact and have difficulty indicating which phoneme is missing. This illusion has been taken as support for the idea that the lexical information modifies the sublexical auditory representation. Another interpretation is that the lexical context simply provides an additional source of information. According to this latter view, there is no reason to assume that the auditory representation was modified.

Repp (1992) carried out a systematic set of experiments to distinguish between these explanations. Basically, he asked the question whether the restoration was localized at the auditory level or at a higher linguistic level. To address this question, subjects were asked to judge the perceived pitch (timbre, brightness) of the extraneous noise that replaced the speech sound. If phonemic restoration modified auditory processing, we would expect these auditory judgments to be influenced by lexical context. The overall result of five experiments was negative: auditory judgments were not modified even though phoneme restoration did occur. A positive influence of a top-down constraint on perceptual report does not necessarily mean that the representation of the bottom-up influence(s) has been modified.

Lexical Context

An influential result reported by Ganong (1980) has generated a series of experiments and some theoretical controversy. His goal was to show that lexical

*Figure 4.3: Observed (points) and predicted (lines) proportion of /d/
identification for -ash and -ask contexts (top panel) and -irt and -urf contexts
(bottom panel) as a function of VOT. (Observed data from Ganong, 1980)*

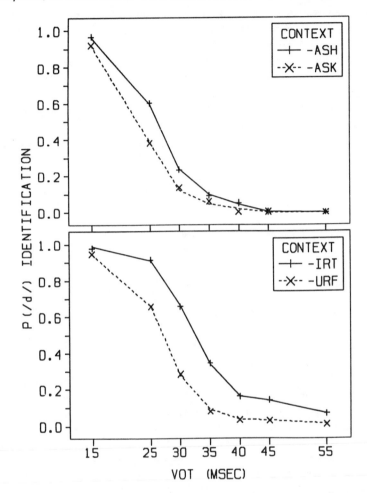

identity could influence phonetic judgments. A continuum of test items was made
by varying the VOT of the initial stop consonant of CVC syllables. The VC was
also varied. For example, subjects identified the initial consonant as /d/ or /t/ in
the context -ash (where *dash* is a word and *tash* is not), or in the context -ask
(where *task* is a word and *dask* is not). Figure 4.3 shows that a lexical effect was
observed because there were more voiced judgments /d/ in the context -ash than
in the context -ask. An important result was that this lexical effect was largest at
the intermediate levels of VOT that were most ambiguous. This result is consistent
with the general principle that the least ambiguous source has the most influence
on perception. Ganong's original results have been replicated by several
investigators (Connine and Clifton, 1987; Pitt and Samuel, 1993).

Summary

We have described several important phenomena characteristic of the speech perception process. Perceptual units of roughly open-syllable size appear to be functional in speech recognition. Research has also shown that multiple sources of information allow recognition to be successful. Evidence for the influence of both bottom-up and top-down sources has been well-documented. Although a top-down contextual source of information can influence perceptual judgment, it does not necessarily modify the representation of other bottom-up sources. Furthermore, these sources trade off with one another in such a manner that one source has the most influence on perception when the other source is ambiguous. With these findings, we now develop and test two extant models of speech recognition.

Computational Models of Speech Perception

Before discussing two representative models of speech perception, it is important to describe some properties of computational models and why they are valuable in the study of language processing. Computational modelling is the formal, quantitative description of behaviour by the interaction of a configuration of component processes. In analogy to explanations in other sciences, complex behaviour should be understood whenever possible in terms of its emergence from the interaction of much simpler processes. In one sense, this is what computational modelling is about. We attempt to help understand the complexity of everyday behaviour in terms of simpler mechanisms working in combination. Computational modelling necessarily involves the processes causing behaviour and not just the behaviour itself. Computational modelling is valuable because it overcomes some powerful constraints on psychological inquiry. Its added value is that models by definition are precisely stated and capable of experimental test, which is essential in empirical science. Verbal theories alone are seldom sufficient to make exact predictions and cannot be easily discriminated from alternative theories.

Models should capture the heart of the theories they implement. Two models representing two theories should be able to contrast the central difference between the theories. The most sensitive tests of psycholinguistic models usually involve specific experiments designed to test the models directly. Existing results seldom provide a critical test of a model unless the design of the experiment just by chance happened to be appropriate for the model test. The two models we develop and test represent two different approaches to computational modelling. In addition, the models make different assumptions about how multiple sources work together to influence speech perception.

Fuzzy Logical Model of Perception (FLMP)

The input to this model consists of multiple sources of information that support speech perception. The throughput involves processes that evaluate and integrate all of these sources to achieve perceptual recognition (Oden and Massaro, 1978). There are many different auditory sources of information or cues that the listener uses to decode the message. Over a dozen different acoustic properties appear to distinguish /igi/ from /iki/ (Lisker, 1978). Perceivers also use information from other modalities in face to face communication. Both lip movements and hand gestures have been shown to aid in speech perception (Massaro, 1987). Finally, perceivers also use situational and linguistic context to help disambiguate the signal. Consistent with our theoretical framework and similar to other approaches (e.g., Pisoni and Luce, 1987), it is assumed that speech is processed through a sequence of processing stages: feature evaluation, feature integration, and decision. Continuously-valued features are evaluated, integrated, and matched against prototype descriptions in memory. An identification decision is made on the basis of the relative goodness-of-match of the stimulus information with the relevant prototype descriptions. Figure 4.4 illustrates the three stages in the

Figure 4.4: Schematic representation of the three stages involved in perceptual recognition. The three stages are shown to proceed left to right in time to illustrate their necessarily successive but overlapping processing. The sources of information are represented by uppercase letters. Auditory information is represented by A_i and visual information by V_j. The evaluation process transforms these sources of information into psychological values (indicated by lowercase letters a_i and v_j). These sources are then integrated to give an overall degree of support for a given alternative p_{ij}. The decision operation maps this value into some response, R_{ij}, such as a discrete decision or a rating

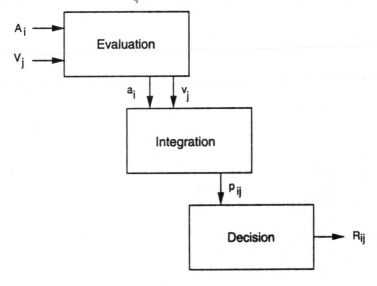

processing of auditory and visual speech. The three stages are shown to illustrate their necessarily successive but overlapping processing. The input corresponds to auditory and visual sources of information (represented by uppercase letters). The evaluation process transforms these into psychological values (indicated by lowercase letters) corresponding to how much each source supports each alternative. The outputs of evaluation are integrated to give an overall degree of support for each alternative. Continuous information is available from each source and the sources are evaluated independently of one another (that is, the output of evaluation of one source is not contaminated by the other source). The output of the integration process is also assumed to provide continuous information. The decision operation maps the output of integration into some response, such as a discrete decision or a rating.

The perceiver maintains in memory summary descriptions of the perceptual units of the language. These summary descriptions are called prototypes and they contain a conjunction of various properties called features. Given some speech input, all prototypes corresponding to the perceptual units of the language are activated to some degree. The features of the prototype correspond to the ideal values that an exemplar should have if it is a member of that category. The exact form of the representation of these properties is not known and may never be known. However, the memory representation must be compatible with the sensory representation resulting from the transduction of the audible and visible speech. Compatibility is necessary because the two representations must be related to one another. To recognize the syllable /ba/, the perceiver must be able to relate the auditory and visual information to some memory of the category /ba/.

Given the necessarily large variety of features, it is necessary to have a common metric representing the degree of match of each feature. The syllable /ba/, for example, might have both visible and audible featural information related to its articulation. These two features must share a common metric to relate them to one another. Fuzzy truth values (Zadeh, 1965) are used as this metric because they provide a natural representation of the degree of match. Fuzzy truth values lie between zero and one, corresponding to a proposition varying between completely false and completely true. The value 0.5 is a completely ambiguous situation, 0.7 is more true than false, and so on. Fuzzy truth values, therefore, provide continuous representations of different types of information. Given that fuzzy truth values couch information in mathematical terms, it is possible to develop a quantitative description of speech perception.

Feature evaluation provides the degree to which each feature in the syllable matches the corresponding feature in each prototype in memory. Feature integration combines the features (the degrees of matches) corresponding to each prototype. Feature integration determines the degree to which each prototype matches the syllable. At decision, the degree of match of each prototype is evaluated relative to all prototypes. This decision operation, called a relative goodness rule (RGR; Massaro and Friedman, 1990), predicts the proportion of times the syllable is identified as an instance of the prototype, or a rating judgment indicating the degree to which the syllable matches the category. In the model, all features contribute to the final value, but with the property that the least ambiguous features have the most impact on the outcome.

The FLMP is not easily pigeon-holed as either symbolic or connectionist in structure. Like symbolic models, its assumptions and operations are fairly transparent. Like connectionist models, it provides a natural account of the use of continuous information and constraint satisfaction given multiple inputs. The closed mathematical form of the model makes it a highly practical and useful theoretical tool. The model is easily tested against empirical results, the outcome of the tests are quickly available, and modification or adjustments are easily instantiated. An application of the model is now illustrated.

A Prototypical Experiment

Given the impressive findings that visible speech from the talker's face influences speech perception, I describe an experiment manipulating auditory and visual information in a speech perception task (Massaro *et al.*, 1993). The expanded factorial design illustrated in Figure 4.5 provides a unique method for addressing

Figure 4.5: Expansion of a typical factorial design to include auditory and visual conditions presented alone. The five levels along the auditory and visible continua represent auditory and visible speech syllables varying in equal physical steps between /ba/ and /da/

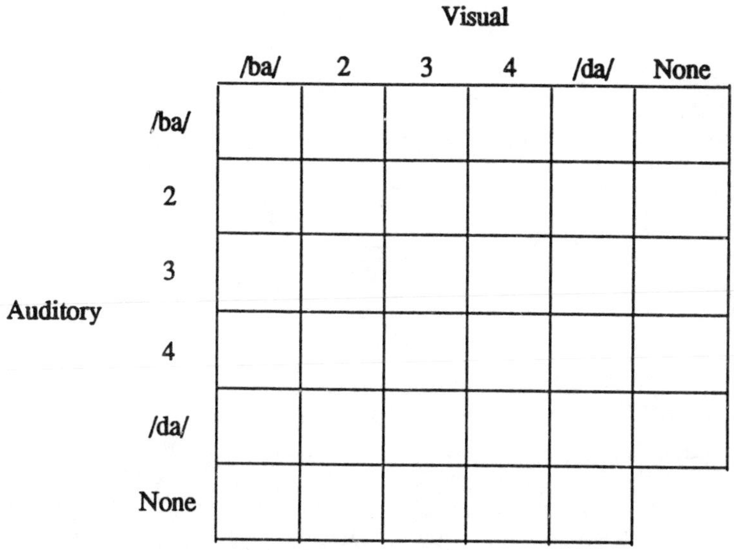

Visual

	/ba/	2	3	4	/da/	None
/ba/						
2						
3						
4						
/da/						
None						

(Auditory labels the rows)

the issues of evaluation and integration of audible and visible information in speech perception. In this experiment, five levels of audible speech varying between /ba/ and /da/ are crossed with five levels of visible speech varying between the same alternatives. The audible and visible speech also are presented alone, giving a total of $25 + 5 + 5 = 35$ independent stimulus conditions. A five-step /ba/ to /da/ auditory continuum was synthesized, by altering the parametric information specifying the first 80 msec of the consonant-vowel syllable. Using an animated face, control parameters are changed over time to produce a realistic articulation of a consonant-vowel syllable. By modifying the parameters appropriately, a five-step /ba/ to /da/ visible speech continuum was synthesized. The presentation of the auditory synthetic speech was synchronized with the visible speech for the bimodal stimulus presentations. All of the test stimuli were recorded on video tape for presentation during the experiment. Six unique test blocks were recorded with the 35 test items presented in each block.

Five college students were subjects in the experiment. They were instructed to listen to and watch the speaker, and to identify the syllable as either /ba/ or /da/. Each of the 35 possible stimuli were presented a total of 12 times during two sessions and the subjects identified each stimulus during a three second response interval.

Figure 4.6: Observed (points) and predicted (lines) proportion of /da/ identifications for the auditory alone (left panel), the factorial auditory-visual (centre panel) and visual alone (right panel) conditions as a function of the five levels of the synthetic auditory and visual speech varying between /ba/ and /da/. The lines give the prediction for the FLMP

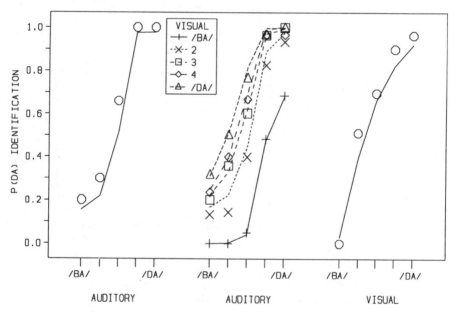

The *points* in Figure 4.6 represent the mean proportion of identifications across subjects. The identification judgments change systematically with changes in the audible and visible sources of information. The left part of Figure 4.6 shows that the likelihood of a /da/ identification increases as the auditory speech changes from /bɑ/ to /dɑ/, and analogously for the visible speech on the right side of Figure 4.6. Each source has a similar effect in the bimodal conditions, relative to the corresponding unimodal condition. In addition, the influence of one source of information is greatest when the other source is ambiguous. The FLMP attempts to replicate these results in a simulation of visual speech recognition. The stages in the model are as follows. The auditory and visual sources of information represent the input to the evaluation process. Both sources are assumed to provide continuous and independent evidence for the alternatives /bɑ/ and /dɑ/. First, these sources of information are translated into truth values corresponding to the degree of support for each of the prototypes. Then, the integration process combines these values to obtain an overall degree of support. Finally, the decision process computes the relative goodness-of-match to each test alternative. The output of the model is the expected proportion of judgments for each alternative. Now let us specify the various steps in some detail.

Defining the onsets of the second (F2) and third (F3) formants as the important auditory feature source and the degree of initial opening of the lips as the important visual feature source, the prototype for /dɑ/ would be:

/dɑ/ : Slightly falling F2-F3 & Open lips.

The prototype for /bɑ/ would be defined in an analogous fashion,

/bɑ/ : Rising F2-F3 & Closed lips.

Each alternative is defined by ideal values of the auditory and visual features. The auditory source supports each alternative to some degree, represented by feature values, and analogously for the visual source. The model requires five parameters for the visual feature values and five parameters for the auditory feature values, for each response alternative.

Given a prototype's independent specifications for the auditory and visual sources, the value of one source cannot change the value of the other source at the prototype matching stage. The integration of the features defining each prototype is evaluated according to the *product* of the feature values. If aD_i represents the degree to which the auditory stimulus A_i supports the alternative /dɑ/, that is, has slightly falling F2-F3; and vD_j represents the degree to which the visual stimulus V_j supports the alternative /dɑ/, that is, has open lips, then the outcome of prototype matching for /dɑ/ would be:

/dɑ/ : $aD_i\, vD_j$

where the subscripts i and j index the levels of the auditory and visual modalities, respectively. The outcome of integration would be computed in an analogous way for the other relevant alternatives. Thus, the feature values representing the degree of support from the auditory and visual information for a given alternative are integrated following the multiplicative rule given by the FLMP.

The decision operation would determine their relative merit leading to the prediction that

$$P(/da/ \mid A_i\, V_j) = \frac{-aD_i\, vD_j}{\displaystyle\sum}$$

where $\sum$ is equal to the sum of the merit of all relevant response alternatives.

The FLMP was fit to the individual results of each of the five subjects. The quantitative predictions of the model are determined by using a parameter estimation program that searches for parameter values that maximize the goodness-of-fit of the model. The model is represented in the program in terms of a set of prediction equations and a set of unknown parameters. By iteratively adjusting the parameters of the model, the program minimizes the squared

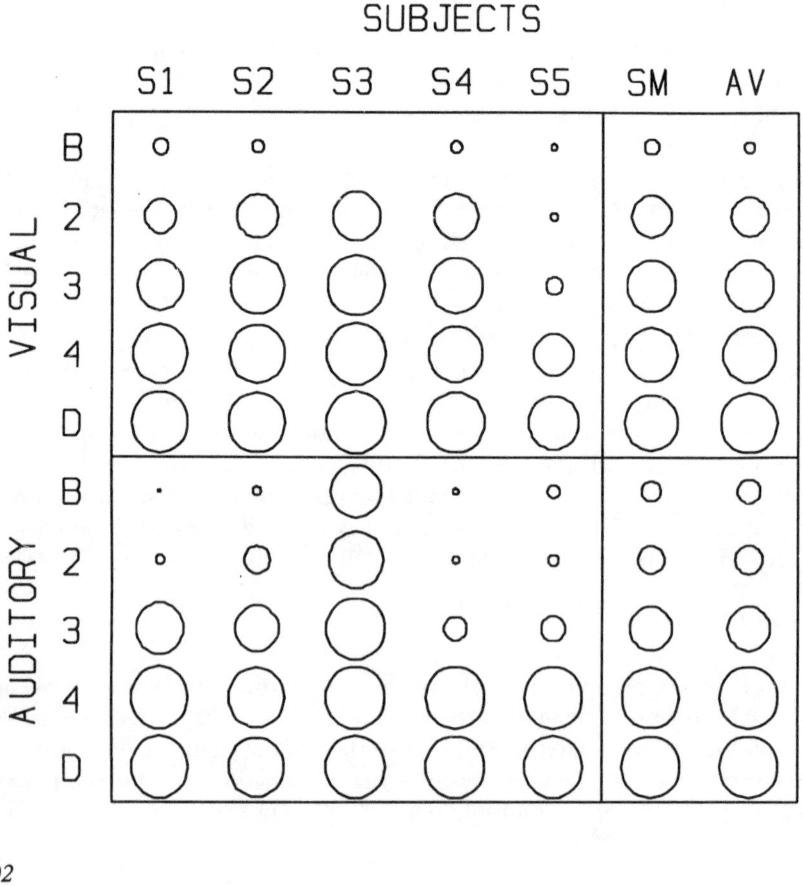

Figure 4.7: Parameter values for five subjects, the mean subject (SM), and the average (AV) of the five subjects for the support of the response alternative /da/ as a function the five levels along the visual-auditory speech continua. The parameter value is given by the area of each circle

deviations between the observed and predicted points. The outcome of the program is a set of parameter values which, when put into the model, come closest to predicting the observed results. The goodness-of-fit of the model is given by the root mean square deviation (RMSD), the square root of the average squared deviation between the predicted and observed values.

The lines in Figure 4.6 give the average predictions of FLMP. The model provides a good description of the identifications of both the unimodal and bimodal syllables (an average RMSD of 0.0731 across the individual subject fits). Figure 4.7 shows the best fitting parameters for each subject. As can be seen in the figure, the parameter values differ for the different subjects but, for each subject, they change in a systematic fashion across the five levels of the audible and visible synthetic speech. The meaningfulness of the parameter values justifies an important distinction between information and information processing. The parameter values represent how informative each source of information is. The integration and decision algorithms specify how this information is processed. This distinction plays an important role in locating several sources of variability in our inquiry. The variability in the information obtained from the auditory and visible speech is analogous to the variability in predicting the weather. There are just too many previous contributions and influences to allow quantitative prediction. In addition, small early influences of speech experience can lead to dramatic consequences at a later time (the butterfly effect in chaos theory). However, once this variability is accounted for (by estimating free parameters in the fit of the model, for example), we are able to provide a convincing description of how the information is processed and mapped into a response. Although we cannot predict a priori how /bɑ/-like a particular level of audible or visible speech is for a given individual, we can predict how the two sources of information are integrated. In addition, the model does take a stand on the evaluation process in the sense that it is assumed that the sources of information are evaluated independently of one another.

TRACE Model

Another computational model that accounts for multiple influences in speech perception is the TRACE model (McClelland and Elman, 1986). Lexical aspects of the model are discussed in Chapter 5, sublexical aspects in the present chapter. In particular, I examine the effects of phonological context on phoneme identification in TRACE and compare them with those in FLMP.

TRACE is one of the interactive activation class of connectionist models in which information processing occurs through excitatory and inhibitory interactions among a large number of simple processing units (see Chapter 3). These units are meant to represent the functional properties of neurons or neural networks. Three levels or sizes of unit are used in TRACE: feature, phoneme, and word (see Figure 5.2 in Chapter 5). Features activate phonemes which activate words, and activation of some units at a particular level inhibits other units at the same level. In addition, an important assumption of interactive-activation models is that activation of higher-order units activates their lower-order units; for example, activation of the /b/ phoneme would activate the features that are consistent with that phoneme.

The TRACE model is structured around the process of interactive activation among units at different layers and also assumes competition among units within a layer. Because of this process, the representation over time of one source of information is modified by the processing of another source of information. TRACE predicts that top-down sources can modify the representation of a bottom-up source of information through the process of interactive activation. Bottom-up activation from the phoneme units activates word units, which in turn, activate the phoneme units that make them up. Interactive activation appropriately describes this model because it is clearly an interaction between the two levels that is postulated. The amount of bottom-up activation modifies the amount of top-down activation, which then modifies the bottom-up activation, and so on.

Tests Between the Models

The FLMP and the TRACE model share a number of assumptions, but also differ on several important dimensions. Speech perception is assumed to be influenced by several sources of bottom-up and top-down information in both models. The units of processing and the nature of processing differ however. The FLMP assumes feature and syllable processing mediate language understanding. In the TRACE model, word recognition is mediated by feature and phoneme recognition. We saw that the evidence supported open syllables rather than phonemes as perceptual units in speech recognition. The TRACE model could easily be changed to accommodate this fact, because the units of processing are relatively arbitrary in the model.

The input is processed on-line in both the FLMP and TRACE, meaning that there is a continuous uptake of information during the speech input. Both models also assume that the system not only has categorical but also continuous information about the speech input (in terms of quantitative feature values). However, TRACE's assumption about interactive activation leads to an approximation of categorical perception at the phoneme and feature level. According to the TRACE model, a stimulus pattern is presented and activation of the corresponding features sends more excitation to some phoneme units than others. These phoneme units in turn activate particular words, which feed down and activate the phonemes of the word units. Similarly, the activation of a particular phoneme feeds down and activates the features corresponding to that phoneme (McClelland and Elman, 1986, p. 47). This effect of feedback produces enhanced sensitivity around a category boundary, exactly as predicted by categorical perception. Unfortunately, the hypothesis that human language processing involves categorical perception has been falsified in several different research situations (Pisoni, 1972; Massaro, 1989). This evidence against categorical perception is, therefore, evidence against the TRACE model.

Context Effects in Speech Perception

The primary difference between TRACE and the FLMP involves the joint effects of bottom-up and top-down information. We illustrate this difference in the models in their interpretation of the phonological context study described earlier. The FLMP can be tested against the results in a straightforward manner. A critical assumption of the application of the FLMP in the phonological constraints study is that the featural information from the glide and the phonological context provide *independent* sources of information. It is assumed that subjects adopt the proto-types /ri/ and /li/ in the task, evaluate and integrate the two sources of information with respect to these prototypes, and make a decision on the basis of the relative

Figure 4.8: Observed (points) and predicted (lines) probability of an r response for three typical subjects as a function of the glide F3 onset level and context (after Massaro and Cohen, Experiment 2, 1983). Predictions are for FLMP

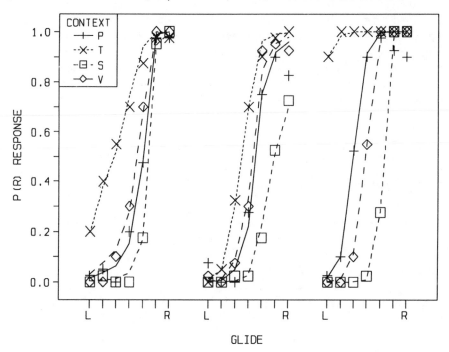

goodness-of-match. Truth values index the degree of support of each source of information for each alternative. Given two independent sources of information, the total degree of match with each prototype is determined by a multiplicative integration of these two sources. The decision operation maps these outcomes of integration into responses by way of a relative goodness rule (Massaro and Friedman, 1990).

In fitting our experimental data to the FLMP model there are 11 free parameters. These include four parameters giving the support for /ri/ from each of the four contexts and seven free parameters giving the support for /ri/ from each of the seven glides. The average fit of the FLMP to the seven individual subjects in terms of the RMSD was 0.055. Figure 4.8 shows the close agreement of the observed and predicted results for three of the subjects.

TRACE was originally formulated as a simulation model without a closed mathematical form. One difficulty in testing between FLMP and TRACE is the somewhat different procedures in testing mathematical and simulation models. Mathematical models allow parameter estimation and provide exact predictions to a set of observations. A measure of goodness-of-fit, such as RMSD, can then be used to evaluate the model. Simulation models, on the other hand, usually specify their parameters in advance, and simulated performance cannot be expected to match actual performance as closely as a fit of a mathematical model. The goal is to see if the simulated results have the same form as the observed, not to test whether they are of the same magnitude.

A simulation of the phonological-context experiment with TRACE was compared to the observed results (Massaro, 1989). A simulation of TRACE involves presentation of a pattern of activation to the units at the feature level. The input is presented sequentially in successive time slices, as would be the case in real speech. The processing of the input goes through a number of cycles in which all of the units update their respective activations at the same time, based on the activations computed in the previous update cycle. These activations are mapped into predicted responses, following McClelland and Elman (1986). Although the results of the simulation showed effects of both the bottom-up and top-down sources of information, the quantitative predictions of TRACE did not follow the

Figure 4.9: Network used in the simulation of the IAC model applied to the phonological constraints experiment of Massaro and Cohen (1983). The inhibitory connections between units within the word, context, and target levels are not shown in the network

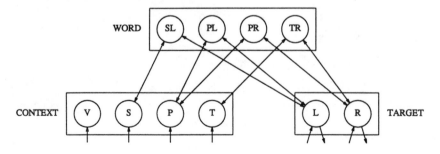

form of the functions given in Figures 4.2 and 4.8. These results might imply that interactive activation, the central premise of TRACE, is not a psychologically plausible mechanism of combining several sources of information.

More recently, several investigators have attempted to place the FLMP and TRACE on more equal footing to allow more direct comparisons. One method that has been used is to reduce the complexity of TRACE by using miniature neural networks. One network designed to predict context effects is shown in Figure 4.9 (Massaro and Cohen, 1991; McClelland, 1991). Three levels of units are assumed: Target, Context, and Word. The Target and Context can be considered to contain units that are activated by the target letter and the contextual letters, respectively. These are analogous to the bottom-up and top-down sources of information in the FLMP. Activation of Context units and Target units activates Word units. Consistent with the TRACE assumption of interactive activation, all units within the Context and Target levels are bidirectionally connected to all Word units. Only the excitatory connections are shown in the figure. Within each of the three levels, each unit also has inhibitory connections to all other units within that level. The Target units R and L are activated to varying degrees by the critical test letter. As in the FLMP, we can assume that changes in the glide will change the activation of the L unit relative to the R unit. The Context units are activated by the different contexts. The Word unit labelled SL corresponds to all words that begin with /sl/, and so on for the other Word units. Because of the interactive-activation assumption, the Word units in turn send their activation downward to the Context and Target units.

In the network, the effects of stimulus and context are combined via the units in the word layer. The activations of Word units are fed back to the Target and Context units, changing their activations in a manner that reflects the activations of both Target and Context units. In this manner, the joint effect of Target and Context are represented in the activations of units in both the Target and Context layers. This passing of activation occurs for a number of cycles until a sufficient amount of activation occurs at the Target units. This activation is then mapped into a response using the RGR. It is also assumed that the activations are mapped into strength values before entering the RGR. The activation a_i of a Target unit is transformed by an exponential function into a strength value S_i,

$$S_i = e^{ka_i}$$

The strength value S_i represents the strength of alternative i. The probability of choosing a particular alternative, $P(R_i)$, is based on the activations of all relevant alternatives, as described by the RGR.

$$P(R_i) = \frac{S_i}{\sum}$$

where $\sum$ is equal to the sum of the strengths of all relevant alternatives. The constant k was set equal to 5.

The simplest model to fit to the study requires 11 parameters: 7 *R* Target value inputs (with the *L* target receiving the additive complement), 4 Context inputs (with the nonselected contexts set to 0).

The simulation of TRACE is completely deterministic: The outcome of a simulation under a given set of conditions will produce the same results each time the simulation is run. The model was fit to the observed data by minimizing the differences between the predicted and observed values. For each of the 28 experimental conditions, a simulation trial was run with a hypothetical set of parameter values, and a goodness-of-fit was computed. As in the fit of the FLMP, the parameter values were changed systematically to maximize the goodness-of-fit of TRACE. As can be seen in the Figure 4.10, TRACE is not capable of describing the influence of the different types of context, and does a poor job describing the results, with an average RMSD value of 0.083, significantly larger than the fit of the FLMP. Given its failure, it is only reasonable to revise the model to attempt to bring it into line with the results.

Figure 4.10: Observed (points) and predicted (lines) probability of an ɾ response for three typical subjects as a function of the glide F3 onset level and context (after Massaro and Cohen, Experiment 2, 1983). Predictions are for the TRACE model with the RGR decision process

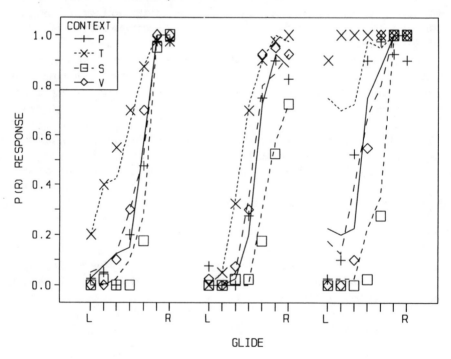

Revised TRACE Model Versus the FLMP

McClelland (1991) placed the blame for TRACE's failure to predict Massaro's results on the decision stage of the model rather than on some other process such as interactive activation. The TRACE model was modified by making the initial processing in the model probabilistic rather than deterministic by adding noise to the input, and changing the RGR decision rule into a best-one-wins (BOW) rule in which the response alternative corresponding to the most active unit would always be chosen (McClelland, 1991). With these two modifications, McClelland (1991) argued that the predictions of TRACE are consistent with the empirical observations and the predictions of the FLMP. However, this new model was not actually tested against any empirical results.

To provide an empirical test of the new TRACE, Massaro ran simulation trials by adding normal noise samples to both the Target and Context input values. For each of the simulated trials, a BOW decision was made on the final target activations. The simulated trials give the predicted proportion of responses at each of the experimental conditions. The fit of this model did not improve on the fit of

Figure 4.11: Observed (points) and predicted (lines) probability of an r response for three typical subjects as a function of the glide F3 onset level and context (after Massaro and Cohen, Experiment 2, 1983). Predictions are for the TRACE model with the BOW decision process

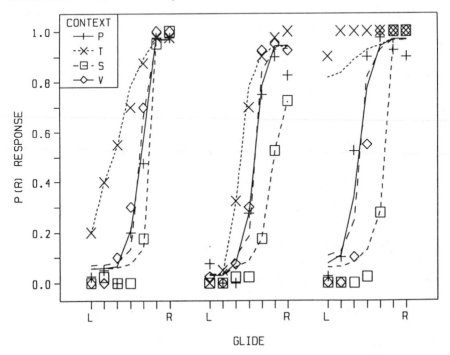

the deterministic TRACE with the RGR decision rule. The RMSD obtained for this model was 0.111, about twice that found for the FLMP. Figure 4.11 shows the fit of this 11 parameter TRACE. A second, 12 parameter TRACE was run (starting with the parameters of the 11 parameter model), which added the standard deviation of the noise as a free parameter. Only a small improvement was seen with an RMSD of 0.099, still significantly poorer than the fit of the FLMP. The TRACE model with intrinsic noise added at each processing cycle also gave a poor description of the results, relative to the FLMP. This model fitting exercise shows that the FLMP gives a better description of the results than TRACE. Thus, we can conclude these results support the FLMP over TRACE. Other results agree with this conclusion by demonstrating that interactive activation appears to be an inappropriate process to account for the influence of context on perception (Massaro and Cohen, 1991).

Epilogue

This chapter has been guided by the assumption that humans use multiple sources of information in the perception of spoken language. The discussion has focused on two psycholinguistically validated yet rather different computational models that incorporate this assumption. Experiments designed within the theoretical framework of the FLMP have covered a broad range of information sources, including bottom-up sources, such as audible and visible characteristics of speech, and top-down sources, such as phonological, lexical, syntactic, and semantic constraints (Massaro, 1987). The results provide important information concerning the sources of information in speech perception, and how these sources of information are processed to support speech perception.

TRACE, like FLMP, has been applied to phenomena on the sublexical domain, for example to categorical perception and the ability to trade cues in the speech signal off against each other in phoneme identification (McClelland and Elman, 1986). TRACE simulates a large number of empirical findings on the perception of phonemes and words and on the interactions of phoneme and word perception. Its application to auditory word recognition is described in depth in Chapter 5. In contrast to the FLMP-model, TRACE is a connectionist model which assumes interactive activation to account for the influence of multiple sources of information in speech perception.

However, the experiments discussed in this chapter raise questions with respect to the assumption that interactive activation is an appropriate mechanism to account for contextual effects in speech perception. At the least, the comparison between the two models has shown that the mathematically complete form of FLMP allows a closer fit to the data.

In the discussion of the psycholinguistic models, the present chapter has focused on the psychological validity of the architecture and processes. Another approach might be characterized as a technical analysis of the effectiveness of certain algorithms that can produce speech recognition by machine. Although the two approaches have been fairly independent, some sharing of empirical results and solutions should be productive. The most widely used technical approach is that of Hidden Markov Models (HMMs). The logic of HMMs in speech recognition is based on conceptualizing the signal in speech as a sequence of states (Rabiner, 1989). The goal is to determine which model best accounts for some observed sequence of states. For example, the states might correspond to a sequence of phonemes or a sequence of smaller segments, and the goal is to determine which word best accounts for the observed sequence.

The three basic problems to be solved by HMMs are computing the probability of an observed sequence for a given model, choosing a state sequence that is optimal given the observation sequence and the model, and adjusting the model's parameters to maximize the probability of an observed sequence. What are the fundamental assumptions in using HMMs? The sequence of observations is assumed to be independent, so that it can be written as a product of individual observations. Furthermore, the probability of being in state t depends only on the state at time $t-1$. Finally, the distributions of individual observation parameters can be represented by a mixture of Gaussian or autoregressive densities.

At this stage, we have seen limited use of HMMs in psychology perhaps because they are not easily applied to empirical studies of speech perception, they are not grounded in psychological processes, and they may not be falsifiable. HMMs are designed to maximize speech recognition whereas most psychological studies are aimed at how the human processing system is influenced by various inputs and processing demands. Given that HMMs are not psycholinguistic models, there is no rationale to apply them to particular empirical investigations. Finally, it can argued that an HMM can always be designed to mimic the results of a particular experiment. Larger HMMs will necessarily provide a better description of the observed sequence of events, violating the principles of good scientific practice (Popper, 1959; Platt, 1964; Massaro, 1987). To bridge the gap with the psycholinguistic work, HMMs will have to be imbued with psychological processes and some constraints will have to be placed on them to make them testable.

References

BAGLEY, W. C. (1900) 'The apperception of the spoken sentence: A study in the psychology of language', *American Journal of Psychology*, 12, pp. 1–130.

BANKS, W. P. and KRAJICEK, D. (1991) 'Perception', *Annual Review of Psychology*, 42, pp. 305–31.

BENNETT, B. M., HOFFMAN, D. D. and PRAKASH, C. (1989) *Observer Mechanics: A Formal Theory of Perception*, San Diego: Academic Press.

COHEN, M. M. (1979) *Three Cues to the Voicing of Intervocali Velar Stops*, Unpublished Master's Thesis, University of Wisconsin, Madison, WI.

CONNINE, C. M. and CLIFTON, C. (1987) 'Interactive use of lexical information in speech perception', *Journal of Experimental Psychology: Human Perception and Performance*, 13, pp. 291–9.

CUTLER, A., MEHLER, J., NORRIS, D. G. and SEGUI, J. (1986) The syllable's differing role in the segmentation of English and French, *Journal of Memory and Language*, 25, pp. 385–400.

CUTLER, A., MEHLER, J., NORRIS, D. and SEGUI, J. (1987) 'Phoneme identification and the lexicon', *Cognitive Psychology*, 19, pp. 141–77.

DEYOE, E. A. and VAN ESSEN, D. C. (1988) 'Concurrent processing streams in monkey visual cortex', *Trends in NeuroSciences*, 11, pp. 219–26.

DUPOUX, E. and MEHLER, J. (1990) 'Monitoring the lexicon with normal and compressed speech: Frequency effect and the prelexical code', *Journal of Memory and Language*, 29, pp. 316–35.

GANONG, W. F. III. (1980) 'Phonetic categorization in auditory word recognition', *Journal of Experimental Psychology: Human Perception and Performance*, 6, pp. 110–25.

GORDON, P. C., EBERHARDT, J. L. and RUECKL, J. G. (1993) 'Attentional modulation of the phonetic significance of acoustic cues', *Cognitive Psychology*, 25, pp. 1–42.

KLATT, D. H. (1976) 'Linguistic uses of segmental duration in English: Acoustic and perceptual evidence', *Journal of the Acoustical Society of America*, 59, pp. 1208–21.

LIBERMAN, A. M., COOPER, F. S., SHANKWEILER, D. P. and STUDDERT-KENNEDY, M. (1967) 'Perception of the speech code', *Psychological Review*, 74, pp. 431–61.

LISKER, L. (1978) 'Rabid vs rapid: A catalog of acoustic features that may cue the distinction', *Haskins Laboratories Status Report on Speech Research, SR-54*, pp. 127–32.

MASSARO, D. W. (1972) 'Preperceptual images, processing time, and perceptual units in auditory perception', *Psychological Review*, 79, pp. 124–45.

MASSARO, D. W. (Ed), (1975) *Understanding Language: An Information Processing Analysis of Speech Perception, Reading, and Psycholinguistics*, New York: Academic Press.

MASSARO, D. W. (1987) *Speech Perception by Ear and Eye: A Paradigm for Psychological Inquiry*, Hillsdale, NJ: Erlbaum.

MASSARO, D. W. (1989) 'Testing between the TRACE model and the Fuzzy Logical Model of Perception', *Cognitive Psychology*, 21, pp. 398–421.

MASSARO, D. W. and COHEN, M. M. (1983) Phonological context in speech perception, *Perception of Psychophysics*, 34, pp. 338–348.

MASSARO, D. W. and COHEN, M. M. (1991) 'Integration versus interactive activation: The joint influence of stimulus and context in perception', *Cognitive Psychology*, 23, pp. 558–614.

MASSARO, D. W. and FRIEDMAN, D. (1990) 'Models of integration given multiple sources of information', *Psychological Review*, 97, pp. 225–52.

MASSARO, D. W. and ODEN, G. C. (1980) 'Speech perception: A framework for research and theory', in LASS, N. J. (Ed) *Speech and Language: Advances in Basic Research and Practice*, Vol. 3, New York: Academic Press, pp. 129–65.

MASSARO, D. W., TSUZAKI, M., COHEN, M. M., GESI, A. and HEREDIA, R. (1993) 'Bimodal speech perception: An examination across languages', *Journal of Phonetics*, 21, pp. 445–78.

MCCLELLAND, J. L. (1991) 'Stochastic interactive processes and the effect of context on perception', *Cognitive Psychology*, 23, pp. 1–44.

MCCLELLAND, J. L. and ELMAN, J. L. (1986) 'The TRACE model of speech perception', *Cognitive Psychology*, 18, pp. 1–86.

MCGURK, H. and MACDONALD, J. (1976) 'Hearing lips and seeing voices', *Nature*, 264, pp. 746–8.

MILLER, G. A. (1962) 'Decision units in the perception of speech', *Institute of Radio Engineers (IRE) Transactions in Information Theory*, 8, pp. 81–3.

NEWMAN, C. W. and SPITZER, J. B. (1987) 'Monotic and dichotic presentation of phonemic elements in a backward recognition-masking paradigm', *Psychological Research*, 49, pp. 31–6.

NOOTEBOOM, S. G. (1992) 'Comment', in TOHKURA, Y., VATIKIOTIS-BATESON, E. and SAGISAKA, Y. (Eds) *Speech Perception, Production and Linguistic Structure*, Tokyo: Ohmsha, pp. 83–5.

ODEN, G. C. and MASSARO, D. W. (1978) 'Integration of featural information in speech perception', *Psychological Review*, 85, pp. 172–91.

PISONI, D. B. (1972) 'Perceptual processing time for consonants and vowels', *Haskins Laboratories Status Report on Speech Research, SR 31/32*, pp. 83–92.

PISONI, D. B. and LUCE, P. A. (1987) 'Acoustic-phonetic representations in word recognition', *Cognition*, 25, pp. 21–52.

PITT, M. A. and SAMUEL, A. G. (1993) 'An empirical and meta-analytic evaluation of the phoneme identification task', *Journal of Experimental Psychology: Human Perception and Performance*, 19, pp. 699–725.

PLATT, J. R. (1964) 'Strong inference', *Science*, 146, pp. 347–53.

POLLACK, I. and PICKETT, J. M. (1963) 'The intelligibility of excerpts from conversation', *Language and Speech*, 6, pp. 165–71.

POPPER, K. (1959) *The Logic of Scientific Discovery*, New York: Basic Books.

RABINER, L. R. (1989) 'A tutorial on hidden markov models and selected applications in speech recognition', *Proceedings of the IEEE*, 77, pp. 257–86.

RAPHAEL, L. J. (1972) 'Preceding vowel duration as a cue to the perception of the voicing characteristic of word-final consonants in American English', *Journal of the Acoustical Society of America*, 51, pp. 1296–303.

REPP, B. H. (1992) 'Perceptual restoration of a "missing" speech sound: Auditory induction or illusion?', *Perception & Psychophysics*, 51, pp. 14–32.

SAVIN, H. B. and BEVER, T. G. (1970) 'The nonperceptual reality of the phoneme', *Journal of Verbal Learning and Verbal Behavior*, 9, 295–302.

SEGUI, J., FRAUENFELDER, U. and MEHLER, J. (1981) 'Phoneme monitoring, syllable monitoring, and lexical access', *British Journal of Psychology*, 72, pp. 471–7.

SEKIYAMA, K. and TOHKURA, Y. (1991) 'McGurk effect in non-English listeners: Few visual effects for Japanese subjects hearing Japanese syllables of high auditory intelligibility', *Journal of the Acoustical Society of America*, 390, pp. 1797–805.

SUMMERFIELD, A. Q. and HAGGARD, M. P. (1974) 'Perceptual processing of multiple cues and contexts: Effects of following vowel upon stop consonant voicing', *Journal of Phonetics*, 2, pp. 279–95.

TYLER, L. K. and WESSELS, J. (1983) 'Quantifying contextual contributions to word-recognition processes', *Perception & Psychophysics*, 34, pp. 409–20.

WARDRIP-FRUIN, C. (1985) 'The effect of signal degradation on the status of cues to voicing in utterance-final stop consonants', *Journal of the Acoustical Society of America*, 77, pp. 1907–12.

WARREN, R. M. (1970) 'Perceptual restoration of missing speech sounds', *Science*, 167, pp. 392–3.

WHALEN, D. H., ABRAMSON, A. S., LISKER, L. and MODY, M. (1993) 'F0 gives voicing information even with unambiguous VOTs', *Journal of the Acoustical Society of America*, 93a, pp. 2152–9.

ZADEH, L. A. (1965) 'Fuzzy sets', *Information and Control*, 8, pp. 338–53.

Chapter 5

Computational Models of Spoken Word Recognition

Uli H. Frauenfelder

Introduction

The listener's ability to identify correctly and almost instantly a word from amongst the tens of thousands of other words stored in the mental lexicon constitutes one of the most extraordinary feats in language processing. This highly efficient *lexical processing* system has received much attention from psycholinguists during the last twenty years. In describing this system, psycholinguists assume the existence of a central store or mental lexicon that serves to keep different types of lexical information (phonological and orthographic as well as semantic and syntactic) in long-term memory. By storing form and meaning information together, the lexicon solves the difficult problem of the arbitrary mapping from form to meaning. Within this framework, three important problem areas can be identified:

1 *The representation problem:* What is the basic lexical entry, what is its internal structure, and how are lexical entries organized in the mental lexicon?
2 *The recognition problem:* How is the intended lexical entry located in the lexicon and the lexical information associated with it accessed on the basis of bottom-up (sensory) and top-down (contextual) information?
3 *The integration problem:* How are the different types of stored lexical information combined and integrated in constructing a meaningful interpretation of the utterance being heard?

The answers to these questions are highly related. The way in which a word is recognized depends upon how it is stored and vice versa. In this chapter we, nonetheless, attempt to limit ourselves to the problem of word recognition, touching on the issues of lexical representation that are relevant for recognition.

Furthermore, the discussion is restricted to *spoken* words (see Chapter 6 for models of *visual* word recognition).

Figure 5.1 presents a rough characterization of the processes and representations that are generally incorporated into models of word recognition. This schematic description includes two different recognition stages, one for the sublexical units of representation and one for words. During the first, the sensory input is segmented and classified to construct a series of successively more abstract (auditory, phonetic, phonological) representations (Pisoni and Sawusch, 1975; Sawusch, 1986). During the second stage, the input representation computed during the first stage makes contact with the internally stored lexical representations. Here, this input representation is matched and aligned with the lexical representation to locate the spoken or target lexical representation and to access the semantic and syntactic information associated with that word.

Figure 5.1: A simplified characterization of the spoken word recognition process involving both sublexical and lexical levels of representation

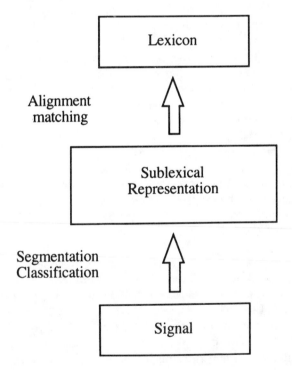

It is striking how closely this characterization of spoken word recognition resembles that proposed by Grainger and Dijkstra for visual word recognition (see Chapter 6). We will see that many of the issues are the same — even though the models proposed to account for word recognition in the two modalities differ, precisely due to the differences in the visual and spoken language inputs. Speech has some special properties that make the study of spoken word recognition particularly challenging.

Speech perception, while presenting no obvious problem for the listener, has been difficult for psycholinguists to understand and for speech engineers to imitate with machines. This difficulty is essentially due to the specific properties of speech (cf., Klatt, 1980 for a discussion). First, speech is produced sequentially at a rate of about 10 speech segments per second. Second, speech is continuous. Unlike written text, there are no systematic spaces or periods of silence to indicate where one word (or segment) ends and the next one begins. Third, speech is overlapping. Due to coarticulation, speech segments are not received in a strictly sequential fashion. Any particular stretch of speech may contain acoustic cues to several adjacent segments. Finally, speech is variable. The same speech sound can manifest itself very differently in the speech stream. Every word takes a different phonetic or phonological shape each time that it is produced depending upon its phonological context or speech rate.

Speech perception research is concerned with determining how and when acoustic and phonetic cues are extracted from the signal and with establishing what kinds of internal representation are constructed on the basis of this information. The reader is referred to Chapter 4 for a more detailed discussion of speech perception and its processing units. However, the issue of sublexical representations and the units that make up these representations are also addressed here, if only briefly, to avoid falling victim to the habitual division of labour between phoneticians and psycholinguists. Research in phonetics has focused traditionally on the acoustic-phonetic analysis of the speech signal and for the most part has not dealt with the problem of how this analysis relates to word recognition and sentence processing. Inversely, psycholinguists have generally concentrated on processing at the higher levels and have tended to neglect the complexities of the acoustic-phonetic input and its analysis. This approach to carving up the scientific problem space is artificial and unproductive. Fortunately, an increasing amount of psycholinguistic research has focused on the nature of the representation(s) that the listener constructs during speech processing and word recognition.

Concerning the processes of word recognition, there appears to be general agreement (Bard, 1990; Marslen-Wilson, 1990) that word recognition involves the activation of a set of lexical candidates and the selection of the target word from amongst this activated set. This view comes quite naturally for speech given its continuous and sequential nature. During most of the time that listeners are processing speech, they have only partial sensory information about any given target word — information that is insufficient to identify it uniquely. They are, nonetheless, continuously generating or activating lexical hypotheses on the basis of this partial information. Given this view of the word recognition process, it becomes important to determine which lexical competitors are activated and how the mismatching competitors are eliminated from contention, that is, from the competitor set in order to identify the intended word.

In the following sections, four leading models of word recognition are described to illustrate the evolution from verbal to computer implemented models. In the section on model evaluation, the predictions of these models with respect to sublexical processing, competitor activation, lexical selection and recognition are discussed and evaluated in the light of existent experimental findings. Diverse problems that arise in the computational modelling enterprise are also presented. Finally, the concluding section considers some implications of computational models for the study of word recognition.

Models of Word Recognition

Our understanding of lexical processing and representation has progressed considerably in the last two decades. Psycholinguistic research in this area has identified a large number of factors that play a role in lexical processing. These factors concern the structural (length, phonological make-up) and distributional (diphone and word frequency) properties of the word being processed and its lexical competitors. In order to include these different factors and their complex interaction in a theoretical model, researchers have been forced to construct models of increasing complexity. It appears that the limits of verbal models are now being reached and that computer technology is required to consolidate and integrate the acquired knowledge. This problem is, of course, not specific to word recognition. In many other scientific disciplines, models implemented upon computers have become an increasingly indispensable tool for studying complex phenomena. As will be shown here, such models have an important contribution to make in characterizing lexical processing and representation.

The four models discussed here represent different points in the evolutionary process from verbal to implemented models. The verbal model, COHORT I (Marslen-Wilson and Welsh, 1978), makes a number of simplifying assumptions about word recognition, which allow it to make several testable predictions about the time-course of word recognition. COHORT II (Marslen-Wilson, 1987) is also a verbal model, but it includes more complex and realistic processing assumptions. However, since COHORT II is not computer implemented, it is difficult to assess exactly what predictions the model makes. In contrast to a verbal model like the COHORT II, the TRACE model (McClelland and Elman, 1986) is computer implemented. It presents the advantages of being able to make precise quantitative predictions about the time-course of spoken word recognition. TRACE also has major limitations, some of which are addressed in a more recent model, SHORTLIST (Norris, 1994). We consider these models in turn to evaluate their contribution to our understanding of spoken word recognition. To organize this discussion we will pay special attention to the answers they give to the following three questions concerning the competitor set:

– What are the activated lexical competitors at any given moment in time?

- How are inappropriate lexical competitors eliminated from the competitor set?
- What is the time-course of word recognition and how is the ultimate choice for the target word over its competitors made?

The COHORT I Model

The original COHORT model (Marslen-Wilson and Welsh, 1978) represents an early attempt at providing systematic answers to these questions. In doing so, this model assumes two successive stages of processing. During the first, all words that exactly match the onset (i.e., the initial one or two segments) of the target word are activated. For example, some words matching the onset /El'/ are *elephant*, *element*, and *electric*. On the basis of this initial contact between a phonemic sublexical representation and the lexicon, a set of competitors or the *word initial cohort* of the target is generated. Words that are not aligned with the onset are not allowed to enter the cohort and hence cannot compete for recognition. Lexically-based segmentation is assumed to ensure that only the words that are aligned with word onsets are introduced into the cohort. Listeners exploit the phonological representation that is the product of lexical access to segment the speech stream. By recognizing words efficiently in a sequential fashion, the listener is assumed to be able to predict the offset of the word being processed before it has been heard completely and then to anticipate the onset of the following word.

The initial activation phase is followed by a stage of deactivation during which the cohort members that mismatch later arriving sensory input are eliminated from the cohort. The number of cohort members decreases as more stimulus information becomes available. Thus, in response to the first question, the cohort model asserts that the competitors at any given point in time are those words that match and are aligned with the target word. The answer to the second question is also simple. The mere presence of other competitors in the cohort prevents the target from being recognized. However, the cohort members do not have any effect upon one another. Hence, neither the number (cohort size) nor the nature (e.g., frequency) of the cohort members affects the time-course of word recognition in this model. It is only the *final cohort member(s)* (i.e., the word(s) matching the target the longest) that determine(s) word recognition. This leads us to the answer to the third question. This model makes precise predictions about the moment at which any word can be recognized in a given lexicon on the basis of an analysis of its cohort members. This recognition point (RP) is assumed to correspond to the word's uniqueness point (UP), i.e., the moment that the word becomes unique with respect to the other words in the lexicon. A given target word spoken in isolation is assumed to be recognized when it is the only word remaining in its cohort. For example, a word like *elephant* heard in isolation, is predicted to be identified at the sound /f/ at which there are no other words in the lexicon sharing its initial part.

By giving simple and clear answers to these three questions, this model can generate precise predictions about the time-course of recognition. The fact that these predictions can be tested and falsified makes this model attractive. However, the model is not very explicit about the representations involved in recognition.

The COHORT II Model

To incorporate some psychologically more realistic assumptions, Marslen-Wilson (1987) proposed a new version of this model, COHORT II. Like its predecessor, the new version presupposes that the competitor set is limited to those candidates that are aligned with the onset of the target word. However, the membership of the cohort is enlarged to include words that mismatch the sensory input to some minimal (but still unspecified) degree. The model is more explicit, however, on the issue of sublexical representations (Lahiri and Marslen-Wilson, 1991). It takes the option of not including an intermediate level of sublexical representation, and of mapping distinctive features extracted from the signal directly onto the lexical entries.

To express the varying degree of match between the input and different competitors, the model appeals to the notion of level of activation. In particular, cohort members vary in activation level as a function of their fit with the input and of their frequency. Unlike the clear binary status of words in the original model (either in or out of the cohort), the identity and status of cohort members is less well-defined in this newer formulation of the model. The model does not specify how the degree of match with the input and word frequency determine activation, since these factors and their relative contribution to lexical activation are difficult to quantify in a verbal model. As a consequence, no precise definition of the competitor set is yet available in this model.

As in the original version, the cohort members exert no direct influence upon the target word or its activation level. However, the decision as to when a particular word is recognized does depend upon the activation level of its competitors. Marslen-Wilson (1990) has suggested that isolated word recognition takes place when the difference in activation between the target word and its most activated competitor has reached a certain criterion. In this way, the most activated cohort members influence the decision phase of the recognition process.

The preceding discussion of the two versions of the COHORT model illustrates a general dilemma confronting efforts to model lexical processing. COHORT I makes clear and testable predictions and therefore has been useful in generating considerable empirical research. However, to do so, it has made several simplifying assumptions. In contrast, COHORT II is a more complex verbal model and presumably fits better with what we know about lexical processing. However, it does not provide direct answers to the questions concerning the competitor set and therefore cannot predict the time-course of word recognition. One way of dealing with this trade-off between complexity and testability is to implement a model on a computer, as was done for the TRACE model.

The TRACE Model

TRACE is an interactive activation model (see Chapter 3) made up of distinctive feature, phoneme and word units that each represent hypotheses about the sensory input. These three types of unit are organized hierarchically. There are bottom-up and top-down facilitatory connections between units on adjacent levels

Figure 5.2: The Interactive Activation model of spoken word recognition TRACE, proposed by McClelland and Elman (1986)

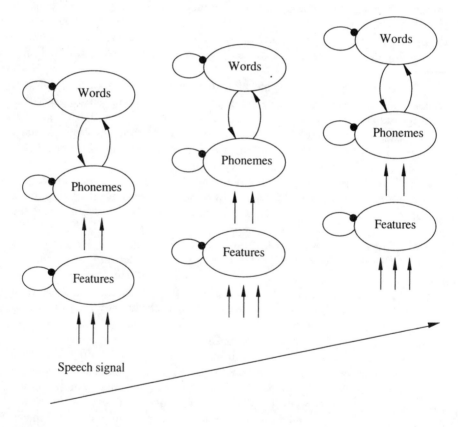

(feature-phoneme, phoneme-word, and word-phoneme) and inhibitory connections between units within levels (feature-feature, phoneme-phoneme, and word-word). Incoming sensory input provides bottom-up excitation of distinctive feature units which in turn excite phoneme units. Phoneme units are activated as a function of their match with the activated distinctive features so that several alternative phonemic units are activated for a given input. As the phonemes become excited, they increase the level of activation of words that contain them. As words receive some activation, they begin to inhibit each other. In addition, as words become activated, they also excite the phonemes that they contain in a top-down fashion. Figure 5.2 illustrates in a simplified fashion the three levels of representation in TRACE as well as the connectivity pattern assumed. The fact that the networks are reduplicated in time is also shown in this figure. Compared with the COHORT I model, TRACE generates a potentially much larger competitor set. The model allows phonemes that mismatch the input in a single distinctive feature to be activated to a limited degree. These phonemes can in turn activate the words that contain them. However, on the basis of a series of simulations, Frauenfelder and Peeters (1994) have demonstrated that these mismatching lexical competitors do not receive much activation and hence play no real role in word recognition. The results showed that — like in COHORT I — the cohort members constitute the only real competitors for word inputs. The situation is different for nonword inputs as will be discussed below.

TRACE diverges from both versions of the COHORT model in its assumption that lexical competitors can exert a direct influence upon the activation level of the target and vice versa. The model incorporates a lateral flow of inhibition between units at the same level. By this mechanism the target word inhibits its competitors, but is also inhibited by them. The degree to which one word inhibits another is a function of the former's activation level: the more a word is activated, the more efficiently it can inhibit its competitors. The dynamics of interactive activation and in particular this inhibition between competitors allows TRACE to keep the actual activated competitor set small and to converge on a single lexical entry despite the mass of lexical candidates that potentially contend for recognition.

Another aspect in which TRACE deviates from both versions of the COHORT model is its assumption of a top-down activation flow from the word to the phoneme level. As a result, the members of the activated competitor set can exert an additional indirect influence upon one another. The activated words provide top-down excitatory feedback to the phoneme units they contain by increasing the latters level of activation. These phoneme units can in their turn again excite the connected word units. For a discussion of lexical to phoneme top-down effects in TRACE, the reader is referred to Chapter 4.

The SHORTLIST *Model*

The SHORTLIST model (Norris, 1994) represents an attempt to improve upon some of the shortcomings of TRACE, in particular, its rather implausible architecture. SHORTLIST involves two distinct processing stages. During the first, a restricted set of lexical candidates, the 'shortlist', is established using both bottom-up excitation and inhibition. Any word — whatever its alignment — can be included in the activated candidate set as long as it matches the input to some preset criterion. Unlike TRACE where all the words are prewired into such a network, the modeller sets an upper limit (e.g., ranging from 3 to 30 words) upon the number of candidates retained. For practical reasons, this shortlist is based upon the match of the input with the phonological form representations of words found in a lexical database. During the second stage, the best fitting words — even those with different alignments — are wired into an interactive activation network similar to that assumed by TRACE. The competition between the lexical items in the shortlist takes place via lateral inhibition, such that the words that best match the input inhibit their competitors most effectively.

More recently, the SHORTLIST model (Norris, McQueen, and Cutler, 1995) has been modified in two important respects. First, a mechanism was introduced to incorporate the Metrical Segmentation Strategy (MSS) developed for the segmentation of English (Cutler and Norris, 1988). Second, the model introduced a recomputation routine so as to prevent highly activated competitors from completely inhibiting later arriving matching words. To introduce prosodic information into the model, the new model boosts the level of activation of words which have a strong initial syllable (not containing a reduced vowel), and decreases the activation of words that are not aligned in their onsets with a strong syllable in the input. By recomputing the activation of the shortlist after each phoneme is received, the model avoids committing itself to the lexical candidates that are activated early and allows later matching words to become activated.

Evaluation of the Models

We have now presented four major models of spoken word recognition. Of course, other computational models of interest have been proposed including those appealing to recurrent networks (Norris, 1990; Content and Sternon, 1994). We have restricted ourselves to this set because of their relative homogeneity and wide use. Moreover, they illustrate nicely the progression from verbal to computational models. In this section, we compare more systematically the specific assumptions of these models and examine how well they account for the available experimental data. We also consider the challenges or difficulties that arise in modelling the different aspects of word recognition.

Sublexical Processing and Units

A central objective in the investigation of sublexical processing is to answer two questions: 1) how is information extracted from the sensory input and mapped onto the lexicon, and 2) which units are computed in the process. With respect to the first question, two general approaches can be distinguished (Frauenfelder, 1992). According to the first, one or more sublexical representations mediates the mapping between the signal and the mental lexicon. The second view holds that no sublexical representation is computed but that the information extracted from the sensory input is mapped directly onto the lexicon. With respect to the second question, many different units of speech perception have been proposed to mediate the word recognition process including: temporally defined spectral templates (Klatt, 1980), distinctive features (Lahiri and Marslen-Wilson, 1991), phonemic segments (Marslen-Wilson and Welsh, 1978; Pisoni and Luce, 1987), demi-syllables (see Chapter 4), and syllables (Mehler, 1981; Segui, Dupoux and Mehler, 1990). It is important to note that the answers to these two questions are at least in part orthogonal since even models that do not postulate intermediary sublexical levels of representations must nonetheless identify units of processing.

The models described above differ in terms of whether they include a sublexical representation (COHORT I, TRACE, and SHORTLIST) or not (COHORT II). COHORT I and SHORTLIST both include some segmental or phonemic representation, while TRACE includes both a distinctive feature and a phoneme level. Only COHORT II explicitly rejects the idea of a sublexical level of representation and assumes that distinctive features are extracted from the input and mapped directly onto the lexical entries.

Experimental Findings on Processing Units

Considerable psycholinguistic research has focused on the nature of the units the listener computes during speech processing. This work is reviewed in Chapter 4. Much less experimental work has been concerned with determining whether these perceptual units are computed pre-lexically so as to mediate word recognition or whether they are the results of post-perceptual processes. This is in part due to the difficulty in establishing the temporal locus of the effects being measured with on-line experiments.

A wide variety of experimental procedures has been used to generate support for one or another of these perceptual units. For example, the perceptual difficulty as a function of the rate of ear switching (Huggins, 1967), the migration of different-sized units in dichotic presentation (Kolinsky, Morais, and Cluytens, 1995) and the effect upon speech perception of backward masks of varying size (Massaro and Oden, 1980) have all been measured. One heavily exploited technique involves the detection of different targets. Studies based on this technique (Mehler *et al.*, 1981; Cutler, *et al.*, 1983, 1986; Bradley, Sanchez-Casas and Garcia-Albea, 1993; Zwitserlood, *et al.*, 1993) have provided evidence for different units across languages. Interestingly, the perceptual units involved vary in a way that is generally compatible with the phonological structure of the language. Although these results present a relatively coherent picture, they have not led to an accepted solution to the access unit debate. However, they do suggest that different types of unit may have to be included in computational models as a function of the language being modelled.

Challenges of Modelling Sublexical Processing

Defining appropriate inputs to computational models presents a formidable but essential challenge since these representational choices determine in large part the adequacy of any modelling enterprise. The use of an input with little physical, physiological and especially psychological reality clearly limits the model's utility at the lexical level. Ideally the model input should possess the important properties of speech. It should be variable. Moreover, it should be presented to the model continuously and sequentially to reflect the manner in which speech is processed. Some of the information corresponding to adjacent segments should become simultaneously available to express coarticulation. Finally, the durational properties of speech should also be captured in the input. Thus, the physical durations of individual segments should ideally correspond to their presentation time in the input, especially if the ultimate aim is to model reaction time data quantitatively.

The most obvious way to satisfy these constraints is to use real speech as input to the model. In this way it is possible to begin the psychological modelling at the earliest point in time with the 'real thing'. However, in adopting this input, the modeller must solve not only the problem of lexical processing, but also that of speech recognition. The difficulties encountered in developing automatic speech recognition programs that can handle multi-speaker, continuous speech input suggest that this approach may still be premature. Errors in the recognition performance of the model's front-end will most likely lead to deficits in the model's performance at the lexical level. As a consequence, it becomes difficult to establish whether poor lexical performance is due to the lexical or the sublexical part of the model.

A commonly adopted alternative is to present computational models with 'mock' input. Mock input generally refers to a symbolic representation of speech — like a phonetic transcription. It should be evident from the preceding discussion that our current understanding of human speech perception has not advanced sufficiently for us to be able to specify a mock input whose content and manner of presentation simulates real speech input exactly. Many of the important issues simply remain open and unresolved. The mock inputs developed until now do not do justice to the complexity of speech and speech processing.

For example, the input to SHORTLIST is a phonemic transcription in which phonological similarity is not expressed. Consequently, no distinction can be made between large and small phonemic mismatches between the input and words. Moreover, the segments are the same length in terms of cycles and do not reflect coarticulation. The input to TRACE is somewhat more realistic since it corresponds to a featural representation in which each phoneme takes on one of nine possible values for seven different acoustic features (e.g., vocalic, diffuse, voiced, etc.). By including a feature level, more than one phoneme is activated by a particular featural input. Moreover, by letting adjacent phonemes receive bottom-up activation from their features, the model can also handle coarticulation indirectly. Nonetheless, the input to this model is still highly simplified and does not take into account several important properties of speech such as its variability, its prosody and its temporal duration. Moreover, the fact that only 13 phonemes are represented severely limits the size of the lexicon that can be handled by the model.

We can expect novel proposals for model inputs to emerge in the future. These will likely incorporate advances in phonological theory and move away from phonemes represented by bundles of features organized strictly linearly. In one such proposal, Shillcock *et al.* (1992) have used an input that is composed of nine elements with physical correlates like nasality, or aperiodic energy. These elements are either binary or tertiary. Another example of research in this direction is found in work by Lahiri and Marslen-Wilson (1991), which restricts the input to distinctive featural information. As the input representations improve and reflect new insights into phonology and speech processing, the performance of the computational models will clearly also improve.

Alignment and Matching: Definition of Competitor Set

This section compares the claims of the four models under scrutiny concerning the membership of the activated competitor set for word and nonword inputs. The make-up of this set for any given model depends upon its assumptions concerning three main factors: the nature of the input units used to contact the lexicon, the manner in which this representation is aligned with the lexical representation, and the assumed nature of the activation flow (bottom-up and lateral). Before considering the individual models, we first examine the latter two factors.

The listener is confronted with the challenge of finding the correct alignment between the input and the lexical representation on the basis of partial or no segmentation information. As noted above, speech is continuous and overlapping and thus contains few pauses to separate phonemes or words. Moreover, word boundaries are not overtly marked in a systematic fashion (Cole and Jakimik, 1980). By alignment we mean that listeners must determine which part of the input representation is correctly matched with which part of the lexical representations. There are a number of different solutions (Frauenfelder and Peeters, 1990) to this alignment problem. These range from exhaustive alignment where all alignments between the input and lexical representations are attempted, to selective alignment based either on information in the signal (phonetic or prosodic) or on lexical (i.e., phonological) information associated with the immediately preceding accessed word(s). Clearly, the number of activated words as well as their degree of activation depends upon the approach taken to the alignment problem.

The specification of the set of activated lexical candidates depends not only upon assumptions concerning the input representation and its alignment with lexical representations, but also upon the nature of the matching process assumed. The majority of word recognition models are based upon the activation metaphor in which the goodness-of-fit between an input representation and a lexical representation is defined in terms of the latter's level of activation. Models diverge, however, in their specification of two aspects of this matching process. First, they disagree on the nature of the activation flow that produces the activation levels of the competitors, with the input representation only activating matching lexical representations, or also deactivating mismatching candidates. Secondly, there is disagreement upon the maximal amount of mismatch that still produces some lexical activation. In some proposals, activation requires an exact fit, whereas in other more tolerant models, the lexical activation varies: the closer and more complete the fit, the greater the activation of the word.

Table 5.1 shows which lexical competitors are assumed to activated by each of the four models. We can see considerable agreement concerning the activated competitors for word inputs. Not surprisingly, all the models assume that lexical competitors (*cohort competitors* — type a) which match and are aligned with the input are activated. In contrast, the models make divergent predictions for the mismatching and misaligned competitors for reasons that will become clearer in the next section.

Whereas mismatching but aligned words (competitor c) are explicitly excluded from the competitor set in COHORT I, the status of these words is less clear in more recent versions of this model. In the first formulation of COHORT II (Marslen-Wilson, 1987), words that do not fully match the bottom-up specification could nonetheless find their way into the cohort. However, on the basis of experimental results, Marslen-Wilson and Zwitserlood (1989) subsequently rejected this possibility and argued that words that mismatch the input at their onset do not become activated. More recently, cohort theory has become more refined in distinguishing between perceptual and post-perceptual processing (Marslen-Wilson, 1994). Lexical activation and recognition still depend upon an exact match with the input independent of lexical status of this input. Mismatch in even a single distinctive feature is assumed to deactivate lexical items. Even then, a word could still be recognized, but this recognition is assumed

Table 5.1: Lexical competitors activated for word input (part) in four word recognition models

Competitors				Models			
type	aligned	matched	example	COHORT I	COHORT II	TRACE	SHORTLIST
compet a	+	+	party	+	+	+	+
compet b	−	+	art	−	−	−	+
compet c	+	−	cart	−	(+)	−	−
compet d	−	−	ark	−	−	−	−

Table 5.2: Lexical competitors activated for nonword input (bart) *in four word recognition models*

Competitors				Models			
type	aligned	matched	example	COHORT I	COHORT II	TRACE	SHORTLIST
compet b	−	+	art	−	−	+	+
compet c	+	−	part	−	−	+	−
compet d	−	−	ark	−	−	+	−

to be mediated by 'second pass' post-perceptual processing.

The activated competitor set of TRACE for word inputs is characterized as being limited to cohort members. This contrasts with the commonly held assumption that TRACE allows mismatching lexical candidates (competitor c) to be activated. This latter claim is intuitively consistent with the model since phonemes that differ minimally (e.g., in one distinctive feature) from the input are activated and can in turn activate the words that contain them. What is generally misunderstood is that these mismatching lexical candidates are too strongly inhibited by the matching target word to become activated. It has been shown (Frauenfelder and Peeters, 1994) that these competitors have virtually no effect upon target recognition. Finally, SHORTLIST differs from both the COHORT and TRACE models in that it predicts the activation of words (competitor b) embedded within target words due to its recomputation mechanism.

Table 5.2 shows which competitors the models predict to be activated by a nonword input. For the COHORT model, no difference in competitor activation is predicted between word and nonword inputs since the operation of bottom-up inhibition and onset alignment is independent of the lexical status of the input. This inhibition prevents the activation of any noncohort lexical competitor. In contrast, TRACE predicts the activation of both mismatching (competitor c) and misaligned (competitor b) candidates by a nonword input when these candidates represent the best and the earliest fit with this input. Indeed, when there is no exact lexical match with the nonword input to dominate and inhibit the partially matching and/or misaligned competitors, these latter competitors have a chance of being activated substantially. The SHORTLIST model differs from the TRACE model in that the candidates that are activated do not vary as a function of the lexical status of the input. Again, it predicts lexical activation for matching competitors that are misaligned.

Experimental Findings on Competitor Activation
This section reviews experimental studies that have examined the initial activation of competitors of different types for word and nonword input sequences.

Activation of Cohort Competitors There is clear evidence that cohort competitors are activated during processing. One study (Zwitserlood, 1989) using the cross-modal semantic priming procedure (Swinney, 1979) showed that the meanings of a target word and its cohort competitor are activated as long as the presented sensory information did not distinguish between them. Thus, given the partial spoken input [kæpt], the meanings of both *captain* and *captive* were activated. This is consistent with all models.

Activation of Mismatching Competitors Another cross-modal semantic priming study (Marslen-Wilson and Zwitserlood, 1989) produced results that suggest that the competitor set is restricted to matching cohort competitors. These authors showed that a spoken word prime that mismatched the target word in its initial phoneme by several distinctive features did not activate the meaning of the latter word (e.g., the word *mat* — phonologically similar to *cat* — did not activate *dog*). This indicates that words differing greatly in their first phoneme do not belong to one another's cohort. Connine, Blasko and Titone (1993) also used the cross-modal priming technique and manipulated the phonological distance between a priming nonword and the target word. The results showed priming by nonwords that were created from words by making small phonological changes in either their onsets or offsets. When the phonological distance was increased, no activation was obtained. These results are consistent with the predictions of the TRACE and SHORTLIST models, rather than COHORT II which predicts no lexical activation of mismatching competitors.

Activation of Misaligned (Embedded) Competitors Shillcock (1990) found that lexical candidates that are embedded non-initially in carrier words are activated during lexical processing. Using the cross-modal priming procedure, he obtained significant priming of a word (e.g., *rib*) by the second syllable (e.g., *bone*) of a bisyllabic target word (e.g., *trombone*). This suggests that the embedded word is activated during the processing of the longer carrier word, a result that is only consistent with the predictions of the SHORTLIST model. In a phoneme monitoring study, Frauenfelder and Henstra (1988) obtained results suggesting the activation of the phonological representation of words embedded in nonwords in a phoneme detection task. This result is consistent with both the TRACE and SHORTLIST models.

Studies like those presented provide important constraints upon models concerning the activated lexical candidates. Unfortunately, however, they are not yet conclusive. More systematic manipulation of the phonological distance separating the input and the lexical competitors as well as the lexical status of the input is still required with a larger variety of experimental procedures.

Challenges of Modelling Lexical Activation

Simulations with computational models make it possible to measure lexical activation and its evolution across time for every word in the model's lexicon. However, a number of difficult problems are raised in modelling this activation. One concerns the problem of how to represent time within the model and how to relate specific lexical hypotheses in the input to this time. The second related problem concerns the ability of the model to scale up from a toy lexicon to a lexicon that is representative of the human lexicon. A final problem stems from the fact that the effects of all independent variables must be expressed in the same terms, that is, activation level.

Representing Lexical Representations in Time The sequential and continuous properties of speech create a major challenge for computational models of spoken word recognition. Indeed, since words can in principle begin at any point in the signal, the model must have the potential of representing every lexical candidate for each incoming input segment and of recording the temporal relation of these candidates to the signal. This problem can be understood by considering which units are activated by inputs containing repeated units (i.e., phonemes, syllables, or words). For instance when a model is confronted by inputs like *cancan*, it must be able to express the fact that the two syllables do not represent the same unit at the same moment in time (cf., the type / token distinction in Chapter 2).

Two main solutions to this problem have been proposed. According to the first, time is represented spatially as in TRACE. For each *time-slice*, this model constructs a complete network in which all the units at every level are represented. Thus, to recognize an input made up of four phonemes, TRACE constructs at least four (in fact, 4 x 6) complete lexical networks and retains the time cycle at which each lexical unit begins. This solution of spatial reduplication is neither psychologically realistic nor efficient. First, since the model cannot record the identity relation between the units expressing the same lexical units at different moments in time, it cannot account for the well-known psycholinguistic phenomenon of repetition priming (Monsell, 1985). Moreover, to recognize a sequence of words, the model must first pre-wire the connections between and within the temporally distinct time slices. This solution is not only implausible but also is very costly from a computational point of view. The number of connections increases dramatically with additional phonemes in the input so that the computational limits of most computers are quickly reached. The addition of words to the lexicon has the same effect, making it impossible to run simulations with larger lexicons (see next section).

An alternative solution to the problem of representing time is provided by recurrent networks (see Chapter 3). These networks present the advantage of not representing time explicitly like in the spatial approach, but rather implicitly in the topology of the network. The recurrent connections provide this network with a memory for the processing of prior segmental and lexical information and for integrating information across time. Moreover, unlike TRACE in which the connection strengths are set by the modeller, these connection strengths are learned by the model through the back-propagation algorithm. Norris (1990) has shown that a simple recurrent network can perform time-invariant word recognition accompanied by behaviour similar to the COHORT model.

Scaling Up to Realistic Lexicons The step from a toy lexicon of a few hundred words to an adult lexicon of 50 000–100 000 words is simply impossible for many computational models. This scaling problem is particularly acute for models like TRACE which reduplicate lexical units. Here the constraints on the size of the lexicon (and on the phoneme inventory) constitute a major limitation. Models with recurrent connections also involve considerable computation and thus are incapable of scaling up to larger lexicons on traditionally available machines. One way of dealing with this problem is to construct reduced lexicons for modelling that nonetheless reflect the distributional properties of the human lexicon. However, this means that all of the stimuli used in an experiment cannot necessarily be included in simulations. The SHORTLIST model was proposed as a practical solution to this scaling problem. By using conventional programming techniques, this model can deal with realistic lexicons and can simulate the experimental materials directly. Moreover, Norris (1994) claims that ultimately these traditional matching procedures will be replaceable by large recurrent networks.

Introducing Multiple Independent Variables The models discussed here appeal to the notion of level of activation to express the strength of any particular lexical or sublexical hypothesis. This means that the influence upon word recognition of each and every relevant variable (like word frequency, word length and degree of match) must be expressed in terms of this single currency. This introduces the difficult problem of determining the relative contribution to lexical activation of each factor in interpreting simulation results and of finding a proper trade-off between the influences of these important variables in programming the model.

To illustrate this problem we can consider the contribution to lexical activation of two variables, word frequency and phonological match. There is evidence (Taft and Hambly, 1986; Marslen-Wilson, 1987) showing word frequency effects, that is, high frequency words are recognized faster than low frequency words matched along other relevant dimensions. To account for this effect, computational models can boost the activation level of the former by assuming higher resting levels, faster rise-times or lower recognition thresholds for the high frequency words.

Problems can arise for models that introduce these frequency effects and that also allow lexical candidates to be activated by small mismatches. These models must be able to prevent high frequency competitors from being falsely recognized when they are close competitors of a low frequency target word. Consequently, the intrinsic activation advantage enjoyed by a high frequency word over a low frequency word must be carefully weighed against the activation differences due to a small phonological mismatch. Models face similar problems when dealing with the trade-off between length (where additional phonemes lead to greater activation) and variables like frequency. It is perhaps not surprising that current simulations with both TRACE and SHORTLIST do not use the word frequency variable despite the fact that it is implemented or could be without difficulty.

Lexical Competition and Selection

The four models discussed here predict that different candidates are initially activated by the sensory input. These models also disagree on how initially

Table 5.3: Patterns of activation flow that characterize the selection mechanisms in four word recognition models

Model	Bottom-up		Top-down		Lateral	
	excitation	inhibition	excitation	inhibition	excitation	inhibition
COHORT I	+	+	−	−	−	−
COHORT II	+	+	−	−	−	−
TRACE	+	−	+	−	−	+
SHORTLIST	+	+	−	−	−	+

activated lexical competitors are subsequently eliminated from the competitor set and how the target word is selected. This is to be expected since the same mechanisms that generate the initially activated candidate set also are responsible for the lexical selection process that reduces the competitor set to the target word. Table 5.3 summarizes the patterns of activation flow that characterize the selection mechanisms in these models. The COHORT and TRACE models appeal to different mechanisms to reduce the competitor set. According to the COHORT model, this is achieved by means of bottom-up inhibition: when mismatching sensory information is received, it decreases the activation of inappropriate lexical units. According to TRACE, competitor set reduction is achieved through a combination of bottom-up activation and lateral inhibition. This inhibition between lexical competitors allows the stronger candidates, and in particular the target, to dominate and eliminate the weaker ones. These two mechanisms are not mutually exclusive but can be combined as in the SHORTLIST model.

Models based upon these two selection mechanisms make divergent predictions concerning the factors that affect the selection process and the time-course of word recognition. For models like the COHORT with bottom-up inhibition, any mismatching sensory input directly decreases the level of activation of the deviant competitors. For models like TRACE, in contrast, this mismatching information only affects word recognition when there are other lexical competitors that are matched and activated by this mismatching input. Such competitors will inhibit the target. If there are no such competitors then the bottom-up mismatch has no effect. Thus, the nature (length and frequency) and number of the competitors affect the level of target activation in TRACE. For COHORT-like models, these factors are essentially irrelevant.

Experimental Findings on Lexical Competition
Defining experiments that test the assumptions of these models concerning lexical competition and selection is not straightforward. This task is complicated by the fact that TRACE and COHORT II make rather similar predictions, as Bard (1990) has pointed out. This is because COHORT II, while excluding competitor inhibition during lexical selection, nonetheless, introduces effects of the competitors into its decision rule. The decision rule establishes the principles for completion of the selection process by determining when the winning (or perceived) lexical entry is identified. By taking the activation level of the most activated competitor into consideration, this model reintroduces effects of competitors like in TRACE.

Nonetheless, some progress has been made in testing these two classes of model by looking for evidence for bottom-up inhibition on the one hand and for competitor inhibition on the other.

Inhibitory Effect of Mismatching Information Mismatching information can have its inhibitory bottom-up effect upon competitor activation at two processing moments. First, this information can prevent a lexical candidate from ever being activated at all if the mismatch comes early, and second, it can deactivate lexical competitors that have been activated by prior matching information. Experiments bearing upon the former effect of mismatching information were considered in the previous section. The question addressed here is whether lexical competitors that have already been activated by matching information are immediately deactivated by mismatching information. Some relevant experiments were conducted by Zwitserlood (1989) who showed that activated candidates were deactivated when mismatching information was received. When additional discriminating sensory information arrived (e.g., the [I] in [kæptI]), the semantic associate of the mismatching competitor (*captain*) was no longer primed, and the competitor was assumed to be deactivated. Unfortunately, it is impossible in this study to determine whether it was the mismatching information that eliminated this competitor or whether the matching competitor (*captive*) inhibited this competitor.

Inhibitory Effects of Competitors To evaluate whether competitors have a direct inhibitory effect upon the activation level of the target words, the competitor environment (number and nature of competitors) is generally manipulated. Inhibitory effects upon the recognition of an embedded word by a single carrier competitor have been shown in an experiment (McQueen, Norris and Cutler, 1993) in which subjects spotted words (e.g., *mess*) embedded non-initially in the word fragments (*domes* as in *domestic*) or nonword fragments (*nemes*). The longer spotting latencies for the words embedded in word fragments suggest not only that words with different alignments (carrier and embedded words) are activated simultaneously, but also that the carrier inhibits the embedded word.

The effects of competitor set size upon word recognition have also been studied to test for competitor inhibition. Marslen-Wilson (1984) showed that subject's latencies to decide that a string was a nonword did not depend upon the number of cohort members just prior to the nonword segment; constant RTs were found independent of cohort size. Conflicting findings were obtained by Jakimik (1979) who obtained evidence for cohort size effects. Slower mispronunciation detection latencies were obtained for nonwords derived from words with a large competitor set (e.g., *complain*) than those with a small set (e.g., *shampoo*). Unfortunately, the stimuli with large cohorts were essentially prefixed, introducing the additional confounding factor of morphological complexity.

A series of experimental studies (Luce, 1986; Goldinger, Luce and Pisoni, 1989; Luce, Pisoni and Goldinger, 1990) examined the role of the number of competitors with another competitor definition, the *N-count* definition. Here, words with a mismatch in any single phonemic position are competitors. Larger competitor sets produced longer auditory lexical decision and word naming times, and also more incorrect perceptual identification. The inhibitory influence of the competitors is consistent with the predictions made by the authors' Neighborhood Activation model (Luce, Pisoni and Goldinger, 1990). This evidence for an influence of competitor set size upon the time-course of word recognition runs counter to the predictions of the COHORT model and against the TRACE model to the extent that the competitors set included non-cohort members. However, to compare these results fairly with the predictions of these models, the effect of cohort and N-count competitors must be teased apart more systematically. More recently, in a word spotting experiment (Norris, McQueen and Cutler, 1995) it has been shown that the latencies to spot an initially embedded word (e.g., *car* in *card*) was a function of the number of overlapping competitors. This provides further evidence in support of the TRACE and SHORTLIST models which both predict effects of competitor set size.

Modelling the Time-Course of Word Recognition

The final problem to be addressed here concerns the moment at which a word is recognized and how this moment can be predicted by computational models. An important asset of computational models based on interactive activation is their ability to produce activation curves for the target word and its competitors. On the basis of these activation values, a decision rule can be used to determine the exact moment at which the word is recognized. According to one type of rule, the criterion rule, the activation level of the target must reach a fixed threshold to be recognized. Alternatively, according to a goodness-of-fit rule, a target is recognized when its activation exceeds that of the other competitor(s) by a predefined amount.

In a study of TRACE's predictions concerning the time-course of word recognition (Frauenfelder and Peeters, 1994), the relation between the simulated recognition points of a group of words and the properties of their competitor set was investigated. The results showed a strong correlation between the recognition point and the uniqueness point (UP). Moreover, in simulations of the gating task, TRACE recognized words on the basis of partial information. More precisely, the amount of input that is both necessary and sufficient for recognition is defined by the location of the UP. However, the words were not actually recognized at the UP, but rather 25–40 cycles (up to 600 ms) later. This lag represents the time required for activation to percolate up to the lexical level via the phonemic level and to meet the recognition criteria. Although the relation between cycles and time remains only approximate and is not motivated psychologically, this large delay distinguishes TRACE from COHORT I in which the word is assumed to be recognized immediately at the UP. It is likely that the true recognition point lies somewhere between these two extreme estimates. The SHORTLIST model has not yet been associated with an explicit decision mechanism so at present makes no predictions concerning recognition points.

Experimental Findings on the Recognition Time-Course

A number of experimental studies have explored the relation between the moment a word is recognized and the properties of its competitor set. In particular, the predictions by COHORT I that a word in isolation is recognized at its UP has attracted considerable experimental attention. Gating studies (Grosjean, 1980; Tyler and Wessels, 1983) have shown that the amount of information required for word identification corresponded closely to the UP defined using phonetic descriptions found in a lexical database. An influence of the location of the UP upon subjects' word recognition performance has also been demonstrated with other more on-line experimental tasks such as phoneme detection (Marslen-Wilson, 1984; Frauenfelder, Segui and Dijkstra, 1990), shadowing (Radeau and Morais, 1990), and gender decision (Radeau, Mousty and Bertelson, 1989). However, in all these studies the fit between the UP and the recognition point is not strong enough to exclude the influence of other variables or even of alternative definitions of the competitor set. In a gender verification experiment (De Ruiter and Frauenfelder, in preparation), the predictive value of the UP was found to be less than that of another definition, *minimal deviation* (Marcus and Frauenfelder, 1985), in which words with the smallest phonological mismatches in any position are included in the competitor set. More research comparing the ability of different competitor definitions to predict the RTs in various experimental tasks is clearly required.

Challenges of Modelling Time-Course of Word Recognition

While it is straightforward to obtain the recognition point for individual words with models like TRACE, it is much more difficult, however, to generalize from this recognition behaviour on individual lexical items to the global patterns. Indeed, the interactive activation mechanism underlying computational models like TRACE leads to complex and even counter-intuitive behaviour as we have seen from the absence of activation of mismatching competitors. Part of the difficulty lies in understanding the complex interaction between the relatively simple processing mechanisms (bottom-up activation, lateral inhibition and top-down activation) underlying interactive activation theory. Furthermore, it is also difficult to establish the extent to which the obtained results are attributable to theoretically motivated assumptions about the model's mechanisms or to mere implementation decisions. Indeed, in implementing these mechanisms, the modeller is forced to make a number of arbitrary choices (e.g., concerning the definition of features, the use of a phoneme level, and the parameter settings) that all can affect the output of the model. Clearly, it is important to determine how much the model's behaviour is really a true reflection of the theory being proposed.

Another difficulty comes from the decision mechanisms which are often simply appended to the output of the model without much theoretical motivation. However, the choice of decision rules is important since it can change the pattern of results obtained as well as the spirit of the model. For instance in the case of the COHORT II model, the use of a goodness rule introduces competition between the target and the most activated competitor, something that is explicitly avoided in the selection process. This rule also leads to double competition in models like TRACE in which there is competition in terms of inhibition during lexical activation and then there is more competition introduced in the decision rule.

Conclusions

Psycholinguistic modelling in the area of spoken word recognition is evolving from verbal to computer implemented models. The present contribution has traced part of this evolution by contrasting four leading interactive-activation models of spoken word recognition. We have shown how their assumptions about the nature and direction of activation flow lead to divergent predictions concerning sublexical processing, lexical activation, selection, and the recognition time-course. Particularly interesting are the contrasting predictions concerning the activation of embedded words as a function of their position and of the lexical status (word vs. nonword) of the carrier items. Also important are the differential effects predicted for phonological mismatch as a function of the lexical status of the sensory input. We have reviewed some preliminary experimental tests that have begun to explore these issues but that unfortunately have not yet produced a convergent picture. It is essential, therefore, that further experiments along the same lines be conducted to test these different assumptions. Such experiments will provide some important additional constraints on models that will help narrow down the immense space of theoretical possibilities.

References

BARD, E. G. (1990) 'Competition, lateral inhibition, and frequency: Comments on the chapters by Frauenfelder and Peeters, Marslen-Wilson, and others', in ALTMANN, G. T. M. (Ed) *Cognitive Models of Speech Processing: Psycholinguistic and Computational Perspectives*, Cambridge, MA: MIT Press, pp. 185–210.

BRADLEY, D. C., SANCHEZ-CASAS, R. M. and GARCIA-ALBEA, J. E. (1993) 'The status of the syllable in the perception of Spanish and English', *Language and Cognitive Processes*, 8, 2, pp. 197–233.

COLE, R. A. and JAKIMIK, J. A. (1980) 'A model of speech perception', in COLE, R. A. (Ed.) *Perception and Production of Fluent Speech*, Hillsdale, NJ: Lawrence Earlbaum.

CONNINE, C. M., BLASKO, D. M. and TITONE, D. A. (1993) 'Do the beginning of words have a special status in auditory word recognition?', *Journal of Memory and Language*, 32, pp. 193–210.

CONTENT, A. and STERNON, P. (1994) 'Modelling retroactive context effects in spoken word recognition with a simple recurrent network', in *Proceedings of the Sixteenth Annual Cognitive Science Society*, Hillsdale, NJ: Lawrence Earlbaum.

CUTLER, A., MEHLER, J., NORRIS, D. G. and SEGUI, J. (1983) 'A language specific comprehension strategy', *Nature*, 304, pp. 159–60.

CUTLER, A., MEHLER, J., NORRIS, D. G. and SEGUI, J. (1986) 'The syllable's differing role in the segmentation of English and French', *Journal of Memory and Language*, 25, pp. 385–400.

CUTLER, A. and NORRIS, D. G. (1988) 'The role of strong syllables in segmentation for lexical access, *Journal of Experimental Psychology: Human Perception and Performance*, 14, pp. 113–21.

DE RUITER, J. P. and FRAUENFELDER, U. H. (in preparation) Neighborhood and frequency effects in spoken word recognition.

FRAUENFELDER, U. H. (1992) 'The interface between acoustic–phonetic and lexical processing', in SCHOUTEN, B. (Ed) *The Processing of Speech: From the Auditory Periphery to Word Recognition*, Berlin: Mouton De Gruyter, pp. 325–38.

FRAUENFELDER, U. and HENSTRA, J. (1988) 'Activation and deactivation of phonological representations', in *Proceedings of the 4th International Phonology Congress, Krems, Austria*.

FRAUENFELDER, U. H. and PEETERS, G. (1990) 'Lexical segmentation in TRACE: An exercise in simulation', in ALTMANN, G. T. M. (Ed) *Cognitive Models of Speech Processing: Psycholinguistic and Computational Perspectives*, Cambridge, MA: MIT Press, pp. 50–86.

FRAUENFELDER, U. H. and PEETERS, G. (1994) *Modelling the Time-Course of Word Recognition*, Manuscript submitted for publication.

FRAUENFELDER, U. H., SEGUI, J. and DIJKSTRA, T. (1990) 'Lexical effects in phonemic processing: Facilitatory or inhibitory?', *Journal of Experimental Psychology: Human Perception and Performance*, 16, pp. 77–91.

GOLDINGER, S. D., LUCE, P. A. and PISONI, D. B. (1989) 'Priming lexical neighborhoods of spoken words: Effects of competition and inhibition', *Journal of Memory and Language*, 28, pp. 501–18.

GROSJEAN, F. (1980) 'Spoken word recognition processes and the gating paradigm', *Perception & Psychophysics*, 28, pp. 267–83.

HUGGINS, A. W. F. (1967) 'Distortion of the temporal pattern of speech by syllable tied alternation', *Language and Speech*, 10, pp. 133–40.

JAKIMIK, J. (1979) *The Interaction of Sound and Knowledge in Word Recognition from Fluent Speech*, Unpublished doctoral dissertation, CMU.

KLATT, D. H. (1980) 'Speech perception: A model of acoustic-phonetic analysis and lexical access', in COLE, R. A. (Ed) *Perception and Production of Fluent Speech*, Hillsdale, NJ: Lawrence Erlbaum, pp. 243–88.

KOLINSKY, R., MORAIS, J. and CLUYTENS, M. (1995) 'Intermediate levels of representation in spoken word recognition: Evidence from word illusions', *Journal of Memory and Language*, 34(1), pp. 19–40.

LAHIRI, A. and MARSLEN-WILSON, W. D. (1991) 'The mental representation of lexical form: A phonological approach to the recognition lexicon', *Cognition*, 38, pp. 245–94.

LUCE, P. A. (1986) *Neighborhoods of Words in the Mental Lexicon* (Research on speech perception technical report No. 6), Bloomington: Indiana University.

LUCE, P. A., PISONI, D. B. and GOLDINGER, S. D. (1990) 'Similarity neighborhoods of spoken words', in ALTMANN, G. T. M. (Ed) *Cognitive Models of Speech Processing: Psycholinguistic and Computational Perspectives*, Cambridge, MA: MIT Press, pp. 122–47.

MARCUS, S. M. and FRAUENFELDER, U. H. (1985) 'Word recognition — Uniqueness or deviation? A theoretical note', *Language and Cognitive Processes*, 1, 2, pp. 163–9.

MARSLEN-WILSON, W. D. (1984) 'Function and process in spoken word recognition', in

BOUMA, H. and BOUWHUIS, D. G. (Eds) *Attention and Performance X: Control of Language Processes*, Hillsdale, NJ: Lawrence Erlbaum.

MARSLEN-WILSON, W. D. (1987) 'Functional parallelism in spoken word recognition', *Cognition*, 25, pp. 71–102.

MARSLEN-WILSON, W. D. (1990) 'Activation, competition and frequency in lexical access', in ALTMANN, G. T. M. (Ed) *Cognitive Models of Speech Processing*, Cambridge, MA: MIT Press, pp. 148–72.

MARSLEN-WILSON, W. D. (1994) 'Issues of process and representation in lexical access', in ALTMANN, G. T. M. and SHILLCOCK, R. (Eds) *Cognitive Models of Speech Processing: The Sperlonga Meeting II*, Hillsdale, NJ: Lawrence Erlbaum.

MARSLEN-WILSON, W. D. and WELSH, A. (1978) 'Processing interactions and lexical access during word-recognition in continuous speech', *Cognitive Psychology*, 10, pp. 29–63.

MARSLEN-WILSON, W. D. and ZWITSERLOOD, P. (1989) 'Accessing spoken words: The importance of word onsets', *Journal of Experimental Psychology: Human Perception and Performance*, 15, 3, pp. 576–85.

MASSARO, D. W. and ODEN, G. C. (1980) 'Speech perception: A framework for research and theory', in LASS, N. J. (Ed) *Speech and Language: Advances in Basic Research and Practice*, New York: Academic Press.

MCCLELLAND, J. L. and ELMAN, J. L. 'The TRACE model of speech perception', *Cognitive Psychology*, 18, pp. 1–86.

MCQUEEN, J. M., NORRIS, D. and CUTLER, A. (1994) 'Competition in spoken word recognition: Spotting words in other words', *Journal of Experimental Psychology: Learning, Memory, and Cognition*, 20(3), 621–38.

MEHLER, J. (1981) 'The role of syllables in speech processing: Infant and adult data', *Philosophical Transactions of the Royal Society, Series B*, 295, pp. 333–52.

MEHLER, J., DOMMERGUES, J., FRAUENFELDER, U. and SEGUI, J. (1981) 'The syllable's role in speech segmentation', *Journal of Verbal Learning and Verbal Behavior*, 20, pp. 298–305.

MONSELL, S. (1985) 'Repetition and the lexicon', in ELLIS, A. W. (Ed) *Progress in the Psychology of Language: Vol. 2*, London: Lawrence Erlbaum.

NORRIS, D. (1990) 'A dynamic-net model of human speech recognition', in ALTMANN, G. T. M. (Ed) *Cognitive Models of Speech Processing: Psycholinguistic and Computational Perspectives*, Cambridge, MA: MIT Press, pp. 87–104.

NORRIS, D. (1994) 'SHORTLIST: A connectionist model of continuous speech recognition', *Cognition*, 52, 189–234.

NORRIS, D., MCQUEEN, J. M. and CUTLER, A. (1995) 'Competition and segmentation in spoken word recognition', *Journal of Experimental Psychology: Learning, Memory, and Cognition*, 21 (5), 1209–28.

PISONI, D. B. and LUCE, P. A. (1987) 'Acoustic-phonetic representations in word recognition', *Cognition*, 25, pp. 21–52.

PISONI, D. B. and SAWUSCH, J. R. (1975) 'Some stages of processing in speech perception', in COHEN, A. and NOOTEBOOM, S. (Eds) *Structure and Processes in Speech Perception*, Heidelberg: Springer, pp. 16–34.

RADEAU, M. and MORAIS, J. (1990) 'The uniqueness point effect in the shadowing of spoken words', *Speech Communication*, 9, pp. 155–64.

RADEAU, M., MOUSTY, P. and BERTELSON, P. (1989) 'The effect of the uniqueness point in spoken word recognition', *Psychological Research*, 51, pp. 123–8.

SAWUSCH, J. R. (1986) 'Auditory and phonetic coding in speech', in SCHWAB, E. C. and NUSBAUM, H. C. (Eds) *Pattern Recognition by Humans and Machines*, New York: Academic Press.

SEGUI, J., DUPOUX, E. and MEHLER, J. (1990) 'The role of the syllable in speech segmentation, phoneme identification, and lexical access', in ALTMANN, G. T. M. (Ed) *Cognitive Models of Speech Processing: Psycholinguistic and Computational Perspectives*, Cambridge, MA: MIT Press, pp. 263–80.

SHILLCOCK, R. C. (1990) 'Lexical hypotheses in continuous speech', in ALTMANN, G. (Ed.) *Cognitive Models of Speech Processing: Psycholinguistic and Computational Perspectives*, Cambridge, MA: MIT Press.

SHILLCOCK, R. G., LINDSEY, J., LEVY, J. and CHATER, N. (1992) 'A phonologically motivated input representation for the modelling of auditory word perception in continuous speech', in *Proceedings of the Fourteenth Annual Conference of the Cognitive Science Society*, Hove: Lawrence Erlbaum, pp. 408–23.

SWINNEY, D. A. (1979) 'Lexical access during sentence comprehension: (Re)consideration of context effects', *Journal of Verbal Learning and Verbal Behavior*, 18, pp. 645–60.

TAFT, M. and HAMBLY, G. (1986) 'Exploring the cohort model of spoken word recognition', *Cognition*, 22, pp. 259–82.

TYLER, L. K. and WESSELS, J. (1983) 'Quantifying contextual contributions to word recognition processes, *Perception and Psychophysics*, 34, pp. 409–20.

ZWITSERLOOD, P. (1989) 'The locus of the effects of sentential-semantic context in spoken-word processing', *Cognition*, 32, pp. 25–64.

ZWITSERLOOD, P., SCHRIEFERS, H., LAHIRI, A. and VAN DONSELAAR, W. (1993) 'The role of syllables in the perception of spoken Dutch', *Journal of Experimental Psychology: Learning, Memory, and Cognition*, 19, 2, pp. 260–71.

Chapter 6

Visual Word Recognition: Models and Experiments
Jonathan Grainger and Ton Dijkstra

Introduction

Reading is facilitated by the fact that, at least in normal text, the boundaries of individualwordsareclearlymarked! The human brain is likely to take advantage of this situation and therefore use these isolated visual patterns as the basic building blocks of the comprehension process. For each word the brain must compute a form representation of the physical signal that is then matched to abstract representations stored in memory. It is this fundamental pattern recognition process, referred to as visual word recognition, that then allows access to the individual word meanings that are integrated in the higher-level processes of sentence comprehension. At least as far as morphologically simple words are concerned, none of the potential sublexical units (i.e., letters or letter clusters) carry meaning, thus implying that meaning can only be accessed via whole-word representations (see Chapter 7 for an analysis of morphologically complex words). Information about the meaning of a given word must be accessed via a preliminary analysis of the formal properties (e.g., orthographic and phonological) of that

Figure 6.1: A general framework for studying visual word recognition (see text for explanation)

FEATURAL DESCRIPTION   STRUCTURAL REPRESENTATION

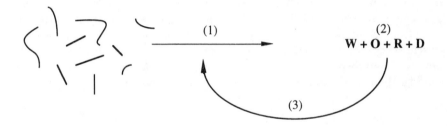

$$W + O + R + D$$

(1)

(2)

(3)

word. This assumption is implicit in practically every model of visual word recognition and explains why the recognition process has dominated psychological enquiry relative to studies of meaning retrieval.

In Figure 6.1 we present a general framework for the study of this recognition process. Written words are visual patterns that reflect light of varying intensity and wavelength. This reflected light falls on retinal receptors that generate neural activity leading to the extraction of featural information by processes common to visual processing in general. This featural information must be transcoded into a form that allows it to be matched to information about the formal properties of words stored in long-term memory. Within such a framework three essential questions arise:

1 What kind of sublexical representations (if any) mediate between featural information and lexical representations in memory?
2 How can one describe the structured lexical representations of written words?
3 Does top-down feedback from higher-level to lower-level representations influence the mapping process?

In the next section we examine some basic empirical results related to the three questions raised with respect to Figure 6.1. Evidence in favour of different types of sublexical representation is examined and the distinction between structural and statistical units introduced. Concerning the lexical level of representation, the effects of word frequency and its interaction with orthographic neighbourhood effects are discussed. At the end of the section the evidence concerning lexical influences on sublexical processing is presented. In the following section a symbolic and a subsymbolic connectionist model of visual word recognition are described and evaluated with respect to the empirical data described previously. As a general conclusion, we offer a global appraisal of each of these modelling approaches, and provide some suggestions for the development of future models of visual recognition.

Some Basic Phenomena in Visual Word Recognition

In this section, we do not aim at an exhaustive review of the results obtained from nearly one hundred years of research on visual word representation. Rather, we select from the literature what appear to be critical data relative to an evaluation of current models of the visual word recognition process. We first consider sublexical processing and then go on to examine processing at the lexical level, and finally we consider the possible influences of the latter on the former.

Sublexical Processing

Orthographic Codes

Surely the simplest means of describing a written word is in terms of its constituent letters (see Figure 6.1). This observation has been implemented in the majority of models of visual word recognition in the form of a preliminary phase of letter coding prior to word recognition (Forster, 1976; Paap *et al.*, 1982; McClelland and Rumelhart, 1981). Is there, however, any empirical evidence that suggests that individual letter representations are indeed coded during visual word recognition and that such coding is a fundamental part of the recognition process? Two principal sources of evidence are examined: unit frequency studies and priming research.

Much of the research investigating effects of sublexical unit frequency in visual word recognition has concentrated not on the single letter, but on letter combinations such as bigrams and trigrams. This particular interest in bigram and trigram frequency is due to the fact that such measures reflect what is referred to as *sequential redundancy*. In other words, the frequency of occurrence of a particular letter sequence in a given language indicates the probability, given the identity of one of the letters, of the other being present. This application of information theory to the study of language comprehension (e.g., Miller, Bruner and Postman, 1954) predicts that sequential redundancy should influence ease of word recognition. Words with high sequential redundancies should be easier to recognize than words with low sequential redundancies. This, however, turned out not to be the case. Gernsbacher (1984), summarizing ten years of research on bigram frequency effects, concluded that the contradictory results in this area could be simply explained on the basis of variations in familiarity of the stimuli at the word level (using rating scales to estimate word familiarity). Although the concept of familiarity and its measurement are themselves problematical, Gernsbacher's study did point out one possible confound with measures of bigram frequency.

What is more problematical, however, is the confound between such informational measures (redundancy or constraint) and measures of familiarity (unit frequency) at the level of sublexical units (cf., Lima and Inhoff, 1985). Constraint and frequency are inversely related, in that a frequently occurring bigram gives you little information about the other possible letters in a given string. When a particular letter or letter cluster appears often at a particular position in a given language (e.g., the sequence WH as an initial bigram in English), this means that readers of English encounter this orthographic pattern often and therefore become familiarized with it. It also means, however, that this particular orthographic pattern occurs in many words and as such is not a good clue as to what the stimulus word is (WH— could be any of the following words: WHERE, WHILE, WHITE, WHISK etc.). Thus, increasing bigram frequency is confounded with decreasing sequential constraint and many of the discrepancies in the experimental literature may be due to an inability to separate out these two factors.

Measures of sequential redundancy can be contrasted with another statistical measure of orthographic structure referred to as spatial redundancy or position-specific letter frequency. This measure reflects the probability that a given letter will be present at a given position in a word of a given length. Studies comparing the relative influence of spatial and sequential redundancy in visual word recognition have generally found stronger support for the former (Henderson, 1982, but see Massaro *et al.*, 1980, for contradictory evidence). This advantage for measures of spatial redundancy can be taken as evidence in favour of the role of individual letter units in visual word recognition. Perhaps the strongest evidence in favour of this position comes from research using letter-in-string detection tasks. Several different varieties of this task have been used, such as Reicher's (1969) two-alternative forced choice paradigm and the letter detection task. In both of these paradigms it has been observed that performance is better for letters with high position-specific frequencies (Mason, 1975; McClelland, 1976; McClelland and Johnston, 1977). Moreover, Grainger and Jacobs (1993) have recently demonstrated that in a partial-word priming paradigm (e.g. *table* primed by TA%LE) it is the positional frequencies of the letters maintained between prime and target (T, A, L, and E, in the above example) that best predicts the size of the obtained priming effects.

However, research by Humphreys, Evett and Quinlan (1990) suggests that this position coding is likely to be more flexible, at least as far as the internal letters of a word are concerned. Thus, for example, Humphreys, Evett and Quinlan (1990) demonstrated that significant positive priming is obtained when prime letters respect their relative position in the target string while violating absolute position (e.g., BVK-BLACK).[1] Moreover, experiments examining letter transposition errors (Estes, Allmeyer and Reder, 1976) and letter migration errors (Mozer, 1983; McClelland and Mozer, 1986) in orthographic displays all converge to suggest that letter position information is coded less precisely than certain models make out. Recently, it has been suggested that context-sensitive coding schemes (e.g., Seidenberg and McClelland, 1989) may provide a better alternative to the position-specific letter detector approach. According to this approach the critical orthographic units subtending visual word recognition are larger than the single letter (typically letter triples or trigrams). There is still no concrete empirical evidence, however, in favour of such abstract statistical entities as units mediating between featural analysis and word recognition. Although, as we see below, there is evidence in favour of the mediating role played by sublexical units above the single letter, most of this evidence suggests structural rather than statistical units.

Indeed, many psycholinguists have attempted to describe visual word recognition as a process whereby some critical processing unit (larger than the single letter and smaller than the whole word) is extracted from the stimulus and subsequently provides access to word representations in memory that share this critical unit (the access code hypothesis). Much of the research testing the role of these hypothetical letter cluster units has used either a divided stimulus paradigm (e.g., gar den) or a priming paradigm (gar-GARDEN). Basically, results in favour of a particular unit would show that target recognition is improved relative to appropriate controls when the division respects the unit or when the prime constitutes such a unit. The evidence available from such research, however, is mixed in terms of its support for different sublexical units (see, for example, Taft, 1979; Lima and Pollatsek, 1983; Jordan, 1986). Seidenberg (1987) has presented a powerful argument against the role of such access code units in visual word recognition by pointing out that the boundaries between such units in a word often correspond to a marked change in bigram frequency across the word (the bigram trough hypothesis).

An alternative line of research in this area has used the illusory conjunction paradigm where subjects are shown briefly presented words written in coloured letters and asked to report the colour of a target letter presented prior to the stimulus word. Prinzmetal and his colleagues have shown that conjunction errors (reporting the colour of the wrong letter) occur significantly more often within syllabic units than across these units (Prinzmetal, Treiman and Rho, 1986). More importantly, Rapp (1992) has shown that this pattern of results can be obtained independently of whether or not syllabic structure was marked by a bigram trough. It therefore appears, after two decades of research on this topic, that the syllable is one structural unit that might possibly subtend the visual recognition of morphologically simple words (see Chapters 4 and 5 for a discussion of the syllable's role in speech recognition). Since the syllable is most naturally defined in terms of the phonological structure of words, this raises the important question as to how phonological information in general might influence the processing of printed words.

Phonological Codes
One of the most important long-standing debates in the visual word recognition literature concerns the role played by phonological information in recognizing printed words. Visual word recognition could be completed successfully without any appeal to phonological information. However, all readers are first and fore-most listeners of a language, and when learning to read written symbols are associated with their phonological equivalents in order to gain access to meaning. The question is therefore whether adult readers recognize what is essentially an orthographic description stored in memory (the orthographic prevalence hypothesis) or some form of phonological description of the written word (the phonologic prevalence hypothesis). According to the latter position (sometimes referred to as the phonological recoding hypothesis; e.g., Rubenstein, Lewis and Rubenstein, 1971) orthographic codes must first be transformed into phonological codes before a word can be recognized and/or meaning representations activated.

Defenders of the phonologic prevalence hypothesis point out that although there is ample evidence for phonological involvement in the visual word recognition process (e.g., Humphreys, Evett and Taylor, 1982; Van Orden, 1987; Perfetti, Bell and Delaney, 1988; Van Orden, Johnston and Hale, 1988; Perfetti and Bell, 1991; Ferrand and Grainger, 1992; Lukatela, Lukatela and Turvey, 1993), there is still no unequivocal evidence in favour of the direct involvement of orthographic codes independently of phonology. In recent experimentation, however, Ferrand and Grainger (1994) evaluated the effects of orthographic priming against appropriate phonological controls. In both priming conditions prime stimuli were pseudohomophones of French target words (i.e., were nonsense letter strings that would typically be pronounced like the target word, an example in English being BLOO-BLUE). One of the categories of pseudohomophone prime shared more letters with the corresponding word targets than the other category. Ferrand and Grainger (1994) found that target recognition was facilitated by increased prime-target orthographic overlap with prime exposures around 30 ms. On the other hand, effects of increased phonological overlap between primes and targets only begin to emerge with prime exposures around 50 ms (Ferrand and Grainger, 1993), while at the same time the effects of orthography disappear and tend toward inhibition. Thus it is now clear that both orthographic and phonological overlap between prime and target stimuli affect target word recognition in both lexical decision (Ferrand and Grainger, 1992, 1993, 1994) and perceptual identification (Perfetti, Bell and Delaney, 1988; Perfetti and Bell, 1991; Grainger and Ferrand, 1994) and that these two effects have distinct time courses (effects of orthography appearing before effects of phonology). These results fit well with previous research showing larger effects of phonological regularity on response times to low frequency words compared to high frequency words in the word naming task (Andrews, 1982; Seidenberg *et al.*, 1984; Waters and Seidenberg, 1985; Jared and Seidenberg, 1991). Since low frequency words take longer to recognize than high frequency words they allow more time for phonological influences to arise before identification is complete.

Research by Van Orden (1987) has shown that the semantic categorization task (*is TULIP a flower?*) is sensitive to phonology. More false positive responses are obtained to targets that are homophones of a real category member (*is ROWS a FLOWER?*) than to corresponding orthographic controls (*is ROBS a flower?*). This was subsequently replicated by Jared and Seidenberg (1991) who further demonstrated that this homophone interference effect only pertained to low frequency words. This differential frequency effect observed by Jared and Seidenberg brings them to reject Van Orden's (1987) proposal that meaning is activated exclusively via phonology. At the same time these results provide further support for the time-course hypothesis according to which phonology will only influence word recognition (and subsequently meaning retrieval) when given sufficient time.

Lexical Processing

The majority of models of visual word recognition developed over the last twenty to thirty years agree that information extracted from the printed string of letters somehow contacts stored representations of words in memory. These models differ essentially in how they describe the matching process and the lexical representations in long-term memory. Although more recent experimental results allow us to reject a large majority of these models, they can all accommodate one basic phenomenon in the visual word recognition literature: the word frequency effect.

Word Frequency

The word frequency effect refers to the observation that words that occur frequently in a given language give rise to faster reaction times and/or lower error rates than words with low frequency counts in tasks such as lexical decision, word naming and perceptual identification. The fundamental role played by word frequency in the word recognition process has been questioned by Balota and Chumbley (1984) (see also McCann, Besner and Davelaar, 1988). These authors suggested that a substantial proportion of the observed effects could be attributed to mechanisms extraneous to the word recognition process (e.g., the decision process in lexical decision or the process of articulatory preparation in word naming). In support of their arguments these authors showed that no significant effects of word frequency are obtained in a semantic categorization task where word recognition is supposedly necessary. This particular result of Balota and Chumbley (1984) has been criticized by Monsell and his colleagues (Monsell, Doyle and Haggard, 1989; Monsell, 1991).

The thrust of the criticism is that the complexity of the decision process involved in Balota and Chumbley's semantic categorization task probably masked effects of word frequency that were in fact present. In support of this, Monsell, Doyle and Haggard (1989) demonstrated significant effects of word frequency in a simpler version of the semantic categorization task. Nevertheless, the work of Balota and Chumbley continues to be widely cited by researchers in the field as a major criticism of the lexical decision task. Future researchers should be wary of such premature conclusions based on a single study. Moreover, significant effects of word frequency have been reported in situations that do not require articulatory and/or decision processes. Thus Inhoff and Rayner (1986) and Vitu, O'Regan and Mittau (1990) have reported effects of word frequency on gaze durations to words in silent text reading. Also, Grainger and Segui (1990) have shown significant effects of word frequency in a progressive demasking paradigm where subjects simply have to press a response button when the target word is identified (target and pattern mask are alternated with increasing target duration and decreasing mask duration on successive cycles). Clearly the evidence at present strongly supports the hypothesis that word frequency has a basic influence on the word recognition process (see Monsell, 1991, for a more detailed examination of word frequency effects leading to the same conclusions).

One of the arguments used by Balota and Chumbley (1984) in their criticism of the lexical decision task is that word frequency effects observed with this task are typically twice the size as those observed in word naming. According to Balota and Chumbley this task difference arises because word naming does not involve a decisional component that is responsible for a large part of the frequency effect observed with the lexical decision task. However, Monsell, Doyle and Haggard (1989) and Grainger (1990) have both reported studies where frequency effects of comparable magnitude are observed with both tasks. On the basis of Grainger's results it would appear that, rather than word frequency, it is the orthographic similarities among words that underlie the difference in effects obtained in the lexical decision and naming tasks. It is to this latter factor that we now turn.

Orthographic Neighbourhoods

Research over the years has demonstrated that words that are orthographically similar to a given target word can affect recognition of the latter. The early work of Havens and Foote (1963) suggested that tachistoscopic recognition thresholds of word stimuli are mainly affected by the frequency of words that are orthographically similar to the stimulus rather than stimulus frequency itself. More recent research suggests that both factors play a fundamental role in visual word recognition.

The majority of recent research in the field has applied the N-count definition of orthographic similarity introduced by Coltheart *et al.* (1977). According to this definition, words that share all but one letter with the stimulus word (respecting position) are called orthographic neighbours of the stimulus. For example, TAN, CAN, BUN, and BAT are all neighbours of the word BAN. Coltheart *et al.* demonstrated that the number of neighbours (N) of a stimulus word had no effect on performance in a lexical decision task, whereas responses to nonword stimuli were adversely affected by increasing N values. More recent experimentation, however, has shown that performance in the lexical decision and word naming tasks can be facilitated in such circumstances but only when the stimuli have low printed frequencies (Andrews, 1989, 1992).

The story is further complicated by research manipulating the printed frequencies of the set of orthographic neighbours compared to the frequency of the stimulus word itself. These experiments have typically shown that high frequency neighbours inhibit the recognition of low frequency words (Grainger *et al.*, 1989, 1992; Grainger, 1990, 1992; Grainger and Segui, 1990) (see Luce, Pisoni and Goldinger, 1990, for similar results in auditory word recognition). One possible solution to these apparently conflicting results has been recently offered Snodgrass and Mintzer (1993) who have shown that either facilitatory or inhibitory neighbourhood effects can be obtained with the same set of stimuli depending on the exact nature of the word recognition task used. When subjects have to report the stimulus word in a perceptual identification task, inhibitory effects of neighbourhood density are observed with low frequency words. When, however, subjects respond before complete stimulus identification (as is possible in the lexical decision task), facilitatory effects of neighbourhood density are obtained with the same set of stimuli. We return to this critical issue in the section on models.

Word Superiority

Ever since Cattell (1866), it has been known that subjects can report more letters from briefly presented words than from unrelated letter strings of the same length. Further experimental evidence for this so-called Word Superiority Effect was provided by Reicher (1969) with a paradigm (two alternative forced choice or 2AFC) that controls for memory loss and word completion strategies. In this paradigm a letter string is presented very briefly and followed immediately by a display of two individual letters, one above and the other below the position of one of the letters in the previously presented string. Thus the stimulus WORD would be briefly presented followed by the letter pair D/K situated above and below the position of the letter D in WORD. Subjects have to decide which of the two letters in the second display were present in the string. The results typically show that letter identification accuracy is better in words than in nonwords or when letters are presented alone (Reicher, 1969; Wheeler, 1970).

The word-letter advantage refers to the recognition advantage of letters in words over isolated letters reported using the 2AFC task (e.g., Reicher, 1969; Wheeler, 1970; Johnston, 1978; Johnston and McClelland, 1980). These results would appear to suggest that words are more perceptible than isolated letters. Recent research by Jordan and De Bruijn (1993), however, has shown that this word-letter advantage disappears or is even reversed (i.e., superior report of isolated letters) when the masking stimulus is the same dimension as the target letter in the isolated letter condition. In previous studies the same size of pattern mask was used for both the word and isolated letter conditions. Jordan and De Bruijn also showed that the word advantage disppears when the masks used for the word stimuli extend past the ends of the stimulus. It would therefore appear from these latest results that under appropriate masking conditions words are not recognized with lower tachistoscopic exposures than single letter stimuli.

The word superiority effect is generally used to refer to the higher accuracy of letter identification in word stimuli compared to letters in pronounceable or un-pronounceable nonword strings (e.g., McClelland and Johnston, 1977). It has often been concluded on the basis of this result that letters are more 'perceptible' in words than in nonwords (e.g., Johnston, 1978). This conclusion implies that our higher-level knowledge of word structure can directly influence the perception of individual letters in a top-down, interactive manner. However, a much simpler explanation can be offered in terms of the global perceptibility of whole-word units compared to pseudoword strings. Subjects can correctly report words at lower tachistoscopic exposures than pseudowords and can therefore deduce the correct letter at the correct position from their knowledge of word spellings (note that none of the different types of control for this type of guessing eliminates the problem). Thus the word-pseudoword advantage correctly refers to the superior recognition of word stimuli over pseudoword stimuli (Carr, 1986; Henderson, 1982) but says nothing about how perceptible individual letters are in these respective stimuli. In other words, the data obtained to date using this paradigm do not address the issue of the presence or absence of top-down feedback from word representations to letter representations during visual word recognition. If, however, one were to demonstrate that the word-pseudoword advantage in letter recognition performance can be observed in conditions where whole-word report is close to zero, then one could satisfactorily conclude that letters are indeed more perceptible in words than in pseudowords. The data at present suggest, on the contrary, that the word-pseudoword advantage in Reicher's 2AFC paradigm is dependent on successful whole-word report (Grainger and Jacobs, 1994).

The Models

The previous sections gave an overview of our knowledge with respect to sublexical and lexical processes and representations involved in visual word recognition. In this section, two different implemented (algorithmic) models of visual word recognition are described. These two models belong to two different classes (as distinguished in Chapter 1). The first model (McClelland and Rumelhart, 1981; Rumelhart and McClelland, 1982) is the prototype of an Interactive Activation model, the second model (Seidenberg and McClelland, 1989) is the prototype of the class of Parallel Distributed Processing models. For more technical aspects of these general classes of models the reader is referred to Chapter 3 of this volume. For a recent presentation of a wider range of models of visual word recognition the reader is referred to Jacobs and Grainger (1994). At the end of the chapter we compare both types of model and formulate expectations and desiderata for future developments of word recognition models.

The Interactive Activation Model of Word Recognition

The Interactive Activation model (IA-model) of visual word recognition (McClelland and Rumelhart, 1981; Rumelhart and McClelland, 1982), shown in Figure 6.2, comprises three different types of unit/node corresponding to linguistic representations at three hierarchically arranged levels. The top level of nodes consist of words, originally 1179 English four-letter words with printed frequencies greater than 1 per million (Kucera and Francis, 1967). The middle level consists of letter nodes, 26 for each spatial position in a four-letter word. The lowest level consists of pairs of nodes that detect the presence/absence of visual features corresponding to the line segments of the Rumelhart and Siple (1974) type font at each letter position. Between nodes from adjacent representational levels both facilitatory and inhibitory connections exist, while connections between nodes at the same level are inhibitory only. Letter nodes are connected to both feature nodes and word nodes. Through their connections, feature nodes can influence the activation of particular letters, while letters can affect word

Figure 6.2: The Interactive Activation model of visual word recognition (McClelland and Rumelhart, 1981). A stimulus word activates featural representations in position-specific processing channels. The activation levels of these feature representations within each channel determines the activation levels of letter representations at each position (see text for more details). Only the excitatory between-level connections are shown, and some of the inhibitory connections within the word level

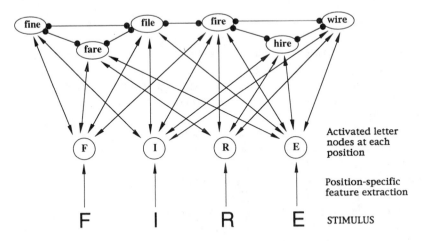

activation, and words letter activation. Depending on parameter settings on the connections, the influence exerted may be inhibitory or excitatory.

When a string of letters is presented to the IA-model, this visual input switches on particular features at each letter position, which subsequently excite letters that contain these features and at the same time inhibit letters for which the features are absent. Each activated letter then excites words in which that letter occurs at the spatial position in question, while all other words and letters in that position are inhibited. Subsequently, all activated words inhibit each other while they excite their component letters. Thus, when a letter string is presented to the model, this gives rise to a complex flow of activation throughout the network which results, after a number of cycles of processing, in an asymptotic activation value in some units at the word and letter levels. When the input is turned off all units slowly decrease in activation level over time as a function of the decay parameters in the model and gradually return to their resting level values.

Sublexical Representations

As will be clear from this description, the current implementation incorporates position-coded letters as the only sublexical unit. The choice of the letter as the basic sublexical unit is supported by the empirical data presented in the section on sublexical processing, though this choice ignores some experimental evidence in favour of the psychological validity of syllabic-type units. Moreover, available research also suggests that the position-specific letter coding in the model is likely to be too extreme (though just how extreme remains to be investigated). The data available at present suggest that the first and last letters of a word are coded quite precisely, whereas position information concerning internal letters is less exact. The model could be modified to accommodate such phenomena by relaxing the specificity of letter-word connections. Thus, the letter R in the stimulus word TRAY would send maximal activation to all four-letter words with R in the second position but also some reduced activation to all four-letter words with R in the third position (e.g., to CART). Effects of positional letter frequency are accommodated by the current model in that a given letter at a given position in a four-letter word will activate all four-letter words that begin with that letter. Since resting level activation of word units is a function of word frequency, the model predicts that it is a (frequency weighted) token count rather than a type count of positional letter frequency that should be the best predictor of word recognition performance. This is indeed what the empirical data presented in the section on sublexical processing show.

Clearly the model falls short with respect to one major aspect of sublexical processing: there is no phonology in the model. An appropriate extension of the model would be to include a layer of sublexical phonological units connected to both the letter and word units (see Ferrand and Grainger, 1992; Dijkstra, Frauenfelder and Schreuder, 1993; Dijkstra, Roelofs and Fieuws, 1995). However, a more complete extension is likely to require the addition of both lexical and sublexical phonology (e.g., Grainger and Ferrand, 1994). We shall return to this point in the General Discussion.

Lexical Processing

The IA-model accommodates the effects of word frequency in visual word recognition through variations in the resting level activations of word units. Words with higher printed frequencies have higher resting level activations and therefore benefit from a headstart compared to low frequency words in the race for identification. More interestingly, however, the effects of varying resting level activation interact with the effects of orthographic overlap among words in a way that allows the model to capture a wide variety of effects reported in the literature. Jacobs and Grainger (1992) have presented detailed simulation results using a semistochastic variant of the IA-model (referred to as SIAM) with French four and five letter lexica. By simply adding a noisy decision criterion set on the dimension of word unit activation, the model can successfully predict not only variations in mean response times obtained in an experiment but also the distributional characteristics of these RTs. Response time in the SIAM is simply the number of processing cycles required for any word unit to reach a critical activation level. As can be seen in Figure 6.3, the model correctly predicts that low frequency words are more subject to neighbourhood interference than are medium frequency words (Grainger and Segui, 1990). On the other hand, as pointed out by Jacobs and Grainger (1992), the facilitatory effects of neighbourhood density reported by Andrews (1989, 1992) are not simulated by SIAM which in fact predicts inhibitory effects of this variable. Interestingly, this is exactly the result obtained by Snodgrass and Mintzer (1993) using a perceptual identification paradigm. It may

Figure 6.3: Observed and predicted response times to low and medium frequency words with (NF+) or without (NF−) high frequency orthographic neighbours. The experimental data are from the progressive demasking task of Grainger and Segui (1990) and the simulation results from Jacobs and Grainger (1992)

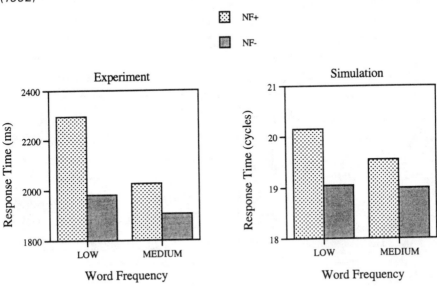

therefore be the case that the facilitatory effects of neighbourhood density observed in the lexical decision task are the result of mechanisms extraneous to the normal process of visual word recognition. In recent developments of the IA model (Grainger and Jacobs, 1994), it has been demonstrated that adding a decision criterion on summed lexical activity in the model allows it to accurately predict effects of neighbourhood density (see Figure 6.4) and the interaction between such effects and nonword foil lexicality. The model also does remarkably well in accommodating data obtained using the masked priming paradigm with very brief prime exposures (e.g., Forster and Davis, 1984; Segui and Grainger, 1990). Simulations with French prime-target word combinations presenting the prime for two cycles immediately followed by target presentation (Jacobs and Grainger, 1992), showed that low frequency targets were inhibited by the prior presentation of a high frequency orthographically related prime, whereas high frequency targets are uninfluenced by a low frequency orthographically related prime. This is exactly the pattern of effects observed in the empirical data (Segui and Grainger, 1990). Interpreted within the framework of the IA-model, this result suggests that, due to their lower resting level activation, low frequency words do not attain a high enough activation level to provoke noticeable interference on target processing under conditions of very brief prime exposures. Further simulation work has demonstrated that the model also successfully simulates the facilitatory effects of partial-word primes discussed in the section on sublexical processing (Grainger and Jacobs, 1993).

Figure 6.4: Observed and predicted response times and error rates to low and high frequency words with either a small or large number of orthographic neighbours. The experimental data correspond to the lexical decision experiment of Andrews (1992) and the simulation results are taken from Grainger and Jacobs (submitted)

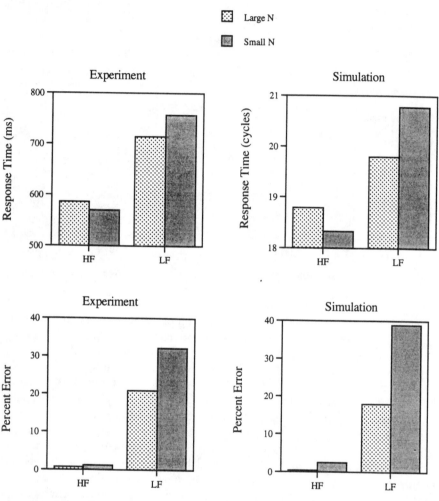

Top-Down Feedback

The IA-model is interactive in the sense that activity at higher levels can influence the processing occurring at lower representational levels. Thus, activation at the word level feeds back to the letter level. For example, a build in activation of the word TRAP will result in a corresponding reinforcement of the activation levels of its component letters T, R, A, and P. This explains the empirical finding (discussed previously) of a word superiority effect (Reicher, 1969), since the facilitatory feedback from word units to letter units is generally stronger for words than for nonwords.

In fact, the original motivation for the IA-model to include word-for-letter feedback in its design was to explain the word superiority effect and related phenomena. However, as pointed out in the section on lexical processing, one can explain these results without appealing to word-letter top-down feedback. In the light of this analysis, Grainger and Jacobs (1994) have presented an alternative explanation of the word superiority effect within the framework of the IA-model, in which responses in the Reicher paradigm are determined by which letter or word representations reach critical levels of activation within the limited processing time available. The results of these simulation studies show that with respect to word superiority over nonword stimuli both the interactive and non-interactive versions of the model do very well. However, it is with respect to the superiority of pronounceable nonword (pseudoword) over unpronounceable nonword strings that word-letter feedback becomes critical in the model. Nevertheless, there is still the possibility that introducing sublexical phonology in the IA-model would allow it to simulate these results without word-letter feedback. Clearly, this is an important point for future empirical and theoretical investigations.

Seidenberg and McClelland's PDP-Model of Word Recognition and Naming

Few researchers would dispute that the word frequency effect is one of the most robust and universally present phenomena in visual word recognition. In fact, many models of word recognition were built around assumptions intended to explain word frequency effects (e.g., Morton, 1969; Forster, 1976). As argued by Monsell (1991), these models have taken a 'synchronic' approach to word recognition, taking word frequency as a characteristic of the 'mature' system, rather than describing how that system came about through experience (a more 'diachronic' approach). The PDP-approach to word recognition takes a very different standpoint here by interpreting frequency of occurrence as a reflection of a lexical system that is dynamically responsive to experience, i.e., that continues to learn with every new presentation of a lexical item.

According to this second type of approach, what is learned by a language user through experience is the relationship between different types of linguistic pattern, e.g., between orthography and semantics, or between present and past tense forms of words. The complicated mappings between the linguistic codes involved are first learned by applying connectionist learning algorithms to distributed network representations for these codes (see Chapter 3). During the learning phase, the network discovers (or rather codes in the weights on its connections) regularities in the mapping between the various codes. The resulting 'experienced' model can then exhibit a rule-following recognition or production performance while at the same time accounting for exceptions. One recent

Figure 6.5: General architecture of Seidenberg and McClelland's (1989) model for word recognition and naming

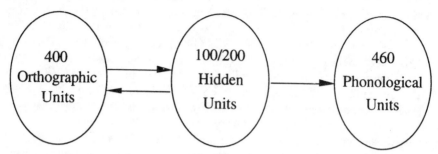

example of the PDP-approach to word recognition that has aroused considerable interest is the computer model of Seidenberg and McClelland (1989). Our brief description of the model (abbreviated as the S&M-model) keeps in mind the empirical data that were reviewed in earlier sections. We focus on the model's performance after training and disregard the learning process (see Chapter 3 on how learning in PDP-models takes place).

The S&M-model was specifically designed to predict performance in the word naming task, and the simulations presented by Seidenberg and McClelland show that it is rather successful on this point. However, since naming performance is not necessarily a good reflection of the processes that are operational when we recognize words during silent reading (cf., Paap *et al.*, 1987), the model's success in simulating word naming may not be particularly informative about its utility as a model of word recognition in general. Here we wish to stress the importance of making a clear distinction between the processes and representations involved in normal word recognition and those involved in specific laboratory tasks such as word naming and lexical decision.[2] In the following sections we give a brief description of the S&M-model and attempt to evaluate its potential as a model of visual word recognition.

In the model, which is graphically represented in Figure 6.5, three types of code or representation are computed: orthographic (O), semantic (S), and phonological (P). Each code is computed as a distributed representation, i.e., a pattern of activation distributed over a number of primitive representational units (cf., a vector, see Chapter 3). At present only the O- and P-units have been implemented. Connections exist between units of different types, but layers of hidden (H) units always mediate between different codes. (The inclusion of 200 H-units in the model enhances the flexibility of the processing capabilities inherent in the network.) Feedback from H-units to O-units, relevant only during learning, is implemented, but not from P-units to H-units. Thus, activity in the phonological network cannot affect that in the orthographic network.

To represent monosyllabic strings of graphemes and phonemes such as words, a variant of Wickelgren's (1969) triple scheme is used. Each item is decomposed and coded into triples of adjacent symbols. For example, the letter string MAKE is orthographically represented by the character triples (or Wickelgraphs) _MA,

MAK, AKE, and KE__, and phonologically by the phoneme triples (or Wickel-phones) __mA, mAk, Ak__ (where A is pronounced as in MAY). In this way, order information is locally conserved. Each triple is not encoded as a separate unit, but as a distributed activation pattern over a whole set of units. In the phonological network, a particular phoneme triple simultaneously activates 16 different P-units, which account for different combinations of the phonetic features of the three triple phonemes. For example, the triple mAk may activate (among others) the P-units [nasal, vowel, stop] and [voiced, vowel, unvoiced]. Each P-unit (of which there are 460 in total) can itself become active during the presentation of many different triples. Thus, the P-unit [nasal, vowel, stop] will not only be activated by the triple mAk but by nAp as well. More or less analogously, in the orthographic network, an O-unit (numbering 400) represents an accidental combination of three letters or of two letters and a begin/end boundary symbol, e.g., one unit may be involved with the character triples [M, A, K] and [N, O,__]. About 20 of these units are activated by each triple. Thus, when an orthographic unit is turned on, it is impossible to determine without further information which of the 1000 (10*10*10) character triples is implicated.

Sublexical Representations

The main representations in the model are the O- and P-units, which provide a coarse context-sensitive coding of linguistic information that is sublexical in nature. In these units still smaller building blocks occur, such as phonetic features and letters (how these basic units are recognized is not specified). Thus, symbolic representations such as letters or syllables are absent in the model. This is problematical in that the model cannot provide any predictions with respect to the large body of data on context effects in letter perception. Moreover, the letter triples implemented in the model cannot handle certain empirical data relative to partial-word priming, e.g., BVK priming BLACK (Humphreys, Evett and Quinlan, 1990). In the preceding example, the prime BVK will activate the triples __BV, BVK, and VK__, none of which are present in the target word BLACK. Also, the particlar O- and P-units that Seidenberg and McClelland chose to implement have since been detected as the source of one major problem in the model, its poor ability to read nonword stimuli compared to human subjects (Besner *et al.*, 1990).

However, Plaut and McClelland (1993) have recently proposed a new coding scheme that produces an excellent simulation of nonword naming data. This new coding scheme distinguishes between onset, vowel, and coda components of monosyllabic words. The input is specified in terms of which particular graphemes are present in each of these components. Thus, the model codes the input string as a set of graphemic representations at three different positions (onset, vowel, coda) which send activation on to hidden units that in turn activate a set of phoneme output units. This new coding scheme allows the model to generalize in a satisfactory manner to nonword reading after training on a word corpus.

Perhaps the most important aspect of the S&M model in contrast to the IA-model is that phonology is included in the form of an important and integrated network. This was of course necessary since the model was principally developed to account for performance in the word naming task. The data reviewed in the section on sublexical processing suggest that this phonology will also affect the word recognition process. However, it should be noted that the S&M-model in its current implementation lacks a feedback route from phonology to orthography, as well as a semantic level of representation. Thus, the effects of phonology in visual word recognition are accounted for in terms of how subjects strategically vary the type of information (orthographic or phonological) used to perform the lexical decision task. This issue is discussed more fully in the following section, which presents some important simulation results on lexical processing related to earlier sections of this chapter (due to space limitations we have to be very selective).

Lexical Processing

The quality of the phonological representation in the P-units is assessed by Seidenberg and McClelland (1989) in their simulation of a number of word naming experiments reported in the literature. The P-units are assumed to be implicated in the construction of an articulatory motor program necessary for the pronunciation of a written word. Given an input word, a Phonological Error Score (PE-score) is computed, which reflects the size of the difference between the obtained phonological activation pattern at the P-units and the correct pronunciation of the input letter string. A lower PE-score is assumed to correspond to a faster naming response and a more accurate pronunciation.

The word frequency effect typically observed in speeded word naming experiments is well simulated by the model. During training, the triples that constitute a word with a high frequency of occurrence exert a considerable effect on the setting of weights on O-H and H-P connections, resulting in better P-output and thus in smaller PE-scores. According to Seidenberg and McClelland such lower scores result in the faster generation of articulatory motor commands for high frequency words. The model also successfully simulates the facilitatory effects of neighbourhood density observed in naming experiments (Andrews, 1989, 1992), and the fact that these neighbourhood effects are robust only for low frequency words. Moreover, the model does an excellent job in accommodating the complex and subtle interactions that are a function of the degree of consistency between the stimulus word's pronunciation and the pronunciations of its orthographic neighbours (Jared, McRae and Seidenberg, 1990). This therefore suggests that the model might well be able to accommodate the complex interactions observed between word frequency and orthographic neighbourhoods in visual word recognition tasks.

The absence of explicit lexical representations in the model clearly creates a major difficulty for the PDP-approach. How can the model simulate human performance in visual word recognition tasks such as lexical decision and perceptual identification? Seidenberg and McClelland (1989) provide one possible mechanism that could be used to make lexical decisions within the framework of their model. An orthographic error score (OE-score) is computed that reflects the difference in O-unit activity generated by the stimulus, and O-unit activity generated by feedback from H-units. For many experimental situations this score was assumed to be a straightforward reflection of the speed of the lexical decision. When the OE-score is lower than a certain criterion, a yes-response is given (the input is a word), when it is higher, a no-response occurs. A score on an item that is either too low or too high results in an error response. The distance from the criterion determines the speed of responding. Lower OE-scores correspond to faster lexical decisions.

However, if an experimental situation occurs in which this strategy would lead to exceptionally high error scores, the subject may resort not only to the OE-score, but also to the PE-score (and to semantic information as well). An example is an experiment in which words and nonwords are orthographically very similar (e.g., TREAK-FREAK). In such a situation the results should become more similar to those obtained with the naming task. Indeed, Waters and Seidenberg (1985) found that low frequency words with regular pronunciations were recognized more rapidly in the lexical decision task than words of equivalent frequency with irregular pronunciations, when strangely spelled items (e.g., ONCE, AISLE, or BEIGE) were included in the stimulus list, but no such effects when these items were deleted.

This account of strategies in the lexical decision task was tested in a model simulation by computing the OE-scores for the word and nonword stimuli in the Waters and Seidenberg (1985) study. The OE-scores produced by the model allowed the setting of a decision criterion that discriminated fairly well between high- and low-frequency regular and exception words (yes-responses) on the one hand and nonwords (no-responses) on the other. However, adding the group of 'strange' words made it impossible to reach an acceptable model performance based on the OE-score only. This is consistent with the findings obtained by Waters and Seidenberg (1985). However, if a combination of OE- and PE-scores had been reported that gave an adequate simulation of the empirical data in this last situation, this would have provided more convincing support for the model.

By relying preferably on OE-scores the present model implements what we have referred to as the orthographic prevalence hypothesis in visual word recognition, the experimental support for which has been previously discussed. However, in its present form the model lacks a plausible mechanism for transforming activity at the level of orthographic nodes into performance in standard word recognition tasks. For example, it seems undesirable that one and the same parameter (the OE-score) would account for both error score/response-choice and reaction time in a task such as lexical decision (even disregarding speed-accuracy trade-off effects). Moreover, since it lacks dynamics, the S&M-model cannot (yet) be applied to priming studies with varying prime exposure durations. Certainly, these are critical points for future developments of this class of model.

Discussion and Conclusions

With respect to visual and auditory word recognition research, it cannot be denied that implemented models are among the most prominent in the field. This can be regarded as a positive and desirable development towards finer grained and more thoroughly specified models of word recognition. While verbal theories allow for qualitative predictions concerning main effects and interactions of experimental factors, computer models can go beyond this to develop quantitative proposals for temporal and structural processing aspects of even individual items (see Chapter 1 for further advantages of implemented models).

Without wishing to disregard other viable approaches to modelling, we must note that the main implemented models available in this area are connectionist in nature, one notable exception being the activation verification model of Paap *et al.* (1982). However, it should be pointed out here that this model has some difficulty (but see Paap and Johansen, 1994), at least in its currently implemented version, in accommodating a number of experimental results (Dobbs, Friedman and Lloyd, 1985; Grainger and Segui, 1990; Segui and Grainger, 1990). It remains to be seen whether future developments of this model will allow it to overcome these difficulties. We would certainly welcome the development of this and other non-connectionist accounts of visual word recognition. Such implementation would require a formalization of how the numerous dimensions on which stimuli may differ (e.g., word frequency, orthographic structure, neighbourhood characteristics, and phonology) all interact to produce the pattern of experimental effects reviewed in this chapter. Clearly, the currently available connectionist models are one step ahead in that they have found an elegant way to deal with the many soft constraints that word recognition involves. Indeed, these models seem to have captured a very fundamental characteristic of the word recognition system, i.e., that of the covariance between the orthographic and phonological subsystems (cf., Van Orden, Pennington and Stone, 1990). A quasiregular mapping between different codes seems to underlie many of the effects reviewed in this chapter, and it is quite parsimonious to assume that this underlying mechanism is one and the same for factors such as word frequency, orthographic-phonological regularity and/or consistency, and neighbourhood characteristics.

With respect to the two models described in this chapter, one critical issue is whether learning is a necessary attribute of an adequate model or not. It could perhaps be argued that any model should restrict its domain of application and that learning is not an indispensible part of a 'synchronous' model. However, the term 'learning' is ambiguous here, since it may be interpreted to correspond to the process of acquiring (representations of) a number of lexical items (and establishing their interrelation) or, alternatively, to the search for an optimal setting of connection weights given a certain lexical space. With respect to the latter aspect, it seems that an adequate word recognition model in the end will have to satisfy multiple constraints provided by many different individual stimulus characteristics. Therefore, parameter setting by hand will probably become very tedious and even practically unfeasible. Learning algorithms, interpreted as optimization routines in optima forma, provide a solution here, even if the learning process itself does not correspond to that of humans. The feasibility of this approach is shown by the S&M-model, in which learning (or, as a better term seems to be, training) results in the recreation of important structural aspects of written and spoken English in the complex pattern of connection weights between orthographic and phonological network nodes (see Norris, 1994, for an alternative approach). However, the extent to which the learning procedures used by such a model have any resemblance to those involved in human learning, remains to be seen.

With respect to structural aspects of modelling, the empirical discussion earlier in this chapter suggests that the choice of sublexical orthographic representations such as individual letters seems defensible and even desirable. Whether orthographic representations larger than letters should be incorporated in a computer model remains unclear. According to Seidenberg and McClelland (1989, 1990), their specific choice of letter-triple representations was not critical for the more general behavioural characteristics of the model, though it did induce single-feature errors. However, they only came to this conclusion after considerable explorations of their model. Therefore, since we do not really know what the implications of a specific choice of representation are, thorough investigation of this issue for any new model is necessary.

Concerning the role of phonology in visual word recognition, it seems clear that models can no longer remain 'stubbornly non-phonological' (Carello, Turvey and Lukatela, 1992). The IA-model clearly falls short in this respect since it cannot account for the growing body of evidence on early phonological effects in visual word recognition. It has been argued (Besner *et al.*, 1990) that the S&M-model cannot very well account for phonological effects with respect to nonword naming either. However, improving the quality of the sublexical phonological representation (by using onset, vowel or coda units) can solve this problem, as was recently shown by Plaut and McClelland (1993). It is not clear, however, how the model would be able to realistically capture effects of phonology in other tasks than naming (e.g., perceptual identification and lexical decision). Furthermore, since there are also data suggesting that orthography plays a role in auditory word recognition (Tanenhaus, Flanigan and Seidenberg, 1980; Dupoux and Mehler, 1992; Dijkstra, Frauenfelder and Schreuder, 1993), it seems that any model of visual word recognition in an alphabetic writing system should include fast bimodal links between orthographic and phonological representations. The S&M-model is insufficiently developed here, since it lacks a feedback route from phonological units back to the hidden units.

With respect to lexical processing, at present we would advocate the use of explicit lexical representations in models of visual word recognition. Arguments of different types can be brought forward to support this view. First, from a linguistic point of view it seems awkward to represent some types of unit (such as letters and features) explicitly, but others (such as words) only implicitly. If we consider current word recognition models as functional models, for which the relationship to neural activity is as yet (and unfortunately) unclear, why should we not make our models more transparent by including words as explicit representations? Furthermore, since only the word as a whole can be related to a meaning representation (see Introduction), it seems necessary and useful to have whole word units mediating between smaller formal units and meaning representations. We also favour the position of integrating word frequency in the core architecture of the model and not only in task-specific components, because, in our opinion, the current empirical evidence favours an early role of frequency in the word recognition process (e.g., Monsell, 1991). Similarly, these core representations and processes must capture the relative frequency with which different spelling patterns map onto particular sounds, a factor that strongly influences the speed with which we read printed words aloud.

A modeller must further face the difficult decisions of whether to include mechanisms of top-down feedback and/or lateral inhibition in the model's architecture. According to Jacobs and Grainger (1992), the empirical evidence available can be accounted for very well by a variant of the IA-model which lacks top-down feedback. While lateral inhibition is implemented in a straightforward way in the IA-model, in the S&M-model competitive processes arise during the training phase and are encoded in the weight variations of the between-level connections. Future research should clarify which choices with respect to model architectures can best be made here, explaining at the same time how different results may arise for different tasks (such as lexical decision, perceptual identification, progressive demasking, and word naming). One final point on our list of model desiderata concerns temporal aspects of word recognition. It would be desirable that the model's internal process could be 'tapped' moment by moment (like in the IA-model) to visualize transient effects of competitors, primes or masks. This point is eloquently made by McClelland (1993), who argues in favour of dynamic types of model.

Collecting appropriate empirical evidence to develop and test new, more generalized multi-task models of word recognition will no doubt be necessary far into the next century. Exciting new data are now available from brain imaging techniques (Posner and Carr, 1992), which may perhaps provide additional constraints for particular models from a hitherto unexpected angle. Although it is too soon to tell which models will survive, we bet they will be implemented ones.

Notes

1 Throughout this chapter we adopt the convention of presenting examples from priming experiments with the example prime stimulus followed by the example target stimulus.

2 Different tasks can be said to functionally overlap in the sense that their performance involves a common set of processes and representations, the core processes, that are (hopefully) also a part of normal word recognition. Accordingly, models of word recognition must specify which processes and representations involved in performing a particular task are task-specific and which are involved in word recognition during normal (extra-laboratory) reading. The concept of functional overlap is explained in more detail in Jacobs and Grainger (1994) and Grainger and Jacobs (1994).

References

ANDREWS, S. (1982) 'Phonological recoding: Is the regularity effect consistent?', *Memory & Cognition*, 10, pp. 565–75.

ANDREWS, S. (1989) 'Frequency and neighborhood size effects on lexical access: Activation or search?', *Journal of Experimental Psychology: Learning, Memory, and Cognition*, 15, pp. 802–14.

ANDREWS, S. (1992) 'Frequency and neighborhood effects on lexical access: Lexical similarity or orthographic redundancy?', *Journal of Experimental Psychology: Learning, Memory and Cognition*, 18, pp. 234–54.

BALOTA, D. A. and CHUMBLEY, J. I. (1984) 'Are lexical decisions a good measure of lexical access? The role of word frequency in the neglected decision stage', *Journal of Experimental Psychology: Human Perception and Performance*, 10, pp. 340–57.

BESNER, D., TWILLEY, L., MCCANN, R. S. and SEERGOBIN, K. (1990) 'On the association between connectionism and data: Are a few words necessary?', *Psychological Review*, 97, pp. 432–46.

CARELLO, C., TURVEY, M. T. and LUKATELA, G. (1992) 'Can theories of word recognition remain stubbornly nonphonological?', in FROST, R. and KATZ, L. (Eds) *Orthography, Phonology, Morphology, and Meaning*, Amsterdam: North-Holland, pp. 211–26.

CARR, T. H. (1986) 'Perceiving visual language', in BOFF, K. R., KAUFFMAN, L. and THOMAS, J. P. (Eds) *Handbook of Perception and Human Performance*, New York: Wiley, pp. 29.1–29.82.

CATTELL, J. M. (1886) 'The time it takes to see and name objects', *Mind*, 11, pp. 53–65.

COLTHEART, M., DAVELAAR, E., JONASSON, J. T. and BESNER, D. (1977) 'Access to the internal lexicon', in DORNIC, S. (Ed) *Attention and Performance*, VI, London: Academic Press.

DIJKSTRA, T., ROELOFS, A. and FIEUWS, S. (1995) 'Orthographic effects on phoneme monitoring', *Canadian Journal of Experimental Psychology*, 49(2), 264–71.

DIJKSTRA, T., FRAUENFELDER, U. H. and SCHREUDER, R. (1993) 'Bidirectional grapheme-phoneme activation in a bimodal detection task', *Journal of Experimental Psychology: Human Perception and Performance*, 19, pp. 931–50.

DOBBS, A. R., FRIEDMAN, A. and LLOYD, J. (1985) 'Frequency effects in lexical decisions: A test of the verification model', *Journal of Experimental Psychology: Human Perception and Performance*, 11, pp. 81–92.

DUPOUX, E. and MEHLER, J. (1992) 'Unifying awareness and on-line studies of speech: A tentative framework', in ALEGRIA, J., HOLENDER, D., JUNCA DE MORAIS, J. and RADEAU, M. (Eds) *Analytic Approaches to Human Cognition*, Amsterdam: Elsevier Science Publishers, pp. 59–75.

ESTES, W. K., ALLMEYER, D. H. and REDER, S. M. (1976) 'Serial position functions for letter identification at brief and extended exposure durations', *Perception & Psychophysics*, 19, pp. 1–15.

FERRAND, L. and GRAINGER, J. (1992) 'Phonology and orthography in visual word recognition: evidence from masked nonword priming', *Quarterly Journal of Experimental Psychology*, 45 (A), pp. 353–72.

FERRAND, L. and GRAINGER, J. (1993) 'The time-course of orthographic and phonological code activation in the early phases of visual word recognition', *Bulletin of the Psychonomic Society*, 31, pp. 119–22.

FERRAND, L. and GRAINGER, J. (1994) 'Effects of orthography are independent of phonology in masked form priming', *Quarterly Journal of Experimental Psychology*, 47 (A), pp. 365–82.

FORSTER, K. I. (1976) 'Accessing the mental lexicon', in WALES, R. J. and WALKER, E. W. (Eds) *New Approaches to Language Mechanisms*, Amsterdam: North-Holland, pp. 257–87.

FORSTER, K. I. and DAVIS, C. (1984) 'Repetition priming and frequency attenuation in lexical access', *Journal of Experimental Psychology: Learning, Memory, and Cognition*, 10, pp. 680–90.

GERNSBACHER, M. A. (1984) 'Resolving 20 years of inconsistent interactions between lexical familiarity and orthography, concreteness and polysemy', *Journal of Experimental Psychology: General*, 113, pp. 256–81.

GRAINGER, J. (1990) 'Word frequency and neighborhood frequency effects in lexical decision and naming', *Journal of Memory & Language*, 29, pp. 228–44.

GRAINGER, J. (1992) 'Orthographic neighborhoods and visual word recognition', in FROST, R. and KATZ, L. (Eds) *Orthography, Phonology, Morphology and Meaning*, Amsterdam: North-Holland, pp. 131–46.

GRAINGER, J. and FERRAND, L. (1994) 'Phonology and orthography in visual word recognition: Effects of masked homophone primes', *Journal of Memory & Language*, 33, pp. 218–33.

GRAINGER, J. and JACOBS, A. M. (1993) 'Masked partial-word priming in visual word recognition: Effects of positional letter frequency', *Journal of Experimental Psychology: Human Perception and Performance*, 19, 5, pp. 951–64.

GRAINGER, J. and JACOBS, A. M. (1994) 'A dual read-out model of word context effects in letter perception: Further investigations of the word superiority effect', *Journal of Experimental Psychology: Human Perception and Performance*, 20, 1158–76.

GRAINGER, J. and JACOBS, A. M. (1995) *A Three-Process Model of Visual Word Recognition and Lexical Decision*, Manuscript submitted for publication.

GRAINGER, J., O'REGAN, J. K., JACOBS, A. M. and SEGUI, J. (1989) 'On the role of competing word units in visual word recognition: The neighborhood frequency effect', *Perception & Psychophysics*, 45, pp. 189–95.

GRAINGER, J., O'REGAN, J. K., JACOBS, A. M. and SEGUI, J. (1992) 'Neighborhood frequency effects and letter visibility in visual word recognition', *Perception & Psychophysics*, 51, pp. 49–56.

GRAINGER, J. and SEGUI, J. (1990) 'Neighborhood frequency effects in visual word recognition: A comparison of lexical decision and masked identification latencies', *Perception & Psychophysics*, 47, pp. 191–8.

HAVENS, L. L. and FOOTE, W. E. (1963) 'The effect of competition on visual duration threshold and its independence of stimulus frequency', *Journal of Experimental Psychology*, 65, pp. 6–11.

HENDERSON, L. (1982) *Orthography and Word Recognition in Reading*, London: Academic Press.

HUMPHREYS, G. W., EVETT, L. J. and QUINLAN, P. T. (1990) 'Orthographic processing in visual word identification', *Cognitive Psychology*, 22, pp. 517–60.

HUMPHREYS, G. W., EVETT, L. J. and TAYLOR, D. E. (1982) 'Automatic phonological priming in visual word recognition', *Memory & Cognition*, 10, pp. 576–90.

INHOFF, A. W. and RAYNER, K. (1986) 'Parafoveal word processing during fixations in reading: Effects of word frequency', *Perception & Psychophysics*, 40, pp. 431–9.

JACOBS, A. M. and GRAINGER, J. (1992) 'Testing a semistochastic variant of the interactive activation model in different word recognition experiments', *Journal of Experimental Psychology: Human Perception and Performance*, 18, pp. 1174–88.

JACOBS, A. M. and GRAINGER, J. (1994) 'Models of visual word recognition: Sampling the state of the art', *Journal of Experimental Psychology: Human Perception and Performance*, 20, 1311–34.

JARED, D., MCRAE, K. and SEIDENBERG, M. S. (1990) 'The basis of consistency effects in word naming', *Journal of Memory & Language*, 29, pp. 687–715.

JARED, D. and SEIDENBERG, M. S. (1991) 'Does word identification proceed from spelling to sound to meaning?', *Journal of Experimental Psychology: General*, 120, pp. 358–94.

JOHNSTON, J. C. (1978) 'A test of the sophisticated guessing theory of word perception', *Cognitive Psychology*, 10, pp. 123–53.

JOHNSTON, J. C. and MCCLELLAND, J. L. (1980) 'Experimental tests of a model of word identification', *Journal of Verbal Learning and Verbal Behavior*, 19, pp. 503–24.

JORDAN, M. I. (1986) 'An introduction to linear algebra in parallel distributed processing', in RUMELHART, D. E., MCCLELLAND, J. L. and the PDP Research Group, *Parallel Distributed Processing: Explorations in the Microstructure of Cognition: Vol. 1. Foundations*, Cambridge, MA: MIT Press, pp. 365–422.

JORDAN, T. R. and DE BRUIJN, O. (1993) 'Word superiority over isolated letters: The neglected role of flanking mask contours', *Journal of Experimental Psychology: Human Perception and Performance*, 19, pp. 549–63.

KUCERA, H. and FRANCIS, W. N. (1967) *Computational Analysis of Present-Day American English*, Providence, RI: Brown University Press.

LIMA, S. D. and INHOFF, A. W. (1985) 'Lexical access during eye fixations in reading: Effects of word-initial letter sequence', *Journal of Experimental Psychology: Human Perception and Performance*, 11, pp. 272–85.

LIMA, S. D. and POLLATSEK, A. (1983) 'Lexical access via an orthographic code: The basic orthographic syllabic structure (BOSS) reconsidered', *Journal of Verbal Learning and Verbal Behavior*, 22, pp. 310–32.

LUCE, P. A., PISONI, D. B. and GOLDINGER, S. D. (1990) 'Similarity neighborhoods of spoken words', in ALTMANN, G. T.M. (Ed) *Cognitive Models of Speech Processing: Psycholinguistic and Computational Perspectives*, Cambridge, MA: MIT Press, pp. 122–47.

LUKATELA, G., LUKATELA, K. and TURVEY, M. T. (1993) 'Further evidence for phonological constraints on visual lexical access: TOWED primes FROG', *Perception & Psychophysics*, 53, pp. 461–6.

MASON, M. (1975) 'Reading ability and letter search time: Effects of orthographic structure defined by single-letter positional frequency', *Journal of Experimental Psychology: General*, 104, pp. 146–66.

MASSARO, D. W., TAYLOR, G. A., VENEZKY, R. L., JASTRZEMBSKI, J. E. and LUCAS, P. A. (1980) *Letter and Word Perception: Orthographic Structure and Visual Processing in Reading*, Amsterdam: North-Holland.

MCCANN, R. S., BESNER, D. and DAVELAAR, E. (1988) 'Word recognition and identification: Do word-frequency effects reflect lexical access?', *Journal of Experimental Psychology: Human Perception and Performance*, 14, pp. 693–706.

MCCLELLAND, J. L. (1976) 'Preliminary letter identification in the perception of words and nonwords', *Journal of Experimental Psychology: Human Perception and Performance*, 1, pp. 80–91.

MCCLELLAND, J. L. (1993) 'Toward a theory of information processing in graded, random, and interactive networks', in MEYER, D. E. and KORNBLUM, S. (Eds) *Attention and Performance XIV: Synergies in Experimental Psychology, Artificial Intelligence, and Cognitive Neuroscience*, Cambridge, MA: MIT Press, pp. 655–88.

MCCLELLAND, J. L. and JOHNSTON, J. C. (1977) 'The role of familiar units in perception of words and nonwords', *Perception & Psychophysics*, 22, pp. 249–61.

McCLELLAND, J. L. and MOZER, M. C. (1986) 'Perceptual interactions in two-word displays: Familiarity and similarity effects', *Journal of Experimental Psychology: Human Perception and Performance*, 12, pp. 18–35.

McCLELLAND, J. L. and RUMELHART, D. E. (1981) 'An interactive activation model of context effects in letter perception: Part I. An account of basic findings', *Psychological Review*, 88, pp. 375–407.

MILLER, G. A., BRUNER, J. S. and POSTMAN, L. (1954) 'Familiarity of letter sequences and tachistoscopic identification', *Journal of General Psychology*, 50, pp. 129–39.

MONSELL, S. (1991) 'The nature and locus of word frequency effects in reading', in BESNER, D. and HUMPHREYS, G. W. (Eds) *Basic Processes in Reading: Visual Word Recognition*, Hillsdale, NJ: Lawrence Erlbaum, pp. 148–97.

MONSELL, S., DOYLE, M. C. and HAGGARD, P. N. (1989) 'Effects of frequency on visual word recognition tasks: Where are they?', *Journal of Experimental Psychology: General*, 118, pp. 43–71.

MORTON, J. (1969) 'Interaction of information in word recognition', *Psychological Review*, 76, pp. 165–78.

MOZER, M. C. (1983) 'Letter migration in word perception', *Journal of Experimental Psychology: Human Perception and Performance*, 9, pp. 531–46.

NORRIS, D. G. (1994) 'A quantitative multiple-levels model of reading aloud', *Journal of Experimental Psychology: Human Perception and Performance*, 20, 1212–32.

PAAP, K. and JOHANSEN, L. (1994) 'The case of the vanishing frequency effect: A retest of the verification model', *Journal of Experimental Psychology: Human Perception and Performance*, 20(6), 1129–57.

PAAP, K., McDONALD, J. E., SCHVANEVELDT, R. W. and NOEL, R. W. (1987) 'Frequency and pronounceability in visually presented naming and lexical decision tasks', in COLTHEART, M. (Ed) *Attention and Performance XII*, Hillsdale, NJ: Lawrence Erlbaum, pp. 221–44.

PAAP, K., NEWSOME, S. L., McDONALD, J. E. and SCHVANEVELDT, R. W. (1982) 'An activation-verification model for letter and word recognition: The word superiority effect', *Psychological Review*, 89, pp. 573–94.

PERFETTI, C. A. and BELL, L. (1991) 'Phonemic activation during the first 40 ms of word identification: Evidence from backward masking and priming', *Journal of Memory & Language*, 30, pp. 473–85.

PERFETTI, C. A., BELL, L. C. and DELANEY, S. M. (1988) 'Automatic (prelexical) phonetic activation in silent reading: Evidence from backward masking', *Journal of Memory & Language*, 27, pp. 59–70.

PLAUT, D. and McCLELLAND, J. L. (1993) 'Generalization with componential attractors: Word and nonword reading in an attractor network', in *Proceedings of the Cognitive Science Society*, pp. 824–9.

POSNER, M. I. and CARR, Th. H. (1992) 'Lexical access and the brain: Anatomical constraints on cognitive models of word recognition', *American Journal of Psychology*, 105, pp. 1–26.

PRINZMETAL, W., TREIMAN, R. and RHO, S. H. (1986) 'How to see a reading unit', *Journal of Memory & Language*, 25, pp. 461–75.

RAPP, B. C. (1992) 'The nature of sublexical orthographic organisation: The bigram trough hypothesis examined', *Journal of Memory & Language*, 31, pp. 33–53.

REICHER, G. M. (1969) 'Perceptual recognition as a function of meaningfulness of stimulus material', *Journal of Experimental Psychology*, 81, pp. 274–80.

RUBENSTEIN, H., LEWIS, S. S. and RUBENSTEIN, M. A. (1971) 'Evidence for phonetic recoding in visual word recognition', *Journal of Verbal Learning and Verbal Behavior*, 10, pp. 647–57.

RUMELHART, D. E. and McCLELLAND, J. L. (1982) 'An interactive activation model of context effects in letter perception: Part II. The contextual enhancement effect and some tests and extensions of the model', *Psychological Review*, 89, pp. 60–94.

RUMELHART, D. E. and SIPLE, P. (1974) 'The process of recognizing tachistoscopically presented words', *Psychological Review*, 81, pp. 99–118.

SEGUI, J. and GRAINGER, J. (1990) 'Priming word recognition with orthographic neighbors: effects of relative prime-target frequency', *Journal of Experimental Psychology: Human Perception and Performance*, 16, pp. 65–76.

SEIDENBERG, M. S. (1987) 'Sublexical structures in visual word recognition: Access units of orthographic redundancy', in COLTHEART, M. (Ed) *Attention and Performance XII: The Psychology of Reading*, Hillsdale, NJ: Lawrence Erlbaum.

SEIDENBERG, M. S. and MCCLELLAND, J. L. (1989) 'A distributed, developmental model of word recognition and naming', *Psychological Review*, 96, pp. 523–68.

SEIDENBERG, M. S. and MCCLELLAND, J. L. (1990) 'More words but still no lexicon: Reply to Besner *et al.* (1990)', *Psychological Review*, 97, pp. 447–52.

SEIDENBERG, M. S., WATERS, G. S., BARNES, M. A. and TANENHAUS, M. K. (1984) 'When does irregular spelling or pronunciation influence word recognition?', *Journal of Verbal Learning and Verbal Behavior*, 23, pp. 383–404.

SNODGRASS, J. G. and MINTZER, M. (1993) 'Neighborhood effects in visual word recognition: Facilitatory or inhibitory?', *Memory & Cognition*, 21, pp. 247–66.

TAFT, M. (1979) 'Lexical access via an orthographic code: The basic orthographic syllabic structure (BOSS)', *Journal of Verbal Learning and Verbal Behavior*, 18, pp. 21–39.

TANENHAUS, M. K., FLANIGAN, H. P. and SEIDENBERG, M. S. (1980) 'Orthographic and phonological activation in auditory and visual word recognition', *Memory & Cognition*, 8, pp. 513–20.

VAN ORDEN, G. C. (1987) 'A ROWS is a ROSE: Spelling, sound, and reading', *Memory & Cognition*, 15, pp. 181–98.

VAN ORDEN, G. C., JOHNSTON, J. C. and HALE, B. L. (1988) 'Word identification in reading proceeds from spelling to sound to meaning', *Journal of Experimental Psychology: Learning, Memory, and Cognition*, 14, pp. 371–85.

VAN ORDEN, G. C., PENNINGTON, B. F. and STONE, G. O. (1990) 'Word identification in reading and the promise of subsymbolic psycholinguistics', *Psychological Review*, 97, pp. 488–522.

VITU, F., O'REGAN, J. K. and MITTAU, M. (1990) 'Optimal landing position in reading isolated words and continuous texts', *Perception and Psychophysics*, 47, pp. 583–600.

WATERS, G. S. and SEIDENBERG, M. S. (1985) 'Spelling-sound effects in reading: Time course and decision criteria', *Memory & Cognition*, 13, pp. 557–72.

WHEELER, D. D. (1970) 'Processes in word recognition', *Cognitive Psychology*, 1, pp. 59–85.

WICKELGREN, W. A. (1969) 'Context-sensitive coding, associative memory, and serial order in (speech) behavior', *Psychological Review*, 76, pp. 1–15.

Chapter 7

Modelling the Processing of Morphologically Complex Words

R. Harald Baayen and Robert Schreuder

Introduction

This chapter reviews a number of linguistic and psycholinguistic computational models of morphological processing. Morphologists study the internal structure of words. For instance, a word such as *antidisestablishmentarianism* can be assigned the following structure:

$$[_N anti + [_N dis + [_N [_N [_A [_N [_V establish_V] + ment_N] + ary_N] + an_N] + ism_N]_N]_N]$$

For English, words with such a complex internal structure are rare. In languages such as Turkish or Greenlandic Eskimo, however, very complex words are far more common. The question with which we are concerned is how the human language processor deals with morphologically structured words of varying complexity. What kinds of mechanism allow listeners to interpret novel as well as familiar complex words? What kind of experimental evidence is available to constrain computational models? What types of morphological operations are attested in human languages? And what requirements do these operations impose on computational models? In this chapter, we first survey the basic linguistic facts that any model should attempt to account for. The following section describes two linguistic computational models, Koskenniemi's (1983) two-level morphology model and Ritchie *et al.*'s (1992) unification-based model. After that, the results of a number of psycholinguistic experiments are summarized, followed by an outline of a number of verbal (not implemented) models of morphological processing, as well as Gasser's (1994a, 1994b) connectionist model for the processing of complex words in the auditory modality. We will see that the complexity of the phenomena involved is such that none of the existing psychological models are able to handle all aspects of morphological processing, and that they are even less able to predict actual experimental reaction times. These and other problems are discussed in the last section.

Some Basic Linguistic Facts

Languages exploit a variety of means for creating morphologically complex words. Often, the means by which morphologically complex words are created involve more complex operations than the simple linear concatenation of morphemes. Hence the modelling of the mapping of form onto meaning in perception cannot depart from the assumption of a simple one-to-one relation between input representations and central representations (*templates*) in the mental lexicon. We review the main linguistic devices by which semantic or syntactic information is morphologically expressed, and discuss the role of phonology. Some of the complexity issues that may be encountered are briefly summarized. Finally, we focus on the semantic aspects of word formation. Throughout our discussion we trace the processing consequences of the linguistic facts discussed.

Morphological Operations

Broadly speaking, we may distinguish between two fundamentally different morphological processes: concatenative and non-concatenative operations. Concatenative operations involve the stringing together of free and bound morphemes. Generally, we distinguish between prefixation, e.g., *re-forest*; suffixation, e.g., *forest-ation*; circumfixation, e.g., Dutch *ge-wandel-d* (past participle of *wandelen*, 'to walk') and compounding, e.g., *door-bell*. The complexity of the resulting words may vary considerably. In English the total number of morphemes that are likely to appear together in one complex word is rather limited. The example in the introduction, from Sproat (1992, p. 44), concerns an English word with seven morphemes, but the maximum number of morphemes registered in the CELEX lexical database of English equals only five, e.g., *de-nation-al-ize-ation*. By way of contrast, Turkish (Altaic) allows words such as *avrupa-ll-las-tlr-ll-a-ml-yacak-lar-dan-sln-lz-dlr*, 'surely you (all) are among those who will not be able to be caused to become like Europeans', with 13 morphemes (Beard, 1992, p. 96) and, somewhat less extreme, *göz-lük-çü-lül-çük-çü*, 'proponent of optometry proponency' (Beard, 1992, p. 94), with six morphemes. Note the affix-based recursion in the last example (. . . *çük-çü* . . .), something that leads to a combinatorial explosion of possibilities that is rarely encountered in Indo-European languages. On the other hand, compounds in English may be of a similar degree of complexity, e.g., *computer communications network performance analysis primer* (Sproat, 1992, p. 41).

Non-concatenative morphological operations involve infixation, root-and-pattern morphology, subtractive morphology, reduplication, subsegmental and suprasegmental morphology and zero-marking. In Tagalog (Austronesian), the infix *-in-* denotes the object which is the result of some action. Characteristically, this infix is inserted not after a morpheme boundary but right after the first consonant of the stem: *sulat*, 'a writing', *s-in-ulat*, 'that which was written' (Schachter and Otanes, 1972).

Root-and-pattern morphology is typical for the semitic languages. It mostly occurs in conjunction with concatenative processes. Consider the Hebrew verb root *šmr*, 'to guard'. In Classical Hebrew, this purely consonantal root is fused with the vowel pattern *a-a* in *šamar-ti*, 'I have guarded', but with a single stem vowel (*-o-*) in *e-šmor*, 'I will guard' (Gesenius and Kautzsch, 1909). These changes in the consonantal and vowel patterns require a fundamentally different parsing technique, even though this kind of morphology can be analyzed as involving concatenation of morphemes in a multi-dimensional representational system (McCarthy 1982).

Subtractive morphology involves the deletion of part of the base in order to mark some semantic operation. In Koasati (Algonquian, Northern Amerindian), to pluralize the subject of a verb one has to delete the last rhyme of the stem: *obakhitip-li-n*, 'he goes backwards', *obakhit-li-n*, 'they go backwards' (Martin, 1988). Note that the rhyme, and hence the deleted segment, will vary from word to word. The absence of a constant segment to meaning association poses a serious problem for any computational theory of word processing (Sproat, 1992).

Reduplication involves the partial or total repetition of a morpheme. Malay (Austronesian) uses total reduplication to express the plural: *kursi*, 'chair', *kursikursi*, 'chairs'. Partial reduplication processes typically depend on the phonological structure of the base word. Samoan (Austronesian) reduplicates the next to last syllable to express plural subjects on verbs: *savali*, 'he travels', *savavali*, 'they travel' (Gleason, 1955).

Subsegmental morphological processes involve the expression of some semantic function by changing some features of a segment of the base. In Nuer (Nilo-Saharan), the phonological feature [*continuant*] distinguishes the negative form of the past participle from its positive counterpart: *jaac* is the negative form of the present participle of the verb 'to hit', of which the past participle is *jaaç* (Lieber 1987).

As an example of a semantic function that is marked by suprasegmental means consider Mono-Bili (Niger-Kongo). In this language the future tense is expressed by a low tone on the verb. The past tense is expressed by a high tone. Thus we have *múrú wó sè*, 'the leopard kiiled him', which contrasts with *múrú wò sè*, 'the leopard will kill him' (Jensen, 1990, p. 74).

Finally, semantic changes are often accompanied by no morphological marking at all. Lieber (1992) argues that two cases of zero-morphology should be distinguished. On the one hand, French instrument-agent nouns such as *essuie glace*, 'windshield wiper', may well involve a semantically specified but phonologically unrealized suffix, given the uniformity of the interpretation of these compounds and the gender they select (masculine: *le*). On the other hand, noun to verb conversion in English, *to book*, expresses such a wide range of meanings that it is implausible to assume that a single (zero) affix is involved. (But see Beard, 1992, for a different view.)

Phonological Issues

When morphemes are combined, various phonological processes may alter their segmental and suprasegmental make-up. Since such processes may significantly complicate the perception process, we present a brief overview of the kinds of change one may encounter.

A first set of changes concerns the form in which particular segments appear. Often the segments at the boundaries of morphemes undergo assimilation (*in-dubitable, im-proper, in-glorious*, the latter pronounced /ŋ/). But assimilation processes may affect segments at longer distances too. A well-known example is vowel harmony. In Hungarian (Finno-Ugric), the exact quality of the vowel of the suffix -*nek*/-*nak* is determined by the vowel quality (front or back) of the stem. Thus we have *öröm-nek*, 'to joy', but *ház-nak*, 'to house' (Jensen, 1990, p. 163). Furthermore, consonants and vowels may be inserted (epenthesis). For instance, in order to avoid a sequence of consonants that is difficult to pronounce, the Latin stem *patr-*, 'father', as in *patris*, 'father (genitive case)' appears with an extra vowel (*pater*) in the nominative case. Segments may also interchange (metathesis), as for instance in Hanunoo (Austronesian), where multiplicative adverbials like 'once' and 'twice' are derived from the corresponding numerals by prefixing *ka-* and interchanging a stem-initial glottal stop with the following consonant: *ka* + '*sa*→*kas'a*, 'once', where -'*sa* is the root of 'one' (Schane, 1973, p. 56). Another kind of phonological change that should be mentioned is final devoicing in some Germanic languages, where stem-final voiced stops and fricatives become voiceless if no other affixes follow: compare Dutch *huizen*, 'houses' with *huis*, 'house'.

A second set of changes concerns the form in which an affix or stem appears. The English nominalizing suffix -*ion* appears as -*ation*, -*ution*, -*ition*, -*tion* and -*ion*, depending on the phonological properties of the stem, although the choice is often morpholexically conditioned (for discussion see Aronoff, 1976). In addition to allomorphy of the affix, allomorphy of stems may complicate matters further. For instance, the Latin stem *cap-* as in *capio*, 'I seize', appears as *cep-* in the perfect: *cepi*, 'I have seized' (for a detailed analysis of stem allomorphy see Aronoff, 1994).

Some of these phonological changes may be perceptually or articulatorily motivated (Schane, 1973, p. 61). For instance, the insertion of a vowel in the nominative of Latin *patr*, 'father', may be articulatory functional, but it complicates the mapping of the various forms in which such stems appear onto their corresponding lexical representations. Similarly, the mismatch between syllable structure and morphological structure for words like Dutch *masten* (/mɑs$tən/ — *mast-en*), 'masts' might be dysfunctional for speech perception, where the perceptually most salient units /mɑs/ and /tən/ do not map onto the morphemes *mast* and *-en*.

Complexity Issues

Let us assume that the perceptual system solves the various phonological and non-concatenative complexities discussed above, and maps the speech input onto the constituent morphemes of a given complex word. At this point problems of another nature may be encountered: how to process long-distance dependencies, how to decide between alternative parsings, and how to handle affixal homonymy.

At first sight, it would seem possible to process a string of morphemes one by one, rejecting a string as soon as two morphemes cannot be legitimately combined. Such a processing algorithm fails, however, for words with so-called long-distance dependencies. Consider the Dutch adjective *on-denk-baar*, 'unthinkable'. Crucially, the prefix *on-* does not attach to verbs: the hypothetical verb *on-denk-en*, 'to unthink', is ungrammatical. It is only after the verb stem *denk* has been integrated with the affix *-baar*, '-able', to result in the adjective *denkbaar* that *on-* is licensed for combination. This example shows that simple left-to-right processing without some form of buffering and look-ahead is doomed to fail.

A problem specific to the recognition of complex words is that often large numbers of possible and competing structural analyses can be assigned. For instance, the Dutch word *belangstellende*, 'interested person', should normally be parsed as *belang-stel-en-d-e*, 'interest-put' followed by suffixes for infinitive, participle, and adjectival inflection, but the reading *bel-angst-ellende*, 'misery of having fear for ringing up' is also possible. According to Heemskerk (1993, personal communication), orthographic complex words in Dutch have on average some three different parsings. The number of different parsings is somewhat reduced for the auditory modality, where stress and syllabification patterns and vowel quality may rule out certain parsings, as for the example given above (/bə$lɑŋ$'stɛl$lən$də/ or /'bɛl$ɑŋst$ɛl$lɛn$də/). It may also happen that a particular string may be either a monomorphemic word or a complex word. For instance, Dutch monomorphematic *beton* generally denotes the building material 'concrete', but phonologically and orthographically identical *be-ton*, 'to mark with buoys', is a less likely but nevertheless established nautical term. Frequency of use and contextual information are crucial for solving ambiguities of this kind.

Affixal homonymy poses yet another problem. In Dutch, the suffix *-te* may attach to verbs to express the singular past tense, e.g., *zwalk-te*, 'roamed', or it may attach to adjectives to form abstract nouns, e.g., *zwakte*, 'weakness'.

According to Beard (1992, p. 78), it is quite common to find productive affixes that serve both derivational and inflectional duties. Within inflection, one and the same affix may be polyfunctional too (-*s* in Dutch and English expresses either the plural or the genitive), and the same holds for derivation (*in-* in Dutch and English expresses either direction, e.g., *intake*, or negation, e.g., *insecure*). Thus identifying the right form does not necessarily lead to a unique correct meaning. The correct meaning can only be established on the basis of the subcategorization properties of the affixes and stems involved.

Semantic Issues

Many complex words, however, are in some way irregular. Such irregularity is especially pervasive at the semantic level in derivation and conversion. One may observe degrees of semantic transparency, ranging from full transparency as in *goodness* to complete opacity, as in *disease*. However, even the slightest unpredictable property of the meaning of the complex word requires the storage of such a property. The number of words with a particular affix that require such storage may be quite substantial. Schreuder and Baayen (1994) observed for a selection of Dutch prefixes that the number of types with at least partially unpredictable readings may amount to 48 per cent of all types with that prefix. In terms of frequencies of use, roughly 70 per cent of all corresponding tokens turn out to be opaque. Such corpus-based calculations show that it may be disadvantageous to force a parsing on each and every input.

Another important distinction is between semantic transparency and semantic complexity. Among the transparent formations, some involve more complex semantic operations than others. For instance, inflectional processes such as pluralization involve a relatively simple semantic operation on the meaning of the stem. Deverbal verb forming processes, on the other hand, may require fairly complex operations on the lexical conceptual structures (Jackendoff, 1991; Lieber and Baayen, 1994) of base and affix. For instance, the Dutch verb *bouwen*, 'to build', is subcategorized for a direct object, the thing being built. Prefixation with *be-*, as in *bebouwen*, 'to build up', gives rise to a verb in which the location on which something is being built appears as the direct object. Such changes in valency patterns introduce additional computational complexity.

Summary

Summing up, the basic linguistic constraints on any computational model of lexical processing are the following. First, the variety of means available for the creation of complex words, both concatenative and non-concatenative, shows that a simple template matching view of morphological processing is inadequate. In as far as these morphological processes are productive, i.e., that they lead to the creation of new words that can be readily understood, they should be taken seriously by any computational model. Second, morphological operations on words may be sensitive to phonological structure. A computational model of lexical processing must include representations for syllables, rhymes, onsets, etc. in addition to bare phoneme sequences. We shall see that this requirement poses considerable problems for almost all computational models. Third, the mapping of form representations on the associated meaning representations may be obscured by phonological processes such as epenthesis and assimilation. Computational models should be able to handle such phonologically conditioned alternations. Fourth, preferential parsings should be given priority in computational models, without giving up the availability in principle of competing, less likely segmentations. Finally, the extent to which semantic opacity pervades the lexicon suggests that lexical storage often takes precedence over parsing.

Linguistic Models

We now turn to describe two operational computational parsing models developed by computational linguists. It is instructive to consider these models in some detail, as they implement efficient algorithms that actually perform the task for which they are designed. By studying these algorithms, one's insight into the complexities involved is enhanced. At the same time, various aspects of these models are relevant for computational modelling in psycholinguistics. In what follows, we describe morphological processing as consisting of three interrelated stages: segmentation (discovering the morphemes), licensing (checking for compatibility of subcategorization), and composition (computation of the syntactic and semantic structure of the complex whole).

Most current linguistic computational models of morphological parsing are designed as shown in Figure 7.1.

Parsing is accomplished in two steps. First, in the segmentation stage, the input is compared with underlying lexical representations in the lexicon. The system attempts to match the input to one or more lexical representations, taking into account phonologically or orthographically determined differences between surface and underlying forms. For instance, the orthographic input *ably* is recognized as *able + ly*. The result of this first step is a set containing one or more flat segmentations, that is, strings of morphemes which match the input given the orthographical and phonological rules of the language. No hierarchical structure is as yet assigned. As we shall see below, the lexicon is assigned a tree-like structure (the so-called L-tree, trie or sieve), and the segmentation process is carried out by a

Figure 7.1: General architecture of linguistic computational models

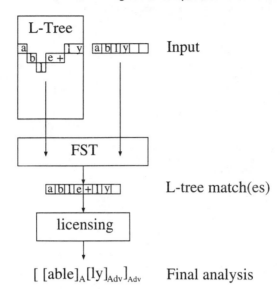

Input

L-tree match(es)

Final analysis

particular kind of finite-state mechanism, the so-called finite state transducer (FST). The first operational parser of this type was called KIMMO, after its creator, Kimmo Koskenniemi (1983). This approach to segmentation is generally known as *two-level morphology*, but might just as well be described as *two-level phonology* (cf., Anderson, 1992).

Once the set of possible flat segmentations has been obtained, the next step, licensing, is to select those segmentations that do not violate the subcategorization properties of the morphemes involved. For instance, the Dutch string *beneveling* can be assigned six flat segmentations, each consisting of a series of legitimate morphemes: *be + neef + eling*, *be + neef + eel + ling*, *be + neef + e + ling*, *been + e + veel + ing*, *be + en + e + veel + ing*, and *be + nevel + ing* (Heemskerk, 1993). Only the last flat segmentation is licensed by the subcategorizations of all morphemes involved, leading to the meaning 'misting up'. Thus the goal of the parsing process is to obtain one (or more) legitimate labelled bracketing(s) for the input, often in combination with a specification of the subcategorization and other syntactic and semantic properties of the analyzed complex word (composition).

In the next two sections we discuss these two steps in more detail.

Segmentation

In KIMMO-like parsers, segmentation is accomplished by means of an *L-tree* or *trie*

Figure 7.2: Scanning the input string sleepily *using an L-tree. The numbers show the successive steps through the L-tree*

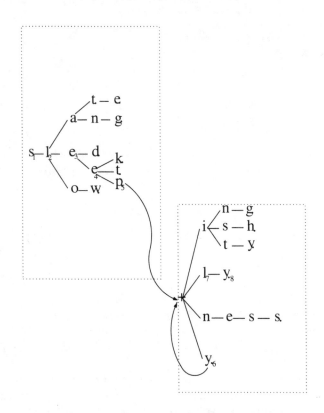

(Knuth, 1973) and a *two-tape finite state transducer* (Koskenniemi, 1983, 1984). An L-tree is a tree structure in which each node is labelled with a particular grapheme or phoneme. To ascertain whether a given string is stored in the L-tree, the input string is scanned from left to right, each successive character being matched with a character in the L-tree, starting at the root. This scanning process is shown for the input string *sleepily* in Figure 7.2. Beginning with the initial *s* matching the letter of the root node of the (partial) L-tree shown here, the successive letters scanned are matched with the available nodes to the right that become available as a path is traced through the L-tree. Nodes in the L-tree are marked when they specify possible word-final segments. In Figure 7.2, a dot marks these end nodes. Thus *sleep* is a legitimate word in the L-tree. In addition, end nodes may contain pointers to one or more so-called continuation lexicons. Figure 7.2 shows part of a possible continuation lexicon. This lexicon is needed for the segmentation of *sleepily*. The numbers in Figure 7.2 show the successive steps through the two L-trees that are required, leading to the segmentation *sleep + y + ly*. Notice, however, that this segmentation does not match the surface form, which does not contain any + symbols nor the grapheme y at the sixth position. It is here that the finite state transducers (FSTs) play a crucial role.

Two-tape FSTs are a class of automata (see Chapter 2) that operate on two sequences of symbols: the symbols of the lexical segmentations (*sleep + y + ly*) and the symbols of the surface string (*sleepily*). An FST accepts or rejects the combination of such strings. They license those mismatches that are brought about by the orthographical and phonological processes in the language. In the simplest case, each of these processes requires its own FST. All FSTs operate in parallel on the successive symbols of the two strings. One of the finite state transducers needed for accepting *sleep + y + ly* as the lexical form of *sleepily* is shown in Figure 7.3. This FST accepts surface *i* as the counterpart of lexical y, allowing the transition from the final *p* of *sleep* in the main L-tree of Figure 7.1 to the y in the L-tree of suffixes. The two-level rule implemented by the FST is the following expression:

(1) $y:i \Rightarrow + :0\_\_ + :0.$

This rule states that the correspondence between lexical *y* and surface *i* is legitimate only when morpheme boundaries precede and follow in the lexical representation. Note that the + :0 symbol pairs specify that a transition in the L-tree is not accompanied by a transition to the next symbol of the surface representation. A FST implementing this rule is shown in Figure 7.3, both in the form of a transition network and in the form of a transition table. State one is both the initial and the (only) final state. This state accepts any pair of symbols (= : =) until a morpheme boundary is encountered (+ :0), in which case the system enters

Figure 7.3: A finite state transducer for accepting sleep+y+ly *as the lexical form of* sleepily

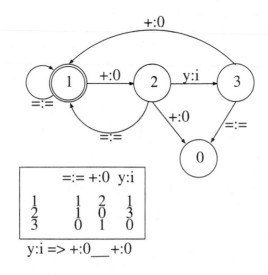

$$y:i => +:0\_\_+:0$$

state two. If the system now encounters the pair y:i, it will enter state three. The only legitimate continuation is the pair + :0, another morpheme boundary, which will return control to the initial state. Any other pair of symbols will put the FST into state 0, the sink state, indicating that the string is not licensed by the FST. Returning to state two, we observe that the symbol pair + :0 will also lead to the sink state (the FST rejects empty morphemes). All other pairs of symbols are allowed at state two, with the FST returning to state one. The reader may verify that this FST will accept strings such as

```
sleep + y + ly      sleep + ish
sleepØiØly          sleepØish
```

The system as shown in Figures 7.2 and 7.3 is greatly simplified. First, by using various continuation lexicons, one may model aspects of morphotactic constraints. For instance, the simplified schema of Figure 7.2 would accept the input string *sleepness*. By having different continuation lexica for the various word categories, many such strings can effectively be ruled out. Long-distance dependencies (*on-denk-baar*), however, cannot be solved in a principled way by means of linked sublexicons (see Sproat, 1992, pp. 91–2). Second, we have illustrated only how one orthographical rule operates in isolation. However, implemented two-level phonologies typically make use of 10 up to 40 FSTs operating in parallel. Special care is required for rules that interact with each other (see Sproat, 1992, pp. 132–43).

Summing up, KIMMO-based segmentation systems can be used to obtain flat segmentations of input strings into their constituent morphemes. Depending on the amount of effort put into the modelling of morphotactics by means of continuation lexicons, the number of different possible flat segmentations for a single input string may be quite substantial (see Heemskerk, 1993). Ideally, one would like a parser to select the correct segmentation from such sets of alternative parsings. In addition, the immediate constituency of the input as well as its word category and argument structure should be computed. A computational framework for accomplishing the tasks of licensing and composition has been developed by Ritchie *et al*. (1987) and Ritchie *et al*. (1992), among others.

Licensing and Composition

The general outline of the approach taken by Ritchie *et al*. (1987, 1992) is sketched in Figure 7.4. A flat segmentation is the input to a so-called *chart parser*, a parsing algorithm that systematically checks through the alternative parses, while keeping track of the previously explored subparses (see Chapter 2). The chart parser makes use of two kinds of information: a lexicon and a set of context-free rules. The lexicon is a list of the morphemes in the language. Each lexical

Figure 7.4: *General outline of a system using a chart parser*

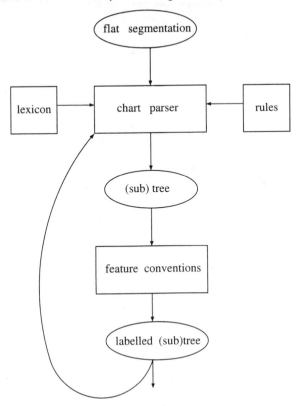

entry consists of a citation field, a phonological field, a syntax field and a semantics field. The entries for the morphemes in our example of a long-distance dependency, *on + denk + baar*, 'unthinkable', would look like this:

(on, /ɔn/, [FIX PRE, BAR – 1, STEM (N +)], NEGATION)
(denk, /dəŋk/, [BAR 0, N – , V +], THINK)
(baar, /baːr/, [FIX SUF, BAR – 1, N + , V + , STEM(N – , V +)], ABLE)

The relevant fields are the citation field, which contains the lexical form of the word as it may appear in the flat segmentation, and the syntactic field, which contains the so-called category of that word. Such categories are defined as unordered sets of feature-value pairs, using the so-called unification formalism. In this approach, the nodes in constituent trees are labelled by such sets of feature-value pairs and not by single terminal or non-terminal symbols (see Shieber, 1986). In the above example, the BAR feature specifies the X-bar level of a (sub)tree (cf., Lieber, 1980; Selkirk 1980). Affixes are assigned the X-bar level – 1, words appear with X-bar level 0. The FIX feature specifies whether a prefix (PRE) or a suffix (SUF) is involved. Word categories are distinguished by means of the features N and V. The STEM feature specifies the word category of the stem to which an affix attaches. Ritchie *et al.* (1992) make use of a rather elaborate feature set, but this allows them to formulate a very simple word grammar. Their English word grammar contains only six context-free rules. The rules for prefixation and suffixation make crucial use of the feature-value pairs mentioned above:

[BAR 0]→[FIX PRE, BAR − 1], [BAR 0]
[BAR 0]→[BAR 0], [FIX SUF, BAR − 1]

The chart parser applies such rules to its input and creates a (binary) tree structure for the first two morphemes in the flat segmentation. Subsequently, a set of so-called feature conventions is applied to this structure, enriching the newly created node with feature-value pairs and checking the compatibility of feature specifications among sister nodes. For instance, the Word-Head Convention specifies that the WHead feature-values (such as N, V) in the mother node should be the same as the WHead feature values of the right daughter. This condition is met by copying the WHead features of the right daughter to the mother. Similarly, the Word Sister Convention stipulates that when one daughter (either right or left) has the feature STEM, the other daughter should contain the feature-value pair specified as the value of the STEM feature. The application of the feature conventions results in either a legal labelled (sub)tree, or in an undefined structure. If the analysis does not exhaust the input, this result is subjected to further processing by the chart parser.

Figure 7.5 illustrates how a complex adjective such as *on + denk + baar* is analyzed. Initially, the chart parser attempts to combine the prefix *on-* with the verb stem *denk*, resulting in the uppermost tree in Figure 7.5. Subsequent application of the Word Sister Convention shows that this combination is not licensed. The chart parser then proceeds to combine the second and third segments of its input, labelling the mother node with the feature-value pair BAR 0. The Word Sister Convention is met, allowing the word category features of the right daughter to percolate to the mother node. The chart parser now combines the initial prefix with the adjective *denkbaar* [N + , V + , BAR 0], as shown in Figure 7.5. This combination is licensed by the Word Sister Convention, and the WHead features of *denkbaar* again percolate upwards by the Word Head Convention. In this way the full structure of the adjective *ondenkbaar* is obtained.

Evaluation

We have described the main features of a computational model of morphological parsing. The basic idea of a two-level approach to segmentation is widely used in current models. The unification approach to licensing and composition of Ritchie *et al.* (1992) is only one of several operational parsing techniques (see e.g.,

Figure 7.5: Word Sister Convention and Word Head Convention in Ritchie et al. (1992)

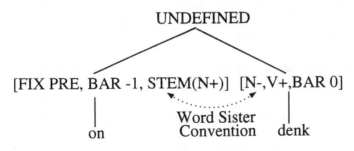

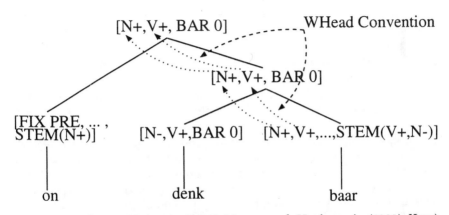

Heemskerk and Van Heuven's (1993) MORPA and Hankamer's (1989) KECI. However, as we see below, it is also an attractive system from a psycholinguistic point of view.

Nevertheless, a number of problems remain to be discussed. Koskenniemi's (1983) two-level morphology assumes that a direct mapping of surface forms onto lexical forms can be achieved without intervening representational levels, contrary to what most phonologists would claim. It remains to be seen whether all morphological and phonological phenomena can in fact be adequately understood without these intermediate representations (see Anderson, 1992, p. 385, but cf., Sproat, 1992, pp. 147–51).

A second set of problems concerns the number of different segmentations and alternative parsings for these segmentations with which one is often confronted. Many initial segmentations will be ruled out by the licensing conditions (feature conventions). Nevertheless, different segmentations may remain possible (*preached*, Ritchie *et al.*, 1992, p. 164). Moreover, one and the same segmentation may lead to different parse trees: the flat segmentation *be + nevel + ing* can be assigned three different labelled bracketings:

[[be + [$_N$nevel]] + ing],   *[[be + [$_V$nevel]] + ing]*,   and   *[be + [$_N$[nevel] + ing]]*
(Heemskerk, 1993). Probabilistic techniques for deciding between alternative analyses are now under development.

Some Basic Psycholinguistic Facts

Having reviewed the linguistic facts that constrain computational models, and having discussed some of the algorithms developed by computational linguists to meet these constraints, we now consider what additional constraints are imposed by psycholinguistic results. We discuss some main lines of evidence concerning the segmentation, licensing and composition stages. For a recent review of the experimental literature, the reader is referred to McQueen and Cutler (in press).

Segmentation

The major research thrust of psycholinguists has been aimed at establishing whether morphological structure plays a role in word recognition. In principle, morphology may be relevant to two representational levels that are generally assumed, the level of modality-specific access representations, and the level of more central, modality-free lexical representations. Most studies have addressed the issue of segmentation at the latter level. A brief overview of experimental results on morphology at this central level is presented first.

Many studies have used the repetition priming paradigm. Repetition priming involves presenting a complex word early in the experiment, to be followed by its base at a specified distance. In the baseline condition no morphologically related word precedes the target. If the base word mediates the recognition of its derivatives, the prior processing of such words should speed up the recognition of the base. Repetition priming effects have been reported for English. Stanners *et al.* (1979) found that the facilitatory effect of regularly inflected verb forms on their stems was as large as the repetition effect of the stem on itself: *walks* primed *walk* to the same extent as *walk* primed *walk*. Similar results are reported for English derivation by Stanners, Neiser and Peinton (1979) and Forster and Davies (1984). These findings are not undisputed, however. Fowler, Napps and Feldman (1985) present evidence that repetition priming effects are episodic rather than lexical (see Henderson, 1989, for a review).

The role of morphology at the central level can also be studied by manipulating word frequency. If the recognition of a complex word involves prior access to its stem representation, and if this stem representation is sensitive to frequency of use, then the summed frequencies of all words containing this stem should be a more reliable predictor of response latencies than the frequency of the surface form itself. Taft (1979) reported faster lexical decision times for words with higher stem frequency and the same surface frequency. When matched on stem frequency, an effect of word frequency remained. These results have been partially replicated by Colé, Beauvillain and Segui (1989) who observed a cumulative frequency effect for derivationally suffixed words in French, but not for prefixed words. Similarly, Bradley (1979) found a cumulative frequency effect for the phonologically transparent English suffixes *-er*, *-ment* and *-ness*, but not for phonologically far less regular *-ion*. Related studies by Lukatela *et al.* (1980) suggest that in Serbo-Croatian, oblique forms are more dependent on cumulative frequency effects than nominative base forms. In sum, there is some, be it not unequivocal, evidence that at least some complex word types require access to a central stem representation.

An experimental technique that sheds light on morphological effects at the level of access representations is phoneme monitoring. This task requires subjects to monitor for a given phoneme and to press a button as soon as this phoneme has been heard. Frauenfelder (personal communication) used this technique to study the speed with which morphemes in Turkish words become available. He obtained evidence that both roots and affixes are immediately accessed as independent units, suggesting that access representations for these roots and affixes are available for the activation of the corresponding central representations.

Additional evidence can be obtained by manipulating the morphological status of nonwords. Laudanna, Burani and Cermele (1994) compared reaction times to nonwords with different types of prefix. One dimension along which prefixes differ is the number of pseudo-prefixed words, the words that appear to contain that prefix, but where no prefix is actually involved (as for instance *re-* in English *reindeer*). As pseudowords by definition lack access and central representations, any effect of a potential morpheme entails the existence of an access as well as a central representation for that morpheme. What they found was that pseudowords containing prefixes with many pseudo-prefixed words in the language required less time to reject than pseudowords with prefixes with few such pseudo-prefixed words. These results suggest that segmentation will not be carried out if there is a high chance of obtaining erroneous results, to our mind a desirable property of the processing system. On the other hand, Taft and Forster (1975) observed longer response latencies for existing words containing a pseudo-prefix compared to controls without pseudo-prefixes, which they take to imply obligatory parsing of all potential prefixes. We will return to this issue below.

Licensing

An important study that has explicitly addressed the issue of licensing in word recognition is that by Caramazza, Laudanna and Romani (1988). These authors explored the role of licensing by presenting subjects with inflected pseudowords of various kinds in a lexical decision task. They compared the reaction times to pseudowords with either an existing stem and a pseudo-affix, a non-existing stem and a real affix, and the combination of a real stem and a real affix that is from an incorrect declension class. Typically, the longest rejection times were obtained for the latter kinds of stimulus. Correct no responses crucially require access to the relevant subcategorization information at a deeper level of processing than simple morpheme identification.

Composition

Relatively few studies have addressed the composition process, that is, the computation of meaning. The existing studies focus on the processing of novel compounds only. Coolen, Van Jaarsveld and Schreuder (1991) obtained evidence suggesting that the semantic interpretation of novel compounds is an immediate and automatic process. This conclusion was based on the observation that it is more difficult for subjects to recognize a compound as novel when that compound has an obvious interpretation. Such interference effects are generally assumed to indicate automatic processing. Furthermore, Coolen, Van Jaarsveld and Schreuder (1991) claim that the combination process is autonomous in the sense that the meaning of a novel compound is constructed from the meanings of its parts in interaction with general world-knowledge rather than by means of analogy-based operations on existing compounds in the lexicon. Although these results show that novel words can be interpreted quickly and efficiently, the exact mechanisms which regulate the interpretation remain unknown.

Psycholinguistic Models

In this section we discuss a number of psycholinguistic models for morphological processing. Most of these models have not been implemented in any way, with the exception of Gasser (1994a, 1994b), whose connectionist model of affix acquisition is a real, operational computational model. The latter model is discussed later, the former models are reviewed below.

The available experimental evidence for morphological processing is, unfortunately, too weak to sufficiently constrain the modelling effort. Hence it is possible for some models of word recognition not to assign any relevance to morphological structure (see e.g., Butterworth, 1983; Seidenberg, 1988), whereas others assume obligatory parsing for every complex word. Here we focus on those models that assume at least some form of morphological processing.

The first model to take morphological structure into account is the prefix-stripping model proposed by Taft and Forster (1975). They hypothesized that prefixes are removed prior to lexical access. The remaining string is used as the access code for a serial search in a so-called access bin. The matching entry in this bin contains a pointer to the list of possible full matches in the master lexicon. This schema was proposed as a way of increasing the efficiency of the serial search for prefixed words. Experiments testing the predictions of this model have led to a series of contradictory results. Even worse, it has been shown that the model is rather unattractive computationally. In fact, the efficiency of a serial search model decreases by roughly a factor of two when a prefix stripping strategy is incorporated, due to the large numbers of pseudo-prefixed word tokens in daily language (from 50 per cent up to 95 per cent for English, depending on one's definition of pseudo-prefixation, see Schreuder and Baayen, 1994).

A more interesting verbal model is the so-called Augmented Addressed Morphology Model (AAM) developed by Burani and Caramazza (1987), Caramazza, Laudanna and Romani (1988), Burani and Laudanna (1993). This model claims that the segmentation phase is generally bypassed in word recognition. All known words, whether morphologically complex or not, have their own access representations in this model. The (modality-specific) access representation of a complex word is linked up to the modality-free central representations of its constituent morphemes. In this central lexicon the representation of the complex whole is computed on-line, although the possibility is left open that very high-frequency complex words may acquire full lexical representations of their own. In order to handle complex neologisms, it is assumed that affixes have access representations in addition to lexical representations. The access route that exploits the full access representations is stipulated to be always faster than the segmentation route. It will be clear that this is a highly underspecified process model. Although Caramazza, Laudanna and Romani are well aware of the importance of phonological and semantic transparency, they have not spelled out what kinds of computation could be involved. The model in its present form is as yet not sufficiently detailed to allow a computational implementation.

A closely related model is the Morphological Race Model (MRM) formulated by Frauenfelder and Schreuder (1992). As in the AAM, two access routes are proposed. Unlike in the AAM, the outcome of the race is not fixed beforehand. In the MRM, both routes operate in parallel, so that it is not excluded that known complex words are nevertheless recognized by the morphological route, that is, by segmentation and subsequent composition. In addition, these authors postulate a mechanism that strengthens the access representations of the constituent(s) that contributed to the winning route. In the case that the direct route is the first to complete access, the resting activation level of the full form access representation of the word is slightly increased. If the parsing route completes first, the resting activation levels of stem and affix access representations are increased. Semantically non-compositional words can be accessed only via the whole-word route. Hence, only the access representations of affixes that participate in many semantically transparent words will obtain high resting activation levels. This is the way in which differences in productivity of affixes are accounted for. The high activation levels of productive affixes enable the system to process both novel complex words and relatively low-frequency transparent words that have been encountered before, but not often enough to allow the whole-word address route to win. However, the MRM is a verbal model that is too unspecified to allow computational modelling.

An extension of the MRM that addresses the role of semantic transparency and its effect on the activation levels of access representations in a more principled way can be found in Schreuder and Baayen (1995). Each of the three recognition stages, segmentation, licensing, and composition, is modelled in some detail using an architecture that combines spreading activation mechanisms with a symbolic parser operating on representations that have reached sufficiently high activation levels. The segmentation of the input into its constituents is accomplished by the spreading activation mechanisms. Licensing and composition are carried out by a unification-based symbolic parser. It is a dual route model in which the routes interactively converge on the correct meaning. The model has three representational levels: the level of access representations, a level of concept nodes, and a level of syntactic and semantic nodes. Activation is allowed to flow back from the semantic and syntactic nodes via the concept nodes to the access representations. This mechanism ensures that semantic transparency is a driving factor in determining the role affixes and stems play in the recognition of morphologically complex words. An *ad hoc* mechanism providing positive feedback for the winning route as in the MRM is no longer necessary. The importance of transparency for the acquisition of affixes and the consequences of differences in age of acquisition for the adult processing system are also stressed.

An Implemented Computational Model

The acquisition of the skill to map form onto meaning for morphologically complex words is studied in detail by Gasser (1994a, 1994b), using connectionist architectures. Interestingly, Gasser does not focus on the issue of whether a single network can accommodate both regular and irregular morphology at the same time, a hotly debated issue in the acquisition literature (Rumelhart and McClelland, 1986; MacWhinney and Leinbach, 1991; Pinker, 1991). Instead, his interest lies with which network architectures are required for the learning of the mapping of form onto meaning in the auditory modality for a wide variety of regular morphological processes (suffixation, infixation, prefixation, circumfixation, deletion, vocalic alternation, and reduplication), and what difficulties specific properties of these morphological processes pose for learning.

Following Norris (1990), Gasser makes use of a recurrent network with three layers to model spoken word recognition. The first layer encodes single phonemes as they become available in time. This phoneme layer is connected to a hidden layer. At each time step, the contents of this hidden layer are copied into a second hidden layer that serves as a short-term memory. At the next time step, the first hidden layer receives input from both the phonological layer and this second hidden layer. In this way the network is enabled to 'remember' the phonemes that were presented to the network at earlier time steps. Finally, the first hidden layer is connected to a semantic layer, where each node represents a full concept. The semantic layer contains two separate sets of units, one set representing the meanings of content words (labelled *stems* in the slightly simplified architecture shown in Figure 7.6), the other the 'grammatical meanings' of affixes (labeled *affixes*). In most of his experiments, Gasser trained the network on a set of 30 roots from a controlled artificial (but linguistically well-motivated) language. Each experiment studied the behaviour of the network for one particular morphological process (prefixation, suffixation, infixation, etc.) The network was trained on 2/3 of the possible combinations. Its performance was evaluated on the remaining — novel — combinations. The networks were trained using conventional backpropagation.

In a first series of experiments, Gasser tested the functionality of the network of Figure 7.6. What he found was that the network has severe difficulties in

Figure 7.6: Gasser's (1994a, 1994b) non-modular connectionist network

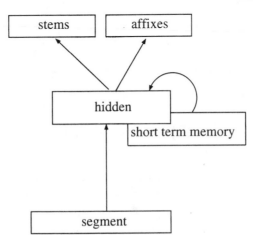

recognizing both the stem and the affix of novel complex words simultaneously. For instance, it performs moderately well for stem recognition for suffixed words, but has great difficulties in getting the suffix right. Conversely, it has no difficulty in recognizing prefixes, but for prefixed words recognition of the stem is abysmal. Apparently, the network has severe problems due to the hidden layer being required to perform two separate tasks at the same time: affix recognition and stem recognition. To avoid overtaxing the hidden layer, Gasser studied a modular network in which stems and affixes have their own hidden layer, as shown in Figure 7.7. Performance for affix recognition improved to nearly 100 per cent for a wide variety of morphological operations, infixation and vocalic alternation being the exceptions. Stem recognition also increased, be it to a much lower level of accuracy (40 per cent–75 per cent). In the case of circumfixation, its performance on root recognition was very poor. Apparently, stem recognition is severely impaired when both the beginning and the end of the stem are 'masked' by affixed segments.

In the system shown in Figure 7.7, the learning of affixes is facilitated by the pre-wiring of the modular structure of the network: the hidden layers are already specialized recognition devices for stems and affixes respectively. Gasser shows that it is, to some extent, possible to let this modular organization arise as part of the learning process. He first trained the net on the recognition of stems. Following this, he added a number of so-called gating units monitoring the connections from the two sets of hidden layers to both stem and affix units. He observed that the network tends to allocate stem recognition to one set of hidden units, and suffix recognition to the other. However, when the network is presented with both prefixes and suffixes, hardly any specialization takes place.

Finally, Gasser shows that the system shown in Figure 7.7 cannot learn rules involving reduplication. He argues that reduplication can be handled only by extending the system with a hidden layer that is geared to recognizing syllables.

Figure 7.7: Gasser's (1994a, 1994b) modular connectionist network

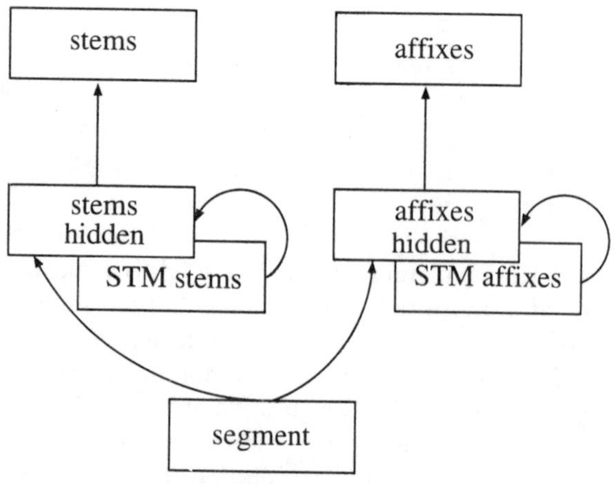

That the recognition system must be allowed to exploit prosodic information is a conclusion that is shared by Sproat, who, in the symbolic domain, shows that a KIMMO-like system by itself cannot adequately handle the complex reduplication patterns of a language such as Warlpiri (Sproat, 1992, pp. 164–70).

It will be clear that the modelling of the acquisition of morphological rules is far from trivial. Gasser's networks appear to be reasonably effective for the learning of a single morphological operation. It is unclear how well this architecture will be able to deal with words with multiple affixes such as *ondenk-baarheid*, 'un-think-able-ness', where on- is not subcategorized for attaching to the verb stem denk, and where the parsing *[[on + [denk + baar]] + heid]* should be selected and not the possible parsing *[on + [[denk + baar] + heid]]*. In addition, it should be noted that languages are often characterized by large numbers of morphologically complex but semantically non-compositional words. If one's goal is to model the acquisition of the full vocabulary and lexical rules of a language, the presence of large numbers of words with affixes that do not allow a regular mapping onto semantics may well cause serious problems for modular networks of this kind, especially in the light of the strong correlation between higher token frequencies and higher degrees of semantic opacity. A number of verb-forming prefixes in Dutch, for instance, are most often encountered in semi-transparent and opaque formations (Schreuder and Baayen, 1994, 1995, see also Lieber and Baayen, 1994). If a learning system is to master the transparent semantics of such affixes, it must do so in an environment that is characterized by a very low signal-to-noise ratio. The large numbers of pseudo-prefixed words observed for English and Dutch lower this signal-to-noise ratio even more. It is as yet unclear which systems that make use of statistical learning can handle distributions of this kind. Nevertheless, Gasser's work is an impressive first step in the computational modelling of morphological processing.

Discussion

The linguistic computational models discussed are clearly superior to the psycho-linguistic models with respect to the range and depth of the linguistic phenomena they cover. Furthermore, compared with Gasser's (1994a, 1994b) model, they perform far better. Nevertheless, in their present form these models are unsatisfactory from a psycholinguistic point of view, for a number of reasons. First consider KIMMO. Koskenniemi (1983, p. 134–6) claims that his model provides a psychologically valid description of morphological processing. However, there are several aspects of this approach that are unsatisfactory. First, in contrast to Gasser's model, KIMMO is not a learning system. All morphological rules are embodied in the transducers once and for all. The question of how a system might acquire such — often intricately interacting — transducers is not answered. Second, the L-tree mechanism is an elegant technical solution for lexical look-up, but it is psycholinguistically implausible. The use of an L-tree predicts that certain classes of nonword should be rejected in much less time than it takes to respond to real words, contrary to fact (Forster, 1989). In addition, word frequency and cumulative frequency effects do not emerge naturally in systems based on the L-tree format. Finally, if lexical access in the auditory modality proceeds on the basis of metrical segmentation strategies as suggested by Cutler and Norris (1988), the idea of a simple left-to-right scan through the word may well be too simplistic.

Next consider Ritchie *et al.*'s (1992) morphological parser for English. An attractive feature of this model is that the number of different morphological rules embodied in the system are kept at a minimum. The main computational burden lies with the computationally relatively simple unification of the lexical representations associated with the morphemes. On the negative side, the model in its present form is designed to parse each and every input string. This property may be desirable from a linguistic (and a practical) point of view, but it is psychologically unsatisfactory, especially for languages such as English where conclusive evidence for an obligatory on-line role for morphological structure has not been obtained. In languages with simple morphologies, high-frequency complex words may very well be recognized using a form of direct access. Furthermore, one would not expect the constituents of semantically opaque words to play a role in production or perception. Finally, note that in this computational approach the way in which the system discovers morphemes and their properties is again left unspecified.

Summing up, it is clear that compared to many of the computational models discussed in the present volume the available psycholinguistic models of morphological processing are underspecified and rudimentary. No operational models predicting reaction times are available. Undoubtedly, this state of affairs can be traced to the complexity of the issues involved. For psycholinguistics, the challenge of building an operational model of morphological processing has yet to be met.

References

ANDERSON, S.R. (1992) *A-Morphous Morphology*, Cambridge: Cambridge University Press.

ARONOFF, M. (1976) *Word Formation in Generative Grammar*, Cambridge, MA: MIT Press.

ARONOFF, M. (1994) *Morphology by Itself: Stems and Inflectional Classes*, Cambridge, MA: MIT Press.

BEARD, R. (1992) *Lexeme-Morpheme Base Morphology. A General Theory of Inflection and Word Formation*, Unpublished manuscript.

BRADLEY, D. (1979) 'Lexical representation of derivational relation', in ARONOFF, M. and KEAN, M.L. (Eds) *Juncture*, Sarasota: Anma Libri, pp. 37–55.

BURANI, C. and CARAMAZZA, A. (1987) 'Representation and processing of derived words', *Language and Cognitive Processes*, 2, pp. 217–27.

BURANI, C. and LAUDANNA, A. (1993) 'Units of representation for derived words in the lexicon', in FROST, R. and KATZ, L. (Eds) *Orthography, Phonology, Morphology, and Meaning*, Amsterdam: Elsevier/North-Holland.

BUTTERWORTH, B. (1983) 'Lexical representation', in BUTTERWORTH, B. (Ed) *Language Production: Vol 2. Development, Writing and Other Language Processes*, London: Academic Press, pp. 257–94.

CARAMAZZA, A., LAUDANNA, A. and ROMANI, C. (1988) 'Lexical access and inflectional morphology', *Cognition*, 28, pp. 297–332.

COLÉ, P., BEAUVILLAIN, C. and SEGUI, J. (1989) 'On the representation and processing of prefixed and suffixed derived words: A differential frequency effect', *Journal of Memory and Language*, 28, pp. 1–13.

COOLEN, R., VAN JAARSVELD, H. and SCHREUDER, R. (1991) 'The interpretation of isolated novel nominal compounds', *Memory and Cognition*, 19, pp. 341–52.

CUTLER, A. and NORRIS, D. G. (1988) 'The role of strong syllables in segmentation for lexical access', *Journal of Experimental Psychology: Human Perception and Performance*, 14, pp. 113–21.

FORSTER, K. I. (1989) 'Basic issues in lexical processing', in MARSLEN-WILSON, W. (Ed) *Lexical Representation and Process*, Cambridge, MA: MIT Press, pp. 75–108.

FORSTER, K. I. and DAVIS, C. (1984) 'Repetition priming and frequency attenuation in lexical access', *Journal of Experimental Psychology: Learning, Memory, and Cognition*, 10, pp. 680–98.

FOWLER, C. A., NAPPS, S. E. and FELDMAN, L. B. (1985) 'Relations among regularly and irregularly morphologically related words in the lexicon as revealed by repetition priming', *Memory and Cognition*, 13, pp. 241–55.

FRAUENFELDER, U. H. and SCHREUDER, R. (1992) 'Constraining psycholinguistic models of morphological processing and representation: The role of productivity', in BOOIJ, G. E. and VAN MARLE, J. (Eds) *Yearbook of Morphology 1991*, Dordrecht: Kluwer, pp. 165–83.

GASSER, M. (1994a) 'Modularity in a connectionist model of the acquisition of morphology', in *Proceedings of the 15th International Conference on Computational Linguistics (COLING '94)*, Kyoto, pp. 214–20.

GASSER, M. (1994b) 'Acquiring receptive morphology: A connectionist model', in *Proceedings of the 32nd Annual Meeting of the Association for Computational Linguistics, Las Cruces*, pp. 279–86.

GESENIUS, W. and KAUTZSCH, E. (1909) *Hebräische Grammatik*, Leipzig: Vogel.

GLEASON, H. A. (1955) *Workbook in Descriptive Linguistics*, New York: Holt, Rinehart & Winston.

HANKAMER, J. (1989) 'Morphological parsing and the lexicon', in MARSLEN-WILSON, W. (Ed) *Lexical Representation and Process*, Cambridge, MA: MIT Press, pp. 392–408.

HEEMSKERK, J. (1993) 'A probabilistic context-free grammar for disambiguation in morphological parsing', in *Proceedings of the 6th Conference of the European Chapter of the Association for Computational Linguistics, Utrecht*, pp. 183–92.

HEEMSKERK, J. and VAN HEUVEN, V. (1993) 'MORPA: a morpheme lexicon-based morphological parser', in VAN HEUVEN, V. and POLS, L. (Eds) *Analysis and Synthesis of Speech, Strategic Research Towards High-Quality Text-to-Speech Generation*, Berlin: Mouton/De Gruyter.

HENDERSON, L. (1989) 'On mental representation of morphology and its diagnosis by measures of visual access speed', in MARSLEN-WILSON, W. (Ed) *Lexical Representation and Process*, Cambridge, MA: MIT Press, pp. 357–91.

JACKENDOFF, R. (1991) *Semantic Structures*, Cambridge. MA: MIT Press.

JENSEN, J. T. (1990) *Morphology: Word Structure in Generative Grammar*, Amsterdam: John Benjamins.

KOSKENNIEMI, K. (1983) *Two-Level Morphology. A General Computational Model for Word-Form Recognition and Production*, Unpublished doctoral dissertation, University of Helsinki.

KOSKENNIEMI, K. (1984) 'A general computational model for word-form recognition and production', in *Proceedings of the 10th International Conference on Computational Linguistics (COLING '84)*, pp. 178–81.

KNUTH, D. E. (1973) *The Art of Computer Programming*, Reading, MA: Addison-Wesley.

LAUDANNA, A., BURANI, C. and CERMELE, A. (1994) 'Prefixes as processing units', *Language and Cognitive Processes*, 9, pp. 295–316.

LIEBER, R. (1980) *On the Organization of the Lexicon*, Unpublished doctoral dissertation, Massachusetts Institute of Technology, Cambridge, MA.

LIEBER, R. (1987) *An Integrated Theory of Autosegmental Processes*, Albany: State University of New York Press.

LIEBER, R. (1992) *Deconstructing Morphology. Word Formation in Syntactic Theory*, Chicago: University of Chicago Press.

LIEBER, R. and BAAYEN, R.H. (1994) 'Verbal prefixes in Dutch: A study in lexical conceptual structure', in BOOIJ, G.E. and VAN MARLE, J. (Eds) *Yearbook of Morphology 1993*, Dordrecht: Kluwer, pp. 51–78.

LUKATELA, G., GLIGORIJEVIC, B., KOSTIC, A. and TURVEY, M. T. (1980) 'Representation of inflected nouns in the internal lexicon', *Memory and Cognition*, 8, pp. 415–23.

MACWHINNEY, B. and LEINBACH, J. (1991) 'Implementations are not conceptualizations: Revising the verb learning model', *Cognition*, 40, pp. 121–57.

MARTIN, W. (1988) 'Subtractive morphology as dissociation', in *Proceedings of the Seventh West Coast Conference on Formal Linguistics*, Stanford: Linguistic Association.

MCCARTHY, J. (1982) *Formal Problems in Semitic Morphology and Phonology* (Doctoral dissertation, Massachusetts Institute of Technology, 1979). Indiana University Linguistics Club.

MCQUEEN, J. M. and CUTLER, A. (in press) 'Morphology in word recognition', in ZWICKY, A. M. and SPENCER, A. (Eds) *The Handbook of Morphology*, Oxford: Blackwell.

NORRIS, D. (1990) 'A dynamic-net model of human speech recognition', in ALTMANN, G. T. M. (Ed) *Cognitive Models of Speech Processing: Psycholinguistic and Computational Perspectives*, Cambridge, MA: MIT Press, pp. 87–104.

PINKER, S. (1991) 'Rules of language', *Science*, 253, pp. 530–5.

RITCHIE, G. D., PULMAN, S. G., BLACK, A. W. and RUSSELL, G. J. (1987) 'A computational framework for lexical description', *Computational Linguistics*, 13, pp. 290–307.

RITCHIE, G. D., RUSSEL, G. J., BLACK, A. W. and PULMAN, S. G. (1992) *Computational Morphology. Practical Mechanisms for the English Lexicon*, Cambridge, MA: MIT Press.

RUMELHART, D. E. and MCCLELLAND, J. L. (1986) 'On learning the past tenses of English verbs', in MCCLELLAND, J.L., RUMELHART, D.E. and the PDP Research Group, *Parallel Distributed Processing: Explorations in the Microstructure of Cognition: Vol. 2. Psychological and Biological Models*, Cambridge, MA: MIT Press, pp. 216–71.

SCHACHTER, P. and OTANES, F. (1972) *Tagalog Reference Grammar*, Berkeley: University of California Press.

SCHANE, S. A. (1973) *Generative Phonology*, Englewood Cliffs: Prentice-Hall.

SCHREUDER, R. and BAAYEN, R. H. (1994) 'Prefix-stripping re-revisited', *Journal of Memory and Language*, 33, pp. 357–75.

SCHREUDER, R. and BAAYEN, R. H. (1995) 'Modelling morphological processing', in FELDMAN, L. (Ed) *Morphological Aspects of Language Processing*, Hillsdale, NJ: Lawrence Erlbaum, pp. 131–54.

SEIDENBERG, M. S. (1988) 'Reading complex words', in CARLSON, S. N. and TANENHAUS, M. K. (Eds) *Linguistic Structure in Language*, Dordrecht: Kluwer, pp. 53–106.

SELKIRK, E. O. (1980) *The Syntax of Words*, Cambridge, MA: MIT Press.

SHIEBER, S. M. (1986) *An Introduction to Unification-Based Approaches to Grammar*, Stanford: Center for the Study of Language and Information.

SPROAT, R. (1992) *Morphology and Computation*, Cambridge, MA: MIT Press.

STANNERS, R. F., NEISER, J. J., HERNON, W. P. and HALL, R. (1979) 'Memory representation for morphologically related words', *Journal of Verbal Learning and Verbal Behavior*, 18, pp. 399–412.

STANNERS, R. F., NEISER, J. J. and PEINTON, S. (1979) 'Memory representation for prefixed words', *Journal of Verbal Learning and Verbal Behavior*, 18, pp. 733–43.

TAFT, M. (1979) 'Recognition of affixed words and the word frequency effect', *Memory and Cognition*, 7, pp. 263–72.

TAFT, M. and FORSTER, K. I. (1975) 'Lexical storage and retrieval of prefixed words', *Journal of Verbal Learning and Verbal Behavior*, 14, pp. 638–47.

Chapter 8

Computational Models of Syntactic Processing in Language Comprehension

Gerard Kempen

Introduction

The pioneers of computational psycholinguistics, who built their earliest models more than twenty years ago, were primarily interested in syntax. Novel computational techniques for analyzing the structure of natural language sentences inspired them to develop parsers that could simulate characteristic phenomena of human sentence processing. Favourite objects of study were *garden-path sentences* that would lead us up the garden path due to strong interpretive biases. Kaplan (1972) introduced *Augmented transition networks as psychological models of sentence comprehension*. At about the same time, Kimball (1973) proposed *Seven principles of surface structure parsing in natural language* which have inspired psycholinguistic parser design for many years.

This chapter takes stock of what has happened since. The next section summarizes the results of experimental psycholinguistic work on the syntactic aspects of sentence comprehension (leaving aside semantic issues). Then, I outline five simulation models of syntactic parsing which have attempted to take such findings into account. The final section presents some conclusions and tries to catch a glimpse of the future.

The Empirical Arena

In this section, I present five groups of syntactic processing phenomena that have been established experimentally. Due to limitations of space I cannot go into procedural details of the experiments nor, with a few exceptions, into the theoretical debates that have accompanied the interpretation of certain sets of data. I refer to Mitchell (1994) for an extensive survey of the empirical literature. I concentrate on clear cases — those areas in the arena where the dust has settled or is settling.

My way of grouping the data and labelling the groups is not entirely conventional. The particular headings I have chosen were guided by the following hypothesis: Processes and mechanisms known to be operative in other cognitive domains, also underlie linguistic performance. The empirical phenomena reflect the way these *dynamic* factors cope with linguistic *structures* of various kinds and varying levels of complexity. This is why I have foregrounded such notions as frequency, priming, recency, control, and capacity at the expense of concepts that denote syntactic configurations such as Minimal Attachment, filler-gap relationship, or various types of clause embedding.

Process Control

Bounded Parallelism

The human syntactic processor does not compute all syntactic structures allowed by an ambiguous input sentence. On the contrary, there is overwhelming evidence that, in the course of processing *structurally ambiguous* sentences, no more than one syntactic representation is constructed (*single-track* processing). Consider the examples of structural syntactic ambiguity in (1) and (2).

(1)   John bought the book that I had been trying to obtain for Susan.
(2)   Welke dokter heeft deze patient bezocht?
    a.   Which doctor has this patient visited?
    b.   Which doctor has visited this patient?

Few readers of (1), for example, will spontaneously realize that *for Susan* can be interpreted as modifying *bought*. And speakers of Dutch consider only one analysis of sentence (2) — usually (2b) where the *Wh*-phrase serves as grammatical subject (Frazier and Flores d'Arcais, 1989). On-line measures of processing load have failed to support the hypothesis that readers or listeners construct and maintain multiple analyses while comprehending such sentences.

Structural syntactic ambiguity originates from the fact that certain constituents may contract several different grammatical relationships. It is to be distinguished from *lexical frame ambiguity* as illustrated by examples (3) and (4). Compare the short version of the sentences (without bracketed string) with the long one.

(3)   Sally found out the answer to the difficult physics problem [was in the book].
(4)   The soldiers warned about the dangers [conducted the midnight raid].

As these examples show, verbs may belong to different *subcategorizations* according to their environments. The lexical item *find out* has two different lexical frames: it can take a noun phrase (NP) as direct object or a complement clause. And *warned* is ambiguous between finite verb and past participle. Gorrell (1991) and MacDonald, Just and Carpenter (1992) obtained evidence for parallel processing. Their data suggest that the alternative lexical frames are both activated and maintained while the ambiguous region is being processed. This observation is in keeping with what is known about processing *semantically* ambiguous lexical items. Multiple meanings are activated initially, but only the contextually appropriate one is retained (Swinney, 1979; Rayner, Pacht and Duffy, 1994).

To sum up, the human syntactic processor avoids the construction of multiple syntactic analyses for complete sentences, although it seems to consider the alternatives offered by syntactically ambiguous lexical items. The upshot is parallelism of a very restricted kind (see Garrett, 1990, for a similar view). I will return to the issue of parallel computing later in the chapter.

Immediacy

In addition to the options discussed so far (namely, single-track or multiple-track processing), there is a third possibility for dealing with syntactic ambiguity. When encountering a syntactically ambiguous region, the parser might adopt a superficial style of analysis and only commit itself to structural decisions that are neutral with respect to the alternative solutions: *minimal commitment* parsing. However, the on-line processing data are at variance with this proposal, as argued at length by Mitchell (1994). (An empirical argument based on Dutch is given by Frazier and Flores d'Arcais, 1989). The human syntactic processor often makes strong commitments without delay. A clear example is provided by the Active Filler Strategy which is responsible for a temporary trouble spot right after *forced* in (5) (cf., Fodor, 1989; Pickering and Barry, 1991).

> (5)   Who could the little child have forced us to sing those stupid French songs for, last Christmas?

The parser needs to find out which lexical frame the preposed *who* belongs to. The first candidate is the direct object slot of *force*. The presence of *us* prevents this, thereby causing a processing problem. This observation suggests that the parser indeed attempts to drop the interrogative pronoun at the first location that seems suitable. The next slot, the one provided by *for*, brings success (compare *For whom could the little child . . .*).

Incremental and Interactive Processing

That language utterances are analyzed syntactically from left to right on a word-by-word basis (rather than, e.g., clause-by-clause) is commonly assumed: *incremental* syntactic processing. Somewhat controversial, though widely accepted, is the further assumption that this characterization also applies to the semantic interpretation of utterances. That is, the unfolding semantic representation is updated at every new content word appearing in the input.

The incremental mode of syntactic analysis and semantic interpretation creates opportunities for *semantic-syntactic interactions*: semantic decisions taken earlier on in the sentence or in previous context sentences may affect subsequent syntactic choices. Under what conditions such influences make themselves felt, and how strong they are, are hotly debated and intensely researched issues. A broad spectrum of opinions has been voiced, based on sometimes conflicting empirical evidence. (For some highlights in the literature, I refer to Frazier, 1978; Crain and Steedman, 1985; Taraban and McClelland, 1988; Altmann, Garnham and Dennis, 1992; Rayner, Garrod and Perfetti, 1992; Britt, 1994; and Trueswell, Tanenhaus and Garnsey, 1994.) What has become clear is that the human syntactic processor is not immune to semantic (conceptual, pragmatic, contextual) factors, rendering the position of full 'autonomy of syntax' untenable. However, at the current state of play it is impossible to draw the contours, let alone the detailed shape, of an empirically well-grounded interactive model.

Lexical Frame Preferences

Lexical frames (or subcategorization frames) express constraints on the shape of possible grammatical environments of a word. This information, which belongs to that word's entry (*lemma*; see Chapter 12) in the mental lexicon, specifies grammatical properties of optional or obligatory complements and modifiers. In the context of examples (3) and (4) above we have already seen that words may have more than one lexical frame associated with them. Moreover, the evidence for bounded parallelism suggests that several lexical frames of a word may be simultaneously active. This does not imply, however, that the syntactic processor treats the alternative frames on equal footing. One of the causes of *garden-pathing* has to do with preference for one lexical frame over another. Such preferences can be assessed in various ways, for example, in sentence production tasks where subjects are given a verb and generate a sentence containing it. Clifton, Frazier and Connine (1984) compared sentences like those in (6).

(6)   a.   The aging pianist taught *his* solo with great dignity.
     b.   The aging pianist taught *with* his entire family.
     c.   The aging pianist performed *his* solo with great dignity.
     d.   The aging pianist performed *with* his entire family.

The verbs *teach* and *perform* have similar lexical frames in that they both allow a transitive or an intransitive frame. However, while *teach* prefers a direct object, *perform* is preferably used intransitively. The underlined words mark the onset of the disambiguating region: from that position onwards, it is clear which of the two frames has to be instantiated. Subjects were presented with such sentences in a word-by-word reading task. Immediately after presentation of the disambiguating word they carried out a visual lexical decision task. Reaction times were longer in sentences with unpreferred lexical frames, i.e., in (6b) and (6c). Giving up the preferred frame apparently increased processing load. A recent study by Shapiro, Nagel and Levine (1993) corroborates this result.

Lexical frame preferences have played an important role in a controversy between *phrase-structure driven* and *lexically driven* models of parsing. The former models hold that the parser constructs an initial syntactic tree on the basis of syntactic phrase-structure rules, guided by parsing strategies such as Right Association and Minimal Attachment. (These concepts are explained in subsequent sections.) Lexical frames are consulted at a later stage and help to confirm or to improve the earlier phrase-structure decisions. In lexically driven models, on the other hand, frame information guides phrase-structure decisions right from the start. They are probably in better agreement with empirical evidence, a few stubborn data notwithstanding (Mitchell, 1987).

Syntactic Frequency

Cuetos and Mitchell (1988) discovered that Spanish readers have a different preference for attaching relative clauses than English readers. The sentences they presented to subjects contained a complex NP with two possible attachment points for a final relative clause. They showed that, while English readers prefer the low attachment point with the relative clause in (7a) modifying *actress*, Spanish readers prefer high attachment with *hermano* modified by the relative clause in (7b). The relative clause does not contain any gender clues.

(7) a. Someone shot the brother of the actress who was on the balcony.
     b. Alguien disparó contra el hermano de la actriz que estaba en el balcón.
     c. Alguien disparó contra el hermano de la actriz que estaba en el balcón *con su marido*.
     d. Alguien disparó contra *la hermana* de la actriz que estaba en el balcón *con su marido*.

In a self-paced reading task, this preference showed up in the viewing times of the passage *con su marido* (*with her husband*) in (7c). These viewing times were longer than in a control condition with *el hermano* replaced by *la hermana* (sister) in (7d). In subsequent experiments it could be verified that the attachment preference indeed reflects the frequency of the two NP constructions in Spanish. Additional correspondences between syntactic frequency and parsing preference have been observed for other constructions and other languages (Gibson and Loomis, 1994; Cuetos, Mitchell and Corley, in press).

Temporal Effects

Syntactic Priming

Facilitation occurs when two or more similar syntactic constructions that share a problematic feature are processed in close temporal succession. Frazier *et al*. (1984) demonstrated this for coordinate structures exemplified by (8) and (9).

(8) Jim believed all Tom's stories [were literally true] and Sue believed Jim's stories [were fictitious].

(9) Mary wrote a long note about her predicament to her mother and Sue wired to her father a telegram requesting more money.

In various trials of a self-paced reading experiment, the bracketed strings of (8) could be present or absent. Without the strings, *Tom's stories* is direct object of *believe*; in the long version with the strings added, this NP is the subject of the embedded complement clause. The long version of the second conjunct was significantly easier to process when the first member was also presented in the long version. No signs of garden-pathing remained. A similar effect obtained when both conjuncts contained a *heavy NP shift* causing the shorter indirect object to precede the longer direct object (cf., Chapter 11). So, (9) was more difficult than its counterpart with *to her mother* immediately following *wrote*. Schuster and MacDonald (1994) have obtained syntactic priming effects in texts where the priming and the primed constructions occurred in different sentences.

Syntactic Recency

The best known and least controversial phenomenon of human syntactic parsing was termed Right Association by Kimball (1973). One of his examples is (10).

(10) Joe said that Martha expected that it would rain yesterday.

The principle predicts that a new constituent will preferably be attached to the lowest possible (most recent, rightmost) non-terminal node of the current syntactic tree. The most likely attachment point for the adverbial phrase (AP) *yesterday* in (10) will be the verb phrase (VP) dominating *rain*. Readings with the AP associated with *expect* and *say* will be increasingly difficult. The principle also predicts that *a mile* in (11) will initially be analyzed as belonging to the subordinate rather than to the matrix (main) clause. Other names for the same or very similar principles are Late Closure (Frazier and Rayner, 1982) and Recency Preference (Gibson, 1990).

(11) Since Jay always jogs a mile seems like a short distance to him.

Constituent Length Effects

One of the experimental manipulations in Frazier and Rayner's (1982) classical eye-tracking study concerned the length of the ambiguous phrase in garden-path sentences. The sentence material contained temporary object-subject ambiguities in preposed subordinate clauses, for example (11), and in object complement clauses, for example, (3). For example, in the short version parallel to (3), the ambiguous region *the answer to the difficult physics problem* was shortened to *the answer*; and in the long version of (11), *a mile* had been replaced by *a mile and a half*. The eye movement data clearly showed that after a long ambiguous region the garden-path effect was larger than after a short one. The short versions of (3) produced only weak signs of garden-pathing. This indicates that ongoing processing is interrupted only beyond a minimum length of the ambiguous region. Another effect of length is discussed below in the context of examples (18a,b).

Working Memory Capacity

The computations performed by the human syntactic processor take place in some working memory — a device for short-term storage of lexical, grammatical and semantic information retrieved from long-term memory or generated in the course of linguistic processing. Capacity limitations of this workspace are often held responsible for language comprehension problems, for example, when sentences become excessively long or when subject and finite verb are far apart, as easily happens in German and Dutch subordinate clauses. Under this heading, I also list the notorious doubly centre-embedded clauses, for example (12c), that are so much harder to understand than the unproblematic single centre-embeddings. Remarkable also are the contrasts between centre-, cross-serial and righthand embeddings, whose comprehensibility increases in this order. Bach, Brown and Marslen-Wilson (1986) have shown that this rank order applies cross-linguistically:

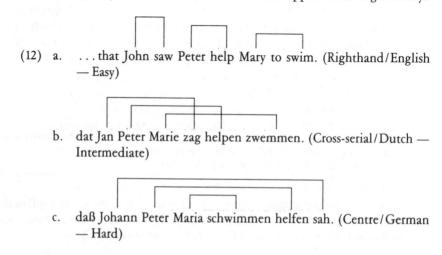

(12) a. . . . that John saw Peter help Mary to swim. (Righthand/English — Easy)

   b. dat Jan Peter Marie zag helpen zwemmen. (Cross-serial/Dutch — Intermediate)

   c. daß Johann Peter Maria schwimmen helfen sah. (Centre/German — Hard)

The Simulation Amphitheatre

Preliminaries

For over twenty years, theory- and computer-minded onlookers — a colourful mixture of psychologists, linguists and computer scientists — have been watching the events in the empirical arena, comfortably seated in the amphitheatre. Only a few of them have descended into the arena to intervene in the spectacle, while the experimental psycholinguists knew they were the stars and most of them preferred to keep it that way. The upshot is that, as we will see, the simulation models do not always bear a close relationship to the empirical facts, and that the course of experimental work has hardly been influenced by results of computer modelling studies.

In this section, I present five different computational models explicitly aiming at psychological plausibility. They all try to simulate some selection of phenomena from the empirical arena. The models are:

1 Augmented Transition Networks (ATNs; Kaplan, 1972, 1975)
2 Shift-Reduce Parsing (Shieber, 1983; Pereira, 1985; Abney, 1989)
3 PARSIFAL (Marcus, 1980)
4 Race-Based Parsing (McRoy and Hirst, 1990), and
5 UNIFICATION SPACE (U-SPACE; Kempen and Vosse, 1989).

ATNs and PARSIFAL have been widely discussed in the literature. Shift-Reduce Parsing is less known in psycholinguistic circles but helps to explain essential properties of PARSIFAL. Race-Based Parsing was inspired by probably the best known non-computational model of the human syntactic processor: Frazier and Fodor's (1978) SAUSAGE MACHINE. The first four models are strictly symbolic (in the sense explained in Chapter 2); the fifth model is *hybrid* in that it mixes symbolic and connectionist features. In order to enhance comparability of the

Table 8.1: Sample grammar associated with sentences (13a,b,c)

1. S→NP VP	6. RRC→Vpass NP	11. PP→Prep NP	16. N→letter
2. NP→Art N	7. VP→Vintr	12. Vintr→fainted	17. N→student
3. NP→PropN	8. VP→Vintr PP	13. Vtr→read	18. PropN→Chrysanne
4. NP→NP PP	9. VP→Vtr NP	14. Vpass→read	19. Prep→to
5. NP→NP RRC	10. VP→Vtr NP PP	15. Art→the	

models, I often use the simple context-free grammar of Table 8.1 to explain the essence of their inner workings. This grammar generates, among other things, the following sentences in (13), adapted from McRoy and Hirst (1990).

(13) a. The student read the letter to Chrysanne.[1]
     b. The student read the letter to Chrysanne fainted.
     c. The student read the letter fainted.[2]

The basic architecture of any syntactic parser is depicted in Figure 8.1. The processor-cum-working memory reads words from the input buffer, consults the lexical, morphological and syntactic information associated with them, and assembles a syntactic structure as output — a complete or fragmentary syntactic tree. The details vary between models, of course. The box drawn with dotted lines denotes an optional semantic/pragmatic component which co-determines the parsing process in parallel with lexical/grammatical information. This would constitute an interactive model. In a syntax-first model, the semantic/pragmatic component would operate upon syntactic structures tentatively proposed by the syntactic processor (serial connection and feedback). In the context of *human* syntactic processing one can safely assume that the grammatical, lexical, and large parts of the conceptual knowledge are stored in long-term memory.

Figure 8.1: Main parser components

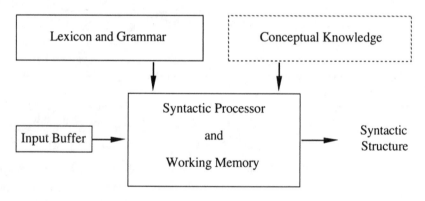

Augmented Transition Networks

In an ATN, the parsing process is represented as a collection of transitions between states (see Chapter 2). The states are usually depicted as labelled nodes, the transitions as directed labelled arcs between nodes. Initial and final states are connected via any number of intermediate states and arcs. Graphs representing the set of permitted transitions embody grammar rules. Words in the input are consumed one by one. Their properties determine how a graph can be traversed. If more than one arc leaves a state, they are tried out sequentially in clockwise direction. An ATN corresponding to the grammar of Table 8.1 is depicted in Figure 8.2.

Figure 8.2: Augmented Transition Network for Analyzing Sentences (13a,b)

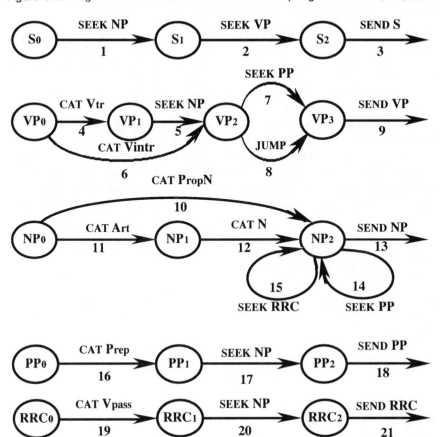

For each of the five phrasal categories S (sentence), NP (noun phrase), VP (verb phrase), RRC (reduced relative clause) and PP (prepositional phrase) there are separate networks which are specialized in parsing Ss, NPs, VPs, RRCs, and PPs. A string is accepted as a sentence if it can move the top ATN from state S_0 to S_2. A string that can bring the NP network from NP_0 to NP_2 is a noun phrase. Arc labels denote condition-action pairs (printed above the arc). CAT arcs specify which word category the next input item should belong to (e.g., Article, Proper Noun, Transitive verb). SEEK arcs are calls to another subnetwork. For instance, SEEK NP causes transfer of control to the NP subnetwork, which then undertakes to interpret (part of) the remaining input as an NP. SEND arcs return control to the 'calling' subnetwork and arc. For example, the S subnetwork opens with a call to the NP subnetwork. If this indeed can recognize an NP in the first part of the input string, then the SEND NP arc leaving state NP_2 transfers control to the S subnetwork, which then moves to state S_1. The last type of arc label (JUMP) indicates that the arc may be traversed for free, without any conditions imposed.

For instance, the JUMP arc in the VP subnetwork renders the PP optional. The numbers below the arcs refer to a (possibly empty) list of actions to be executed when the arc is traversed — usually bookkeeping operations needed to put together part of a tree. For instance, Action 1 in the S-network assigns the role of Subject to the recognized NP. An excellent source of further information is Winograd (1983).

How does this ATN fare with sentence (13b)? Would it yield a garden-path effect? Let us consider Figure 8.3a, which shows the arcs traversed until hitting upon the final word *fainted*. At that point a Sentence has been accepted although the input has not yet finished. This induces a rather complex *backtracking* operation (this concept is explained in Chapter 2). It turns out that a wrong path was taken almost at the beginning. If, within the first instantiation of the NP-network, after *student*, arc 15 had been chosen instead of arc 13, everything would have fallen out well. This is illustrated in Figure 8.3b. The reader who handparses the sentence will notice that it is the ordering of outgoing arcs which causes the garden-path. Simply scheduling both SEEK arcs leaving NP$_2$ before the Send arc will pre-empt the need to backtrack here. But of course, in that case sentence (13a), without *fainted*, becomes problematic.

Figure 8.3: ATN parsing of sentence (13b). Backtracking operations are not shown

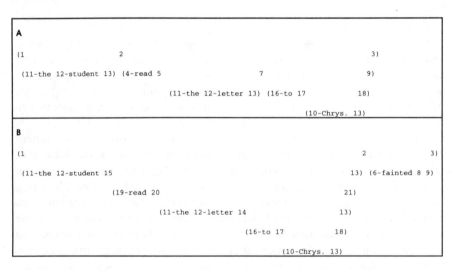

Wanner (1980) describes a general arc ordering scheme intended to account for two interpretation biases that in those days were hardly disputed: Minimal Attachment and Right Association (see also Frazier and Fodor, 1978; and Fodor and Frazier, 1980). Right Association has survived until the present day (previously it was rechristened Syntactic Recency). The Minimal Attachment principle predicts that in cases of syntactic ambiguity the structure with fewer

Figure 8.4: Minimal Attachment (a) and Non-Minimal Attachment (b,c) analyses of (13a) according to the original sample grammar of Table 8.1. The analysis shown in (d) is based on a modified sample grammar without left-recursive rules

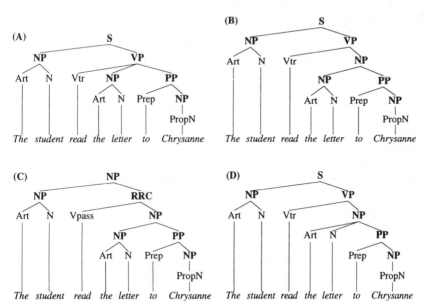

nodes will be preferred. Sentence (13a) provides an illustration. Figure 8.4a shows the Minimal Attachment analysis, with the PP attached to the VP. In Figure 8.4b, the PP modifies the object NP. The latter analysis requires one more node, thus violating Minimal Attachment. The principle also accounts for the garden-path character of (13b). Figure 8.4c shows that analyzing (13a) as a Noun Phrase, i.e., as the subject of (13b), also costs one more node than the Minimal Attachment analysis in Figure 8.4a. Wanner proposes to schedule CAT arcs before SEEK arcs, and both of these before JUMP and SEND arcs. (JUMP and SEND arcs need not be ordered because Wanner assumes they never leave the same state.) Modifying Figure 8.2 accordingly, i.e., scheduling SEEK arcs 14 and 15 in the NP subnetwork before SEND arc 13, indeed yields Right Association: *to Chrysanne* will become attached to the NP rather than to the VP (*letter to Chrysanne* instead of *read . . . to Chrysanne*). However, Wanner's proposal cannot manage with Minimal Attachment. The problem is rooted in the presence of *left-recursive* rules in the sample grammar, i.e., rewrite rules where the first symbol at the righthand side is identical to the lefthand symbol.[3] Examples are rules 4 and 5 in Table 8.1: *NP→NP PP* and *NP→NP RRC*. A straightforward conversion of rule 4 leads to the network of Figure 8.5. This ATN, however, gets easily trapped in infinite recursion. Consider a parser that consists of the ATN of Figure 8.2 with the NP subnetwork replaced by Figure 8.5. How will it deal with garden-path sentence (13c)?

Figure 8.5: ATN with left-recursion (cf., Rule 4 of Table 8.1)

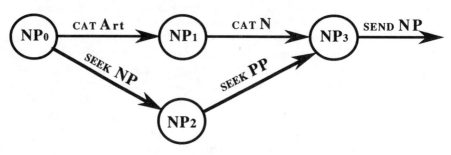

After the VP subnetwork has identified *the letter* as direct object NP, the verb *fainted* poses a problem. This triggers a backtracking operation, causing the processor to traverse the SEEK NP arc that leaves NP_0. A new instantiation of the NP net is created, which again interprets *the letter* as an NP. The parser, now in state NP_2, cannot proceed any further since *fainted* is not a preposition. Backtracking to state NP_0 now triggers another instantiation of the NP net, which falls into the same trap as its predecessor — and so on indefinitely.

The lesson to be learned from this example is to avoid left-recursion in ATNs (see also Winograd, 1983). The NP network depicted in Figure 8.2, which does not suffer from this problem, nevertheless has another drawback. It does not match rules 4 and 5 of the sample grammar. Instead, it corresponds to non-left-recursive rules (4') *NP→Art N PP+* and (5') *NP→Art N RRC+*. (The plus sign indicates that the constituent involved may occur more than once.) Now consider the alternative sample grammar that results from replacing the original rules 4 and 5 by 4' and 5'. The Minimal Attachment principle no longer predicts a preference for interpreting *to Chrysanne* as a VP rather than as an NP modifier. The two attachments cost the same number of nodes: compare Figures 8.4a and 8.4d.

The conclusion must be that Wanner's (1980) proposal cannot provide a viable account of Minimal Attachment preferences. However, from a present-day perspective this is not a serious disadvantage. Already for some time the principle is under heavy fire from experimental corners (see Mitchell, 1994). The experimental results it is supposed to cover were sometimes difficult to replicate, or can be explained on different grounds (e.g., Lexical Frame Preferences or Syntactic Frequency). The odds are that the Minimal Attachment Principle will be abandoned and its duty taken over by a combination of dynamic factors.

Successful attempts to confront ATNs with a more encompassing set of empirical data have not been reported in the literature. Probably the biggest disadvantage of ATNs is their rigid top-down control structure which leaves little room for typically bottom-up phenomena such as Lexical Frame Preferences or Syntactic Priming. Bottom-up parsing techniques are clearly gaining the upper hand.

Shift-Reduce Parsing

The technique of Shift-Reduce parsing has been developed by computer scientists in the context of parsing programming language expressions. The basic ingredients are three data structures: *input buffer, push-down stack*, and *control table*. The input buffer contains the string of words to be processed and is scanned from left to right. The stack is a linear arrangement of symbols, initially empty, which functions as a working memory for saving intermediate results. The control table is a procedural embedding of the grammar rules. It specifies which actions must be taken when certain syntactic conditions are met.

The actions decreed by the control table are of two kinds: *shifts* and *reductions*. A shift is executed by removing the leftmost word waiting in the buffer and placing it on top of the stack, thereby pushing down any other symbols residing on the stack. A reduction is like applying a grammar rule in reverse. For

Table 8.2: Control table corresponding to the sample grammar in Table 8.1

	Art	N	NP	PP	Prep	PropN	RRC	S	VP	Vintr	Vpass	Vtr	#	Chrys	fainted	letter	read	student	the	to
0	1		2			3		4						Sh, 5					Sh, 6	
1		7														Sh, 8		Sh, 9		
2			10	11		12	13	14	15	16					Sh, 17		Sh, 18			Sh, 19
3													NP		NP		NP			NP
4													†							
5													PropN		PropN		PropN			PropN
6																Art		Art		
7													NP		NP		NP			NP
8													N		N		N			N
9													N		N		N			N
10													NP		NP		NP			NP
11	1		20			3								Sh, 5					Sh, 6	
12													NP		NP		NP			NP
13													S							
14			21	11									VP							Sh, 19
15	1		22			3								Sh, 5					Sh, 6	
16	1		23			3								Sh, 5					Sh, 6	
17													Vintr							Vintr
18														Vtr Vpass					Vtr Vpass	
19														Prep					Prep	
20			10	11		12			15				PP		PP		PP Sh, 24			PP Sh, 19
21													VP							
22			10	11		12			15				RRC		RRC		RRC Sh, 24			RRC Sh, 19
23			25	11		12			15				VP				Sh, 24			Sh, 19
24														Vpass					Vpass	
25													VP NP		NP		NP			NP

example, instead of *rewriting* the symbol NP as Art N in accordance with the second rule of the sample grammar, we *reduce* the sequence Art N to NP. More precisely, if the topmost stack symbol is N and the one underneath Art, then these two are removed and replaced by the single symbol NP — the new top symbol on the stack. In terms of the rewrite rules in Table 8.1, a reduction causes one or more stack symbols which correspond with the right-hand side of a rewrite rule, to be substituted by the left-hand side of that rule. It will be clear that a reduction is a bottom-up operation.

In LR(1) parsing, a special variety of Shift-Reduce parsing, undigested input words waiting in the buffer may be referenced in addition to stack symbols. This constitutes a kind of look-ahead which helps to select the best possible next action. In LR(1) parsing, only the first word waiting in the input buffer may be inspected.

At any point in time, the fact that certain relevant events have occurred earlier during the parse is encoded by the current parser state. States are pushed onto the stack, just like the input words. The most recently assigned state on the stack counts as the current state. The action prescribed by the control table is determined by three conditions: the current state, the stack top symbol and (possibly) the look-ahead item.

Table 8.2 is a control table corresponding to the sample grammar in Table 8.1.[4] In the leftmost column, the possible states of the parser are designated by integer numbers (0–25). Their order is of no particular importance.[5] The next 12 columns (Art–Vtr) refer to the topmost symbol on the stack, the 8 rightmost columns to the first word in the input buffer (# is end of input). Cell contents indicate actions to be performed. Numbers indicate the transition from one state to the next. For example, if the parser is in state 0 and an Art is the topmost symbol on the stack, the current state is changed to 1. Syntactic categories in the cells prescribe reductions and Sh indicates a shift. If a cell contains two lines, there is a reduce-reduce or shift-reduce conflict. The dagger in row 4 means *accept*.

Table 8.3 shows how the LR(1) parser deals with example (13b). Each row corresponds to a step in the parsing process. The leftmost column represents the stack, with the top pointing to the right. The middle column shows the first few undigested words in the input buffer waiting to be processed. The rows of the right-hand column specify the action dictated by the control table in response to the configuration of stack top, stack state and look-ahead in the same row. For instance, the first row shows the parser in its initial state (#0), with an empty stack (Ø). State #0 together with the first buffer item triggers action 'Shift, →6'. (See the first cell in the *the*-column of Table 8.2. The triggering elements of the current configuration are underlined in Table 8.3.) The processor eliminates *the* from the buffer, pushes it onto the stack, and enters state #6. The effects of this action are visible in the second row of Table 8.3. Current state #6 in combination with look-ahead item *student* elicits a reduction step (Rd Art). This causes *the* to be replaced by Art, corresponding to rule 15 of the sample grammar. At the same time, the processor enters state #0 again.

The remainder of this section will deal with ambiguity, following some of the ideas expressed by Pereira (1985). The action in the tenth row of Table 8.3 shows

Table 8.3: Shift-Reduce parsing of example (13b)

Vpass.	Stack	Input Buffer	Action
	Ø-<u>0</u> <u>the</u> student read...	Shift,→6
	Ø-0 the -<u>6</u> <u>student</u> read the...	Rd Art
	Ø-<u>0</u> <u>Art</u> student read the...	→1
	Ø-0 Art-<u>1</u> <u>student</u> read the...	Shift, →9
	Ø-0 Art-1 student-<u>9</u> <u>read</u> the letter...	Rd N
	Ø-0 Art-<u>1 N</u> read the letter...	→7
	Ø-0 Art-1 N-<u>7</u> <u>read</u> the letter...	Rd NP
	Ø-<u>0</u> <u>NP</u> read the letter...	→2
	Ø-0 NP-<u>2</u> <u>read</u> the letter...	Shift,→18
	Ø-0 NP-2 read-<u>18</u> <u>the</u> letter to...	*RdVtr*/Rd Vpass
	Ø-0 NP-<u>2 Vtr</u> the letter to...	→16
	Ø-0 NP-2 Vtr-<u>16</u> <u>the</u> letter to...	Shift,→6
	Ø-0 NP-2 Vtr-16 the-<u>6</u> <u>letter</u> to Chrysanne...	Rd Art
	Ø-0 NP-2 Vtr-<u>16 Art</u> letter to Chrysanne...	→1
	Ø-0 NP-2 Vtr-16 Art-<u>1</u> <u>letter</u> to Chrysanne...	Shift,→8
	Ø-0 NP-2 Vtr-16 Art-1 letter-<u>8</u> <u>to</u> Chrysanne fainted #	Rd N
	Ø-0 NP-2 Vtr-16 Art-<u>1 N</u> to Chrysanne fainted #	→7
	Ø-0 NP-2 Vtr-16 Art-1 N-<u>7</u> <u>to</u> Chrysanne fainted #	Rd NP
	Ø-0 NP-2 Vtr-<u>16 NP</u> to Chrysanne fainted #	→23
	Ø-0 NP-2 Vtr-16 NP-<u>23</u> <u>to</u> Chrysanne fainted #	Shift,→19
	Ø-0 NP-2 Vtr-16 NP-23 to-<u>19</u> <u>Chrysanne</u> fainted #	Rd Prep
	Ø-0 NP-2 Vtr-16 NP-<u>23 Prep</u> Chrysanne fainted #	→11
	Ø-0 NP-2 Vtr-16 NP-23 Prep-<u>11</u> <u>Chrysanne</u> fainted #	Shift,→5
	Ø-0 NP-2 Vtr-16 NP-23 Prep-11 Chrysanne-<u>5</u> <u>fainted</u> #	Rd PropN
	Ø-0 NP-2 Vtr-16 NP-23 Prep-<u>11 PropN</u> fainted #	→3
	Ø-0 NP-2 Vtr-16 NP-23 Prep-11 PropN-<u>3</u> <u>fainted</u> #	Rd NP
	Ø-0 NP-2 Vtr-16 NP-23 Prep-<u>11 NP</u> fainted #	→20
	Ø-0 NP-2 Vtr-16 NP-23 Prep-11 NP-<u>20</u> <u>fainted</u> #	Rd PP
	Ø-0 NP-2 Vtr-16 NP-<u>23 PP</u> fainted #	→25
	Ø-0 NP-2 Vtr-16 NP-23 PP-<u>25</u> <u>fainted</u> #	Rd NP
	Ø-0 NP-2 Vtr-<u>16 NP</u> fainted #	→23
	Ø-0 NP-2 Vtr-16 NP-<u>23</u> <u>fainted</u> #	Fail

what happens when lexical ambiguity cannot be resolved by look-ahead. (Other cases of lexical ambiguity *are* solvable by look-ahead. For instance, *that* followed by *books* will be a subordinating conjunction rather than a demonstrative pronoun; e.g., *You know that books can be heavy*.) The word *read* is ambiguous between transitive (active) and passive verb (Vtr or Vpass), and the control table offers two possible reductions. In order to solve this reduce-reduce conflict the processor has recourse to external information, e.g., the relative frequencies of *read*'s lexical frames. I have assumed that *read* in this particular passive construction (exemplified by *the student was read the letter* rather than by *the letter was read to the student*) is less common than *read* as transitive active verb. This selects the reduction corresponding to grammar rule *Vtr→read*. This choice will turn out to have fatal consequences. The control table entry corresponding to bottom row configuration 'state #23, *fainted*' is empty, indicating parser failure. In other words, the processor has been led up the garden path.

Sentence (13a) gives rise to a happier course of events. Table 8.4 shows the parsing steps after *Chrysanne* has been shifted onto the stack. The seventh row reveals a reduce-reduce conflict, namely, between rule 10 (*VP→Vtr NP PP*) and rule 4 (*NP→NP PP*) of the sample grammar. The former replaces three stack symbols, the latter only two. Pereira (1985) recommends selecting the 'longer' option if one desires Minimal Attachment. The former reduction indeed corresponds to Figure 8.4a.

Pereira's (1985) second advice concerns shift-reduce conflicts. Consider the course of events when *read* is analyzed as a Vpass and *the letter* as an NP (Table 8.5). The control table offers a choice between shifting look-ahead item *to* onto the stack, or a reduction according to grammar rule *RRC→Vpass NP* (see last line of Table 8.5). The shift option has the advantage of yielding Right Association: the PP *to Chrysanne* will become attached as the sister of *the letter* rather than as a higher node. Pereira has shown that solving shift-reduce conflicts in favour of shifting guarantees Right Association (see also Shieber, 1983).

Control Table 8.2 contains cells that leave a choice between two or more possible actions. If the LR parser indeed explores several or all of these options in parallel or sequentially, the parser is non-deterministic. In contrast, if an LR control table does not contain a cell that specifies more than one possible action, the parser is said to be *deterministic*. Adding *conflict resolution strategies* changes a non-deterministic parser into a deterministic one. From a psycholinguistic point of view this is an attractive move because, as we have seen in the section on process control, the human syntactic processor avoids parallel (multiple-track) processing. Garden-path phenomena, however, imply that our parsing mechanism is not fully deterministic for they induce backtracking, that is, sequential exploration of alternative syntactic options. I return to this issue in the next section.

Table 8.4: Shift-Reduce parsing of example (13a): final part

Stack	Input Buffer	Action
Ø-0 NP-2 Vtr-16 NP-23 Prep-11 Chrysanne-5	#	Rd Prep
Ø-0 NP-2 Vtr-16 NP-23 Prep-11 PropN	#	→3
Ø-0 NP-2 Vtr-16 NP-23 Prep-11 PropN-3	#	Rd NP
Ø-0 NP-2 Vtr-16 NP-23 Prep-11 NP	#	→20
Ø-0 NP-2 Vtr-16 NP-23 Prep-11 NP-20	#	Rd PP
Ø-0 NP-2 Vtr-16 NP-23 PP	#	→25
Ø-0 NP-2 Vtr-16 NP-23 PP-25	#	*Rd VP*/Rd NP
Ø-0 NP-2 VP	#	→13
Ø-0 NP-2 VP-13	#	Rd S
Ø-0 S	#	→4
Ø-0 S-4	#	†

A psychological phenomenon that seems to pose a problem for Shift-Reduce parsers is *incremental* analysis. Take rule 10 of the sample grammar in Table 8.1:

Table 8.5: Shift-Reduce parsing of example (13b): correct analysis replacing the last nine steps shown in Table 8.3

Stack	Input Buffer	Action
Ø-0 NP-2 read-18	the letter to...	RD Vtr/*Rd Vpass*
Ø-0 NP-2 Vpass	the letter to...	→15
Ø-0 NP-2 Vpass-15	the letter to...	Shift,→6
Ø-0 NP-2 Vpass-15 the-6	letter to Chrysanne...	Rd Art
Ø-0 NP-2 Vpass-15 Art	letter to Chrysanne...	→1
Ø-0 NP-2 Vpass-15 Art-1	letter to Chrysanne...	Shift,→8
Ø-0 NP-2 Vpass-15 Art-1 letter-8	to Chrysanne fainted...	RD N
Ø-0 NP-2 Vpass-15 Art-1 N	to Chrysanne fainted...	→7
Ø-0 NP-2 Vpass-15 Art-1 N-7	to Chrysanne fainted...	Rd Np
Ø-0 NP-2 Vpass-15 NP	to Chrysanne fainted...	→22
Ø-0 NP-2 Vpass-15 NP-22	to Chrysanne fainted...	Rd RRC/*Shift,→19*

VP→Vtr NP PP. The corresponding reduction can be executed only after the parser has identified all three VP subconstituents. Up to that point, the constituents are just waiting on the stack while their role in the sentence structure is left undecided. An incremental parser, on the contrary, will attempt to assign every subconstituent, if not every single word, a grammatical function without delay. Abney (1989) has proposed an extension of LR(1) parsing, called Licensing-Structure parsing, intended to remedy this problem. However, this model has recently come under attack from an empirical angle (Hemforth, Konieczny and Strube, 1993). A theoretical solution to the incremental analysis problem for LR parsers has been proposed by Shieber and Johnson (1993).

PARSIFAL

Although natural language is fraught with ambiguity, and this chapter with talk about garden-paths, it is a fact that people seldom become consciously aware of having misparsed a sentence. PARSIFAL is an attempt at designing a single-track parser which fails at exactly those sentential positions where people become consciously aware of having been misled, and only then undertakes to reanalyze the sentence (backtracking). If a parse fails (presumably due to a garden-path), an external reanalysis/recovery mechanism is activated which diagnoses the situation and puts the parser back on track. In other words, PARSIFAL's design aimed at exactly mirroring the degree of determinism[6] of the human syntactic parser.

Marcus described his work on PARSIFAL in his 1977 Ph.D. dissertation, which was published in 1980. Here I can only render the bare essentials of the parser, ignoring the reanalysis component which helps it to recover from garden-paths. PARSIFAL employs a stack and condition-action rules not unlike normal Shift-Reduce parsers.[7] Its most important distinguishing feature concerns the treatment of look-ahead, which is not restricted to the first undigested input word. The input buffer is conceived of as a row of cells, and the three left-most cells are accessible for look-ahead. Initially, each cell is occupied by a single word. However, the buffer is allowed to include non-terminal symbols from the grammar, e.g., NP or VP. This is needed, for instance, in cases such as (14),

(14) a. Have the new students taken the exam today?
     b. Have the new students take the exam today.

where the processor has no way of telling whether *have* is an auxiliary or a main verb without first inspecting the verb following *the new students*. If this second verb is an infinitive, *have* is a main verb; if it is a past participle, then *have* is auxiliary. Since most native speakers of English appear to parse these sentences without being garden-pathed, the look-ahead must include *take(n)*. But the NP in-between *have* and *take(n)* is already three words long, so *take(n)* is inaccessible to the processor. Expanding the look-ahead to four or even more words does not solve the problem because the intervening NP can be arbitrarily long. Marcus' solution, in principle, amounts to activating a second instantiation of the parser, assigning it to find an NP in the remaining string, and inserting the complete NP into the first buffer cell (cf., Berwick and Weinberg, 1984, p. 280). After this intermediate operation (called *attention shifting* by Marcus), the first look-ahead item comprises the complete NP rather than its leading edge *the*; and *take(n)*, promoted to the second buffer cell, is within the processor's scope.

Although the model has attracted a great deal of attention, from an empirical point of view it was not very successful. Pritchett (1992, p. 44ff) lists some of the mismatches between predicted and observed garden-paths. Sentence (15) is short enough to fit into the input buffer but causes problems nevertheless. Similarly, in (16) the distance between *her* and *would* is small enough for the processor to decide that *her* is a personal rather than a possessive pronoun.

(15) Boys hit cry. (Boys who are hit cry.)
(16) Without her money would be hard to come by.

At the end of his book, Marcus himself admits that the size of the look-ahead buffer may vary among individuals, and a few years later the model is substantially revised so as to improve the empirical coverage (see Marcus, Hindle and Fleck, 1983). Pritchett (1992), however, points out that problems remain. Finally, as to the nature of syntactic-semantic integration, Marcus argues that deterministic parsing not only allows but even necessitates an interactive model. The condition-action rules must be sensitive to semantic and pragmatic factors if premature structure building is to be avoided. This aspect has not been implemented, however.

SAUSAGE MACHINE and Race-Based Parsing

In the late 1970s, Frazier and Fodor developed a well-known parsing model called the SAUSAGE MACHINE (see Frazier and Fodor, 1978; Fodor and Frazier, 1980). Taking this model as their point of departure, McRoy and Hirst (1990) developed a computational sentence processor called Race-Based Parsing that accounts for a considerably wider range of empirical phenomena than any of the models discussed so far. Before going into Race-Based Parsing, I first outline the essence of the SAUSAGE MACHINE.

SAUSAGE MACHINE
The SAUSAGE MACHINE consists of two cascaded parsing stages during which the same grammar is used. In Stage 1, input words are parsed, resulting in relatively simple phrases or clauses. These chunks are shunted to Stage 2 which combines them to complete sentences. Although their inputs are very different, the stages operate similarly. Their working memories are both limited to about six units (words and phrases/clauses respectively), and they abide by the same, now familiar parsing principles of Minimal Attachment and Right Association. There is no feedback from the second to the first parsing stage.

Minimal Attachment is invoked to account not only for various garden-paths such as (3) and (13b) but also for the difficulty of understanding multiple centre embedded clauses. The difficulty of (17) is supposed to stem from a tendency to interpret the initial NPs as a coordination (*The woman, the man, the girl, and...*).

(17)   The woman the man the girl loved met died.

An attractive feature of the SAUSAGE MACHINE is its capability to explain certain interactions between the parsing principles. For instance, in the preferred interpretation of (18a), the final PP is attached to the VP rather than to the NP. This preference is reversed in (18b).

(18)   a.   John read the letter to Mary.
       b.   John read the note, the memo and the letter to Mary.

The reason is that the words of (18a) fit into the working memory of Stage 1, which therefore can parse the sentence as a whole while satisfying the principle of Minimal Attachment. But (18b) is too long. The first stage only sees *John read the note, the memo*, parses this as a clause, and shunts it to Stage 2. Spotting then *and the letter to Mary*, Stage 1 can only parse this fragment as a single NP because the verb *read* is out of sight. Stage 2 accepts this input and appends it unchanged to the clause received earlier. Notice that this course of events presupposes the assumption of determinism.

Frazier and Fodor (1978) provide few details concerning the style of parsing employed by their SAUSAGE MACHINE. They suggest that the attachment of an incoming lexical item depends on the outcome of a *race*. In particular, the processor explores in parallel various ways of relating the new item to the already existing structure, and the first alternative meeting with success is favoured. A mechanism of this sort could be responsible for the Minimal Attachment preferences. Non-minimal attachment requires accessing more grammar rules, which presumably takes more time.

The assumption of parallel computing involved here does not contradict the notion of bounded parallelism that has been previously advocated as a plausible form of process control in the human syntactic processor. This is because, after the winner of a race has been selected, all its competitors are thrown away. It may be useful to introduce a distinction between *local* and *global* parallelism. The latter involves parallel exploration of alternative attachments of individual input items without choosing a winner and destroying the losers. That is, some or all of the alternative analyses are kept until the end of the sentence or a disambiguation point has been reached. Local parallelism means that one of the explored attachment alternatives is selected as best, at least provisionally, and all traces of the competitors are removed.

Race-Based Parsing

McRoy and Hirst (1990) adopted the basic idea of processing races in a modified form. For each of the attachment alternatives they calculate a *time cost*, and the winning (cheapest, fastest) one will the guide further processing. Furthermore, time cost not only depends on number of grammar rules involved in an attachment. Other cost determining factors are Priming, Distance (Right Association or Recency), Lexical Frame Preferences and Semantic Preferences. The resulting architecture is interactive in the sense of the section on process control.

The central component of the Race-Based Parser is the *Attachment Processor*. Consulted by Stage 1 or Stage 2 to suggest a suitable attachment point for a new item (a word or a phrase/clause), it calls on syntactic, semantic/pragmatic and lexical procedures (so-called hypothesizers) to suggest possible alternatives and their associated time costs, and commands tree formation routines to actually carry out the lowest-cost attachment.

McRoy and Hirst (1990) illustrate their model by tracing through the processing of sentence (13a). From their account, I select the steps which are of greatest interest in the present context. The sentence is short enough to be fully processed by Stage 1. When *read* is processed, the lexicon suggests both the Vtr and the Vpass options. One of the hypothesizers reports that the latter option will be more costly because building a reduced relative clause takes more time than a finite clause (six versus three cost units; the authors admit that the numbers are somewhat arbitrary). Attaching *read* as a transitive verb leads the parser to predict an object NP. This expectation is fulfilled by the next word. The article *the* is attached to the tree, thereby creating the expectation of a noun. After *letter* has been attached accordingly, the highly ambiguous *to* is considered next. The option of *to* as a complementizer (e.g. . . . *to pass the time*) is very expensive (eleven units). For the preposition *to*, the hypothesizers offer various possibilities: as a modifier to *letter* (four units), as a modifier to *read* (eleven units; the distance to *read* is larger than to *letter*), and as the indirect object. The latter option has a time cost of only three units because it fulfils *read*'s semantic expectation of a Beneficiary argument. The end result is a parse which conforms to the preferred interpretation of (13a). Incidentally, notice that the choice in favour of the VP rather than the NP attachment was not dictated by Minimal Attachment in the original sense but by expectations raised by lexical frame information.

I cannot go into further detail of the time cost calculations or the actual implementation. The outline presented here suffices to show that Race-Based Parsing, given appropriate time cost functions, in principle can account for psycholinguistic phenomena related to syntactic recency, semantic-syntactic interaction, priming, and lexical frame preferences. The two latter effects are simulated by allotting fewer time cost units to, respectively, recently processed constructions and preferred lexical frames. Moreover, unlike any of the previous models, the implementation includes a rudimentary revision component which allows recovery from mild parsing failures.

However, the model's basic architecture is at variance with MacDonald, Just and Carpenter's (1992) finding concerning lexical frame ambiguity, discussed previously in the context of examples (3) and (4). In terms of example (13a), input item *read* will lead to the selection of either the Vtr or the Vpass option; the fact that this word has two entries in the lexicon rather than one, does not slow down the parallel exploration of attachment alternatives. Nor does it affect the complexity of subsequent processing because the traces of the losing option are immediately erased. Saving losing options would go against the grain of the overall architecture and its source of inspiration, the SAUSAGE MACHINE.

The UNIFICATION SPACE

The UNIFICATION SPACE model, proposed by Kempen and Vosse (1989; see also Vosse and Kempen, 1991), proceeds from a chemical synthesis metaphor. The molecules entering into bonds are lexical trees with nodes as potential attachment points. For every word of the language the lexicon specifies at least one lexical tree, each having one or more attachment points (see Figure 8.6). Two trees dominating different words of a sentence may combine into a larger tree by merging attachment points, a process called unification (Figure 8.7). The selection proceeds on a probabilistic basis. The unification probabilities p(U) between two nodes depend on various lexical, syntactic and semantic/pragmatic factors: certain node pairs make better unification partners than others. The determinants of 'goodness-of-fit' are summarized in one variable called *Strength*. Probabilities p(U) correlate positively with Strength.

In contrast with the foregoing models, attachments may break up, that is,

Figure 8.6: Lexical trees corresponding to the words of examples (13a,b). Attachment points are printed in bold

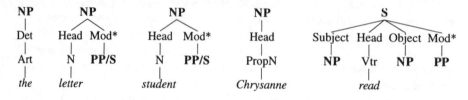

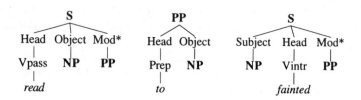

Figure 8.7: Two possible unifications of some of the lexical frames of Figure 8.6

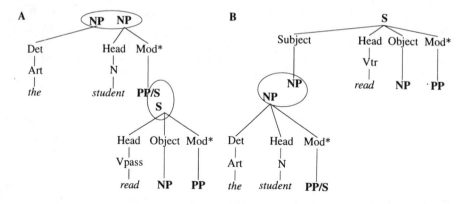

unifications may be cancelled so that the nodes become available for other, possibly stronger unifications. Break-up probabilities p(B) correlate negatively with Strength. It follows that candidates forming a good partnership are more likely to unify and less likely to break up: the stronger a unification, the longer it will survive. The consequence is that, as time proceeds, more and more nodes will find a strong and stable unification partner, and more and more lexical trees will cluster together. As soon as this search/optimization process has settled down, the sentence has been parsed. If the result is a tree that spans the whole sentence, the parse is successful. In fact, the model delivers at most one such tree for a grammatical sentence, in accordance with the characteristic of single-track processing. Parsing has failed if the result consists of several disconnected trees, each dominating only part of the sentence. Ideas from Simulated Annealing (see Chapter 3), a thermodynamic optimization technique, are used to improve the likelihood of obtaining fully connected trees for sentences of varying length and grammatical composition.

As shown in Figure 8.6, there is a tree for every lexical frame associated with a word. The root and the non-lexical terminals of a tree are attachment points. An asterisk on a Modifier node indicates that this node and the branch it belongs to may occur zero or more times. Only identically labelled nodes are allowed to unify, e.g., the roots of the trees for *the* and *student*, or the S nodes that dominate Vpass and modify *student*, respectively. As to the concept of unification, Kempen and Vosse (1989) use a non-recursive form of feature unification; one of its duties is to check agreement (number, person, gender, etc.) between unification partners.

It is important to note that all rules of syntax are encoded in the lexical trees and the unification operation. The Segment Grammar formalism adopted in the UNIFICATION SPACE model (for some details see Chapters 2 and 11) therefore belongs to the class of *lexicalized* grammars together with, e.g., Tree Adjoining Grammar (cf., Rambow and Joshi, 1994).

While input words are read from the buffer one by one, the lexical tree(s) associated with each of them enter(s) the UNIFICATION SPACE (U-SPACE for short). The 'free' nodes (attachment points) start hunting for suitable unification partners without delay. However, due to the probabilities p(U) and p(B), the attachments may never be considered final. The possibility of a break-up always lurks as long as the process has not come to a halt.

The dynamics of the model depend to a large extent on the level of *activation* of syntactic nodes.[8] Upon entry into U-SPACE, every node of a lexical tree is assigned an activation level. The entry levels correlate positively with frequency in the language and with the language users' preference (if that is something different). Activation is supposed to decrease by a constant fraction per time unit (the *decay* parameter). Activation has a strong positive influence on probabilities p(U). This causes the more active nodes to be the more likely unification partners. In other words, active nodes are more avid explorers of the search space. However, due to the unremitting decay of activation levels, the avidity of all nodes is bound to decrease and the system will come to rest.

Empirical predictions are derivable from average parsing times and proportions of successful parses when a sentence is presented to the model many times (Monte Carlo simulation method). Input sentences that consume more processing cycles or give rise to more parsing failures, are predicted to be harder to understand for human language users. The model's interpretive biases reveal themselves in the alternative parse trees delivered during a Monte Carlo run: preferred analyses will turn up in greater proportions. Kempen and Vosse (1989) report successful simulations of an interesting range of psycholinguistic phenomena. The Syntactic Recency effect follows from the higher levels of activation of more recently launched lexical trees. Lexical Frame Preferences and

Syntactic Priming are modelled in terms of varying entry level activations. The garden-path character of example (13b) results from the low frequency of *read* occurring in that particular lexical frame. The comprehensibility ranking of three types of embedded clause (cf., examples 15a,b,c) was 'pre'dicted correctly. The U-SPACE belongs to the class of interactive models due to the semantic/pragmatic contribution to the Strength parameter.

Notwithstanding these successes, various problems remain to be solved. For instance, constituent length effects do not fit into the 1989 version of the model nor do the syntactic frequency phenomena reported by Cuetos and Mitchell (1988).

Conclusions and Outlook

A fair conclusion from the preceding survey of syntactic processing models is that the gulf between requirements and achievements, although slowly and steadily narrowing down, is still looming large. Neither the experimentalists nor the modellers are to be blamed for this. The models were under construction *while* the empirical domain was being opened up through increasingly sophisticated machinery so that, of necessity, they have been aiming at moving targets.

Recent developments are the discovery that syntactic processing problems and preferences are sensitive to statistical factors, and the spread of dynamic modelling techniques in the wake of connectionist successes. Since statistical trends are readily expressible in dynamic terms, one may expect a keen interest of experimentalists in dynamic modelling of human syntactic processing. Another reason why dynamic models may hold great attraction for experimental psycholinguists is the *graded* nature of their empirical predictions, as opposed to merely *all-or-none* (binary) predictions allowed by most structural models. Examples of dynamic models are not only Race-based Parsing and the UNIFICATION SPACE but also more recent neural network models (e.g., Stevenson, 1993a, 1993b; Henderson, 1992).

Dynamic/stochastic models are not without danger, though. Because they tend to contain quite a few numerical parameters, they run the risk of losing predictive power in as far as their behaviour is potentially tweaked to any desired pattern. They may also fail to meet linguistic demands with respect to descriptive or explanatory power. To my judgment, none of these dangers is threatening the dynamic models described or quoted in this chapter; they are firmly rooted in modern syntactic theory.

What will be the main concerns of computational modellers in the years to come? Central topics will undoubtedly include the design of computational architectures that account for semantic-syntactic interactions and for statistical effects in empirically justifiable ways. The behaviour of these systems should be tested in the context of considerably larger grammars and lexica than the toy versions that current models have to make do with. Another topic — of utmost importance but hardly explored — is the relation between syntactic processes in sentence comprehension and those in sentence *production*. Finally, it is my personal conviction that progress in these areas presupposes a multidisciplinary research setting with combined experimental-psychological, computational and linguistic expertise.

Notes

1   This sentence is ambiguous: *to Chrysanne* can modify either *read* or *the letter*.
2   The verb *read* in (13b,c) opens a reduced relative clause (RRC; cf., *The student who was read the letter, fainted*). I disregard the semantically odd analysis of *the letter (to Chrysanne) fainted* as an object complement clause (*The student read that the letter fainted*).
3   For a more general definition of left-recursion see, e.g., Aho and Ullman (1972).
4   Algorithms for converting a grammar to a control table are discussed by Aho and Ullman (1972).
5   The numbers are assigned by the algorithm that constructs the control table. There is no relationship between these numbers and those on the ATN arcs in Figure 8.2.
6   If the reanalysis/recovery component is not considered to belong to the parsing mechanism proper, PARSIFAL may be said to be fully deterministic.
7   Although PARSIFAL is an independent development, Berwick and Weinberg (1984, p. 185ff.) have shown that it may be viewed as a special kind of Shift-Reduce parser. I will follow their lead.
8   For a characterization of activation-based models, see Chapter 3.

References

ABNEY, S. P. (1989) 'A computational model of human parsing', *Journal of Psycholinguistic Research*, 18, pp. 129–44.

AHO, A. and ULLMAN, J. (1972) *The Theory of Parsing, Translation and Compiling*, Englewood Cliffs, NJ: Prentice-Hall.

ALTMANN, G. T. M., GARNHAM, A. and DENNIS, Y. (1992) 'Avoiding the garden-path: Eye movements in context', *Journal of Memory and Language*, 31, pp. 685–712.

BACH, E., BROWN, C. and MARSLEN-WILSON, W. (1986) 'Crossed and nested dependencies in German and Dutch: A psycholinguistic study', *Language and Cognitive Processes*, 4, pp. 249–62.

BERWICK, R. C. and WEINBERG, A. S. (1984) *The Grammatical Basis of Linguistic Performance*, Cambridge, MA: MIT Press.

BRITT, M. A. (1994) 'The interaction of referential ambiguity and argument structure in the parsing of prepositional phrases', *Journal of Memory and Language*, 33, pp. 251–83.

CLIFTON, C., FRAZIER, L. and CONNINE, C. (1984) 'Lexical expectations in sentence comprehension', *Journal of Verbal Learning and Verbal Behavior*, 23, pp. 696–708.

CRAIN, S. and STEEDMAN, M. (1985) 'On not being led up the garden path: The use of context by the psychological syntax processor', in DOWTY, D., KARTTUNEN, L. and ZWICKY, A. (Eds) *Natural Language Parsing: Psychological, Computational, and Theoretical Perspectives*, Cambridge: Cambridge University Press.

CUETOS, F. and MITCHELL, D. C. (1988) 'Cross-linguistic differences in parsing: Restrictions on the use of the Late Closure strategy in Spanish', *Cognition*, 30, pp. 73–105.

CUETOS, F., MITCHELL, D. C. and CORLEY, M. M. B. (in press) 'Parsing in different languages', in CARREIRAS, M., GARCIA-ALBEA, J. and SEBASTIAN-GALLES, N. (Eds) *Language Processing in Spanish*, Hillsdale, NJ: Lawrence Erlbaum.

FODOR, J. D. (1989) 'Empty categories in sentence processing', *Language and Cognitive Processes*, 4, pp. 155–209.

FODOR, J. D. and FRAZIER, L. (1980) 'Is the human sentence parsing mechanism an ATN?', *Cognition*, 8, pp. 417–59.

FRAZIER, L. (1978) *On Comprehending Sentences: Syntactic Parsing Strategies*, Unpublished Doctoral Dissertation, University of Connecticut.

FRAZIER, L. and FLORES D'ARCAIS, G. B. (1989) 'Filler driven parsing: A study of gap filling in Dutch', *Journal of Memory and Language*, 28, pp. 331–44.

FRAZIER, L. and FODOR, J. D. (1978) 'The SAUSAGE MACHINE: A new two-stage parsing model', *Cognition*, 6, pp. 291–325.

FRAZIER, L. and RAYNER, K. (1982) 'Making and correcting errors during sentence comprehension: Eye movements in the analysis of structurally ambiguous sentences', *Cognitive Psychology*, 14, pp. 178–210.

FRAZIER, L., TAFT, L., ROEPER, T., CLIFTON, C. and EHRLICH, K. (1984) 'Parallel structure: A source of facilitation in sentence comprehension', *Memory and Cognition*, 12, pp. 421–30.

GARRETT, M. F. (1990) 'Sentence processing', in OSHERSON, D. N. and LASNIK, H. (Eds) *An Invitation to Cognitive Science*, Cambridge, MA: MIT Press.

GIBSON, E. (1990) 'Recency preference and garden-path effects', in *Proceedings of the 12th Cognitive Science Society*.

GIBSON, E. and LOOMIS, J. (1994) 'A corpus analysis of recency preference and predicate promixity', in *Proceedings of the 16th Annual Conference of the Cognitive Science Society*, Hillsdale, NJ: Lawrence Erlbaum.

GORRELL, P. (1991) 'Subcategorization and sentence processing', in BERWICK, R. C., ABNEY, S. P. and TENNY, C. (Eds) *Principle-Based Parsing: Computation and Psycholinguistics*, Dordrecht: Kluwer Academic Publishers.

HEMFORTH, B., KONIECZNY, L. and STRUBE, G. (1993) 'Incremental syntax processing and parsing strategies', in *Proceedings of the 15th Annual Conference of the Cognitive Science Society*, Hillsdale, NJ: Lawrence Erlbaum.

HENDERSON, J. (1992) 'A connectionist parser for stucture unification grammar', in *Proceedings of the 30th Annual Meeting of the Association for Computational Linguistics*.

KAPLAN, R. M. (1972) 'Augmented transition networks as psychological models of sentence comprehension', *Artificial Intelligence*, 3, pp. 77–100.

KAPLAN, R. M. (1975) 'On process models for sentence analysis', in NORMAN, D. A., RUMELHART, D. E. and the LNR RESEARCH GROUP (Eds) *Explorations in Cognition*, San Francisco, CA: Freeman.

KEMPEN, G. and VOSSE, Th. (1989) 'Incremental syntactic tree formation in human sentence processing: A cognitive architecture based on activation decay and simulated annealing, *Connection Science*, 1, pp. 273–90.

KIMBALL, J. (1973) 'Seven principles of surface structure parsing in natural language', *Cognition*, 2, pp. 15–47.

MacDONALD, M. C., JUST, M. A. and CARPENTER, P. A. (1992) 'Working memory constraints on the processing of syntactic ambiguity', *Cognitive Psychology*, 24, pp. 56–98.

MARCUS, M.P. (1980) *A Theory of Syntactic Recognition for Natural Language*, Cambridge, MA: MIT Press.

MARCUS, M.P., HINDLE, D. and FLECK, M.M. (1983) 'D-Theory: Talking about talking about trees', in *Proceedings of the 21st Annual Meeting of the Association for Computational Linguistics*.

McROY, S.W. and HIRST, G. (1990) 'Race-based parsing and syntactic disambiguation', *Cognitive Science*, 14, pp. 313–53.

MITCHELL, D.C. (1987) 'Lexical guidance in human parsing: Locus and processing characteristics', in COLTHEART, M. (Ed) *Attention and Performance XII: The Psychology of Reading*, Hillsdale, NJ: Lawrence Erlbaum.

MITCHELL, D.C. (1994) 'Sentence parsing', in GERNSBACHER, M.A. (Ed) *Handbook of Psycholinguistics*, San Diego, CA: Academic Press.

PEREIRA, F.C.N. (1985) 'A new characterization of attachment processes', in DOWTY, D.R., KARTTUNEN, L. and ZWICKY, A.M. (Eds) *Natural Language Parsing: Psychological, Computational, and Theoretical Perspectives*, Cambridge: Cambridge University Press.

PICKERING, M. and BARRY, G. (1991) 'Sentence processing without empty categories', *Language and Cognitive Processes*, 6, pp. 229–59.

PRITCHETT, B.L. (1992) *Grammatical Competence and Parsing Performance*, Chicago: University of Chicago Press.

RAMBOW, O. and JOHSI, A. (1994) 'A processing model for free word-order languages', in CLIFTON, C., FRAZIER, L. and RAYNER, K. (Eds) *Perspectives on Sentence Processing*, Hillsdale, NJ: Lawrence Erlbaum, pp. 267–301.

RAYNER, K. GARROD, S. and PERFETTI, C.A. (1992) 'Discourse influences during parsing are delayed', *Cognition*, 45, pp. 109–39.

RAYNER, K. PACHT, J.M. and DUFFY, S.A. (1994) 'Effects of prior encounter and global discourse bias on the processing of lexically ambiguous words: Evidence from eye fixations', *Journal of Memory and Language*, 33, pp. 527–44.

SCHUSTER, S. and MACDONALD, M.C. (1994) 'Syntactic priming and syntactic ambiguity resolution', Poster presented at the Seventh CUNY Conference on Human Sentence Processing, New York.

SHAPIRO, L.S., NAGEL, H.N. and LEVINE, B.A. (1993) 'Preferences for a verb's complements and their use in sentence processing', *Journal of Memory and Language*, 32, pp. 96–114.

SHIEBER, S.M. (1983) 'Sentence disambiguation by a shift-reduce parsing technique', in *Proceedings of the 21st Annual Meeting of the Association for Computational Linguistics*.

SHIEBER, S. and JOHNSON, M. (1993) 'Variations on incremental interpretation', *Journal of Psycholinguistic Research*, 22, pp. 287–318.

STEVENSON, S. (1993a) 'A competition-based explanation of syntactic attachment preferences and garden path phenomena', in *Proceedings of the 31st Annual Meeting of the Association for Computational Linguistics*.

STEVENSON, S. (1993b) 'Establishing long-distance dependencies in a hybrid network model of human parsing', in *Proceedings of the 15th Annual Conference of the Cognitive Science Society*, Hillsdale, NJ: Lawrence Erlbaum.

SWINNEY, D.A. (1979) 'Lexical access during sentence comprehension: (Re)consideration of context effects', *Journal of Verbal Learning and Verbal Behavior*, 18, pp. 654–60.

TARABAN, R. and MCCLELLAND, J.L. (1988) 'Constituent attachment and thematic role assignment in sentence processing: Influences of content-based expectations', *Journal of Memory and Language*, 27, pp. 597–632.

TRUESWELL, J.C., TANENHAUS, M.K. and GARNSEY, S.M. (1994) 'Semantic influences on parsing: Use of thematic role information in syntactic ambiguity resolution', *Journal of Memory and Language*, 33, pp. 285–318.

VOSSE, Th. and KEMPEN, G. (1991) 'A hybrid model of human sentence processing: Parsing right-branching, center-embedded and cross-serial dependencies', in *Proceedings of the Second International Workshop on Parsing Technologies*.

WANNER, E. (1980) 'The ATN and the SAUSAGE MACHINE: Which one is baloney?', *Cognition*, 8, pp. 209–25.

WINOGRAD, T. (1983) *Language as a Cognitive Process: Volume I. Syntax*, Reading, MA: Addison-Wesley.

Chapter 9

Discourse Comprehension Models
Alan Garnham

Introduction

In ordinary language comprehension, computation of the syntactic structure of sentences is never an end in itself, but part of the process of deriving meaning. Furthermore, the meanings of the individual sentences of a text or discourse[1] must be combined, incrementally, to determine what the speaker or writer wishes to convey. The processes that derive the meanings of individual sentences (or utterances) and combine them into a whole must take account of their (linguistic and nonlinguistic) context, and must often make use of relevant background knowledge.

In the first two decades of modern psycholinguistics, to about 1980, there was considerable unclarity about the nature and goals of discourse comprehension. A clear account of the scope of semantics and of the difference between semantics, pragmatics and world knowledge was lacking. Consequently, it is hardly surprising that claims about *semantic interpretation* and the construction of *semantic representations* were confusing, or worse. In David Marr's (1982) terms, psycholinguists did not have a *computational theory* of discourse comprehension.

This problem has to some extent been solved by the notion of *mental models* (Johnson-Laird, 1980, 1983; Garnham, 1987) of which mental models of discourse, or *discourse models* (Johnson-Laird and Garnham, 1980; see also, Stenning, 1978; Webber, 1979), are a special case. People talk and write about things in the real world, or sometimes in an imaginary world. They often talk about specific situations, though they may talk about more abstract matters. Thus, the representations that they construct during comprehension are representations of bits of the world, not representations of the text itself. In addition, the discourse model constructed by one participant has to include (at least partial) models of the other participants, so that, for example, the appropriate referring expressions can be chosen (Johnson-Laird and Garnham, 1980). Suppose someone has read the entertainments page in today's newspaper, and I ask:

Are you interested in seeing the film showing at the Gaumont?

I can expect them to give a specific interpretation to the definite noun phrase *the film showing at the Gaumont*, because they know I'm talking about *Duck Soup*, say. Another person might give the definite description only, what Donnellan (1966) called an *attributive* interpretation (*the film showing at the Gaumont, whatever it is*). However, although the broader notion of a discourse model is needed in a complete theory of comprehension, research has focused mostly on the mental representation of situations that texts are about, and not on the other participants' beliefs.

The notion of a discourse model is most obviously applicable to the comprehension of narrative or descriptive texts about concrete situations. In such cases the things represented are people, objects, places, times and so on, and relations between them, including those that arise from their participation in events, actions, states and processes. Crucially, the things represented are, for example, objects, and not words used to describe objects, or general concepts that objects fall under. So, a definite description such as *the scissors* will be interpreted as referring to an entity represented in the discourse model. The relation between this representation in this particular discourse model and the more permanent mental representations of words (such as *scissors*), and their corresponding general concepts, is not well understood, and leads to complications in interpreting the results of certain kinds of experiment. For example, what is the relation between a pair of scissors being represented in a discourse model and a response to the word *scissors* in a priming experiment? It has often been assumed that speeded responding to a word indicates that some entity not explicitly mentioned in a text has been encoded into a model. For example, speeded response to *scissors* following *The woman cut the paper* might suggest that the implicit instrument, a pair of scissors, has been encoded into the discourse model. However, since the scissors in the model are a representation of an object, whereas the subjects' task is to respond to a word, this conclusion is unsafe.

In abstract texts the distinction between a general concept and things that fall under it is only sometimes relevant. For example, in a text about Tahitians, a reference to *their religion* refers to a specific example of the abstract concept of religion. But a text may be about religion in general, and may refer to that abstract concept. The same is true in concrete domains — we can talk about cars in general as well as about particular cars. Nevertheless, even when the discussion is general, the notion of a discourse model is still applicable. Abstract texts are about abstract domains, and relations between abstract entities are independent of particular attempts to describe them.

In an account of discourse comprehension, we need to take seriously Marr's notion that a computational theory specifies the (mathematical) function, or input-output mapping, that a cognitive system computes. To specify a function, it is necessary to characterize its inputs and outputs. The output of the comprehension system is a discourse model, together with a specification of the role that the model should play for the speaker (e.g., providing information, or representing an action that might be performed). It is hard to give a definitive account of the representations that the discourse comprehension system produces. However, specifying the input to the discourse model construction system is even more difficult, for two reasons. First, the unit of input is not clear. For example, there is evidence for both word-by-word incremental processing (e.g., Marslen-Wilson, 1975) and for end-of-sentence wrap-up effects (e.g., Mitchell and Green, 1978). Different aspects of discourse models may be computed from linguistic units of different sizes. Second, particularly for spoken language, the input is noisy. It contains, pauses, hesitations, false starts, slips of the tongue, and so on. Whether the input is 'cleaned up' by a preprocessor, or whether what appears to be noise is, in fact, an aid to interpretation remains to be clarified (Smith and Clark, 1993).

Psycholinguistic Investigations of Discourse Comprehension

The broad characterization of discourse comprehension given above was derived primarily from a priori considerations. However, a theory of discourse comprehension must also account for a variety of empirical phenomena. In particular, it must specify the details of the processes that combine information that is explicit in the text with general and specific information about the world, the context in which spoken discourse is understood, and the pictures, diagrams and tables that accompany written text. This section outlines some of the most important of these phenomena.

Representations Constructed in Discourse Comprehension

Before the notion of a discourse model was developed, it was often claimed that texts were represented by structured sets of propositions. Although there are many different notions of *propositional representation*, most psycholinguists have assumed that such representations reflect the linguistic structure of the text. However, while empirical findings show that readers and listeners construct short-lived representations of form, such representations need not be identified with propositional representations. On the one hand they contain information, for example, about the location of information on the page, which is not propositional in the standard psycholinguistic sense. Indeed, such superficial representations contain many types of information. On the other hand, there are serious problems in explaining how propositions can be extracted from text and how they can represent meaning (see e.g., Garnham, Oakhill and Johnson-Laird, 1982).

It is relatively easy to demonstrate that the representation of a text does not reflect its superficial form, particularly in the spatial domain. For example, early work on memory for one-dimensional spatial arrays described by sentences such as *The lion is to the left of the bear; the bear is to the left of the moose* (e.g., Potts, 1974) showed that the structure of an array's representation corresponds to that of the array itself rather than that of the sentences used to describe it. Similar findings have been obtained with 2-dimensional arrays (Ehrlich and Johnson-Laird, 1982; Mani and Johnson-Laird, 1982). Many other studies also show that spatial relations are encoded in a way that cannot be explained in terms of the sentences that express them (e.g., Glenberg, Meyer and Lindem, 1987; Morrow, Greenspan and Bower, 1987; Franklin and Tversky, 1990; Bryant, Tversky and Franklin, 1992). Such findings appear to suggest that spatial relations are represented *analogically*, or even that spatial mental models are *image-like*. However, detailed consideration of the findings shows that the second of these ideas is incorrect, and that the first must be treated with caution. Spatial mental models, unlike images, need not have a perspective built into them (Franklin and Tversky, 1990), and they almost certainly do not reflect the 3-dimensional Euclidean geometry of space.

Inference

Texts do not contain complete information about the situations they describe. More importantly, they do not always contain enough explicit information for the reader or listener to form a coherent representation of the relevant situation. In such cases, *bridging inferences* (Clark, 1977), or other inferences necessary for a coherent interpretation, must be made if the text is to be properly understood. In other cases, information not stated in the text may be so obvious that it is encoded into a mental representation of the events described, even if it is not needed to establish coherence. For example, if people eating dinner cut their food, they are almost certainly using knives, even if that fact is not stated.

These observations lead to questions about when and how extratextual information is combined with information from the text itself in order to create a mental model. Answering these questions is complicated by the fact that people read, and listen, for different reasons. Sometimes they may fail to interpret a text coherently, and yet still fulfil their goals — if they are seeking a particular piece of information, for example. At other times they may undertake detailed textual analysis. Nevertheless, it is plausible to postulate a common mode of reading in which inferences needed to interpret a text coherently, and those that require only a minimal amount of effort, are made. There are several ways an inference might be made with little or no effort. The mental representation of the meanings of individual words can be complex, and using those representations to build sentence meanings might bring inferences for free. For example, Garnham and

Oakhill (1988, pp. 733–4) suggested that a mental model of dressing automatically includes clothes. Thus, *The clothes were made of pink wool* is read as quickly after *dressing the baby* has been mentioned as after an explicit mention of the clothes (Garrod and Sanford, 1981; but see Sanford and Garrod, 1981, pp. 103–5, for a slightly different interpretation).

The spatial domain provides another illustration of how inferences might be a by-product of constructing a representation. When spatial relations between a set of items are described, those relations not explicitly mentioned are represented in the same way as those that are. Thus, in Potts' (1974) work on one-dimensional arrays, relations that were not mentioned, but which were easy to read off an array-like representation (because the objects were well-separated) were verified more quickly than relations that were explicitly mentioned, but which were harder to read from the array. The phenomenon of *noticing* (Glenberg and Langston, 1992) similarly indicates 'free' inferencing. Relations between objects that are close together are more readily available that those between distant objects, even when the objects were never mentioned together.

Apart from inferences that come for free because of the way representations are constructed, it is difficult to find unequivocal evidence for inferences that do not contribute to the coherent interpretation of texts. Even inferences to highly probable case-fillers (e.g., spoons as instruments for stirring coffee) may not be routinely made.[2] Thus, the idea that inferences not necessary for coherence are made, if the relevant background knowledge is readily available, has to be treated with caution. If the knowledge that spoons are used to stir coffee is not readily available, the term *readily available* is being used in a technical sense, and independent criteria are needed for determining when information is readily available.

Inferences needed to establish a coherent representation of a text are almost certainly made routinely (Haviland and Clark, 1974, and many subsequent studies). And, except in the cases discussed above where they come for free, they take time, and they are made in a backwards direction, only when both pieces of information to be integrated have been read. This idea is consistent with the notion that few, if any, elaborative inferences are made. If elaborative inferences were computed, backwards bridging inferences would not be necessary to link together pieces of information in the text. For example, if a spoon was inferred as the instrument of:

John stirred the coffee.

it would be available as the referent of *the spoon* in:

The spoon was dirty and tainted it.

and no bridging inference would be needed.

Understanding Anaphoric Expressions

Many links between pieces of information in a text are local — they connect adjacent or near adjacent clauses. One of the principal devices indicating such links is anaphora (pronouns, ellipses, etc.). Anaphoric expressions are typically shorter than the fuller expressions that they replace, but their interpretation is more complex. For example, in:

I met a man at the conference.

He told me about a new theory of discourse comprehension.

He is considerably shorter than *the man I met at the conference*, yet it maps much less directly onto the earlier part of the sentence. However, fuller expressions are often cumbersome, or even unacceptable, so the brevity of anaphors must compensate for complications in interpreting them.

The interpretation of anaphors sometimes depends on inference. For example, in:

John lent a hamper to Bill because he was organizing a picnic.

knowledge about picnics and hampers, and about lending, determines that *he* in the second clause refers to Bill. However, in the similar sentence:

Sue lent a hamper to Bill because he was organizing a picnic.

the gender of the pronoun is sufficient. The matching of *he* and Bill can be described as an inference. It depends on knowledge about the names Sue and Bill — that one is given to females and the other to males. However, a more complex inference is needed to resolve the pronoun in the gender ambiguous version of the sentence, and under some circumstances it takes longer (see e.g., Garnham, Oakhill and Cruttenden, 1992).

Anaphoric expressions do not always *refer* to something that has been mentioned, or that is salient in the context. Definite pronouns standardly do (e.g., *he* in the sentences above refers to Bill, mentioned in the first clause). Other pronouns, such as *one* refer to an item of the same kind as one already mentioned.

I like Sue's dress and I want one for Christmas.

Anaphors can be classified in another way. Some, definite and indefinite pronouns for example, take their meaning from a representation of a situation. It does not matter whether what they refer to has already been mentioned. Others, the ellipses proper, are devices for avoiding repetition, and get their meaning indirectly by being linked to another (usually preceding) piece of text (Sag and

Hankamer, 1984). This distinction is linguistically straightforward. It does not, however, translate simply into a psychological theory of anaphoric processing (see Garnham and Oakhill, 1987, 1989; Carreiras, Garnham and Oakhill, 1993).

Global Links

In addition to local links established by anaphora and other devices, there are global links that may not depend directly on local ones. For example, the first part of a story may set out the main character's goal, and subsequent parts may detail attempts to fulfil that goal. In addition, the point of a story may require the story's content to be related to something outside itself. Texts have not been properly understood until these internal and external relations have been computed. Nevertheless, such relations may not be computed as a matter of course in normal reading. A reader may, for example, miss the point of an allegory, or have to work hard to find it, engaging in problem solving rather than straightforward discourse comprehension.

It is likely that readers compute relations between, for example, characters' goals and attempts to fulfil them, even when those relations are not explicitly signalled locally. Indeed, texts with clear overall structure are easier to understand than those that lack it (Garnham, Oakhill and Johnson-Laird, 1982). One view is that readers have special knowledge about types of text — grammars or schemas to which texts of particular types conform. An alternative view (Garnham, 1983, 1991) is that most of the structure in texts reflects structure in what the texts are about, and that sensitivity to this structure is another instance of the use of background knowledge in comprehension.

Nonliteral Meaning

In some kinds of discourse, academic journal articles for example, the information the speaker or writer intends to convey is straightforwardly related to the literal meaning. The work of Paul Grice (1975) brought to psycholinguists' attention the fact that such cases are atypical. In one of Grice's best known examples, a statement about an establishment's location:

There's a filling station round the corner.

communicates to someone standing by a car that is out of fuel where some can be bought. The process of *conversational implicature*, which constructs intended meaning from literal meaning, is a central aspect of discourse comprehension.

As this example shows, conversational implicature is needed even in very ordinary conversations. According to Grice, it is also essential for understanding figures of speech, such as metaphor and irony. On this view, a listener works out the literal meaning of metaphor, determines that it does not convey a sensible message, and so constructs a different meaning that makes sense in the context. This view implies that nonliteral uses of language should take longer to understand than appropriately matched literal uses. Some early experimental results supported this view (e.g., Clark and Lucy, 1975). Later evidence, however, goes against it (see e.g., Cacciari and Glucksberg, 1994; Gibbs, 1994).

Coordination in Conversational Interaction

Clearly written text is, for most people, difficult to write. Ordinary conversation is easy to engage in, but it is full of hesitations, repetitions, false starts, and repairs. These phenomena complicate theories of discourse understanding, though they do not usually prove problematic for those engaged in conversation. Listeners must, in some sense, be discounting the disfluencies, so they can extract the intended message. However, the disfluencies may themselves help in understanding what is said (Smith and Clark, 1993).

In determining the message conveyed, conversationalists have one great advantage over readers. If they do not understand, they can ask for clarification. Indeed, asking for clarification is one aspect of the complex coordination in conversation, which led Clark to identify it as a species of *joint action*. Another is the joint establishment of who or what is being referred to (see e.g., Clark and Wilkes-Gibbs, 1986; Clark and Schaefer, 1987). Theories of discourse comprehension that focus on written texts inevitably ignore this coordinating aspect of comprehension. According to Clark, they do so at their peril, since face-to-face conversation is the most basic type of language use. However, detailed theories of this aspect of comprehension have not yet been developed.

Models of Discourse Understanding

The representation of a text reflects the structure of the part of the (real or imaginary) world to which it corresponds. Theories of comprehension that embody this idea are most naturally presented symbolically, even if they are not implemented as computer programs. Indeed, many of the structures in discourse models are of the kind that have proved problematic for connectionist accounts (see e.g., Fodor and Pylyshyn, 1988). Nevertheless, the interpretation of a text is determined by information from many sources: syntax, lexical semantics, discourse semantics, pragmatics, background knowledge. If these sources are thought of as providing *local constraints* on interpretation, the relaxation techniques used to generate overall interpretations of, for example, visual scenes using multiple local constraints (e.g., Waltz, 1975; Marr, 1982) might find application in computational models of discourse understanding.

Although sometimes dubbed *connectionist*, models such as Waltz's and Marr's do not have distributed representations (in the connectionist sense) and they *do* employ symbols, for example, to represent line junctions, or components of the primal sketch. Such models have a *hybrid* architecture (see also Chapter 3, where these models are called *local connectionist*). In psycholinguistics, relaxation-like techniques have been used, for example, in interactive activation models, which propagate partial constraints on the identity of a printed word until a stable interpretation is reached. These models also have a hybrid architecture, in which the nodes have interpretations that are naturally glossed symbolically (e.g., G in the third position in a word). The application of these ideas to cognitive, rather than perceptual phenomena has been labelled *symbolic connectionism* (Holyoak, 1991). In the applications Holyoak has in mind, the 'nodes' in the network are more complex than those in the interactive activation models. Similarly, in Kintsch's (1988) construction-integration model of discourse comprehension, nodes representing the meanings of simple sentences are linked into a network, around which activation is passed. Kintsch's model is discussed below, as well as a model proposed by Sharkey (1990) which is a somewhat more thoroughgoing connectionist model.

Models of Discourse Comprehension: A Brief History

Models of discourse comprehension have been proposed in both AI (artificial intelligence) and psycholinguistics. In AI, Winograd's (1972) SHRDLU was for many years a dominant influence, although its performance in the toy domain of the Blocksworld never scaled up. SHRDLU used a rudimentary discourse model, and performed impressively on, among other things, pronoun interpretation. For example, if at some point, the topic of conversation was a large green block, SHRDLU could correctly interpret the command *Pick it up*. SHRDLU used comparatively sophisticated knowledge of the syntax and semantics of English. Its reliance on such knowledge, particularly syntactic, contrasted with Schank's MARGIE, SAM and other programs written by his Yale group (see e.g., Schank, 1975, for an early account), where syntax in the ordinary sense was almost altogether absent. In these programs, understanding was driven by expectations based on (primarily verb) semantics, or general knowledge of common situations, encoded in *scripts* (see also Chapter 2). Schank's programs processed a wider range of texts than Winograd's, but in a less sophisticated way. Schank was also one of the principal proponents of the idea that comprehension should be assessed by paraphrases and question answering, rather than, for example, by analyzing what information ought to be present in a representation of a text. In principle, the two approaches should converge. In practice, selective choice of questions and superficial assessments of paraphrases, allowed many important questions to be overlooked.

In psycholinguistics, the principles of (i) *text representations* corresponding to situations, (ii) *constructive processing* (combination of information explicit in the text with background knowledge), and (iii) *integrative processing* (combining information from different parts of the text), were set out by Bransford in the early 1970s (e.g., Bransford and Franks, 1971; Bransford, Barclay and Franks, 1972). However, Bransford did not incorporate his ideas into a computational model. The construction of a more detailed psychological theory of discourse comprehension was left to proponents of a different approach, one that saw comprehension as the construction of a set of propositions representing the meaning of the text (Kintsch, 1974).

Propositions correspond roughly to the meanings of simple sentences, though a proposition may be expressed by an adjective, so that:

The red ball hit the window

expresses two propositions, *The ball hit the window* and *The ball was red*. Propositions are often expressed in bracketed notation, where a predicate is followed by its arguments, e.g., (*hit*, *ball*, *window*) and (*red*, *ball*). A satisfactory automatic procedure for deriving propositions from text has never been devised. One reason is that proponents of propositional representations pay little attention to questions about reference or, more generally, to questions about the relation between language and the world. In early work, it was assumed that, once propositions had been derived, they could be combined on the basis of argument overlap. When questions about how language relates to the world are taken seriously, it becomes apparent that their resolution cannot be postponed until 'propositional meaning' has been extracted. The elements of meaning supposedly encoded into propositions must be extracted from texts, but constructing a propositional representation is not necessarily a stage on the way to constructing a mental model (though cf., Johnson-Laird, 1983).

Kintsch and van Dijk (1978) proposed a model of comprehension that takes a set of propositions derived from a text, and uses them to build a coherent semantic representation. For example, the following sentence:

A series of violent, bloody encounters between police and Black Panther Party members punctuated the early summer days of 1969.

is broken down by Kintsch and van Dijk into the following propositions:

1 (SERIES, ENCOUNTER)
2 (VIOLENT, ENCOUNTER)

3 (BLOODY, ENCOUNTER)
4 (BETWEEN, ENCOUNTER, POLICE, BLACK PANTHER)
5 (TIME: IN, ENCOUNTER, SUMMER)
6 (EARLY, SUMMER)
7 (TIME: IN, SUMMER, 1969)

These propositions are incorporated into a hierarchical *coherence graph* by a cyclical process that operates on a few propositions at a time. The actual number is determined by working memory limitations, and may be about 10. The principal determinate of coherence is referential — coherent texts refer to the same people, objects etc. more than once. According to Kintsch and van Dijk, referential coherence depends on argument overlap between propositions. This can easily be verified in Figure 9.1 for the seven propositions listed above, where 1–5 share the

Figure 9.1: Coherence graph for the seven propositions in the example from Kintsch and van Dijk (1978)

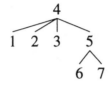

encounter argument, and 5–7 the *summer argument*. If there are no common arguments between the propositions in working memory on any one cycle, the full representation of the text in long-term memory has to be searched for information that can be used to establish connections. At the end of each cycle, some propositions (four in one simulation) remain in working memory. One method of selecting propositions favours those on the *leading edge* of the graph (i.e., the most recent proposition at each level in the hierarchy). Propositions not retained remain attached into the coherence graph, which represents the *microstructure* of the text in long-term memory. Subsequent operations create a more compact *macrostructure*, 'by deleting or generalizing all propositions that are either irrelevant or redundant and by constructing new inferred propositions' (Kintsch and van Dijk, 1978, p. 372). The more cycles a proposition stays in working memory, the better it is remembered.

The model was greatly elaborated by van Dijk and Kintsch (1983). Two of the major changes were the recognition that argument overlap alone cannot explain local coherence, and that a text must be represented by a *situation model* 'of the events, actions, persons, and in general the situation, a text is about' (van Dijk and Kintsch, 1983, pp. 11–2), as well as by a set of propositions.

Coherence graphs encode hierarchical relations between the parts of a text. New propositions are typically subordinated to propositions already in the graph with which they share arguments, because they give further details about items that have already been mentioned. These details are more poorly remembered (and less likely to be included in summaries) than information stored higher up the hierarchy, because they rarely remain in working memory for long. Story grammars (e.g., Mandler and Johnson, 1977; Thorndyke, 1977), which attempt to analyze story structure in the same way that sentence grammars analyze sentence structure, also attempt to identify hierarchical structure in texts — in this case a structure based not on argument overlap, but on predefined 'grammatical' relations between parts of a text. A story grammar-based theory of comprehension would hold that people have knowledge of the rules by which stories can be structured, and a parsing device that assigns structures to particular stories. The problems with this idea are well documented (e.g., Garnham, Oakhill and Johnson-Laird, 1982; Garnham, 1983). It is both unworkable, because there is no way of deciding, before a story has been understood, what component of a story is encoded in a particular sentence, and unnecessary, because most of the structure in stories is a reflex of structure in the world. Identifying structure in stories is a special case of using knowledge about the world to understand texts.

Unfortunately, the way knowledge about the world is used in text comprehension is not well understood. The two main questions are how knowledge is structured in long-term memory, and how it is retrieved. Schank and Abelson's (1977) scripts are a special case of a type of memory structure called a *schema* (see Chapter 2). Scripts encode information about the sequences of simpler events that make up a complex event, such as a visit to a restaurant. Frames, another type of schema, encode information about structured objects. The *car* frame contains knowledge that cars have engines, so a text such as:

I crashed my car. The engine had to be replaced.

is coherent, even though there is a definite reference (*the engine*) to an object that has not been explicitly mentioned.

A generalization of the idea that frames and scripts are used in comprehension is found in Sanford and Garrod's (e.g., 1981) theory, recently renamed *scenario mapping* (Sanford and Moxey, 1995). Sanford and Garrod have a more sophisticated, but less formal account of knowledge structures in long-term memory. They claim that these *scenarios* are accessed by information in the text, and that entities mentioned in the text are mapped directly into roles provided by the scenarios. Texts should be constructed so that the appropriate scenarios are accessed at the right times, otherwise incorrect mappings will be made. The surprise elicited by one of their best known texts (Sanford and Garrod, 1981, p. 114) is compatible with this idea.

John was on his way to school.

He was terribly worried about the maths lesson.

He thought he might not be able to control the class again today.

It was not a normal part of a janitor's duties.

However, the surprise need not be explained by an explicit mapping of John into a schoolboy role when the first sentence is read. An alternative account would be that, when the third sentence is read, a clash arises between the information that the main character has to control a class, and the information, perhaps only accessed at that point, that most of the people going to school are likely to be pupils.

Sanford and Garrod (1981, p. 129) suggest that the usual basis for scenario selection is the mention of an action central to the scenario, together with a reference to a character who plays a role in that action. However, they recognize that the previous discourse and prior knowledge of the people mentioned in a text can impose constraints on what scenarios are relevant.

One problem with schema theories is that they focus on stored knowledge, rather than the use of rules to compute structures. It is unlikely that all of the structure in texts corresponds to structures stored in memory. So, although a story grammar account of comprehension is incorrect, the idea that some of the knowledge used to understand stories is rule-based is not. For example, the main goal, subgoals, and attempts to fulfil them found in a particular story are likely to conform to general principles, but not to a particular prestored pattern. Similarly, the complex sets of causal and intentional relations that underlie even simple narratives differ from text to text in a way that precludes their being prestored. Such causal networks (e.g., Trabasso and van den Broek, 1985) are probably computed on-line, though most of the evidence for this view is indirect (Myers, 1990), and may reflect processes happening after a text has been read. Bloom *et al.* (1990) provide an exception to the general use of off-line measures. Fletcher and Bloom (1988) suggested a revision of Kintsch and van Dijk's (1978) model in which the leading edge strategy is replaced by one in which states of affairs that have not yet produced consequences are retained in working memory. This model was applied by Bloom *et al.* (1990) to on-line measures of reading causal texts.

Kintsch's Construction-Integration Model

Kintsch presents a new model of discourse comprehension, the *construction-integration* model, with a hybrid architecture that 'represents a symbiosis of production systems and connectionist approaches' (1988, p. 164). Kintsch contrasts his model with expectation-driven, or *top-down*, accounts of comprehension (such as Schank's). He claims that it is difficult, in such accounts, to find a compromise between precise detail and flexibility in the long-term memory structures that encode the expectations. Generally speaking, the more detail, the greater the likelihood of generating incorrect predictions about a particular text.[3]

In the construction-integration model, long-term memory has a less regimented structure. It is a set of concepts and propositions (in Kintsch's, 1974, sense), linked by positive or negative associations. Furthermore, long-term memory structure does not impose structure on text representations directly. Rather, a set of associated concepts and propositions from the text and long-term memory is assembled into a network corresponding, at first loosely, to the meaning of the text (the construction phase). Activation-passing processes then adjust the activation levels of the elements of the network so that consistent ideas boost one another's activation, whereas isolated propositions and concepts lose their activation and drop out of the representation (the integration phase). Construction and integration processes may be interleaved in the comprehension of a particular text.

The model assumes that the concepts corresponding to the main content words of a text are activated, and propositions are constructed from the output of a parser. It does not give an account of how propositions are derived. Kintsch does provide examples of propositional representations of texts. For example, in a study of word sense disambiguation (Till, Mross and Kintsch, 1988), subjects read sentences such as:

> The townspeople were amazed to find that all the buildings had collapsed except the mint.

Kintsch (1988, p. 172) gives the following propositional representation for this text.[4]

1 TOWNSPEOPLE
2 AMAZED[TOWNSPEOPLE,P3]
3 COLLAPSE[P4]
4 ALL-BUT[BUILDING,MINT]
5 BUILDING
6 MINT

In the initial construction phase, concepts and propositions from this sentence are combined with ones from long-term memory. For each text concept and proposition, a small number of strong associates from long-term memory are selected. For example, MONEY and CANDY are added to the network, because they are strong associates of MINT, though for different senses — no decision has yet been made about the intended sense of the ambiguous word *mint*. The proposition

7 ISA[MINT,BUILDING]

(*A mint is a building*) is also selected as an associate of MINT. The next operation is to link the enlarged set of concepts and propositions into its own network where associative strengths range from −1 to +1. Propositions from the text have positive associative strengths which decrease with distance apart in the text. So, in one simulation, propositions next to each other (e.g., 2 and 3) are connected with a strength of 0.9, whereas propositions separated by one, two, or more others are connected with strengths of 0.7, 0.4 and 0, respectively. Concepts and propositions from long-term memory are connected to their text associates with a strength of 0.5. So the MINT-MONEY connection is 0.5, for example.

At this point integration processes can start. The concepts and propositions from the text have an initial activation level of one sixth, and those from long-term memory, zero.[5] These activation levels are repeatedly adjusted according to the strengths of the connections between the concepts and propositions, using matrix arithmetic, until the network reaches a steady state. Highly activated nodes at the end of this process constitute a representation of the discourse, which may be refined by further construction and integration. In this initial phase, the text propositions attained activation levels between about 0.1 and 0.15, and the associates around 0.02, so that MONEY and CANDY were equally activated (see Figure 9.2). However, if concepts and propositions from long-term memory inherit their prior associative strengths, and integration is restarted, not only are the associates differentially activated, but some of them attain activation values close to those of the text propositions. For example, the long-term MONEY-CANDY connection was set to −1, so that MONEY and CANDY inhibit each other, and the ISA[MINT,BUILDING] to KILL[BUILDING,TOWNSPEOPLE] to 0.5, since they share an argument (BUILDING).[6] When the activation levels had restabilized, MONEY, associated with the intended meaning of *mint*, had an activation level of about 0.07, whereas CANDY was deactivated, as shown in Figure 9.2. The reason is that, in this text, the CANDY meaning of the word *mint* is not supported by links between the text and long-term memory (except MINT-CANDY), whereas the

Figure 9.2: The changing meaning of MINT in the example from Kintsch (1988). Numbers on the x-axis refer to propositions in the text

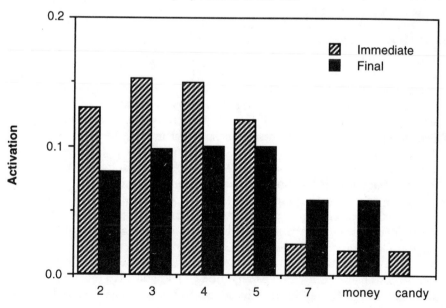

MONEY meaning is supported by a (sub)network of several connections.

In the reaction time data of Till, Mross and Kintsch (1988), inferred concepts and propositions are not activated for at least 500 ms, whereas simple associates are activated in about 350 ms. Kintsch (1988), therefore, assumes that inferred topics are constructed relatively late. Although he provides no account of how topics are established, he suggests that, for the text above, the concept EARTHQUAKE and the proposition CAUSE[EARTHQUAKE,P3] are added to the representation of the text. They have connection strengths of 0.5 with the text propositions that underlie the inferences, and initial activation levels of 0. After further cycles of activation passing, they reached activation levels of around 0.05.[7] The text representation now contains the information that the collapse of the buildings (except the mint) was caused by an earthquake.

Sharkey's Connectionist Model of Text Comprehension

Sharkey (1990) proposes an account of text comprehension, which he contrasts with Kintsch's (1988), and which is more thoroughgoingly connectionist. However, the model contains nodes representing semantic microfeatures, words, and propositions. These nodes are naturally given symbolic labels, so some of the *representations* in the model are not distributed. Sharkey describes three aspects of his model — a knowledge net, a lexicon, and an interface between them — and presents simulations of them. He claims that the three components 'interfaced gracefully' (Sharkey, 1990, p. 510), though this claim does not appear to be based on an overall simulation.

In constructing his knowledge net, Sharkey, like Kintsch, begins with Schank and Abelson's (1977) scripts. Like Kintsch, he worries about their lack of flexibility, and about the fact that they provide no mechanism for predicting the time-course of effects of knowledge on comprehension.

In Sharkey's model, knowledge is stored in a set of *macro-units*, which correspond roughly to Schank's (1982) *memory organization packets* (MOPs). MOPs are a response to the lack of flexibility of scripts, but they remain symbolic. They represent subsequences of actions that recur in many scripts. For example, the *sitting in the waiting room* MOP is common to the scripts for *going to the doctor* and *going to the dentist*. In MOP theory, scripts are not prestored in memory, but assembled on-line to understand particular texts.

Since macro-units correspond to MOPs, sets of them correspond to scripts, with some shared between scripts. For example, Sharkey posits a STAND IN LINE macro-unit, which might be activated by texts about going to the bank or to the cinema. Other macro-units needed for a text about a bank visit are: ENTER BANK, WRITE CHEQUE, TRANSACT WITH BANK TELLER, GET MONEY (Sharkey, 1990, p. 497). Connections between macro-units might be either hard-wired (Sharkey, Sutcliffe and Wobcke, 1986), or learned by a standard connectionist procedure. The network completes patterns of activation corresponding to scripts when part of a pattern (i.e., some of the macro-units) is activated by propositions explicit in a text. Propositions are encoded in *micro-units*, whose connections to the macro-units can also be learned, with stronger connections generated by more frequent presentation, simulating more central script events. Examples of (schematic) propositions that might have low, medium, and high strength connections to STAND IN LINE are the following (where X is the person that the text is about):

Low: X moved forward.
Medium: X went to the back of the line.
High: X stood in line.

After training, snippets from script-based texts activate constellations of macro-units corresponding to appropriate scripts. Typically a text proposition activates one macro-unit directly, and directly activated macro-units activate others by pattern completion. Sharkey (1990, pp. 496–7) describes the processing of a stylized text:

Go to the bank. Give cheque to bank teller. Leave the bank.

These three 'propositions' are encoded in three micro-units. They activate the ENTER BANK, TRANSACT WITH BANK TELLER, and GET MONEY macro-units, respectively. By pattern completion, these macro-units activate the set of units corresponding to the VISIT TO THE BANK script (ENTER BANK, STAND IN LINE, WRITE CHEQUE, TRANSACT WITH BANK TELLER, GET MONEY). Since activation flows back from the macro-units to the micro-units, the model explains false recognition and intrusions in recall. Propositions related to the script, but not presented, will have comparatively high activation values. So, a WRITE THE AMOUNT OF MONEY ON THE CHEQUE micro-unit will be strongly connected to the WRITE CHEQUE macro-unit, and will be activated by the backward flow of activation.[8] Because Sharkey's model is based on connectionist principles, it makes predictions about the time-course of activation-passing and, hence, about the time-course of script activation and deactivation. Unlike the original script theory, the model, therefore, explains how script-based effects vary over time — for example, the fact that, at points of transition in texts, two scripts are active simultaneously (Sharkey and Mitchell, 1985).

In Sharkey's model, there is a problem about how to characterize the micro-units (and their links to macro-units), since texts can express indefinitely many propositions, not all of which have links with preestablished knowledge encoded in the macro-units and *their* interrelations. In the simulation, each micro-unit corresponds to a fixed proposition. In discussing the interface between the lexicon (which lies outside the scope of this chapter) and the knowledge net, and in particular *propositional effects* on word recognition, Sharkey (1990, p. 505ff.) addresses this problem. He assumes that, in a realistic system, there will be a fixed number of propositional nodes. Thus a single node has to represent different propositions at different times. The nodes are linked, perhaps via word nodes, to nodes representing *semantic microfeatures*, which encode lexical meaning.[9] An initial set of connection strengths can be learned in the same way as the initial set of connection strengths between micro- and macro-units.

Sutcliffe (1992, p. 52) suggests the following microfeatures as representing (part of) the meanings of *book* and *food*.

book	**food**
small__size	small__size
made__of__paper	made__of__organic__material
is__common	is__common
found__in__bookshops	found__in__foodshops
found__in__offices	found__in__kitchens
found__in__homes	found__in__homes
is__functional	is__functional
involves__information	is__edible
is__aesthetically__pleasing	is__aesthetically__pleasing

Each microfeature has a *centrality* value for each concept it is used to analyze, a value that will differ from concept to concept. Microfeatures can be autoassociated into clusters that correspond to the meanings of words, and words in text can then produce patterns of activation in the microfeature nodes. Sharkey suggests that word nodes can act as an interface between the lexicon and the rest of the comprehension system. In a sentence of more than one word, each content word will be represented by a different set of microfeatures. Sharkey says little about how different words contribute to the meaning of a proposition (e.g., *John read the book*). One possibility (Sutcliffe, 1992) is that different microfeature networks process information from different parts of the sentence: subject, verb, object, for example, in *John read the book*. Thus, just as the Interactive Activation model (see Chapter 3) has separate subnetworks for letters in different positions in a word, Sharkey's model could have separate microfeature (and word) networks for the subject, verb, and object of proposition.

When fully assembled, the model would, therefore, work as follows. When a new clause is read, its content words activate microfeature and word nodes in a number of subnetworks. Propositional nodes are then activated via the existing connections with the microfeatures. In addition, the propositional nodes activate macro-units (and hence constellations of them corresponding, roughly, to scripts). They may also receive top-down activation from macro-units. After several cycles of activation passing, one proposition node should be the most active. This part of the processing, in which a single propositional node becomes active, is called the *selection stage*. However, the meaning of the current piece of text may not have exactly the same microfeatural analysis as represented by the preestablished links between the activated propositional node and the microfeatures. So selection of a proposition is followed by one in which the node becomes *associated* with the active microfeatures by a rapidly acting weight-changing process.

Critique of the Kintsch and Sharkey Models

Psycholinguistic models of discourse comprehension should fulfil two functions. First, they should provide an account of what it is to understand a discourse. Second, they should model data from psychological experiments. Traditionally, mathematical models in psychology, the precursors of computational models, have fulfilled the latter function. In domains that involve complex mental computations, such as discourse comprehension, parameter-setting models are unlikely to reflect the complexity of the underlying processes, and the parameters have to be interpreted as reflecting properties of complex and unanalyzed subdevices. The advent of AI and, later, cognitive science has shown how complex cognitive processes can be modelled in detail. However, traditional AI models do not readily explain reaction time data. Furthermore, AI modelling has been criticized (Marr, 1982) for failing to provide an analysis of cognition at the right level, what Marr calls *computational theory*. A computational theory results from task analysis, which determines the mathematical function a device computes, and why it computes that function. By combining a computational theory with an analysis of the *algorithms and systems of representation* that the device uses, and the hardware on which it *implements* them, Marr argued that a model of the system could be devised that would provide both a detailed analysis of what the device did, and a model of its working in real time, which would be able to account for psychological data.

Psychological models of discourse comprehension tend to ignore its complexities. They do so by relying on intuitive understanding of what texts mean. So a partial representation of meaning may suggest a fuller analysis than the model provides. For example, the propositions WEED[LUCY, GARDEN] and VEGETABLE[GARDEN] appear to capture the meaning of *Lucy weeded the vegetable garden*, but how do we know they do not mean *Lucy weeded the garden, which was a vegetable*, for example? An example of the omission of information from representations is found in both Kintsch's and Sharkey's assumptions about the links between information in long-term memory. In both models these links are associations, with possibly modifiable strengths. However, the relation of association is not sufficient to model links between pieces of information conveyed by texts. One piece of information may be strongly (or weakly) linked to other pieces in various ways. For example *John hit his brother* may be linked to *John bruised his brother* as cause, but to *John is a naughty boy* as evidence. Behaviourists, and empiricist philosophers before them, assumed that all links between pieces of information were of the same kind, but the cognitive revolution of the 1950s and 1960s demonstrated that this idea is incorrect.

A related problem arises in considering what constitutes a representation of the meaning of a text. Sharkey does not address this issue, since the activated propositions (and the relations between them) are not stored permanently. Kintsch explicitly identifies the representation with an interrelated set of activated nodes. However, since the only relation between nodes is association, he has no means of representing such things as the temporal structure of events. To use a well-known example, the information that Kintsch might represent as the associated propositions MARRY[JOHN, MARY] and PREGNANT[MARY] will be different depending on whether the state described in the second held before or only after the event described in the first. Similarly, although Sharkey's model processes the sentences of a text in order, it has no means of capturing aspects of meaning that depend on order. Furthermore, although clusters of macro-units correspond to scripts, there is no representation of the order in which the subevents of, say, a visit to a bank occur.

What is valuable about connectionist, or hybrid, models is the ease with which they model, at least qualitatively, the temporal course of comprehension. It must be hoped that this strength will carry over into models that are representationally more adequate.

Discourse Models Revisited

The notion of a discourse model, which can readily be embodied in a computer program, can be regarded as a part of a computational theory in Marr's (1982) sense — a theory that specifies what discourse comprehension comprises. Thus a theory based on discourse models does not attempt to 'explain' comprehension by providing a mechanism that satisfies indirect criteria, such as answering questions about a text, or paraphrasing it. Neither is its primary goal to explain reaction time data. Rather, it tries to give an analysis of what it is to comprehend a text, of what information has been mentally encoded by someone who has correctly understood it. In Marr's view, modelling that is not guided by an understanding of the processes being modelled, at the computational level, is severely disadvantaged.

Discourse comprehension has, as an essential component, a mapping from words[10] to representations of situations in the real or an imaginary world. In addition, the status of the situations must be computed. A description presents new information; a question, a request for information; a command, a demand to bring a situation about. Representations derived from texts are similar to those in long-term memory. So, a theory of discourse understanding depends on a relatively full account of types of memory structure. It must be stressed that it is no easy matter to give such an account, for it requires assumptions about folk ontology — the kinds of entity we take the world to be made up of — and about folk theories of the everyday world (of causation, intention, time and space, argumentation, and morality). To take just one example, in representing information about a spatial layout we may not represent space as a 3-dimensional Euclidian manifold. The space of everyday experience is (approximately) Euclidian. But we do not know how that space is represented mentally, or whether it is always represented in the same way.

More mundanely, we can be sure that discourse models (and long-term memory) contain representations of people and objects. But do they contain unitary representations of actions, or are actions represented 'merely' as people, objects, and the relations between them. Such questions can be answered: Kamp's (1979; Kamp and Rohrer, 1983) work on tense suggests that actions must, for some purposes, be treated as wholes. However, answering these questions is not a trivial matter, and should not be taken lightly. Some aspects of discourse comprehension may be explained by a gross measure of the associative strength between the different pieces of information in a text, but associative strength cannot, in general, provide an account of what information must be in the mental representation.

Notes

1 I use *text* and *discourse* interchangeably. Where a claim applies only to written text or only to spoken discourse that fact should be obvious from the context.
2 Since the findings that support this claim come partly from priming experiments, it can only be regarded as tentative.
3 Flexibility might be achieved by encoding information in a rule-based format, rather than in fixed structures.
4 Kintsch uses capital letters for concepts (as opposed to words). P3 in proposition 2 refers to proposition 3.
5 The total activation in the network always sums to one.
6 Kintsch assumes that if concepts or propositions are related in both the text and the knowledge base, the strengths add together, up to a maximum of 1.
7 Since the total activation is 1, and more concepts and propositions are now activated, the average activation level is lower. EARTHQUAKE and CAUSE [EARTHQUAKE,P3] were comparatively highly activated for nontext concepts and propositions.
8 How this micro-unit might come to be in the network is not explained.
9 Sharkey acknowledges his failure to deal with syntax. His proposal sounds uncomfortably like the failed compositional semantics of Katz and Fodor (1963), whose projection rules simply created larger sets of semantic features from smaller ones.
10 By using the term 'words' I do not intend to endorse any particular view about the relation between syntax and interpretation.

References

BLOOM, C. P., FLETCHER, C. R., VAN DEN BROEK, P., REITZ, L. and SHAPIRO, B. P. (1990) 'An on-line assessment of causal reasoning during comprehension', *Memory and Cognition*, 18, pp. 65–71.

BRANSFORD, J. D., BARCLAY, J. R. and FRANKS, J. J. (1972) 'Sentence memory: A constructive vs. interpretive approach', *Cognitive Psychology*, 3, pp. 193–209.

BRANSFORD, J. D. and FRANKS, J. J. (1971) 'The abstraction of linguistic ideas', *Cognitive Psychology*, 2, pp. 331–50.

BRYANT, D. J., TVERSKY, B. and FRANKLIN, N. (1992) 'Internal and external spatial frameworks for representing described scenes', *Journal of Memory and Language*, 31, pp. 74–98.

CACCIARI, C. and GLUCKSBERG, S. (1994) 'Understanding figurative language', in GERNSBACHER, M. A. (Ed) *Handbook of Psycholinguistics*, San Diego, CA: Academic Press, pp. 447–77.

CARREIRAS, M., GARNHAM, A. and OAKHILL, J. V. (1993) 'The use of superficial and meaning-based representations in interpreting pronouns: Evidence from Spanish', *European Journal of Cognitive Psychology*, 5, pp. 93–116.

CLARK, H. H. (1977) 'Bridging', in JOHNSON-LAIRD, P. N. and WASON, P. C. (Eds) *Thinking: Readings in Cognitive Science*, Cambridge: Cambridge University Press, pp. 411–20.

CLARK, H. H. and LUCY, P. (1975) 'Understanding what is meant from what is said: A study in conversational conveyed requests', *Journal of Verbal Learning and Verbal Behavior*, 14, pp. 56–72.

CLARK, H. H. and SCHAEFER, E. F. (1987) 'Collaborating on contributions to conversation', *Language and Cognitive Processes*, 2, pp. 19–41.

CLARK, H. H. and WILKES-GIBBS, D. (1986) 'Referring as a collaborative process', *Cognition*, 22, pp. 1–39.

DONNELLAN, K. (1966) 'Reference and definite descriptions', *Philosophical Review*, 75, pp. 281–304.

EHRLICH, K. and JOHNSON-LAIRD, P. N. (1982) 'Spatial descriptions and referential continuity', *Journal of Verbal Learning and Verbal Behavior*, 21, pp. 296–306.

FLETCHER, C. R. and BLOOM, C. P. (1988) 'Causal reasoning in the comprehension of simple narrative texts', *Journal of Memory and Language*, 27, pp. 235–44.

FODOR, J. A. and PYLYSHYN, Z. (1988) 'Connectionism and cognitive architecture', *Cognition*, 28, pp. 3–71.

FRANKLIN, N. and TVERSKY, B. (1990) 'Searching imagined environments', *Journal of Experimental Psychology: General*, 119, pp. 63–76.

GARNHAM, A. (1983) 'What's wrong with story grammars', *Cognition*, 15, pp. 145–54.

GARNHAM, A. (1987) *Mental Models as Representations of Discourse and Text*, Chichester: Ellis Horwood.

GARNHAM, A. (1991) 'Where does coherence come from: A psycholinguistic perspective', *Occasional Papers in Systemic Linguistics*, 5, pp. 131–41.

GARNHAM, A. and OAKHILL, J. V. (1987) 'Interpreting elliptical verb phrases', *Quarterly Journal of Experimental Psychology*, 39A, pp. 611–27.

GARNHAM, A. and OAKHILL, J. V. (1988) '"Anaphoric islands" revisited', *Quarterly Journal of Experimental Psychology*, 40A, pp. 719–35.

GARNHAM, A. and OAKHILL, J. V. (1989) 'The everyday use of anaphoric expressions: Implications for the "mental models" theory of text comprehension', in SHARKEY, N. E. (Ed) *Models of Cognition: A Review of Cognitive Science, Vol. 1*, Norwood, NJ: Ablex, pp. 78–112.

GARNHAM, A., OAKHILL, J. V, and CRUTTENDEN, H. (1992) 'The role of implicit causality and gender cue in the interpretation of pronouns', *Language and Cognitive Processes*, 7, pp. 231–55.

GARNHAM, A., OAKHILL, J. V. and JOHNSON-LAIRD, P. N. (1982) 'Referential continuity and the coherence of discourse', *Cognition*, 11, pp. 29–46.

GARROD, S. C. and SANFORD, A. J. (1981) 'Bridging inferences and the extended domain of reference', in LONG, J. and BADDELEY, A. D. (Eds) *Attention and Performance IX*, London: Lawrence Erlbaum, pp. 331–46.

GIBBS, R. W. (1994) 'Figurative thought and figurative language', in GERNSBACHER, M. A. (Ed) *Handbook of Psycholinguistics*, San Diego, CA: Academic Press, pp. 411–46.

GLENBERG, A. M. and LANGSTON, W. E. (1992) 'Comprehension of illustrated text: Pictures help to build mental models', *Journal of Memory and Language*, 31, pp. 129–51.

GLENBERG, A. M., MEYER, M. and LINDEM, K. (1987) 'Mental models contribute to foregrounding during text comprehension', *Journal of Memory and Language*, 26, pp. 69–83.

GRICE, H. P. (1975) 'Logic and conversation', in COLE, P. and MORGAN, J. M. (Eds) *Syntax and Semantics 3: Speech Acts*, New York: Academic Press, pp. 41–58.

HAVILAND, S. E. and CLARK, H. H. (1974) 'What's new: Acquiring new information as a process in comprehension', *Journal of Verbal Learning and Verbal Behavior*, 13, pp. 512–21.

HOLYOAK, K. J. (1991) 'Symbolic connectionism: Toward third-generation theories of expertise', in ERICSSON, K. A. and SMITH, J. (Eds) *Towards a General Theory of Expertise: Prospects and Limits*, New York: Cambridge University Press, pp. 301–35.

JOHNSON-LAIRD, P. N. (1980) 'Mental models in cognitive science', *Cognitive Science*, 4, pp. 71–115.

JOHNSON-LAIRD, P. N. (1983) *Mental Models: Towards a Cognitive Science of Language, Inference, and Consciousness*, Cambridge: Cambridge University Press.

JOHNSON-LAIRD, P. N. and GARNHAM, A. (1980) 'Descriptions and discourse models', *Linguistics and Philosophy*, 3, pp. 371–93.

KAMP, H. (1979) 'Events, instants and temporal reference', in BAUERLE, R., EGLI, U. and VON STECHOW, A. (Eds) *Semantics from Different Points of View*, Berlin: Springer Verlag, pp. 376–417.

KAMP, H. and ROHRER, C. (1983) 'Tense in texts', in BAUERLE, R., SCHWARZE, C. and VON STECHOW, A. (Eds) *Meaning, Use, and Interpretation of Language*, Berlin: Walter de Gruyter, pp. 250–69.

KATZ, J. J. and FODOR, J. A. (1963) 'The structure of a semantic theory', *Language*, 39, pp. 170–210.

KINTSCH, W. (1974) *The Representation of Meaning in Memory*, Hillsdale, NJ: Lawrence Erlbaum.

KINTSCH, W. (1988) 'The role of knowledge in discourse comprehension: A construction-integration model', *Psychological Review*, 95, pp. 163–82.

KINTSCH, W. and VAN DIJK, T. A. (1978) 'Towards a model of text comprehension and production', *Psychological Review*, 85, pp. 363–94.

MANDLER, J. M. and JOHNSON, N. S. (1977) 'Remembrance of things parsed: Story structure and recall', *Cognitive Psychology*, 9, pp. 111–51.

MANI, K. and JOHNSON-LAIRD, P. N. (1982) 'The mental representation of spatial descriptions', *Memory and Cognition*, 10, pp. 181–7.

MARR, D. (1982) *Vision: A Computational Investigation into the Human Representation and Processing of Visual Information*, San Francisco, CA: Freeman.

MARSLEN-WILSON, W. D. (1975) 'Sentence perception as an interactive parallel process', *Science*, 189, pp. 226–8.

MITCHELL, D. C. and GREEN, D. W. (1978) 'The effects of context and content on immediate processing in reading', *Quarterly Journal of Experimental Psychology*, 28, pp. 325–37.

MORROW, D. G., GREENSPAN, S. L. and BOWER, G. H. (1987) 'Accessibility and situation models in narrative comprehension', *Journal of Memory and Language*, 26, pp. 165–87.

MYERS, J. L. (1990) 'Causal relatedness and text comprehension', in BALOTA, D. A., FLORES D'ARCAIS, G. B. and RAYNER, K. (Eds) *Comprehension Processes in Reading*, Hillsdale, NJ: Lawrence Erlbaum, pp. 361–75.

POTTS, G. R. (1974) 'Storing and retrieving information about ordered relationships', *Journal of Experimental Psychology*, 103, pp. 431–9.

SAG, I. A. and HANKAMER, J. (1984) 'Toward a theory of anaphoric processing', *Linguistics and Philosophy*, 7, pp. 325–45.

SANFORD, A. J. and GARROD, S. C. (1981) *Understanding Written Language: Explorations in Comprehension Beyond the Sentence*, Chichester: John Wiley & Sons.

SANFORD, A. J. and MOXEY, L. M. (1995) 'Aspects of coherence in written language: A psychological perspective', in GERNSBACHER, M. A. and GIVON, T. (Eds) *Coherence in Spontaneous Text*, Philadephia, PA: John Benjamins, pp. 161–87.

SCHANK, R. C. (1975) *Conceptual Information Processing*, Amsterdam: North-Holland.

SCHANK, R. C. (1982) *Dynamic Memory*, Cambridge: Cambridge University Press.

SCHANK, R. C. and ABELSON, R. P. (1977) *Scripts, Goals, Plans and Understanding*, Hillsdale, NJ: Lawrence Erlbaum.

SHARKEY, N. E. (1990) 'A connectionist model of text comprehension', in BALOTA, D. A., FLORES D'ARCAIS, G. B. and RAYNER, K. (Eds) *Comprehension Processes in Reading*, Hillsdale, NJ: Lawrence Erlbaum, pp. 487–514.

SHARKEY, N. E. and MITCHELL, D. C. (1985) 'Word recognition in a functional context: The use of scripts in reading', *Journal of Memory and Language*, 24, pp. 253–70.

SHARKEY, N. E., SUTCLIFFE, R. F. E. and WOBCKE, W. R. (1986) 'Mixing binary and continuous activation schemes for knowledge access', in *Proceedings of the American Association for Artificial Intelligence, Philadelphia, Vol. 1*, Los Altos, CA: Morgan Kaufman, pp. 262–6.

SMITH, V. L. and CLARK, H. H. (1993) 'On the course of answering questions', *Journal of Memory and Language*, 32, pp. 25–38.

STENNING, K. (1978) 'Anaphora as an approach to pragmatics', in HALLE, M., BRESNAN, J. W. and MILLER, G. A. (Eds) *Linguistic Theory and Psychological Reality*, Cambridge, MA: MIT Press, pp. 162–200.

SUTCLIFFE, R. F. E. (1982) 'Representing meaning using microfeatures', in REILLY, R. G. and SHARKEY, N. E. (Eds) *Connectionist Approaches to Natural Language Processing*, Hove, Sussex: Lawrence Erlbaum, pp. 49–73.

THORNDYKE, P. W. (1977) 'Cognitive structures in comprehension and memory of narrative discourse', *Cognitive Psychology*, 9, pp. 77–110.

TILL, R., MROSS, E. F. and KINTSCH, W. (1988) 'Time course of priming for associate and inference words in a discourse context', *Memory and Cognition*, 16, 4, pp. 283–98.

TRABASSO, T. and VAN DEN BROEK, P. (1985) 'Causal thinking and the representation of narrative events', *Journal of Memory and Language*, 24, pp. 612–30.

VAN DIJK, T. A. and KINTSCH, W. (1983) *Strategies of Discourse Comprehension*, New York: Academic Press.

WEBBER, B. L. (1979) *A Formal Approach to Discourse Anaphora*, New York: Garland Publishing.

WINOGRAD, T. (1972) 'Understanding natural language', *Cognitive Psychology*, 3, pp. 1–191.

WALTZ, D. (1975) 'Understanding line drawings of scenes with shadows', in WINSTON, P. H. (Ed) *The Psychology of Computer Vision*, New York: McGraw-Hill, pp. 19–92.

Part III
Models of Language Production

Chapter 10

Discourse Planning: Empirical Research and Computer Models

Jerry Andriessen, Koenraad de Smedt and Michael Zock

Introduction

Discourse, be it written or spoken, consists generally of more than a single sentence. Production of a multisentential discourse requires *planning*, or a series of choices that guide subsequent verbal production. Discourse planning involves the creation and elaboration of communicative goals, and the application of strategies for the selection and organization of content, taking into account the situation and the available linguistic resources. This chapter focuses on aspects of planning that pertain to producing coherent discourse, and on computational models to perform this planning process.

In the introduction we discuss some of the problems faced by a producer of an extended piece of discourse. The list is not exhaustive, but it captures the most important issues in discourse planning and shows how they are interrelated. Later we will review experimental evidence pertaining to discourse planning. An important part of this discussion addresses written rather than spoken discourse. It is shown that our understanding of the whole process is far from complete. We believe that computational models may help to discover what pieces of the puzzle are lacking and how the different pieces may fit together. Next, we present some of the computational models that have been developed for discourse planning. It should be noted that none of these systems has been developed as a psychological model, hence none of them should be evaluated strictly on that basis. However, it appears that computational work is progressing towards the point where implementation and testing of psychological models of discourse planning will become feasible.

Some Problems and Phenomena in Discourse

Contextualization

The purpose of discourse production is to perform an act of communication, to realize an intention by linguistic means (Austin, 1962; Searle, 1979). The first problem that a discourse producer has to solve is how to develop intentions into a set of goals realizable in the current context. Bronckart (1985) calls this process *contextualization*. Driven by the intentions of the discourse producer (e.g., *I want to write a letter that leads to an invitation for a job interview*), the contextualization process causes reflection on goals to take into account situational constraints. Many courses on writing (e.g., Flower, 1981) include heuristics for working out a *discourse plan* before actual writing starts. These heuristics include tactics for brainstorming, and making inventories and schematic outlines. Contextualization leads to the creation of an orientation that guides the activities in discourse production. Beginning writers often lack such an orientation. They start a paper without knowing what to include, what to omit, how to provide adequate background information, and how to put into perspective what is most important. Hence they often provide unnecessary details while leaving out crucial general information (Barnard *et al.*, 1989).

Tailoring the Message to the Audience

Early writing is based on experience with oral conversation. Partners in a dialogue provide feedback which indicates their information needs. In contrast, writing is a monologic activity in which a writer must anticipate the interpretation process of a specific audience. The characteristics of such an audience guide the discourse planning strategies needed. Texts written for a lay audience require more general information and explanation of the domain than texts written for experts. The latter may expect more of an in-depth analysis and require less general information. Young writers tend to overlook the demands of a specific audience (e.g., Roussey and Gombert, 1992).

Discourse Types

Among the different types of discourse, the following four have received most attention: *description, narration, argumentation* and *exposition*. Each of these discourse types is generally associated with a pragmatic goal and a canonical structure. For example, Toulmin's (1958) model of the structure of *argumentations* decribes how an opening statement of opinion needs to mention certain supportive evidence, which then crystallizes to a conclusive statement. Such a global structure fosters (but does not prescribe) the organization of the discourse. Different structures are often required for different purposes. A persuasive discourse should minimally include a point of view and some supportive evidence. Further options include counterarguments, which then have to be refuted, as in (1a). If the same information is to be presented in a neutral rather than persuasive manner, arguments for and against a point of view could be presented alongside (1b).

(1) a. People should go abroad on holidays. Being abroad is important to broaden your mind. Going abroad is costly, but there are usually affordable offers.

b. Going abroad on holidays has advantages and disadvantages. On the one hand, being abroad broadens your mind. On the other hand, it is costly, even though there are usually affordable offers.

Thematic Progression and Linearization

Decisions on what to say necessarily involve decisions on *linearization* of information. When a discourse is to convey a complex image or thought, it must be broken down into an ordered set of separate utterances for communicative purposes. The writer must present the content elements in a suitable order and add linguistic cues that enable the reader to re-create the initial whole. For example, a *definition* may be linearized in the following way: One starts by mentioning the general class of an object, then lists some subtypes, and finally describes the functions of the object and its components.

The linear structure of texts shows a *thematic progression* in which the different themes or topics should be linked without abrupt shifts. Compare the difference between sentences (2b) and (2c) as continuations for (2a) in the following example by Brown and Yule (1985):

(2) a. The Prime Minister stepped off the plane.
b. Journalists immediately surrounded her.
c. She was immediately surrounded by journalists.

Brown and Yule claim that there is a preference for (2c) as the continuation sentence, rather than (2b). Their explanation is that readers prefer to maintain the same topic. The choice for (2b) would entail a shift of topic.

Moreover, ordering may not only affect ease of processing but also interpretation, as illustrated in example (3) from Levelt (1981).

(3)　a.　She married and became pregnant.
　　　b.　She became pregnant and married.

Reference and Cohesion

A given object may be referred to in different ways, depending on the set of alternatives from which it must be distinguished. If a speaker wants to refer to a big black ball in a situation where the alternative object is a big white ball, the referring expression may be *the black one* or *the black ball* (Levelt, 1989). In other situations the same object may be referred to as the *big one*, *the ball*, or simply the pronoun *it*.

A sentence within a discourse can generally be understood by its links to other sentences, as shown in the following example, taken from Halliday and Hasan (1976, p. 14). The meanings of *he* and *so* in (4b) can only be captured by reference to their *antecedents*, which are in (4a).

(4)　a.　Did the gardener water my hydrangeas?
　　　b.　He said so.

Anaphora, such as *he*, *so*, and *it*, are *cohesive* devices. Halliday and Hasan define *cohesion* as a semantic relationship between two textual elements in which one is interpreted by the other. Clear cohesive ties are essential for the interpretation of discourse. Especially young writers appear to have problems with proper reference (Bartlett, 1984), as evident from sentences like (5).

(5)　John got into an argument with Charlie. Then he hit him and knocked him down.

Another type of cohesion is established by using connectors like *and*, *but*, *then*. Such cue words relate what is about to be said to what has been said before. Furthermore, they instruct the reader how to link the different pieces of information (temporally, causally, etc.). Still another way of establishing cohesion is to repeat words or semantically related items, as in (6).

Coherence

Example (6) shows a piece of discourse that is cohesive but not *coherent*:

(6)   My daughter works in a library in Amsterdam. Amsterdam has a museum of modern art. Collectors of modern art are often yuppies. Yuppies don't like punks. The punk phenomenon originated in Great Britain in the seventies.

To understand a piece of discourse, the reader or listener must construct a coherent mental representation of that discourse. This requires not only solving problems of reference, as sketched above, but also finding a general frame of interpretation. This frame guides inferences that link different parts of the discourse, based on knowledge of the world. Such a frame is absent in (6). In contrast, example (7), taken from Roberts and Kreutz (1993), is hardly cohesive but still coherent.

(7)   The storm took the vacationers by surprise. The clothes took hours to dry.

The writer relies on the reader's interpretation that the vacationers' clothes got wet from the rain during the storm. The reader is assumed to know that storms usually involve rain which causes clothes to get wet. Furthermore, *storms* and *clothes* occur at the beginning of the sentence, so that inferences related to these concepts can readily be made. Writers and readers are both usually cooperative in handling such inferences.

Research on Discourse Planning

Many theories of language production assume some rough distinction between preverbal planning activities and the verbal production of sentences. Preverbal activities include contextualization of the communicative goal, selection and organization of the message. According to the language user framework proposed in Chapter 1, the Conceptualizer component produces preverbal messages. These serve as input to the Formulator or realization component, which prepares the syntactic frame and the word material of the sentences under construction (see Chapters 11, 12 and 13). Only recently, in the 1980s, conceptualizing has become an important subject of psycholinguistic research.

In this section, we take a closer look at some important theoretical aspects of discourse planning. We start by sketching a picture of current research on written discourse production by novice and expert writers. Next, psycholinguistic theories of discourse planning are discussed. Since the subject represents a fairly recent branch of psycholinguistics, no complete model or theory can as yet be provided. We therefore focus on some empirical phenomena that seem to be central to the domain. Finally, we present linguistic approaches to discourse structure.

Computational Psycholinguistics

Compared to psycholinguistics, linguistics in a sense approaches the problem from the opposite side, by attempting to analyze discourse in terms of its structure rather than in terms of cognitive operations performed over time.

Writing Research

Embedded in a tradition of *problem-solving* research (Newell and Simon, 1972; Ericsson and Simon, 1984), many models of writing are based on the analysis of verbal protocols. These protocols are recorded on assignments during which subjects must carry out a particular task while they are simultaneously *thinking aloud* and explain what they are doing. On the basis of the analysis of the resulting text, notes and thinking-aloud protocols, researchers have constructed models of writing as a problem solving activity (Flower and Hayes, 1980; Cooper and Matsuhashi, 1983; de Beaugrande, 1984; Bereiter and Scardamalia, 1987). In various ways, these models comprise the problems, processes, and strategies that are supposed to capture the essence of writing. Thus, writing research provides general descriptions of the processes involved in written-discourse production. A problem in reviewing writing research is that different authors often divide the process and its units in different ways.

The most frequently cited model of writing is that by Flower and Hayes (1981). Though the model is not procedural in nature, it can be used as a framework that describes, at a high level, the activities going on during composition. According to Flower and Hayes, writing involves three interacting processes: *planning, translating*, and *reviewing*. Here we only discuss their notion of planning. Planning involves the retrieval of knowledge from memory and its organization according to the goals of the writer. The planning process is constrained by the writers knowledge as well as by the writing context. Its main output is a *text plan*, i.e., something like an outline. The resulting plan does not need to correspond to the final surface form of the text, because it may be vague, quite incomplete, and diverse, yet it is often precise enough to guide the discourse producer in the complex task of writing (Flower and Hayes, 1984). *Expert planning* can be distinguished from *novice planning* by four features (Hayes and Flower, 1986):

1 During planning, expert writers include an initial task representation and a body of goals that guide and constrain their efforts to write.
2 This body of goals can be represented as a hierarchical structure, including top-level goals, plans and subgoals.
3 The network of goals is a dynamic structure: it is built and developed and sometimes radically restructured at the top levels while the writer composes and responds to new ideas or to the text. Modifying writing goals may be essential for good writing.

4 Experts tend to develop far more elaborated networks with more connections and integration among goals than novices.

Other authors characterize beginning and expert writing in terms of two qualitatively different production modes, respectively called knowledge-telling and knowledge-transforming (Bereiter and Scardamalia, 1983, 1987). *Knowledge-telling* involves text generation through primarily linear processes. The writing of a prototypical knowledge-teller is based on an initial task representation, which signals a relevant discourse type, which triggers a highly canonical schema (narrative, persuasive, etc.). The task representation also provides topic associations that act as probes to retrieve content from memory. Because discourse is generated as a direct consequence of this retrieval process, the coherence of the produced texts is supposedly directly related to the organization of topical information in memory (McCutchen and Perfetti, 1982; Scardamalia and Paris, 1985). What is crucially lacking in knowledge telling is purposeful reflection on the content and form of the discourse. A knowledge-teller engages in sentence-to-sentence operations, primarily guided by local topic associations (*what to say next?*). Instruction in awareness of discourse functions does not change this behaviour (Scardamalia and Paris, 1985).

The second production mode, *knowledge-transforming*, can be characterized by an inclusion in the writing process of reflective operations that transform intentional, structural, and gist representations. These operations correspond to the restructuring in adult planning as characterized by Hayes and Flower (1986) (see item 3 above). Analysis of thinking-aloud protocols has shown that mature writers plan by globally working through a writing task at an abstract level before working through it at a more concrete level. During the text production process, problems are tackled both at the level of content (*what do I mean?*) and at the level of form (*how do I say it?*). Reflection on both levels during composition leads to the transformation of content and form, giving rise to new thoughts.

A psycholinguistic theory of discourse planning must therefore account for the fact that experts of discourse production perform problem solving in at least two domains: at the ideational level (content determination and organization of ideas) and the rhetorical level (determination of linguistic forms according to communicative goals). The two domains mutually interact, whereby ideas give rise to linguistic planning, while the resulting linguistic forms provoke further reflection on ideas. Expert writing is not a one-shot process, but involves reflection and revision on all relevant aspects of the assignment. Therefore, planning structures seem to be required which can be adapted and modified on the fly. Planning processes appear to take place at all levels of production, from the construction of pragmatic plans to the preparation of articulatory sequences. To what extent the various levels are autonomous or interdependent remains an open question (Fayol, 1991). Finally, there is a fundamental difference between expert and novice writing with respect to the nature of planning. Planning by beginners is opportunistic and driven by local constraints, while expert planning is strategic: the writer's goals determine the generation and organization of content.

The general distinction in terms of writing activities of beginning and expert writers is useful. As we shall see below, some computational models embody characteristics of beginner's writing, including essentially linear processes guided by a highly canonical schema. Some aspects of expert writing, including explicit modelling of intentions and hierarchical planning, have also been subjects of computational modelling. However, what is meant by dynamic restructuring has yet to be specified. The nature of the processes involved, and the information sources that serve as their inputs and outputs, are as yet unclear. It is generally acknowledged that the way the task is initially represented is a crucial factor in determining subsequent activities, but it is unknown what this initial task representation exactly contains. Furthermore, it is even unclear what a discourse model should look like (see Chapter 9 for a more detailed discussion of this issue). Proposals from various sources incorporate the individuals goals, socio-cultural conventions, abstract (hierarchical, propositional) representations of content, or a *hearer model* or *user model* expressing the speaker-writers ideas about the hearer-reader (e.g., Van Dijk and Kintsch, 1983; Bereiter and Scardamalia, 1987; Levelt, 1989; Hermann and Grabowski, 1994). To avoid an extensive discussion concerning the nature of the discourse model, we focus on the processes of planning and come back to the structural issue only later, when we discuss computational modelling.

Macroplanning and Microplanning

Psycholinguistic notions of discourse planning are generally based on the spoken mode. Moreover, the data often involve dialogues, where the specification of consecutive discourse actions is highly dependent on the direct interaction with the hearer. In monologues, such as in a lecture or a news story, planning may be a more conscious activity, the resulting discourse plan more elaborate, and its execution better controlled (Van Dijk and Kintsch, 1983). In the analysis of dialogues, the focus has been more on individual utterances than on the discourse structure as a whole. Thus, less consideration has been given to higher-level speaker goals which underlie multiple, purposefully interrelated utterances (Paris, 1991; Redeker, 1992). Nevertheless, many insights from psycholinguistic approaches to discourse are clearly relevant to text writing as well.

From the psycholinguistic perspective, Levelt (1989) distinguishes between *macroplanning* and *microplanning. Macroplanning* is a hierarchically structured activity which involves the elaboration of some global communicative goal into a series of subgoals, and the retrieval of relevant information instrumental for realizing each of these subgoals. Van Dijk and Kintsch (1983, p. 266) distinguish between pragmatic goals (e.g., *I want you to take my advice*) and their semantic specification (e.g., *I don't want you to go to Nigeria*). Microplanning assigns the right propositional shape to the information, as well as the perspective (topic, focus) from which the speaker views the situation and by which the speaker guides the addressee's focus of attention. The output of microplanning has been described by Van Dijk and Kintsch (1983) as a *micro speech act*, whose definite selection depends on local pragmatic coherence constraints and features of the actual local context.

In the following paragraphs, we focus essentially on macroplanning processes. We discuss the planning processes from several viewpoints. It should be noted that no serial order is implied in the execution of these processes, since the flow of planning activities in discourse generation involves repeated, recursive and maybe even simultaneous execution of several processes (see, e.g., Goldman-Eisler, 1968; Butterworth, 1980; Matsuhashi, 1987).

Pragmatic Factors in Discourse Planning

Discourse production is guided by a number of pragmatic factors, on which speakers and listeners implicitly agree during communication. Cooperation is a basic ingredient for the establishment of coherence, i.e., the recognition of the fact that different pieces of a discourse are somehow related. A three-year-old child describing a picture scene seems to move from detail to detail in a more or less random way. As she inspects the picture for details to be announced, salient features that catch her attention are reported immediately. Associations that come to her mind may sometimes lead to sidetracking, distracting the flow of speech by details of her personal experience. Such discourse can only be understood by a very cooperative listener who knows the person. Deutsch and Pechmann (1982) examined the way speakers select information for making reference to objects. Speakers describing arrays with many objects do not simply move from one object to the other, pointing out all the details. Rather, they mention only a few objects, and the speaker relies on the addressee's cooperation to pose further questions if the referent cannot fully be identified. Especially younger children tend to exploit such cooperativeness (Levelt, 1989). Speakers try to establish the mutual belief that the object reference is understood well enough for the current purposes (Clark and Wilkes-Gibbs, 1986). The source of coherence is therefore not the discourse itself, but has to be found in the interaction between speaker and addressee.

Important cooperative principles for interaction have been formulated by Grice (1975) as *maxims*, e.g., *be polite*, *be concise*, and *be as clear as possible*. Another important pragmatic factor in the establishment of coherence is *presupposition* (Seuren, 1985). Presupposition can be defined as the logical assumptions underlying utterances. Thus after hearing *Martians appeared again last night*, the hearer may assume that (according to the speaker) Martians had already appeared before.

Semantic Macroplanning

After our discussion of pragmatic goals, we now turn to the macroplanning of their semantic content. A well-known concept that might figure as a plan for translating intentions into content subgoals is the *schema*. Schemata are structured packets of generic knowledge that furnish much of the content needed to interpret, explain, predict, and understand events (Mandler, 1984; Graesser, Singer, and Trabasso, in press; see also Chapter 9). Besides acting as a filter for determining what information is relevant given some discourse goal, they serve as a device for the organization of content.

There is some empirical evidence supporting the importance of schematic knowledge in *narrative* writing. According to Trabasso, Van den Broek and Suh (1989), a narrative is based on a schema with different components (*setting*, *event*, *internal response*, *goal*, *attempt*, and *outcome*) which are supposed to be causally connected. Recognizing the different components of the narrative in (8) is left as an exercise to the reader.

(8) a. It was winter.
     b. Mary wanted to surprise her mother.
     c. She went to the shop and bought a sweater.
     d. Her mother was very pleased.

According to Trabasso and Nickels (1992), coherence in narration is achieved when people are able to relate everyday knowledge to the protagonists' behaviour in order to infer their goals and plans according to the narrative schema. The content and the structure of a narration is the result of an interaction between a person's model of physical and psychological causation (e.g., wearing warm clothes causes people not to be cold in winter) and the events to which it is applied.

By analyzing the presence and nature of goal-plan structures from the perspective of each character in stories by children of several ages, Trabasso and Nickels (1992) were able to show how children from three years onward progressively move from simple descriptions of states to stories consisting of actions and later to explanations of actions carried out according to a goal plan. Using a sentence selection assignment, involving local planning of next sentences, Andriessen (1991) showed that coherence, defined in terms of intentional and purposeful action of the story characters, was related to the subjects' (10–12 years old) proficiency in reasoning about their decisions and to the quality of their revisions of sentences.

A familiar background knowledge structure (such as a schema) may be easily retrieved from memory for use in discourse production. A well-organized representation solves many problems of selection and organization of discourse, allowing the main focus of the discourse producer to be on what to say next. We see, later, a specific use of schemata in computational models of discourse generation. However, we should bear in mind that, no matter how useful schemata may be, they do not work in all situations. In particular, the writer's representation of the content to be expressed may not be organized well enough to fit in a single schema (Andriessen, 1991, 1994).

Linearization

In addition to content selection, there is the problem of determining in what order the different content elements will be presented. To deal with this problem of linearization, speakers apply a number of principles, such as mentioning causes before results, or earlier events before later ones. In several experiments, Levelt (1981, 1982a, 1982b, 1989) studied such principles in the following way. Subjects were asked to describe orally spatial grid-like networks which were put on the table in front of them. These networks consisted of differently coloured dots, connected by horizontal and vertical arcs (see Figure 10.1). The subjects were asked to start their descriptions at a node indicated by an arrow, and to proceed so as to enable the hearer to draw the network correctly on the basis of their tape-recorded description.

Figure 10.1: The network on the left is traversed in the order ABCDBEF, following the stack principle, and that on the right as ABCDEBFG, preserving connectivity

Analyzing these results, Levelt distinguished between *content-related* and *process-related* determinants of the ordering of information. The content-related determinants derive from the so-called principle of natural ordering, in this case a spatial ordering. Linear spatial structures seem to have a natural order, imposed for the listeners sake: the connective sequence of loci from source to goal (Klein, 1979, 1982). It is also known that preserving chronological order is one of the earliest rhetorical skills in children (Clark, 1970). Process-related determinants of linearization concern the complexity of information and the bookkeeping abilities of the speaker. Levelt discusses the principle of *connectivity*, which predicts that a speaker will go over a pattern as much as possible without lifting the 'mental pencil'. Speakers rarely violated the connectivity principle for string-like patterns. Connectivity is a general ordering principle in perception and memory. Ehrich and Koster (1983) found a high degree of connectivity in the description of play furniture arrangements in a doll house.

Linde and Labov (1975, p. 924) studied apartment descriptions. The subjects described their own apartments in terms of 'imaginary tours which transform spatial lay-outs into temporally organized narratives'. The narrative tour begins at the front door, just as it would if the interviewer were to arrive for the first time at the apartment. Levelt (1989) notes that these descriptions conform to a second process-related principle of linearization, the stack principle, which states that speakers always tend to return to the last node in the waiting line. Levelt's final principle is that of minimal load: when confronted with alternative branches, speakers prefer continuations which involve the least memory load. In other words, do the simplest thing first.

Put briefly, linearization of discourse has been found to follow certain cognitive principles: preserve natural order, continue the path as long as possible, return to the last digression point, and minimize memory load. While these ideas are attractive, they have only been studied in well-structured domains and tasks. In other words, they merely determine what to say next.

Topic and Focus

Elements of a message (the output of the conceptualization process) usually fulfil certain thematic roles (e.g., actor, source, goal, beneficiary). Thematic roles differ in their importance, saliency, and/or centrality to the discourse producer. Certain roles can be put in the (mental) foreground, others in the background. This perspective is what distinguishes, e.g., the sentences in (9).

(9)　　a.　Mary bought the book from John.
　　　　b.　The book was bought from John by Mary.

The saliency of certain discourse elements varies over time. What the discourse is about at each moment in time is called the *discourse topic*. Normally, an utterance will relate to the discourse topic (as we have seen, this will promote coherence), but sometimes a speaker or writer may want to change the topic. Such changes need to be explicitly marked (Grosz and Sidner, 1985). The fragment of information in the centre of attention (often containing new information on a topic) is called the *focus*.

Investigating focus, Grosz (1977) implemented a set of mechanisms for the interpretation of definite noun phrases in a computer program that participated in a dialogue about a task. These mechanisms bring entities into focus as the discourse moves to a subtask, and move the main task back into focus when the subtask is completed. For doing so, the program uses a stack of focus spaces, containing the entities that discourse participants focus on during a specific discourse segment. The focusing techniques allow the correct prediction of the anaphoric referent of a definite noun phrase such as *the screw* when the screw in a wheelpuller has been brought into focus. Appelt and Kronfeld (1987) use the mechanisms for focusing in the generation of referring expressions. McKeown (1982, 1985) and McDonald (1983) adapt the focusing algorithms to generate pronouns in text. Below we see a specific use of these focusing techniques in computational modelling.

Semantic microplanning consists of deciding what to say (in the immediate context) and from what point an event is viewed (perspective). It should be noted, however, that thematization pertains not only to microplanning, as it also involves what theme to select in the clause to follow. As this choice goes beyond the immediate or local context, thematization is also part of macroplanning, i.e., what to say in the global context.

Local planning has been investigated in the context of argumentative discourse by Andriessen, *et al.* (in press). In a sentence selection paradigm, an initial and a final statement of an argumentative text were presented, and the subjects were asked to insert six arguments in between. The first and last statements expressed contrastive points of view concerning a topic (e.g., *The car is very practical* and *So, the train is more practical than the car is*, respectively). The polarity of the arguments was varied (in favour of or against the car or train) as well as the means of presentation of the sentences to be selected (6 out of 24, presented at once, or 6 times 1 out of 4). In this way, it was investigated whether the subjects (10–14 years old) preferred arguments in favour of the first sentence (indicating local planning) or the last (indicating global planning). It appeared that subjects produced better argumentative sequences, containing more kinds of arguments in a more plausible order, when all possible arguments were presented to them at once. When they received consecutive groups of four sentences, local planning predominated. The tendency for subjects of this age to continue earlier themes was also observed in narrative sentence selection (Andriessen, 1991).

Rhetorical Structure Theory

Complementary to observations about how people deal with discourse production tasks are descriptive linguistic approaches. These analyze the result of discourse production in terms of the functions of its components (for an overview see Maier and Hovy, 1991).

An important line of research in this area is Rhetorical Structure Theory (RST), which has inspired several computational modelling approaches for discourse generation. The goal of RST is to describe text organization in terms of *rhetorical relations*, such as *purpose*, *enablement*, *circumstance*, *background*, *motivation*, etc. Rhetorical relations indicate which role a given part (segment) plays with respect to the whole.

On the basis of an analysis of a wide variety of texts, Mann and Thompson (1987) derived some 25 rhetorical relations. Texts can be characterized by these relations at different levels: a relation may hold between its basic elements (clauses) as well as between larger chunks (paragraphs). Relations are typically signalled by special cue words. For example, the PURPOSE relation is usually signalled by phrases such as *in order to*, *so that*, etc.

The rhetorical relation is embedded into the fundamental unit of RST, the *schema* (not to be confused with McKeown's notion of schema, see below). A schema is composed of three elements: a *nucleus*, a *satellite* and a *relation*, where the relation specifies the satellite's role with regard to the nucleus. An example is the MOTIVATION schema that can be applied to (10). RST relations are conventionally depicted as arcs between the nucleus and the satellite, e.g., in Figure 10.2.

(10) a. Come to the party at my new house. (nucleus)
     b. I've got lots of tasty Belgian beers. (satellite)

Figure 10.2: RST representation of the motivation relation

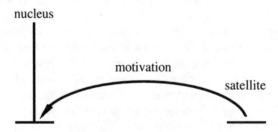

Come to the party at my new house   I've got lots of tasty Belgian beers

A rhetorical relation is defined in terms of its *effects* and *constraints*. The effects specify the result a given relation shall have on the hearer (in terms of communicative goals). For example, providing a MOTIVATION may stimulate the hearer for some action, by increasing the hearer's desire. The constraints specify under which conditions a given relation holds or may be used. For example, MOTIVATION is only applicable if the nucleus expresses an action. An example of the definition of this relation is provided in (11), based on Moore and Paris (1993).

(11) *relation name*:   MOTIVATION
     constraints on nucleus: Presents an action (unrealized with respect to the nucleus) in which the hearer is the actor.
     constraints on satellite: None.
     constraints on N + S combination: Comprehending the satellite increases the hearer's desire to perform the action expressed in the nucleus.
     effect: The hearer's desire to perform the action presented in the nucleus is increased.

Schemata are unordered: satellite and nucleus can appear in any order in the schema. Furthermore, they can be used recursively: a text fragment (or *text span*) serving as the nucleus or satellite of one schema may itself be decomposed into a nucleus and satellite, using another schema. A text can thus be represented as a tree structure. In order to avoid uncontrolled growth, control strategies or constraints are needed that dictate when a satellite should appear or not, how often, and when it should be expanded as some other schema.

RST addresses coherence in terms of rhetorical relations. While this approach has successfully inspired many models of discourse generation, some weaknesses have become apparent. A first limitation is that RST relations have very weak semantics, merely indicating what general effects a given relation will have upon the hearer. Unlike an outline showing the topical structure of discourse and the writer's flow of thought, an RST-tree discloses little of what a text is about. An RST-tree is like a macrostructure stripped of its content. For a complementary line of research where topic trees are built up bottom-up by using domain-specific and background knowledge, see Zock (1986).

A second problem is that the chosen relations should be cognitively basic and reliably applicable to any discourse segment. Otherwise, the list of possible relations could grow indefinitely long and become very complex. Sanders, Spooren and Noordman (1992) present a taxonomy of discourse relations in terms of cognitive primitives, such as the polarity of the relation and the semantic or pragmatic character of the link between the units. As an alternative, Knott and Dale (1994) investigate the use of explicit linguistic markers as a basis for the classification of coherence relations. The validity of these approaches in the context of discourse generation has not yet been shown.

A third problem with RST is its assumption that between two segments only one relation may hold. This is clearly wrong: many of them can signal more than one relation and can do so in a single token (Shiffrin, 1987). For example, (10) can be analyzed in terms of other relations, such as background or evidence. A more principled proposal to deal with different kinds of relation is the Parallel-Components Model (Redeker, 1992), based on the idea that multiple relations exist between utterances:

1 The ideational structure conveys the meaning of the discourse;
2 The rhetorical structure expresses a hierarchy of intentions;
3 The sequential structure signals coordination and subordination of discourse segments.

For example, a causal relation (ideational) may be used as evidence (rhetorical) for a claim or argument. This relation may constitute a structurally coordinated or subordinated segment (sequential) in the discourse.

Conclusion

While writing research up to now has provided a general characterization of discourse production, the relations between process and product are as yet very unclear. One of the main tasks for the future is to characterize strategies for discourse generation at several grain sizes (discourse and planning units) and in several domains of problem solving (rhetorical and ideational), and also to specify how these interact during planning. Computational approaches may be heuristically applied in simulations of discourse planning, in order to organize and observe the different factors involved in discourse, thus helping in the construction of a coherent and complete theoretical framework.

Computational Models of Discourse Planning

So far, no computational psycholinguistic models are available that cover all aspects of discourse production discussed in the previous section. To date, computational approaches have especially addressed *structural* aspects of the discourse generation problem. No attempt has been made to simulate the actual writing process. The aim of most computational models is to construct working systems dealing with discourse structure in terms of schemata for canonical discourse types (e.g., McKeown, 1982, 1985), schemata for rhetorical relations (RST), speaker intentions and pragmatic constraints (e.g., Hovy, 1988; Jameson, 1990; Moore and Paris, 1993), and focus constraints (e.g., McCoy and Cheng, 1991). Issues concerning the interaction between topic selection and organization have not been addressed. Most systems simply take a message representation and find a way of expressing it.

In the discussion of the models that follow, we point out which processes are included and what kind of data are generated. Our selection of models is based not only on their current theoretical relevance in the field, but also on the clarity of their description and their potential for generating further research. Their inspiration comes from linguistics and Artificial Intelligence, rather than from psycholinguistics. This being so, no evaluation based on psycholinguistic criteria is attempted here. In the final section, we try to place these models in the virtual space of 'things to do'.

Schemata for Discourse Planning: McKeown's TEXT

TEXT (McKeown, 1982, 1985) was one of the first systems to automatically produce paragraph length discourse. The system was built as a front-end to a naval data base. By communicating with the system, the user can get information about ships and weapons. McKeown analyzed texts that people produced to identify, describe, and compare objects. This analysis showed that people tended to reach a certain discourse goal by providing the same kind of information in a stereotypical way and in a rigid order.

These discourse strategies are typically composed of *rhetorical predicates*. They describe the relations (of similar grain size as RST relations) holding between two text units. Some examples of predicates are the following:

- IDENTIFICATION: identify the object as a member of some generic class or provide distinguishing attributes; e.g., *This beer is a Belgian beer.*
- CONSTITUENCY: present the constituents of the item; e.g., *This beer contains pure malt.*
- ATTRIBUTIVE: present properties of the object being defined; e.g., *This beer is dark brown.*

The combination of predicates appearing in texts with the same discourse structure is identified as a discourse strategy and can be formally represented as a *schema* (not to be confused with an RST schema). For example, a strategy where the CONSTITUENCY predicate is prominent is represented in the schema in (12), where {} indicates optionality, / indicates alternatives, + indicates 'at least once', *'any number of times', and ; means 'either'.

(12) {Identification}
      Constituency
      Attributive* / Cause-Effect*
      {Depth-identification / Depth attributive
          {Particular-Illustration / Evidence}
          {Comparison; Analogy}} +
      {Attributive / Explanation / Attributive / Analogy}

Considerable freedom exists within a schema; as can be seen from the example, portions may be omitted or repeated when necessary. Each entry in the schema can be filled by an instantiated predicate or a full schema with the same name. This flexibility allows schemata to be embedded, which provides for a hierarchical account of text structure. Each schema could be associated with one or more discourse goals. For example, the CONSTITUENCY SCHEMA could be used in order to *define* or to *describe a concept*.

Incorporating these schemata, TEXT can answer three types of request made by users: requests for a definition of an object (*define*), for a description of an object (*describe*) and for the comparison of two objects (*compare*). When asked to define or describe an object, TEXT chooses between two strategies. According to the quantity of information available in the database it will choose either the CONSTITUENCY schema (which details subparts) or the IDENTIFICATION schema (which gives defining characteristics). To generate the content of a response, TEXT follows the steps defined by the selected schema. The predicates of the schema dictate what kind of information to look for in the database.

Suppose the user requested a definition by asking *What is a guided missile?* Based on the user's question, TEXT would select a relevant subset of the knowledge base. For the current example, the system would select attributes, relations, subordinates and superordinate information of the notion *guided missile*. How the knowledge base is traced in order to determine what to say next is dictated by the *process strategy* (Paris and McKeown, 1987) which follows the structure of the knowledge base closely. Next, according to the discourse goal (define, describe, or compare) and the amount of information available in the relevant knowledge pool, a schema is chosen. Walking through the schema, TEXT instantiates the rhetorical predicates by using information from the selected subset of the knowledge base. When applied to a knowledge base on guided missiles, the constituency schema may lead to the text in (13).

(13) (IDENTIFICATION) A guided projectile is a projectile that is self-propelled.

(CONSTITUENCY) There are two types of guided projectile in the ONR database, torpedoes and missiles.

(IDENTIFICATION) The missile has a target location in the air or on the earth's surface.

(IDENTIFICATION) The torpedo has an underwater target location.

(EVIDENCE) The missile's target location is indicated by the DB attribute DESCRIPTION and the missile's flight capabilities are provided by the DB attribute ALTITUDE.

(EVIDENCE) The torpedo's underwater capabilities are provided by the DB attributes under DEPTH (for example, MAXIMUM OPERATING DEPTH).

(ATTRIBUTIVE) The guided projectile has DB attributes TIME TO TARGET & UNITS, HORZ RANGE & UNITS and NAME.

One principle of linearization is that one should avoid side-tracking. TEXT accounts for this principle by using *focus* rules, which choose the information that ties in best with the text produced so far. McKeown takes the focus rules introduced by Sidner (1983) as a starting point and reorders the three basic focus moves as follows:

1 Change focus to a recently introduced element.
2 Maintain current focus.
3 Return to the previous focus.

It should be added that this is not only an additional means of determining content, but also a means of controlling surface form (pronouns), as can be seen in example (14), in which the topic shifts in different ways (14a–c) according to the three rules, respectively.

(14) John is a good friend of mine. He told me that he was looking for a flat.
    a.   It shouldn't be too expensive.
    b.   He looked at the adds.
    c.   I know him for more than 20 years.

Schemata, as used in TEXT, have a number of interesting features. First of all, they are easy to build and use. Second, they may be defined for each type of paragraph to be generated by a specific application. For each clause typically appearing in such a paragraph, a predicate is incorporated into the schema that represents the type of information in the clause. To use a schema, the conditions of use of the predicates must be evaluated (taking into account focus), the appropriate material in the data base should be found, and the relevant material must be passed on to the realization component. Schemata are equivalent to what Levelt (1989) calls macroplans. Third, besides being useful on the macrolevel, schemata are also useful on the microlevel. The process strategy and the focusing rules adhere to the principles for linearization discussed previously. In fact, Paris and McKeown (1987) point out that their process strategy resembles that identified by Linde and Labov (1975; see also above) for apartment descriptions.

Unfortunately, schemata also have a number of shortcomings. One limitation on their use is the fact that they do not specify the role of each part with regard to the whole. Schemata merely describe what comes next. In this respect, they are equivalent to what Bereiter and Scardamalia (1987) call knowledge telling. Regardless of the number of optional and repeating predicates, the same question will invariably produce the same kind of answer, irrespective of the user's expertise or interest. The instantiation of the predicates in schemata is only driven by what is found in the knowledge base. This indicates that McKeown's communicative goals are not properly contextualized. The complex planning required for knowledge transforming is therefore far beyond the capabilities of TEXT. From another perspective, a schema can be viewed as the result of a compilation process where the rationale for all the steps in the process has been compiled out (Moore and Swartout, 1991). Because of this compilation, schemata provide an efficient but inflexible way to produce multisentential texts for achieving generic discourse purposes. A more flexible approach to planning is discussed in the next section.

Rhetorical Relations: Hovy's Structurer

As we have seen, RST is a descriptive theory of the organization of natural language texts. An RST description of a text is a hierarchical structure (consisting of clauses, sentences, paragraphs) that characterizes the text in terms of basic rhetorical relations holding between the parts of the text. The definition of each RST relation includes constraints on the two entities being related and on their combination, as well as a specification of the effect which the speaker attempts to achieve on the hearer's beliefs. Because RST provides an explicit connection between the speaker's intention and the rhetorical means to achieve those intentions, RST offers a more flexible approach to planning (Hovy, 1991; Moore and Paris, 1993) than the use of McKeown's schemata.

In order to be applicable to text generation, RST relations must be implemented in a discourse planner. Hovy (1988) was the first to operationalize a subset of RST relations into plans, by representing them as NOAH-like plan operators (Sacerdoti, 1977). Operators are named after their corresponding RST relation, e.g., SEQUENCE, a simplified example of which is given in (15) below.

(15)	Results	(SEQUENCE-OF ?PART ?NEXT)
	N + S requirements/subgoals	((NEXT ACTION ?PART ?NEXT))
	Nucleus requirements/subgoals	(TOPIC ?PART)
	Satellite requirements/subgoals	(TOPIC ?NEXT)
	Nucleus growth points	(CIRCUMSTANCE-OF ?PART ?CIRC)
		(ATTRIBUTE-OF ?PART ?VAL)
		(PURPOSE-OF ?PART ?PURP)
	Satellite growth points	(ATTRIBUTE-OF ?NEXT ?VAL)
		(DETAILS-OF ?NEXT ?DETS)
		(SEQUENCE-OF ?NEXT ?FOLL)
	Order:	(NUCLEUS SATELLITE)
	Relation-phrases:	("" "then" "next")

The intended effect of the RST relation is mapped into the *results*-field of the operator, while the constraints of the RST relation are mapped into *requirements/subgoals*, which are treated as semantic preconditions based on the knowledge of the hearer. So-called *growth points* are included which signal appropriate spots for conveying additional material. The inclusion of growth points was motivated by an extensive analysis of relevant texts and interviews with domain experts. Below we describe how all this is put to work in discourse planning.

Plan operators of the kind we just described are called *relation/plans* in Hovy's (1991) text planner or Structurer. The domain Hovy uses is a naval application in which the Structurer, together with PENMAN, a surface generator (Mann and Matthiessen, 1985; Penman Natural Language Generation Group, 1989), are part of a larger system that presents database information about U.S.

Figure 10.3a: Nucleus and satellite of the sequence relation

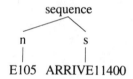

Figure 10.3b: Tree growth at the nucleus of the sequence relation

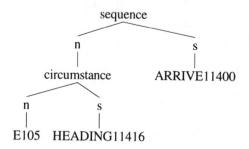

Figure 10.3c: RST generated Navy text

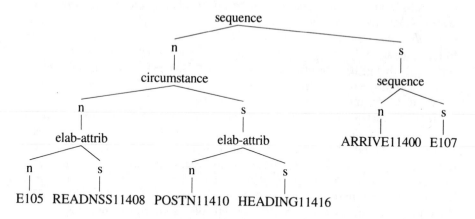

Navy vessels to a user by means of maps, tables, and text (Arens *et al.*, 1988). The database consists of a network of assertions about entities and actions. When a goal is posted (by a host system), the Structurer tries to find a relation/plan whose results-field matches this goal. The output of the Structurer is a hierarchical structure, called the paragraph tree (Figure 10.3d), which contains the discourse relation/plan as the top goal, and retrieved data-base elements as the bottom leaves.

Figure 10.3d: Joint RST and focus generated Navy text

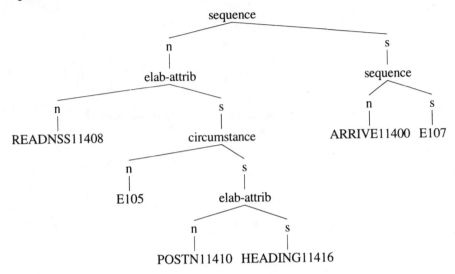

Consider an example (based on Hovy, 1991, 1993), in which the user asks for the next position of a particular vessel (called Knox) in the database. To the Structurer, this goal is represented in the following way: (BMB SPEAKER HEARER (POSITION-OF E105 ?NEXT)), which can be put in plain language as: *Achieve the state in which the hearer believes that it is the intention of the speaker that they mutually believe that the event E105 is followed by some other event.* In what follows, we simplify this goal by leaving out the BMB-part. The Structurer thus starts with this goal, simplified as (POSITION-OF E105 ?NEXT) which matches the results-field of the relation/plan SEQUENCE, shown in (15). In the match, ?PART is bound to E105, and with this binding, the Structurer begins searching for an appropriate nucleus, as the core of the message to be expressed. To accomplish this, it searches for input entities in the database that match the first requirement, which is the combined nucleus and satellite requirements (i.e., line 2 in (15)). The database input contains the information that the arrival of the vessel (ARRIVE11400) is the next action. This becomes bound to ?NEXT, which then becomes the satellite of the SEQUENCE relation/plan (line 4 in (15)), while E105 is the nucleus (Figure 10.3a). Next, the growth points are considered. Suggestions for additional input material related to the nucleus are considered in the Nucleus growth point field: these call for circumstances, attributes, and purpose. These act as subgoals the planner must try to achieve. A similar set is associated with the satellite. The first growth point to be considered (i.e., line 5 in (15)) is (CIRCUMSTANCE-OF ?PART ?CIRC). This appears to match the results-field of the CIRCUMSTANCE relation/plan (not shown). In the same way as for the sequence relation/plan, a match is sought for the variable ?CIRC. In this case the database provides the heading of the ship (HEADING11416). The found CIRCUMSTANCE relation between E105 and HEADING11416 thus fulfils the growth-point goal of the original SEQUENCE nucleus, which causes the tree to grow at this point. The nucleus E105 is moved down to become the nucleus of the newly formed CIRCUMSTANCE relation, where HEADING11416 becomes the satellite. The whole CIRCUMSTANCE relation then replaces the original nucleus in the SEQUENCE (Figure 10.3b).

Put briefly, the propagation of remaining growth points eventually leads to further growth of the paragraph tree (Figure 10.3c). The whole process stops when no satisfiable goals remain posted or the input is exhausted, regardless of whether at the end some growth points may remain unsatisfied. After adding the relation's characteristic cue words (line 12 in (15)) or phrases to the appropriate input entries and setting the appropriate syntactic constraints, the tree structures are transmitted to PENMAN for surface generation (16a). Notice that one of the *relation-phrases* in the last line of (15) is used.

Text planning with RST has enjoyed several enrichments. Consider, for example, the surface form in (16a), which looks rather odd. For example, the repeated use of the pronoun *it* does not seem natural. A speaker or writer would probably have used the words *the ship* or *the vessel*. Furthermore, with regard to coherence, the text introduces first the circumstance (condition) of the Knox and then enumerates a sequence of events. While this may be structurally appropriate, it fails to group semantically related material concerning the direction: *to head SSW*, and *to be en route to Sasebo* (see Maybury, 1992, pp. 80–1).

(16) a. Knox, which is C4, is en route to Sasebo. Knox, which is at 18N 79E, heads SSW. It arrives on 4/24. It then loads for 4 days.

   b. With readiness C4, Knox is en route to Sasebo. It is at 18N 79E, heading SSW. It will arrive on 4/24. It will load for 4 days.

To overcome some of these problems, Hovy and McCoy (1989) enriched RST in order to promote coherence, by using *discourse focus trees* (McCoy and Cheng, 1991). In this way, the initial text could be improved to (16b). To this end, the focusing rules used by TEXT were extended by representing the topics in the discourse as nodes in a tree, which is built up and traversed as the discourse progresses. McCoy and Cheng identified some general constraints for hopping from one node to the next, according to the conceptual types of node. For example, if the current focus is on an object, the next focus may be one of its attributes or actions. Hovy and McCoy describe how an RST paragraph tree and a focus tree can be constructed in parallel. During the expansion of a node in the RST discourse structure, the Structurer disregards questions with respect to the ordering of the growth points, collecting all the potential candidate relations and their associated database inputs. Each candidated relation is then checked against the currently legal focus shifts in the Focus Tree.

To recapitulate, Hovy's Structurer transforms RST into a text planner which allows more versatile planning than the schemata in TEXT, thanks to the use of growth points. The use of independent relation/plan operators explicitly links intentions and rhetorical relations in a hierarchy. Each RST relation/plan is simultaneously a basic rhetorical operator (microplan) which can be incorporated into a schema as well as a generalized schema (macroplan) for building a specific type of paragraph. Furthermore, Hovy (1993) argues that a text planner where RST relation/plans are combined with intraclause planning rules (such as those proposed by Appelt, 1985) and focusing rules (McCoy and Cheng, 1991) offers fine grained control over smaller spans of text than schemata. This also allows control over various syntactic aspects, such as relative clauses, the use of the tense, and the combining of several clauses into a single sentence.

Moore and Paris: Planning of Explanations

Hovy's text Structurer orders the inputs from the domain according to the constraints on the RST relations. It looks for some coherent way to organize the text so that all of the information in the input is included according to the requirements of the plan operators. The lack of a distinction between content selection and organization ignores the possibility that the same content domain may be used for different goals, which may mandate different items to be selected. Conversely, the availability of content may affect the discourse production strategy. For instance, the decision to present an example depends, among other things, upon the speaker's knowledge of such an example.

Furthermore, Hovy's system lacks higher order goals that allow the system to explain why it behaves as it does. The rhetorical relations serve at the same time as communication plans and as discourse structuring relations. In other words, communication goals can only be stated directly in terms of rhetorical relations. Moore and Swartout (1991) argue for a separation of *intentional* and *rhetorical* relations as well as for the primacy of communicative intentions. This is motivated by the fact that there is no one-to-one mapping between intentions and rhetorical relations. Moore and Pollack (1992) present an example (17) to illustrate this point:

(17) S: (a) Come home by 5:00.
          (b) Then we can go to the hardware store before it closes.
      H: (c) We don't need to go to the hardware store.
          (d) I borrowed a saw from Jane.

At the informational level, utterance (17a) is a CONDITION for (17b). Getting to the hardware store before it closes depends on H's coming home, but at the intentional level S may be trying to increase the ability of H to perform the act described in (17b). It is thus an ENABLEMENT, if S believes that H does not realize that the store closes early tonight. On the other hand, S may be trying to motivate H to come home early, say because S is planning a surprise party for H (MOTIVATION). H's reaction (17c–d) requires further motivation.

Example (17) shows that intentions and rhetorical relations do not map one-to-one. In particular, it illustrates that a generation system cannot simply rely on the information to be conveyed, while disregarding the speakers underlying intentions. It is only on the basis of the intentions underlying (17a) and (17b) that the speaker can decide how to subsequently respond to (17c) and (17d).

Moore and Paris (1993) describe a Text Planner that constructs explanations, in the context of a prototype expert system called Program Enhancement Advisor (PEA), which gives advice to beginning LISP programmers. The Text Planner is based on the intentions (goals) of the speaker at each moment of discourse production and finds the linguistic means available for realizing these intentions. We describe some details of this Text Planner, first examining the goals represented in the text plan and subsequently the operation of the operators.

Moore and Paris distinguish two types of goal to be reached by the discourse producer: communicative goals and linguistic goals. *Communicative goals* represent the speaker's intentions to affect the beliefs or goals of the hearer. Given a goal representing the speaker's intention, the planner tries to find the linguistic resources available for achieving that goal by *posting linguistic goals*. The latter lead to the generation of text and are of two types: speech acts and rhetorical goals. *Speech acts*, such as INFORM or RECOMMEND, map straightforwardly into utterances that form part of the final text. *Rhetorical goals*, such as MOTIVATION and CIRCUMSTANCE (compare RST relations) cannot be achieved directly but must be refined into one or more subgoals, which may be further communicative goals or speech acts.

Plans are utilized by the same style of hierarchical planner as Hovy's RST-based Structurer. The plan language provides *operators* which implement both general and specific strategies. The effect of an operator is defined in terms of a communicative or linguistic goal; constraints on the operator are listed as conditions which should be true for the operator to have the intended effect; furthermore, an operator specifies a nucleus (the most essential subgoal) and satellites (additional subgoals). As examples, operators for RECOMMEND and MOTIVATION are given in (18) and (19), respectively.

(18) NAME: RECOMMEND-ENABLE-MOTIVATE
      EFFECT: (GOAL ?hearer (DO ?hearer ?act))
      CONSTRAINTS: (Nucleus)
      NUCLEUS: (RECOMMEND ?speaker ?hearer ?act)
      SATELLITES: (((COMPETENT ?hearer (DONE ?hearer ?act))
           optional)
           (PERSUADED ?hearer (GOAL ?hearer (DO ?hearer ?act))
           optional))

English paraphrase:
      To make the hearer want to do an act,
      IF this text span is to appear in the Nucleus position, THEN

　　　1　Recommend the act
　　　　AND optionally,
　　　2　Achieve the state where the hearer is competent to do the act
　　　3　Achieve the state where the hearer is persuaded to do the act

(19)　EFFECT: (PERSUADED ?hearer (DO ?hearer ?act))
　　　CONSTRAINTS: (AND (STEP ?act ?goal)
　　　　　　　　　　　　　(GOAL ?hearer ?goal)
　　　　　　　　　　　　　(MOST-SPECIFIC ?goal)
　　　　　　　　　　　　　(CURRENT FOCUS ?act)
　　　　　　　　　　　　　(SATELLITE)
　　　NUCLEUS: (FORALL ?goal (MOTIVATION ?act ?goal)
　　　SATELLITE: none

English paraphrase:
To achieve the state in which the hearer is persuaded to perform an act,
IF the act is a step in achieving some goal(s) of the hearer,
　　　AND the goal(s) is/are the most specific along any refinement path
　　　AND the act is the current focus of attention
　　　AND the planner is expanding a satellite branch of the text plan
THEN motivate the act in terms of these goal(s).

The planning process begins when a communicative goal is posted, for example *Make the hearer set a cup of coffee*. When a goal is posted, the planner searches its library for all operators whose *effect* field matches the goal. To make this search more efficient, plan operators are stored in a discrimination network based on their effect field. When the plan operator in (18) is selected, it posts its nucleus as a discourse subgoal, in this case RECOMMEND. This goal is defined as a speech act, which maps directly into a specification for the sentence generator. The two satellites, however, require further operators, among which the one in (19), indicating that the communicative goal of persuading can be achieved by using the rhetorical strategy MOTIVATION.

　　　Note the explicit representation of various knowledge sources that are included in the constraints of (19). The first constraint (STEP ?act ?goal) says that there must be some domain goal(s) for which the act is a step in achieving. Satisfying this goal requires the planner to search the expert system's domain knowledge for such goals. The second constraint (GOAL ?hearer ?goal) specifies that if any such domain goal(s) exist, they must be goals of the user. For this, the system must inspect the user model. The last two constraints refer to the evolving text plan. They state that the operator can only be used if the act is in focus and that a satellite branch of the current text plan is expanded.

Planning proceeds by selecting one operator among those whose constraints are satisfied. Once a plan operator has been selected, it is recorded in the current plan node and the others are recorded as untried alternatives. The planner then expands the plan by posting its nucleus and required satellites as subgoals to be refined. For each subgoal, candidate operators are again selected and the planning process is repeated.

The planner maintains an agenda of pending goals to be satisfied. New subgoals for the nucleus and satellites are collected in a list, which is added to the front of the agenda. In this way, the text plan is built in a depth first manner (see Chapter 2). When a speech act is reached, no further elaboration of the plan at that point is necessary, but instead, the system constructs a specification that directs the realization component PENMAN which formulates the utterance. As the planner examines each of the arguments of the speech act, new goals may be posted as a side effect. Whether optional satellites are expanded depends on a parameter representing *verbosity* (terse or verbose) in the system. In terse mode, no optional satellites are expanded, whereas in verbose mode, each satellite is checked against the user model, and those that add to the user's knowledge are expanded.

Summing up, Moore and Paris extended the work on RST-based planning in various principled ways. While using plan-based operators resembling those of Hovy's Structurer, they also take the important distinction between communicative and linguistic goals as a new point of departure. The Text Planner described by Moore and Paris has a set of 150 operators that can answer questions like *Why?*, *Why . . . conclusion? Why are you trying to achieve goal? Why are you using this method? Why are you doing act? What is a concept? What is the difference between concept1 and concept2? Huh?* etc. The planner is implemented into several knowledge base systems and two intelligent tutoring systems (Rosenblum and Moore, 1993). Work in progress on the system includes, among other things, the use of focus and the implementation of dialogue management strategies. The problem of phrasing utterances for different types of users and situations is also being investigated (Paris, 1991).

Evaluation and Conclusion

Computational models for coherent text generation can only be evaluated according to psycholinguistic criteria when they incorporate explicit mechanisms for selecting and organizing what to say, as well as devices to translate these intentions into semantic and pragmatic plans. When, in addition, mechanisms are included for monitoring and revising both ideas and text, thereby allowing answers to questions about the reasons for producing a piece of discourse, the status of the model can be evaluated with respect to theories of writing. When neither is the case, we can only evaluate the internal characteristics of the model.

For example, we can investigate what types of discourse the system is able to generate. Of course, such an exercise may still generate interesting ideas concerning the mechanisms involved in discourse planning.

Despite the relative lack of empirical evidence, computational work is in progress, yielding interesting results with respect to several aspects of discourse planning. We have focused our discussion on three approaches (McKeown's TEXT, Hovy's Structurer, and Moore and Paris' Text Planner), but many more are worth mentioning. For example, the work by Dale (1992) on the generation of referring expressions, the work of Endres-Niggemeyer, Maier and Sigel (1994) on developing an expert system for abstracting and that by Jameson (1990) on the selection of information, thereby dealing with conversational maxims. It seems that computational approaches will soon be in a position to test specific questions about discourse planning. It is unfortunate that relevant testable hypotheses based on psycholinguistic models are lacking.

The systems that we have discussed show a progress from more or less prepackaged plans to dynamic text structuring to a more explicit link between communicative goals and linguistic means. As a consequence, the output of computational text planning steadily improves. In particular, progress has been made with respect to the tailoring of texts to specific users and the coherence of multisentence paragraphs. It remains to be seen whether these approaches model the richness that characterizes human discourse planning. The interaction between communicative goals and linguistic goals in Moore and Paris' Text Planner is at least reminiscent of the interaction between the ideational and rhetorical domains which characterizes knowledge transforming.

Furthermore, it seems hard to move from a descriptive theory of text structure to a theory of multisentence paragraph planning. Text planning systems may solve problems, but they may do so in a different way from human writers. Moreover, an open-ended task such as discourse planning may offer a wealth of qualitatively different strategies for problem solving. Only a few of these strategies have been studied so far. If current systems were used as a testbed for the evaluation of alternative strategies for planning discourse, some new insights could be expected.

Currently prominent text planners crucially hinge on the use of RST-inspired planning operators. The status of these operators is questionable, not only from a psychological perspective. Hovy (1993) discusses an attempt to assemble a core library of discourse relations. It is assumed that these should at least be described in intentional, structural, semantic and rhetorical terms. However, since the context of use generally determines their nature and specificity, a closed set of such operators may, in fact, not exist (Grosz and Sidner, 1985; Polanyi, 1988).

Dealing with the flexibility that characterizes human discourse generation may require better theories of planning, text coherence, and knowledge representation than are currently available. Computational research is gradually moving from the descriptive to the procedural phase. That is still a long way from modelling strategies.

References

ANDRIESSEN, J. E. B. (1991). *Minimal Strategies for Coherent Text Production*. Doctoral dissertation. Utrecht: Instituut voor Sociaalwetenschappelijk Onderzoek, Rijksuniversiteit Utrecht (ISOR).

ANDRIESSEN, J. E. B. (1994). 'Episodic representations in writing and reading', in EIGLER, G. and JECHLE, Th. (Eds) *Writing: Current trends in European research*, Freiburg: Hochschulverlag, pp. 71–83.

ANDRIESSEN, J. E. B., COIRIER, P., ROOS, L., PASSERAULT, J. M., BERT-ERBOUL, A. (in press). 'Thematic and structural planning in constrained argumentative text production', in VANDENBERGH and RIJLAARSDAM, G. (Eds) *Current Trends in Writing Research: What is Writing?*, Amsterdam: Amsterdam University Press.

APPELT, D. E. (1985). 'Planning English referring expressions', *Artificial Intelligence*, 26, pp. 1–133.

APPELT, D. E., and KRONFELD, A. (1987). 'A computational model of referring', in *Proceedings of the 10th International Joint Conference on Artificial Intelligence, Milan*, pp. 640–7.

ARENS, Y., MILLER, L., SHAPIRO, S. C., and SONDHEIMER, N. K. (1988). 'Automatic construction of user-interface displays', in *Proceedings of the 7th Conference of the American Association for Artificial Intelligence, St. Paul*, pp. 808–13.

AUSTIN, J. L. (1962) *How To do Things with Words*, Oxford: Clarendon.

BARNARD, Y. F., ANDRIESSEN, J. E. B., BLÄCKER, T., and ERKENS, G. (1989). 'Fostering reflection on organizational functions of text segments during expository paper composition', *3rd EARLI Conference, Madrid*.

BARTLETT, E. J. (1984). 'Anaphoric reference in written narratives of good and poor writers', *Journal of Verbal Learning and Verbal Behavior*, 23, pp. 540–52.

BEREITER, C., and SCARDAMALIA, M. (1983) 'Does learning to write have to be so difficult?, in FREEDMAN, I. P. Y. A. (Ed) *Learning to Write: First Language, Second Language*, New York: Longman, pp. 20–33.

BEREITER, C., and SCARDAMALIA, M. (1987) *The Psychology of Written Composition*, Hillsdale, NJ: Lawrence Erlbaum.

BRONCKART, J. P. (1985) *Le Fonctionnement des Discours: Un Modèle Psycholinguistique et une Méthode d'Analyse*, Neuchatel: Delachaux et Nestlé.

BROWN, G., and YULE, G. (1985) *Discourse Analysis*, Cambridge: Cambridge University Press.

BUTTERWORTH, B. (1980) 'Evidence from pauses in speech', in BUTTERWORTH, B. (Ed) *Language Production: Vol. 1. Speech and Talk*, London: Academic Press, pp. 155–75.

CLARK, E. V. (1970) 'How children describe events in time', in FLORES D'ARCAIS, G. B. and LEVELT, W. J. M. (Eds), *Advances in Psycholinguistics*, Amsterdam: North-Holland.

CLARK, H. H., and WILKES-GIBBS, D. L. (1986) 'Referring as a collaborative process', *Cognition*, 22, pp. 1–39.

COOPER, C. R., and MATSUHASHI, A. (1983) 'A theory of the writing process', in MARTLEW, M. (Ed) *The Psychology of Written Language*, New York: Wiley, pp. 3–39.

DALE, R. (1992) *Generating Referring Expressions*, Cambridge, MA: MIT Press.

DE BEAUGRANDE, R. (1984) *Text Production: Towards a Science of Composition*, Norwood, NJ: Ablex.

DEUTSCH, W., and PECHMANN, T. (1982) 'Social interaction and the development of definite descriptions' *Cognition*, 11, pp. 159–84.

EHRICH, V., and KOSTER, C. (1983) 'Discourse organization and sentence form: The structure of room descriptions in Dutch', *Discourse Processes*, 6, pp. 169–95.

ENDRES-NIGGEMEYER, B., MAIER, E., and SIGEL, A. (submitted) 'How to implement a naturalistic model of abstracting: Four core working steps of an expert abstractor'.

ERICSSON, K. A., and SIMON, H. A. (1984) *Protocol Analysis: Verbal Reports as Data*, Cambridge, MA: MIT Press.

FAYOL, M. (1991) 'From sentence production to text production: Investigating fundamental processes', *European Journal of Psychology of Education*, 6, 2, pp. 101–20.

FLOWER, L. F. (1981) *Problem-Solving Strategies for Writing*, New York: Harcourt Brace Jovanovich.

FLOWER, L. and HAYES, J. R. (1980) 'The dynamics of composing: Making plans and juggling constraints', in GREGG, L. and STEINBERG, E. R. (Eds) *Cognitive Processes in Writing*, Hillsdale, NJ: Lawrence Erlbaum, pp. 39–58.

FLOWER, L., and HAYES, J. R. (1981) 'Plans that guide the composing process', in FREDERIKSEN, C. H. and DOMINIC, J. F. (Eds), *Writing: The Nature, Development and Teaching of Written Communication, Vol. 2*, Hillsdale, NJ: Lawrence Erlbaum, pp. 39–58.

FLOWER, L. and HAYES, J. R. (1984) 'Images, plans, and prose: The representation of meaning in writing', *Written Communication*, 1, 4, pp. 120–60.

GOLDMAN-EISLER, F. (1968) *Psycholinguistics: Experiments in Spontaneous Speech*, New York: Academic Press.

GRAESSER, A. C., SINGER, M. and TRABASSO, T. (in press) 'Constructing inferences during narrative text comprehension', *Acta Psychologica*.

GRICE, H. P. (1975) 'Logic and conversation', in COLE, P. and MORGAN, J. L. (Eds) *Syntax and Semantics 3:* Speech Acts, New York: Academic Press, pp. 41–58.

GROSZ, B. (1977) *The Representation and Use of Focus in Dialogue Understanding*, (Technical report 151), Menlo Park, CA: SRI International.

GROSZ, B. J. and SIDNER, C. L. (1985) 'Discourse structure and the proper treatment of interruptions', in JOSHI, A. (Ed) *Proceedings of the 9th International Joint Conference on Artificial Intelligence, Los Angeles, Vol. 2*, Los Altos, CA: Morgan Kaufmann, pp. 832–9.

HALLIDAY, M. A. K. and HASAN, R. (1976) *Cohesion in English*, London: Longman.

HAYES, J. R. and FLOWER, L. (1986) 'Writing research and the writer. *American Psychologist*, 41, pp. 1106–13.

HERMANN, T. and GRABOWSKI, J. (1994) 'Pre-terminal levels of process in oral and written language production', in QUASTHOFF, U. (Ed), *Aspects of Oral Communication*, Berlin: De Gruyter.

HOVY, E. H. (1988) *Generating Natural Language Under Pragmatic Constraints*, Hillsdale, NJ: Lawrence Erlbaum.

HOVY, E. H. (1991) 'Approaches to the planning of coherent text', in PARIS, C. L., SWARTOUT, W. R. and MANN, W. C. (Eds), *Natural Language Generation in Artificial Intelligence and Computational Linguistics*, Boston: Kluwer Academic Publishers, pp. 83–102.

HOVY, E. H. (1993) 'Automated discourse generation using discourse structure relations', *Artificial Intelligence*, 63, pp. 341–85.

HOVY, E. H. and McCOY, K. F. (1989) 'Focusing your RST: A step towards generating coherent mutisentential text', in *Proceedings of the Annual Conference of the Cognitive Science Society, Ann Arbor, MI*, pp. 667–74.

JAMESON, A. (1990) *Knowing What Others Know. Studies in Intuitive Psychometrics*, (Technical report 90–10), Nijmegen: Nijmegen Institute for Cognition and Information, University of Nijmegen.

KLEIN, W. (1979) 'Wegauskunfte', *Zeitschrift fur Literaturwissenchaft und Linguistik*, 9, pp. 9–57.

KLEIN,, W. (1982) 'Local deixis in route directions', in JARVELLA, R. J. and KLEIN, W. M (Eds) *Speech, Place and Action: Studies in Deixis and Related Topics*, Chichester: Wiley.

KNOTT, A. and DALE, R. (1994) 'Using linguistic phenomena to motivate a set of coherence relations, *Discourse Processes*, 18, pp. 35–62.

LEVELT, W.J.M. (1981) 'The speakers linearization problem', *Philosophical Transactions of the Royal Society of London*, 295, pp. 305–15.

LEVELT, W.J.M. (1982a) 'Linearization in describing spatial networks', in PETERS, S.and SAARINEN, E. (Eds), *Processes, Beliefs, and Questions*, Dordrecht: Reidel.

LEVELT, W.J.M. (1982b) 'Cognitive styles in the use of spatial direction terms', in JARVELLA, R.J. and KLEIN, W.M. (Eds) *Speech, Place and Action: Studies in Deixis and Related Topics*, Chichester: Wiley.

LEVELT, W.J.M. (1989) *Speaking: From Intention to Articulation*, Cambridge, MA: MIT Press.

LINDE, C. and LABOV, W. (1975) 'Spatial networks as a site for the study of language and thought', *Language*, 51, pp. 924–39.

MAIER, E. and HOVY, E.H. (1991) 'Organising discourse structure relations using metafunctions', in HORACEK, H. and ZOCK, M. (Eds) *New Concepts in Natural Language Generation*, London: Pinter, pp. 69–86.

MANDLER, J.M. (1984) *Stories, Scripts and Scenes: Aspects of Schema Theory*, Hillsdale, NJ: Lawrence Erlbaum.

MANN, W.C. and MATTHIESSEN, C. (1985) 'A demonstration of the NIGEL text generation computer program', in BENSON, R. and GREAVES, J. (Eds) *Systemic Perspectives on Discourse*, Norwood, NJ: Ablex, pp. 50–83.

MANN, W.C. and THOMPSON, S.A. (1987) 'Rhetorical structure theory: Description and construction of text structures', in KEMPEN, G. (Ed) *Natural Language Generation: New Results in Artificial Intelligence, Psychology and Linguistics*, Dordrecht: Nijhoff (Kluwer), pp. 85–95.

MATSUHASHI, A. (1987) 'Revising the plan and altering the text', in MATSUHASHI, A. (Ed) *Writing in Real Time*, Norwood, NJ: Ablex, pp. 197–223.

MAYBURY, M.T. (1992) 'Communicative acts for explanation generation', *International Journal of Man-Machine Studies*, 37, pp. 135–72.

McCOY, K.F. and CHENG, J. (1991) 'Focus of attention: Constraining what can be said next' in PARIS, C.L., SWARTOUT, W.R. and MANN, W.C. (Eds) *Natural Language Generation in Artificial Intelligence and Computational Linguistics*, Boston: Kluwer Academic Publishers, pp. 103–24.

McCUTCHEN, D. and PERFETTI, C.A. (1982) 'Coherence and connectedness in the development of discourse production', *Text*, 2, pp. 113–39.

McDONALD, D. (1983) 'Description directed control: its implications for natural language generation', *Computers & Mathematics*, 9, pp. 111–30.

McKEOWN, K. (1982) 'The TEXT system for natural language generation: An overview', in *Proceedings of the 20th Annual Meeting of the Association for Computational Linguistics, Toronto*, pp. 113–20.

McKEOWN, K.R. (1985) *Text Generation: Using Discourse Strategies and Focus Constraints to Generate Natural Language Text*, Cambridge: Cambridge University Press.

MOORE, J.D. and PARIS, C.L. (1993) 'Planning text for advisory dialogues: Capturing intentional and rhetorical information', *Computational Linguistics*, 19, pp. 651–94.

MOORE, J.D. and POLLACK, M.E. (1992) 'A problem for RST: The need for multi-level discourse analysis', *Computational Linguistics*, 18, pp. 537–44.

MOORE, J.D. and SWARTOUT, W.R. (1991) 'A reactive approach to explanation: Taking the user's feedback into account', in PARIS, C.L., SWARTOUT, W.R. and MANN, W.C. (Eds.) *Natural Language Generation in Artificial Intelligence and Computational Linguistics*, Boston: Kluwer Academic Publishers, pp. 3–48

NEWELL, A. and SIMON, H.A. (1972) *Human Problem Solving*, Englewood Cliffs, NJ: Prentice Hall.

PARIS, C.L. (1991) 'Generation and explanation: Building an explanation facility for the explainable expert systems framework', in PARIS, C.L., SWARTOUT, W.R. and MANN, W.C. (Eds.) *Natural Language Generation in Artificial Intelligence and Computational Linguistics*, Boston: Kluwer Academic Publishers, pp. 49–82.

277

PARIS, C. L. and McKEOWN, K. R. (1987) 'Discourse strategies for descriptions of complex physical objects', in KEMPEN, G. (Ed) *Natural Language Generation: New Results in Artificial Intelligence, Psychology and Linguistics*, Dordrecht: Nijhoff, pp. 97–115.

PENMAN NATURAL LANGUAGE GENERATION GROUP (1989) *The PENMAN User Guide*, Information Science Institute, University of Southern California, Marina Del Rey, CA.

POLANYI, L. (1988) 'A formal model of the structure of discourse', *Journal of Pragmatics*, 12, pp. 601–38.

REDEKER, G. (1992) *Coherence and Structure in Text and Discourse*, Unpublished manuscript, Tilburg University.

ROBERTS, R. M. and KREUTZ, R. J. (1993) 'Nonstandard discourse and its coherence', *Discourse Processes*, 16, 4, pp. 451–64.

ROSENBLUM, J. and MOORE, J. (1993) 'Participating in instructional dialogues: Finding and exploiting relevant prior explanations', in BRNA, P., OHLSSON, S. and PAIN, H. (Eds) *Proceedings of the 5th World Conference on Artificial Intelligence in Education, Edinburgh*, pp. 145–52.

ROUSSEY, J.-Y. and GOMBERT, A. (1992) 'Ecriture en Dyade d'un Texte Argumentatif par des Enfants de Huit Ans', *Archives de Psychologie*, 60, pp. 297–315.

SACERDOTI, E. (1977) *A Structure for Plans and Behavior*, Amsterdam: North-Holland.

SANDERS, T. J. M., SPOOREN, W. P. M. and NOORDMAN, L. G. M. (1992) 'Towards a taxonomy of coherence relations', *Discourse Processes*, 15, pp. 1–35.

SCARDAMALIA, M. and PARIS, P. (1985) 'The function of explicit discourse knowledge in the development of text representation and composing strategies', *Cognition and Instruction*, 2, pp. 1–39.

SEARLE, J. R. (1979) *Expression and Meaning: Studies in the Theory of Speech Acts*, Cambridge: Cambridge University Press.

SEUREN, P. A. M. (1985) *Discourse Semantics*, Oxford, Blackwell.

SHIFFRIN, D. (1987) *Discourse Markers*, Cambridge: Cambridge University Press.

SIDNER, C. L. (1983) 'Focusing in the Comprehension of definite anaphora', in BRADY, J. M. and BERWICK, R. C. (Eds) *Computational Models of Discourse*, Cambridge, MA: MIT Press, pp. 267–330.

TOULMIN, S. (1958) *The Uses of Argument*, Cambridge: Cambridge University Press.

TRABASSO, T. and NICKELS, M. (1992) 'The development of goal plans of action in the Narration', *Discourse Processes*, 15, pp. 249–76.

TRABASSO, T., VAN DEN BROEK, P. and SUH, M. (1989) 'Logical necessity and transitivity of causal relations in stories', *Discourse Processes*, 12, pp. 1–25.

VAN DIJK, T. and KINTSCH, W. (1983) *Strategies of Discourse Comprehension*, New York: Academic Press.

ZOCK, M. (1986) *Le Fil d'Ariane ou les Grammaires de Texte Comme Guide dans l'Organisation et l'Expression de la Pensée en Langue Maternelle et/ou etrangère*, Paris: UNESCO.

Chapter 11

Computational Models of Incremental Grammatical Encoding

Koenraad de Smedt

Introduction

In formulating a sentence, speakers must take into account not only what they want to say and the context in which they are saying it, but also the grammar of the language they are speaking. *Grammatical encoding* is the casting of a message into a linguistic plan that conforms to the grammar of a language. Together with *phonological encoding*, it is part of a module called the *Formulator* which occupies a central place in the blueprint of the speaker drawn by Levelt (1989, p. 9; see also Chapter 1). The input to the Formulator consists of preverbal messages generated by the *Conceptualizer*. I assume that this input is given as *conceptual structures*, without making detailed assumptions about their form, except that they consist of conceptual entities and relations. The output of the Formulator is a phonetic plan that can control the articulation processes.

Grammatical encoding comprises both the selection of lexical material and the organization of this material in a syntactic framework. The present chapter concentrates on the latter aspect, while lexical selection is dealt with in Chapter 12. The assembly of a syntactic framework involves structural choices that are subject to various restrictions imposed by the grammar but are also sensitive to various performance factors which presumably originate in situational and architectural characteristics of the speaker's cognitive system. Some of these factors are explained in the next section. But first, I briefly touch upon three grammatical restrictions which play a role in this chapter: subcategorization, word order, and the use of markers such as inflection and function words.

First, the syntactic form of sentences is to some extent determined by certain characteristics of the chosen words. More specifically, it is assumed that words are *categorized* in the lexicon according to what parts of speech they are. The English word *dream*, for example, is categorized as a verb or a noun, but it cannot be used as an article nor as a preposition. Furthermore, words are *subcategorized* according to the way they can be complemented to form a complete utterance. For example, certain verbs take *that*-clauses as direct objects, as in *I dreamt that I could fly*, whereas others take *to-infinitives* instead, as in *I wanted to fly*. This subcategorization is not predictable from the meaning, so that an interdependence between word choice and syntactic planning must be assumed.

Second, spoken or written utterances are necessarily linear in form. Words and phrases cannot always be put in the same order as that in which the corresponding ideas have come to the speaker's mind. In English, word order is rather fixed and canonical linear patterns may convey meaningful distinctions. The question *Was she late?* has a different word order than the assertion *She was late*. Other variations may be stylistically marked: *Late she was*, or may simply be wrong: *She late was*. Still, the syntax of English allows some freedom of choice in the left-to-right order of words. We can say either *Yesterday she was late* or *She was late yesterday*. Consequently, we can ask the question how such choices are accounted for in a performance model of sentence production.

Third, markers such as inflection (see also Chapter 7) and the use of function words, including articles, prepositions, and auxiliaries, are prescribed by the grammar to express certain aspects of meaning. For example, the feature *plurality* is normally expressed in English by a suffix that makes the difference between *horse* and *horses*, and the feature *definiteness* is marked with an article in *the horses*. The use of these markers is governed by rules which seem arbitrary and language-dependent. Russian, for example, has no articles at all. Moreover, the use of these markers is dependent on other parts of the planned utterance. English has a rule for *subject-verb agreement* (SVA) which requires finite verbs to agree in person and number with their subjects: *He walks* vs. *They walk*. The computation of agreement presupposes knowledge about grammatical functions, such as *subject*, which the speaker must somehow identify in the sentence plan.

Summing up, planning an utterance involves choices that take into account several grammatical restrictions, of which I have mentioned word order, the use of inflexion and function words, and subcategorization. These restrictions generally presuppose structural knowledge about word groups (such as noun phrases) rather than single words. Moreover, word groups and sentences can involve several levels of embedding. Language production therefore seems to require representations and processes that manipulate hierarchically organized syntactic units. It is generally accepted that sentence planning involves hierarchical representations, usually depicted in the form of tree shaped graphs (see also Chapter 8), and yields a frame with ordered slots for words. The structural knowledge expressed in a graph allows features like gender, number, etc., to be assigned to words where appropriate, in order to allow the computation of inflected phonological forms at a subsequent level of the language production process.

Given a conceptual input, a grammar, and a lexicon, the speaker has all the necessary knowledge to start building the linguistic form of an utterance. But how does the speaker go about it? From a computational viewpoint, grammatical encoding can be viewed as the satisfaction of multiple constraints. The final utterance must be both well-formed according to the grammar and composed of existing words that fit in the syntactic structure. It must, of course, also express the conceptual input as precisely as possible. Choices on one level may conflict with choices on another level. Furthermore, all the information from the various sources of knowledge may not necessarily be accessible at the same moment. The process needs to cope with certain limits of its computational resources, for example, the size and extent of working memory. Consequently, it should not be surprising that errors and hesitations are quite common in on-line speech production. Still, the language production process generally succeeds in the timely generation of utterances that convey the intended meaning. These high demands presuppose some amount of sophisticated planning that is supposed to proceed in an *incremental* (piecemeal) way. The goal of this chapter is to consider some computational models that provide an account of syntactic representation and processes for incremental language production.

The next section presents a selection of linguistic and psycholinguistic phenomena, leading to the formulation of some important problems and assumptions in grammatical encoding. Then the chapter zooms in on the incremental mode of sentence production. A number of computational models which account for this processing mode are discussed in detail. Although the models have been developed for different languages (Dutch, German or English) and sometimes aim at giving an account of specific word order phenomena in that language, a comparison can be made. This is done in the final section.

Phenomena and Assumptions in Grammatical Encoding

What clues can we find for a psychologically plausible architecture for grammatical encoding? Some indications can be found in studies of speech errors and dysfluencies. Even if spontaneous speech generally appears to be uttered relatively smoothly, closer inspection reveals some performance problems. Speakers make short pauses, repeat themselves, make mistakes, correct themselves, stop in mid-sentence, start all over, etc. Some of these phenomena can be seen as indicating the difficulties and limitations of syntactic processing. Other clues can be found in regular variations in the forms of utterance. Even if the grammar prescribes the linguistic form of our utterances, it also allows certain degrees of freedom. For example, we can choose between active and passive sentences, or between alternative word orderings. Such choices are neither entirely random, nor completely predictable from the underlying message or the context of the utterance, but seem partly to reflect certain performance aspects. Put briefly, empirical work suggests that variation in the forms of utterance, as well as error and hesitation, commonly reflect variations in the processing of linguistic information (for example, Garrett, 1980; Bock, 1982; 1986; Bock and Warren, 1985; Stemberger, 1985). Some of the processing factors which may exert such influences are discussed below. For a wider overview of observational and

experimental evidence about the syntactic component in speech planning, I refer
to Bock and Levelt (1994) and Bock (1995, a).

Conceptual and Lexical Guidance

If one hypothesizes the need for syntactic plans in sentence production, then one
of the main questions is how to co-ordinate word selection and syntactic planning.
There are occasions when the production process may be driven by syntactic
patterns which follow directly from the content and structure of the message to be
transferred. A definition, for example, is likely to be built on the syntactic pattern
An X is a Y that Z. In addition, there is evidence for correspondences between the
meaning of a verb and its subcategorization (Fisher, Gleitman and Gleitman,
1991). Whether a verb is transitive or not, for example, is somewhat predictable
from the kind of action it expresses. This seems to suggest that syntactic plans can
be created on the basis of the meaning to be expressed. However, if this is done
without regard for the specific words to be inserted, this would still give rise to un-
grammaticalities. Consider the sentence patterns in (1), which are constrained by
the different subcategorizations of the verbs *replace* and *substitute*, even if these
verbs are very similar in meaning.

> (1)   a.   Cecile replaced/*substituted Greek literature with Spanish.
>   b.   Cecile *replaced/substituted Spanish literature for Greek.

It makes sense to assume that lexical knowledge guides the construction of a
syntactic structure (Kempen and Hoenkamp, 1987). This guidance could be
accomplished by *lemmas*, lexical entries associating meaning with words in an
abstract syntactic plan (see Chapter 12). For example, there is a lemma associating
the verb *substitute* with its meaning and with a syntactic plan where it is followed
by a direct object (expressing the replacement) and a prepositional clause with *for*
(expressing the replaced item).

While lexical choice thus seems to determine the syntactic structure, it seems
reasonable to assume that lexical choice is at the same time constrained by the
given syntactic context. Speech errors, in particular blends or fusion errors, suggest
that lemmas may compete during grammatical encoding. In utterance (2), for
example, it seems that *understanding* and *compassion* are both available, but it is
not possible to integrate both in the current syntactic structure.

> (2)   ...that one would get understanding for this compa...
>   uh...compassion for this character.[1]

The notion of the lemma is complemented by the notion of the *lexeme*, which
defines a particular phonological word form suitable for a given syntactic context.

The separation of semantic-syntactic information in lemmas on the one hand and morpho-phonological information in lexemes on the other hand has been assumed by various authors who suppose that lexical access is a two-stage process (Garrett, 1980; Levelt and Maassen, 1981; Kempen and Huijbers, 1983; Levelt and Schriefers, 1987). The first stage is the selection of lemmas (see Chapter 12) which are configured into a syntactic structure during grammatical encoding (present chapter); the second stage is the retrieval of lexemes during phonological encoding (see Chapter 13).

Performance Factors in Word Order and Syntactic Choice

Incremental Production

Spontaneous speech is to some extent planned *incrementally*, that is, in a piecemeal way. According to a stage model as outlined in Chapter 1, a message must be delineated before lemmas for it can be retrieved and before it can be grammatically encoded. But this kind of seriality does not necessarily apply to the whole sentence. It would be odd if speakers always first conceptualized the complete content for the next sentence, then retrieved all lemmas, then created a syntactic structure, next computed the phonetic string for the whole utterance and only then started uttering the first word. Instead, there is evidence that sentences are not always planned in their entirety before speakers start to articulate them. Experimental work by Lindsley (1975, 1976), Levelt and Maassen (1981) and Kempen and Huijbers (1983) suggest that while there is some planning ahead, speakers start articulating their utterance not long after the first words (but not yet the whole sentence) can be produced. This is in line with some earlier studies on hesitations in speech (e.g., Boomer, 1965; Goldman-Eisler, 1968; Brotherton, 1979).

More recent empirical work with picture description tasks has focused on the effect of *conceptual* and *lexical accessibility* on incremental production (Bock and Warren, 1985; Kelly, Bock and Keil, 1986; McDonald, Bock and Kelly, 1993). The hypothesis is that variations in the syntactic structure of sentences, other things being equal, are partly determined by the ease of retrieving the words' conceptual content and the lemmas to express this content. Among other things, assignments of grammatical functions, such as subject and direct object, would be affected by the ease of finding a lexical representation consistent with the intended meaning. Similarly, Pechmann (1989) Schriefers and Pechmann, 1988; but see Pechmann, 1994) hypothesized that variations of word order, e.g., *a white big triangle* rather than the preferred *a big white triangle*, will be partly determined by the ease of accessing the words' conceptual content in a given context. Experimental results point in this direction, although the evidence is not conclusive.

There are several ways of viewing incremental production. One way allows various stages of sentence production to run in parallel by letting one module start processing before the previous one has completely finished. This approach, called *pipelining* in computer science, was first proposed for sentence production by Kempen and Hoenkamp (1987) and has been implemented in a number of computer models discussed below. Other models are not pipelined, but are incremental in the sense that small amounts of work are being done in successive small amounts of time. One such model, discussed below, lets grammatical encoding proceed stepwise by choosing successive words to be incorporated in the utterance one by one, while all conceptual inputs and all linguistic knowledge act together.

Syntactic Weight

Ross (1967) coined the term 'heavy-NP shift' to describe the phenomenon in English where a long or *heavy* noun phrase (NP) tends to appear in sentence-final position, as in (3a). Hawkins (1994) found that the length of the NP (counted in words in written English) is less important than its length relative to other constituents which could occupy sentence-final position, for example the prepositional phrase (PP) *to Claire* in (3).

(3) a. I introduced to Claire *some friends that Alex had brought along*.
     b. I introduced *some friends that Alex had brought along* to Claire.

More specifically, at equal weight there is a clear preference for the normal NP PP order in (3b), but as the relative NP weight increases, this preference diminishes and NP movement to final position becomes more likely. De Haan and Van Hout (1986) have found similar *weight* phenomena in a statistical analysis of postmodifying clauses, including relative clauses, in a corpus of written English.

Hawkins (1990) proposes an account of weight phenomena in terms of the ratio of immediate constituents (ICs) to words in a sentence. The assumption is that having longer constituents toward the end improves the IC-to-word ratio early in the sentence. This is viewed as an advantage for sentence comprehension. However, it hardly explains the phenomenon from the viewpoint of the speaker. On-line experiments by Stallings, MacDonald and O'Seaghdha (1994) suggest that heavy-NP shift facilitates both comprehension and on-line production.

No definitive explanation has been proposed so far. Assuming that heavy constituents place extra demands on processing and memory resources, they may be 'overtaken' by competing constituents which are lighter, or they may be postponed to a point in the utterance where overall processing demands are low. However, processing preferences directly based on surface features such as relative length seem difficult to integrate in a theory of incremental production, because the length of a constituent may not yet be known when its utterance is initiated. Alternatively, heavy constituents may be expressing less accessible complex concepts.

Persistence

Syntactic persistence is the spontaneous repeated use of a particular syntactic construction across successive sentences. This effect has been reported in natural conversation (Kempen, 1977) but has also been found in a controlled context. Priming experiments suggest that the choice of a particular syntactic plan can be positively biased by prior activation of an instance of such a plan. Bock (1986) conducted experiments with a picture description task where subjects who first produced a prime sentence with a given structure were asked to describe a picture of a conceptually unrelated event. Subjects who had just produced the prepositional dative sentence (4a) were more likely to describe a subsequently shown picture as (4b) than by using the double-object dative (4c). The opposite pattern was also found for the double-object dative (4d) as a prime.

(4)   a.   The governess made a pot of tea for the princess.
      b.   A clerk is showing a dress to a man.
      c.   A clerk is showing a man a dress.
      d.   The governess made the princess a pot of tea.

A similar tendency was observed for active vs. passive sentences. These findings suggest not only that there is competition between alternative structural realisations, but also that recently used structures are at an advantage in this competition. Recently used structures may be more *activated* than competing than less recently used structures (see Chapter 3 for an explanation of the activation metaphor, and Chapter 8 for the use of activation in models of syntactic analysis).

Syntactic Coherence and Repairs
Errors affecting the *correctness* and *syntactic coherence* of the utterance occur relatively often in spontaneous speech. Word exchange errors, as in (5), provide the basis for an argument that different parts of the sentence are simultaneously present during sentence planning (Garrett, 1980). In computational terms, this argues for allowing different branches of the syntactic tree structure to be constructed in parallel.

(5)   We all sing around and . . . stand around and sing.

One type of syntactic incoherence is the *apokoinou*, where the middle of a sentence goes with both the first and the last part of a sentence. For example, in (6a), the first part, between braces, is in itself grammatical, and so is the overlapping final part between square brackets; however, the sentence as a whole is incoherent. Such utterances are sometimes treated as *non-retracing repairs* (De Smedt and Kempen, 1987), because they can be seen as a kind of repair that is uttered without a correction marker and often without hesitation, in contrast to syntactic rearrangements which appear as normal retracing repairs (6b).

(6)   a.   {So we get as [an added bonus to this approach} is a system which . . .]
      b.   It smells a little . . . a little citrusy is what it smells like.

Spontaneous apokoinous might be explained in computational terms as the intrusion of competing syntactic frames into a syntactic structure of which the less recent elements have 'decayed'. The most recently uttered constituent is used as a hook to attach a new sentence pattern. The phenomenon could also be seen as evidence for the simultaneous exploration of several syntactic structures. However, even if they imply the construction of several parallel structures, the various alternative structures need not be active at the same point in time, but could be active in succession, as already suggested above by their treatment as non-retracing repairs.

Structural Dependency in Subject-Verb Agreement

The morphology of a word may be structurally dependent on features of other words. In *subject-verb agreement* (SVA) in English, the inflexion of the verb is under the control of the features of the subject noun, in particular its features number and person. How do speakers implement dependencies that span multiple words or constituents? The presence of a noun with diacritical parameters different from the subject, in a position close to the verb, may promote errors against SVA, as in (7).

(7) a. *The producer of the latest films were in financial trouble.
      b. *The producer who made the films were in financial trouble.

Such errors have been labelled *attraction errors* or *proximity concord* by some authors (for example, Quirk, *et al.*, 1972), reflecting the fact that the more recent noun plays a role as an attractor. Recency in itself, however, does not explain the fact that SVA errors are more frequent across *phrases* (7a) than across *clauses* (7b), as found in error eliciting experiments (Bock and Miller, 1991; Bock and Cutting, 1992; Bock, 1995b). It was further found that only in the phrase condition did the error frequency increase with phrase length, which means that processes responsible for agreement are most sensitive to the diacritical parameters of noun phrases within the same clause. Bock and Cutting conclude that the ability to maintain information in working memory seems necessary to implement dependencies that span multiple words or constituents, and, more importantly, sentence production seems to rely on a hierarchical architecture where clauses are separate planning units. Vigliocco, Butterworth and Semenza (1995) share this view but argue against an autonomous syntactic module because they found morpho-phonological and semantic effects on SVA errors in several languages. Furthermore, an asymmetry between singular and plural has often been found.

AI-Based Models

The previous section briefly reviewed some important phenomena and assumptions with respect to grammatical encoding. We now turn our attention to computational models. A wealth of implemented computer models for sentence production has emerged from the Artificial Intelligence, Computational Linguistics and Cognitive Science traditions.[2] Some of these models are hardly or not at all related to psycholinguistic insights into sentence production. No known computer model takes into account all of the phenomena described above, let alone the remaining phenomena in the literature that are not discussed here. Many computational models, however, do address the incrementality issue explicitly. Several incremental models based on an AI paradigm will be discussed in detail in this section.

IPG

Incremental Procedural Grammar (IPG; Kempen and Hoenkamp, 1987; Levelt, 1989) is a computational model for sentence production which claims that human sentence production involves parallel activity in the different modules responsible for *conceptualizing, formulating* and *articulating*. Each of these modules takes the output of the previous one as its input, but the modules can be organized so that they operate on different pieces of input concurrently, as illustrated in Figure 11.1. The scheme shows *intercomponent* parallelism, i.e., the simultaneous activity of the various modules. This allows the Formulator to begin producing a sentence before the Conceptualizer has completely defined all of its content. In addition, the overlapping lines in the Formulator stage show *intracomponent* parallelism, i.e., the simultaneous processing of fragments within a module. This allows several branches of the syntactic structure to be computed in parallel.

IPG is a model with a *procedural* architecture (see Chapter 2), implemented on a computer and tested with a grammar for Dutch. Syntactic planning is

Figure 11.1: Schematic view of incremental generation in IPG

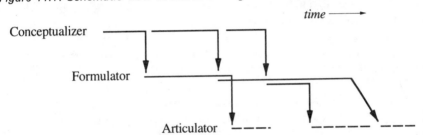

executed by procedures which in turn call other procedures to do part of their job. A distinction is made between categorial procedures, which plan syntactic categories such as a noun phrase (NP), a noun (N), a sentence (S), a verb (V), etc., and functional procedures, which plan syntactic functions such as subject (Subj), direct object (Obj), etc. IPG claims that the choice of these procedures is largely controlled by the grammatical properties of the lemmas which are retrieved to express a given meaning.

As an example, consider the Dutch lemmas for *zien* (see) and *willen* (want), shown in (8a,b). Both are verb (V) lemmas which require slots for a subject (Subj) and a direct object (Obj). Examples (8c,d) are instances of nominal (N) lemmas.

(8) a. V (nil, <Lexeme (zien) >)
         Subj (Path (actor:), < >)
         Obj (Path (object:), < >)
     b. V (nil, <Lexeme (willen) >)
         Subj (Path (actor:), < >)
         Obj (Path (object:), < >)
         ObjCompl
     c. N (nil, <Lexeme (Chris) >)
     d. N (nil, <Lexeme (film) >)

Each lexical specification consists of a conceptual pointer (possibly *nil*), and lexeme (between angled brackets, possibly empty). The specifications in the verbal lemmas cause calls to the dedicated subprocedures named V, Subj and Obj. They also indicate what parts of the message are to be associated with the Subj and Obj procedures. More generally, syntactic procedures are always specialized according to the kind of constituent they produce, and they operate within the constraints that the lemmas impose on their syntactic and conceptual environment. An example of a lexically specified syntactic constraint is the feature ObjCompl in (8b), which signifies that the object complement is an infinitival clause.

As a simple example of how incremental production proceeds, consider the generation of the Dutch sentence (9). The conceptual structure serving as input consists of conceptual entities representing objects, actions, events, etc. in the message to be expressed, linked by conceptual relations, sometimes called *case relations* or *thematic roles*, for example *actor, possessor, location*, etc. This structure is referenced by a conceptual pointer (*cp*) as shown in (10). Furthermore, suppose that the conceptual structure is not accessible all at once, but that initially only the concept in (10a) is accessible, and at successive time intervals the expansions in (10b,c) become available.

(9) Chris heeft de film willen zien. (Chris has wanted to see the film)

(10) a. cp = Chris
     b. cp = want (actor: Chris) (aspect: perfect)
     c. cp = want (actor: Chris) (object: see (actor: Chris) (object: film))
                  (aspect: perfect)

To start the grammatical encoding of a sentence, an initial procedure for the main sentence (S) is set up with the appropriate conceptual pointer as its argument, as in (11).

(11)   S (cp, < Main >)

IPG presupposes that a lemma is selected that satisfies the conceptual structure (see Chapter 12 for models of lemma selection). Lemma (8c) satisfies the conceptual specifications in (10a). This lemma gives rise to a categorial procedure N which attempts to become active in the context of S. However, N cannot be directly called by S, because it first needs to be assigned a grammatical function. According to the grammar, N can be the head of an NP; consequently, a categorial procedure NP is created that will call a functional procedure Head, which will in turn call N. Furthermore, an NP is by default the subject of an S, so a functional procedure Subj is created. This gives rise to the initial procedure calling hierarchy in (12).

(12)   (13)

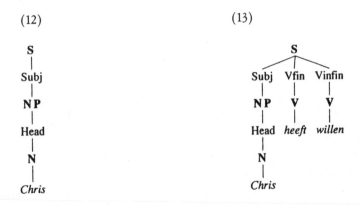

IPG uses iteration as a basic procedural mechanism to model incrementality. Each procedure repeatedly checks for the next conceptual expansion and processes it. Suppose, for example, that the next expansion of the conceptual structure is that in (10b). Suppose furthermore that lemma (8b) is retrieved and creates the necessary subprocedures. Subj is a functional procedure which can be called directly by S. Moreover, it is already present, and its conceptual structure is consistent with the (*actor:*) specification in the lemma. The perfect aspect gives rise to the addition of a procedure V for an (auxiliary) verb. V is a categorial procedure and must first be assigned a grammatical function. In this case, V is a finite verb, and therefore a procedure VFin is created. Another V procedure for the main verb is spawned and it is assigned the grammatical function Vinfin because it is a non-finite verb. The current state is reflected in (13). In the final iteration, the *cp* in (10c) becomes accessible. Skipping further details, structure (14a) represents the eventual results of expansion of the procedure call hierarchy with an Obj branch. This structure is still unordered.

(14)   a.   b.

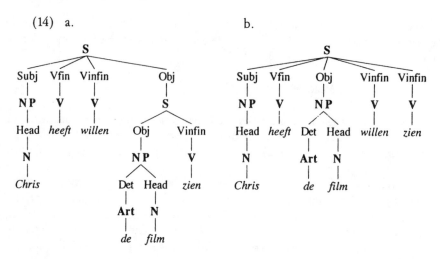

Now let us consider IPG's treatment of word order, and in particular the discontinuity in (9) which has not been explained so far: The verb *willen* apparently breaks up the subclause *de film zien*. In IPG, each subprocedure computes a value as its output which represents the syntactic constituent that has been produced, and normally this value is returned to the calling procedure. Categorial procedures determine the left-to-right position of the constituents they receive from the functional procedures. As a result, subclauses and other hierarchically embedded structures are kept together in the linear order of the resulting sentence. But the model also contains mechanisms for a value return that is exceptional, as for the discontinuity at hand.

This exception is due to the influence of a piece of information coded as ObjComp1 in lemma (8b) which allows for an infinitival clause. Such clauses may exhibit the kind of discontinuities mentioned, which are commonly known as *clause union*. The exceptional lexical information responsible for this structure specifies that the constituents of the lower S are to be returned to the next higher S. The positions assigned to the *raised* constituents by the higher S break up their grouping, so that the discontinuity arises, as illustrated in (14b). IPG implements this value return mechanism by using the scope of variables in the procedure hierarchy.

The incremental mode of generation in IPG has its consequences for word order. Categorial procedures assign newly constructed material a position as early in the utterance as possible within limits of grammaticality. A sentence may, for example, start out with *Yesterday* . . . if that part of the conceptual structure underlying this word is the first which is accessible. This initial utterance might be completed as *Yesterday* . . . *Chris has seen the film*. In different circumstances, the concept underlying *yesterday* may become accessible much later, resulting in *Chris has seen the film* . . . *yesterday*. Clearly, each iteration of the looping procedures should take care to continue adding to a syntactically coherent sentence, rather than producing a succession of disconnected utterances. Measures to this effect include certain syntactic adaptations, including a shift to the passive voice. Suppose that the object role is accessible before the actor, then the previous example might be uttered as *The film... was seen by Chris yesterday.* In this regime, clearly there may be occasions when early choices lead to partial utterances that cannot be completed with the newly incoming input, representing a case where the speaker has 'talked himself into a corner'. For instance, it may not be possible to continue *The film...* to express the fact that Chris has wanted to see the film.

Summing up, incremental production is modelled in IPG by expanding the conceptual structure presented as input to the Formulator at each iteration. The more accessible parts of the conceptual structure are assumed to enter the Formulator sooner and are processed during earlier iterations. They are at an advantage to be realized at an earlier position in the sentence and to take preferential grammatical functions. IPG proposes intercomponent and intracomponent parallelism, even if these forms of parallelism have only partially been implemented. The procedural approach opens up the possibility of accounting for linguistic phenomena not in terms of grammar rules but in terms of the computational properties of the syntactic processor (compare Marcus, 1980, for a similar approach to parsing). Indeed, IPG explains some grammatical constructs, including conjunction and locality constraints on raising, not so much in terms of explicit grammar rules but in terms of computational properties of the processor.

IPF

The Incremental Parallel Formulator (IPF; De Smedt, 1990, 1994) has taken the work in IPG several steps further, especially with respect to the timing of the input, the implementation of parallelism, and the grammar formalism. Variations in conceptual accessibility are modelled by letting conceptual *fragments* enter the Formulator one by one, rather than as cumulative expansions of a single conceptual structure. These input fragments are assumed to be small and correspond roughly to a single word or thematic role. Moreover, they enter the Formulator at precisely specified time intervals. For example, a typical input sequence for the generation of the Dutch sentence (15a) could be (15e). Note that (15b,c,d) are some of the possible variants of the sentence.

(15)   a.   Chris heeft vandaag de film gezien. ('Chris has today the film seen')

     b.   Vandaag heeft Chris de film gezien. ('Today has Chris the film seen')

     c.   Chris heeft de film gezien vandaag. ('Chris has the film seen today')

    d. De film heeft Chris vandaag gezien. ('The film has Chris today seen')

    e. concept CHRIS
       (wait 5 time units)
       concept SEE (+ perfective)
       (wait 3 time units)
       thematic role ACTOR between CHRIS and SEE
       (wait 5 time units)
       concept TODAY
       (wait 2 time units)
       thematic role MODIFIER between TODAY and SEE
       (wait 4 time units)
       concept FILM (+ definite)
       (wait 3 time units)
       thematic role OBJECT between FILM and SEE

IPF presents a detailed implementation of both intercomponent and intracomponent parallelism that goes beyond the iterative control structure of IPG. The moment when each individual conceptual fragment (either a concept or a thematic role) enters the Formulator can be precisely specified in the input by means of the *wait* instructions in (15e). For each incoming conceptual fragment, the Formulator immediately spawns a computational process that may overlap in time with any other active processes and may compete with them. Because there is no central controlling mechanism, grammatical encoding is performed in a parallel and distributed fashion. However, all processes share the same memory, so that together they build parts of a single coherent syntactic structure. IPF does not model the syntactic structure as a hierarchy of procedures, as IPG does, but rather as a heterarchy. It allows a more flexible order in which various parts of the utterance are computed. In particular, IPF takes the following requirements formulated by Kempen (1987a) seriously:

1 Because it cannot be assumed that conceptual fragments which are input to the Formulator are chronologically ordered in a particular way, it must be possible to expand syntactic structures from the bottom-up as well as from the top down.

2 Because the size of each conceptual fragment is not guaranteed to cover a full clause or even a full phrase, it must be possible to attach individual branches to existing syntactic structures, including the addition of sister nodes.

3 Because the chronological order in which conceptual fragments are attached to the syntactic structure does not necessarily correspond to the linear precedence in the resulting utterance, word order should be assigned incrementally by exploiting grammatical variations on the one hand and should contain mechanisms to avoid ungrammaticality on the other hand.

The incremental grammar which Kempen (1987a) proposes has later been called Segment Grammar (SG; De Smedt and Kempen, 1991). This grammar is distributed: it consists of a set of *syntactic segments*, which are representations of separate grammatical relations to which features and word order constraints are added. By virtue of its organization, the grammar not only specifies which sentences are grammatical, but also which *partial* structures are grammatical if continued. The constituents of a sentence with their grammatical relations (somewhat different from those in IPG) are represented in *functional structures*. An example of a functional structure and the segments from which it is made up are shown in Figure 11.2.

Figure 11.2: Syntactic segments and functional structure for sentence (15a)

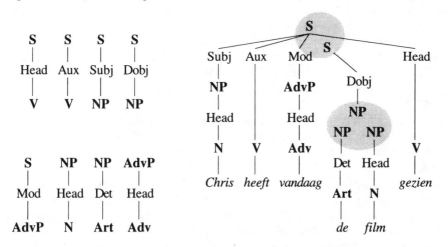

A functional structure is formed by incrementally adding segments by means of a general *unification* operation which merges two nodes into one. Because unification is not restricted to expanding the tree in a particular direction, the tree can be expanded top-down as well as bottom-up and breadthwise as well as depthwise. As an illustration, the unifications resulting from the last two increments of (15e) are highlighted by means of a grey background in Figure 11.2. The penultimate increment selects an *NP-Head-N* segment for *film* and attaches the definite article *de* in an *NP-Det-Art* segment. Finally, the conceptual increment for the thematic role *object* causes insertion of the *S-Dobj-NP* segment.

Unification is an information combining operation proposed by Kay (1979, 1984) and is used in several grammar formalisms (see Chapter 2). Segment Grammar uses a unification operation which combines two nodes into one node having the features of both. Corresponding feature values should match. For example, a singular NP node can only unify with another NP node that is also singular. If one of the nodes is singular and the other undetermined with respect to singular or plural, the new node becomes singular. This feature matching enforces syntactic constraints such as subject-verb agreement.

Word order is computed incrementally by constructing an ordered constituent structure on the basis of the functional structure. Like IPG, the SG grammar used in IPF allows the construction of a constituent structure which is not necessarily isomorphic with the functional structure, thus providing for the incremental production of discontinuous constituency (De Smedt and Kempen, in press).

Especially important for incremental production is the way in which choices are made between alternatives in word order, as between (15a,b,c,d). In IPF these are naturally explained as the outcome of a race between constituents. Because in the input (15e), the concept for *Chris* is the first one accessible, it has a higher chance of occupying a position early in the sentence. If the input is reordered and its fragments passed on to the Formulator at different times, other word orders such as (15b,c,d) may emerge, due to a similar principle as in IPG, that constituents try to occupy the earliest position in the sentence that is still free as well as grammatically permissible. Computer simulations of IPF have demonstrated that such variation in word order indeed occurs. Assuming that the *topic* of a sentence is relatively more conceptually accessible, then the IPF processing strategy can account for the fact that the topic is often fronted (Bock, 1982; Bock and Warren, 1985; Levelt, 1989).

IPF underwrites Kempen and Hoenkamp's (1987) proposal to let an incremental mode of production trigger not only marked word order variations, but also lexico-syntactic operations such as *passivization*. Thus, for example, the passive voice in *The film has been seen by Chris* may be due to timing effects. Abb, Herweg and Lebeth (1993) focus on the incremental generation of passive sentences, and work out the assumptions of IPG and IPF in the context of the SYNPHONICS model for German sentence production. Their approach differentiates explicitly between two types of condition that can trigger the incremental production of passives as opposed to actives.

The first condition which may give rise to passive sentences is indeed related to *prominence* and *timing*. A prominent conceptual fragment may be made available to the Formulator prior to the event in which it plays a role, even if its thematic role in that event is not yet specified. The SYNPHONICS Formulator is guided by heuristic principles including the following: 'Integrate phonologically filled material as soon as possible into the highest and leftmost position available in the current utterance fragment'. According to this heuristic, similar to one in IPG and IPF, the phrase expressing the prominent fragment (*the film* in our example) is inserted into the most prominent syntactic position and by default assigned the nominative case. So far, no specific information about the fragment's thematic role has been used. At a later moment, however, such information becomes available, and lemma selection is then restricted not only by the conceptual content, but also by the syntactic structure produced so far. In the present case, lemma retrieval must choose a lemma for *see* that allows the patient to be subject (because it has already been assigned the nominative case). This is exactly the property of the passive form of this lemma.

The second case is triggered by *agent backgrounding*, a condition where the agent of an action is unknown, defocused or backgrounded. In this condition, lemma retrieval results in the choice of a passivized lemma, which is subcategorized as taking over all but the first argument (which would the subject of the active voice). In this way, a passive sentence can be realized without the agent.

To summarize, IPF is a further development of IPG. In the parallel distributed architecture of IPF, incrementality is gradual, because the time span between successive inputs can be made to vary. The more time there is between successive inputs, the more time each grammatical encoding process has to 'get ahead' of the next ones and the more the effects of incremental processing will show up in the form of the utterance.

POPEL

POPEL (Finkler and Neumann, 1989; Neumann and Finkler, 1990; Reithinger, 1991, 1992) is a language generation system consisting of two main modules: a Conceptualizer POPEL-WHAT, and a Formulator POPEL-HOW. The system is not explicitly meant as a simulation of human language production. Rather, it is meant to be used in a human-computer interface where written dialogue is combined with other interaction modes including gestures. Still, its architecture shares the assumptions of other, psychologically motivated approaches, including incrementality, and intercomponent as well as intracomponent parallelism. This need not be surprising. On the contrary, it illustrates the point that nature inspires technology. I am restricting this section to an explanation of how the incremental generation of German topicalization constructions is realized in POPEL-HOW.

The input to the model is an intentional goal, for example, to make the hearer believe a state of affairs. The conceptual knowledge representing this state of affairs can be represented in a graph consisting of nodes representing concepts

Figure 11.3: A conceptual graph in POPEL

and links labelled with roles, for example the graph in Figure 11.3. The information in this graph can in fact be realized in two separate sentences (16c, 17d). The Conceptualizer, which selects concepts for formulation, operates independently from the Formulator. It incorporates a user model and a dialogue model, among other things, to guide its selection of what to formulate next. The selection process has knowledge about standard schemata to structure a message (see Chapter 10). However, if the actual dialogue requires cohesion in a text (see Chapter 10), the default selection sequence may be overridden, and conceptual elements that connect to the previous discourse are selected and activated first. They trickle down the cascade, and if the grammar rules allow for it, are verbalized first.

Take as an example the incremental generation of the sentences in (16) and (17), which together express the knowledge in the graph of Figure 11.3. There is no marker in the whole system that says that a particular concept is in focus and has to be put in front. Rather, the surface position and form is dependent on the prominence of the concept, as apparent from its position in the activation cascade. That is, concepts which are most prominent and reside in immediate memory are put first in the cascade. For instance, the word *dort* is prominent in (17), when uttered immediately after (16), where its referent *Völklingen* has just been mentioned.

(16) a. Ein Mann fährt . . . (A man rides)
     b. Ein Mann fährt mit einem Motorrad . . . (A man rides on his motorbike)
     c. Ein Mann fährt mit einem Motorrad nach Völklingen. (A man rides on his motorbike to Völklingen)

(17) a. Dort . . . (There)
     b. Dort kauft er . . . (There he buys)
     c. Dort kauft er einer Frau . . . (There he buys for a woman)
     d. Dort kauft er einer Frau ein Kochbuch. (There he buys for a woman a cookbook)

In contrast to IPG and IPF, POPEL assumes a bi-directional flow of information between the main processing components. At several points during the production of these sentences, feedback information is passed from one level to the previous one. During the production of (16a), for example, the Formulator initially receives only the concept DRIVE, which is realized as a verb. Because the Formulator cannot express this verb without a subject, it passes a request upward so that the Conceptualizer knows which concept to provide. Next, the concept PERS-1 is provided by the Conceptualizer but found unsatisfactory by the Formulator because it needs a more specific reference to find an appropriate word. Such a reference is found via the *name* role, yielding the concept MAN, which is passed down the cascade. The restrictions at the intermediate knowledge levels, both conceptual and syntactic, are responsible for the rest of the story. They are not discussed here.

Through incremental processing, discourse context has a substantial effect on word order and lexical choice. In (17a), for example, the anaphoric adverb *dort* (there) is chosen rather than a full NP to refer to a recently focused concept, and it comes early in the utterance. The influence of discourse on the form of the utterance is even more evident from the examples (18) and (19), which are produced by POPEL right after (16) and (17) and with the same intentional goals. The changed context is taken into consideration, which leads to adaptations in lexical choice and word order in the sentences and even the order of the sentences themselves. Thus, the organization of content to be expressed is determined by what is topic, implemented by time differences rather than by standard schemas.

(18)   Das kauft er ihr in Völklingen.

(19)   Dorthin fährt er mit dem Motorrad.

To summarize, POPEL both selects and formulates the concepts that currently get the highest attention before others. The surface realization is adapted to the decisions made by the selection processes. POPEL's use of time spans between conceptual inputs that are incrementally passed on to the Formulator is essentially the same as that in IPG and IPF. A major difference is the provision for feedback in the form of requests from the Formulator to the Conceptualizer. This feedback implies that the Formulator is not passively waiting for input from the Conceptualizer, but takes an active role in requesting concepts necessary for a suitable utterance.

The work on POPEL is currently being followed by work on a more ambitious model called TAG-GEN (Harbusch, Finkler and Schauder, 1991; Finkler and Schauder, 1992). First, this project aims at investigating how incremental input affects further components of the language production process after grammatical encoding. Second, it is based on a different grammar formalism, Tree Adjoining Grammar (TAG; Joshi, 1987). Third, a prototype of this model has been implemented as a parallel system running on a network of computers. And finally, the model is able to realize a limited number of self-repairs when needed by incremental input, for example, *Peter plays . . . Peter and Mary play ball*, when Mary is added as a second agent at a later time.

A Connectionist Model: FIG

The Flexible Incremental Generator (FIG; Ward, 1992) is a connectionist model, somewhat similar to the interactive activation model proposed by Stemberger (1985), and also similar in some respects to the connectionist model by Kalita and Shastri (1987).

FIG strongly deviates from the preceding models due to its connectionist architecture. Perhaps the most striking difference is that it does not explicitly construct syntactic structures at any point during sentence production. Incremental sentence production is viewed as the selection of consecutive words to be uttered, one at a time. Syntactic, lexical and other knowledge mediate the choice of appropriate words at appropriate times, but there is no global structure representing the current syntactic state of affairs.

The linguistic and other knowledge in FIG consist of an associative network with nodes representing conceptual, lexical, and syntactic knowledge. The input to FIG is not substantially different from that in the other models: it is formed by a graph of nodes representing conceptual *notions* (with labels ending on *n*) linked together by thematic *roles* (with labels ending on *r*). As an example, Figure 11.4 depicts the conceptual nodes necessary for sentence (20). However, in contrast to the previous models, FIG feeds all information in the network as a whole into the Formulator. In addition, topicalization is not modelled by timing differences, but by an explicit marker *topic_n* in the input.

(20)   The old woman went to the stream to wash clothes.

Figure 11.4: An input to FIG

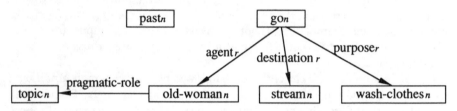

The computational mechanism responsible for the production of a sentence is based on spreading activation (see Chapter 3). Initially each conceptual node is given a certain amount of activation. The activation then starts spreading through the system, eventually reaching syntactic nodes (called *constructions*) and words. At appropriate intervals, the word with the highest current activation is selected to

Figure 11.5: Selected paths of activation just before output of the

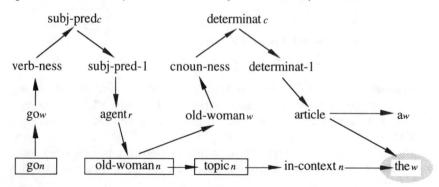

be uttered as the next word of the sentence. This activation and selection process is repeated until every concept in the input has been expressed. In this way, sentence production proceeds word by word from left to right.

Figure 11.5 illustrates some paths of activation from concepts, mediated by other conceptual and syntactic nodes, to the first word to be uttered, which will be the article *the*. The nodes include words (with labels ending on *w*) and syntactic constructions (with labels ending on *c*) representing phrases and clauses. In FIG, the activation level of a word represents its current relevance at each time. Therefore, words which are syntactically and conceptually appropriate must be strongly activated at the right moment. In FIG, the representation of the current syntactic state is distributed across the nodes representing phrases and clauses. As an example, a piece of the network in Figure 11.5 is given in somewhat more detail in Figure 11.6, with numerical weights to be multiplied by the activation values flowing on the links. In this network, the constituents of the node *determinat$_c$* are encoded in their positional order as *determinat-1* and *determinat-2*. The current relevance of each constituent in a phrase or clause is determined by the use of *cursors* that move from one constituent to the next. The cursor acts as a filter so that only the currently relevant constituent receives activation. In the network shown in Figure 11.6, for example, the cursor initially points at the first

Figure 11.6: Use of the cursor in a syntactic construction

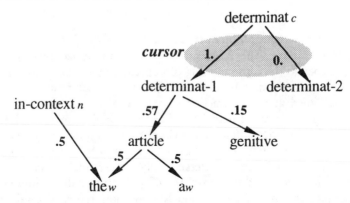

constituent, which is linked to the article and genitive nodes. The cursor puts a weight of 1. on activation flowing to the current constituents, so that activation passes freely, but puts a weight of 0. on the other constituents, which effectively cuts off the flow of activation. After either an article or the genitive has been emitted, the cursor moves to the second node, and so on. Optional constituents will be skipped when there is no concept to activate them. More specifically, the next constituent which receives conceptual activation will become the most highly activated and will be emitted.

Summing up, FIG operates incrementally in the sense that it produces words in time one by one in a strictly left-to-right order. Computation in FIG is guided by the sequencing of its output rather than that of its input. FIG uses local conceptual and syntactic activation patterns to consider many words in parallel and select the appropriate word at the right time. Even if this model does not explicitly construct a syntactic structure, the operations of the cursors implicitly follow the constraints of a distributed grammar that underlies this model.

Evaluation of the Models

It is difficult to compare the models on their actual results, because none of them make predictions that are specific and quantified enough to be tested empirically. Rather, the models illustrate that incremental production itself, as a processing mode, is not only computationally possible but also computationally advantageous, which could be interpreted as a theoretical indication of psychological plausibility. This section mainly compares the theoretical assumptions and computational architectures of the different approaches.

Incremental Production and Computational Parallelism

All models link incremental production to a form of computational parallelism, but in different ways. The AI-based models try to realize every part of the utterance as soon as the corresponding conceptual input becomes available. Each successive conceptual input triggers some grammatical encoding activity in the Formulator, aimed at the production of a piece of the utterance — although sometimes a piece must be held back due to constraints of the grammar and lexicon. Parallelism is dependent on the chunks of conceptual input that are being processed at the same time. In contrast, FIG is driven by the appropriateness of words at each given point in the utterance, where the available conceptual input, the words in the lexicon and the constraints of the grammar all act simultaneously.

Consequently, the AI-based models show how sentence production can already get under way with an incomplete conceptual input, and how variations in the timing of this input are linked to variations in the shape of the resulting utterance, including fine grained effects on word order, as hypothesized by Pechmann (1989). In addition, IPG implements the assumption that early constituents take preferential grammatical roles (Bock and Warren, 1985). In contrast, FIG uses explicit, separate markers in the input, for example $topic_n$.

Even so, it is not unthinkable that the two views of incrementality could be combined. Ward (personal communication) claims that providing FIG with all necessary concepts for a whole sentence is not strictly necessary and that the model could be adapted to process conceptual input in a piecemeal way. This might perhaps be achieved by activating the nodes of the conceptual input each at different moments in time. How this would interfere with the existing syntactic choice mechanism has not yet been investigated.

A final remark on this matter is that the models presented here hardly take into account how pragmatic factors interact with incremental production. It is not shown, for example, how the demands of incremental production are compatible with the need to manipulate the hearer's attention (McCoy and Cheng, 1991). Only POPEL contains some cohesive devices. The other models assume that any pragmatic considerations will be reflected either in the timing of input to the Formulator or by means of special markers. For example, a focused element in the preverbal message may be given prominence in IPF by passing it to the Formulator earlier than other elements. However, it has not been systematically shown that this would be adequate for handling pragmatic phenomena beyond single sentences.

Other Psycholinguistic Phenomena and Assumptions

None of the models account very well for the other word order phenomena such as variations due to weight and persistence. The IPF model could perhaps be adapted to take into account some measure of processing load. Because grammatical encoding is distributed among separate competing processes that each have their own running time, the complexity of grammatical processing for each constituent could in principle be brought to bear upon the moment when the constituent is integrated in the utterance, and thereby be given a left-to-right position. However, as mentioned before, it seems difficult to reconcile this scheme with incremental processing, because an incremental Formulator prefers to integrate a constituent in the current syntactic structure before its surface features have been completely determined. To model syntactic persistence, FIG seems to offer the possibility of preactivating 'persistent' syntactic constructions before conceptual input is given.

Similarly, the FIG model accounts for speech errors when, due to the contextual or other influences, the activation of an unintended element exceeds that of an intended one, in a way similar to that proposed by Dell (1986; see also Chapter 13). However, it is unclear whether such errors would be similar to the kinds of error in human speech. Dell uses a system of categorized slots and other mechanisms to ensure that errors meet certain constraints; FIG does not seem to have such stringent provisions.

None of the models accounts for the characteristics of SVA errors. With respect to these errors, Vigliocco, Butterworth and Semenza (1995) criticize modular achitectures, in particular IPG, because in these architectures agreement is computed at a separate syntactic level, before and independently of the retrieval of the lexeme of the head noun in the subject NP. This is at odds with cross-linguistic studies indicating that the morpho-phonological marking of the subject head noun affects the rate of SVA errors. Also, some even more marked effects remain altogether unexplained, in particular, the assymmetry between singular and plural errors, and a semantic effect involving distributivity and collective nouns.

The AI-based models and FIG differ in their assumptions with respect to cognitive constraints. FIG represents the syntactic state of affairs locally, whereas the other models keep a large structure in memory for an extended length of time. The latter has been exploited in a model of agrammatism, which, according to Kolk (1987), could result from the speaker's adaptation of some kind of memory impairment. Kolk simulates agrammatism by using a version of IPG implemented with production rules that have a limited time span, so that parts of large structures decay over time. Admittedly, there are other ways to conserve memory in hierarchical models, for example, by narrowing the scope of planning at each level (narrowing to the clause during the assignments of functions, or to the phrase during the assignment of positions), but this has not been implemented.

Modularity and Interaction

In all models, parallelism is a direct architectural basis for incremental production. Computational simultaneity is deemed necessary for explaining word exchanges (Garrett, 1980). In addition to being psychologically plausible, a parallel mode of processing is more efficient than a serial mode if each processing module is immediately triggered by any fragment of characteristic input. In the AI-based models, there is a parallel operation of modules (intercomponent parallelism) as well as parallel operation on different inputs (intracomponent parallelism), with the number of simultaneous processes of the order of the number of conceptual inputs. This kind of parallelism is more efficient than a serial mode insofar as the processing of several inputs overlap. FIG presupposes an interactive rather than a modular architecture, with a more fine-grained, massive parallelism, where each node in the network, either conceptual, syntactic or lexical, spreads activation simultaneously. This kind of parallelism promotes efficiency by collapsing the various processing stages.

The information in the modular language production models generally flows from the conceptual to the lexical and syntactic levels. POPEL makes use of feedback between the Formulator and the Conceptualizer. Levelt's (1989) arguments against such feedback are supported by (heavily discussed) empirical and simulation results (Levelt *et al.*, 1991). Like Reithinger, Rubinoff's (1992) generator IGEN implements a bi-directional flow of information between the Conceptualizer (which he calls the *planner*) and the Formulator (the *linguistic* component). But in contrast, the feedback in IGEN mainly pertains to word choice rather than syntactic needs. For example, a general concept *rain* can be expressed by various words, including *drizzle* and *pour*, but the Conceptualizer may not know in advance which details of the meaning it should provide in order to allow a suitable choice. The Formulator therefore provides the Conceptualizer with annotations about possible words, some of which may satisfy secondary plans at the conceptual level more than others. Thus lexical choice arises as an interplay between the two components.

Within the Formulator, the interaction between lemma retrieval and syntax that the various models assume does not seem to be limited to phenomena such as passivization. Nogier and Zock (1992) view lemma retrieval as a matching operation where both semantics and syntax are highly relevant. Their proposed interaction between lexical choice and syntax suggests that even if grammatical encoding is largely conceptually and lexically driven, lexical choice is also partly syntax driven.

To conclude and sum up the discussion in this chapter, there are a number of computer models of grammatical encoding that are sophisticated from a computational point of view. They have been useful to visualize and test some theories of incremental syntactic processing. However, they have not produced any easily quantifiable results. Up to now, computer models have mainly aided in globally showing that some ways of organising a grammar and syntactic processes are more effective and may be psychologically more plausible than others.

Notes

1 The speech errors in this chapter were recorded during spontaneous speech.
2 Overviews of seminal work from these traditions can be found in Kempen (1989) and McDonald (1992). For proceedings of workshops on computer models for natural language production in general, we refer to volumes edited by Kempen (1987b), Zock and Sabah (1988), Dale, Mellish and Zock (1990), Paris, Swartout and Mann (1991), Dale *et al.* (1992), and Horacek and Zock (1993). Much of this work uses the term *generation* rather than production.

References

ABB, B., HERWEG, M. and LEBETH, K. (1993) 'The incremental generation of passive sentences', in *Proceedings of the Sixth Conference of the European Chapter of the ACL*, Morristown: Association for Computational Linguistics, pp. 3–11.

BOCK, J. K. (1982) 'Toward a cognitive psychology of syntax: Information processing contributions to sentence formulation', *Psychological Review*, 89, pp. 1–47.

BOCK, J. K. (1986) 'Syntactic persistence in language production', *Cognitive Psychology*, 18, pp. 355–87.

BOCK, J. K. (1995a) 'Sentence production: From mind to mouth', in MILLER, J. L. and EIMAS, P. D. (Eds) *Handbook of Perception and Cognition. Vol. 11: Speech, Language and Communication*, Orlando, FL: Academic Press, pp. 181–216.

BOCK, J. K. (1995b) 'Producing agreement', *Current Directions in Psychological Science*, 8, pp. 56–61.

BOCK, J. K. and CUTTING, J. C. (1992) 'Regulating mental energy: Performance units in language production', *Journal of Memory and Language*, 31, pp. 99–127.

BOCK, J. K. and LEVELT, W. J. M. (1994) 'Language production: Grammatical encoding', in GERNSBACHER, M. A. (Ed) *Handbook of Psycholinguistics*, Orlando, FL: Academic Press, pp. 945–84.

BOCK, J. K. and MILLER, C. A. (1991) 'Broken agreement', *Cognitive Psychology*, 23, pp. 45–93.

BOCK, J. K. and WARREN, R. (1985) 'Conceptual accessibility and syntactic structure in sentence formulation', *Cognition*, 21, pp. 47–67.

BOOMER, D. (1965) 'Hesitation and grammatical encoding', *Language and Speech*, 8, pp. 148–58.

BROTHERTON, P. L. (1979) 'Speaking and not speaking: Processes for translating ideas into speech', in SIEGMAN, A. W. and FELDSTEIN, S. (Eds) *Of Speech and Time: Temporal Speech Patterns in Interpersonal Contexts*, Hillsdale, NJ: Lawrence Erlbaum.

DALE, R., HOVY, E., RÖSNER, D. and STOCK, O. (Eds) (1992) *Aspects of Automated Natural Language Generation*, Berlin: Springer.

DALE, R., MELLISH, C. and ZOCK, M. (Eds) (1990) *Current Research in Natural Language Generation*, London: Academic Press.

DE HAAN, P. and VAN HOUT, R. (1986) 'Statistics and corpus analysis: A loglinear analysis of syntactic constraints on postmodifying clauses', in AARTS, J. and MEIJS, W. (Eds) *Corpus Linguistics II: New Studies in the Analysis and Exploitation of Computer Corpora*, Amsterdam: Rodopi, pp. 79–97.

DELL, G. S. (1986) 'A spreading-activation theory of retrieval in sentence production', *Psychological Review*, 93, pp. 283–321.

DE SMEDT, K. (1990) 'IPF: An incremental parallel formulator', in DALE, R., MELLISH, C. and ZOCK, M. (Eds) *Current Research in Natural Language Generation*, London: Academic Press, pp. 167–92.

DE SMEDT, K. (1994) 'Parallelism in incremental sentence generation', in ADRIAENS, G. and HAHN, U. (Eds) *Parallel Natural Language Processing*, Norwood, NJ: Ablex, pp. 421–47.

DE SMEDT, K. and KEMPEN, G. (1987) 'Incremental sentence production, self-correction and co-ordination', in KEMPEN, G. (Ed) *Natural Language Generation: New Results in Artificial Intelligence, Psychology and Linguistics*, Dordrecht: Nijhoff (Kluwer Academic Publishers), pp. 365–76.

DE SMEDT, K. and KEMPEN, G. (1991) 'Segment Grammar: A formalism for incremental sentence generation', in PARIS, C. L., SWARTOUT, W. R. and MANN, W. C. (Eds) *Natural Language Generation in Artificial Intelligence and Computational Linguistics*, Boston: Kluwer Academic Publishers, pp. 329–49.

DE SMEDT, K. and KEMPEN, G. (in press) 'Discontinuous constituency in Segment Grammar', in VAN HORCK, A. and BUNT, H. (Eds) *Discontinuous Constituency*, Berlin: Mouton/Walter de Gruyter.

FINKLER, W. and NEUMANN, G. (1989) 'POPEL-HOW: A distributed parallel model for incremental natural language production with feedback', in *Proceedings of the 11th International Joint Conference on Artificial Intelligence, Detroit*, pp. 1518–23.

FINKLER, W. and SCHAUDER, A. (1992) 'Effects of incremental output on incremental natural language generation', in *Proceedings of the 10th European Conference on Artificial Intelligence, Vienna*, Chichester: Wiley, pp. 505–7.

FISHER, C., GLEITMAN, H. and GLEITMAN, L. (1991) 'On the semantic content of subcategorization frames', *Cognitive Psychology*, 23, pp. 331–92.

GARRETT, M. F. (1975) 'The analysis of sentence production', in BOWER, G. H. (Ed) *The Psychology of Learning and Motivation, Vol. 9*, New York: Academic Press, pp. 133–77.

GARRETT, M. F. (1980) 'Levels of processing in sentence production', in BUTTERWORTH, B. (Ed) *Language Production: Vol. 1, Speech and Talk*, London: Academic Press, pp. 177–220.

GOLDMAN-EISLER, F. (1968) *Psycholinguistics: Experiments in Spontaneous Speech*, New York: Academic Press.

HARBUSCH, K., FINKLER, W. and SCHAUDER, A. (1991) 'Incremental syntax generation with tree adjoining grammars', in BRAUER, W. and HERNÁNDEZ, D. (Eds) *4th International GI Congress on Knowledge Based Systems, Munich*, Berlin: Springer, pp. 363–74.

HAWKINS, J. A. (1990) 'A parsing theory of word order universals', *Linguistic Inquiry*, 21, pp. 223–61.

HAWKINS, J. A. (1994) *A Performance Theory of Order and Constituency*, Cambridge: Cambridge University Press.

HORACEK, H. and ZOCK, M. (Eds) (1993) *New Concepts in Natural Language Generation*, London: Pinter.

JOSHI, A. (1987) 'The relevance of tree adjoining grammar to generation', in KEMPEN, G. (Ed) *Natural Language Generation: New Results in Artificial Intelligence, Psychology and Linguistics*, Dordrecht: Nijhoff (Kluwer Academic Publishers), pp. 233–52.

KALITA, J. and SHASTRI, L. (1987) 'Generation of simple sentences in English using the connectionist model of computation', in *Proceedings of the 9th Annual Conference of the Cognitive Science Society, Seattle*, Hove: Lawrence Erlbaum, pp. 555–65.

KAY, M. (1979) 'Functional grammar', in *Proceedings of the 5th Annual Meeting of the Berkeley Linguistic Society*, pp. 142–58.

KAY, M. (1984) 'Functional unification grammar: A formalism for machine translation', in *Proceedings of COLING84, Stanford*, Morristown: Association for Computational Linguistics, pp. 75–8.

KELLY, M. H., BOCK, J. K. and KEIL, F. C. (1986) 'Prototypicality in a linguistic context: Effects on sentence structure', *Journal of Memory and Language*, 25, pp. 59–74.

KEMPEN, G. (1977) 'Conceptualizing and formulating in sentence production', in ROSENBERG, S. (Ed) *Sentence Production: Developments in Research and Theory*, Hillsdale, NJ: Lawrence Erlbaum, pp. 259–74.

KEMPEN, G. (1987a) 'A framework for incremental syntactic tree formation', in *Proceedings of the 10th IJCAI, Milan*, Los Altos, CA: Morgan Kaufmann, pp. 655–60.

KEMPEN, G. (Ed) (1987b) *Natural Language Generation: New Results in Artificial Intelligence, Psychology and Linguistics*, Dordrecht: Nijhoff (Kluwer Academic Publishers).

KEMPEN, G. (1989) 'Language generation systems', in BÁTORI, I. S., LENDERS, W. and PUTSCHKE, W. (Eds) *Computational Linguistics: An International Handbook on Computer Oriented Language Research and Applications*, Berlin: Walter de Gruyter, pp. 471–80.

KEMPEN, G. and HOENKAMP, E. (1987) 'An incremental procedural grammar for sentence production', *Cognitive Science*, 11, pp. 201–58.

KEMPEN, G. and HUIJBERS, (1983) 'The lexicalization process in sentence production and naming: Indirect election of words', *Cognition*, 14, pp. 185–209.

KOLK, H. (1987) 'A theory of grammatical impairment in aphasia', in KEMPEN, G. (Ed) *Natural Language Generation: New Results in Artificial Intelligence, Psychology and Linguistics*, Dordrecht: Nijhoff (Kluwer Academic Publishers), pp. 377–91.

LEVELT, W. J. M. (1989) *Speaking: From Intention to Articulation*, Cambridge, MA: MIT Press.

LEVELT, W. J. M. and MAASSEN, R. (1981) 'Lexical search and order of mention in sentence production', in KLEIN, W. and LEVELT, W. (Eds) *Crossing the Boundaries in Linguistics*, Dordrecht: Reidel, pp. 221–52.

LEVELT, W. J. M. and SCHRIEFERS, H. (1987) 'Stages of lexical access', in KEMPEN, G. (Ed) *Natural Language Generation: New Results in Artificial Intelligence, Psychology and Linguistics*, Dordrecht: Nijhoff (Kluwer Academic Publishers), pp. 395–404.

LEVELT, W.J.M., SCHRIEFERS, H., VORBERG, D., MEYER, A.S., PECHMANN, T. and HAVINGA, J. (1991) 'The time course of lexical access in speech production: A study of picture naming', *Psychological Review*, 98, pp. 122–42.

LINDSLEY, J.R. (1975) 'Producing simple utterances: How far ahead do we plan?', *Cognitive Psychology*, 7, pp. 1–19.

LINDSLEY, J.R. (1976) 'Producing simple utterances: Details of the planning process', *Journal of Psycholinguistic Research*, 5, pp. 331–51.

MARCUS, M. (1980) *A Theory of Syntactic Recognition for Natural Language*, Cambridge, MA: MIT Press.

McCOY, K.F. and CHENG, J. (1991) 'Focus of attention: Constraining what can be said next', in PARIS, C.L., SWARTOUT, W.R. and MANN, W.C. (Eds) *Natural Language Generation in Artificial Intelligence and Computational Linguistics*, Boston: Kluwer Academic Publishers, pp. 103–24.

McDONALD, D. (1992) 'Natural language generation', in SHAPIRO, S. (Ed) *Encyclopedia of Artificial Intelligence (2nd ed.)*, New York: Wiley, pp. 983–97.

McDONALD, J.L., BOCK, J.K. and KELLY, M.H. (1993) 'Word and world order: Semantic, phonological, and metrical determinants of serial position', *Cognitive Psychology*, 25, pp. 188–230.

NEUMANN, G. and FINKLER, W. (1990) 'A head-driven approach to incremental and parallel generation of syntactic structures', in *Proceedings of the 13th International Conference on Computational Linguistics, Helsinki, Vol. 2*, pp. 288–93.

NOGIER, J.-F., and ZOCK, M. (1992) 'Lexical choice as pattern matching', *Knowledge Based Systems*, 5, pp. 200–12. (Also in NAGLE, T., NAGLE, J., GERHOLZ, L. and EKLUND, P. (Eds) *Current Directions in Conceptual Structures Research*, Berlin: Springer, pp. 413–35.)

PARIS, C.L., SWARTOUT, W.R. and MANN, W.C. (Eds) *Natural Language Generation in Artificial Intelligence and Computational Linguistics*, Boston: Kluwer Academic Publishers.

PECHMANN, Th. (1989) 'Incremental speech production and referential overspecification', *Linguistics*, 27, pp. 89–110.

PECHMANN, Th. (1994) *Sprachproduktion: Zur Generierung Komplexer Nominalphrasen*, Opladen: Westdeutscher Verlag.

QUIRK, R., GREENBAUM, S., LEECH, G. and SVARTVIK, J. (1972) *A Grammar of Contemporary English*, London: Longman.

REITHINGER, N. (1991) 'POPEL — A parallel and incremental natural language generation system', in PARIS, C.L., SWARTOUT, W.R. and MANN, W.C. (Eds) *Natural Language Generation in Artificial Intelligence and Computational Linguistics*, Boston: Kluwer Academic Publishers, pp. 179–99.

REITHINGER, N. (1992) 'The performance of an incremental generation component in multi-modal dialog contributions', in DALE, R., HOVY, E., RÖSNER, D. and STOCK, O. (Eds) *Aspects of Automated Natural Language Generation*, Berlin: Springer, pp. 263–76.

ROSS, J.R. (1967) *Constraints on Variables in Syntax*, Doctoral dissertation, Massachusetts Institute of Technology (available from Indiana University Linguistics Club).

RUBINOFF, R. (1992) 'Integrating text planning and linguistic choice by annotating linguistic structures', in DALE, R., HOVY, E., RÖSNER, D. and STOCK, O. (Eds) *Aspects of Automated Natural Language Generation*, Berlin: Springer, pp. 45–56.

SCHRIEFERS, H. and PECHMANN, Th. (1988) 'Incremental production of referential noun phrases by human speakers', in ZOCK, M. and SABAH, G. (Eds) *Advances in Natural Language Generation, Vol. 1*, London: Pinter Publishers, pp. 172–9.

STALLINGS, L., McDONALD, M.C., and O'SEAGHDHA, P.G. (1994) 'What's heavy in heavy-NP shift?', *Abstracts of the 7th Annual CUNY Conference on Human Sentence Processing*, p. 32.

STEMBERGER, J.P. (1985) 'An interactive activation model of language production', in

ELLIS, A. W. (Ed) *Progress in the Psychology of Language, Vol. 1*, London: Lawrence Erlbaum, pp. 143–86.

VIGLIOCCO, G., BUTTERWORTH, B. and SEMENZA, C. (1995) 'Computing subject-verb agreement in speech: The role of semantic and morphological information', *Journal of Memory and Language*, 34, 186–215.

WARD, N. (1992) 'A parallel approach to syntax for generation', *Artificial Intelligence*, 57, pp. 183–225.

ZOCK, M. and SABAH, G. (Eds) (1988) *Advances in Natural Language Generation: An Interdisciplinary Perspective*, London: Pinter.

Chapter 12

Computational Models of Lemma Retrieval
Ardi Roelofs

Introduction

Suppose a speaker wants to produce the utterance *These birds drink*. This requires, among other things, accessing in memory the words *bird* and *drink*. Psycholinguists assume that the process of lexical access consists of two major steps, called lemma retrieval and phonological encoding (e.g., Garrett, 1975; Kempen and Huijbers, 1983; Dell, 1986; Kempen and Hoenkamp, 1987; Levelt, 1989, 1992). Lemma retrieval is the process by which a message concept (e.g., BIRD) is mapped onto a lemma. A lemma is a representation of the meaning and the syntactic properties of a word. For instance, the lemma of the word *bird* specifies the conceptual conditions for the appropriate use of the word, and indicates, among other things, that the word is a noun. Importantly, lemmas do not make explicit phonological information. The retrieval of lemmas from memory is a crucial step in the process of grammatical encoding (see Chapter 11). The building of a phrasal, clausal, or sentential structure (e.g., making the noun *bird* the head of the noun phrase *these birds*) requires the syntactic information that lemmas contain. Furthermore, lemma retrieval mediates between message encoding and the second stage of lexical access, phonological encoding, both in the production of connected speech and in the production of single words. For example, in object naming, a word's lemma is used in mapping a lexical concept (e.g., BIRD) onto the appropriate word form (i.e., /bɜrd/). Phonological encoding is the process by which phonological information about a word is recovered from memory and used to compute the phonetic shape of the word (see Chapter 13).

The distinction between lemma retrieval and phonological encoding is based on a large variety of empirical findings (for an overview, see e.g., Levelt, 1989). Some classical evidence comes from errors in spontaneous speech. The distinction explains, for example, the difference in distribution between word and sound exchanges. Word exchanges such as *The tall dog beats the boy* typically involve items of the same lexical category and occur across phrasal boundaries. By contrast, sound errors such as *The ball toy beats the dog* typically do not respect lexical category and occur within a phrase. Other evidence comes from controlled speech production experiments. For example, different frequency effects are obtained from accessing lemma information (such as grammatical gender) and from accessing word-form information (Jescheniak and Levelt, 1994). Furthermore, during lexical access, lemma information is available before word-form information (Schriefers, Meyer and Levelt, 1990).

Lemma retrieval is an extremely efficient process. First, lemmas are retrieved very fast. In normal conversation, a speaker can easily retrieve up to two lemmas per second, but speeding up to five lemmas poses no difficulty (Levelt, 1989). Of course, in producing connected speech, lemmas may be retrieved in parallel. Thus, the number of words per second does not reveal the speed of retrieval of a single lemma *per se*. Studies of object naming, however, suggest that the retrieval time for a lemma can be as small as 100–150 ms (Levelt *et al.*, 1991). Second, lemmas are retrieved very accurately. If a speaker wants to express a concept, and the mental lexicon contains a lemma for the concept, then typically that lemma is retrieved and no other. In an object naming experiment, a subject accesses a wrong lemma on only a small percentage of the trials. In normal conversation, a speaker fails to retrieve the right lemma roughly once per 2,000 words (Levelt, 1989). This is a great achievement given the vastness of the mental lexicon — it is conjectured that a speaker has an active vocabulary of some 30,000 words (Levelt, 1989). The efficiency of the retrieval of lemmas poses a challenge to a model builder. Any computational model proposed for lemma retrieval should be able to explain the speed and accuracy of retrieval, referred to by Levelt and Flores d'Arcais (1987) as the criteria of *speed* and *convergence*.

Convergence in lemma retrieval cannot be taken for granted, as the following examples demonstrate. The word *parent* is called a hyperonym of *father*, and *father* is called a hyponym of *parent*. If the conceptual conditions for the application of a word such as *father* are met, then those of its hyperonyms such as *parent* are automatically satisfied as well. A father may be referred to as a *parent*. Why, then, does the retrieval process not recover both the intended word and its hyperonyms (Levelt, 1989)? Or consider words that express disjunctive concepts. For example, *sibling* means BROTHER OR SISTER. If the conceptual conditions for *sibling* are satisfied, then those of *brother* or those of *sister* are satisfied too, and vice versa. Why does the lemma retrieval process not deliver both the word and its hyponyms? As a final example, take the word *father* and the phrase . . . *male parent*, which express the same underlying conceptual content. How does the retrieval process know whether a speaker wants to produce a single word instead of a phrase, or vice versa?

In this chapter, I briefly review the major computational models of lemma retrieval in the literature and highlight some important issues concerning the memory representation and the retrieval algorithm for lemmas. For instance, what is the nature of message concepts, the input representations to the retrieval process? In particular, are message concepts conceptually decomposed or not? If messages are decomposed, do lemmas contain semantic tests which, in lemma retrieval, are applied to the input representations testing for these conceptual components? If such tests are involved, are they applied in series or in parallel? It is indicated where the models stand with respect to these issues. I evaluate the models with respect to the criteria of speed and convergence, and discuss whether they are in accordance with relevant empirical findings.

As we will see, all models except one fail to meet the convergence criterion. As a consequence, the comparison between models and experimental results in this chapter is to a large extent carried out for one (i.e., the converging) model only. In this respect, the chapter is somewhat biased. However, this reflects the state of the art. At present, the best one can do is to evaluate empirically the converging model together with the suggestions that have been put forward to solve the convergence problems for the other models. Also, I restrict myself to existing models and attempted solutions — no new models and solutions are advanced. Furthermore, the chapter concentrates on the task domain of the retrieval of single lemmas, as it occurs in typical experimental tasks in language production research. I do not address such important issues as, for example, the role of conceptual context in lemma retrieval or the retrieval of lemmas in the production of connected speech (for an extensive discussion of such issues, see e.g., Levelt, 1989; Bierwisch and Schreuder, 1992; Roelofs, 1994).

Before describing the models, it is useful to go into the structure of lemmas in somewhat more detail (for an extensive description, see Levelt, 1989). As indicated, a lemma is a representation of the meaning and the syntactic properties of a word. For example, the lemmas of the words *bird* and *drink* describe the conceptual conditions for the appropriate use of these words. In addition, the lemma of *bird* indicates that this word is a noun, and the lemma of *drink* says that the word is a verb. A verb's lemma also makes explicit the word's functional structure, that is, the way it maps conceptual arguments (e.g., actor, theme) onto syntactic functions (e.g., subject, object). Typically, several morphosyntactic parameters of a lemma can be set. For a noun, there is a parameter for its number (i.e., singular and plural). For a verb, there are, in addition, parameters for the word's tense (e.g., past, present), person (i.e., first, second, third), mood (e.g., indicative), and so forth. The parameter values play an important role in phonological encoding, the construction of an articulatory program for the word. For example, in encoding the word form of *drink* with the morphosyntactic parameters set to third person, plural, and present tense, the corresponding morpheme and the speech segments /d/, /r/, /I/, /ŋ/, and /k/ have to be retrieved (see Chapter 13). The morphological and phonological composition of a word is specified in the form lexicon, which can be accessed via the word's lemma. Also, the form inventory is used in accessing lemmas during spoken language comprehension (see Chapter 5). Via a specification of the orthography of the word, a lemma can be accessed in visual language comprehension (see Chapter 6). Thus, a lemma can be accessed by meaning as well as by form (for a detailed description, see Roelofs, in preparation). In language production, lemma access is based on meaning.

Major Computational Models

The process of lexical access has not received as much attention in the study of language production as it has in the study of language comprehension. Furthermore, models of lexical access in speaking primarily address the process of phonological encoding. Although typically some assumptions are made about lemma retrieval, only a few models address this process in depth. The most detailed computational models of conceptually driven lemma retrieval are discrimination nets (Goldman, 1975), decision tables (Miller and Johnson-Laird, 1976), logogens (Morton, 1969),[1] and spreading-activation networks (Dell and O'Seaghdha, 1991, 1992; Roelofs, 1992a, 1992b, 1993, in preparation). The basic idea behind these models is simple. Below, I briefly describe the models. Some of their shortcomings will immediately become clear.

Discrimination Nets

The discrimination nets proposed by Goldman (1975) are binary trees with non-terminal nodes that represent semantic tests and terminal nodes that represent lemmas. To retrieve a lemma for a message concept, semantic tests are applied to the concept, starting with the test at the root of the tree. If the concept passes the test, control moves to the left daughter node; if not, control moves to the right one. Tests are run until a terminal node is reached.

Figure 12.1: Illustration of a discrimination net

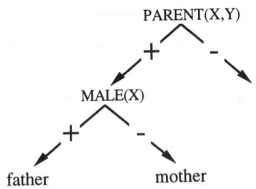

Figure 12.1 illustrates the way a binary discrimination net operates. The figure shows a discrimination net with a test for PARENT(X,Y) at the root, followed by a test for MALE(X), which leads to the lemma nodes of *father* and *mother*. Assume a speaker wants to express the concept FATHER, which is presumed to be

represented within the message by the conceptual features MALE(X) and PARENT(X,Y). First the test for PARENT(X,Y) at the root of the tree will be applied to the message concept. This test will evaluate to True (+), thus the left branch will be taken. Next, the test for MALE(X) will be applied. This test will also evaluate to True, and therefore the lemma node of *father* will be reached. Note that if the outcome of the last test had been False (−), then the lemma of *mother* would have been reached. But what if the speaker wants to express the concept PARENT? How is the lemma of *parent* represented and recovered? This poses a difficulty to this model. For someone to be a parent it is irrelevant whether that person is a male or female — both a mother and a father can be referred to as *parent*. Therefore, the MALE(X) test cannot be appropriately used for *parent*. What, then, is the test for *parent*? Perhaps, the inclusion of a feature that indicates whether gender is relevant would enable convergence to take place. Then, when the tests for PARENT(X,Y) and this feature evaluate to True, *parent* would be reached. Of course, such a proposal is *ad hoc* because for the problem of disjunctive terms and the word-to-phrase synonymy problem other solutions have to be found.

Decision Tables

Decision tables (Miller and Johnson-Laird, 1976) are access matrices where the row margins represent semantic tests, the matrix columns stand for outcome patterns on a series of such tests, and the column margins represent lemmas. An entry of a matrix can contain the value True (+), False (−), or can be blank. The latter indicates that the outcome of a test is irrelevant. Semantic tests are applied in parallel to each concept a speaker wants to express, and the pattern of outcome triggers a particular lemma.

Figure 12.2: Illustration of a decision table

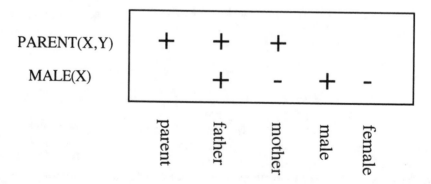

Figure 12.2 illustrates the way a decision table works. Horizontally, the semantic tests for PARENT(X,Y) and MALE(X) are depicted, and vertically the lemmas for *parent, father, mother, male,* and *female* are shown. The table specifies, for example, that triggering the lemma of *father* requires both the test for PARENT(X,Y) and the test for MALE(X) to evaluate to True (+). Note that in contrast to a binary discrimination net, the representation of the meaning of *parent* is straightforward. The lemma of *parent* has simply a blank for the outcome of the MALE(X) test, indicating the irrelevance of the result of this test. Assume again that a speaker wants to express the concept FATHER. Then, both the MALE(X) test and the PARENT(X,Y) test will evaluate to True. The outcome pattern for *father* will thus be satisfied, but the condition for the retrieval of, for example, *parent* will simultaneously be satisfied as well. The only requirement for triggering this lemma is that the PARENT(X,Y) test evaluates to True, the outcome of the MALE(X) test is irrelevant. Consequently, if a speaker wants to verbalize FATHER, both the lemma of *father* and the lemma of *parent* will be retrieved, thereby violating the convergence criterion. Thus, although decision tables can easily represent hyperonyms, they cannot cope with hyperonymy in the actual retrieval of words (Levelt, 1989). For the same reasons, they cannot handle disjunctive concepts and word-to-phrase synonymy. The major problem posed by disjunctive terms (e.g., *sibling*) is that the satisfaction of a disjunction of conceptual conditions (e.g., BROTHER OR SISTER) implies that the condition of at least one of the disjuncts is met. A decision table cannot deliver a disjunctive term without producing its hyponyms, and it cannot deliver a word that has a disjunctive hyperonym without producing the hyperonym. The problem posed by word-to-phrase synonymy is that a decision table cannot know whether to deliver *male* and *parent* instead of *father*, or vice versa, when the tests for MALE(X) and PARENT(X,Y) evaluate to True. Therefore, a decision table fails as a model of lemma retrieval.

Logogens

A logogen (Morton, 1969) is a device counting how many of a word's conceptual features are present in the message. When the count surpasses a critical threshold the logogen will fire, thereby making the word available. In lemma retrieval a set of conceptual features is switched on, and the logogen that fires first will be selected. Figure 12.3 illustrates the working of a system of logogens for lemma retrieval. The conceptual features MALE(X), PARENT(X,Y), and FEMALE(X) are depicted at the top, the logogens for the lemmas of *male, father, parent, mother,* and *female* are shown at the bottom. The arrows from conceptual features to logogens indicate which features are relevant to a particular logogen. For example, the conceptual features PARENT(X,Y) and MALE(X) are the features relevant to *father*. Note that to represent the values True, False, and Irrelevant, the feature

Figure 12.3: Illustration of a system of logogens and a featural spreading-activation net

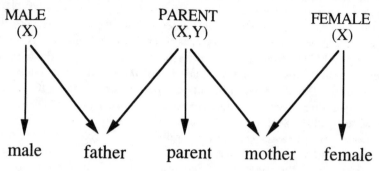

FEMALE(X) is needed in addition to the feature MALE(X), because turning MALE(X) *on* or leaving it *off* cannot encode three values. In retrieving the lemma of *father*, the features MALE(X) and PARENT(X,Y) are turned on. Consequently, the logogen of *father* will exceed threshold, because all the relevant features are present. However, similar to a decision table, hyperonymy poses difficulty (Levelt, 1989). The set of features relevant to a word includes those relevant to its hyperonyms. Therefore, in switching the features MALE(X) and PARENT(X,Y) on, the logogen of *parent* will also exceed threshold and fire too (*parent* requires PARENT(X,Y) to be on and nothing else). For the same reasons, a system of logogens cannot handle word-to-phrase synonymy, nor can it cope with disjunctive concepts. Thus, similar to a decision table, a system of logogens cannot explain how the retrieval process converges onto the appropriate words in memory.

Spreading-Activation Nets

Spreading-activation networks come in two varieties: featural nets and non-decompositional nets. Featural nets have much in common with logogens. In such a net, conceptual feature nodes are directly connected to lemma nodes (cf., Dell and O'Seaghdha, 1991, 1992).[2] By contrast, in a non-decompositional net, conceptual features are indirectly connected to lemma nodes, via independent nodes for lexical concepts (Collins and Loftus, 1975; Roelofs, 1992a, 1993). Lemma retrieval begins by activating the set of conceptual feature nodes (in a featural net) or the lexical-concept node (in a non-decompositional net) making up the to-be-verbalized concept. The activation is not all-or-none (as was the case in the logogen model), but is real valued. Nodes then spread a proportion of their activation towards the associated lemma nodes. This proportion is the same for all nodes, that is, there is a general spreading rate. Finally, after a certain period of time (e.g., depending on the speaking rate), the highest activated lemma node (or the first node exceeding a response threshold) is selected.

Featural Spreading-Activation Networks

I illustrate the working of a featural spreading-activation net by using Figure 12.3 again. The top layer represents conceptual feature nodes, the bottom layer consists of lemma nodes, and the arrows indicate the connections between the feature nodes and the lemma nodes. For example, the nodes for PARENT(X,Y) and MALE(X) are connected to the lemma node of *father*. The connections are usually taken to be bi-directional (i.e., from features to lemmas and from lemmas back to features or 'interactive') so that the network can also be used for language comprehension (cf., Dell and O'Seaghdha, 1991, 1992).

In verbalizing the concept FATHER, the feature nodes MALE(X) and PARENT(X,Y) are activated. The activation then spreads towards the lemma nodes (and back again), activating the lemma node of *father*, among other things. Often, activation is assumed to spread according to

$$(1) \qquad a(m,s+1) = a(m,s)(1-d) + \sum_{n} r\, a(n,s)$$

where $a(m,s)$ is the activation level of node m at time step s, and d is a decay rate with $0 < d < 1$ (e.g., Dell and O'Seaghdha, 1991, 1992; Roelofs, 1992a, 1993). The rightmost term denotes the amount of activation m receives between s and $s+1$, where $a(n,s)$ is the output of neighbour n (equal to its level of activation). The factor r indicates the spreading rate. Figure 12.4 illustrates the behaviour of the network by showing activation curves for the lemma nodes. The curves were obtained by using the spreading equation with parameter values (taken from Dell and O'Seaghdha, 1991, 1992) $d = 0.4$ and $r = 0.1$, and an external input to the feature nodes of size 1.0.

In contrast to a decision table and a system of logogens, there is no hyperonym problem, as shown by the activation plots of Figure 12.4. In activating the conceptual features MALE(X) and PARENT(X,Y) to express FATHER, the lemma of the word *parent* will not be selected. Although the lemma nodes of the hyperonyms of *father* such as *parent* will be activated, they will not be activated as high as the node of *father*. Both conceptual features for FATHER (i.e., MALE(X) and PARENT(X,Y)) will send a proportion of their activation to *father*, but only one of these features (i.e., PARENT(X,Y)) will activate *parent*. Thus, *father* will have a higher level of activation than its hyperonyms. According to this model, lemmas are selected on the basis of their level of activation (e.g., Dell, 1986). The retrieval process suffers, however, from a hyponym problem, because all features that activate a word will also activate the word's hyponyms. As can be seen, the network produces incorrectly *mother* and *father* for PARENT, and *father* for MALE. In verbalizing PARENT, *mother* and *father* will end up with a higher level of activation than *parent* due to a reverberation of activation from FEMALE(X) and MALE(X) via the backward links. The same holds for the verbalization of MALE, where the level of activation of *father* exceeds that of *male* due to the feedback of activation from PARENT(X,Y). Finally, consider the situation with two message concepts, MALE and PARENT, requiring that two lemma nodes are selected to

Figure 12.4: Activation curves for the interactive featural spreading-activation net

FEATURAL

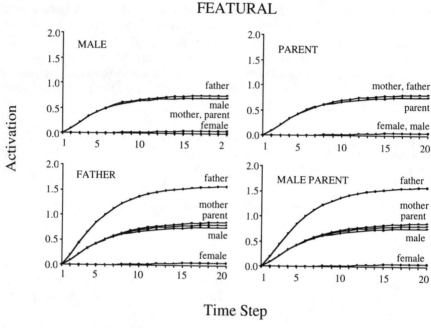

Time Step

produce the phrase ... *male parent*. Figure 12.4 shows that the system will incorrectly select the lemmas of *father* and *mother*, since they are the two lemmas with the highest activation.

Of course, there is nothing in the featural approach that requires a general spreading rate *r* (i.e., equal weights on the links between feature nodes and lemma nodes). Thus, perhaps the hyponym problem can be solved by abandoning the assumption of a general spreading rate. Instead, one could put appropriately tuned weights on the links between conceptual feature nodes and lemma nodes. To prevent the problem, the weights have to be set (e.g., during a learning process, see Chapter 3) such that in activating the conceptual feature nodes of a word, its lemma node will receive more activation than the nodes of the word's hyperonyms and hyponyms. This ought to hold for all words in the lexical network. However, tuning weights is insufficient to solve all convergence problems. Again, the problem of disjunctive terms remains unresolved. Also, the word-to-phrase synonymy problem cannot be handled by the same mechanism. For example, if MALE(X) and PARENT(X,Y) are connected to the lemma nodes of *father*, *male*, and *parent* such that activating these components can retrieve *father* as well as *male* and *parent*, then activating the components will retrieve all these terms. To solve this problem, one might perhaps assume that a single verbalization and building the phrase are accomplished on the basis of different patterns of activation over the feature nodes. That is, by assigning different activation patterns to MALE PARENT and FATHER. Alternatively, one might assume

Figure 12.5: Illustration of a non-decompositional spreading-activation net

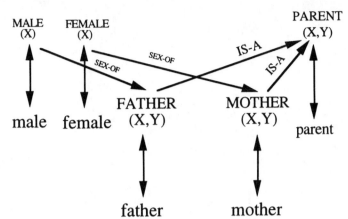

that retrieving *male parent* without accessing *father*, and vice versa, is achieved by nodes that stand for combinations of components (i.e., a node for MALE PARENT). Of course, both solutions would amount to giving up decomposition. To conclude, a general solution to the convergence problems requires more than tuning weights.

Non-Decompositional Spreading-Activation Networks

Figure 12.5 illustrates how a non-decompositional spreading-activation net works (Roelofs, 1992a, 1993). In contrast to a featural network, each lexical concept (e.g., FATHER, MOTHER, PARENT) is represented by an independent node in the net. The conceptual properties of the concept FATHER are specified by labelled links (pointers) between its lexical concept node FATHER(X,Y) and other concept nodes in the network. For example, FATHER(X,Y) is linked to PARENT(X,Y) by an IS-A link, and MALE(X) is connected to FATHER(X,Y) by a SEX-OF link. In expressing the concept FATHER, the activation level of the lexical-concept node FATHER(X,Y) is enhanced. Thus, the crucial difference with a featural network is that lemma retrieval starts with the activation of FATHER(X,Y), and not with activation of the features MALE(X) and PARENT(X,Y). These features provide background information about FATHER, but are not directly engaged in the lemma retrieval process.

Figure 12.6 illustrates the behaviour of the network by showing the activation curves for the lemma nodes in the verbalization of FATHER, PARENT, MALE, and MALE PARENT. Similar curves are obtained with other connectivity patterns at the conceptual level. The parameter values (taken from Roelofs, 1992a, 1993) were $d = 0.60$, $r = 0.25$ for the conceptual connections, and $r = 0.19$ for the connections between lexical-concept nodes and lemma nodes. The external input to the lexical-concept nodes was of size 4.91. Consider the verbalization of FATHER. After activating FATHER(X,Y), activation will spread towards the lemma nodes, and the first node whose activation level exceeds that of the other nodes by some critical

Figure 12.6: Activation curves for the non-decompositional spreading-activation net

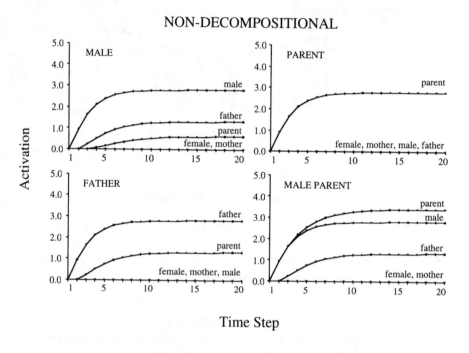

NON-DECOMPOSITIONAL

Time Step

amount (e.g., 1.5) is selected. As can be seen in Figure 12.6, the first node reaching the response threshold will be the node of *father*. Although the lemma node of *parent* will be co-activated due to the IS-A link between FATHER(X,Y) and PARENT(X,Y), the *parent* node will receive only a proportion of a proportion of the activation of FATHER(X,Y), whereas the lemma node of *father* will get a full proportion. For the same reasons, the process correctly delivers *parent* for PARENT, *male* for MALE, and *male* and *parent* instead of *father* when MALE and PARENT are the intended concepts (and MALE(X) and PARENT(X,Y) are made part of the message). This example demonstrates that a non-decompositional spreading-activation net can cope with the hyperonym problem, the hyponym problem, and the word-to-phrase synonymy problem (for mathematical proof, see Roelofs, 1994).

The decompositional models suffer from the convergence problems in lemma retrieval because the set of conceptual features of a concept (e.g., BIRD, FATHER) contains that of its superordinates (e.g., ANIMAL, PARENT) as a proper part. The non-decompositional model seems to be confronted with a convergence problem too, albeit in message encoding rather than in lemma retrieval. In a non-decompositional approach, set inclusion may be prevented by adhering to some form of economy in organizing the conceptual network. In particular, there should be no full redundancy in the storage of features with concepts in memory.

Then, some properties shared by a concept and its superordinate are not stored with the concept but only with the superordinate. The concept inherits these properties from its superordinate via an IS-A link (cf., Collins and Loftus, 1975). In this way, set inclusion is prevented and convergence in the selection of lexical concepts in message encoding may be achieved (for details, see Roelofs, 1992b).

Evaluation of the Models

The models of lemma retrieval can be characterized along a number of dimensions. A first dimension concerns the nature of the input to the retrieval process. As indicated, with respect to the input, the models take either a *de-compositional* or a *non-decompositional* stance. A non-decompositional approach assumes that the lemma of a word such as *father* is retrieved on the basis of the abstract representation FATHER(X,Y). For a lemma of a word in the language there is a corresponding element in the vocabulary for the specification of messages (cf., Fodor *et al.*, 1980; Roelofs, 1994). By contrast, decompositional models assume that the lemma of a semantically complex word (i.e., a word whose meaning can be further analyzed into more elementary concepts) is retrieved on the basis of a number of primitive concepts. For example, the lemma of *father* is retrieved on the basis of MALE(X) and PARENT(X,Y). Thus, each element for the specification of messages is typically linked to several lemmas (cf., Bierwisch and Schreuder, 1992). PARENT(X,Y) is associated to both *father* and *parent*. All models described above are decompositional except the one proposed by Roelofs (1992a, 1993), in which lemmas are accessed from independent lexical-concept nodes in a lexical network by means of the spreading of activation.

The models can be further classified on the basis of whether they distinguish between *conceptual representations* on the one hand and *semantic representations* (word meanings) on the other (cf., Jackendoff, 1987). Models that make this distinction assume that the input representation (i.e., the message concept) and the semantic part of a lemma are mentally realized by separate, independent representations. This holds for discrimination nets and decision tables. Here, lemmas contain semantic tests (making up a semantic representation) to be applied to the message concept (making up a conceptual representation). By contrast, in a logogen system and in a spreading-activation net, the message concept and the word meaning are embodied by one and the same representation. The representations of the conceptual features or the lexical-concept node make up both the message concept *and* the word meaning.

Discrimination nets and decision tables are *symbolic* models (for a definition, see Chapter 2). They involve mental operations (i.e., the semantic tests) on structured mental representations (i.e., the conceptual structures making up the messages). Logogens are *connectionistic* in that no structure sensitive operation is involved but only a process of counting (cf., Chapter 3). That is, they involve the accumulation of discrete inputs until a selection threshold is exceeded. The same holds for the featural spreading-activation model of Dell and O'Seaghdha (1991, 1992), except that the accumulation involves real-valued inputs. The general framework adopted by Dell (1986), however, is a *hybrid* one. For example, in grammatical encoding a selected lemma is associated to the first empty slot of a syntactic frame. This is clearly a structure sensitive process, involving such notions as *first*, *slot*, and *frame*. The non-decompositional spreading-activation model of Roelofs (1992a, 1993) is also a hybrid one for the same reasons. In addition, in that model the links between the nodes are labelled, following a computational tradition starting with the work of Quillian in the mid-1960s (for a review, see Collins and Loftus, 1975). The lexical network is made up by structured representations, such as IS-A(FATHER, PARENT) and LEXICAL_CATEGORY(father, NOUN). The labels on the links do not play a direct role in lemma retrieval, but are relevant for grammatical encoding processes. For example, in selecting a noun as opposed to a verb in the construction of a phrase, the formulation processes have to access the information specified by the category link and node. Also, the labels play a role in the retrieval of conceptual information from semantic memory in language comprehension and in message encoding (e.g., Collins and Loftus, 1975).

In the logogen model and the featural spreading-activation model, lemma nodes are *local* computational units. Each lemma node represents a single lemma. A lexical concept such as FATHER is represented by its component conceptual features, in the connectionist literature often referred to as *microfeatures* and in the symbolic literature as *semantic markers*. Each microfeature or marker is assumed to be represented by a single node in the network. Thus, similar to the lemma nodes, conceptual features are represented in a local way. Instead, the conceptual features may be represented in a *distributed* manner (see Chapter 3). Then, each node would be involved in the representation of several conceptual features, and each conceptual feature would be represented by several nodes. A conceptual feature is then represented by an activation pattern over a set of nodes (i.e., an activation vector). The unit of computation of the system at the representational level is the activation pattern.

Finally, the models differ in whether they assume that semantic tests are applied (or conceptual features are activated) in *series* or in *parallel*. The discrimination nets assume a serial ordering of the tests. Each test is applied to the message concept after the test has received the control of its immediate predecessor. The decision tables presume parallel testing. Similarly, in a logogen system and in a featural spreading-activation net, conceptual features will be activated simultaneously.

The speed of access makes a serial accessing mechanism an unattractive option (Levelt, 1989). In a discrimination net, the lemma access time will be equal to the sum of the latencies of the semantic tests leading to the lemma. Thus, the speed depends on the number of tests. A much more attractive option is a parallel accessing mechanism such as a decision table. Here, the slowest semantic test determines the retrieval speed. The lemma retrieval latency will be equal to the maximum of the latencies of the tests to be satisfied for the lemma. In case each lexical concept is linked to a single lemma, the retrieval latency will be short too.

Empirical Tests of the Models: Retrieval Speed

At first sight, one can derive strong empirical predictions from the models about the speed of lemma retrieval (for an extensive discussion of latency predictions from models, see McGill, 1963; Townsend and Ashby, 1983; Luce, 1986). For example, if the tests for a word are a proper superset of the tests for the word's hyperonyms, and the time to retrieve a lemma equals the sum of the latencies of the semantic tests, then words should be retrieved more slowly than their hyperonyms. Unfortunately, however, the failure of the decompositional models to handle hyperonymy makes such empirical tests problematic in that the retrieval of the correct word on an experimental trial is a problem for these models right from the start.

By contrast, the non-decompositional spreading-activation model does not suffer from the convergence problems. Consequently, it has been possible to put the model to a number of empirical tests. In testing this model, the so-called picture-word interference paradigm was used (for a review of this paradigm, see Glaser, 1992). In recent years, this experimental paradigm has become one of the major tools in the study of lexical access in language production (e.g., Schriefers, Meyer and Levelt, 1990). Subjects have to name pictured objects (e.g., they have to say *bird* to a pictured bird) while trying to ignore so-called distractor words. A distractor word is a written word superimposed on the picture or a spoken word presented via headphones. The speed of retrieval of the target lemma is affected depending on, among other things, the temporal relationship (the stimulus onset asynchrony or SOA) and the content relationship between picture and word. Usually, the distractor is presented just before (e.g., -400, -300, -200, or -100 ms), simultaneously with, or right after (e.g., $+100$, $+200$, $+300$, or $+400$ ms) picture onset, and is either semantically related to the pictured object (e.g., distractor *fish* in a pictured bird) or semantically unrelated (e.g., distractor *shoe*). Alternatively, the subjects are asked to refer to the picture or to the word printed in the picture by producing a hyperonym — called, respectively, picture categorization and word categorization. For example, they have to say *animal* to a depicted bird, while trying to ignore the word printed in the picture. Or they have to say *animal* to the word *bird* and ignore the picture. Typically, one observes semantic inhibition (i.e., naming latencies are slower for the related condition than for the unrelated one) at SOAs between -100 and $+100$ ms for picture naming, semantic facilitation (i.e., naming latencies are faster for the related condition than for the unrelated one) at SOAs between -400 and -100 ms for picture categorization, and even more semantic facilitation at SOAs between -400 and $+200$ ms for word categorization. The panels A, B, and C of Figure

Figure 12.7: SOA functions of the semantic effect from distractors in picture naming, picture categorization, and word categorization. Real data (filled squares) and the predictions by the non-decompositional spreading-activation model (empty squares). [Real data in (A), (B), and (C) are from Glaser and Düngelhoff, 1984; real data in (D) are from Roelofs, 1992]. A positive value means an inhibitory effect from a distractor word, and a negative value indicates a facilitatory effect

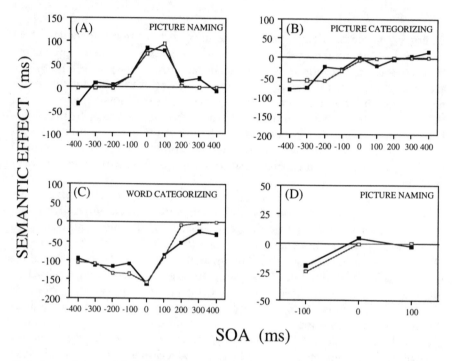

12.7 show the empirical SOA curves of the semantic effect for picture naming, picture categorization, and word categorization obtained by Glaser and Düngelhoff (1984). The panels depict for each SOA (in ms) the mean latency in the semantically related condition minus that in the unrelated condition (in ms). Thus, a positive value indicates semantic inhibition, and a negative value indicates semantic facilitation.

The panels also show the SOA curves for the three tasks as derived from the non-decompositional spreading-activation model by computer simulation. The simulations used the activation equation (with the parameter values) given above and networks consisting of lemma nodes and lexical-concepts nodes as shown in Figure 12.5. There were two different semantic fields, each typically consisting of a superordinate (e.g., ANIMAL(X)) and two subordinates (e.g., BIRD(X) and FISH(X)), which were connected to each other and to their lemma nodes in a bi-directional manner. The presentation of a picture and a word was simulated by assigning external activation to the corresponding concept node and lemma node, respectively, representing the output from picture and word perception. The external input was provided using the appropriate SOA, with the duration of a time step taken to be 25 ms. The probability of actual selection of the target node in any time step was assumed to be equal to a ratio. The numerator of the ratio was formed by the activation level of the target node. The denominator was equal to the sum of the activation levels of the target and all the other lemma nodes. On the basis of the spreading equation and the selection probability, the mathematical expectation of the retrieval time of the target lemma was computed for each SOA and distractor type. Figure 12.7 depicts for each SOA the theoretically expected retrieval time in the semantically related condition minus that in the unrelated condition. For details of the simulations, I refer to the original publications (i.e., Roelofs, 1992a, 1993). As can be seen in Figure 12.7 (and has been shown by a statistical χ^2 measure of fit), the fit of the model to the data is good.

The non-decompositional spreading-activation model explains the semantic effects as follows. If *fish* is superimposed as distractor on a pictured bird, the activation from the picture and from the distractor word will converge in the network on the lemma node of the distractor word *fish*. This is because BIRD(X) and FISH(X) are connected in the network through links which are bi-directional (unlike in the *father* example). If *shoe* is superimposed, there will be no such convergence of activation — BIRD(X) and SHOE(X) are not connected. As a result, *fish* will be a stronger competitor to the target lemma than *shoe*. This is what the SOA curve in panel A of Figure 12.7 shows. According to the model, distractor lemmas will only be competitors if they are potential responses in the experiment (this was the case in the picture-naming experiment just described). Thus, in a categorization experiment where subjects respond by using hyperonyms such as *animal*, the distractors *fish* and *shoe* should be no competitors because they are no longer potential responses. Instead, a facilitatory effect from *fish* should be obtained, because *fish* will prime the lemma of *animal* via the conceptual links in the network, whereas *shoe* will not. This prediction is supported by the experimental data, as shown in panel B and C of Figure 12.7. A prediction along the same line is that distractors such as the hyperonym *animal*, the cohyponym *fish*, and the hyponym *robin* should facilitate the naming response (*bird*) if the pictured bird is the only animal to be named in the experiment. Then, the distractors are not permitted responses, and therefore they will not be a competitor to the target lemma. Thus, they should lead to facilitation if they are semantically related, as we saw for the categorization experiments. This prediction is confirmed by the empirical data, shown in panel D of Figure 12.7. The panel depicts the mean semantic effect per SOA for distractor words such as *animal*, *fish*, and *robin* (there was no difference in effect between hyperonym, cohyponym, and hyponym distractors). To conclude, the non-decompositional spreading-activation model gives a good account for several important findings on the speed of lemma retrieval. Importantly, these findings were obtained with a number of different experimental tasks, which cross-validates the model.

Recently, Bierwisch and Schreuder (1992) suggested that the hyperonym problem may be solved within a decompositional model by an inhibitory link between a word and its hyperonyms. For example, in the logogen model, the logogen of a word may have inhibitory connections to the logogens of its hyperonyms. Then, if the logogen of a word exceeds threshold, it inhibits the logogens of its hyperonyms (e.g., *father* inhibits *parent*). Consequently, only one logogen will fire, as required by the convergence criterion.

Of course, such a proposal is *ad hoc* since for the solution of the word-to-phrase synonymy problem and the problem of disjunctive terms other mechanisms have to be found. Furthermore, an inhibitory link may cause additional problems. In retrieving *male parent* by MALE(X) and PARENT(X,Y), *father* (activated by these conceptual features) will inhibit its hyperonyms *male* and *parent* (the targets of retrieval) too.

Nevertheless, it is an empirical question whether such inhibitory links exist. An inhibitory link between a word and its hyperonyms has clear consequences. It implies, for instance, that the naming of a pictured object should be inhibited by a distractor that is a hyponym of the picture name. For example, *robin* should inhibit the retrieval of *bird* (relative to an unrelated hyponym as distractor). Similarly, *bird* as distractor should inhibit the retrieval of *animal*. It is irrelevant whether the distractor is a potential response in the experiment, because the inhibitory link is assumed to be hard-wired in the mental lexicon. As we saw earlier, picture-word interference experiments using these types of distractor have been conducted. The results were clear-cut: No inhibitory effect from hyponyms on the retrieval of a word is obtained. Instead, the retrieval of the lemma of *bird* is facilitated by the distractor word *robin*, and the retrieval of the lemma of *animal* is facilitated by the word *bird*. This holds for nouns (see panels B, C, and D of Figure 12.7) as well as for verbs (Roelofs, 1993). For example, the retrieval of *laugh* is facilitated by *chuckle*. Clearly, an inhibitory link between a word and its hyperonyms is not the answer to the hyperonym problem.

Alternatively, one may implement a principle of *specificity*, as proposed by Levelt (1989, 1992). This principle says that of all lemmas whose conceptual conditions are satisfied, the most specific one is selected. For example, if BIRD triggers *bird*, *animal*, and so forth, then *bird* will be selected because it is the most specific term. The principle might be incorporated in a decision table. Then, of all the lemmas that match the concept, the one with the most specific condition would be given preference. Similar to an inhibitory channel, however, a specificity principle predicts an inhibitory effect from hyponym distractors on the retrieval of the picture name. In case of a distractor hyponym (e.g., *robin*), the distractor word would be preferred to the name of the picture (*bird*) because it is more specific. Note, however, that the principle may be reconciled with the empirical findings if its domain of application is restricted to the lemmas that are permitted responses in the experiment. Then, although *robin* is more specific than *bird*, it is not considered for selection because it is not a permitted response in the experiment.

There are, however, other problems with a specificity principle. Although the principle solves the hyperonym problem, it fails on the word-to-phrase synonymy problem. Also, it cannot handle the retrieval of words that express disjunctive concepts. For example, if a speaker wants to verbalize SIBLING (i.e., BROTHER OR SISTER), the conceptual conditions of *brother* or of *sister* will be satisfied too. Consequently, the latter terms will be selected because they are more specific. And if a speaker wants to say . . . *male parent*, the principle of specificity leads to retrieval of *father* and not to retrieval of *male* and *parent*.

Conclusion

In this chapter, I have reviewed the major existing computational models of lemma retrieval: discrimination nets, decision tables, logogens, and featural and non-decompositional spreading-activation nets. I have shown that, first, the decompositional proposals for lemma retrieval fail to solve the convergence problem, which is composed of several subproblems — how to avoid retrieving hyperonyms and hyponyms along with or instead of the intended words, and how to correctly retrieve either a word or a synonymous phrase. Second, I have shown that the non-decompositional model satisfies the speed and convergence criteria and accounts for several major empirical findings on conceptually driven lemma retrieval. These findings concerned the time course of the inhibitory and facilitatory influences of semantic relatedness in the picture-word interference paradigm. This poses a challenge to a builder of computational models — to develop a decompositional model for lemma retrieval that meets the computational criteria and accounts for the data in a more parsimonious way.

Notes

1 Originally, discrimination nets, decision tables, and logogens were proposed as models for lexical access *per se*, without making the distinction between lemma retrieval and phonological encoding. This distinction originates from more recent research.
2 Dell and O'Seaghdha do not make a case for a featural representation of word meaning; their featural approach was one of convenience. I refer to their model because it is a computational model and gives a good description of feature-based lemma retrieval within a spreading-activation framework.

References

BIERWISCH, M. and SCHREUDER, R. (1992) 'From concepts to lexical items', *Cognition*, 42, pp. 23–60.

COLLINS, A. M. and LOFTUS, E. F. (1975) 'A spreading-activation theory of semantic processing', *Psychological Review*, 82, pp. 407–28.

DELL, G. S. (1986) 'A spreading-activation theory of retrieval in sentence production', *Psychological Review*, 93, pp. 283–321.

DELL, G. S. and O'SEAGHDHA, P. G. (1991) 'Mediated and convergent lexical priming in language production: A comment on Levelt *et al.* (1991) 'Psychological Review, 98, pp. 604–14.

DELL, G. S. and O'SEAGHDHA, P. G. (1992) 'Stages of lexical access in language production', *Cognition*, 42, pp. 287–314.

FODOR, J. A., GARRETT, M. F., WALKER, E. C. T. and PARKES, C. H. (1980) 'Against definitions', *Cognition*, 8, pp. 263–367.

GARRETT, M. F. (1975) 'The analysis of sentence production', in BOWER, G. H. (Ed) *The Psychology of Learning and Motivation*, New York: Academic Press.

GLASER, W. R. (1992) 'Picture naming', *Cognition*, 42, pp. 61–105.

GLASER, W. R. and DÜNGELHOFF, F.-J. (1984) 'The time course of picture-word interference', *Journal of Experimental Psychology: Human Perception and Performance*, 10, pp. 640–54.

GOLDMAN, N. (1975) 'Conceptual generation', in SCHANK, R. (Ed) *Conceptual Information Processing*, Amsterdam: North-Holland, pp. 289–371.

JACKENDOFF, R. (1987) *Semantics and Cognition*, Cambridge, MA: MIT Press.

JESCHENIAK, J.-D. and LEVELT, W. J. M. (1994) 'Word frequency effects in speech production: Retrieval of syntactic information and phonological form', *Journal of Experimental Psychology: Learning, Memory, and Cognition*, 20, pp. 824–43.

KEMPEN, G. and HOENKAMP, E. (1987) 'An incremental procedural grammar for sentence formulation', *Cognitive Science*, 11, pp. 201–58.

LEVELT, W. J. M. (1989) *Speaking: From Intention to Articulation*, Cambridge, MA: MIT Press.

LEVELT, W. J. M. (1992) 'Accessing words in speech production: Stages, processes and representations', *Cognition*, 42, pp. 1–22.

LEVELT, W. J. M. and FLORES D'ARCAIS, G. B. (1987) 'Snelheid en uniciteit bij lexicale toegang [Speed and uniqueness in lexical access], in CROMBAG, H. F.M., VAN DER KAMP, L. J. Th. and VLEK, C. A. J. (Eds) *De Psychologie Voorbij*, Lisse: Swets & Zeitlinger, pp. 55–68.

KEMPEN, G. and HUIJBERS, P. (1983) 'The lexicalization process in sentence production and naming: Indirect election of words', *Cognition*, 14, pp. 185–209.

LEVELT, W. J. M., SCHRIEFERS, H., VORBERG, D., MEYER, A. S., PECHMANN, T. and HAVINGA, J. (1991) 'The time course of lexical access in speech production: A study of picture naming', *Psychological Review*, 98, pp. 122–42.

LUCE, R. D. (1986) *Response Times: Their Role in Inferring Elementary Mental Organization*, New York: Oxford University Press.

MCGILL, W. J. (1963) 'Stochastic latency mechanisms', in LUCE, R. D., BUSH, R. R. and GALANTER, E. (Eds) *Handbook of Mathematical Psychology, Vol. 1*, New York: Wiley, pp. 309–60.

MILLER, G. A. and JOHNSON-LAIRD, P. N. (1976) *Language and Perception*, Cambridge, MA: Harvard University Press.

MORTON, J. (1969) 'The interaction of information in word recognition', *Psychological Review*, 76, pp. 165–78.

ROELOFS, A. (1992a) 'A spreading-activation theory of lemma retrieval in speaking', *Cognition*, 42, pp. 107–42.

ROELOFS, A. (1992b) *Lemma Retrieval in Speaking: A Theory, Computer Simulations, and Empirical Data*, Doctoral dissertation, NICI Technical Report 92–08, University of Nijmegen.

ROELOFS, A. (1993) 'Testing a non-decompositional theory of lemma retrieval in speaking: Retrieval of verbs', *Cognition*, 47, pp. 59–87.

ROELOFS, A. (1994) 'Word retrieval in speaking: A case for conceptually non-decomposed access', Manuscript submitted for publication.

ROELOFS, A. (in preparation) 'From lexical concept to articulatory program: A theory of lexical access in spoken word production'.

SCHRIEFERS, H., MEYER, A. S. and LEVELT, W. J. M. (1990) 'Exploring the time course of lexical access in language production: Picture-word interference studies', *Journal of Memory and Language*, 29, pp. 86–102.

TOWNSEND, J. T. and ASHBY, F. G. (1983) *Stochastic modeling of elementary psychological processes*, Cambridge: Cambridge University Press.

Chapter 13

Computational Models of Phonological Encoding

Gary S. Dell and Cornell Juliano

Introduction

Phonological encoding in language production, the process through which the sounds of words are retrieved, ordered, and organized for articulation, is an ideal candidate for computational modelling. In the first place, there already exists a widely supported general theory of production, and the role of phonological encoding in it. The essence of this *standard theory* is that sentence production requires the construction of a conceptual representation of the sentence and at least two other representations — one which emphasizes syntactic relations among words, and one which specifies their sound structure and serial order. Moreover, these representations are assembled in advance of articulation, with greater advance planning associated with the earlier syntactic-level representation than with the later phonological representation. The theory was initially developed by Garrett (1975) and has since been extended and refined by a number of researchers (e.g., Shattuck-Hufnagel, 1979; Bock, 1982; MacKay 1982, 1987; Kempen and Huijbers, 1983; Levelt, 1983; Stemberger, 1985, 1990; Dell, 1986; Kempen and Hoenkamp, 1987; Schriefers, Meyer and Levelt, 1990; Levelt *et al.*, 1991; Meyer, 1991; Bock, Loebell and Morey, 1992; Roelofs, 1992). A compelling synthesis of the original standard theory and some of the further developments was provided by Levelt (1989). The two computational models described in this chapter (Dell, 1986; Dell, Juliano and Govindjee, 1993) come out of the tradition of this theory although, as will be seen, they are at odds with some of its assumptions.

A second reason that phonological encoding in production is suited to modelling is that, compared to other aspects of comprehension and production, it is easy. In fact, computational models of phonological encoding have been restricted to the seemingly straightforward task of *lexeme* retrieval. The lexeme is the phonological form of a word. As described in Chapters 11 and 12, the production of a word can be broken down into a sequence of stages. Beginning with the concept to be expressed, the initial stage maps the concept to a *lemma*, an abstract representation of the word as a grammatical entity. The subsequent mapping from lemma to lexeme constitutes lexeme retrieval. In focusing on lexeme retrieval, the developers of models of phonological encoding have elected to set aside both the issue of how the lemmas are chosen and ordered and those aspects of phonological encoding that span units larger than the word, such as prosody. Lemma retrieval models have been developed (see Chapter 12), but computational models that deal with the production of prosody from a psycholinguistic perspective have not.

A final consideration in modelling phonological encoding is that there are many empirical phenomena that can serve as modelling goals. Most of these phenomena concern *speech errors* or *slips of the tongue*, specifically, the kinds of error that occur, their frequency of occurrence, and factors that influence their likelihood. These error data, which are obtained both from controlled experiments (e.g., Baars, Motley and MacKay, 1975; Stemberger, 1991) and from analyses of natural errors (e.g., MacKay, 1970; Fromkin, 1971), provide a multidimensional source of constraint and, in some cases, have been used as targets for quantitative data fitting (e.g., Dell, 1986; Martin *et al.*, 1994). One drawback of error data is that one can question the extent to which the operation of the production system, when it makes an error, is related to the system's error-free production (Levelt *et al.*, 1991). While no one would claim that the production of slips and that of error-free utterances are unrelated, the generalization from a characterization of utterances with errors, only, to one of all utterances requires some degree of faith. Consequently, it is desirable to model both correct and incorrect performance, and to consider experimental data concerning the time to produce correct utterances and data from secondary tasks designed to probe the nature of correct performance (e.g., Schriefers, Meyer and Levelt, 1990; Levelt *et al.*, 1991; Meyer, 1991). The models that we are presenting here have, to some extent, tried to account for the probability of both correct and errorful utterances, but have not modelled findings involving production time or performance in secondary tasks.

Speech Errors and Phonological Encoding

A natural categorization of speech errors is based on the size of the slipping unit. Saying *heft lemisphere* for *left hemisphere* involves the misordering, in particular, the exchange of phonological segments. This is an example of a phonological, or sound error. Errors involving speech sounds or groups of speech sounds can be distinguished from lexical errors in which whole words or morphemes slip (e.g., Fromkin, 1971; Garrett, 1975). Errors such as *I have to fill my gas up with car*, a word exchange, or *Liszt's second Hungarian restaurant* (for *Rhapsody*), a word substitution, are lexical errors. In the standard theory, phonological errors occur during phonological encoding and most lexical errors occur during either lemma retrieval or during the association of lemmas with slots in a syntactic representation. Given our focus on phonological encoding, we consequently have more to say about phonological errors, although we will be concerned with the possible influence of phonological variables on lexical errors.

Below are some of the error effects that the computational models of phonological encoding seek to reproduce.

Effects Concerning the Size of Slipping Units

The most common phonological errors involve the substitution, movement, deletion, or addition, of a single phonological segment. Estimates of the percentage of phonological errors that involve single segments run from 70 per cent to 90 per cent (Nooteboom, 1969; Shattuck-Hufnagel and Klatt, 1979). It is somewhat surprising that well-motivated phonological units such as the syllable and the phonological feature tend not to slip. For example, only 3 per cent of Shattuck-Hufnagel's (1983) phonological exchanges involved the exchange of non-morphemic syllables, and 1 per cent involved the unambiguous exchange of phonological features. These facts have led most theorists to assume that phonological segments are the units that are manipulated during phonological encoding.

Effects Concerning the Movement of Sounds

Most phonological errors (e.g., around 70 per cent, Garnham *et al.*, 1981) appear to have a *contextual* source. When one sound replaces another, or is erroneously added to a word without replacing anything, the sound occurs in a nearby word. In these errors, sounds are said to 'move' and the errors are called contextual or movement errors, or simply, misorderings. For example, in an exchange such as *heft lemisphere*, the /h/ and /l/ each moved to the other's locations. Although exchanges are often viewed as the prototypical misordering (e.g., Shattuck-Hufnagel, 1979; Dell, 1986), complete exchanges are less common than anticipatory substitutions (e.g., *heft hemisphere*) or perseveratory substitutions (e.g., *left lemisphere*). Among normal speakers, anticipatory errors predominate (Nooteboom, 1969).

Effects Concerning Similarity

In substitution errors, the target and replacing sounds are usually very similar, sharing most of their phonological features. Sixty to eighty per cent of substitution errors share all but one feature (MacKay, 1970; Stemberger, 1983). Thus, in the error *reading list* being spoken as *leading list*, the anticipated sound /l/ is quite similar to the target /r/. Also the environment of the slipping sounds tends to be similar (MacKay, 1970; Dell, 1984). For example, in *heft lemisphere*, the exchanging sounds are both word-initial and are followed by the vowel /E/. Similarity effects also occur with lexical errors. In particular, word substitutions often involve the replacement of a target word with either a semantically related word (*elbow* spoken as *knee*), a phonologically related word (*population* for *pollution*), or both (*cat* for *rat*). Word substitutions exhibiting both kinds of similarity appear to be especially likely when the number of opportunities for such errors is taken into account (Dell and Reich, 1981; Harley, 1984; Martin, Weisberg and Saffran, 1989; del Viso, Igoa and Garcia-Alba, 1991).

Effects Concerning Familiarity

Phonological errors are less likely on common words, sounds, and syllable structures (Stemberger and MacWhinney, 1986; Dell, 1990; Stemberger, 1990, 1991). At the same time, phonological errors have a tendency to create familiar sequences of segments (Motley and Baars, 1975) and to exhibit the *lexical bias effect*, a tendency to make words over pronounceable nonwords (Baars, Motley and MacKay, 1975; Dell and Reich, 1981; see, however, del Viso, Igoa and Garcia-Alba, 1991). For example, the chance of the error *barn door* for the target *darn bore* is enhanced because *barn* and *door* are words. There is also evidence for a related *semantic bias effect* on phonological errors. Motley and Baars (1976) elicited initial-consonant misorderings and found that the probability of erroneously producing phrases such as *wet gun* for targets such as *get one* is increased if subjects had recently read semantically related phrases, e.g., *damp rifle*. In general, there is a bias for both correct and erroneous utterances to favour familiar or contextually appropriate sequences of sounds and words. Many 'Freudian' influences on errors can be attributed to these familiarity effects.

Effects Concerning Within-Word Phonological Structure

There are four strong error effects that reveal the rule-governed hierarchical structure of words: the *phonotactic regularity effect*, the *consonant-vowel category effect*, the *syllabic constituent effect*, and the *initialness effect*. Because these effects are central to one of the models that we discuss, we present them in some detail.

Phonotactic Regularity Effect
Phonological errors only rarely create nonoccurring sound sequences. For example, saying *dlorm* for *dorm* violates English phonotactics because /dl/ is not an acceptable syllable onset. This error did in fact occur (Stemberger, 1983), but such violations are unlikely. Stemberger reported 37 violations, which constituted less than 1 per cent of his phonological error corpus. The adherence of errors to the phonotactic patterns of the language was first noted by Meringer and Mayer (1895) and was called the 'first law' of speech errors by Wells (1951). It is a strong constraint on any theory of phonological encoding and has been attributed to the active use of phonotactic rules (e.g., Fromkin, 1971).

Consonant-Vowel Category Effect
In single-segment substitution errors, vowels replace vowels, and consonants replace consonants. This constraint appears to be even stronger than the phonotactic regularity effect. MacKay (1970) found no exceptions in his analysis of exchange errors and Shattuck-Hufnagel and Klatt (1979) claimed that exceptions were 'rare'. There are cases in which syllabic consonants and vowels replace one another (e.g., *Mexicle* for *Mexico*, Shattuck-Hufnagel, 1986) but a clear exception such as *and* being spoken as *ano* would seem to be highly unlikely (Stemberger, 1983). The consonant-vowel category effect can either be viewed as the result of segmental dissimilarity or as a specific constraint involving the consonant and vowel categories. The two models presented below each adopt one of these perspectives.

Syllabic Constituent Effect
Although most errors involve single segments and consonant clusters, there are occasional slips in which an adjacent vowel and consonant are replaced. When this happens, the sequence is more likely a VC than a CV in the English and Dutch corpora that have been examined. For example, saying *get* for *cat* would be less likely than saying *cod* for *cat*. Shattuck-Hufnagel (1983) found that 6 per cent of phonological exchange errors were VCs and 2 per cent were CVs; Stemberger (1983) and Nooteboom (1969) also reported that VC slips outnumbered CV slips. These effects are seen as revealing a hierarchical structure to the syllable. A VC sequence often corresponds to a hypothesized sub-syllabic constituent, the *rhyme*, and hence VC errors can be viewed as the slip of a single higher order unit. The division of the syllable into onset and rhyme is an important aspect of phonological structure, obtaining its motivation from the distribution of sounds and stress placement in languages of the world (see, e.g., Goldsmith, 1990). There is also considerable psycholinguistic data in support of rhyme-like units (e.g., MacKay, 1972; Treiman, 1983; Fowler, Treiman and Gross, 1993).

Initialness Effect

Initial consonants are more likely to slip than noninitial ones. There are two related effects. First, there is a strong tendency for word-initial consonants to slip. About 80 per cent of consonant misordering errors occur with word onsets. In nonmovement errors, the percentage is smaller (40–50 per cent) but is nevertheless substantially greater than what would be expected if all sounds were equally likely to slip (Shattuck-Hufnagel, 1986). Second, there may be a tendency for syllable-initial consonants (*onsets*) to slip more than syllable-final ones (*codas*), but this has proved to be hard to establish because of the confounding of syllable and word position and the fact that there are more opportunities for onset than coda slips. The initialness effect can be attributed to the hierarchical structure of the word or syllable (e.g., MacKay, 1972; Shattuck-Hufnagel, 1986). For example, if CVC syllables consist of two syllabic constituents, an onset and a rhyme, the predominance of onset slips over coda slips can be attributed to the fact that the onset is more of a constituent than the coda is. Alternatively, the initialness effect could be a consequence of sequential retrieval.

The remaining three sections of this chapter present the characteristics of the standard theory of production and the two computational models. Both computational models are based on the connectionist paradigm (see Chapter 3). They are a general *interactive activation* model of retrieval (Dell and Reich, 1981; Dell, 1986, 1988; Peterson, Dell and O'Seaghdha, 1989; Martin *et al.*, 1994) and a *parallel-distributed-processing* (PDP) model of single-word phonological encoding (Dell and Juliano, 1991; Dell, Juliano and Govindjee, 1993).

Standard Theory

Figure 13.1 illustrates three important features of the standard theory. First, producing an utterance consists of building several internal representations of it. Our interest lies in the syntactic and phonological representations. Second, these representations are assumed to be built by a *frame-and-slot* mechanism (Garrett, 1975; Shattuck-Hufnagel, 1979; see also Chapter 2). At each level, a hierarchical frame with labelled slots is assembled, and then linguistic units are inserted into the slots. At the syntactic level, lemmas are put into slots in a syntactic frame. The phonological level is analogous. Speech sounds are inserted into the slots of a frame that represents the grouping of the sounds into suprasyllabic units, syllables, and syllabic constituents such as onset and rhyme. The third important characteristic of the standard view is that the levels access information sources in a modular fashion. The frame-and-slot aspect of the standard theory enables it to dissociate linguistic structure, represented by the frame, from linguistic content, the items that go into the slots. This dissociation gives the theory a mechanism for many kinds of speech error. In particular, various substitutions and misorderings are assumed to occur when incorrect items are inserted into the slots. For example,

Figure 13.1: Syntactic and phonological representations in the standard model
(from Dell, Juliano and Govindjee, 1993)

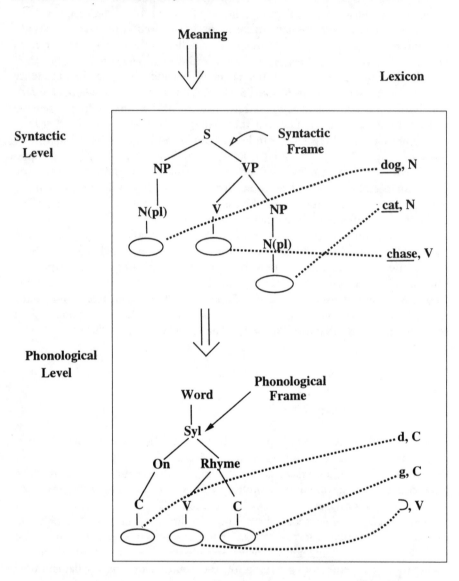

exchanges occur when two intended items go into each others slot's. This could happen either at the syntactic level (*fill up the gas with car*) or the phonological level (*darn bore* spoken as *barn door*). If an item that is not intended anywhere in the utterance is retrieved and finds a frame slot, a *noncontextual* substitution happens. *Liszt's second Hungarian restaurant* would be an example at the syntactic level and *garn bore* at the phonological level. Deletions, additions, and deletion addition combinations (also called *shifts*) require the postulation of error mechanisms within the frame but, in general, the standard theory gives an excellent account of the variety of error types that occur (see Shattuck-Hufnagel, 1979).

The modularity feature of the standard theory enables it to make predictions about the relations that hold between target and intruding items. Specifically, word errors should only be influenced by syntactic and semantic information and not phonological information, while the reverse should apply for phonological errors. To a large extent, this is true. In the *gas . . . car* example, the exchanging words are both nouns and are not similar in form aside from syllable structure. The *darn bore* sound error involves phonologically similar sounds, but, unlike the word error, does not involve target words of the same syntactic class. In general, word-level errors obey a syntactic class constraint, while phonological errors do not, thus providing support for the modularity feature of the standard theory (Garrett, 1975).

However, the modularity of the standard theory does not receive support from a closer scrutiny of the speech error data. There seem to be phonological influences on word-level errors and nonphonological factors can affect sound errors. Consider the *Liszt's second Hungarian restaurant* error. The error exhibits the syntactic class constraint and shows an associative influence of the phrase *Hungarian restaurant*. Yet it also reveals an effect of word form; *restaurant* and *Rhapsody* are metrically similar and begin with /r/. This is not an isolated example. Analyses of substitutions from natural error corpora (Dell and Reich, 1981; Harley, 1984; del Viso, Igoa and Garcia-Alba, 1991) and experimental tasks (Martin, Saffran and Weisberg, 1989) support the claim that errors exhibit multiple influences, including semantic and phonological effects. This suggests that phonological and semantic factors are simultaneously active during the assignment of lemmas to slots in the syntactic frame, contrary to the modularity feature of the standard theory. Similarly, it appears that sound errors can reflect nonphonological factors. The lexical bias and semantic bias effects mentioned earlier show that sound misorderings are more likely when the outcome of the error is meaningful. Again, this is at odds with strict modularity.

According to Dell and Reich (1981) and Dell and O'Seaghdha (1991), the data, on balance, support a view of lexical access in production as 'globally modular' but 'locally interactive'. It is globally modular in that one can distinguish the processing of lemmas and lexemes. Lemma processing clearly precedes that of lexeme processing, and lemma selection and ordering, unlike that involving lexemes, are very strongly dependent on syntactic category. At the same time, there is some degree of interactiveness revealed in error data showing that phonological and nonphonological information sources are simultaneously active during the processing of lemmas and lexemes. While there are accounts of these non-modular effects based on post-access monitoring that preserve the idea of purely discrete stages (e.g., Levelt *et al.*, 1991), it is our view that the interactive activation approach presented in the next section provides a good account of the interactive error effects within a globally modular framework. Furthermore, the interactive activation approach provides for explanations of many other error effects.

The Interactive Activation Approach

The model that we summarize here is that of Dell (1980, 1986, 1988, 1990; Martin *et al.*, 1994; see also Peterson, Dell and O'Seaghdha, 1989). Others have also presented models of production that deal with phonological encoding from an interactive activation perspective (MacKay, 1982, 1987; Stemberger, 1982, 1985, 1990, 1991; Harley, 1984, 1993; Berg, 1988; Houghton, 1990; Schade 1992). To a large extent, these other models exhibit many of the desirable features that the model we are discussing possesses. Of the other models, those of Houghton (1990), Schade (1992), and Harley (1993) have at least one computational implementation, and we briefly discuss some of the advances that these models have made over the original implementations by Dell.

Overview of the Model

Figure 13.2 illustrates the architecture of Dell (1986) by showing a moment in the production of the sentence *Some swimmers sink*. Like the standard model, there are separate syntactic and phonological representations. The figure also shows a morphological level, but this is not discussed. Each representation consists of a hierarchical frame with slots to which items are linked. However, these items are found in a separate lexical network consisting of units for semantic features or concepts, words (lemmas), and phonological units. The connections are excitatory and allow for a bi-directional spread of activation. So, an activated word unit will tend to excite phonological units (*top-down spreading*) and an activated phonological unit will tend to excite word units (*bottom-up spreading*). Activation levels are positive real numbers and are determined by external sources and a linear activation updating function with a decay factor. The production of a word involves the following six steps.

1   The semantic unit(s) of the concept-to-be-lexicalized receive(s) external input.
2   Activation spreads through the network as determined by the activation updating rule.
3   The most highly activated word unit of the appropriate syntactic category is selected. Selection entails the linkage of this unit to the appropriate slot

Figure 13.2: The spreading activation model of Dell (1986). The figure shows a moment in the production of the sentence Some swimmers sink

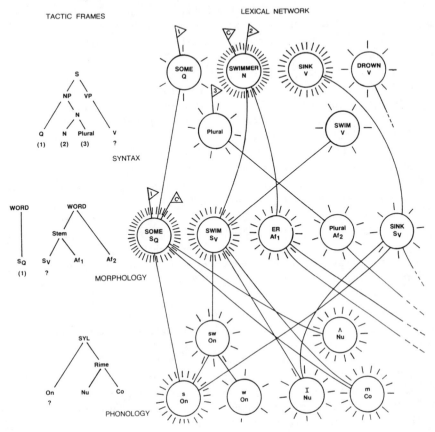

in the developing syntactic frame. This is analogous to the insertion of the lemma symbol into a frame slot in the standard model.

4 When a word is ready for phonological encoding, its unit is given a triggering jolt of activation. For multi-word utterances, the timing of this jolt is controlled by the syntactic frame slot that the unit is linked to.

5 Activation continues to spread as before, but because of the extra activation from the jolt, the appropriate phonological units become significantly activated.

6 The most active phonological units are selected and linked to slots in an assembled phonological frame.

Large-scale implementations of the model have dealt only with steps 4–6, although some smaller models have been developed for the entire sequence (Dell and O'Seaghdha, 1991; Martin *et al.*, 1994)

Because activation spreads continually and bi-directionally, phonological units become activated during the process of lemma selection (step 3) and semantic units become active during the selection of phonological segments (step 6). Consequently, the main difference between this model and the standard theory is that spreading activation creates an interactive, rather than a modular system. The lexical network allows information to leak from one linguistic level to another.

The bi-directional spread of activation explains a variety of speech error phenomena, most importantly the familiarity effects presented above. Consider lexical bias, the tendency for sound errors to create words. The model creates this effect because spreading activation pushes the activation of units at adjacent levels into consistent patterns. For example, any pattern in which the segments /k/, /æ/, and /t/ are highly active is a consistent one, because their activation reverberates with the word unit for *cat*. If activated segments do not correspond to a single word, spreading activation tends to change the pattern until it does. This produces the lexical bias effect in the model. The tendency for errors to create words that are related to surrounding words, such as *Hungarian restaurant* for *Hungarian Rhapsody*, is another example of how spreading activation creates familiarity effects. The bottom-up spread of activation from the word unit *Hungarian* contacts the stored concept *Hungarian restaurant*, thus increasing the activation on the word *restaurant* and, hence, the chance that it is selected and linked to the noun slot of the syntactic frame.

Spreading activation between adjacent levels of processing is also the model's mechanism for similarity effects. Consider the *restaurant — Rhapsody* error again. When the intended word unit *Rhapsody* is active, it activates its sounds, including /r/. The activation from /r/ then spreads in a bottom-up fashion to all /r/-initial words including *restaurant*, and the combination of this activation and that from the familiar phrase, *Hungarian restaurant* greatly increases the chance that *restaurant* is selected. This joint influence of similarity and familiarity enables the model to account for a variety of error effects, particularly effects that were problematic for the standard theory's modularity assumption.

Simulations

The particular simulations that have been developed with Dell's interactive activation model give a fair account of the variety of phonological error phenomena, but also illustrate some of the problems of the approach. Dell (1986) presented two simulations. The first was one in which there were units for morphemes, syllables, syllabic constituents, phonemes, and features, and whose vocabulary consisted of 50 two-syllable words which were treated as monomorphemic. Each intended morpheme unit was given a standard jolt of activation and the next intended one was primed with half of the standard jolt. Activation initially spread preferentially to the unit for the first syllable, and then to the second syllable. After a fixed number of time steps, determined by the speech rate, the most highly activated onset, vowel, and coda unit were selected, thereby encoding a syllable. Onset and coda units represented singleton consonants, consonant clusters, or special null-onset or null-coda units. Parameters were set so that single words were spoken without error at a speech rate of three time steps per syllable. The model was tested by having it say two-word strings at various speech rates. Gaussian noise proportional to a node's activation level was added in during each time step.

The errors generated by the first simulation exhibited the proper size and movement characteristics of phonological errors. With respect to the size of the slipping units, errors mostly involved single phonemes (66–90 per cent), feature and syllable errors were unlikely (syllables 0–2 per cent; features 0 per cent), and VC errors (5–20 per cent) outnumbered CV errors (2–6 per cent). These relative frequencies, which roughly agree with human data (e.g., Nooteboom, 1969; Shattuck-Hufnagel, 1983), reflect the following characteristics of the model: The model includes units for each level of the hierarchy, but selection is only based on the activation levels of units that are potential onsets, vowels, and codas. Consequently, most slips involve single phonemes because most onsets, vowels, and codas in English are single phonemes. The VC vs. CV effect arises because the VC is usually a syllable rhyme and there is a unit for it in the lexical network. The presence of the unit leads to a positive correlation in the activation levels of the vowel and coda that it connects to. With respect to the kinds of movement error that occurred, the model produced anticipations, perseverations, exchanges and shifts, with exchanges and shifts being less likely than the others. These types and their proportions resulted from a complex interplay of activation decay, anticipatory priming, and a self-inhibitory process in which each selected phonological unit temporarily sets its activation to zero when it is selected.

The relative proportions of all error types from the simulation agreed with the error corpora with one notable exception: The model tended to produce more deletions than additions and the data (e.g., Nooteboom, 1969) are exactly opposite. Deletions and additions in the model occurred when onset or coda units were replaced with units representing a different number of consonants. The model's tendency to delete arose because units with fewer consonants (e.g., null-onset and null-coda units, or singleton consonants) are more frequent in the vocabulary and, hence, tend to replace the less common units that represent consonant-clusters. We suggest that the model's use of null onsets and codas and (or) consonant cluster units may be faulty. In general, the model's representational assumptions about syllable structure are cumbersome, and force each syllable into an onset-vowel-coda structure. In addition, the model must use different nodes for the same sound when it is an onset and when it is a coda — an inelegant treatment of the serial order of subsyllabic units (Dell, 1988; Houghton, 1990; Meyer, 1991).

The model's ability to account for the structural effects that we listed above is mixed. To a large extent, these effects are built into the model's representational assumptions, rather than emerging in more interesting ways from its processing assumptions. The model's errors are phonotactically regular because it is specified that each selected syllable consist of any legal onset, followed by any vowel, followed by any legal coda. This pretty much guarantees that the output will be phonotactically regular. Similarly, vowels replace vowels, and consonants replace consonants in the model because each syllable-position slot only accepts onsets in onset slots, vowels in vowel slots, and codas in coda slots. The tendency for slips to involve onset consonants (see the initialness effect) is not present in the model at all. The model encodes the three positions of the syllable simultaneously and thus there is nothing to differentiate the onset from the coda.

A second simulation (Dell, 1986) simplified the network to include CVC words only. This was done to examine familiarity and similarity effects due to spreading activation, while setting aside representational issues associated with syllable order and structure. This simulation only included a morpheme and a phoneme level and was set up to simulate the conditions of an experiment that

Figure 13.3: Rate of initial consonant misordering errors as a function of word vs. nonword outcome and deadline (from Dell, 1986). The obtained data are from an experiment using a deadline to manipulate the speech rate and the predicted are from the second simulation in Dell (1986). Both the data and the model show that lexical bias increases as speech slows

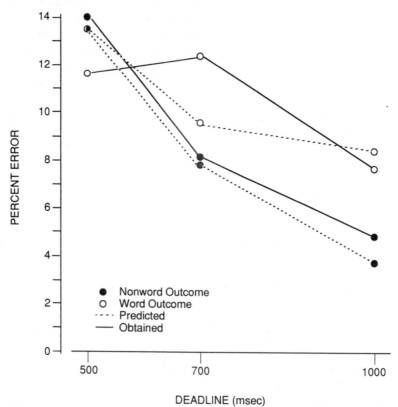

examined the lexical bias effect and the influence of environmental similarity on initial consonant misorderings in CVC words. The experiment also manipulated the speech rate because the model predicts that the familiarity and similarity effects on errors are tied to spreading activation and activation takes time to spread. Here we focus on one such predicted effect: Lexical bias should increase as speech slows. When there is less time available for activation to reverberate, there is less of a tendency to transform the activation pattern into words. The results of the experiment supported the prediction. At fast speech rates, there was no tendency for initial consonant misorderings to create words over nonwords. As speech slowed, however, errors became less likely and lexical bias emerged. Figure 13.3 shows the findings and a fit of the model to the data. In general, the model was able to give a good account of the effects of familiarity and speech rate on the various types of initial consonant misordering (see Dell, 1986). Also, unlike the previous simulation, the second simulation fit actual error probabilities rather than relative error frequencies and, hence, mimicked the proportion of correct responses as well as error responses.

It is important to keep in mind that the second simulation did not implement exactly the same theory as the first one. It is able to produce strong lexical bias effects precisely because morphemes and phonemes are directly linked. In the previous model, which was more structurally complex, morphemes were two or three links away from the primary syllabic constituents of onset, vowel, and coda. Consequently, one can ask whether the first simulation's ability to handle basic quantitative features of the errors is wholly consistent with the second simulation's ability to handle familiarity effects such as lexical bias (see Levelt *et al.*, 1991). In other terms, what exactly are the representational assumptions behind this interactive activation approach to phonological encoding? As we shall see, some recent implemented models and theory, including the PDP model presented later, have moved toward eliminating intermediate syllable and syllabic constituent nodes, and assume a fairly direct mapping between words or morphemes and either phonological segments or phonological features.

Recent Developments

Later implementations of interactive activation models of phonological encoding extended the paradigm in several respects. These extensions produced models that are more similar to interactive activation models in other domains (e.g., Grossberg, 1978; McClelland and Rumelhart, 1981) and less similar to traditional spreading activation models (e.g., Anderson, 1983). In particular, most new models use nonlinear activation functions in which activation values are bounded (e.g., Peterson, Dell and O'Seaghdha, 1989; Houghton, 1990; Eikmeyer and Schade, 1991; Schade, 1992; Harley, 1993). Along with this, the recent models emphasize inhibitory as well as excitatory connections (see Schade and Berg,

1992). Nonlinear models that use inhibition can settle into stable nonzero activation patterns, unlike the linear/excitatory model of Dell, which has the undesirable feature that the activation pattern must be examined within a particular time window after the input jolt of activation to achieve effective retrieval.

One model, that of Houghton (1990), nicely uses lateral inhibition and nonlinear activation functions to solve the within-word serial order problem. Word units excite phoneme units, such that the first unit is most active, then the second, and so on. Then each phoneme node excites a counterpart node in a separate layer of the network, called a *competitive filter*. In the filter, strong lateral inhibition causes all but the most active phoneme to be inhibited, thus selecting the first phoneme. This phoneme is then removed from the pool by inhibition and the filter is reloaded. Now, the second phoneme wins the competition in the filter, and so on. In this way, serial order is stored directly in the connection weights from words to phonemes and there is no need for separate nodes for onset and coda consonants. Moreover, this kind of model can account for data showing that phonological encoding within the syllable involves the left-to-right activation of sounds (e.g., Meyer, 1991; Meyer and Schriefers, 1991) and, consequently, may have the potential to explain initialness effects on speech errors.

Another development in interactive activation models of phonological encoding concerns learning. How are the networks set up to begin with? The model of MacKay (1987) has explicit rules for forming new nodes and for modifying connection weights. Houghton's (1990) network described above actually learned the connection weights between the word and phoneme layers by a supervised procedure that uses a Hebbian learning rule (see Chapter 3).

A final development concerns implementations of the structural frames by interactive activation. Dell (1986) did not explicitly implement the frame or tree structures of the model through spreading activation. Yet, there are good reasons to suppose that these structures both receive and send activation to nodes in the lexical network (Bock, 1982; MacKay, 1982, 1987; Stemberger, 1985, 1990, 1991). Schade (1992; see Eikmeyer and Schade, 1991; Berg and Schade, 1992) implemented phonological frames as activated sequences of linguistic-category nodes (e.g., *onset*) that send activation to members of the categories. This controls the serial order of the actual phonemes that are retrieved by spreading activation. This method does, however, still require separate nodes for onsets and codas.

Conclusions: Interactive Activation Approaches

Interactive activation models of phonological encoding give good accounts of many speech error effects, particularly those effects that we have ascribed to the interactive flow of activation such as similarity and familiarity effects. They are also, in our view, broadly consistent with other experimental work. However, as a group, the implemented models still largely deal only with the problem of lexeme retrieval and, even there, have not really come to grips with the complexities of phonological structure, and speech error effects that arise out of this structure. In addition, although some recent implementations are more sophisticated and can therefore lay claim to a degree of computational adequacy, the trend has been away from attempting to simultaneously account for a lot of psycholinguistic data, in favour of a focus on one or two phenomena. Thus the recent developments using extensive lateral inhibition, learning procedures, and new ways of producing serial order and structural frames, have not been applied to the range of phenomena that earlier implemented and unimplemented models were.

The PDP model outlined in the next section (Dell and Juliano, 1991; Dell, Juliano and Govindjee, 1993) represents an attempt to deal with a number of effects within the context of a learning model. Most importantly, the goal is to deal with error effects that arise out of phonological structure.

PDP Model

In the standard theory and the interactive activation approach, it has been assumed that there is a distinction between linguistic structure and linguistic content. This was implemented in the distinction between rule-governed frames and the items that go in the frame slots. The PDP model of Dell, Juliano and Govindjee (1993) is an attempt to show that some of the error data that are cited as revealing aspects of phonological rules and frames can be explained by a mechanism in which there are no separate frames. Specifically, the model learns to map between distributed representations of words and sequences of phonological features. The principal goal of the model is to account for the phonological error data listed above. These effects, which they call *phonological frame constraints*, include the phonotactic regularity effect, the consonant-vowel category effect, the syllabic constituent effect, and the initialness effect. Here we will also consider this model's ability to handle other error effects as well.

The PDP model illustrates one of the most well-known and controversial claims associated with PDP models, namely that they obviate the need for explicit, separately stored rules (e.g., Rumelhart and McClelland, 1986; Elman, 1989; Seidenberg and McClelland, 1989). In language processing, it is common for these models to assume that knowledge about linguistic structure (e.g., rules or frames) is not stored separately from linguistic content (e.g., words and sounds). Rather, structural or rule-like effects emerge from how the individual items, in this case words, are stored. Each item is represented in a distributed and composite fashion with the result that items are superimposed on the same set of connection weights. When a particular item is processed, one is effectively processing many other items as well. This massed influence of the other items enables the model to be sensitive to the general characteristics of the set, that is, to reflect their structure.

General Architecture

Like the NETtalk model of Sejnowksi and Rosenberg (1986) and Seidenberg and McClelland's (1989) reading model (see Chapter 6), the PDP model learned to pronounce words through an error-correcting learning rule, *backpropagation* (Chapter 3; Rumelhart, Hinton, and Williams, 1986). Figure 13.4 shows the basic design. The model starts with an *input* representation of the lemma coded as a pattern of activation (1's and 0's) across lexical input units. Activation is passed through weighted connections to a *hidden* layer, and finally to an *output* layer of ·18 units, one unit for each phonological feature. When fully trained, the model should activate the output feature nodes corresponding to each segment of the input word, one segment at a time. The sequential aspect of the model is indebted to previous work on *recurrent networks* by Jordan (1986) and Elman (1990). Jordan presented a general model for producing sequential output in the PDP framework and applied it to the problem of coarticulation in speech. His proposal was that the input layer should contain both an invariant *plan* and a *state* or *context* representation derived from the network's output during the sequential execution of the plan. In the present model, the plan is the lexical input units and the state is a set of *external feedback* units, which are copies of the output resulting from the production of the previous segment. Elman (1990) explored a related architecture in which the state representation was a copy of the most recent activations of the hidden units. The PDP model includes this kind of state representation as well, which in Figure 13.4 is labelled *internal feedback*. Thus, both the output and hidden unit activations are copied to units in the input layer. In other respects, the model was a standard backpropagation architecture: The activation of a unit was a logistic function of its input, hidden and output units had a bias, there was a momentum factor in the weight changes (always 0.5), and prior to training, weights were initialized to randomly distributed values between

Figure 13.4: The PDP architecture with both internal and external context units. Each elongated rectangle represents a set of units (from Dell, Juliano and Govindjee, 1993)

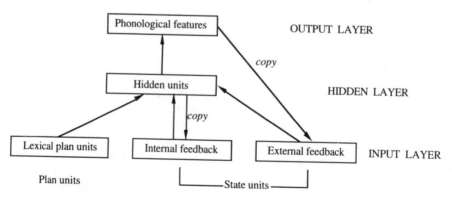

– 0.1 and 0.1. The learning rate parameter was fairly large, varying between 0.25 and 1.0 across the various models that were produced. Other assumptions of the model derived directly from its sequential nature. Given a lexical input, say some encoding of the word *cat*, the network's goal was to output the features of the first segment /k/, then /æ/, then /t/, and then it should stop, which was defined as outputting a *null segment* (activation of 0.5 on all features). Weight change via backpropagation occurred after the attempted production of each segment, including the null segment. When the encoding of a word began, the external-feedback state units were initialized to the null segment, and the internal-feedback units were initialized to zero. After the model's approximation to the first segment was produced, the activation values of the output units were copied to the external feedback units, and the values of the hidden units were copied to the internal feedback units. Following this, the forward spread of activation attempted to produce the second segment, and so on until the word was finished.

Simulations

Dell, Juliano and Govindjee (1993) presented three sets of simulations. For all three sets, the model's mispronunciation errors were examined to see if they exhibited the four phonological constraints listed above. In the first, 24 models were trained on small vocabularies, while varying a number of features of the models. In these simulations, the model's slips resulted from incomplete training-training was stopped before all of the segments were correctly produced. The second set of simulations used models trained on small vocabularies until performance was perfect. Errors were then generated by adding varying amounts of noise to the connection weights. In the third set of simulations, larger vocabularies were trained, for example, the 412 English words consisting of three segments or less.

Simulation Set 1

Eight versions of the model were derived by combining two different training vocabularies with two different kinds of input representation and with two different kinds of state representation. These factors are explained below.

Training Vocabulary
Two vocabularies, each comprising 50 English words, were prepared. Both were samples from the set of 308 three-segment three-letter words in Kucera and Francis (1967). Table 13.1 gives both vocabularies and some of their statistical

Table 13.1: Characteristics of training vocabularies

Frequent Vocabulary

ago	car	had	men	sat
and	cut	has	met	set
any	did	him	nor	son
art	end	his	not	ten
ask	far	hot	old	try
bad	for	its	one	use
bed	get	job	put	war
big	god	let	ran	was
but	got	lot	red	yes
can	gun	man	run	yet

88.9% of tokens of 3 segment/letter words in Kucera/Francis (1967)
82% CVC's
mean number of words per CV 1.16
mean number of words per VC 1.88

Infrequent Vocabulary

arm	fat	kid	pat	tip
bag	few	let	pot	tom
bus	gas	lid	rid	top
cap	gin	lot	rub	van
cat	her	map	rug	vet
cow	hit	mud	sad	web
dan	how	net	sin	win
dog	ivy	nut	sit	won
dot	jet	oil	sim	yin
elm	joy	out	tin	zen

8% of tokens
88% CVC's
mean number of words per CV 1.15
mean number of words per VC 1.53

properties. The *frequent* vocabulary was made of very common words from the set. These 50 words accounted for 88.9 per cent of the tokens of the occurrences of the 308 words in the corpus. In contrast, the *infrequent* vocabulary's 50 words accounted for 8.0 per cent of the tokens. It turned out that the frequent vocabulary was not only representative of English in the sense that it contained common words, but also in two other respects. First, there were nearly twice as many word types per VC than per CV in the frequent vocabulary, while this asymmetry was less pronounced in the infrequent vocabulary. English vocabulary, in general, has the characteristic that its VC sequences are more redundant than its CV sequences. Second, the frequent vocabulary contained a variety of consonant cluster types — nasal-stop, /s/-stop, stop-/s/, stop-liquid, and liquid-stop. The infrequent vocabulary had fewer clusters, overall, and only liquid-nasal and /fj/. Given that the error pattern should reflect the entire stored vocabulary in a PDP architecture, Dell, Juliano and Govindjee (1993) expected the more representative vocabulary to be associated with a more realistic error pattern.

Input Representations

Two methods of representing the lemma in the lexical input units were compared. In the *random* coding, each word was a randomly sampled pattern of 1's and 0's across 30 input units. Because it is random, this coding is unrelated to the phonological form of the word and, hence, reflects the assumption that the lemma is a syntactic/semantic representation. The second kind of input representation, the *correlated* coding, was based on the word's orthography. Each letter was assigned an arbitrary 5-digit binary code which appeared, where appropriate, in units 1–5 for initial letters, 6–10 for second letters and so on. The correlated coding, therefore, was associated with only 15 input units. According to Dell, Juliano and Govindjee (1993), the correlated coding is less like the lemma and more a form of underlying phonological representation, at least in the sense that the representation is highly, but imperfectly, correlated with the sequence of features to be retrieved.

State Representations

The state units enable the production of sequential output by keeping track of where the model is in the sequence. Dell, Juliano and Govindjee (1993) compared an *internal-external* architecture in which both the output and hidden units activations were copied onto state units, with an *internal-only* architecture in which only the hidden units' values were copied back. They expected the internal-external architecture to be associated with an error pattern that is more indicative of the frame constraints because this architecture emphasizes the immediately prior context to a greater extent than the internal-only architecture. Because most phonological rules of English reflect contingencies between adjacent segments, one might expect greater sensitivity to these rules when more contextual information is available. It should be noted that an external-only architecture is not capable of sequencing when there are repeated items (Jordan, 1986; Elman, 1990). To see this, consider how such a model would produce *pop* (/p/ /a/ /p/ null). After /p/ has been produced at output, its features would be copied back to the state units, representing the state of just having produced a /p/. But this state is uninformative as to which /p/ and, consequently, the model does not know whether to next produce /a/ or null. When the state contains the values of hidden units, as in the internal-only or internal-external architectures, repeated items are not a problem, at least in principle (Elman, 1990). The internal state that leads to the production of initial-/p/ can be different from the state that leads to that of final-/p/. We should note that Jordan's (1986) model used external feedback only, but avoided the repetition problem by giving each state unit a memory; its activation was a combination of the corresponding output unit's and its own previous activation.

Training

Three models were created for each of the eight versions (2 vocabularies × 2 input codings × 2 architectures), each of the 24 models starting from a different set of initial weights. Training involved repeated sweeps through the vocabulary, each sweep, or *epoch*, consisting of a presentation of all 50 words in a random order. Training continued until between 90 and 95 per cent of the segments were correctly produced. The output pattern for a segment was deemed to be correct if it was closer in Euclidian space to the pattern for the desired segment than to that for any other segment. In all cases, this level of correctness was achieved within 200 epochs.

Error Analysis

When a model's output, after training, was closer to a segment other than the correct segment for any of the four sequential positions (including the null segment), an error was recorded. The 24 models yielded 376 errors. Table 13.2

Table 13.2: Errors from a single model

ask	æsk	→	ætk*
big	bɪg	→	bɛd
did	dɪd	→	dæd
far	fɔr	→	vɔr
for	fɔr	→	vɔr
him	hɪm	→	hɛn
his	hɪz	→	hɛz
job	jɑb	→	jɑd
not	nɑt	→	nʌt
old	old	→	ʌnd
put	put	→	pʌt
sat	sæt	→	θæt
set	sɛt	→	θɛt
son	sʌn	→	θʌn
ten	tɛn	→	nɛn
use	juz	→	jɔz

Phonotactic violations are followed by an asterisk

gives all of the errors for the first model that was trained. Before we discuss how well the errors fit the four frame constraints, it is useful to consider how well the models' errors exhibit other known characteristics of phonological errors. To a first approximation, the models' errors involved the right-sized units (segments as opposed to larger units), and they were properly sensitive to similarity. The errors in Table 13.2 illustrate these features: 13 of the 16 errors are segmental, and 3 involve a VC unit; seven of the single-segment substitutions are one feature off, five are two features away, and one differs by three features. However, because the models' errors were noncontextual, they were not able to reproduce any of the effects listed previously, concerning the movement of sounds. We return to this shortcoming in the general discussion of the PDP model. With regard to familiarity effects on errors, Dell, Juliano and Govindjee (1993) suggest that this kind of PDP model is consistent with the fact that speech errors tend to occur on less familiar elements and tend to create familiar ones (facts listed above), but presented only limited simulation data on the question. They analyzed a model trained on 412 words and found that the errors occurred on uncommon syllable types and tended to create common types.

The main goal of the modelling effort was to see if the four frame constraints emerge from the superpositional storage of sequences of features. Dell, Juliano and Govindjee's conclusion was that the models did exhibit these effects, but that some versions of the model were better than others. We first consider the average effects for all 24 models, then contrast the eight versions. In all analyses, we compare percentages that index the constraint from the models to standards derived from the speech error literature.

Phonotactic Regularity Effect
Across the 24 models, 92.6 per cent of the errors were phonotactically legal (see Table 13.3 for examples of illegal slips). This percentage can be compared to a finding of 99 per cent legal slips from Stemberger's (1983) English error corpus. In fact, Dell, Juliano and Govindjee noted that one illegal error produced by the model, *atk* for *ask*, actually occurred in Stemberger's corpus. An experimental speech production experiment by Meyer and Dell (in preparation), in which a limited set of phonotactic constraints of Dutch was examined, found that 97.7 per cent of the errors obeyed the constraints. The models' percentage, although good, is not quite up to the standards based on human errors.

Table 13.3: Examples of phonotactic violations

ivy	→	avɪ	illegal word-final vowel
any	→	ɛnɪ	illegal word-final vowel
ask	→	ætk	illegal cluster
old	→	ʌtd	illegal cluster
job	→	ʒɑd	illegal word-initial consonant
try	→	trɑh	illegal word-final consonant
few	→	fɛʌ	two vowels in a row
his	→	æɛz	two vowels in a row
arm	→	ɔrmm	English has no double consonants
oil	→	ʌjl	ʌj does not occur in the English dialect used for comparison

Consonant-Vowel Category Effect
Substitution errors in the models respected the category (Consonant or Vowel) of the target sounds at a very high rate: 97.6 per cent. That is, it was highly unusual for a consonant to replace a vowel or vice versa. One of the few violations obtained was /æ/ replacing /h/ in the word *his*. Given claims from the speech error literature that violations either do not occur or are rare (see the consonant-vowel category effect above), Dell, Juliano and Govindjee somewhat arbitrarily adopted a standard of 99.5 per cent adherence to the constraint and noted that the average model's behaviour was slightly worse than this standard.

Syllabic Constituent Effect
When the models' substitution errors involved an adjacent consonant and a

vowel, the errors were more often substitutions of a VC sequence than a CV sequence, thus exhibiting the syllabic constituent effect. 5.6 per cent of all errors were VCs and 2.1 per cent were CVs. These percentages are strikingly close to the 6 per cent VC and 2 per cent CV reported above by Shattuck-Hufnagel (1983). However, Shattuck-Hufnagel's percentages are based on exchange errors and so do not constitute an ideal standard. But, there are no standards for VC and CV rates based on nonmovement errors, so we will follow Dell, Juliano and Govindjee and stick to the 6 per cent and 2 per cent standards from Shattuck-Hufnagel.

Initialness Effect

Single-consonant substitutions in the models corresponded to syllable-onsets 61.6 per cent of the time. This occurred in spite of the fact that there were more codas than onsets in the vocabularies (47.4 per cent onsets/52.6 per cent codas). Because the words in the vocabularies were so short, most syllable-onset errors were also word-onset errors, so it is not possible to tell whether the models' initialness effects are word- or syllable-based, or both. Estimates of the strength of the initialness effect in natural error corpora vary with the kind of error and the size of the word. Given that the training words were only three segments long and that the resulting errors were noncontextual, a standard was chosen from Shattuck-Hufnagel (1986) that was based on noncontextual errors in monosyllabic words. This standard was 62 per cent onset errors. So, again, the average model is close to the standard.

In conclusion, the average model from Dell, Juliano and Govindjee exhibited errors that adhered to the general frame constraints. Why is this? They claim that two principles determine the model's error pattern, *similarity* and *sequential bias*. When one sound replaces another, it tends to be similar to the intended sound and, at the same time, tends to create a sequence that reflects the statistical structure of the vocabulary.

Each of the frame constraints is a manifestation of similarity and (or) sequential bias. The phonotactic regularity effect is a product of both of these forces. It is in the nature of phonotactic patterns that if the sequence of segments AB is acceptable, then A'B and AB' tend to be acceptable as well (where segments X and X' are similar segments). Because the model tends to replace segments with similar ones, the sequences tend to be acceptable. Sequential effects also play a role in keeping errors phonotactically legal. AB will be replaced by AC to the extent that AC or a similar sequence AC' is represented in the vocabulary. In general, the models' errors do not stray very far from the sequential schemata that reflect the covariances among adjacent or nearly adjacent feature patterns in the vocabulary. Although these schemata are generalizations in much the same way that rules are generalizations, the model has no separately stored rules or frames that enforce adherence to phonotactic patterns, as is the case with some of the interactive activation models of phonological encoding.

The consonant-vowel category effect arises from similarity. Vowels and consonants are simply very different sounds. Hence, the PDP model explains this constraint quite differently than the interactive activation model, which assumed that frame slots were labelled as to whether they hold vowels or consonants. The syllabic constituent and initialness effects derive from the model's sensitivity to sequential structure. In the vocabularies used with the model, particular VC sequences tended to recur to a greater extent than particular CV sequences. As a result, VC combinations become more unit-like. Segments that co-occur with high frequency may give rise to emergent behaviours that mimic the effect of explicitly assigning a node to a higher order grouping. Recall that in the interactive activation model of Dell (1986), VC units that corresponded to rhymes did have an explicit node assigned to them. The initialness effect in the PDP model derives from the fact that there is more uncertainty about sounds at the beginning of the word. At the beginning, the context units always have null values and, hence, are less effective at pointing to the correct initial sound. Later on in the word, the context units exhibit a pattern that is more specific to that word and thus are better retrieval cues. Note that this explanation of the initialness effect identifies it as a word-onset rather than a syllable-onset effect. This is consistent with the data for English according to Shattuck-Hufnagel (1986). However, we note that one analysis of Spanish errors (Berg, 1991) makes a strong case for a syllable-onset rather than word-onset characterization of initialness effects in errors, at least in Spanish.

In addition to their analysis of the behaviour of the average model, Dell, Juliano and Govindjee compared the eight versions of the model using statistical techniques designed to evaluate how the versions differed in their adherence to the frame constraints. It was found that when the frequent vocabulary was used, and when the state representation included internal and external feedback, the errors followed the frame constraints more closely. The nature of the input representation, whether it was random or correlated, had no effect.

Figure 13.5 illustrates the effects of vocabulary and state representation by contrasting the standard and obtained percentages for the frame constraints. We collapsed over the input representation factor, reducing eight versions to four:

1 frequent/internal-external
2 frequent/internal-only
3 infrequent/internal-external and
4 infrequent/internal only.

The models trained on the frequent vocabulary with the internal-external state representation did very well. The match with the standards is quite good. If the state representation is only based on internal feedback, the models do reasonably well, but the percentage of errors that are phonotactically regular falls off in comparison to models with internal and external feedback. As one might expect, adherence to this constraint is aided by a more extensive representation of immediate context.

The figure also shows models trained with the infrequent vocabulary. Here, adherence is not as good. Both the phonotactic and consonant-vowel constraints are not well met and, interestingly, the syllabic constituent effect is not either.

Figure 13.5: Comparison between frame constraint percentages from seven types of model and standard percentages from the speech-error literature

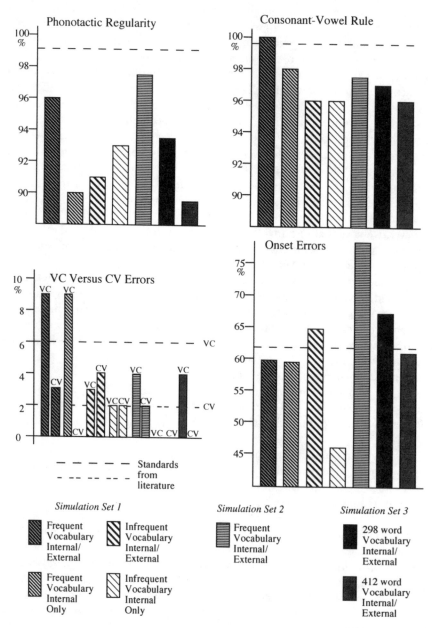

Clearly, a model's ability to reproduce the frame constraints depends on having the right sort of vocabulary. This can be most easily appreciated with regard to the syllabic constituent effect. The frequent vocabulary has greater redundancy in its

VCs than its CVs and this was reflected in a preponderance of VC errors. The infrequent vocabulary has less of an asymmetry in its VCs and CVs and did not have a greater proportion of VC than CV errors. In sum, the simulations in the first set show that not all the models are equally good, but that it is possible to achieve very human-like performance on the frame constraints. The model must have a solid encoding of the context, as in the internal-external models, and a representative vocabulary. Whether the input representation is correlated or random did not have much effect and thus shows some degree of generality to the model.

Simulation Set 2

There is something a little odd about comparing the models' errors, which result from incomplete training, to adult speech errors, which reflect temporary glitches in a fully trained system. Dell, Juliano and Govindjee (1993) suggested, however, that errors resulting directly from the learning process and those due to temporary difficulty are similar. To support this claim, they carried out a second set of simulations in which models were trained until they could correctly pronounce all the words in their vocabulary, and then errors were induced by adding noise to the connection weights. They viewed this noise as reflecting interference from surrounding words and external contexts. These models used the internal-external architecture, the correlated input representation, and the frequent vocabulary. We summarize their findings here (also see Figure 13.5).

When normally distributed noise was added to the connections between hidden and output units, the errors followed the frame constraints. Two models were repeatedly lesioned with varying amounts of noise creating 291 errors. The errors were phonotactically regular 97.9 per cent of the time and followed the consonant-vowel category constraint 97.6 per cent of the time. 3.8 per cent of the errors were VCs and 2.1 per cent were CVs. Finally, 78 per cent of the consonant errors involved onsets. In addition, the tendency for errors to be phonotactically regular increased as error likelihood decreased. For example, when the standard deviation of the noise was 0.15, 91.9 per cent of the attempted segments were correct and 96.1 per cent of the errors were phonotactically regular. With a noise standard deviation of 0.05, errors were less likely (98.3 per cent correct segments) and 100 per cent of them were phonotactically regular. It is worth noting that even the model with the 0.05 noise standard deviation is somewhat less accurate than human speakers. According to Hotopf (1983), people make a slip every 300 words. Other estimates (e.g., Garnham *et al.*, 1981) are that people are even more accurate.

Simulation Set 3

Dell, Juliano and Govindjee (1993) also examined models trained with larger vocabularies. One set of models was trained on all 298 one-syllable words from Kucera and Francis (1967) that were three segments and three letters in length. The internal-external architecture with the correlated input representation was used except that network size was increased to 40 hidden and 30 input units. Furthermore, external-context units were given a memory based on 20 per cent of their activation level from the previous time step. The strictness of the backpropagation teacher was varied across training, as well. For the first 50 epochs, an output of greater than 0.6 or less than 0.4 was acceptable for units whose targets were 1 and 0, respectively. This was increased to 0.7 and 0.3 for the next 50 epochs, and so on until the teacher was as strict as possible (1.0 and 0). Three models were trained resulting in 99.1 per cent correct segments. Performance on the frame constraints was acceptable with the exception of the syllabic constituent effect: 93.8 per cent of errors were phonotactically regular, and 96.9 per cent obeyed the consonant-vowel category effect; 66.7 per cent of the consonant errors involved onsets. However, no VC or CV errors were obtained.

Another set of models was trained on all 412 words that are three letters long. This included some one- and two-segment words, and some two-syllable words. Four models were trained, reaching a level of performance of 96.1 per cent correct segments. With the exception of the phonotactic regularity effect, which was only at 89.3 per cent, the other frame constraints were exhibited: 96.1 per cent of the errors followed the consonant-vowel category constraint; 3.9 per cent were VCs and none were CVs; 61.2 per cent of the consonant errors involved onsets. It was noted that most of the phonotactic violations involved the substitution of a lax vowel for a word-final tense vowel in one- or two-segment words. For example *she*→/SI/, *fee*→/fI/, *eye*→/E/. These are legal syllables, but violate English phonotactics as word-final syllables. They suggested that the phonological theory behind the model's features, in which long vowels are segments bearing the feature *tense*, may be in error. More recent phonological theory treats long vowels as occupying two rather than one segmental slot. In addition, the relatively poor performance on the phonotactic constraint for the 412-word models, suggests that these kinds of network may be increasingly challenged to the extent that they must deal with patterns that apply to words of different lengths.

The Problem With Movement Errors

The PDP model is able to account for many of the relevant speech error facts. However, it falls short of both the standard theory and the interactive activation models in one very important respect. It does not produce movement errors. Dell,

Juliano and Govindjee (1993) discuss various ways in which contextual influences could be introduced. For example, the lexical input pattern for word i, could have some influence from that of word i−1 or word i+1. In principle, this would produce anticipatory and perseverative tendencies in the model's errors, although it remains to be seen whether these would be the correct tendencies. But one very large problem remains. The PDP model simply does not produce exchanges. A perturbation in the model's output that causes a later sound to replace an earlier one would not lead to a corresponding perturbation for the originally replaced sound to then substitute for the original replacing sound. The very existence of exchanges argues for a distinction between slots and items that go into them (Shattuck-Hufnagel, 1979). Until the PDP model can produce these kinds of effect, the models that distinguish between structure and content will enjoy the advantage.

The PDP model can, however, be taken as a demonstration that sequential biases and similarity are powerful principles in explaining error patterns. In fact, we argue that the general frame constraints simply reflect the sequentially-defined similarity structure in the lexicon, and not phonological frames, at least not directly. Furthermore, we interpret the model's success in its limited domain as evidence that there is something right about its central assumption: Phonological speech errors result from the simultaneous influence of the words stored in the system, in addition to the words in the intended utterance. The PDP model creates this simultaneous influence through the superimposition of all words on the same set of connections.

Conclusions

Both the interactive activation and PDP approaches account for several error phenomena. Which is better, though? On balance, the interactive activation models win because the PDP model's inability to produce exchanges is a serious omission. Moreover, the interactive activation models handle more phenomena and are, at present, better integrated with, and informed by, linguistic theory, insofar as they use phonological frames. At the same time, there are appealing features of the PDP model. Its account of error effects is quite simple. They result from the massed influence of the vocabulary. Moreover, because of its learning rule, the PDP model could be applied to facts about change as a function of experience, both the short-term changes that might be measured in an experiment and developmental changes.

The challenge to computational psycholinguistics remains to explain the storage and retrieval of phonological structure and content in production. We think that future models will need to make use of both frame-like structures, as in the interactive activation models, and the kind of superpositional storage that characterizes the PDP model. That is, there are a sufficient number of good features of both approaches to invite the conclusion that some synthesis would be desirable.

Regardless of how phonological structure is ultimately treated, we are persuaded of three things. First, a model must distinguish between words as syntactic entities or lemmas, and words as phonological entities or lexemes. Second, although the processing of lemmas and lexemes can be distinguished, we believe that the data support a degree of interaction between these levels of processing. Finally, a successful model of phonological encoding must recognize the sequential nature of production.

References

ANDERSON, J. R. (1983) *The Architecture of Cognition*, Hillsdale, NJ: Lawrence Erlbaum.

BAARS, B., MOTLEY, M., and MACKAY, D. (1975) 'Output editing for lexical status in artificially elicited slips of the tongue', *Journal of Verbal Learning and Verbal Behavior*, 14, pp. 382–91.

BERG, T. (1988) *Die Abbildung des Sprachproduktionprozess in einem Aktivations-flussmodell*, Tübingen: Niemeyer.

BERG, T. (1991), 'Phonological processing in a syllable-timed language with pre-final stress: Evidence from Spanish speech error data', *Language and Cognitive Processes*, 6, pp. 265–301.

BERG, T., and SCHADE, U. (1992) *The Role of Inhibition in a Spreading Activation Model of Language Production, Part 1: The Psycholinguistic Perspective*. Unpublished manuscript.

BOCK, J. K. (1982) 'Towards a cognitive psychology of syntax: Information processing contributions to sentence formulation', *Psychological Review*, 89, pp. 1–47.

BOCK, J. K., LOEBELL, H. and MOREY, R. (1992) 'From conceptual roles to structural relations: Bridging the syntactic cleft', *Psychological Review*, 99, pp. 150–71.

DELL, G. S. (1980) *Phonological and Lexical Encoding in Speech Production: An Analysis of Naturally Occurring and Experimentally Elicited Slips of the Tongue*, Unpublished doctoral dissertation, University of Toronto.

DELL, G. S. (1984) 'The representation of serial order in speech: Evidence from the repeated phoneme effect in speech errors', *Journal of Experimental Psychology: Learning, Memory and Cognition*, 10, pp. 222–33.

DELL, G. S. (1986) 'A spreading activation theory of retrieval in language production', *Psychological Review*, 93, pp. 283–321.

DELL, G. S. (1988) 'The retrieval of phonological forms in production: Tests of predictions from a connectionist model', *Journal of Memory and Language*, 27, pp. 124–42.

DELL, G. S. (1990) 'Effects of frequency and vocabulary type on phonological speech errors', *Language and Cognitive Processes*, 5, 4, pp. 313–49.

DELL, G. S. and JULIANO, C. (1991) 'Connectionist approaches to the production of words', in PETERS, H. F. M., HULSTIJN, W. and STARKWEATHER, C. W. (Eds) *Speech Motor Control and Stuttering*, Amsterdam: Elsevier, pp. 11–35.

DELL, G. S. and O'SEAGHDHA, P. G. (1991) 'Mediated and convergent lexical priming in language production: A comment on Levelt *et al.*' *Psychological Review*, 98, pp. 604–14.

DELL, G. S., JULIANO, C. and GOVINDJEE, A. (1993) 'Structure and content in language production: A theory of frame constraints in phonological speech errors', *Cognitive Science*, 17, pp. 149–95.

DELL, G. S. and REICH, P. A. (1981) 'Stages in sentence production: An analysis of speech error data', *Journal of Verbal Learning and Verbal Behavior*, 20, pp. 611–29.

DEL VISO, S., IGOA, J. M. and GARCIA-ALBA, J. E. (1991) 'On the autonomy of phonological encoding: Evidence from slips of the tongue in Spanish', *Journal of Psycholinguistic Research*, 20, pp. 161–85.

EIKMEYER, H.-J. and SCHADE, U. (1991) 'Sequentialization in connectionist language-production models', *Cognitive Systems*, 3, 2, pp. 128–38.

ELMAN, J. L. (1989) 'Structured representations and connectionist models', in *Proceedings of the 11th Annual Conference of the Cognitive Science Society*, Hillsdale, NJ: Lawrence Erlbaum, pp. 17–25

ELMAN, J. L. (1990) 'Finding structure in time', *Cognitive Science*, 14, pp. 213–52.

FOWLER, C. A., TREIMAN, R. and GROSS, J. (1993) 'The structure of English syllables and polysyllables', *Journal of Memory and Language*, 32, pp. 115–40.

FROMKIN, V. A. (1971) 'The non-anomalous nature of anomalous utterances', *Language*, 47, pp. 27–52.

GARNHAM, A., SHILLCOCK, R. C., BROWN, G. D. A., MILL, A. I. D. and CUTLER, A. (1981) 'Slips of the tongue in the London-Lund corpus of spontaneous conversation', *Linguistics*, 19, pp. 805–17.

GARRETT, M. F. (1975) 'The analysis of sentence production', in BOWER, G. H. (Ed) *The Psychology of Learning and Motivation*, San Diego, CA: Academic Press, pp. 133–75.

GOLDSMITH, J. A. (1990) *Autosegmental and metrical phonology*, Oxford: Basil Blackwell.

GROSSBERG, S. (1978) 'A theory of human memory: Self-organization and performance of sensory-motor codes, maps, and plans', in ROSEN, R. and SNELL, F. (Eds), *Progress in Theoretical Biology*, San Diego, CA: Academic Press, pp. 233–374.

HARLEY, T. A. (1984) 'A critique of top-down independent levels models of speech production: Evidence from non-plan-internal speech errors', *Cognitive Science*, 8, pp. 191–19.

HARLEY, T. A. (1993) 'Phonological activation of semantic competitors during lexical access in speech production.', *Language and Cognitive Processes*, 8, pp. 291–309.

HOTOPF, W. H. N. (1983) 'Lexical slips of the pen and tongue', in BUTTERWORTH, B. (Ed) *Language Production*, Vol 2, San Diego, CA: Academic Press, pp. 147–99.

HOUGHTON, G. (1990) 'The problem of serial order: A neural network model of sequence learning and recall', in DALE, R, MELLISH, C. and ZOCK, M. (Eds) *Current research in natural language generation*, London: Academic Press, pp. 287–319.

JORDAN, M. I. (1986) 'Attractor dynamics and parallelism in a connectionist sequential machine', in *Proceedings of the Eighth Annual Conference of the Cognitive Science Society*, Hillsdale, NJ: Lawrence Erlbaum, pp. 531–46.

KEMPEN, G. and HOENKAMP, E. (1987) 'An incremental procedural grammar for sentence formulation', *Cognitive Science*, 11, pp. 201–58.

KEMPEN, G. and HUIJBERS, P. (1983) 'The lexicalization process in sentence production and naming: Indirect election of words', *Cognition*, 14, pp. 185–209.

KUCERA, H. and FRANCIS, W. N. (1967) *Computational Analysis of Present-Day American English*, Providence, RI: Brown University Press.

LAPOINTE, S. and DELL, G. S. (1989) 'A synthesis of some recent work in sentence production', in CARLSON, G. and TANENHAUS, M. K. (Eds) *Linguistic Structure in Language Processing* Dordrecht: Kluwer, pp. 107–56.

LEVELT, W. J. M. (1983) 'Monitoring and self-repair in speech', *Cognition*, 14, pp. 41–104.

LEVELT, W. J. M. (1989) *Speaking: From Intention to Articulation*, Cambridge, MA: MIT Press.

LEVELT, W. J. M., SCHRIEFERS, H., VORBERG, D., MEYER, A. S., PECHMANN, T. and HAVINGA, J. (1991) 'The time course of lexical access in speech production: A study of picture naming, *Psychological Review*, 98, pp. 122–42.

MacKay, D. G. (1970) 'Spoonerisms: The structure of errors in the serial order of speech', *Neuropsychologia*, 8, pp. 323–50.

MacKay, D. G. (1972) 'The structure of words and syllables: Evidence from errors in speech', *Cognitive Psychology*, 3, pp. 210–27.

MacKay, D. G. (1982) 'The problems of flexibility, fluency, and speed-accuracy trade-off in skilled behaviors', *Psychological Review*, 89, pp. 483–506.

MacKay, D. G. (1987) *The Organization of Perception and Action: A Theory for Language and Other Cognitive Skills*, New York: Springer-Verlag.

Martin, N., Dell, G. S., Saffran, E. and Schwartz, M. F. (1994) 'Origins of paraphasias in deep dysphasia: Testing the consequence of a decay impairment of an interactive spreading activation model of lexical retrieval', *Brain and Language*, 47, pp. 609–60.

Martin, N., Weisberg, R. W. and Saffran, E. M. (1989) 'Variables influencing the occurrence of naming errors: Implications for a model of lexical retrieval', *Journal of Memory and Language*, 28, pp. 462–85.

McClelland, J. L. and Rumelhart, D. E. (1981) 'An interactive activation model of context effects in letter perception: Part I. An account of basic findings', *Psychological Review*, 88, pp. 375–407.

Meringer, R. and Mayer, K. (1895) *Versprechen und Verlesen*, Stuttgart: Goschensche.

Meyer, A. S. (1991) 'The time course of phonological encoding in language production: Phonological encoding inside a syllable', *Journal of Memory and Language*, 30, pp. 69–89.

Meyer, A. S. and Dell, G. S. (in preparation) 'An experimental analysis of positional and phonotactic constraints on phonological speech errors'.

Meyer, A. S. and Schriefers, H. (1991) 'Phonological facilitation in picture-word interference experiments: Effects of stimulus onset asynchrony and types of interfering stimuli', *Journal of Experimental Psychology: Learning, Memory, and Cognition*, 17, pp. 1146–60.

Motley, M. T. and Baars, B. J. (1975) 'Encoding sensitivities to phonological markedness and transition probability: Evidence from spoonerisms', *Human Communication Research*, 2, pp. 351–61.

Motley, M. T. and Baars, B. J. (1976) 'Semantic bias effects on the outcomes of verbal slips', *Cognition*, 4, pp. 177–88.

Nooteboom, S. G. (1969) 'The tongue slips into patterns', in Sciarone, A. G., van Essen, A. J., and van Raad, A. A. (Eds) *Leyden Studies in Linguistics and Phonetics*, The Hague: Mouton, pp. 114–32.

Peterson, R. R., Dell, G. S. and O'Seaghdha, P. G. (1989) 'A connectionist model of form-related priming effects, in *Proceedings of the 11th Annual Conference of the Cognitive Science Society*, Hillsdale, NJ: Lawrence Erlbaum, pp. 196–203.

Roelofs, A. (1992) 'A spreading-activation theory of lemma retrieval in speaking', *Cognition*, 42, pp. 107–42.

Rumelhart, D. E., Hinton, G. E. and Williams, R. J. (1986) 'Learning internal representations by error propagation', in Rumelhart, D. E. and McClelland, J. L. (Eds) *Parallel Distributed Processing: Explorations in the Microstructure of Cognition: Vol. 1. Foundations*, Cambridge, MA: MIT Press, pp. 318–64.

Rumelhart, D. E. and McClelland, J. L. (Eds) (1986) *Parallel Distributed Processing: Explorations in the Microstructure of Cognition: Vol. 1. Foundations*, Cambridge, MA: MIT Press.

Schade, U. (1992) *Konnektionismus – Zur Modellierung der Sprachproduktion*, Opladen: Westdeutscher Verlag.

Schade, U. and Berg, T. (1992) 'The role of inhibition in a spreading activation model of language production. II. The simulational perspective', *Journal of Psycholinguistic Research*, 6, pp. 435–62.

Schriefers, H., Meyer, A. S. and Levelt, W. J. M. (1990) 'Exploring the time-course of lexical access in production: Picture-word interference studies', *Journal of Memory and Language*, 29, pp. 86–102.

SEIDENBERG, M. S. and McCLELLAND, J. L. (1989) 'A distributed developmental model of visual word recognition and naming', *Psychological Review*, 96, pp. 523–68.

SEJNOWSKI, T. J. and ROSENBERG, C. R. (1986) *NETtalk: A Parallel Network that Learns to Read Aloud* (Technical Report EECS-86/01). Baltimore, MD: Johns Hopkins University.

SHATTUCK-HUFNAGEL, S. (1979) 'Speech errors as evidence for a serial-order mechanism in sentence production', in COOPER, W. E. and WALKER, E. C. T. (Eds) *Sentence Processing: Psycholinguistic Studies Presented to Merrill Garrett*, Hillsdale, NJ: Lawrence Erlbaum, pp. 295–342.

SHATTUCK-HUFNAGEL, S. (1983) 'Sublexical units and suprasegmental structure in speech production planning', in MACNEILAGE, P. F. (Ed) *The Production of Speech*, New York: Springer, pp. 109–36.

SHATTUCK-HUFNAGEL, S. (1986) 'The representation of phonological information during speech production planning: Evidence from vowel errors in spontaneous speech', *Phonology Yearbook*, 3, pp. 117–49.

SHATTUCK-HUFNAGEL, S. and KLATT, D. (1979) 'The limited use of distinctive features and markedness in speech production: Evidence from speech error data', *Journal of Verbal Learning and Verbal Behavior*, 18, pp. 41–55.

STEMBERGER, J. P. (1982) *The Lexicon in a Model of Language Production*, Unpublished doctoral dissertation, University of California, San Diego.

STEMBERGER, J. P. (1983) *Speech Errors and Theoretical Phonology: A Review*, Bloomington, IN: Indiana University Linguistics Club.

STEMBERGER, J. P. (1985) 'An interactive activation model of language production', in ELLIS, A. W. (Ed) *Progress in the Psychology of Language, Vol. 1*, Hillsdale, NJ: Erlbaum, pp. 143–86.

STEMBERGER, J. P. (1990) 'Wordshape errors in language production', *Cognition*, 35, pp. 123–57.

STEMBERGER, J. P. (1991) 'Apparent anti-frequency effects in language production: The addition bias and phonological underspecification', *Journal of Memory and Language*, 30, pp. 161–85.

STEMBERGER, J. P. and MACWHINNEY, B. (1986) 'Frequency and the lexical storage of regularly inflected forms', *Memory and Cognition*, 14, pp. 17–26.

TREIMAN, R. (1983) 'The structure of spoken syllables: Evidence from novel word games', *Cognition*, 15, pp. 49–74.

WELLS, R. (1951) 'Predicting slips of the tongue', *Yale Scientific Magazine*, 3, pp. 9–30.

Chapter 14

Modelling Approaches in Speech Production

Lou Boves and Bert Cranen

Introduction

Normal children have virtually no problems learning the pronunciation of their native language. Yet, from a purely motoric point of view, speaking is probably the most complex of human motor processes. For a person older than twelve to fourteen years, mastering the pronunciation of a second language is extremely tedious and often the result leaves much to be desired. It is interesting that in second language learning, pronunciation is the part which is least likely to result in performance comparable to native. If it comes to syntax and semantics, second language learners may well reach a level of performance exceeding that of many native speakers.

Speech production can be studied and modelled at several different levels:

- the higher levels of (psycho)linguistics, in terms of linguistic representations and psycholinguistic processes,
- the articulatory level, in terms of the motor processes and movements of the articulatory organs, the *articulators*,
- the acoustic level, in terms of the physical signal, and, perhaps surprisingly,
- the perceptual level, in terms of the way the signal is perceived, the *percept*.

In this chapter we focus on the articulatory and acoustic levels. The higher levels of speech production are treated in Chapters 10 to 13. Here we assume that concepts have already been encoded as a series of basic phonological units, probably of the size of *phonemes*.

At the peripheral (physical) level, a complete theory of speech production must account for the transformation of the linguistic representation of an utterance into motor commands that cause all articulators (e.g., tongue, jaw, lips, velum, cf., Figure 14.1) to execute the right movements at the right times. Speech production is an incredibly complex process. Some hundred muscles are involved, and over ten bony structures (Lenneberg, 1967). In normal conversational speech we produce between 10 and 15 phonemes per second. Controlling the production of over ten complex movements per second *individually* is far beyond the processing capacity of the human neuromuscular system. Psychologists have developed a number of theories to account for the control of the complex motor activity in skilled movements like speech production. All these theories involve some degree of preplanning.

Although linguists are used to describing speech in the form of sequences of abstract discrete units (phonemes), there are numerous articulatory and acoustic measurements which prove that the actual realization of speech sounds is a smooth continuous process in the output of which there are absolutely no such things as sharp boundaries between discrete units. If anything, speech is much more like cursive handwriting than like Roman print. Surprisingly, phonetics appears to have no generally accepted term that only refers to the articulatory representation of phonemes; the term *speech sound* is used both to refer to articulation and to its acoustic product. In this chapter the term speech sound is also used with two meanings. Due to the smooth and continuous movements of the articulators, speech sounds are heavily influenced by their neighbours. It does not take much practice to feel that uttering the /k/ sound in *keep* is quite different from uttering the corresponding sound in *cope*. Thus, in addition to explaining how we manage to produce so many sounds per second, a theory of speech production must also account for the large differences between the realizations of the same phoneme due to different phonetic contexts.

For a long time phoneticians have thought that a complete account of speech production could be given at the level of articulation. It was assumed that the transformation from articulation to audible sound was automatic, completely predictable by the acoustic theory of speech production (Fant, 1960; Flanagan, 1972). However, modern articulatory and acoustic research has shown that the situation is much more complex. Sounds which are not distinguishable from an auditory point of view can be produced with very different articulatory postures. But it is also true that apparently insignificant changes in articulation can result in sounds which are easily distinguished. Thus, models of speech production are not complete without an account of the transformation of articulatory gestures to acoustic signals.

There is an additional reason why we think that speech acoustics must be included in a theory of speech production: with the exception of very rare cases (like articulatory experiments), humans articulate to produce sounds that are meant to convey some meaning to one or more listeners. And in all normal speech communication the audio signal is the only reliable link between speaker and listener. Articulation aims at producing sound; without the resulting sound it is a useless waste of energy. Thus, we cannot but divide our attention in this chapter over two very complex processes (control of articulatory movement and sound generation). Neither of these processes can be treated in great detail. In what follows we first discuss articulatory phonetics and then acoustic phonetics. Next, we turn to computational modelling of speech production. We discuss two main approaches, the articulatory synthesis class of models (in particular the task-dynamics model) and terminal analogue synthesis. The chapter closes with comments on trends that can be seen in present day research and an outlook towards the future.

Introductory Phonetics

Characterization of Speech Sounds in the Articulatory Domain

Most linguists agree that the phoneme is the smallest unit needed to describe speech. Informally, phonemes are those sounds that serve to distinguish between words in a given language. The set of phonemes can be different between languages. For instance, in Japanese the /l/ and /r/ sounds (which in English distinguish word pairs like *erect* and *elect*) have no phonemic status: in Japanese there are no minimal pairs which differ only because one member contains an /r/ sound at the position where the other has an /l/. Some languages may not use a given sound at all. French, for instance, does not have the word-initial consonants in the English words *this* and *think*. Linguists have described languages that use as few as three and as many as fifteen vowels (Disner, 1983; ten Bosch, 1991).

Phonemes are characterized by a set of so-called *distinctive features*. These distinctive features are conventionally formulated in articulatory terms, although it has been attempted to define feature in the acoustic or perceptual domain (Jakobson, Fant and Halle, 1963). Whereas phonemes are abstract linguistic constructs, speech sounds are physical events, created when part of the energy in the expiratory air flow from the lungs, through the windpipe (trachea), throat (pharynx) and mouth and/or nose is converted into acoustic energy (cf., Figure 14.1). This acoustic energy must be generated somewhere and somehow: there must be a sound source. All languages use three sound sources. The first source is located in the *larynx*, where the vocal folds are. When adjusted properly, the vocal folds vibrate due to energy exchange between the tissues and the expiratory air flow (Titze, 1988). These vibrations cause the opening between the vocal folds, i.e., the *glottis*, to close periodically. The resulting periodic modulation of the air flow is the source of the class of speech sounds known as *voiced*. This type of sound production is called *phonation*. The frequency of the vocal fold vibrations is mainly determined by the length and mechanical properties of the tissues (which can be changed by adjusting the laryngeal muscles) and by the pressure difference between the trachea and the vocal tract. The raw sound generated at the glottis is moulded into speech sounds in the tube above the glottis, formed by throat,

Figure 14.1: Cross-section of speech production apparatus

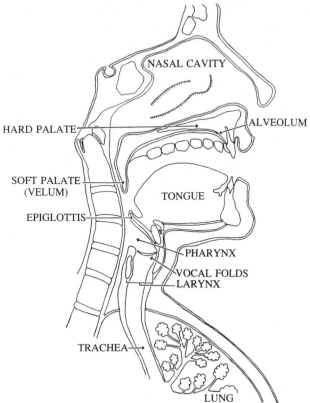

mouth and nasal cavity, in technical terms the *vocal tract*. It is easily verified by introspection that the position of the tongue is quite different for the vowels /i/ (as in *sea*), /ɑ/ (as in *father*) or /u/ (as in *book*).

The second essential sound source in speech production can be located almost everywhere in the vocal tract. If the cross-sectional area of the tract is made small enough, the air flow becomes turbulent. In auditory terms, turbulent air flow corresponds to noise. Noise sources are involved in the unvoiced continuant sounds, like the word-initial /s/ in the word *sound*. In addition to purely voiced and purely unvoiced sounds there is a set of sounds that involve both the periodic glottal source and a noise source. The most prominent members of this class are the voiced fricatives, like the /z/ in the word *zoo*.

Finally, there is the class of the so called plosives, where the sound source consists in the sudden release of pressure behind a total constriction at some place in the vocal tract. Plosive sound generation can be combined with vocal fold vibration, as in the voiced /b/ in *bond*. Vocal fold vibration is absent in the /p/ of *pond*.

Articulatory characteristics pertaining to the three ways in which speech sounds are produced are summarized by the term *manner features*. Obviously, three manner features are not enough to distinguish the 45 or so phonemes of an arbitrary language. A complete classification of speech sounds requires that place of articulation is specified in addition to manner. A constriction, e.g., for a plosive, can be at the lips, at the alveolar ridge or at the soft palate. Place features are handled differently by different scientists, but these details need not concern us here. Conventionally, place features are treated separately for vowels and consonants (e.g., Catford, 1977).

Phonetics text-books tend to describe speech sounds in isolation. This is in line with conventional phonology, which considered phonemes essentially as static, invariant units. But in actual speech, sounds are always produced in context. Moreover, transitions between sounds are smooth, and they are so by necessity, because the articulators cannot move with infinite speeds and acceleration. Last but not least, actual articulatory movements for one sound are influenced by neighboring sounds (cf., the different /k/ articulations mentioned above). This discrepancy between the smooth, continuous and context-dependent movements of the articulators on the one hand and the discrete, static and invariant nature of the underlying linguistic units on the other has posed many problems, none of which has been completely solved today. Implementing and testing computational models of speech production is one way of attempting to shed light on these problems. Below we describe a number of different ways in which such modelling might be attempted. Before we can do that, we must first look into the basics of sound production in the vocal tract.

Characterization of Speech Sounds in the Acoustic Domain

Speech production involves two essentially independent processes, namely a source that generates the raw sound, and the vocal tract that modifies it into recognizable speech sounds. In the acoustic domain speech production can, by analogy, be viewed as a process in which the auditory colour of a source sound is shaped by a filter (cf., Figure 14.2). This analogy has led to the ubiquitous linear source-filter model of acoustic speech production (Fant, 1960; Flanagan, 1972). Acoustic descriptions of (speech) sounds can be given in two, intimately linked, domains. Physically, the sensory impression of sound is caused by minute, but rapid fluctuations in the air pressure. The visual display of the pressure-versus-time signal is called an *oscillogram*. Because sounds are time-pressure signals, it seems natural to describe them in terms of this time-domain pattern. However, if we are interested in the auditory sensation caused by acoustic signals, a description of the sounds in terms of pure tones may be more attractive. Every sound can be analyzed in terms of a sum of sinusoidal signals, where each sine wave has its own frequency, amplitude and phase. The mathematical technique to decompose a signal into sinusoids is called *Fourier analysis*. A description of a signal in terms of sinusoids is said to be in the spectral domain, i.e., it specifies the different

Figure 14.2: Schematic account of the linear source-filter model of acoustic speech production

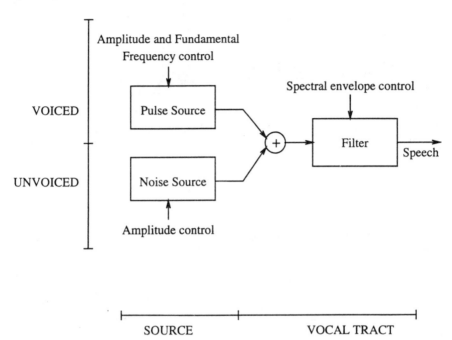

frequency components. The graphical display of the amplitudes of the spectral components is called an *amplitude spectrum*, that of the phases of the spectral components a *phase spectrum*. Because the phase of the sinusoids is relatively unimportant from a perceptual point of view, a significant data reduction can be obtained: one only needs to present the amplitude spectrum.

As is the case for articulatory descriptions of speech sounds, acoustic descriptions of vowels are often expressed in different terms from consonants. In the spectral domain vowels are easily characterized by their formants. Formants are energy concentrations at specific points on the frequency axis. Physically, formants are related to resonances of the vocal tract. Experiments have shown that most vowels can be recognized by their first (lowest) two formants, numbering these energy concentrations going from low to high frequency. Formant 1 (F1) and 2 (F2) suffice to identify the vowel. Some continuant consonants, like the /w/ and the /l/, can also be characterized by formant patterns. Consonants, and especially plosives and affricates which are inherently dynamic, are not easily described in terms of formant patterns. In many situations a time-domain description of consonants is to be preferred. Figure 14.3 shows oscillogram and spectrum of two speech sounds, a vowel in Figure 14.3a,b and a voiceless fricative in Figure 14.3c,d. The oscillogram of the vowel shows a repetitive pattern, that also appears in the spectrum in the form of equally spaced local maxima. The periodic structure of the time domain signal is related to the vocal fold vibration, as is the

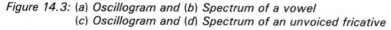

Figure 14.3: (a) *Oscillogram and* (b) *Spectrum of a vowel*
(c) *Oscillogram and* (d) *Spectrum of an unvoiced fricative*

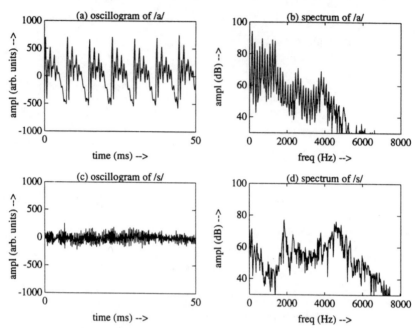

regular fine structure in the spectrum. The contribution of the vocal tract to the identity of the speech sound shows up in the oscillogram in the form of the fine structure of the pressure variation within each period. Voiceless speech sounds (Figure 14.3c,d) are characterized by a more random behaviour. There is no repetitive structure in the time-domain signal and the fine structure of the time-domain signal is extremely difficult to characterize. The absence of the periodic structure in the time domain shows up in the frequency domain in the absence of equidistant local maxima. The best way to characterize the envelope of the spectrum is by saying that there are two gross relative maxima in the high frequencies, although it can be maintained that some of the spectral minima (anti-resonances, anti-formants or zero's) are relevant as well, at least from a physical point of view.

Speech signals are in an essential way non-stationary. In order to capture the change of signal characteristics over time, a three-dimensional representation is required, with time, frequency and amplitude/power as axes. Conventionally, time is displayed along the horizontal, and frequency along the vertical axis, while the amount of energy is coded by means of a gray scale (the larger the energy the blacker). Since time and frequency are dual quantities, the resolution along the time and frequency axes are inversely proportional. This three-dimensional display is known as the *sonagram* or *spectrogram*. Figure 14.4 shows the sonagram of the Dutch utterance *Dit is een sonagram* ('This is a sonagram'), spoken by an

Figure 14.4: SONAGRAM of the utterance Dit is een sonagram ('*This is a sonagram*')

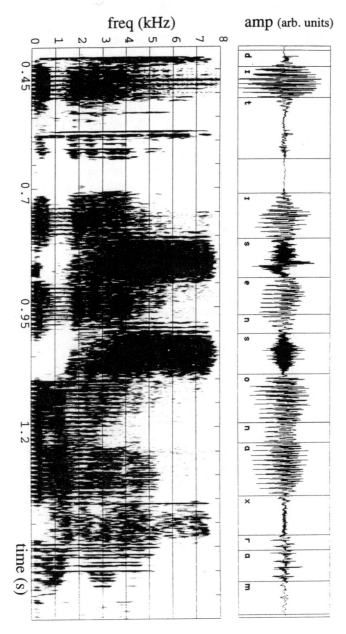

adult male. The time resolution is chosen in such a way that the distinction between voiced and unvoiced sounds is reflected in the presence or absence of vertical striations. The sonagram has been tremendously important for speech research. Sonagrams made it practical to study formant changes over time. Hypotheses derived from these pictorial displays could be tested by checking whether a prescribed articulatory configuration did indeed give rise to the predicted formant pattern and whether artificially generated sounds with known formant patterns would indeed give rise to the predicted vowel percepts. Cooper, Liberman and Borst (1951) were the first to succeed in generating understandable speech from stylized spectrograms (i.e., formant tracks). Fant (1960) and Flanagan (1972) were among the pioneers who showed that formant patterns can indeed be predicted from articulatory configurations measured in the mid-sagittal plane (the vertical cross-section of the head cutting right between the eyes).

Modelling Speech Production

Now that we have presented the basic concepts of both speech articulation and speech acoustics, the scene is set for an attempt to model speech production in a more formal way. It should be clear by now that a comprehensive model of speech production would involve at least two sub-models, one explaining the way in which linguistic input commands control the articulators and a second that accounts for the transformation of articulatory configurations into audible speech. Contrary to what the extremely simplified descriptions of articulation and speech acoustics given above may have suggested, anatomically, physiologically and physically realistic models are extremely complex. Actually, at present they are far beyond our present knowledge and understanding. What we have is so crude an approximation that it cannot even pass as a caricature.

In modelling speech production what we should really try to accomplish is audible output that sounds like naturally produced human speech. Each goal that is set lower requires acknowledgment that we are still falling short of a complete understanding of the processes we are trying to model. Human speech is produced to convey information; thus, it is very probable that humans, in producing speech, consider (probably unconsciously) what the listener needs to comprehend the message. Carefully and clearly articulated speech is not always necessary. In many circumstances a considerable part of the words in a message tolerate sloppy pronunciation without endangering intelligibility. A comprehensive model of speech production should be able to model that sloppy behaviour in a convincing way.

One extremely difficult problem in modelling speech production is the fact that we have no way of knowing what exactly is the input that controls the articulators. Linguistic theorizing leads to the hypothesis that speech consists of a sequence of abstract phoneme-sized units. All presently existing computer models of speech production take for granted input in the form of discrete units. Thus, each such model must cope in some way or another with the transformation of timeless, discrete input into articulator movements which are continuous in both time and space (cf., also Levelt, 1989).

Theories of Speech Motor Control

Speech motor control has not only attracted attention of speech scientists. A large number of psychologists have approached the problem, sometimes trying to apply theories developed for other complex motor behaviour, like typing (Sternberg *et al.*, 1980). Their work has resulted in the *motor programming theory*, which postulates that articulation of words and phrases is controlled by a motor program that is assembled in advance and executed in the brain and that organizes the actions of the individual muscles. According to the motor programming theory, the discrete and timeless phonemes constituting the linguistic description of an utterance do not surface in the measurable neurophysiological processes. Commands necessary to produce speech sounds overlap in time, as do the motions of the articulators in fluent speech production. This overlap is voluntarily brought about as a result of assembling the motor program before the actual articulation starts. One argument supporting this view is the observation that the time between visual presentation of a word or phrase to be read aloud and the first indications of the actual start of articulation is a function of the number of sounds to be spoken: if the stimulus consists of a monosyllabic word, articulation starts much sooner than with a polysyllabic word (Meyer, 1990). One seemingly inevitable consequence of the motor programming theory is that the motor commands underlying the production of a phoneme become dependent on the neighbouring phonemes that seem to lose their identity to a large extent.

In this chapter we focus our attention on another theory, known as *action theory* or *task-dynamics*, mainly because the work of the research group at Haskins Labs (New Haven, Connecticut) has elaborated that theory into a model that really does produce speech from abstract discrete phonemic input. Task-dynamics theory is much too complicated to give a precise account in the space available here. It is a special instance of articulatory synthesis, a general term for a number of approaches discussed in a later section. More or less comprehensive descriptions can be found in Saltzman and Munhall (1989), Perkell (1991), Fowler (1993). Task-dynamics solves the problem of transforming timeless phonemes into temporal movements by replacing the static distinctive features from conventional phonetics and phonology by *abstract gestures*, which are inherently dynamic. Gestures are specified in terms of constrictions in the vocal tract that must be formed by appropriate movements of the articulators. Thus, gestures are not identical to movements. The gesture for the closure of the vocal tract for the production of the alveolar plosive /t/ only specifies that the tip of the tongue must get in firm contact with the alveolar ridge. The exact movement that is needed to reach that goal will depend on the position of the tongue tip during the sound(s) preceding the /t/. Many gestures involve multiple articulators (since the position of the tongue is dependent on the position of the lower jaw, a gesture like tongue raising will also involve the jaw). In a similar vein, some phonemes require multiple coordinated gestures (e.g., the nasal /n/ requires simultaneous velum lowering and alveolar closure).

Task-dynamics assumes two levels of coordination, one between gestures involved in neighbouring sounds and another between the articulators involved in the production of the sounds. This coordination allows the articulators to reach their goal irrespective of the point of departure (which may be dependent on the previous phoneme) and irrespective of the direction of movement necessary to arrive in time at the configuration needed for the following phoneme. One of the most compelling arguments in favour of task-dynamics comes from experiments in which the movements of one major articulator are impeded at random points in time. If, for instance, the lower jaw is prevented from moving upward for the production of a /p/ sound, this impediment is counteracted within 30 to 40 milliseconds by increased displacement of the lips, resulting in the complete lip closure that is necessary. Compensatory movements with such a short delay cannot possibly result from active replanning of the movement pattern; they can only be explained by assuming that the coordinated set of articulators 'know' that complete lip closure must somehow be accomplished. The task-dynamics model succeeds in saving the concept of phonemes as invariant units, despite the absence of observable invariance at any level of speech production.

Input for a task-dynamics model is the so-called *gestural score*. If gestures can be defined as constrictions that must be formed in an abstract vocal tract, the gestural score can be considered as the activation pattern for the abstract gestures. Abstract gestures only have a time dimension; there is no way — and no need – for specifying gesture strength. The gestural score drives an abstract vocal tract, or perhaps better, a number of abstract model articulators. From the position in space of these model articulators a mid-sagittal view of a vocal tract is derived, which in its turn is converted into vocal tract cross-sectional areas. In the latter process the simplifying assumption is made that the cross-sectional area can be approximated by a series of cylindrical tubes. Conventional acoustic theory of speech production, finally, is used to generate audible speech signals from vocal tract cross-sectional area configurations (cf., Figure 14.5). Although task dynamics uses terms like *stiffness* in converting gestural scores to articulator positions, it must be stressed that these terms do not refer to actual physical properties of articulators. In effect, task dynamics only specifies the kinematics of articulation, i.e., the movements of some abstract articulators in time and space. The theory does not yet provide an account for the dynamics of articulation simply because it would be practically impossible, due to our lack of knowledge about the real physical properties of the articulators. By making such crude abstractions, however, task dynamics succeeds in implementing a complete peripheral speech production system, thereby showing how the processes of converting discrete and

Figure 14.5: The task dynamics model of speech production

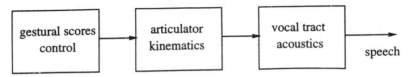

invariant input units to continuous and context-dependent audible sounds could be accomplished. Therefore, the task-dynamics model can be considered as a fully-fledged articulatory synthesizer. A broader overview of articulatory synthesis is now presented.

Articulatory Synthesis

Articulatory synthesis is a cover term for a number of approaches, which have in common that they try to generate acoustic speech signals by simulating articulatory movements and subsequently predicting the acoustic output by simulating the aerodynamic and acoustic processes in the human vocal tract. For this chapter the commonalities of these approaches are more important than the differences.

Each articulatory synthesizer has three main components: a voice source model, one or more noise source models and a vocal tract model.

Modelling the Voice Source

The physical principles governing vocal fold vibration and its acoustic effects are only partially understood. The best-known model of vocal fold vibration is the one published by Ishizaka and Flanagan (1972). They modelled each vocal fold as two solid masses coupled by a spring. It appears that this model is capable of modelling the most eye-catching aspects of vocal fold behaviour. However, it constitutes such a crude stylization that it can hardly serve as a physiologically realistic vocal fold model. In particular, the fact that the air gap between the folds is always rectangular and the lack of a provision to simulate *abduction* (the articulatory gesture by which the vocal folds are moved apart, e.g., in preparation for a voiced-unvoiced transition) in a realistic way, suggest that a more refined model is needed to control the voice source in a physiologically transparent way (Titze, 1988).

Another factor which complicates realistic modelling of glottal air flow is that this flow (which is the primary acoustic excitation of the vocal tract) is itself *not* independent of the vocal tract shape. The flow through the glottis is determined by the pressure difference across the glottis. This pressure difference, however, is not only determined by the static pressures in the subglottal cavity and the vocal tract. Pressures due to standing waves (resonances) in the cavities below and above the glottis add to that pressure difference, and the strength of the resonances depends on the strength of the acoustic excitation caused by the glottal pulses.

Noise Source Models

Noise sources are even more difficult to model. Noise can be generated by two processes: aerodynamic theory predicts that turbulence will occur when the air flow is forced through a narrow constriction or when it impinges on a sharp boundary (e.g., the frontal teeth) (Shadle, 1990). The exact spectral characteristics of a noise source depend crucially on minute details of the geometry of the cavities in which it is generated.

Modelling the Vocal Tract

The acoustic effects of the vocal tract are governed by the physical equations that describe sound propagation in cavities with varying cross-sectional areas (relating acoustical pressure and air particle velocity at each point along the tract). In a first approximation the acoustics of speech production can be modelled by assuming plane wave propagation along the longitudinal axis of the vocal tract. If one is willing to assume that the vocal tract wall is equally stiff everywhere, it is sufficient to know the cross-sectional area of the tube at regular distances of, say, 0.5–1.0 cm. The vocal tract length of an adult male is approximately 17 cm, requiring 20–40 parameters.

The usual procedure in articulatory synthesis is to select a small number of parameters to describe the position of a set of moving articulators. Cross-sectional area is then computed from the shape of the articulators and their positions. For example, in the articulatory synthesizer of Coker (1972) seven parameters determine the cross-sectional area of the vocal tract (see Figure 14.6). Actual cross-sectional areas are computed from these parameters by clever interpolation routines. However, several other proposals for articulatory parameters have been made (cf., Lindblom and Sundberg, 1971; Mermelstein, 1973; Ladefoged and Lindau, 1979; Maeda, 1979), and each proposal implies different constraints for the set of tract configurations which result from interpolation of the parameters between the targets for consecutive sounds. In the implementation of the task-dynamics model at Haskins Labs a relatively straightforward procedure is used for the conversion of vocal tract shapes to acoustic speech signals. Effectively, a computer implementation of the classical acoustic theory of speech production is used (Fant, 1960). Although that theory does indeed account for the basic aspects of speech production, it abstracts away from many details, some of which may be quite important for the production of natural sounding connected speech.

Critical Remarks

As has been explained above, articulatory synthesis as implemented by the task-dynamics model involves crude simplifications, both at the level of (the control of) movements of articulators and at the level of the conversion of vocal tract shapes to acoustic output. These simplifications prohibit a meaningful evaluation of the model in terms of real human speech production (cf., Perkell, 1991).

Figure 14.6: Articulatory synthesis according to Coker (1972). Seven parameters determine the cross-sectional area of the vocal tract: the position of the tongue body (requiring an X and Y coordinate), the lip protrusion (L), the lip rounding (W), the place (R) and degree (B) of constriction at the tongue tip and the degree of velar coupling (N)

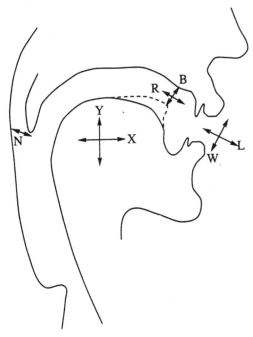

At the articulatory level the choice of the abstract model articulators combined with the procedure for converting the position of these abstract articulators to vocal tract shapes determines not only the details of each individual vocal tract configuration, but implicitly also the way in which tract shapes are interpolated between the target configurations for consecutive sounds. One might assume that it should not be too difficult to evaluate the accuracy of the task-dynamics model in predicting humanlike vocal tract kinematics, but unfortunately this assumption is wrong. Measurement data of tract shapes in connected speech are virtually non-existent. What we have are crude estimates of vocal tract shapes in simple vowel-consonant-vowel (VCV) utterances, obtained from tracking the position of little gold pellets attached to the tongue via an X-ray microbeam scanner (Johnson, Ladefoged and Lindau, 1993). One important conclusion which must be drawn from the research with the X-ray microbeam is that vocal tract shape kinematics differs considerably between subjects who produce the same VCV utterance. Thus, the best we can hope to achieve is that the model behaviour fits the behaviour of a specific class of subjects. It may be possible to simulate other subjects' classes by changing the stiffness parameters of the abstract articulators, but for the time being it remains to be seen whether a single subject's trajectories can be approximated with sufficient accuracy.

If we take the claim seriously that speech is generated to be understood, the concept *sufficient accuracy* should probably be operationalized by requiring that the resulting speech is at least intelligible and preferably also natural sounding. This brings us to the second source of simplification and uncertainty, the mapping of vocal tract shapes on acoustic output. There are a number of observations which make modelling the acoustic-articulatory relation cumbersome. First, there is an infinite number of tract shapes that give rise to the same formant pattern (Atal *et al.*, 1978). In other words, the study of articulation by solely observing the acoustic signal involves a one-to-many mapping which makes a simple inverse transformation impossible. Second, the magnitude of an acoustic effect of a perturbation of the vocal tract tube depends on the exact position where that perturbation takes place. There are certain regions where a substantial change of the cross-sectional area has barely an effect, while in other regions even a small perturbation shifts the formant pattern appreciably. These non-linear sensitivity characteristics are probably exploited by humans to give the speech production a quantal nature (Stevens, 1972). This complicates the parameterization of the vocal tract shape, since one cannot assume that small deviations in vocal tract shape will always have small acoustic effects. Especially during dynamic changes of the vocal tract when going from one sound to the next, all intermediate shapes should be physiologically realistic and produce acoustically correct transitions so that the sound produced is recognized as a phonetically correct concatenation of phonemes.

Recent work using Magnetic Resonance Imaging (MRI) has shown that the assumption that the vocal tract cross-sectional area can be approximated by a series of cylindrical tubes must be called into question. Baer *et al.* (1991) have shown that there are significant discrepancies between measured formant frequencies and the formant frequencies predicted by the acoustic theory of speech production from detailed cross-sectional area patterns obtained from three-dimensional MRI scans. McGowan (1994) failed to recover the articulatory movements which controlled the Haskins speech synthesizer from the acoustic output when a small amount of random noise was added to the acoustic output.

In conclusion, fundamental knowledge about speech production processes is still very incomplete. In the physical domain it is not clear what features of the speech sound must be attributed to source or vocal tract. In the articulatory domain (where measurement data are relatively scarce) there is still a lot of uncertainty about how best to parameterize articulator positions and movements. Consequently, the ideal of a model explaining all relevant relations between the acoustic, articulatory, and phonetic domain is still far away. Existing articulatory synthesis models are research tools and certainly have not reached a stage where their acoustic output can compete with that of terminal analogue synthesis. Further development of articulatory models awaits measurement data that combine vocal tract geometry with acoustic measurements.

Terminal Analogue Synthesis: An Acoustic Approach

Motivating Terminal Analogue Synthesis

Even if preplanning seems to be inevitable in fast-skilled movements, several kinds of feedback must also play an essential role in speech production. Although an external acoustic feedback loop is arguably too slow to be a major factor in the control of articulation, there is ample evidence that some form of acoustic feedback is essential in maintaining speech quality. One such finding shows that if a person becomes deaf, due to some incident, after having learned to speak, the quality of the articulation deteriorates measurably over time. One can only explain this finding by assuming that the deterioration is caused by the fact that speech production can no longer be monitored auditorily. Therefore, it is likely that the targets that we try to reach in the production of speech sounds are also specified in terms of their perceptual properties.

Another argument in favour of an acoustic-auditory specification of speech sounds is that the sounds babies and children make during language acquisition differ substantially from the linguistically identical sounds of adults talking to the child. This is due to the fact that the acoustic properties of the mouth and throat of the child are different from an adult, simply because the overall dimensions are different. During maturation the relative sizes of throat and mouth cavity change. Because there is a direct relation between vocal tract shape and acoustic output, these maturation effects will force the adolescent to adapt the articulation, in order to maintain a suitable acoustic output. And because exact equality of the output sound during and after the maturation process may be physically impossible, one is almost forced to assume that 'suitability' is defined in terms of the linguistic identity of the speech sounds, which in communicative situations is checked by the listeners' reactions. In this process, the speaker is perhaps the most important listener, since (s)he is the only one who can determine whether the reactions of other listeners are in accordance with what was meant.

Last but not least, we must reiterate an argument made before: speech is produced to be heard and understood by the listener. Apart from the very incomplete visual picture one can get by observing the speaker's face, the listener has no access to the speech production mechanism other than via the sounds that are produced. Therefore it is difficult to conceive of a successful and robust communication like speech which does not specify information in terms of the signal in the transmission medium.

Recently, several techniques have been developed to convert written text into synthetic speech, without bothering about the details of articulation and vocal tract shape to sound conversion (Allen, Hunnicut and Klatt, 1987). Although these systems were *not* designed with the intention to serve as psycholinguistic models of speech production control, it is nevertheless interesting to investigate to what extent they incorporate knowledge about speech and speech production that is also relevant from a psycholinguistic point of view. For the purpose of this chapter we are not concerned with the intricacies of converting conventional spelling into a phonemic representation comparable to the abstract phonemes

Figure 14.7: Terminal analogue synthesis normally implements the basic source/filter model of acoustic speech production

Figure 14.7: Terminal analogue synthesis normally implements the basic source/filter model of acoustic speech production

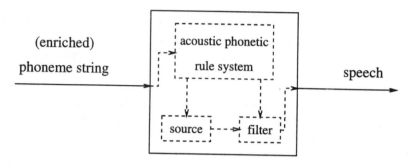

which form the input for the task-dynamics model. We simply assume that such input can be provided. In the following sections we describe the system developed in our laboratory to convert a phoneme string into natural sounding speech.

Types of Terminal Analogue Synthesis

The goal of terminal analogue synthesis is to generate synthetic speech waveforms which can be decoded correctly by a human listener, i.e., a listener must recognize the linguistic message represented by the input phoneme string (cf., Figure 14.7). In addition, the output speech should sound natural (i.e., humanlike). The term *terminal analogue* refers to the fact that the analogy with human speech only exists at the output terminal of the synthesizer. No claims are made with respect to the anatomical, physiological or physical reality of the processes internal to the synthesizer. All terminal analogue synthesizers implement the basic source/filter model of acoustic speech production in one way or another. Moreover, all terminal analogue systems comprise an explicit acoustic description of a full set of basic sound units. Until recently, that description was always parametric, i.e., what was stored was a recipe for synthesizing speech sounds. We distinguish two methods, formant based synthesis and diphone concatenation.

In *formant based synthesis*, the basic units are allophones, specified in terms of default target values for a number of synthesizer control parameters, usually formant frequencies and bandwidths, voiced/unvoiced status, etc. Explicit acoustic phonetic rules must be invoked to compute the transitions between the target values for phonemes n and $n+1$. Below, we consider *rule driven formant synthesizers* as the type of terminal analogue synthesis which is most useful for psycholinguistic experiments.

Terminal analogue synthesizers employing *diphone concatenation* try to sidestep the very difficult problem of explicitly specifying the parameter transition rules. This is done by storing a full set of parameter tracks obtained from human productions of transitions from one phoneme to the next (*diphones*). In psycholinguistic terms, this means that the basic units of speech production are not the 50 or so phonemes of a language, but rather the $50*50 = 2500$ diphones. It should be said, however, that to our knowledge the engineers who developed diphone synthesis systems have never made claims with respect to the mental reality of diphones. Recently, diphone concatenation systems have been developed that are not parametric, but store time-domain signals for each diphone (Charpentier and Moulines, 1989).

Rule Based Formant Synthesis

The rule based formant synthesis system under development at our laboratory has two types of input, namely the string of phonemes (enriched by intonation commands) which specifies the linguistic message, and a table of default acoustic parameter values for the complete set of phonemes. Before attempting to compute suitable interpolations between target values for consecutive phonemes, the targets themselves are adapted to account for the influence of the surrounding sounds. Our system assumes that the adaptations due to coarticulation are in a way automatic, determined by the mechanical limitations of (and perhaps also by the control strategy for) the articulators. Coarticulatory adaptations are effected by means of an elaborate set of explicit rules. Another set of rules then computes the exact parameter tracks connecting the adapted targets.

Although the source/filter approach suggests a relation between synthesizer architecture and the physiology of speech production, one should be aware that this relation is very remote. The rule developer has a large amount of freedom in the choice of whether spectral details known to occur in real speech are modelled in the source or in the filter. For instance, the steep spectral roll-off in voiced continuant consonants can be obtained by changing the spectrum of the voice source or by narrowing the bandwidth of the first formant resonator. Although rule developers are encouraged to take the physiology of speech production into account whenever that is possible, there is little that can prevent them from ignoring this suggestion (Boves, 1992). It has been our experience, however, that the auditory quality of the synthetic speech improves considerably if physiologically unrealistic rules are replaced by rules which comply with knowledge about the physiology of speech production. To reiterate the example given above: after the implementation of voice source rules for continuants (and removal of rules narrowing the first formant bandwidth), the intelligibility and naturalness of the synthesizers output were judged to be significantly improved.

Modelling the Excitation in a Formant Based Synthesizer In older synthesizers the source for voiced speech sounds is modelled so that its energy distribution approximates the average spectrum of real glottal pulses, i.e., a spectrum with a slope of approximately −6 dB/octave. Usually this is accomplished by passing a Dirac Delta pulse through a second order low pass filter. This model assumes that all spectral structure beyond a smooth roll-off is due to the vocal tract. However, in real human speech the voice source contribution to the shape of the spectrum is more complex. This is reflected in the voice source model implemented in our synthesizer, namely the model developed by Klatt and Klatt (1990). The excitation source consists of two components: a periodic signal which has approximately the same shape as real glottal flow pulses, and a random component. From a phonetic point of view, the periodic component of the voice source is described by four parameters, namely the period duration T0, the Open Quotient (the interval in a glottal period during which the vocal folds are apart, allowing air to flow into the vocal tract), the pulse amplitude, and the high frequency spectral slope. These parameters are easily incorporated into a mathematical model.

The random component serves as the excitation for unvoiced sounds; it is also used in voiced fricatives and plosives. Last but not least, it is also used to simulate breathy voices. The random component is implemented by means of a Gaussian noise generator. This model is too simplistic to account for all possible noise sources in the vocal tract, but our understanding of the acoustics of speech production is not sufficiently advanced to warrant the added complexity of more elaborate models.

Modelling the Filter in a Formant Synthesizer Those aspects of the speech signal not accounted for by the source must be modelled in the filter, in our model a cascade of resonators and anti-resonators, each characterized by a centre frequency and a bandwidth. The overall filter characteristics are controlled via the characteristics of the individual resonators and anti-resonators. The centre frequency determines which frequency is amplified (or attenuated) most. The bandwidth specifies how selectively the resonator responds to a certain input frequency.

Although the spectrum envelope of most speech sounds can be approximated quite accurately by means of a cascade of resonators, we included an equal number of anti-resonators in our vocal tract filter, because we want to adhere as closely as possible to the physics of natural speech production. The resonator-only model of the vocal tract is only accurate (if ever) during the production of oral vowels. In all other speech sounds, the vocal tract acts as a combination of resonators and anti-resonators. Even if in stationary sounds the contribution of the anti-resonators can be modelled by clever changes in the parameters of the resonators, it appears that this 'abuse' of resonators can have very adverse perceptual effects during sound transitions.

Finding the Rules for Controlling Source and Filter In order to generate natural sounding speech, one cannot just concatenate speech sounds (although diphone concatenation can yield excellent quality speech). The acoustic characteristics of synthetic speech must reflect the continuous changes in the real vocal tract. Therefore, in addition to a set of target values for all synthesizer parameters (for instance, formant frequencies and bandwidths), the duration of the transition from one set of target values to the next must also be specified. Moreover, both target and transition parameters are sensitive to the phonetic identity of the surrounding sounds, and to their position in a prosodic unit. These rules try to model observations made in natural speech. It has been our experience that the specifications of the transitions between neighbouring sounds especially should not be modelled after average values obtained from the speech of a (large) number of talkers. Much better synthetic speech quality is obtained if one models the speech of a single speaker. In specifying target values the use of averages across speakers is less detrimental. This suggests that target formant values may vary quite a lot (which is inevitable, due to anatomical differences between speakers) but that transitions — even if they are different between speakers — carry a lot of essential information.

Designing rules for high-quality formant based synthesis is all but trivial. Although there is much information about acoustic properties of speech sounds, this information must be used with discretion. The problem is complicated by the fact that the synthesizer has a large number of control parameters that are not orthogonal. To reiterate, some spectral effects observed in natural speech can be obtained in several ways, which do not have to be mutually exclusive. Overall spectral slope is a good case in point: it can be controlled via the voice source, by means of widening the bandwidth of the first formant, and by cleverly manipulating anti-resonances. It is our strategy to model the effect via the parameters that are most likely to correspond to the actual physics of speech production.

Critical Remarks

From the point of view of psycholinguistic theory the single most important drawback of terminal analogue synthesis is probably the distance it creates between its internal mechanism for converting discrete phonemic input to continuous output speech and the way in which humans accomplish that feat (provided they really do). The terminal analogue approach does not care about that relation; it bothers only about efficient ways to generate speech that is intelligible and natural enough for use in practical applications. Yet, for some psycholinguistic research, the neglect may become a definite advantage, because the output speech can be of very high quality while there is still tight control over all parameters. This has allowed the use of terminal analogue synthesis in numerous experiments addressing the perceptually relevant aspects of the speech signal.

It is difficult to compare rule based formant synthesis with diphone concatenation. It is probably fair to say that the best systems that store diphones in the form of time-domain signals (Pitch Synchronous Overlap Add or PSOLA systems, cf., Charpentier and Moulines, 1989) can reach a level of intelligibility and naturalness that has not yet been attained by rule based systems. It is not true, however, that diphone systems in general outperform rule based systems. Moreover, PSOLA systems make manipulation of formant parameters extremely difficult.

It is of some interest to note that diphone systems solve the problem of converting discrete and invariant input into continuous and context dependent output in a completely different way to rule based terminal analogue systems. Diphone systems can be characterized as data driven systems: all knowledge which is necessary to effect the conversion is stored in the representation of the basic building blocks. Rule based systems, on the other hand, require very large numbers of explicit rules for the same purpose. The number of rules may grow beyond reasonable limits, if separate rules are needed for each sequence of sounds; and if these rules have to be adapted, for example, to different speaking rates or different speaking styles the number really explodes. When the number of rules is of the same order as the number of diphones the distinction between rule based and data based systems becomes fuzzy.

Evaluating Articulatory and Terminal Analogue Synthesis

From what has been said so far it may seem that articulatory synthesis is inherently superior to terminal analogue synthesis. In an abstract sense this may well be true. It does not mean, however, that articulatory synthesis is necessarily a better vehicle for testing psycholinguistic hypotheses about speech production. This is due to a number of limitations inherent in the presently available articulatory synthesis systems. Although it is perfectly possible to generate time courses for several articulators departing from a phonemic input representation, it is extremely difficult to test the appropriateness of these contours in any way other than by actually synthesizing the utterance and have subjects judge its adequacy. Unfortunately, the acoustic theory employed (or invoked) in this synthesis contains so many approximations and simplifications that failure to synthesize acceptable speech does not necessarily imply that the linguistic, phonological and phonetic theory underlying the synthesis is faulty. Even if subjects judge the utterances favourably, that can at best be taken as an indication that the underlying theory is probably not completely wrong. It can certainly not be construed as evidence that an alternative theory must be wrong, because it is quite possible that equally acceptable auditory judgements could have been obtained from synthesis departing from quite different parameter tracks.

Quality of Model Input

On the surface, terminal analogue and articulatory synthesis seem to use the same input representation, i.e., some prosodically enriched phonemic (allophonic) representation of the utterance to be spoken. At a somewhat deeper level, however, the input representations are fundamentally different. The allophone symbols are just names; the parameter sets specifying the allophones make for the real substance. In terminal analogue synthesis the allophone units are specified in terms of acoustic parameters. In an articulatory synthesizer, on the other hand, the basic units are specified in terms of the default positions of a small number of key articulators. Consequently, the input representation for articulatory synthesis is much more parsimonious.

In many rule based formant synthesizers, the allophone units constituting the input also seem to be represented in the form of articulatory features. These features can be mapped onto the articulatory parameters used in articulatory synthesis. Also, it has been stressed that in our rule based formant synthesis articulatory knowledge is taken into account whenever possible. However, differences between the interpretation of the input representations remain. In our rule system, features can only be used in their conventional abstract phonological interpretation, i.e., as a set of possible descriptive contrasts (a vowel is either *rounded* or it is not); the feature value (+ or −) for *round* determines whether or not a vowel takes part in some rule, and when it does, it can give rise to a change in the value of some specific acoustic parameter, e.g., the frequency of F1 of the following consonant. It cannot, however, lead to a representation where the feature *round* of some sound is given a fractional value between 0 and 1. Thus, even in the articulatory domain, the rule developer is still required to express the eventual effect of articulatory gestures in terms of the acoustic synthesizer parameters. This is different from an articulatory synthesizer, where it is quite possible to represent the information that coarticulation between /u/ and /p/ may lead to a lesser degree of lip rounding than coarticulation between /u/ and /k/, and where this degree can be expressed on a ratio scale.

Types of Internal Representation

Modern powerful terminal analogue synthesizers typically employ a very large number of parameters to specify the acoustic properties of the basic allophone units. On the one hand, these extremely rich representations allow one to model virtually every detail that could conceivably occur in natural speech. On the other hand, the parameters are mutually independent, despite the fact that their acoustic consequences are not orthogonal. This allows one to generate sounds which could never have been produced by a human speech apparatus. Viewed this way, the redundant parameter specification is a hindrance rather than an asset. In reaction to this 'overkill' of degrees of freedom, it has been suggested that synthesis rules should not be defined in terms of individual parameters, but rather in terms of higher level articulatory concepts, that predict the acoustic parameter values on the basis of their relation to anatomically and physiologically realistic behaviour of the articulators (Stevens and Bickley, 1991). Such an articulatory theory of speech acoustics, if it ever materializes, would essentially eliminate the problem of too large a number of degrees of freedom in the acoustic domain, by tying sets of parameters together on the basis of their predicted covariation as articulators move.

In this context it is necessary to elaborate on articulatory modelling. Despite its superficial anatomical realism, task dynamics abstracts away from many essential mechanical and physiological properties of the human speech production apparatus. From our own experience, with computer implementations of voice source models, it appears that every actual implementation that intends to be physiologically and physically realistic will have to face the same curse of dimensionality, the same overkill of degrees of freedom, as the terminal analogue synthesizers. The elastic properties of the vocal fold tissue alone yield so many free parameters, that almost any, even quite unrealistic, glottal waveform can be generated. It may well be possible to go to an even higher level of abstraction, allowing us to cope with the dimensionality problem in articulation, but for the time being the number of unsolved problems is far larger than the number of computationally feasible solutions.

Psychological Reality of Processing Assumptions

It appears that the psychological reality of the models employed in speech synthesis is at best remote. The task-dynamics model abstracts away from the mechanical and physiological properties of the articulators, while terminal analogue synthesis explicitly denies any claim towards any other reality than the acoustic quality of the output signal. Moreover, neither articulatory nor terminal analogue synthesis can, or intends to, account for the role of auditory feedback in human speech production. Even worse, it is not apparent how feedback could be integrated in existing models and architectures.

Articulation is so complex — and so badly understood — that we will have to be content with very incomplete models for a long time to come (cf., Perkell, 1991). In addition to the linguistic input, speech production involves physiological, physical and acoustic processes, neither of which is sufficiently understood. If one is willing to limit the analysis to movements and positions of a small number of easily observable articulators (the jaw and the lips, for instance) fast progress may be made. However, we have argued that the specification of trajectories for these and other articulators, even if they fit some set of measurement data, cannot be construed to support psycholinguistic theories about the control of articulation beyond extremely limited conditions. Moreover, due to the many-to-many mapping between articulation and acoustics, one must always take account of the possibility that another set of articulatory trajectories could have produced perceptually identical speech output.

This conclusion is not a pledge to give up on phonetic and psycholinguistic research on speech production. On the contrary, modern measurement techniques like MRI are likely to allow us to obtain substantial articulatory data in the future. Combined with the availability of the computing power needed to carry out principled simulations of air flow and pressure distributions in the larynx and in the vocal tract, these techniques should lead to significant progress. It must be expected, however, that it will take a long time, and a lot of creativity, to bridge the gap between the physiological, physical and acoustic knowledge on the one hand, and psycholinguistic theory on the other. For the time being, psycholinguistic theorizing should be extremely cautious and careful in using results from speech synthesis experiments as arguments pro or contra a theory.

Connectionist Approaches

During the late 1980s and the early 1990s, connectionist models have attracted a lot of attention in speech recognition research. Studies of speech production based on connectionist models seem to be extremely rare. We will not go into the attempts to solve the grapheme-to-phoneme mapping problem for languages like English or Dutch using neural networks, because that issue is outside the focus of this chapter. We will only say a few words about connectionist approaches to speech signal generation. We are not aware of serious attempts to employ neural networks in terminal analogue synthesis, although in principle it might be possible to train networks to generate smooth parameter interpolations fom discrete input representations. In the framework of the task-dynamics model, attempts have been made to train neural networks for the mapping of model articulator trajectories onto the formant tracks (Laboissiere, Schwartz and Bailly, 1992).

The fact that it proves possible to solve the vocal tract to acoustics mapping problem using neural networks should certainly be taken as one more argument in favour of the modelling power of these networks. However, one should be aware that it is still data which are modelled, not underlying articulation, let alone underlying articulatory control, because of the lack of physical and physiological realism of the underlying models. From our own research in articulatory synthesis it has appeared that the acoustics-to-articulatory inversion, which is implicit in the training of the networks, is extremely ill-conditioned, if not ill-posed, given our present knowledge of the physics and acoustics of speech production (Cranen and Schroeter, 1994). Minor changes in the assumptions about the physics of sound production or minor changes in the objective function to be optimized may lead to major changes in the optimal parameters. Under these circumstances even the most cautious psycholinguistic interpretation of connectionist modelling of articulation may prove to be premature, for exactly the same reasons that more conventional approaches to articulatory modelling are prone to misinterpretation.

Conclusions

Colleagues who have read draft versions of this chapter have said that the tone is somewhat pessimistic; we ourselves prefer the adjective *realistic*. Implicit in what is written above is the message that we have made substantial progress in understanding speech production and in simulating speech with computer models. Speech synthesis is actually being used in information services over the telephone and in reading aids for the visually impaired. Our knowledge of the physiology and physics of speech production has advanced at a rapid pace over the last couple of decades, and the development of new measurement equipment that can safely be used for large scale studies holds promise for continuous progress at an even faster pace. Yet, it is important to emphasize that our knowledge of speech production is still essentially incomplete, and that we can be certain that essential parts will remain poorly understood for a long time to come, even at the level of relatively peripheral processes. We do not dare to predict when it will be possible to formulate theories about the exact neural representation of the linguistic input that can be tested with conclusive experiments.

Probably the most important reason to think that complete understanding of speech production is not to be expected in the near future is the sheer complexity of the process. This process involves neural control (unknown and very difficult to investigate) of a very large number of bones and muscles (with mechanical and physiological properties which are almost impossible to measure in vivo as long as one respects certain ethical rules) which convert air flow energy into acoustic energy (in ways that are amenable to experimental investigations, but at a very high cost). Of course, all this should not stop us from building models and testing those aspects which allow experimental verification in one way or another. We see excellent possibilities for comprehensive computer simulation studies, which will certainly contribute considerably to our knowledge and understanding of speech production.

References

ALLEN, J., HUNNICUT, M.S. and KLATT, D. (1987) *From Text to Speech*, Cambridge: Cambridge University Press.

ATAL, B.S., CHANG, J.J., MATHEWS, M.V. and TUKEY, J.W. (1978) 'Inversion of articulatory-to-acoustic transformation in the vocal tract by a computer sorting technique', *Journal of the Acoustical Society of America*, 63, pp. 1535–55.

BAER, T., GORE, J.C., GRACCO, L.C. and NYE, P.W. (1991) 'Analysis of vocal tract shape and dimensions using magnetic imaging: Vowels', *Journal of the Acoustical Society of America*, 90, pp. 799–828.

BOVES, L. (1992) 'Considerations in the design of a multi-lingual text-to-speech system', *Journal of Phonetics*, 19, pp. 25–36.

CATFORD, J.C. (1977) *Fundamental Problems in Phonetics*, Bloomington, IN: Indiana University Press.

CHARPENTIER, F. and MOULINES, E. (1989) 'Pitch-synchronous waveform manipulation techniques for text-to-speech systems using diphones', in *Proceedings of Eurospeech-'89, Paris*, pp. 13–9.

COKER, C.H. (1972) 'Speech synthesis with a parametric articulatory model', in FLANAGAN, J.L. and RABINER, L.R. (Eds) *Speech Synthesis*, Stroudsburg: Dowden, Hutchinson, and Ross, pp. 135–9.

COOPER, F.S., LIBERMAN, A.M. and BORST, J.M. (1951) 'The interconversion of audible and visible patterns as a basis for research in speech perception', in *Proceedings of the National Academy of Science, Vol. 37*, pp. 318–25.

CRANEN, B. and SCHROETER, J. (1994) *Physiologically Motivated Modelling of the Voice Source in Articulatory Analysis/Synthesis*, Manuscript submitted for publication.

DISNER, X. (1983) 'Vowel quality: The relation between universal and language specific factors', *UCLA WPP*, 58, Los Angeles: University of California.

FANT, G. (1960) *Acoustic Theory of Speech Production*, The Hague: Mouton.

FLANAGAN, J. L. (1972) *Speech Analysis, Synthesis, and Perception*, Berlin: Springer.

FOWLER, C. A. and SALTZMAN, E. (1993) 'Coordination and coarticulation in speech production', *Language and Speech*, 36, 171–95.

JAKOBSON, R., FANT, G. and HALLE, M. (1963) *Preliminaries to Speech Analysis: The Distinctive Features and Their Correlates*, Cambridge, MA: MIT Press.

JOHNSON, K., LADEFOGED, P. and LINDAU, M. (1993) 'Individual differences in vowel production', *Journal of the Acoustical Society of America*, 94, pp. 701–14.

KLATT, D. H. and KLATT, X. (1990) 'Analysis, synthesis, and perception of voice quality variations among female and male talkers', *Journal of the Acoustical Society of America*, 87, pp. 820–57.

LABOISSIERE, R., SCHWARTZ, J.-L. and BAILLY, G. (1992) *Motor Control for Speech Skills: A Connectionist Approach*, Rapport de Recherche de l'ICP, Nr. 2, pp. 19–31.

LADEFOGED, P. and LINDAU, M. (1979) 'Where does the vocal tract end?', *UCLA WWP*, 45, Los Angeles: University of California, pp. 32–8.

LENNEBERG, E. H. (1967) *Biological Foundation of Language*, New York: Wiley.

LEVELT, W. (1989) *Speaking: From Intention to Articulation*, Cambridge, MA: MIT Press.

LINDBLOM, B. and SUNDBERG, J. (1971) 'Acoustic consequences of lips, tongue, jaw and larynx movements', *Journal of the Acoustical Society of America*, 50, pp. 1166–79.

MAEDA, S. (1979) 'Un modèle articulatoire basé sur une étude acoustique', *Bulletin de l'Institut de Phonétique de Grenoble*, 8, pp. 35–55.

McGOWAN, R. (1994) 'Recovering articulatory movement from formant frequency trajectories using task dynamics and a genetic algorithm: Preliminary model tests', *Speech Communication*, 14, pp. 19–48.

MERMELSTEIN, P. (1973) 'Articulatory model for the study of speech production', *Journal of the Acoustical Society of America*, 53, pp. 1070–82.

MEYER, A. (1990) 'The time course of phonological encoding in language production: The encoding of successive syllables of a word', *Journal of Memory and Language*, 29, pp. 524–45.

PERKELL, J. (1991) 'Models, theory and data in speech production', in *Proceedings of the XIIth International Congress of Phonetic Sciences*, pp. 182–91.

SALTZMAN, E. L. and MUNHALL, K. G. (1989) 'A dynamical approach to gestural patterning in speech production', *Ecological Psychology*, 1, pp. 333–82.

SHADLE, C. H. (1990) 'Articulatory-acoustic relationships in fricative consonants', in HARDCASTLE, W. J. and MARCHAL, A. (Eds) *Speech Production and Speech Modelling*, Dordrecht: Kluwer Academic Publishers.

STERNBERG, S., MONSELL, S., KNOLL, R. L. and WRIGHT, C. E. (1980) 'The latency and duration of rapid movement sequences: Comparisons of speech and typewriting', in COLE, R. (Ed) *Perception and Production of Fluent Speech*, Hillsdale, NJ: Lawrence Erlbaum, pp. 469–505.

STEVENS, K. N. (1972) 'The quantal nature of speech: evidence from articulatory-acoustic data', in *Human Communication: A Unified View*, MacGraw-Hill, pp. 51–66.

STEVENS, K. N. and BICKLEY, C. A. (1991) 'Constraints among parameters simplify control of Klatt formant synthesizer', *Journal of Phonetics*, 19, pp. 161–74.

TEN BOSCH, L. (1991) *On the Structure of Vowel Systems — Aspects of an Extended Vowel Model Using Effort and Contrast*, Unpublished doctoral dissertation, University of Amsterdam.

TITZE, I. R. (1988) 'The physics of small-amplitude oscillation of the vocal folds', *Journal the Acoustical Society of America*, 83, pp. 1536–52.

Chapter 15

Computer Models of Handwriting

Lambert R. B. Schomaker and Gerard P. Van Galen

Introduction

Although nowadays many of us prefer keyboard-driven text processors above pencils to 'engrave' our thoughts in written form, handwriting is still one of the more practised and convenient forms of communication. As a goal for the computer modeller, handwriting is a special challenge because this skill involves many stages of the human cognitive machinery, from conceptualization and formulation to the continuous displacement of a pencil in time, resulting in the permanent representation of discrete letters, words, sentences, and text in the form of an ink trace. Here we focus on models of the pencil trajectory formation. In Figure 15.1, a typical record is shown of the velocity profiles for the horizontal and the vertical movement dimension of writing. The handwritten production of the words *formal models* was recorded by means of an electronic digitizer.

The designer of a computer model for the simulation of the natural production of connected, cursive script needs to integrate principles of *symbolic* processes within the handwriting process with *subsymbolic* processes that generate consecutive writing strokes. The symbolic processes concern the manipulation of discrete linguistic representations. Examples of typical symbolic processes are the transformation from letter code to letter shape (allograph) and the subsequent concatenation of these letter shapes. The *subsymbolic* processes control the actual movement and are of a more continuous nature than the symbolic processes. Never are two renditions of the same type of letter identical from a spatial and kinematic perspective. The spatial and temporal features of the final trace that forms a letter depend not only on the position in a word, the preceding and following allographs, but also on the semantic, lexical, and phonological processes that concur with the production of script in real time (Van Galen, 1991).

Figure 15.1: *An original handwriting sample recorded with an XY digitizer, (a) spatial pattern; (b) horizontal pen-tip velocity; (c) vertical velocity; (d) absolute velocity. The signal was low-pass filtered at 20 Hz*

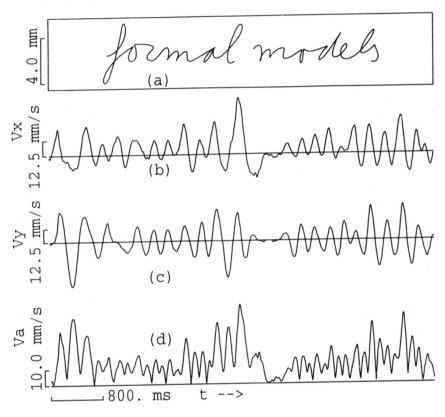

Aim of the Chapter

This chapter introduces computer modelling of handwriting in which both symbolic and subsymbolic aspects of handwriting are addressed. Because so far, only few researchers have addressed both aspects in modelling, we have to borrow to a large extent from our own work in the field. We do not aim only to mimic the visual appearance of the handwriting ink trace, but also to simulate the trajectory formation processes which determine the pen-tip movement in time. To this end, first a theoretical framework is presented in which psychological knowledge and constraints for such a handwriting model are explored. Following this theoretically oriented section, two approaches towards the design of working models of handwriting production are discussed at some length. The first of these approaches emphasizes especially the concatenation of allographs following a symbolic/

algorithmic procedure. In the second approach, two sample models are portrayed in which the subsymbolic features of stroke generation are simulated through the application of neural network theory.

Handwriting Research and Modelling

Compared to speech, handwriting has a slow production rate. Experienced writers produce about five letter strokes per second and thus, dependent on the complexity of the allographs to be written, two to three letters per second. However, the actual rate is influenced by the level of skill, development, age, linguistic complexity of the text, and other cognitive and neuropsychological factors. As an acquired skill, handwriting is taught in most school systems over a period of five to six years, and evolves only gradually during the writer's lifetime. Fundamental knowledge about production mechanisms of handwriting is relevant to the design of computer algorithms for the automatic *recognition* of connected cursive handwriting (Schomaker, 1991), as well as to the design of working models for the *production of script*, which is the core topic of this chapter.

Recent years have witnessed a steep increase in empirical and theoretical knowledge with respect to the handwriting process. Progress in the field has been inspired by technological advances which enabled the recording of pen movements with high temporal and spatial accuracy (Teulings and Maarse, 1984). Apart from that, the flourishing of interest in language processes in general has stimulated research in the handwriting domain as well (Thomassen and Van Galen, 1992).

Many authors have tried to model the handwriting process (Plamondon and Maarse, 1989). Denier van der Gon, Thuring and Strackee (1962) simulated the writing of letters by a machine which combined the vertical and horizontal excursions produced by two electrically driven step motors that could be varied in amplitude and relative phase. Already this simple electromechanical device produced smooth, natural looking letters and letter sequences. The experiment showed that simple on-off coding leads to smooth movement due to physical damping properties. Many other researchers have built on this basic idea of trajectory formation with biomechanically more refined principles of stroke production and stroke concatenation. Vredenbregt and Koster (1971) added variable degrees of noise to the input function which led to an individualized and natural appearance of the machine's script. These handwriting simulation models, which by their simple nature can easily be implemented on the computer, may be termed *peripheral* models. In essence, they mimic only the final and peripheral steps in the chain from intention to trajectory formation.

Other investigators, mostly from the psychological discipline, have concentrated on portraying the more *central* and cognitive steps involved in the production of script. Most models developed in this field of research are not computational but primarily descriptive in nature. Ellis (1982) used a large body of neuropsychological data to defend a modular nature of the cognitive processes of writing. According to Ellis, writing may be partly considered to follow the top-down path through the same processes as those involved in reading. Typical for writing are the motor processes involved in letter formation, size and slant control, and their anatomical and biomechanical implications. In this context, Ellis mentioned modular steps such as allograph retrieval and graph production. Ellis did not specify any details about the production of letters at the level of trajectory formation. Van Galen (1991) explored especially the *motor processes* involved in handwriting. In his model of the writing process, which partly inspired the computer models that are discussed later, a modular architecture of processes is defended as well. The notion of modularity is used here to refer to a feature of the architecture of a model of human cognition, which does not necessarily mirror exactly the anatomical structure of the brain. Grapheme selection (i.e., letter code identification), allograph selection (i.e., letter form retrieval), overall size control, and muscular implementation are the basic processes in the model of the motor side of the writing machinery.

A significant proportion of handwriting studies centred around the pen tip kinematics, while abstracting from the intricate anatomical and biomechanical processes that drive pen tip movements (Thomassen, Keuss and Van Galen, 1984; Plamondon, Suen and Simner, 1989; Plamondon and Leedham, 1990). We follow this tradition and concentrate on modelling pen tip movements instead of simulating anatomical details of finger and hand movements that generate pen displacement. Also, pen tip movement can be accurately measured with modern digitizer equipment. However, keep in mind that this approach focuses only upon a reduced and specific aspect of the handwriting process. Many more factors, notably the forces exerted on the joints and on the writing surface (Schomaker and Plamondon, 1991), play an essential and partly independent role. Nevertheless, the challenge to build a working model of handwriting currently has its capital interest in the motor side, and therefore we concentrate on these motor aspects.

Psychomotor Aspects of Handwriting: A Brief State of the Art

Three research questions, directly relevant for the architecture of any (computer) model of handwriting, and guiding much of the psychological research in the field, are addressed in the next three sections (for overviews see Van Galen, 1991; Thomassen and Van Galen, 1992).

What Kind and Number of Processing Modules Contribute to Handwriting?

Early research on handwriting followed the main stream of motor performance research in general. Inspired by early notions of the concept of abstract motor programs, Van Galen and Teulings (1983) investigated whether letter form and letter size are controlled by independent mechanisms. Empirical support for such a modular view on form and size control was found in reaction time (RT) experiments in which subjects were requested to write down a visually presented stimulus as quickly as possible. The form or the size of the stimulus over consecutive trials was repeated or alternated. Repetition and change of *form* turned out to have different effects on RT than *size* variation. In later experiments (Van Galen and Teulings, 1983), the same question was explored, this time following Sternberg's (1969) additive factors paradigm. The basic assumption underlying this paradigm is that, if two experimental variables in a choice RT experiment have additive (statistically independent) contributions to the total statistical variance in a data set, these factors are processed in at least two independent and serially organized modules. The logic does not specify the order of this seriality nor does it say anything about the role of variables left out of consideration. Empirical arguments were found for the independence of retrieving graphemic letter codes (spelling), the processing of allographic letter form (motor programming), the control of letter scale (parameterization), and, finally, the recruitment of appropriate groups of motor units in effector limbs (muscular initiation).

Corroborative evidence for a modular view was supplied by an extensive body of neuropsychological studies (Ellis, 1982; Caramazza, Miceli and Villa, 1986; Black, Behrmann and Hacker, 1989). Neuropsychological evidence was found in the so-called *double dissociation* phenomenon, i.e., two groups of patients were able to perform handwriting either under one or the other of two task conditions, but not both. In particular, Ellis (1982) found that one group of patients could write meaningful but irregularly spelled words correctly but were unable to write (or spell) nonsense words. Another group of patients could easily write meaningless phoneme sequences but could not spell or write irregularly spelled meaningful words. Ellis concluded that phoneme-to-grapheme conversion and the retrieval of irregular spellings from a spelling lexicon occurs within two independent neural processing stages, each of which can be affected by neural damage.

What Are the Basic Units of Processing Involved in Handwriting?

Closely related to the question of whether distinct processes contribute to the production of handwriting is the topic of basic unit(s) of processing. Early simulation models have often assumed that units of a fixed length (strokes, letters, or even complete words) are the units of processing. The handwriting process is, however, more complex than that. Teulings, Thomassen and Van Galen (1983) studied the effects of precueing the identity of a forthcoming writing target on the time to initiate the first pen movement. If the identity of a complete letter was precued to the subject, the RT decreased by about 100 ms. Precueing only the form of the *initial* stroke of a forthcoming letter had no effect on RT. Apparently, in presetting the motor system for an upcoming handwriting response, complete letters are the appropriate programming units. Hulstijn and Van Galen (1988) articulated this conclusion showing that RT effects in handwriting tasks are highly sensitive to the degree of practice and the meaningfulness or abstractness of the writing task. Based on these experiments, Van Galen (1991) proposed that the preparation of handwriting is not a unitary process. Instead, programming and execution of a written message proceed along different independent steps. Each of these processing steps is realized by a different processing module. Further, each module is characterized by its own grain size of processing units. Earlier modules (i.e., earlier in time relative to the real-time deliverance of the written trace) process more abstract and more extensive portions of the message as measured against the time scale of the complete message. At the same time, the codes which are activated (or produced) by an earlier module are assumed to form the input for the next lower module. The latter accepts the input with a grain size which is smaller, and characteristic for that particular processing stage. So, for example, the spelling module accepts sentence phrases word by word and transcodes each word letter by letter into its output. Subsequently, the motor programming module accepts letter by letter and transcodes each letter into a stroke production pattern. Still later, muscular initiation processes evoke the muscle contractions which are appropriate for the given biomechanical situation.

Is the Handwriting Process Strictly Serial or Also Parallel?

So far, we have discussed evidence in favour of a serial nature of the handwriting process. The higher, more abstract modules work on global task elements and deliver their output to the lower modules. At the output level, the generation and concatenation of strokes is obviously a serial process. However, there is clear psychological evidence that handwriting production has many features of a parallel process as well. The most direct evidence of this is that chronometric aspects of the production of script are simultaneously influenced by all current task demands. Writing time for a particular task segment is affected by such diverging variables as spelling difficulty, allographic choice, motor complexity of oncoming letters, and features of spacing and lineation. Van der Plaats and Van Galen (1990) studied the delay of the tip of the pen during the spacing between two words. Spacing time was influenced by both the effective width of the spacing and the

the motor complexity of the first letter after the space. The movements producing the writing trace are simultaneously influenced by various processing loads such as lexical status, phonological structure, motor complexity, and spatial arrangement (Van Galen, 1990, 1991). This indicates that several processing stages are active in parallel.

There is ample evidence that demands of a differing nature (linguistic, psychomotor, biomechanical) have *combined* effects on writing trajectories. At the same time, a specific *order* of the manifestation of task demands has been demonstrated. Larger representational units (e.g., words) affect the production speed of writing segments over a larger temporal range than smaller units at lower levels (e.g., letters and strokes). With respect to letters, repetition and letter length were shown to influence writing trajectories at a range of only two or one letters ahead of the target letter. With respect to the smallest units studied (letter strokes) it appeared that repetitions and difficult stroke alterations led to an increase of writing time of only the difficult strokes themselves (Van Galen *et al.*, 1989). A possible solution for these seemingly conflicting data on parallelism and seriality was suggested by Van Galen (1991) in his assumption of the *ordered parallelism* of the writing system. It implies that in a natural writing task all modules are active in parallel but different modules work on different chunks of the message and work with units of different grain sizes, as explained above (cf., Levelt, 1989).

Five Elements for a Handwriting Model

Having reviewed the evidence which guided thinking on psychomotor modelling of handwriting, we now list the requirements for a handwriting model as suggested by Van Galen (1991). Next, these requirements are used to sketch the outline of a modular model, which serves as a framework for the discussion of the computer models discussed in later sections. The following five features are considered essential to a realistic model of handwriting production.

1 *Modularity.* The handwriting process involves several different processing modules, each of which addresses specific (e.g., semantic, lexical, allographic, geometrical, etc.) aspects of production.
2 *Seriality.* The architecture of these modules is serial (and thus hierarchical in a particular aspect) in the sense that the output of each stage forms the input for the next lower stage. The serial nature of the architecture is not necessarily 'hard-wired'. The serial correspondences may hold during the execution of an overlearned handwriting process, but the modules may be engaged in a different connectivity in other tasks and in the case of interruptions or shifts of attention.
3 *Size of Processing Units.* From the higher stages of the processing

architecture down, generality decreases and specificity increases. At a high cognitive level, phoneme-to-grapheme translation modules, often in concerted action with a lexically based spelling module (Ellis, 1982; Portier, Van Galen and Thomassen, 1993), generate the ensemble of letter codes (graphemes) which form the correct (or incorrect) spelling of a word. At an intermediate, psychomotor level, motor programming processes

Figure 15.2: A general psychomotor model of handwriting. The central column describes, from top to bottom, the consecutive processing modules which are involved in writing performances. The right-hand column refers to the changing type and extent of the representations on which the processing modules work. The left-hand column indicates the relevant contextual constraints at each processing level. The shaded area denotes the levels addressed by the models in this chapter. The symbolic model deals with allograph concatenation (upper part), the neural-network models deal with allograph representation (lower part)

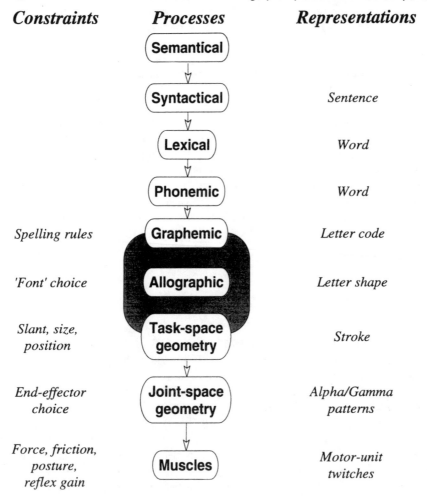

Constraints	*Processes*	*Representations*
	Semantical	
	Syntactical	*Sentence*
	Lexical	*Word*
	Phonemic	*Word*
Spelling rules	**Graphemic**	*Letter code*
'Font' choice	**Allographic**	*Letter shape*
Slant, size, position	**Task-space geometry**	*Stroke*
End-effector choice	**Joint-space geometry**	*Alpha/Gamma patterns*
Force, friction, posture, reflex gain	**Muscles**	*Motor-unit twitches*

activate concatenations of goal trajectories which represent the shape of an allograph. Here, letter strokes and their assembly into allographs form smaller processing units than letter codes. At the lower and more peripheral end of the chain, processing units are small and numerous. Here, high-frequent neural commands evoke thousands of muscle twitches which generate forces that drive the pen tip to its realization of a stroke trajectory.

4 *Parallelism.* All modules are engaged in processing activities simultaneously. However, higher modules are further ahead of real-time output than lower modules. This concurrent processing goes on in all modules concerned, as far as the memory characteristics of individual modules permit.

5 *Transient Buffering.* The necessary buffering of information during a particular processing stage may be operationalized as a time-constant of representation decay (cf., Chapter 3). Each module may have its own typical decay constant related to its role in the overall structure. Transient buffering accommodates time frictions between information processing activities in different modules. A module lower in the hierarchy can produce a series of short-lasting representations at its output, derived from a single, longer-lasting input representation.

Figure 15.2 depicts the handwriting process as proposed by Ellis (1982) and Van Galen (1991). The vertical organization of the processes in the central column of Figure 15.2 corresponds to their assumed serial ordering. Arrows express input-output relations between neighbouring levels. The left-hand column shows possible contextual constraints which influence processing at a specific level. Contextual influences may occur at all levels, although in the figure they are indicated for the five lowest levels only. In the right column the units of representation at the different levels are indicated.

Limitations of the Framework

One obvious limitation of the modelling framework is that it does not explicitly represent feedback processes in any form. Empirical studies on the role of visual control have investigated how handwriting is produced without seeing the hand or script. Under these circumstances, the production rate is delayed and the shapes are somewhat distorted (Smyth and Silvers, 1987; Van Galen *et al.*, 1989; Van Doorn and Keuss, 1992). Smyth and Silvers (1987) primarily attributed the overall monitoring of word and letter order to visual control, and not to the real time realization of pen movements. In line with this assumption, removing visual feedback was found to result in slow variations of the baseline within words, and abrupt errors after each pen-lifting movement between words (Schomaker, 1991).

A further phenomenon is the typical stroke-counting error, yielding, e.g., <m > or <w > with too many strokes. These phenomena show that a good model of handwriting should make room for at least some degree of afferent feedback. For example, the orientation of the line of script could be updated at the start of each oncoming letter on the basis of the collective orientation of the immediately preceding letters. This constraint would ascertain that a chosen lineation at the beginning of a line is maintained through feedback, just as the experimental results suggest.

Discussion and Outlook

The empirical findings discussed above have substantially influenced psychological theorizing of handwriting as a psychomotor skill. The psychomotor approach as such, however, is not complete and detailed enough to construct a computational model. First, the approach is near to silent about the biomechanical details of the trajectory formation process proper. Although the model by Van Galen (1991) proposes a muscle initiation stage, no further clues are provided as to how human handwriting is performed in a dynamically changing mechanical context. Outside the field of experimental psychology, and more specifically in biomechanics and engineering, an abundance of models addresses the issue of pentip trajectory formation. Extensive overviews are given by Plamondon and Maarse (1989) and Teulings (1993). However, as already said before, many of these models focus on biomechanical aspects only. Models which are embedded in a multi-level theory of complex motor function are lacking. In the further sections of this chapter we report on attempts to bridge this gap. The aim of this excursion is to show that, eventually, the integration of cognitive and psychomotor knowledge with trajectory formation principles may contribute to a more natural simulation of the handwriting skill.

From Theory to Computer Models

The psychological framework of handwriting processes, depicted in Figure 15.2, suggests a number of the steps in the production of handwriting. An intention to write a message (semantic level) is transformed into words (lexical and syntactic level). After the identification of letters in a word (spelling or graphemic level) the writer selects specific letter shape variants (allographs). An allograph is selected according to a syntax (e.g., capital letter forms are selected at the start of a new sentence), according to individual preferences (e.g., connected script or print letters) or just according to random choice (e.g., many people use alternate forms for *r* and *t* and *s* in an unpredictable or semi-predictable fashion, see Van der Plaats and Van Galen, 1991).

Below the allograph selection level, allographs are transformed into abstract stroke production patterns and, ultimately, into the real-time kinematics of characteristic up and down pen movements. Teulings, Thomassen and Van Galen (1986) demonstrated that both the spatial and temporal characteristics of error-free, non-hesitant handwriting tend to show a high degree of invariance for a given writer. However, the spatial characteristics are more invariant than the temporal characteristics. It seems that the handwriting production system capitalizes on producing stable *spatial* results, in order to facilitate visual processing by the reader. Indeed, for a given writer, handwriting is highly consistent, regardless of the limb or type of pencil used (Raibert, 1977; Maarse, Schomaker and Teulings, 1988). Therefore, we assume that the writing system stores *spatial representations* of allographs, residing in some long-term memory. These spatial allograph representations (paths) have to be transformed into spatial-temporal representations (target trajectories).

Furthermore, a single allograph is linked to its neighbours by connecting strokes and/or pen-up movements. Studies on the kinematics of within-letter strokes and between-letter (connecting) strokes have shown that, especially in children, connecting strokes are more demanding than letter strokes proper, notwithstanding identical curvature and direction (Meulenbroek and Van Galen, 1989).

For the purpose of modelling, it is useful at this point to distinguish between (a) descriptions of the *chaining* process of basic movement segments, and (b) descriptions of the *shaping* process of an individual movement segment. The distinction is not always sharp and depends on the definition of *movement segment*. The shaping functionality typically requires implicit knowledge of the biomechanics of the output system, yielding neural activity that compensates for unwanted biomechanical side-effects or making effective use of the properties of the output device. Hierarchically, shaping is of a lower level than chaining, i.e., a chaining module drives a shaping module. The distinction between chaining and shaping becomes evident in handwriting, where overlearned basic patterns (allographs) are chained and subsequently shaped into fluent movements. In comparison, the occurrence of coarticulation effects in speech can be described as shaping being affected by the chaining process. In contrast, anticipation and perseveration errors in handwriting, typing, and speech indicate problems in the chaining process itself.

From Abstract Goal Trajectories to Muscle Activation

So far, the biomechanical details of the 'articulation' of the segments and the joints of the limb that moves the pencil have not been discussed. Until the stage of specifying a particular sequence of letter strokes, the output of the model is a target trajectory in three-dimensional space, or two-dimensional space if only the inscriptions on the paper surface are considered. There is empirical evidence that humans plan movements in a three-dimensional (or two-dimensional) representation of the outside world and not in terms of an intracorporal joint space (Hollerbach and Flash, 1981; Morasso and Tagliasco, 1986). The ecological significance of the principle is that the planning of movements is bound to the same spatial representation that locates objects and obstacles in perception. Planning of movement in task space is not the 'focus of control' (Schomaker, 1991) in all aspects of the writing task. Consider, for instance, the task of holding the pen between thumb and forefingers. Here, the focus of control lies more on the forces (torques) in the joints, to ensure a stable grip on the pen. However, we assume that for the main task of generating letter shapes, the planning of movement produces an idealized pen tip trajectory in the two-dimensional XY-plane of the paper, rather than a plan representation in joint space.

As evident in natural handwriting as well as in the framework, the representation of a goal trajectory can still be moulded geometrically (translation, rotation, shearing, size adjustment) depending on the parameter settings at the level of Task-Space Geometry (cf., Figure 15.2). The allowable transformations are bounded, however, because not all possible parameter values can lead to a successful transform. Consider, for instance, writing upside down, which is not easy without training.

Still lower levels in the motor system must handle the problem of the conversion from three-dimensional internalized space to n-dimensional joint space, such that the performing limb will follow the prescribed trajectory and forcing pattern in external three-dimensional space. This is known as the problem of *inverse kinematics* and *inverse dynamics* transformations. Currently, a number of models for this transform are known, some of them based on neural network theory, others on cost minimization (Albus, 1975; Thomassen, Meulenbroek and Tibosch, 1991; Meulenbroek *et al.*, 1993). The lowest and last stage is the specification of the excitation pattern for the alpha and gamma motorneuron pools of the involved muscles. It is only at this stage that biomechanical damping (read filtering) through stiffness and viscosity of the muscles and limbs takes place.

In the following sections, two approaches to computational modelling, each addressing a separate level of processing, are compared with respect to their merits. The first approach follows the *computational symbolic* tradition, while the second approach, represented by two models, takes stock of the *connectionist* paradigm.

A Computational Model of Stroke Formation and Letter Concatenation

The computational model discussed in this paragraph (Schomaker, Thomassen and Teulings, 1989) is situated within the *symbolic/algorithmic* paradigm (see Chapter 2). The model is centred around the process of concatenating allographs in cursive script, which is formalized as a Cursive Connections Grammar. The trajectory formation stage is represented by a sparse parameterization of single strokes. No theoretical assumptions are made about the underlying neural patterning. The problem of linking the discrete, symbolic processing stage with the continuous, subsymbolic stage is solved by choosing discrete anchor points in time, corresponding to symbols, whereas the continuous nature of the simulated pen tip movement is the result of the parameterization of the shape of the trajectory between these anchor points. In terms of the framework presented in Figure 15.2, the present model specifically addresses the allographic level and the task-space geometry level.

With this model we investigated whether a symbolic algorithm can *regenerate* recorded handwriting movements in a naturalistic manner, as well as *generate* new samples of script according to the spatial-temporal characteristics of a particular individual. In the latter case, the model analyzes the recorded writing movements of an experienced writer, and subsequently is able to generate a completely new text, written in the cursive handwriting style, retaining the temporal characteristics for this subject. Most handwriting models are *re*generative, thus addressing only a limited domain of the modelling of handwriting (see Teulings, 1993). Notable exceptions are models by Edelman and Flash (1987) and Morasso, Mussa Ivaldi and Ruggiero (1983), which are generative as well as regenerative.

Given that the present model is concerned with the handwriting of an experienced adult writer, it has access already to a number of well-defined, stable spatial representations of allographs. *Input* to the model consists of chains of allograph symbols for lower and uppercase letters, blanks and an occasional period or comma. These symbols are viewed as referring to internal abstract categories available within the neural system. *Output* of the model consists of specifications of planar target trajectories of the pen tip. Penlifting movements are reduced to a binary signal (pen up/down). By means of a feedback mechanism, a constant orientation of the baseline relative to the generated target trajectory is maintained. We now discuss the model in more detail, first dealing with the quantitative aspects of stroke formation within allographs, and then handling the concatenation of neighbouring letters.

The Quantitative Level of the Symbolic Model: Stroke Parameterization

Already in early simulation studies it became apparent that the timing of movement units is an essential determinant of handwriting (Denier van der Gon, Thuring and Strackee, 1962; Vredenbregt and Koster, 1971). When we look at the vertical and horizontal velocity components of natural script, we see a pattern of low-frequency content, near-sinusoidals of varying amplitude and period, only disturbed by a moderate amount of noise (see velocity profiles in Figure 15.1). Sometimes the zero crossings in both signals coincide; sometimes the horizontal component (Vx) lags behind the vertical component (Vy), and vice versa (see Figure 15.3). We consider trajectory formation as a process of chaining discrete

Figure 15.3: Three variants of up and down strokes and their relative timing (t) in the velocity domain (Vx and Vy). Looking at the upward stroke, which starts at the left in each pattern, the following basic types of strokes can be discerned: (a) obtuse clockwise, ending with Vx lagging behind Vy; (b) sharp ending, no delay; (c) obtuse counter-clockwise, looping with the next stroke, Vx leads Vy in time (Schomaker, 1989)

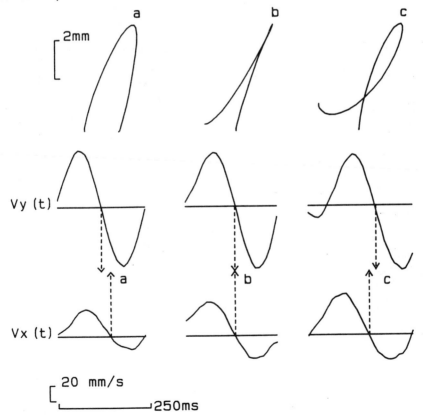

Figure 15.4: An overview of the data structures and the data processing modules of the symbolic model, depicting the flow of information from grapheme codes to pen-tip displacement functions

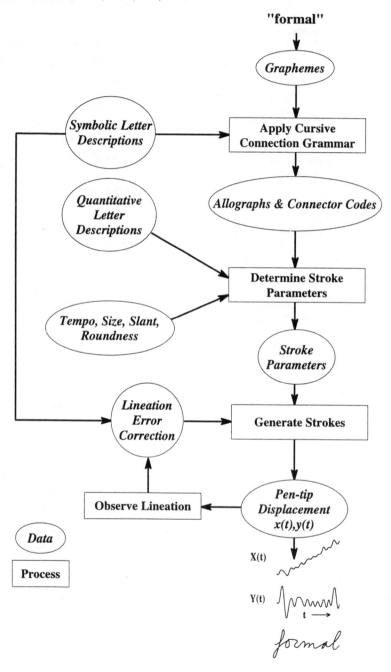

strokes (Morasso, Mussa Ivaldi and Ruggiero, 1983). However, unlike Morasso, Mussa Ivaldi and Ruggiero's stroke definition, which is essentially in terms of circle segments, we define a stroke as a pair of momentum impulses. The basic shape of such a momentum impulse along a single axis (horizontal/vertical) is (nearly) sinusoidal in the velocity domain. In the resulting absolute velocity curve, the typical monophasic curve of a handwriting stroke is produced, and the depth of the velocity minima at begin and end depends on the relative timing of the sinusoids. Figure 15.3 shows examples of up and down strokes in handwriting, which were extracted from larger samples of text written by a single writer. The depicted phenomenon forms the basis for a stroke parameterization which describes shape on the basis of relative movement timing. The spatial up stroke is produced by horizontal and vertical momentum impulses with a specified onset time, amplitude and duration. For reasons of simplicity, a representative variety of strokes was encompassed by using only four parameters per stroke: relative horizontal displacement (dX), relative vertical displacement (dY), duration (T), and shape factor (C). On the basis of the shape factor C and duration T, an estimate of the delay (phase shift) between the zero velocity crossings of the horizontal and vertical movements can be computed, which determines the curvature of the stroke.

Using an 'alphabet' of prototypical strokes, characters can be composed as sequences of vectors of the four parameters in time. Figure 15.4 gives a flowchart of data structures and processing modules relevant to the model. The incoming data are allograph symbols that are converted stepwise into a quantitative form.

The Generation of Connecting Strokes

For generating connections between letters, the model first inserts symbols for connecting strokes and pen-lifting strokes between the allographs. This is done by the Cursive Connections Grammar (CCG). The CCG can be understood as a simple grammar consisting of rewrite rules (compare phrase structure rules in Chapter 2). Following is a small sample of such rules (< ALPHA > stands for a symbol belonging to the set of alphabetic symbols, < * > stands for any symbol).

```
< ALPHA > < ALPHA >   : = =  < ALPHA > < CONNECTOR > < ALPHA >
< ALPHA > < PENUP >    : = =  < ALPHA > < ENDSTROKE > < PENUP >
< ALPHA > < PUNCT >    : = =  < ALPHA > < ENDSTROKE > < PUNCT >
< PENUP > < ALPHA >    : = =  < PENUP > < BEGINSTROKE > < ALPHA >
< ENDSTROKE > < * >    : = =  < ENDSTROKE > < PENUP > < * >
< * > < PUNCT          : = =  < * > < PENUP > < PUNCT >
```

Connecting strokes (referred to as < CONNECTOR > above) normally start at about the base line or descender line. They complete the shape of the current letter and span the horizontal distance to the next letter while initializing its shape. The rules shown above insert connecting strokes between two alphabetics, append small ending strokes at the verge of a pen-up movement, and lift the pen before a punctuation sign. The CCG is recursively applied to an incoming pair of symbols and it inserts new symbols until no further rules are applicable.

To substitute the initially inserted connection symbols, the CCG consults a qualitative (ordinal) description of allographs: the Symbolic Letter Description. This is a grid of available spatial vertical and horizontal starting and end levels, and levels of curvature, for each individual allograph recorded from samples of script. For instance, consider the generation of the connecting stroke between <d> and <e> in the word <models> when it is cursively written. The Symbolic Letter Description of the <d> contains information that a <d> ends on the baseline, with a counter-clockwise turning direction. The Symbolic Letter Description of the <e> contains information that an <e> starts counter-clockwise, the top of the loop being at the corpus or middle line. Thus, going from a <d> to an <e> requires a connecting stroke from <base-line> to <mid-line>, <counter-clockwise> (together represented as <b-m-n>), and with <normal-progression>. With these pieces of information, the CCG is able to infer the symbolic description of the required connecting stroke. For example, the input text string *formal models* is transformed by the CCG into the following output:

<i-u-n> <f> <b-m-s-c> <o> <m-m-s-c> <r> <b-m-p-c>
<m> <b-m-s> <a> <b-u-n> <l> <b-bplus-s-c>
<SPACE> <i-m-p-c> <m> <b-m-s-c> <o> <m-m-s>
<d> <b-m-n> <e> <b-u-n> <l> <b-m-p-c> <s>
<SPACE>

In this example, the codes referring to letters are in bold enlarged font. The connecting strokes are coded by starting level, end level, end shape, a horizontal progression code if the movement deviates from the modal horizontal spacing, and a pen-up code if the stroke is in the air, producing no visible ink. The first initial stroke <i-u-n> means 'from an intermediate vertical-level (*i*), to the upper vertical-level (*u*), counter-clockwise (*n*), with a normal horizontal spacing'. As a second example, <b-m-s-c> means 'from the baseline (*b*) to the middle line (*m*), with a sharp ending (*s*), horizontally closer than normal (*c*)'. Space limitations do not allow for a detailed explanation of all eighteen codes, but one shape code worth mentioning is *p* for clockwise stroke movement. The shape codes *p,s,n* refer to shapes as in the upward strokes in Figure 15.3a, 15.3b and 15.3c, respectively.

Stroke Parameterization and Generation

The symbol chains, representing allographs and connecting strokes are passed onto the next process, the stroke parameterization process. During this process the symbol chains are further refined and converted into sequences of stroke parameters, that are biased by the global setting of the tempo, size and shape factors. The refinement is achieved by consulting the Quantitative Letter Description (a look-up table), which is more accurate but less general than the Symbolic Letter Description. Each letter code is expanded into a series of within-letter stroke symbols, each of which is represented by a stroke parameter vector. The resulting chain of stroke parameter vectors originating from letters and connection strokes is illustrated in Table 15.1. The third and final process, stroke

Table 15.1: Stroke parameter vectors as derived by the symbolic model after consulting the Quantitative Letter Description. Each row represents one stroke. dX and dY represent displacement in the horizontal and vertical direction respectively. C is the shape factor and T is the duration of the stroke. See text for further explanation

Stroke	Code	dX	dY	C	T
1	<i_u_n>	6.2	4.6	-0.222	140
2	<F>	-6.8	-10.5	-0.040	135
3	<F>	3.5	7.2	-0.400	125
4	<F>	-0.9	-2.1	-0.421	95
5	<b_m_s_c>	4.1	2.5	0.000	100
6	...	...	...	...	...
7	...	...	...	...	...

generation, involves the distribution of available time for a spatial stroke among momentum impulses along the X and Y axis according to the required size and shape. The output of stroke generation is monitored by a process which uses the Symbolic Letter Descriptions as a lineation reference. This is necessary because the position data have to be updated in the correct cells of a memory of the lineation that has actually been produced until now. If an already generated stroke deviates too much from the current state of the lineation memory, programming of the size of the subsequent stroke is adjusted. To simulate a proportionally decreasing effect of the position of already written letters, the lineation memory is of the exponentially decaying type.

An Empirical Test of the Symbolic Model

The model was tested on the data of a cursive writer (male, right-handed, age 44).

Parameters for the generation of new script by the model were derived from a full page of handwriting produced by the subject on a digitizer tablet. The Symbolic Letter Descriptions were created semi-automatically by determining the stroke starting and end points for each recorded letter with the help of a handwriting data editor. The Symbolic Stroke Description structure was also created semi-automatically, by quantizing the stroke parameters on the basis of the shape of

Figure 15.5: A comparison of six replications of the word computer. *From left to right: spatial pattern, horizontal velocity and vertical velocity. A human writer produced the samples 1–3. Sample 4 represents a newly generated word by the symbolic model and is the most important in this context. Sample 5 and 6 are regenerated variants of the original human-written sample 1, testing the parameterization method, sec*

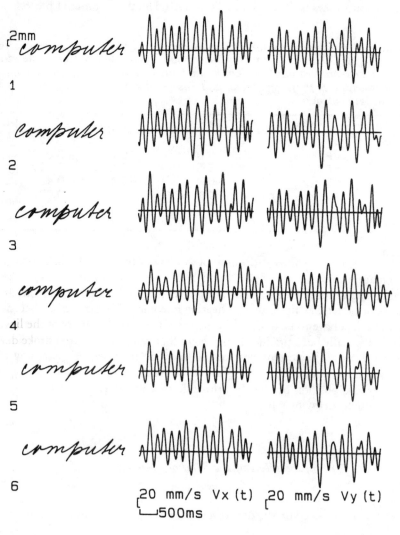

their histograms (e.g., horizontal 'ink density'), yielding discrete lineation codes.

It was found that for connecting strokes a limited number of parameter categories was sufficient to arrive at a realistic (re)generation, whereas parameter values within letters had to be much more accurate. For the writer under study, three levels of the shape parameter of individual strokes were chosen to describe the connecting strokes: *counter-clockwise* as in a connecting stroke leading to <e>, *sharp* as in a connecting stroke leading to <i>, and *clockwise* as in a connecting stroke leading to <m>. For the horizontal progression between letters, a categorization in three levels appeared to be sufficient: *close*, *normal*, and *far*.

A number of replications of the word *computer* were used to test the model on regeneration and generation of handwriting (Figure 15.5). Schomaker, Thomassen and Teulings (1989) report high correlations between parameter values of regenerated and newly generated samples of script. Replications of words by a human writer correlate in the range 0.97–0.99 with respect to vertical stroke size. The model generates words with a vertical stroke size showing the same correlation of 0.97–0.99 with human writing. Horizontal stroke size, within-human, correlates from 0.74–0.99 between different word replications. The model correlates with these words from 0.72–0.93. With respect to stroke duration, the correlations are lower. Vertical stroke duration is correlated 0.29–0.52 within-human, 0.17–0.72 between human and model. Horizontal stroke duration is correlated 0.35–0.94 within-human, 0.38–0.61 between human and model. Figure 15.6 shows a longer sample of script generated by the model. At first sight, the result looks natural. There are no evident artificial-looking shape repetitions. A given letter may differ in shape according to the context (e.g., <e> or <a>). Thus, even with a parsimonious parameterization, a reasonable approximation of the subject's handwriting in the spatial and temporal domain is obtained. In the spatial domain, between-letter context effects similar to those in the original handwriting are present. The lineation grid enables the model to maintain a horizontal baseline and to generate an estimate of the vertical position of the next pen-down position for new words.

Figure 15.6: A simulated handwriting sample produced by the symbolic stroke concatenation model. The parameters were calculated from the handwriting of another writer than in Figure 15.1. The text is not to be interpreted seriously

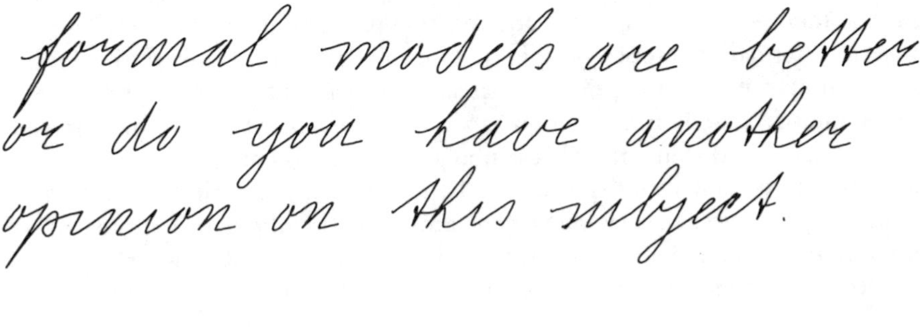

Limitations of the Symbolic Model

Closer observation of the data records reveals some peculiarities. Not all connecting strokes look fully appropriate. Moreover, horizontal progression between words is a little coarse. In some strokes, finally, inflection points might be expected (Schomaker and Thomassen, 1986). The connecting strokes are generic, i.e., the model treats the <m>-<e> transition in the same way as the <n>-<e> transition. This does not seem to be justified in all cases. Presumably, the human writer makes use of more varied stored connecting strategies for different allograph contexts. To implement such flexibility into the model, transition constraints should be added to the CCG and the Symbolic and Quantitative stroke definitions should be updated. Alternatively, it might be that writers perform more on-line computation of stroke parameterization. If so, the Stroke Generator module should be made more sensitive to the current stroke context.

Schomaker, Thomassen and Teulings (1989) noted a number of additional limitations of the model. One fundamental limitation is that the model never produces natural *writing errors*, e.g., fusion of strokes at the stroke concatenation level, or noise at the stroke formation level. At the level of stroke formation, the occurrence of errors could perhaps be handled by adding some specified degree of noise as derived from probability density functions of spatial error in human handwriting. Also, noise can be added to the parameter values. In fact, work is in progress to add stochastic properties to a symbolic model derived from the current model (Charraut and Hay, 1993). However, errors on the graphemic, allographic and stroke selection level do not emerge from the model and must be formalized explicitly in order to be elicited by the model. A final limitation of the model is its inability to infer the most appropriate stroke codes for completely new and unknown transitions.

From Descriptive, Symbolic to Neuromorphic, Subsymbolic Models

The two connectionist models described in this section focus on a lower level in the general framework, i.e., not the concatenation or chaining of characters, but the trajectory formation proper (shaping). One model is a variant of the Jordan recurrent network (see Chapter 3), whereas the other model is an illustration of a new approach, based on the neuron as a *spike oscillator*. These two models were developed out of discontent with a symbolic formalization method which requires all details to be described explicitly by the model, and has little or no emerging 'natural' properties, such as movement errors. In the alternative approach, we built trainable neural network models. The architecture of massively parallel connectionist models resembles the structure and functioning of neurons of the human brain in some respects, which is why we call them *neuromorphic*. Moreover, such models are well fit to simulate the dynamics of natural learning processes over time. We do not think that there is a specific functionality within the earlier symbolic model which cannot in principle be handled by a connectionist approach. As an example, there is no reason why the Cursive Connections Grammar cannot be modelled using a multi-layer perceptron (MLP) trained by the backpropagation learning algorithm (see Chapter 3). Such a connectionist model is likely to generalize to new unseen letter transitions, as opposed to a symbolic model which has to be reprogrammed explicitly. In this chapter, however, our connectionist modelling attempts address a still lower level, i.e., the allograph shaping in handwriting.

We should briefly pay attention to the *temporal patterning* of the writing process. Both chaining of movement segments and their shaping take place along the time axis. Originally, the time axis was ignored in many neural network models. Schomaker (1991) argued that many connectionist models are inherently static (non-temporal) and the addition of a time delay only partly solves the problem of temporal patterning. For instance, time-delay neural networks (e.g., TRACE, cf., McClelland and Elman, 1986) suffer from the limitation of a fixed-time window. Both temporal input and output patterns for a real information processing system may be of varying duration and thus difficult to handle. As another solution to this problem, Jordan (1985) and Elman (1988) proposed recurrent network architectures within the MLP approach. We follow Jordan's approach in the first model discussed below, in which the horizontal and vertical movements of the pen tip are modelled.

This section also illustrates the feasibility of a very different approach. Many neural network models ignore some essential time-related features of real biological networks. Biological neurons are pulse oscillators, producing action potential trains by a stochastic point process in time, whereas artificial neurons as used in a perceptron are mostly only level reservoirs. Apart from specific physiological modelling studies, there is only a limited number of general network models based on pulse oscillators (Torras i Genis, 1986; Tam and Perkel, 1989). A pulse oscillator model that handles pen tip displacement is discussed as the second model in this section.

General Features Needed in a Motor Pattern Generator

Before describing the specific models in detail we introduce a few more terms to describe the functionality of a subsymbolic movement pattern generator. In the production of motor patterns, four basic events or phases can be identified in chaining and in shaping. First, there is a *system configuration* stage, also known by such terms as motor programming, coordinative structure gearing, preparation, movement planning, schema build-up, etc. It involves the determination of the pattern, and the end effector system to be used for the task at hand. Second, there must be a signal *releasing the pattern* at the correct time (*start of pattern event*). Third is the phase of *pattern execution*, of which the duration must be monitored. The actions that are performed during this phase depend on information about the elapsed time, the distance from a spatial target position or force target value, and even on the number of motor segments produced. An incorrect representation or implementation of this stage leads to errors as in stuttering and the doubling error in the production of strokes in the cursive handwriting of *m* and *w*. An easy demonstration is the cursive writing of the word *minimum* without dots at normal or slightly accelerated speed while keeping the eyes closed. Fourth, there must be a *stopping signal* (*end of pattern event*), which appears essential in recurrent networks, because otherwise the network will go on producing a learned repetitive pattern (e.g., *aabaab*) endlessly. Similarly, for non-repetitive patterns, a recurrent network may indulge in infinite chaotic babbling after correctly reproducing a pattern. The same problem may occur in pulse oscillator networks. A version of the NETtalk model for pronouncing English words (Sejnowski and Rosenberg, 1986) displayed a similar problem after reading the last input character. It initially pronounces the word correctly and subsequently babbles in an erratic way until the end of the artificially predefined time window.

There are basically two solutions to represent the execution-of-pattern phase and the end-of-pattern event. First, there is an autonomous solution, chosen in the recurrent network model below, which assumes that a stop signal is generated within the pattern generator itself. Second, there is a nonautonomous solution based on feedback. Here, peripheral sensory or central efference-copy information is used to determine the relative position within the pattern or the end of the pattern (Bullock and Grossberg, 1988). In the spike oscillator model, we assume that the feedback comes from a higher level than the model itself.

A final feature of the natural production of movement is that muscular activation signals are contaminated by noise. Any plausible neurally inspired model should be able to tolerate a moderate amount of noise on single unit activations.

We now describe the two types of connectionist model. The models are not completely comparable, but are different illustrations of neuromorphic principles for motor articulation.

A Recurrent PDP Network Model

Our model is trained to produce horizontal and vertical pen-tip velocity functions, coded as two real values on two output nodes, one for the x-velocity and one for the y-velocity. The model uses a Jordan (1985) type network, where the output of a three-layer network is fed back to some nodes of the input layer. The network architecture is modified to handle graded continuous functions acting as a

Figure 15.7: A version of the Jordan (1985) recurrent network, modified to handle graded time functions. For explanation see text

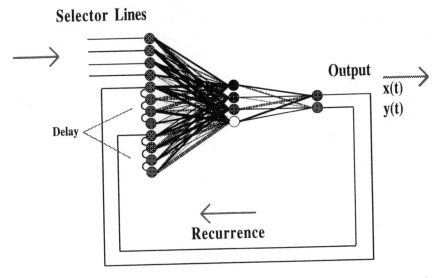

recursive filter, providing a temporal context, by saving the last two output values produced in time for each output channel. Apart from the delayed output information, the input layer is fed by a selector pattern arriving from four channels from a higher level outside the model. This pattern corresponding to a letter is presented to the model once and is coded as arbitrary binary values on four nodes of the input layer.

As can be seen in Figure 15.7, the input representation from the higher processing level is presented for a given time period on the Selector Lines (upper left). The aim is to produce a complex motor pattern on the output, on the basis of a simple input representation. The input activations are propagated towards the output units via the hidden layer. The essence of the Jordan-type recurrent network is the feedback of the output state at a previous time t-1 to separate input nodes (lower left), for inclusion with the current forward processing sweep at time t. In the proposed modification, not only the output states at t-1, but also at delays t-2, etc. are present at the input, yielding a longer output state history pattern which is used in each forward processing sweep. Since the model is used to simulate handwriting, a separate x and y output unit is needed (right), to produce the two-dimensional pen-tip trajectory x(t), y(t). Therefore, two delay lines at the input are present to contain earlier values of x(t) and y(t).

The system-configuration phase, which determines the movement pattern selection, is not modelled. The start-pattern phase is signalled by a switch from relaxation (0.1) to maximal activation (0.9) of one of the four input channels which selects the movement pattern to be produced. To provide the model with an autonomous solution for the detection of the end-of-pattern phase, the activation of the relevant selector channel exponentially decays during the duration of the movement. In other words, no external signalling of the end-of-pattern phase is necessary, because the time constant of the decay is chosen such that the selector activation is lower than 0.2 at the end of the movement pattern. Training is done using a standard backpropagation algorithm (see Chapter 3). Single unit activation levels contained 0.1 per cent of added noise from a uniform distribution.

Tests of the Recurrent Network Model

The model was tested in a simulation experiment with training sets consisting of the pen-tip movement signals Vx(t) and Vy(t) of isolated cursive characters of a single writer, sampled at 100 Hz. The letters used here were manually isolated from whole words by means of a handwriting editor program. The beginning and end of a pattern were padded with zeros (relaxed state) corresponding to a 50 ms real-time duration.

The performance of the network was tested in two modes. In the feedforward *teacher-forced* mode, we presented the original samples from the training set to the context input nodes. This is similar to testing in a normal network. In contrast, in the *free-running* mode, the input values were copied from the output nodes at earlier times. After training the recurrent network with 2 000 presentations of the Vx and Vy pattern of an *a*, the network never showed a legible approximation of the handwriting in the free-running mode. For the allographs *e* and *f*, the learning history was irregular. The pattern degenerated rapidly. Only after over 10 000 training epochs was it possible to teach an *a* to a recurrent network. In this case, the state space trajectory was robust and allowed for up to 5 per cent noise on the selector channel in the free run. Experiments with other letters from the alphabet produced comparable results. In contrast, the teacher-forced operation led to the faithful reconstruction of the handwriting pattern, as could be expected from a normal MLP model trained by backpropagation.

Figure 15.8 illustrates this performance difference in more detail. Three time function graphs are shown in the left part of the figure. The bottom time function

Figure 15.8: The characteristic behavior of the recurrent network model for handwriting described in the text. For explanation see text

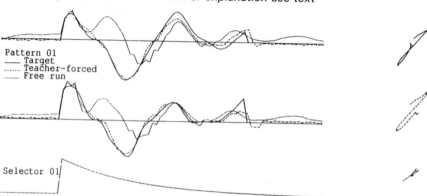

shows the input signal at one of the selector lines of the network. A decaying time function provides the system with a measure of the pattern's duration. The top and middle time function represent the vertical and horizontal pen-tip velocity, respectively. The solid line in each of the time functions represents the target signal as recorded from a human writer. The dashed line represents the output of the model when error-free feedback input is provided representing knowledge of previous Vx and Vy data. Since this feedback must be given by an external trainer, the dashed line is said to represent a 'teacher-forced' run. This type of simulation tests the quality of performance with the exclusion of the internal feedback signal, as if the network were a non-recurrent multilayer perceptron. The dotted line represents the output of a 'free run' of the model where all recurrent feedback is provided by the network itself.

In the right part of Figure 15.8 actual spatial patterns of the cursive letter *f* are represented, corresponding to the target letter *f* (top), the spatial output of the 'teacher-forced' run (middle), and the free run (bottom). The output signal of the teacher-forced run (dashed line) matches the target signal reasonably well, as evidenced from the resulting *f* (middle right). However, testing the network in free run mode results in poor performance (dotted line, bottom right). Problems arise because small disturbances in the input may be amplified by the feedback, leading to chaotic behaviour. In this case, the spatial output does not even come close to the actual target *f* (represented at the upper right). However, depending on the pattern, and after very long training, better results are sometimes obtained (see Schomaker, 1991).

A Pulse Oscillator Ensemble Model: The NiN Net

The *pulse oscillator ensemble model* is concerned with the training of X and Y pen-tip displacement functions to a network of Neuron/Inter-Neuron (NiN) pairs (see Figure 15.9). The basic assumption of the NiN ensemble approach is similar to that of a Jordan-type network, in the sense that the onset of a simple activation pattern (on/off) at the input leads to a complex output pattern in time. The neurons used in the NiN net are spike oscillators which will start firing at a steady rate, once activated by external input. This is similar to physical relaxation oscillators where constant accumulation of energy leads to sudden relaxation (dissipation of energy) each time a threshold is reached. However, in an NiN net the interaction of two oscillators may lead to more complex firing behaviour. In particular, when the output of a particular neuron is fed to an interneuron which inhibits our initial neuron, burst-like spiking patterns result. The NiN combination is present at all levels of the biological neural system. The NiN ensemble model can be best explained by comparing it to Fourier signal composition, which reconstructs a given signal by adding up a limited set of sine waves of differing frequency, amplitude and phase. In the NiN ensemble model,

Figure 15.9: A schematic description of a Neuron-Inhibitory Interneuron network. On the left, 'Selector Lines' are shown, depicting the origin of the external ON/OFF pattern. Within the rectangle, an ensemble of four NiN pairs is shown. A single NiN pair consists of a neuron (left, diagonal shading), the output of which is fed back via an inhibitory interneuron (right, stippled), and sent to the common output via a weight matrix W_{ik}. In the insets, typical spiking patterns are shown. Note the 'bursting' which is typical for a NiN, assuming proper neuron parameters. On the right part of the figure, the weight matrix and output units are shown, similar to the architecture of a perceptron in a PDP model. In the described model, the NiN cell parameters are drawn at random, once, and only the weight matrix W_{ik} is trained

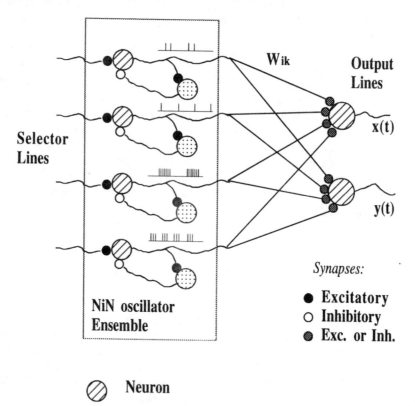

the same idea is exploited, using spike burst patterns as the basic signal constituent instead of the sine wave.

When a group of NiN pairs, each having a typical spiking pattern, starts responding to a common external *on* signal, the combined resulting activation of these units can be moulded by a weight matrix to approach the shape of an arbitrary time function. In our case, this time function will be a short fragment of handwriting movement. In theory, this idea can also be explored without the inhibitory interneurons, but by adding the inhibitory interneurons, a wider spectral distribution is obtained due to the bursting patterns. Consequently, a smaller number of oscillators is necessary than in the case of single-neuron oscillators.

The NiN pairs are mutually independent in the current version of the model which consists of 400 NiN oscillators. The parameters for the neurons are drawn from a uniform probability distribution bounded by reasonably extreme parameter values, and are not modified during the training for this initial experiment. Single unit activation levels contained 0.1 per cent added noise from a uniform distribution.

The System Configuration phase, which determines the movement pattern selection, falls outside the scope of the model. The start pattern phase, execute pattern phase, and end pattern phase are determined by activating the Neurons of a set of NiN pairs, and releasing the activation at the end of the pattern (square wave). This on-off signal, given artificially here, is assumed to be provided by a higher level. The firing behaviour of each neuron (including interneurons) follows a general model by Perkel *et al.* (1964, in Torras i Genis, 1986). Training is achieved by an experimental Hebb-type training rule based on the correlation between single NiN activity and the error between target time function and obtained time function (see Schomaker, 1992, for details). Next, low-pass filtering

Figure 15.10: Simulation results for the six letters a,b,c,d,e,f after 500 presentations to the NiN network. For each panel, the top time function trace is X(t), next trace is Y(t). Target and output pattern can be distinguished by looking at the abrupt ending of the target as opposed to the smooth ending of the network output. In each panel, the left pattern represents the target letter, right is the shape of the output letter

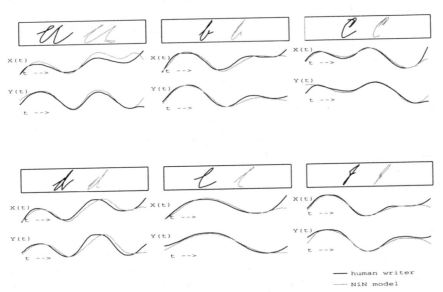

(with a cut-off frequency of 10 Hz) is used to simulate a virtual 'muscle' system (Teulings and Maarse, 1984).

Test of the NiN Network

A simulation study with the model showed that the training of the NiN network requires only 500 epochs to produce acceptable simulation of the pen tip movement, which is much less than the recurrent network requires. Training histories for six cursive letters < a,b,c,d,e,f > reached learning asymptotes after some 300 presentations. However, the learning rule does not always lead to convergence. Due to the Hebbian term in the learning rule, the size is not always approximated correctly. Figure 15.10 shows the simulation results for the six letters. The amplitudes of X(t) and Y(t) output were normalized to the amplitude of the target pattern. The error is larger at the end of the pattern than in the middle, due to the low-pass filtering of the output.

Evaluation of the Subsymbolic Models

Although theoretically the recurrent multi-layer perceptron is an attractive model in the present context, it did not display a convincing functionality and naturalness. The learning speed was very slow. At the same time, it was impossible to store more than one pattern in a single recurrent network, which reduces its suitability as the basis for both chaining and shaping in a non-toy model. Dedicated learning rules may alleviate these problems to some extent, but only at the risk of introducing new degrees of freedom which may be even less realistic from the physiological point of view. Summing up, the training of the recurrent network appears similar to forcing an essentially static system to display temporal behaviour.

In contrast, the NiN pulse oscillator ensemble model displayed rapid learning behaviour. Even if the Hebbian learning rule did not always lead to convergence, there are a large number of untried optimization methods still to be explored. The accuracy of pattern reproduction in the NiN model depends on the distribution of the neuron parameters in the ensemble. In the present experiment, these parameters were fixed, but fine tuning can theoretically be obtained by adapting the parameters (Torras I Genis, 1986), apart from adapting a set of NiNs to a pattern through a weight matrix. Other interesting features of the NiN network are the natural oscillation and the influence of the general activation level on the average firing rate, allowing for pace modulation (higher activation levels result in faster writing). Also, doubling of a movement segment can be produced by a single NiN oscillator. The fact that the NiN unit is a pulse oscillator running in time, and that it exploits non-linear dynamics creates a functionality not easily reproduced in a standard PDP or interactive activation model. Much more work is needed with respect to its physiological credibility, learning rules, and its capacities in terms of faithfully modelling motor parameter invariance. Obviously, any neural network model of pattern production in motor behaviour should display a functionality that exceeds the mere storage and retrieval of a pattern. The NiN network presented here is a promising first step towards a better exploitation of temporal characteristics of individual neurons in connectionist modelling.

General Discussion

The aim of the chapter is to demonstrate that recent advances in the modelling of handwriting production are successful in simulating realistic features of natural script. Empirically based insights into the cognitive and motor components of the human writing system are adopted as much as possible in the models discussed here. We distinguished between higher cognitive processes like formulation, spelling, allograph selection on the one hand and typical motor processes like motor pattern retrieval, parameterization and muscle innervation on the other hand. We further developed the cognitive model to implement biomechanical, trajectory formation aspects as well. To this end, two different approaches to the modelling of handwriting were discussed, one approach leaning on a symbolic frame of reference and one building on principles of subsymbolic, connectionist modelling. Interesting results were obtained with the subsymbolic, connectionist NiN network.

Evaluating the state of the art, we think that modelling, both symbolic and subsymbolic, has the advantage of making processing steps explicit. However, caution is necessary. Using the concept of a modular processing hierarchy possibly oversimplifies the functioning of a realistic biological system. In the latter, the interactions between processing stages are certainly more continuous and reciprocal than a strictly serial model allows. Subsymbolic connectionist modelling is attractive, because of its potential for natural generalization (as opposed to the necessarily explicit rules in symbolic modelling) and because of the inherent emergence of errors. However, the empirical results were only partly satisfying. Training smooth time functions to a recurrent multi-layer perceptron appeared to be very difficult, though not impossible. With respect to the proposed neural-oscillator network it seems that its value will become more apparent if the model can be extended to allow scaling, both along the time axis and the amplitude axis.

Alternative Models

The architecture of the current models is based on the concept of a continuous flow of small chunks of information through a hierarchically constructed set of operations. The opposite view would consider a sequence of operations on larger information units such as complete words or sentences. From a theoretical as well as from an empirical point of view, there are arguments against such an alternative approach. In the first place, it would be a severe limitation if the model would operate word by word only. It is well known that the human writer can write cursive words that are dictated by spelling letter by letter. The same would be impossible if the task were to correctly *pronounce* the task words. In the models discussed, processing at the level of words is necessary for the selection of correct spelling but once the graphemes (letters) are selected, motor articulation is influenced by the immediate neighbouring letters only. This picture seems to deviate from the much wider context effects on pronunciation in speaking.

On closer view, however, there are features of natural script that resemble context effects in speech. One of these is the overall decreasing size contour towards the end in words, but also in single syllables (Kao, 1983). Explanations have been given in terms of the increasing stiffness of the hand and wrist when the end of the natural extension range of these anatomical structures is reached. More cognitive interpretations hold that in most languages, final letters in words and syllables are more redundant than letters at more initial positions. Whatever the definite answer might be, it is obvious that in the models discussed here, context effects of this type have not been simulated. Nevertheless, it may be clear that the subsymbolic variants in particular easily allow for implementation of, for example, overall scaling factors. Their architecture, which works with small chunks of information at a time, allows for the insertion of context-dependent processing steps at all levels within the hierarchy.

Questions for Further Research

In both areas of modelling, the symbolic and the subsymbolic, the demand for empirical validation is strong. Future computer models will have to incorporate additional levels of the handwriting task, both in the direction of the lexical stages and higher, and in the effector control stage and lower. An intriguing question which was already touched upon above is how *errors* originate at the multiple levels of the writing architecture, from spelling to stroke chaining. Some errors are simply re-iterations of a processing step and can easily be mimicked in a model. Much more difficult are complex errors like transpositions and replacements of letters across complete words or syllables, e.g., writing *New Yersey* instead of *New Jersey*. Probably due to a competing spelling variant (*New York*), the subject substitutes *Y* for *J*, but correctly capitalizes the letter. Psychological research on errors (Ellis, 1982) has shown that the origin of an error may be at widely different levels of the writing system. This makes it highly probable that cross-talk between higher and lower processing levels is as natural as the occurrence of errors themselves. It would be a real challenge for future modelling endeavours to provide for forward and backward cross-talk in the model.

A final comment should be made on the presumably parallel nature of the human writing system. In the description of the psychological framework we have stressed the *ordered parallelism* of the system, in the sense that processing modules are serially organized but work simultaneously on different parts of the message to be written. The empirical basis for this assumption is that the real-time production of writing strokes is affected by the combined effects of higher and lower order processing demands. As a consequence, a naturalistic model of the process implies parallel computing procedures to simulate this feature. At present, however, only few applications of parallel computing are known to be used in simulation studies. At an overall level, the algorithms discussed above are organized as serially structured models in which processing steps are performed one at a time, even though within the processing modules of the neuromorphic models, simultaneous activation is simulated.

In psychological theories, the concept of parallelism is intimately related to the concept of *processing resources*. The overall pacing of the task is regulated by the sum of the processing resources needed at a particular moment in time. If the demands on processing resources are increased, the system slows down. Although it is not really understood how a biological system can take care of its simultaneous processing loads, the resource concept is widely accepted to describe the phenomenon. A working model, however, confronts its designer with the task of implementing variation of concurrent task demands into working mechanisms of trajectory formation. A possible, easily implementable solution is proposed by Van Galen, Van Doorn and Schomaker (1990) who assume that increased processing demands during task performance lead to higher levels of irradiant neuromotor noise and, therefore, are equivalent to decreasing signal-to-noise ratios in the processing system. In a computer model of the writing process, the processing complexity of earlier steps could be reflected by a decreasing amount of noise that is transferred to following processing steps. The decreased signal-to-noise ratios at the lower levels of the model would lead to longer processing times, as found in experiments with human task performance.

Recent progress in symbolic and subsymbolic modelling made it possible to mimic several aspects of human behaviour in a quasi-naturalistic manner. The question remains: what do the models teach us about the real system? An answer to this question is only to be given by further research on natural handwriting tasks in combination with theoretically inspired modelling experiments.

References

ALBUS, J. S. (1975) 'A new approach to manipulator control: The cerebellar model articulated controller (CMAC)', *Journal of Dynamic Systems, Measurement, Controls*, 94, pp. 220–7.

BLACK, S. E., BEHRMANN, K. B. and HACKER, P. (1989) 'Selective writing impairment: Beyond the allographic code', *Aphasiology*, 3, pp. 265–77.

BULLOCK, D. and GROSSBERG, S. (1988) 'Neural dynamics of planned arm movements: Emergent invariants and speed-accuracy properties during trajectory formation', *Psychological Review*, 95, pp. 49–90.

CARAMAZZA, A., MICELI, G. and VILLA, G. (1986) 'The role of the (output) phonological buffer in reading, writing, and repetition', *Cognitive Neuropsychology*, 3, pp. 37–76.

CHARRAUT, D. and HAY, L. (1993) 'A stochastic generator for handwriting synthesis', in *Proceedings of the 6th International Conference on Handwriting and Drawing*, Paris: Ecole Nationale Superieure des Telecommunications, pp. 201–3.

DENIER VAN DER GON, J. J., THURING, J. P. and STRACKEE, J. (1962) 'A handwriting simulator', *Physics in Medicine and Biology*, 6, pp. 407–14.

EDELMAN, S. and FLASH, T. (1987) 'A model of handwriting', *Biological Cybernetics*, 57, pp. 25–36.

ELLIS, A. W. (1982) 'Spelling and writing (and reading and speaking)', in ELLIS, A. W. (Ed) *Normality and Pathology in Cognitive Functions*, London: Academic Press, pp. 113–46.

ELMAN, J. L. (1988) *Finding Structure in Time*, (CRL Technical Report 8801), La Jolla: University of California, San Diego, Center for Research in Language.

HOLLERBACH, J. M. (1981) 'An oscillation theory of handwriting', *Biological Cybernetics*, 39, pp. 139–56.

HOLLERBACH, J. M. and FLASH, T. (1981) *Dynamic Interactions Between Limb Segments During Planar Arm Movement*, (AI Memo No. 635), Boston: Massachusetts Institute of Technology, Artificial Intelligence Laboratory.

HULSTIJN, W. and VAN GALEN, G. P. (1988) 'Levels of motor programming in writing familiar and unfamiliar symbols', in COLLEY, A. M. and BEECH, J. R. (Eds) *Cognition and Action in Skilled Behaviour*, Amsterdam: North-Holland, pp. 65–85.

JORDAN, M. I. (1985) *The Learning of Representations for Sequential Performance*, Doctoral dissertation, University of California, San Diego.

KAO, H. S. R. (1983) 'Progressive motion variability in handwriting tasks', *Acta Psychologica*, 54, pp. 149–59.

LEVELT, W. J. M. (1989) *Speaking: From Intention to Articulation*, Cambridge, MA: MIT Press.

MAARSE, F. J., SCHOMAKER, L. R. B. and TEULINGS, H.-L. (1988) 'Automatic identification of writers', in VAN DER VEER, G. C. and MULDER, G. (Eds) *Human-Computer Interaction: Psychonomic Aspects*, New York: Springer, pp. 353–60.

McCLELLAND, J. L. and ELMAN, J. L. (1986) 'Interactive processes in speech perception: The TRACE model', in McCLELLAND, J. L., RUMELHART, D. E. and the PDP Research Group (Eds) *Parallel Distributed Processing: Explorations in the Microstructure of Cognition: Volume 2. Psychological and Biological Models*, Cambridge, MA: MIT Press, pp. 59–121.

MEULENBROEK, R. G. J., ROSENBAUM, D. A., THOMASSEN, A. J. W. M. and SCHOMAKER, L. R. B. (1993) 'Limb-segment selection in drawing behavior', *Quarterly Journal of Experimental Psychology*, 46, pp. 273–99.

MEULENBROEK, R. G. J. and VAN GALEN, G. P. (1989) 'The production of connecting strokes in cursive script: Developing co-articulation in 8 to 12 year-old children', in PLAMONDON, R., SUEN, Y. C. and SIMNER, M. L. (Eds) *Computer Recognition and Human Production of Handwriting*, Singapore: World Scientific, pp. 273–86.

MILLER, J. (1990) 'Discreteness and continuity in models of human information processing', *Acta Psychologica*, 74, pp. 297–318.

MORASSO, P., MUSSA IVALDI, F. A. and RUGGIERO, C. (1983) 'How a discontinuous mechanism can produce continuous patterns in trajectory formation', *Acta Psychologica*, 54, pp. 83–98.

MORASSO, P. and TAGLIASCO, V. (1986) *Human Movement Understanding*, Amsterdam: North-Holland.

PERKEL, D. H., SCHULMAN, J. H., BULLOCK, T. H., MOORE, G. P. and SEGUNDO, J. P. (1964) 'Pace maker neurons: Effects of regularly spaced synaptic input', *Science*, 145, pp. 61–3.

PLAMONDON, R. and LEEDHAM, G. (Eds) (1990) *Computer Processing of Handwriting*, Singapore: World Scientfic.

PLAMONDON, R. and MAARSE, F. J. (1989) 'An evaluation of motor models of handwriting', *IEEE Transactions on Systems, Man and Cybernetics*, 19, pp. 1060–72.

PLAMONDON, R., SUEN, C. Y. and SIMNER, M. L. (Eds) (1989) *Computer Recognition and Human Production of Handwriting*, Singapore: World Scientific.

PORTIER, S. J., VAN GALEN, G. P. and THOMASSEN, A. J. W. M. (1993) 'Phonological and orthographic demands in the production of handwriting', *Acta Psychologica*, 82, pp. 251–74.

RAIBERT, M. H. (1977) *Motor Control and Learning by the State Space Model'*, Doctoral Dissertation, Massachusetts Institute of Technology.

RUMELHART, D. E. and NORMAN, D. A. (1982) 'Simulating a skilled typist: A study of skilled cognitive-motor performance', *Cognitive Science*, 6, pp. 1–36.

SCHOMAKER, L. R. B. (1991) *Simulation and Recognition of Handwriting Movements*, Doctoral Dissertation, TR NICI 91-03, Nijmegen University, The Netherlands.

SCHOMAKER, L. R. B. (1992) 'A neural-oscillator model of temporal pattern generation', *Human Movement Science*, 11, pp. 181–92.

SCHOMAKER, L. R. B. and PLAMONDON, R. (1991) 'The relation between pen force and pen point kinematics in handwriting', *Biological Cybernetics*, 63, pp. 277–89.

SCHOMAKER, L. R. B. and THOMASSEN, A. J. W. M. (1986) 'On the use and limitations of averaging handwriting signals', in KAO, H. S. R., VAN GALEN, G. P. and HOOSAIN, R. (Eds) *Graphonomics: Contemporary Research in Handwriting*, Amsterdam: North-Holland, pp. 225–38.

SCHOMAKER, L. R. B., THOMASSEN, A. J. W. M. and TEULINGS, H.-L. (1989) 'A computational model of cursive handwriting', in PLAMONDON, R., SUEN, C. Y. and SIMNER, M. L. (Eds) *Computer Recognition and Human Production of Handwriting*, Singapore: World Scientific, pp. 153–77.

SEJNOWSKI, T. J. and ROSENBERG, C. R. (1986) 'Parallel Networks that Learn to Pronounce English Text', *Complex Systems*, 1, pp. 145–68.

SMYTH, M. M. and SILVERS, G. (1987) 'Functions of vision in the control of handwriting', *Acta Psychologica*, 65, pp. 47–64.

STERNBERG, S. (1969) 'The discovery of processing stages: Extension of Donders' method', *Acta Psychologica*, 30 (*Attention and Performance II*, W. G. Koster, Ed.), pp. 276–315.

TAM, D. C. and PERKEL, D. H. (1989) 'A model for temporal correlation of biological neuronal spike trains', *Proceedings of the IEEE International Joint Conference on Neural Networks 1989, Vol. I*, pp. 781–6.

TEULINGS, H.-L. (1993) 'Handwriting movement control. Chapter E, Part II: Particular Skills', in KEELE, S. W. and HEUER, H. (Eds) *Handbook of Perception and Action, Vol. 3: Motor Skills*, London: Academic Press.

TEULINGS, H.-L. and MAARSE, F. J. (1984) 'Digital recording and processing of handwriting movements', *Human Movement Science*, 3, pp. 193–217.

TEULINGS, H.-L., MULLINS, P. A. and STELMACH, G. E. (1986) 'The elementary units of programming in handwriting', in KAO, H. S. R., VAN GALEN, G. P. and HOOSAIN, R. (Eds) *Graphonomics: Contemporary Research in Handwriting*, Amsterdam: North-Holland, pp. 21–32.

TEULINGS, H.-L., THOMASSEN, A. J. W. M. and VAN GALEN, G. P. (1983) 'Preparation of partly precued handwriting movements: The size of movement units in handwriting', *Acta Psychologica*, 54, pp. 165–77.

TEULINGS, H.-L., THOMASSEN, A. J. W. M. and VAN GALEN, G. P. (1986) 'Invariants in handwriting: The information contained in a motor program', in KAO, H. S. R., VAN GALEN, G. P. and HOOSAIN, R. (Eds) *Graphonomics: Contemporary Research in Handwriting*, Amsterdam: North-Holland, pp. 305–15.

THOMASSEN, A. J. W. M., KEUSS, P. J. G. and VAN GALEN, G. P. (Eds) (1984) *Motor Aspects of Handwriting: Approaches to Movement in Graphic Behaviour*, Amsterdam: North-Holland.

THOMASSEN, A. J. W. M., MEULENBROEK, R. G. J. and TIBOSCH, H. J. C. M. (1991) 'Latencies and kinematics reflect graphic production rules', *Human Movement Science*, 10, pp. 271–90.

THOMASSEN, A. J. W. M. and VAN GALEN, G. P. (1992) 'Handwriting as a motor task: Experimentation, modelling and simulation', in SUMMERS, J. J. (Ed) *Approaches to the Study of Motor Control and Learning*, Amsterdam: North-Holland, pp. 113–44.

TORRAS I GENIS, (1986) 'Neural network model with rhythm-assimilation capacity', *IEEE Transactions on Systems, Man, and Cybernetics*, 16, pp. 680–93.

VAN DER PLAATS, R. E. and VAN GALEN, G. P. (1990) 'Effects of spatial and motor demands in handwriting', *Journal of Motor Behaviour*, 22, 361–85.

VAN DER PLAATS, R. E. and VAN GALEN, G. P. (1991) 'Allographic variability in adult handwriting', *Human Movement Science*, 10, pp. 291–300.

VAN DOORN, R. R. A. and KEUSS, P. J. G. (1992) 'The role of vision in the temporal and spatial control of handwriting', *Acta Psychologica*, 81, pp. 269–86.

VAN GALEN, G. P. (1984) 'Structural complexity of motor patterns: A study on reaction times of handwritten letters', *Psychological Research*, 46, pp. 49–57.

VAN GALEN, G. P. (1990) 'Phonological and motoric demands in handwriting: Evidence for discrete transmission of information', *Acta Psychologica*, 74, pp. 259–76.

VAN GALEN, G. P. (1991) 'Handwriting: Issues for a psychomotor theory', *Human Movement Science*, 10, pp. 165–91.

VAN GALEN, G. P., MEULENBROEK, R. G. J. and HYLKEMA, H. (1986) 'On the simultaneous processing of words, letters and strokes in handwriting: Evidence for a mixed linear and parallel model', in KAO, H. S. R., VAN GALEN, G. P. and HOOSAIN, R. (Eds) *Graphonomics: Contemporary Research in Handwriting*, Amsterdam: North-Holland, pp. 5–20.

VAN GALEN, G. P., SMYTH, M. M., MEULENBROEK, R. J. G. and HYLKEMA, H. (1989) 'The role of short-term memory and the motor buffer in handwriting under visual and non-visual guidance', in PLAMONDON, R., SUEN, C. Y. and SIMNER, M. L. (Eds) *Computer Recognition and Human Production of Handwriting*, Singapore: World Scientific, pp. 253–72.

VAN GALEN, G. P. and TEULINGS, H.-L. (1983) 'The independent monitoring of form and scale parameters in handwriting', *Acta Psychologica*, 54, pp. 9–22.

VAN GALEN, G. P., VAN DOORN, R. R. A. and SCHOMAKER, L. R. B. (1990) 'Effects of motor programming on the power spectral density function of finger and wrist movements', *Journal of Experimental Psychology: Human Perception and Performance*, 16, pp. 755–65.

VREDENBREGT, J. and KOSTER, W. G. (1971) 'Analysis and synthesis of handwriting', *Philips Technical Review*, 32, pp. 73–8.

Notes on Contributors

Ton Dijkstra (PhD 1990) is a senior staff member at the Nijmegen Institute for Cognition and Information (The Netherlands). He investigates monolingual and bilingual visual and auditory word recognition, but makes occasional side trips to other domains such as morphological and sentence processing and language production. As a firm believer in the heuristic value of modelling, he currently explores the possibilities of a bilingual interactive activation model. With Gerard Kempen as a coauthor he has published two Dutch books on Psycholinguistics, one of which is translated into German.

Koenraad de Smedt is Professor of Computational Linguistics at the University of Bergen (Norway). He has worked previously at the Universities of Nijmegen (PhD 1990) and Leiden (The Netherlands). He has published in the areas of natural language generation, linguistic knowledge representation and language engineering. His main research interest lies in the modelling of human incremental sentence generation.

Walter Daelemans is a researcher at Tilburg University (The Netherlands) and associate professor at the University of Antwerp (Belgium), teaching Computational Linguistics and Artificial Intelligence courses. In 1987, he earned a PhD (University of Leuven) with an object-oriented model of Dutch morphology and phonology and its applications in language technology. His current research interests are in Machine Learning of Natural Language, and knowledge representation techniques for natural language processing.

Jaap Murre wrote a PhD thesis on neural network modelling at Leiden University in 1992. After working at the MRC — Applied Psychology Unit in Cambridge until 1995, he now holds a fellowship of the Netherlands Royal Academy of Arts in Sciences at the University of Amsterdam. Previous publications concern the quantitative neuroanatomy of neural networks and their implementation in parallel neurocomputers (monograph: 'Learning and Categorization in Modular Neural Networks', 1992). His present work focuses on connectionist modelling of memory, learning, and amnesia, and on models of recovery from brain damage.

Rainer Goebel has worked on artificial neural networks for visual processing and rule acquisition. Until 1994, he was at the University of Braunschweig (Germany) writing his thesis about a large-scale oscillatory neural network model of perceptual organisation, selective attention, and object recognition. He is now working at the Max Planck Institute for brain research in Frankfurt/Main and studies neural mechanisms of vision using functional magnetic resonance imaging. In 1994, he received the Heinz-Billing award for developing a powerful neural network simulation program.

Dominic W. Massaro is a Professor and Chair of Psychology in the Program in Experimental Psychology at the University of California, Santa Cruz. He has been a Guggenheim Fellow, a University of Wisconsin Romnes Fellow, a James McKeen Cattell Fellow, and an NIMH Fellow. His research interests (which have resulted in several books) include perception, memory, cognition, learning, and decision making. His current research is on the development and theoretical and applied use of a completely synthetic and animated head for speech synthesis. He is a past president of the Society for Computers in Psychology and the current book review editor of the *American Journal of Psychology*.

Uli Frauenfelder is Professor of Psycholinguistics at the University of Geneva and the director of its Logopedie school. He completed his PhD at the EHESS in Paris, and did a post-doc at MIT. Before coming to Geneva, he worked at the Max-Planck Institute for Psycholinguistics in Nijmegen. His principal research interests lie in the processes of speech perception and spoken word recognition, but more recently he has worked on problems related to language disorders, simultaneous interpretation, and language acquisition.

Jonathan Grainger is Research Director at the Centre for Research in Cognitive Psychology at the University of Provence (Aix, France). He completed his PhD at René Descartes University in Paris, and has published widely in the area of visual word recognition. He has recently co-edited a special issue of the *Journal of Experimental Psychology: Human Perception and Performance*, on modelling visual word recognition.

Harald Baayen studied linguistics at the Free University of Amsterdam. In 1989, he completed his PhD thesis on statistical and psychological aspects of morphological productivity. Since 1990, he has held post-doc positions at the Max Planck Institute for Psycholinguistics in Nijmegen. His research interests include general linguistics, morphological theory and the psycholinguistics of morphological processing in perception and production, as well as lexical statistics in literary and linguistic corpus-based computing.

Robert Schreuder studied Psychology at Nijmegen University, and obtained his PhD in 1978. From 1978 to 1984, he worked as a senior research fellow at the University of Leiden. In 1980–1981, he held a post-doc position in the Psychology

Department of Stanford University. From 1984 onwards, he has been Head of the Interfaculty Research Unit for Language and Speech, University of Nijmegen. Since 1985, he has held a Professorship in Language Behavior. His research interests include the mental lexicon, reading, word recognition, lexical statistics, and morphology.

Gerard A.M. Kempen is Professor of Cognitive Psychology at the University of Leiden. As a member of the Experimental and Theoretical Psychology Unit and the Graduate Research Institute for Experimental Psychology, he is studying syntactic aspects of human sentence comprehension and production, and computer-based teaching of grammar and writing. From 1976 to 1992, he was Professor of Psycholinguistics at the University of Nijmegen, where he had received his PhD in 1970. Since 1980, he has initiated and supervised various applied research projects dealing with the computational treatment of Dutch.

Alan Garnham is Reader in Experimental Psychology in the Laboratory of Experimental Psychology, University of Sussex at Brighton (UK). His principal research interests are in text comprehension and syntactic processing. He has published widely on these topics, and has written or edited seven books, including *Psycholinguistics: Central Topics* (Methuen, 1985), *Mental Models as Representations of Discourse and Text* (Ellis Horwood, 1987), and *Discourse Representation and Text Processing* (with Jane Oakhill, 1992, Erlbaum).

Jerry Andriessen is assistant professor in Educational Sciences at the University of Utrecht (The Netherlands). He lectures on topics involving Learning with New Media and Intelligent Tutoring Systems. He completed a PhD on sentence selection strategies in narrative writing by beginners. His current research is on local planning processes in writing, especially in argumentative text production, and on learning with new media applications, especially in telematics.

Michael Zock (CNRS — LIMSI France) investigates the modelling of the cognitive processes underlying language generation and builds tools that help people learn to speak a language. He has participated in international projects, has organized exchange programmes and workshops, and has led tutorials and lecture courses in psychology, computational linguistics and Artificial Intelligence all over the world (e.g. in Eastern Europe, Japan, and Canada). He has edited several books on natural language generation and has recently received the 'UNAM School of Psychology Twentieth Anniversary Award'.

Ardi Roelofs is a staff member of the Max Planck Institute for Psycholinguistics (Nijmegen, The Netherlands). He obtained his PhD from Nijmegen University and held a post-doc position at MIT. His main research interest concerns language production (e.g. lemma retrieval, morphology, and phonological encoding). His work involves computational modelling and experimentation.

Gary S. Dell is Professor in the Department of Psychology and the Beckman Institute at the University of Illinois at Urbana-Champaign. He held previous faculty appointments at Dartmouth College and the University of Rochester. He has published many articles dealing with language production and comprehension and has a particular interest in developing connectionist models of normal and impaired linguistic performance.

Cornell Juliano is a graduate student in the Brain and Cognitive Sciences Department at the University of Rochester. His research in language processing and connectionist modelling explores the extent to which certain psycholinguistic phenomena may be explained as emergent properties of a language system that is sensitive to systematic regularities found in the linguistic environment.

Louis Boves obtained his PhD in Linguistics from Nijmegen University (The Netherlands) in 1984. His research interests include a wide range of topics in speech signal processing and in phonetics, as applied to automatic synthesis and speech recognition. Since 1993, he has been Professor for Speech Technology in the Department of Language and Speech of Nijmegen University.

Bert Cranen achieved his masters degree in Electrical Engineering in 1979. His main research interest has been in modelling the human voice source properties. His doctoral thesis, published in 1987, was entitled 'The acoustic impedance of the glottis — Measurements and Modelling'. Since 1985, he has been a senior lecturer at the Department of Language and Speech at the University of Nijmegen (The Netherlands).

Lambert Schomaker is a senior researcher at the Nijmegen Institute of Cognition and Information (NICI, The Netherlands). His PhD dissertation is titled 'Simulation and Recognition of Handwriting Movements' (1991). He is involved in a number of research projects in pattern recognition of handwriting and the development of multimodal user interfaces. He is a coordinator of the UNIPEN project of on-line handwriting databases and recognizer benchmarking. His main research interests lie in the area of neural networks and hybrid modelling.

Gerard P. van Galen is senior researcher at the Nijmegen Institute for Cognition and Information (NICI), Division of Motor Function and Rehabilitation. His primary research interests are in the field of human motor control. After his thesis on focal versus ambient information processing and single-channelness (1971), he specialized in complex motor skills such as speech, handwriting, and drawing. His main publications are on psychological models of handwriting. Recently he coordinated several research projects on biomechanical and neuropsychological aspects of motor tasks.

Index